𝓑

GRAHAM ROBB

FRANCE

An Adventure History

PICADOR

First published 2022 by Picador
an imprint of Pan Macmillan
The Smithson, 6 Briset Street, London EC1M 5NR
EU representative: Macmillan Publishers Ireland Ltd, 1st Floor,
The Liffey Trust Centre, 117–126 Sheriff Street Upper,
Dublin 1, D01 YC43
Associated companies throughout the world
www.panmacmillan.com

ISBN 978-1-5290-0762-6

1 3 5 7 9 8 6 4 2

A CIP catalogue record for this book is available from the British Library.

Map artwork by Global Blended Learning, re-drawn from originals by Graham Robb

Typeset in Janson Text by Palimpsest Book Production Ltd, Falkirk, Stirlingshire
Printed and bound by CPI Group (UK) Ltd, Croydon, CR0 4YY

Visit **www.picador.com** to read more about all our books
and to buy them. You will also find features, author interviews and
news of any author events, and you can sign up for e-newsletters
so that you're always first to hear about our new releases.

FOR MARGARET

Contents

PART THREE
The Third, Fourth and Fifth Republics

List of Illustrations

Section One

12. Parisian women heading for Versailles 'to bring back some bread and the King', 1789. (incamerastock / Alamy Stock Photo)
13. The Mistral wreaking havoc on the Col des Tempêtes, just below the summit of Mont Ventoux, 1827. (Cliché Bernard Cousin. UMR TELEMME, Maison méditerranéenne des Sciences de l'Homme, Aix-en-Provence, France)

Section Two

14. The mill town of Rouen from the cemetery of Bonsecours, c. 1850. ('Rouen, vue prise du cimetière de Bon-Secours', Bibliothèque municipale de Rouen (Est. topo. g-3884))
15. Louis-Napoléon Bonaparte, 'Prince-President' of the French Republic. Daguerreotype, c. 1850. ('Portrait de Napoléon III, en buste, de trois-quarts, à gauche', Bibliothèque nationale de France, Rés. Eg8-560)
16. 'Madame H…' (Harriet Howard), the President's consort, by Henriette Cappelaere, 1850. (RMN-Grand Palais, domaine de Compiègne / image RMN-GP.)
17. Rulers of Gaul and France depicted on coins and one seal. (Philippe Auguste).
18. Narcisse Pelletier, 'the White Savage', in Constant Merland's *Dix-sept ans chez les sauvages* (1876).
19. Anatole Roujou, geologist and Darwinian anthropologist, c. 1872. (Archives départementales du Cantal, 28 J 2/445, fonds Alphonse Aymar).
20. Stage One of the second Tour de France (Paris to Lyon, 2–3 July 1904), somewhere between Moulins and Roanne. (Presse Sports / Welloffside (23350)).
21. Reims after four years on or near the Western Front, by a member of the American Red Cross, 20 May 1919.
22. Maréchal Pétain on a propaganda poster for the Vichy puppet government by Bernard Villemot, 1943. (Bridgeman Images / DACS)
23. Mont Aiguille in the Vercors, pictured in *Les Sept Miracles de Dauphiné* (Grenoble, 1701).
24. Outside the offices of *Charlie Hebdo* on 16 October 2017.
25. One of the early leaders of the Gilets Jaunes movement, Priscillia Ludosky, at a Gilets Jaunes demonstration in Paris, 20 January 2019. (ERIC FEFERBERG / AFP via Getty Images)

List of Maps

About This Book

This is a history of the region on the western edge of the Asian continent which is currently referred to as France. It begins in the earliest days for which written records exist and ends in the distant future. The scenes of wars and revolutions, from the plains of Provence to the slums and boulevards of Paris, may be familiar; some of the protagonists are well known in a real or legendary form – Caesar, Charlemagne, Louis XIV, Napoleon Bonaparte, General de Gaulle. Many other events, places and people have never before appeared in a history of France.

Historical explorations are unpredictable. This book was to have opened with the indigenous legend of the origins of Gaul, which predates the Roman conquest (58–51 BC). The protohistorical tale of a wandering hero led to a discovery which grew into a book on the scientifically advanced civilization of the Iron Age Celts. The discovery was confirmed by a decoded ancient map in a second book, dictated by other, equally compelling circumstances.*

By then, ten years had passed since the cloud shape of a social, political and geographical history of France had come into view on the mental horizon. Several expeditions had been undertaken in libraries and on the ground. I was happy to note that the idea was already a decade old. Another four full years would be spent writing the book I had come to think of as a slow history ('slow' as in 'slow food').

Despite the mortal disadvantages, the passing of time is the writer's friend. To recover rather than simply tabulate the past calls for some reliable means of self-estrangement besides the miraculously mnemonic bicycle and the inspirational wine which first reached Gaul by the Mediterranean, the Rhone and the highway that was created by trans-humant herds and upright apes between the Pyrenees and the Alps.

✻

---

* *The Ancient Paths* (US title, *The Discovery of Middle Earth*), 2013; *The Debatable Land*, 2018.

The walls of the room in which this book was written are bare apart from a relief map of France and neighbouring territories published by the Institut Géographique National. The map is exactly one millionth the size of the real land mass, which is nothing compared to the compaction that would be required to fit two thousand years of history into a single volume. On this map, I have marked in white correction fluid all the routes which Margaret (my wife) and I have cycled, omitting the journeys made by train and – in times almost beyond recall and scarcely worth recalling – by car.

The map used to reassure me that I had seen quite a lot of the country beyond Paris, including many grim and graceless towns and regions which no informed tourist would deliberately visit. Before the continent rediscovered the plague walls and *cordons sanitaires* of previous centuries, the total distance covered in western Europe was approaching thirty thousand miles, most of which had been ridden within the borders of modern France. Now, the map looks like a record of things unseen, even from a distance. Assuming an average eye-span of five miles either side of the white line, that still leaves a vast expanse of *terra invisa*.

In the early days, we travelled to particular areas, and then, by ever more circuitous routes, to particular periods. Gentle cycling for weeks on end gave the scrolling landscapes a binocular intensity and deepened the journey's fourth dimension. The gathering and sorting of precise local information in preparation for each journey always took longer than the journey itself.

With their amnesia-inducing blur of facts and dates, general histories soon proved no more useful than small-scale maps which depict only major roads and railway lines. I longed for the authors of those histories to leave the express train at any randomly chosen spot, to engage with a native, living or dead, to share an enigmatic meal, to ponder inexplicably relevant minor details, and especially to ask more questions.

Eventually, everything sounded so familiar that it was hard to believe that this was the real past. I imagined the existence of a 'French History' kit which allowed serviceable examples of the genre to be swiftly assembled. In the rush to reach the chosen terminus, entire provinces and populations were erased by speed and one place looked much like another. Physical geography was often absent, left to some other dimension or discipline. Some histories of 'France' never strayed beyond the outer boulevards of Paris, except when driven out by war. In one case, 'women' were sectioned off and dealt with in a framed box. Each period lived in strict chronological lockdown and was permitted to interact only with itself and its immediate neighbours.

❁

The Discovery of France (2007) described the charting and colonizing of France from the Revolution to the First World War. This only slightly longer book, spanning nearly ten times as many years, demanded a more symphonic or operatic arrangement. I looked for a closer match of experience and history, knowing how much otherwise unmemorable information can adhere to one intimate encounter with a person or a place.

The marshalling of historical data is unthinkable without conventions and some recognizable uniformity, but it is a sad adventure that offers no hope of getting lost. Sooner or later, the data takes on the characteristics of its uniform. In this rigid state, it can serve as the raw material of propaganda or a politician's speech. Tactical deviations from the prevailing forms of presentation can then impart an air of suspect foreignness to historical truths.

The identity papers and luggage labels of any outlandish or seemingly delusive details can be inspected in the notes and references in the back pages. Along with primary documents in the languages of Gaul, Francia, Occitania and France, scholarly studies of specific events and people are the foundation of this book. Scholarship provides the authors of general histories with well-made roads to the past. It also reveals the unfathomable voids on either side of the carriageway and conveys that thrilling sense of ignorance which gives exploration its *raison d'être*.

Previously . . .

The history of France begins like the crackle of a wireless or the flickering of a film strip so decayed that it is hard to tell whether this is supposed to be an adventure story or a record of events which actually took place.

A man dressed in a lion skin is driving a herd of cattle across a plain. Behind him, the pyrocumulus clouds of a forest fire or the fogs of a distant ocean are billowing over a jagged range of mountains. As he strides along with the sun in his eyes, the skies darken and the scene is obliterated by a hail of stones. When daylight returns, that scarred footage from the Iron Age shows the unmistakeable sight of the pebble-strewn plain of the Crau and the Rhone at its delta spreading out into the Mediterranean.

To the Greek and Roman writers who recorded the fragments of a Gaulish legend, the traveller was Herakles/Hercules. To Hannibal, whose army marched in his footsteps from the Pyrenees to the Alps in 218 BC, he was the sun god, Melqart. Five centuries later, Christians re-carved his graven images into semblances of Saint Christopher. But to the tribes who had come from the east in the sixth century BC and who told this story to their children and then to their oppressors, the herdsman and the Celtic princess he impregnated in the fertile interior were the grandparents of their multi-ethnic nation.

The name of this founder of the land that became France was Ogmios. In the extinct language of the Gauls, 'Ogmios' meant 'guide' or 'man of the roads', because wherever he walked, a safe pathway appeared.

✴

The fabled birth of a nation on the shores of the Western Ocean belongs to protohistory, but the legend itself is real: its geographically coherent scenes can be spliced together from fragments preserved by twenty different ancient authors.

Ogmios himself may once have existed as a late Bronze Age prophet or cattle-rustling warlord. His phantom footsteps fell on familiar, solid ground. In the dry lowlands traversed by the Heraklean Way, sherds of Gaulish pottery and tile can still be picked up and the route can be retraced from the alluvial plain of the Crau to the vineyards of the Rhone, then up into the chaotic country where the sun carves deep gullies of shade into the limestone.

On reaching the impassable wall of the Alps, he felled a pine forest, set fire to the trunks and brash and waited for the miracle. The rock exploded and a portal opened up. Through that portal, numberless armies, traders, fugitives, slaves and brides from either side of the mountains travelled to and from Gaul and Italy. When the Roman proconsul who became the destroyer and the historian of Gaul marched with five legions through that wide pass on his way to the Provençal Alps in the spring of 58 BC, the road was already several centuries old.

PART ONE

Ancient Gaul to the Renaissance

1

The Hedge

A tall man with piercing black eyes was staring at an impenetrable hedge. The year was 57 BC; the hedge stood near a riverbank in northern Gaul; the man was Julius Caesar.

This was the second year of a potentially lucrative war against Rome's transalpine neighbours. The first campaign had been fought in the southern half of Gaul, where the barbarians lived in beautifully walled hilltop towns served by roads and bridges. Now, the legions were marching through an unexplored land inhabited by 'wild men of great courage'. The wind brought the smell of a boundless ocean and the water clocks showed the summer days growing longer.

Like so much else in Outer Gaul, the hedge was too exotic for an educated Roman to form an accurate impression of it. In his annual report to the Senate, Caesar would have to describe it in some detail in order to explain to the senators exactly how a Roman army came to find itself thwarted and intimidated by vegetation.

A tidy and punctilious man, Julius Gaius Caesar manipulated Latin with precision and economy, just as he wielded the comb, the shears and the razor, ruthlessly plucking out any superfluous hairs. But the language of civilization offered only the pastoral word *saepes*, which denoted a small barrier or fence of twigs and foliage.

> There, as of old, your neighbour's bordering *saepes*
> Oft shall lull you with the hum of the bees
> Which sip its willow flowers.*

---

* Virgil, *Eclogues*, i.

Those gargantuan Gaulish *saepes* had not been created to keep live-stock out of gardens and cornfields: they were there to neutralize the Roman cavalry and to serve the enemy as a cloak of invisibility. The best way to describe the hedge for a Mediterranean reader would be to define the manner of its construction:

> They cut notches in tender saplings, then bend the dense branches which the trees fling out on either side and thread them through with brambles and thorns. The resulting hedges provide them with a wall-like fortification through which it is impossible not only to pass but also, indeed, to see.

✿

Caesar was the first Roman commander to enter this far-flung region to the west of the lower Rhine. The only fully Romanized part of Gaul was the province of Gallia Transalpina, founded in 121 BC and later renamed Gallia Narbonensis. A narrow strip of land along the Mediterranean coast, bounded by the Alps, the Jura, the Cévennes and the Pyrenees, it provided a safe corridor between Spain and Italy along which Gaulish gold, wheat and slaves could be channelled to Rome.

The rest of Gaul was a vast hinterland stretching away to the northern ocean. One third of it was occupied by the tribes known collectively as Belgae. It was not even certain that Belgica formed a true part of Gaul: the Belgic tribes had Celtic names but claimed to be the sons and grandsons of Germanic invaders. No merchant was allowed to cross its borders, especially if he dealt in wine and other Roman luxuries which the Belgae believed had weakened the moral fibre of the tribes who lived along the Rhone and the Seine.

Most of what appeared to be known about the region was hearsay, yet the rumours were all too credible. A year before, at Vesontio (Besançon), Caesar had seen his soldiers quaking with fear and almost mutinous after listening to the tales of spies and traders. Men who had encountered Germanic tribesmen on their travels or in battle had found them brave and disciplined and 'prodigiously large in body'. 'They had often been unable to withstand the sight of their coun-tenance and their staring eyes.' Legionaries who claimed to be unafraid of a human enemy felt an insidious dread of Nature, which, like its feral offspring, seemed to conspire against the Romans: they feared 'the narrowness of the roads and the vastness of the forests'.

Beyond the Rhine, according to Greek and Roman travellers and geographers, the sunless Hercynian Forest, which was as old as the world itself, ran so far to the east that it could not be crossed in under sixty days, and then only by following the flight of the forest bird which shed its luminescent feathers in the gloom. In the far north, where Caesar had led his eight legions, another great forest, the Arduenna, 'the largest in all of Gaul', was said to be 'more than five hundred miles wide'. This was the eroded mountain range now called the Ardennes, which straddles the Franco-Belgian border.*

The land of monstrous hedges lay on the western rim of the Arduenna. Deep in the forest, in 'out-of-the-way locations' and 'latebris' (lurking places), the Gauls convened their war councils. The Arduenna was a bandits' lair the size of a country. Invisible paths led by labyrinthine routes to secret valleys and ravines. In certain parts of the inner forest, there were dense plantations of oak and yew where human sacrifices were performed by Druids, a priestly caste of scientists and intellectuals. The weavers of military-strength hedges could also fashion pliant willow stems into 'enormous effigies, the limbs of which they fill with living men before setting them on fire'.

Nearer the coast, the forest was defended by morasses and a peculiar terrain which was neither land nor sea. The ocean tides formed temporary islands which looked like shipwrecked vessels in the fog, and then the surging waves would send giant oaks and their understorey sailing dangerously out into the shipping lanes, their crooked limbs spread like rigging.

✻

As the legions advanced through Outer Gaul that early summer, the threat of the northern warriors appeared to have been exaggerated. Some of the more sophisticated tribes – the Aedui of the Morvan, the Treveri of Trier, the Remi of Reims – had diplomatically pledged allegiance to Caesar. Having attended the latest war council, the Remi were able to provide him with impressive statistics on the size of the Belgic armies. According to the Gaulish census, a total of

---

* See Map 1: The geography, resources and curiosities of ancient Gaul.

298,000 soldiers belonging to fifteen different tribes were ready to take up arms against the Romans.

Thus far, only one battle had been fought. Belgic warriors had besieged the Remian town of Bibrax, twenty miles north-west of Reims, but the Romans had easily prevailed. Seemingly indifferent to their losses, the Belgae had observed the tactics of the Romans, retreated to their camp – which, to judge by the smoke of their fires seen at a distance of two miles, was fully eight miles wide – then returned home to fight on their own ground. Three other tribes had since surrendered to Caesar, most recently the Ambiani of Amiens.

In that fertile part of northern Gaul, the legions had rested for a week or so, consuming the grain and livestock, and imposing an early harvest on their hosts, who would suffer a hard winter. Then they set off across the plains of Picardy and marched east for three days until they reached the edge of the Ambiani's territory.

After crossing the deserted buffer zone, they entered the dominion of a different people. The Nervii were said to be 'the most barbarous and remote of the Belgic tribes'. To a Roman eye, the marshes and thickets were signs of brutish neglect, but the well-engineered hedges showed that Nature had been assisted rather than abandoned. The ground became wetter and the long baggage-trains called *impedimenta* were living up to their name.

On the third day, some Gaulish prisoners informed Caesar that a river called the Sabis lay ten miles to the east. Scouts were sent ahead and reported back that the Nervii were lying in wait on the far side of the river. They had been joined by their Belgic neighbours, the Atrebates and the Viromandui, and were expecting the forces of the Aduatuci to arrive at any moment.

The Romans pushed on to the river and, cresting a ridge, stationed themselves on the upper slopes of a low hill. From there, Caesar was able to examine the barrier-hedges which had been planted in strategic positions, presumably several years before, like a trap set for a gigantic beast. The hill ran steeply but evenly down to the river. As he later ascertained, the river was very wide but no more than waist deep. On the opposite bank, a hill with a similar gradient rose from the valley. On the Roman side, between the foot of the hill and the river, there was a clear, flat area about two hundred feet wide.

A few sentries on horseback were spotted along the riverbank, but 'the higher part of the hill was so densely wooded that it was hard to see into the interior'. If a bank of woodland is kept under observation, a human presence will eventually be betrayed by the wheeling of a bird of prey, the clatter of a wood pigeon or a breeze which affects only one or two branches. But no sight or sound gave the Romans any clue that sixty thousand warriors were lurking in the forest.

*

The battle that was about to be fought on the banks of the Sabis between sunrise and sunset has lost its place in history. This obscure act of genocide on a summer's day in the late Iron Age is the earliest recorded event in the two-thousand-year-long saga which saw the centres of European power shift from the Mediterranean to the North Sea. It was here that a Roman army first fought hand to hand with warriors who lived on the edge of the Oceanus Germanicus.

In the vanished world of small places where most people lived their lives, this is also the first ordinary location to be plucked from the infinite mass of earthly detail. Nothing proclaims its importance: there are no commemorative plaques, let alone a visitor centre; the only hint of carnage is the name of the Rue de l'Abattoir. No monument or settlement distinguished the site in 57 BC and no Celtic or Roman remains have been found. It was chosen by the chaos of war and would have slipped into oblivion along with all the other people and places of protohistory if Julius Caesar had not described it with such myopic concentration that it can still be identified today.

The legions arriving from the region of Amiens had reached what is now Hautmont, a suburb of the industrial town of Maubeuge, six miles from the Belgian border. They camped on the edge of a wood which belongs to the profusely littered but still ecologically valuable Mormal massif.

Some of the native trees on the rising ground above the River Sambre are probably remnants of the Arduenna Forest, but the hedges which shield the houses of Hautmont are privet and conifer – species that would have been familiar to the Romans but not to the Nervii. The hedges are tended by householders armed, in defiance of injury and futility, with hedge trimmers, leaf blowers and chainsaws. The ArcelorMittal steel factory has planted itself on the conveniently flat ground which extends two hundred Roman feet from the river. Cycling to Hautmont in the spring of 2018, I was surprised to see how swiftly the modern scene could fade when confronted with the muscular evidence of the original topography.

In studying *De Bello Gallico*, Napoleon Bonaparte was puzzled by Caesar's tactics. The camp was still being fortified and the baggage-trains dragged into position when Caesar sent a squadron of cavalry with archers and slingers splashing across the river towards the wooded hill. No one had been ordered to scout the woods and plumb the dark interior. As the advance guard reached the other bank, a band of half-naked warriors rushed out at the cavalry then vanished into the trees 'where no one dared to follow'.

From the rim of the plateau, near the upper end of the present-day Rue du Vélodrome, the Romans would have seen only the wall of vegetation, but for the Nervii, with the sun at their backs, the deciduous woodland offered countless observation posts from which to track the glint of Roman armour. Scanning the top of the opposite hill, they spotted the leading baggage-train lumbering into the camp from the west.

> With such incredible speed that they seemed to be almost simultaneously in the woods, in the river and close at hand, they rushed up the hill to our camp which the men were busy fortifying.
>
> . . .
>
> There was no time to attach the insignia or even to don helmets and remove the shield covers . . . The view, moreover, was obstructed, as I previously pointed out, by the very thick hedges which were in the way.

Inexplicably, Caesar had launched an attack on an unseen enemy before all the troops and their *impedimenta* had arrived. The camp was overrun and the legions nearly surrounded. In his annual bulletins, Caesar rarely confessed to incompetence, but he knew that, in this case, the senators would be able to compare his report with other eyewitness accounts.

For a reason he had yet to discover, news in Gaul travelled faster than a Roman messenger could ride. The Treverean auxiliaries saw the cavalry and infantry flee in all directions like mice from a nest and sensibly ran away. They rode through the Arduenna Forest until they reached the Moselle. Once back in their chief *oppidum* near Trèves

(Trier), they informed their Senate that the Romans had suffered a shambolic defeat. From there, by the Saar and the Rhine, word would soon reach Rome. In the circumstances, Caesar could hardly pretend that victory over the Nervii had been a foregone conclusion.

※

With the enemy now close at hand, he was able to observe the tactics of warriors from another world:

> So great was their courage that when those in the front rank fell, the men behind stepped onto their prostrate forms and fought on from their bodies. And when they in turn had been hacked down and the heap grew higher, the survivors used the mound of corpses as a platform from which to throw darts at our men and to hurl back the spears which they snatched out of the air.

Even in that mayhem of his own making, unnerved by the alien terrain and a suicidal foe, Caesar had an eye for ethnological detail. Throughout his eight summers of campaigning and three winters of recuperation in Gaul, he collected intelligence on the civilization he had come to plunder and destroy. He had local informants, a travelling library and a Gaulish friend, Diviciacus the Aeduan, a Druid intellectual and politician who had addressed the Roman Senate. Faced with the Belgic corpse-rampart, he knew that he was witnessing the military potential of a belief in reincarnation – for a Celtic warrior, death in battle was the doorway to a new life, and 'the dread of death is thereby negated'. He also knew the Celtic name of his opposite number and its ominous connotations: 'The Nervii rushed towards the camp under the command of their supreme leader, Boduognatos.'

Boduo-gnatos or 'Crow-born' was the Son of the Crow. In its other forms, 'branos' and 'brennos', the all-seeing, never-dying Crow was familiar to Romans in the guise of two great Celtic generals: the Brennos whose army had entered Rome in 387 BC and massacred its population, and the Brennos who had ravaged the temple of Delphi in 279 BC. In the collective memory of Romans, the Celts were the ancestral threat which hovered over the fortress peaks of the Alps.

That Celtophobia is evident everywhere in Caesar's account. With their pan-Gallic federations, democratic institutions, meritocratic education system and advanced vehicular technology, the Celtic tribes were in several ways more sophisticated than the Romans. They, too, traced their descent from the Trojans and a demi-god who appeared to be an avatar of Hercules. But in Caesar's patrician mind, they belonged to a primeval wasteland. His vision of Gaul was a waking nightmare: private, habitable space was infinitely contracted and accessible only by 'unknown and hidden routes', while all around, distance and time expanded to the edges of creation.

The towns of the Gauls, called *dunon* in Celtic and *oppida* in Latin, were perched on hilltops from which entire regions could be mapped and memorized in a moment. Caesar himself spent several months in the wealthy Aeduan town of Bibracte, with its panorama embracing the Alps and the Massif Central. But in the reports later published as *De Bello Gallico*, views are either restricted by vegetation or narrowly focused on the smoke of enemy campfires and the dust of an approaching horde.

The continent-spanning legends of the Gauls and the geometrical organization of their *oppida* suggest a mastery of space which the Romans lacked, sometimes to a ludicrous degree. Roman maps were so poor that, without the aid of native scouts, Caesar sometimes had little idea where he was in relation to the mountain ranges of Gaul and the road back to Rome. Why he believed that the territory of the Carnutes (the region of Chartres and Orléans) formed 'the central region of the whole of Gaul' remained a mystery until, after reconstructing the chaotic Roman map of Gaul from Ptolemy's coordinates and written descriptions, I saw Carnutia exactly where Caesar imagined it to be, in the middle of the misshapen land mass. (Fig. 1.)

The vocal telegraph of the Gauls could transmit a complex message in several directions at once over one hundred and sixty Roman miles at a speed of fifteen miles an hour. This implies a precisely surveyed network of listening posts covering about two hundred thousand square miles. Away from the main arteries, Roman messaging was crude by comparison. Three years after the Battle of the Sambre, in a neighbouring district of Belgica, two of Caesar's generals and their troops were tricked into entering a wooded ravine: warriors emerging from 'a hidden place' cut them off at both ends. When news finally reached him, Caesar sent orders to a third beleaguered general, Quintus Cicero. His letter was 'written in Greek characters' in case it was intercepted – a questionable ruse, since the Gauls used the Greek alphabet. The messenger was supposed to circumvent the blockade of Cicero's fort by attaching the missive to the thong of a spear. Creeping as close to the camp as he dared, he flung the spear. It stuck high up in one of the watchtowers and remained there unnoticed for nearly three days.

In the dreamlike spaces of Outer Gaul, the meticulous description of a particular location provided a certain psychological comfort: at least one minuscule part of the map could be magnified into an exact picture of reality. In the miniature world of the battle scene – two hills, a riverbank, some hanging woodland and a maze of hedges – Caesar knew exactly where he was.

✻

While the Nervii were impaling Romans on their own spears, the two legions led by Caesar's second-in-command, Titus Labienus, had crossed the river and occupied the enemy's camp. 'From that higher spot they gained a view of what was going on in our own camp.' The whole battle could now be comprehended at a glance – the panicked horses, the encirclement of the overcrowded camp, the Nervii springing from the spongy morass of their comrades' corpses. At Caesar's side, the men of the Seventh Legion turned their backs on the Twelfth to form a double front.

Only from the top of the Rue d'Alsace and Rue de la Fontaine is there a clear line of sight to the Roman position, between the hedges and brick houses of Hautmont. From somewhere near that vantage point, 'sacrificing everything to speed', Labienus sent the Tenth Legion clattering down the hill and up the other side. Cars entering the precipitous street from left and right and the sweeping bend at the supermarket car park before the bridge make it easy to imagine the fear and the force of the charge.

Bravery and renewed resolve may have played a role in the reversal of fortunes, as Caesar says, but his account of the later stages of the battle suggests a more decisive factor. Even without artillery, a wooded area fought over by forty thousand Romans and seventy thousand Gauls (including the Nervii's allies) would have been ravaged and exposed. The dénouement clearly implies enhanced visibility. This was the key to the Roman victory, and perhaps it was here on the banks of the Sambre that Caesar discovered the solution to the problem of the impenetrable hedges.

The enemy to be vanquished above all was the Gaulish terrain. The following year, late in the season, just before the first storms of autumn, Caesar was fighting the Belgic tribes who lived in the rolling country of fields and forest between the Pas-de-Calais and Flanders. The final engagement took place somewhere north of Amiens. Like their Nervian neighbours, the Menapii and Morini rushed from 'their uninterrupted expanse of forest', attacked the legions and retreated into the woods. 'Some of our men were lost as a result of pursuing them too far into those tangled abodes.' Then Caesar ordered his soldiers to exchange their swords for axes, and they set about the job of felling the silent army of trees. 'In only a few days, a great open space was cleared with incredible speed.'

With Nature disarmed, the human threat could more easily be neutralized. On the banks of the Sambre, the legions completed their victory with a massacre. While the killing proceeded, Caesar was deciding what to do with the women, the old men and the children who had taken refuge in the flood plains and the swamps. In a single day, the Nervii had lost 'all but three of their six hundred senators'; the sixty thousand warriors were reduced to 'scarcely five hundred able to bear arms'.

'In order to be seen to show clemency to those who were wretched and begging for mercy', Caesar spared the survivors. He could afford to be merciful because, in any case, according to the post-battle estimates, 'the race and name of the Nervii had been well nigh eradicated'.

☙

There are photographs of helmeted soldiers trudging through the rutted mud on the outskirts of Maubeuge. The wrecked landscape is almost treeless – precisely the kind of fighting conditions that Caesar would have wanted. In August 1914, Maubeuge, which guarded a key invasion route to Paris and the Marne, was besieged by the German First Army. The wooded hills on either side of the Sambre where Caesar had annihilated the Nervii in 57 BC were one of the main centres of resistance. After two weeks of bombardment, large numbers of French soldiers (variously estimated at thirty, forty and fifty thousand) were taken prisoner. But as General Joffre reported at an inquiry into the catastrophic surrender, the Germans would have broken through the line much sooner were it not for the men of Maubeuge who, 'at the first call to arms, had left their families and firesides and rushed to the aid of the fatherland'.

A generation after Caesar reduced the united tribes of Gaul to slavery and murdered approximately one million people, most of the hilltop *oppida* of the Gauls were abandoned for new towns in the plain. A well-maintained system of long-distance roads made it look as though the inexplorable tracts of forest and mire evoked in *De Bello Gallico* had ceased to exist. (Fig. 2.) The Gaulish villages, cosily surrounded by cool and shady woods, as Caesar had observed, were subsumed into the large estates called *villae*. Rectangular wheat fields, usually unhedged and unfenced, ran perpendicular to the roads that would carry the surplus wealth away to Rome. When travellers saw the smoke of a great fire in the distance they would think of burning stubble rather than rampaging barbarians.

Long after the pacification of Gaul, when the old Celtic language was dying out and could be heard only in forgotten, isolated places, and when the Druids who escaped the imperial purges taught at universities instead of officiating in groves of oak, even the Gallo-Roman citizens who took pride in their Celtic ancestry knew little of the ancient ways. The natives of the land once referred to by the Romans as Gallia Comata ('Hairy Gaul') were associated, as they are today, with mysticism and magic. To the Romans, they were an enigmatic people, just as the Romans in turn would be a mystery to generations who grew up in the ruins of their temples and amphitheatres.

Caesar himself would come to be seen as a hero of legend, a builder of roads and castles who had brought civilization to a benighted world. Most of the ancient fortified sites called 'Camp de César' had actually been small or medium-sized *oppida* of the pre-Roman period. They tend to be found on low hilltops, near rivers and away from any later settlement.

The Gauls' understanding of the landscape is hard to recapture without an aerial view. These 'Caesar's Camps' can sometimes be identified on a map, but on the ground, they can be surprisingly elusive. I have sometimes been standing in the camp itself, checking the coordinates, when the arc of an earth bank gradually became perceptible and the roundness of the Gaulish *oppidum* emerged from the jumble of mounds and vegetation.

In the absence of walls and foundations, the historical treasure of these sites is the location itself with its comfortable adaptation to the topography and its unexpected vistas. If the ground is bare or stony, there may be fragments of pottery and scatters of pebbles used in slingshots. It is not unusual to hear wingbeats or the scurrying of a creature that has made its home in a thorny hedge. Since the Gauls rarely built in stone, these living hedges are practically the only Gaulish structures to have survived for two thousand years.

•

2

A Home in Gaul

For a wealthy family in late-Roman Gaul, choosing a home in the country was, in theory, a simple affair. The villa had to be near a well-made road so that slaves and provisions could be brought in. There should be a vineyard unchoked by barbarous brambles, sweet-smelling gardens with trellises and arbours and a waving sea of wheat. Hardly any new villas were being built, but the second-hand residence should at least be in a solid state of repair, preferably endowed with original features such as Italian marble cladding, built-in glazed bookcases and functioning baths or, failing that, a warm spring where a vapour pit could be dug under a roof of wattled hazel and filled with red-hot stones.

Estates in Gaul were on the large side – sometimes more than two thousand acres – which meant that, in remote or hilly regions, they were exposed to wandering bands of thieves. Some were designed to withstand a siege, others were defended by the difficulty of finding them. The rural domains of Gaulish aristocrats were widely scattered and their visitors often came from far away. Local maps were non-existent and if the main roads had become impassable, it could be hard to provide clear directions, as a guest invited to two neighbouring villas on the edge of the Cévennes politely hinted in a letter written in the early 460s:

> Sharp-eyed scouts had been posted to look out for us, not only on the public roads but also on the winding shortcuts and the sidetracks used by shepherds, so that it was quite impossible for us to slip past the friendly ambush.

Satisfying all these criteria – comfort, security, elegance and productivity – was practically out of the question. It was advisable, in fact, to abandon the dream of rustic tranquillity and to acquire a suburban property, just far enough from town to escape the smells of tanneries and the effects of any civil disorder such as a slaves' revolt. Much of the Gaulish countryside was now in the hands of barbarian Visigoths, Burgundians and Franks, who had either fought as allies of Rome or been invited to colonize farmland that would otherwise be ravaged by even wilder barbarians from east of the Rhine. (Fig. 3.)

The towns themselves, where political power resided, were re-assuringly Gallo-Roman. Their high-ranking inhabitants proudly proclaimed their Celtic ancestry: major cities such as Lutetia, Durocortorum and Augustonemetum had regained their tribal iden-tities and were now called Parisius, Remis and Arvernus. As Roman citizens, Gaulish nobles were, by definition, Christian. The quaint customs of their forefathers had long since been abandoned. No visitor would now expect to find his Gaulish host festooned with heavy gold jewellery, insisting on sharing his own bed and showing off the severed head of an enemy preserved in cedar oil. The beautiful timber mansions and temples of the ancient Gauls were just a memory. Their *aedificia* (houses or villas) were mentioned twenty-three times in Caesar's *Gallic War*, and in thirteen cases, the noun was attached to the verb *incendere* (to burn). But it was not unusual for a modern house to contain echoes of past splendour in porticoes and painted walls and even mosaics depicting mythical heroes grappling with savage beasts or Christian martyrs suffering unspeakable torments with a smile.

The public buildings were in a state of barely arrested decay. Not even the former capital of Gaul, Lugdunum (Lyon), could mirror the luxurious grandeur of Caesar's Rome. But since the Eternal City had been vandalized by Alaric and his Goths in 410, Gaul was probably the safest part of the tottering empire. With its ancient traditions of internal migration and inter-tribal cooperation, it was well equipped to reach an accommodation with barbarians.

In 414, when this tale of two very different ideal homes begins, Goth and Roman had lain down together in an uneasy peace. Alaric's successor Ataulf had crossed the Alps from Italy with an army of Goths. But Ataulf, it was said, had wearied of his own people's 'un-bridled barbarism', and so, instead of turning southern Gaul into a Gothic kingdom, he had married the half-sister of the Roman emperor Honorius at Narbonne. In one form or another, the empire would persist. As though to anoint the alliance, a rival emperor, Jovinus, who had been supported by some prominent Gaulish aristocrats, was obediently disposed of by the Prefect of the Gauls, who made a point of personally cutting off his head.

✿

In this long evening of the Roman Empire, when more than half of Gaul was occupied by trouser-wearing Goths with little interest in Latin culture, villas could still be found on the outskirts of Narbonne which a land agent would have had no difficulty selling to a discerning customer. On a shady terrace with a glass of Falernian wine to hand or some acceptable local substitute, it was possible to imagine that Rome's power had never dwindled. The Gallo-Roman poet and diplomat Sidonius Apollinaris described the home of his friend Consentius, nine miles west of Narbonne, between the coastal lagoons and the first undulations of the Corbières hills. The year was 478, but the prose and the vision it yearningly evoked in flattering exaggerations belonged to a period when the sun of the empire was still rising over the fertile lands between the Ocean and the Alps.

> Situated near town, river and sea, it yields a rich crop of visitors and food with which to feed them. When first approached, it has a charming aspect, with very high walls artistically constructed in accordance with all the rules of architectural symmetry. Then there are the chapel, the majestic porticoes and the baths which can be seen shining from afar, as well as fields and streams, vineyards and olive groves, the entrance court and esplanade, and a most delightful hill. In addition to the abundant store of furniture, there is the treasure of a well-stocked library. When the master himself is in residence, devoting himself equally to the pen and the plough, it would be hard to say which is better cultivated: the land or its owner's mind.

A hundred years after Sidonius celebrated this idyllic domain, the villa was abandoned. Nothing now remains of Consentius's paradise but a corrupted place name – 'Conscience' – attached to a farmhouse and a piece of ground, a straight road running through the vines, and the fragments of dinner plates and wine amphorae which sometimes come to the surface of the stony soil.

✿   ✿   ✿

Not long after the marriage of Ataulf the Goth and Placidia the emperor's half-sister, a man and his wife, with their servants, slaves, tenant farmers and men-at-arms, left the craggy fortress-town of Segustero (Sisteron) and headed into the high, hilly region above the left bank of the Durance.

Segustero was a former tribal capital near the border of the old Roman provinces of Gallia Narbonensis and Alpes Maritimae, which now formed part of the Diocese of Vienne. It was served by a road which ran from the Mediterranean to the Rhone, but to the east, there were no roads and scarcely any signs of settlement.

Tracing the torrents up through a puzzle of gorges and ravines, in the deep shadows under dazzling walls of limestone, they came to a narrowing pass. This is the point at which a walker who intends to spend the night in a civilized place might decide to turn back. Here, in the early fifth century, a cart track was pickaxed through a cliff, then lost to landslips for over a thousand years.

When I first saw it in 2008, I mistook it for a modern replica: skilfully carved into a rippling rock face, a long inscription records a house removal which took place in about 414. Unvandalized after sixteen hundred years, the inscription can be read quite easily with a slight craning of the neck.

CLAUDIUS POSTUMUS DARDANUS, A NOBLE OF PATRICIAN RANK, FORMER CONSUL OF THE PROVINCE OF VIENNE, KEEPER OF THE OFFICE OF REQUESTS, HEAD OF THE IMPERIAL COUNCIL AND PRAETORIAN PREFECT OF THE GAULS, AND HIS WIFE, NEVIA GALLA, A MOST HONOURABLE AND NOBLE WOMAN, FURNISHED THE PLACE WHOSE NAME IS THEOPOLIS WITH ROADS CUT THROUGH BOTH SIDES OF THE MOUNTAIN AND GAVE IT WALLS AND GATES. THESE WORKS WHICH THEY CARRIED OUT ON THEIR OWN LAND WERE INTENDED FOR THE SECURITY OF ALL.

In that lonely spot where the only sounds are the cries of eagles and the skittering of stones falling from the bare slopes, this trumpeting of Roman dignity is like an eerie echo of something unheard. The clue to a mysterious Theopolis or 'City of God' lying somewhere to the east might have been dreamt up by a Gallo-Roman Jules Verne were it not for the fact that Claudius Postumus Dardanus existed: this was the man who had personally executed the usurper Jovinus. As

Prefect of the Gauls, he was the second most powerful official in the empire, and his wife Nevia was probably a relative of the emperor's half-sister Placidia.

So little is known of this twilight age that the wealth of information on a particular moment in an anonymous location looks like a practical joke. Why, after retiring from duty, did Dardanus acquire a seemingly worthless estate in the untravelled hills between Sisteron and Digne? When he and his wife might have lived in luxury, why did they have a track cut through solid rock to make their home in stony highlands where vines and olives would struggle to survive and the corn would shrivel before it ripened? And where – and what – in that wilderness was 'the place whose name is Theopolis'?

Dardanus had at his disposal the best intelligence sources. He is unlikely to have feared reprisals for his execution of Jovinus, but he knew that shortly after the marriage ceremony, Ataulf had fallen out with the Roman emperor. Eighty miles to the south, Emperor Honorius's commander-in-chief was blockading the Mediterranean ports with ten thousand mercenary Huns. Barbarians threatened Gaul from without and within. As Dardanus felt the quaking of the empire at his feet, he might have wanted to flee the approaching tide of anarchy. But there were many other, more convivial places where he and his family could have sheltered from the storm.

By an extraordinary stroke of luck, two other clues to this obscurest of late-Roman odysseys have survived. We happen to know that, at that pivotal moment in his life, Dardanus had begun to consider the official religion a matter of urgent, personal concern. As an experienced administrator, he naturally applied for information to the best authorities. His letters must have been taken by a foot messenger either to Segustero or Dinia (Digne) and then by the imperial post to Bethlehem in Judea and Hippo Regius in Numidia.

The first was addressed to Jerome of Stridon, who had translated the Bible into Latin, and the second to the theologian Augustine of Hippo. The letters have been lost, but the substance of his queries can be deduced from the replies he received. Like house-hunters before and since, but in his case quite literally, the former Prefect of the Gauls was looking for paradise on earth.

✵

The former province of Alpes Maritimae was one of the least Romanized parts of Gaul. It seemed to exist in a different age. The Trophy of Augustus (c. 6 BC), the ruin of which still towers above the sea on the former border of Italy and the Roman Province, listed the names of forty-five 'conquered Alpine tribes', but at least twenty-five other tribes were missing from the list. Some, such as the Capillati (the 'Hairy Ones'), were known only by the name that was given to them by the Romans. Others belonged to the Ligurian race which predated the civilization of the Celts. The scantily mapped hinterland was still yielding sightings of uncontacted 'half-savages' in the 1830s:

> They have sometimes been seen, perched atop a lofty crag, leaning
> on a stick, scarcely moving, and clad from head to foot in animal
> skins . . .

Seen from a distance or suddenly jutting out of a contorted land-scape, certain rock formations have an appearance of weirdness which tends to give rise to chilling folk tales and eyewitness reports of alien visitations. In the early fifth century, as the towns and cities became unsafe, habitations created by wind erosion and volcanic extrusion attracted monks in search of a refuge or a *locus* where heaven seemed to communicate directly with the earth. Caverns deserted since the Stone Age were converted into hermitages. Thirty miles south-east of 'Theopolis', the Grand Canyon of the Verdon, which remained unknown to the outside world until 1905, had a scattering of troglodytic recluses clinging to its dizzying verandas. In that mazy terrain, a man with engineers and labourers at his disposal had a wide choice of retreats.

Beyond the inscribed stone, after another four miles of gradual ascent, the wind grows stronger and the tang of thyme and fennel no longer hangs in the air. The eastern horizon then reveals the pinnacles and chasms of the Alps: they look like a frozen ocean at the ends of the earth. The land falls away to the south and there are two curiously shaped bluffs resembling the half-scrolls of a Celtic 'pelta' design. This is all that remains of a steep-sided outcrop which a document of 1030 calls the Castellum Dromone (now the Rocher du Dromon).

The crescent-shaped crags could be mistaken for the monumental gateway of a city that was never built. There is just enough pasture beneath the rock and on the hillsides opposite to feed a small community. Traces of a minor *oppidum* of the first to third centuries have been found, but there is no sign of the 'walls and gates' and no other inscription to confirm the suspicion that this natural ruined castle was once a fortification of Theopolis.

❉

Dardanus had been brought to this numinous place by a mixture of coincidence and deduction. He had noticed references in the Psalms to a 'City of God' or, in Greek, 'Theopolis': 'the city of God, in the mountain of His holiness'; 'the city of God, the holy place of the tabernacles of the Most High'. In all his experience of the wide empire, he had never learned of its whereabouts, but since it was mentioned in the sacred texts, there was every reason to believe that it existed.

He was especially intrigued by the words spoken by Jesus on the cross to the penitent thief almost four centuries before: 'Verily I say unto thee, Today shalt thou be with me in paradise.' Was the paradise of which Jesus spoke the same as Heaven, or was it somewhere else, and if so, where? Was it related to the 'promised land' sought by the Jews? The inscription implies that, when Dardanus learned of its existence, the place in the hills *'cui nomen Theopolis est'* already bore that beguiling name. He may have wondered whether, in this quiet corner of Gaul where hermits made their homes, he had stumbled on the gateway to another world or even found the true City of God.

Augustine and Jerome knew that the sober judgements of scholarship might come as a sad disappointment to this excited seeker after truth who was also a man of sweeping influence. Addressing him as 'the most noble of Christians and most Christian of nobles', Jerome gently suggested that the promised land which, to Jews, was a geographical reality, was not to be found on earth. However – since a purely allegorical reading might be deemed heretical – he did not absolutely deny its physical presence. Augustine similarly conceded that when Jesus talked of 'paradise', he might have been thinking of a particular location in the lower world.

Their letters were not entirely discouraging . . . With the empire on the brink of collapse, it took no great leap of the mind to visualize a cataclysmic end to civilization and to believe that somewhere in its ruins might be found the first signs of a kingdom of heaven on earth.

❉

The reality that cannot be doubted is the place itself. I saw it again in 2015 after finding a description of the area published by the provost of a local monastery in 1664. This was the account which first revealed the existence of the inscribed stone. Archaeologists and treasure-hunters have concentrated on the atmospheric Rocher du Dromon, but the provost, knowing the ins and outs of the landscape and the propensities of hermits, believed Theopolis to have been located in the environs of a hermitage called Trenon, 'where there are the remains of a very large town, and gold and silver coins are every day discovered'.

On the Trenon mountain opposite the Rocher du Dromon, a rough track leads to the site of the hermitage, which was last shown on a map in 1814. Now, there are only thorn bushes and bare rocks, but there is, quite unexpectedly, a magnificent view, extending far down the lower valley of the Durance towards Aix-en-Provence and the port of Marseille.

From that natural watchtower, a powerful man in a crumbling empire watched for the coming of Christ or an army of Huns swarming up the valley towards the Rhone and the city of Lugdunum. As the southern horizon turned red, that crepuscular state of the world might have been the thickening of night or the glimmer of a new dawn.

The 'remains of a very large town' seen by the provost in 1664 were probably used to build the neighbouring village of Saint-Geniez and the Chardavon monastery. No other inscribed stones have come to light, but names are subject to slower processes of erosion, and it is not quite as remarkable as it might seem that a clue to the original Theopolis is embedded in the place itself. Below the mountain where the hermitage stood, wedged into a side valley, there was once a hamlet called Theous. A small farm now bears the name. Dardanus might have heard the name or seen it written and, as wishful thinking worked its wonders, drawn his own conclusions.

'Theous' may well contain the Greek for 'god' (*theos*). In the fifth century BC, some traders from the Greek colonies on the Mediterranean coast might have established an outpost in the hills above the Durance. But a more likely origin of the name is the Celtic word '*tauus*' or '*tauius*'. Since Gaulish was on the verge of extinction, only a scholar familiar with the ancient tongue could have told Dardanus that the meaning of that word which held such promise was 'silent'.

✷   ✷   ✷

One morning in 467, fifty years after Dardanus and his wife immured themselves in the 'City of God', Sidonius Apollinaris, the proud son and grandson of prefects of Gaul, was leaving his native town of Lugdunum on a hundred-mile journey to his estate near Arvernus, formerly known as Augustonemetum. The estate had come to him by marriage to the teenage Arvernian princess, Papianilla, whose father, Avitus, had reigned briefly over the Western Roman Empire. Now that the old tribal territory of the Arverni was an isolated enclave of the empire, with the Vandals called Burgundians to the east and Visigoths in every other direction, Gallo-Roman aristocrats were more than ever inclined to consider themselves the true heirs and defenders of civilization.

The usual dawn fog must have lifted since, when his horse reached the top of Fourvière hill and he looked down towards the confluence of the Rhone and the Saône, he could clearly see the old cemetery with its burial mounds, both pagan and Christian, flattened by years of rain and snow. Some men were hard at work with spades: he could make out a patch of black earth where the soil had been disturbed.

On such a splendid morning, despite the dilapidation of Lugdunum and the neglected graveyard of his ancestors, the glory of Rome still seemed to shine. His grandfather Apollinaris had been buried there. He remembered his tales of Jovinus, the emperor who had been brought to power by the noblest of Gallo-Roman families, and of his executioner Dardanus, whom his grandfather had execrated as 'the sum of all vices'.

It struck him all at once: it was on the very spot where the men were digging that his grandfather had been laid to rest. He wrote to his nephew the following morning from a staging post on the road to Arvernus:

> I put my horse to a gallop and raced across the intervening space
> – o'er flat and steep at equal speed – impatient at the slightest delay.
> The cries I sent before me stopped them in their insolence even
> before I had reached the scene. Caught in the act, the villains were
> still wondering whether to stand or run away when I was upon them.

This desecration of a tomb by ignorant slaves was an insult to the family and a baleful sign of the times: if such crimes went unpunished, there would be no peace even for the pious dead. He saw the black sods piled up on the untended grave and his outrage was sharpened by a pang of conscience: neither he nor his father had ever thought to restore the collapsed mound or to mark the site with a stone.

Unless he happened to be travelling with ropes, lead weights and a wooden frame, the process of torturing the offenders would have occasioned some delay. Because Sidonius later became Bishop of Arvernus and a saint of the Catholic Church, the phrase '*torsi latrones*' has been delicately translated, 'I gave the villains a trouncing'. But the word '*torsi*' ('I tortured' or 'put to the rack') is unambiguous. A Roman law, which had been adopted by the Visigoths, required violators of tombs to be tortured and put to death, whether or not they had been following orders. His only misgiving was that he had acted without informing their master, the Bishop of Lugdunum, who was notorious for his leniency to inferiors. Fortunately,

> this just and holy man not only absolved me, he praised me for my righteous rage, declaring that in the eyes of our forefathers a deed of such audacity would have merited death.

The Bishop's discreet hint that torture belonged to a time of heathen savagery went unremarked.

Later on the same day, in a roadside tavern, Sidonius composed a long verse epitaph for his grandfather. He pictured himself (with all due modesty) as Alexander sacrificing to the shade of Achilles, and as Caesar paying homage to his presumed ancestor, Hector of Troy. Of course, the epitaph would also have to stress his grandfather's Christian credentials: 'after governing the Gauls', 'he was the first of his race to purify his brow with the sign of the Cross and his limbs with the water of baptism'.

Sidonius instructed his nephew to have the lines engraved on a slab of polished marble and to make sure that the stonemason spelled everything correctly. Arvernians were at last 'abandoning the scabrous Celtic dialect', but the Latin spoken in Gaul was still 'blighted with the mould of vulgar barbarisms'.

His duty fulfilled, his thoughts could turn to the goal of his journey, Avitacum, 'a name which sounds sweeter to my ears than my own father's name because it came to me with my wife'. Another day on the great west road would bring him within sight of the mountains where the Gauls had held out against the armies of Caesar. Then would come the busy outskirts of Arvernus and, beyond the city, between a steep hill and a serpentine lake, the estate where his wife and children were waiting to greet him.

✻

Reading the only surviving letter from Sidonius to his 'affectionate' wife Papianilla, one suspects that the daughter of the last Gaulish Roman emperor sometimes wondered whether she had drawn the short straw in the marriage lottery. 'I am sure you were never quite so gratified by any of my own honours', he wrote to her on the occasion of her brother's promotion to the rank of patrician. Ecdicius was the sort of soldier who would cheerfully lead a small band of trusted men against a whole army of barbarians.

As a diplomat and courtier, Sidonius took a softer approach. To him, a barbarian in whom a spark of interest in Latin culture could be kindled was preferable to a barbaric Roman like the hated Dardanus – the man who had fled a just punishment and disappeared into parts unknown. Shortly after his marriage, Sidonius had met the Visigothic king Theodoric II at his spartan court in Toulouse and, bravely enduring the lumbering conversation and the lack of music, wine and second helpings, had perfected the noble art of losing convincingly at board games: 'I am glad to be beaten by him when I have a favour to ask.'

Papianilla's impatience with her unheroic husband can hardly have been eased by the obsequious mini-epic he had written in praise of Emperor Majorian, the Roman general who had deposed her father. When Sidonius reluctantly accepted the post of Bishop of Arvernus in 469, she would be driven to distraction by his bishoply behaviour. Having never shown any interest in the moral teachings of Christianity, he began to act like a candidate for sainthood. According to Gregory of Tours,

> He would often remove silver dishes from his house without telling
> his wife and bestow them on the poor. And whenever she found out,
> she would be scandalized, and he would bring the dishes back and
> then go and give the paupers their equivalent value in money.

Now in his late thirties with no official function, he was spending a great deal of time at home. He played ball games and went hunting, composed poems in the classical style and corresponded with like-minded friends. He lived in his own little Roman Empire like a man slumbering peacefully in a collapsing building. Instead of treating the Avitacum estate as a power base, he used it as a holiday retreat.

One day during the summer heatwave, and for several days thereafter, Papianilla found him in the north-facing drawing-room writing to a friend.

> The ice is melting on the Alps; the parched earth is covered with the scribble of gaping cracks . . . We are all perspiring in fine linen and silks.

He was inviting the friend to Avitacum, but, as usual, he wrote with an eye to publication. The letter would be a well-crafted example of the epistolary art, bejewelled with erudite allusions to his favourite authors. While Papianilla's brother was campaigning against Visigoths, her husband was conversing with posterity. He was painting a verbal self-portrait of the Gallo-Roman noble in his domestic kingdom, seated in the comfort of a well-stocked mind with the scrolls and codices on their wooden shelves, savouring the best that this beleaguered remnant of the empire could offer. How much of this famous evocation was the description of a fantasy, I discovered quite by chance.

The villa, he wrote, lies at the foot of a mountain and faces north and south, with baths to the south-west. More than half the letter was taken up by the bath complex: 'the sobbing of hot water as it surges through the supple lead pipes', the brilliant light of the *tepidarium* 'which makes the bashful bather feel something more than naked', the *frigidarium* with its cone-shaped roof of tiles and simple stone instead of pretentious marble, the *piscina* or *baptisterium* where 'a stream enticed from the brow of the hill' roars deafeningly through the mouths of sculpted lions.

Bathed and perfumed, the visitor then has a choice of pleasant rooms. After the ladies' dining-room, a portico on the east side overlooks a long, curving lake. Then comes the winter dining-room with its arched oven, followed by another dining-room offering a panoramic view of the lake. To fill the idle moments between each course, the guests can watch 'the small boats furrowing the ever-changing field' and the fishermen spreading their trout nets. Maids, nurses and valets are always close at hand, snoozing but not asleep. After the meal and a stroll down to the wooded banks and the little lakeside harbour, the guests recline in the summer drawing-room while the chirp of cicadas, the twittering of swallows, the tinkling of cow-bells and the peeping of the shepherds' seven-holed pipes 'lull you into ever deeper slumbers' . . .

But I shall say no more, lest this letter's end become so distant that 'twould be autumn ere thou finished.

❖   ❖   ❖

It was impossible to resist this invitation to a luxurious Gallo-Roman villa, and so, a year after cycling to 'Theopolis', I added the presumed site of Sidonius's domain to another itinerary. The detour to Avitacum would fit nicely with a trip to Arvernus (Clermont-Ferrand) and the neighbouring mountain *oppidum* of Gergovia, where the Gauls had won a famous victory over Caesar. Using ancient texts to plan an expedition usually generates an adventure of some kind. There is, obviously, a risk that when the visitor arrives fifteen centuries late, the place will turn out to be unpleasant, boring or even dangerous, but in this case, there seemed to be general agreement that Avitacum is now the pretty holiday village of Aydat with its boating lake and its eleventh-century church of Saint Sidonius.

As we lunched by the peaceful lake in the noon-day sun, picturing Sidonius and Papianilla feeding the ducks, the vision faded: had that feeble rivulet which supplies the Lac d'Aydat ever 'foamed white against rocky barriers and plunged into the lake as it won clear of the crags'? There would have to have been some seismic rearrangement of the landscape, but the last volcanic eruptions in these parts occurred nearly nine thousand years ago.

Ever since the Auvergne began to market itself to tourists, the lovely Lac d'Aydat has been judged the best match for Sidonius's domestic Eden. But the topography is radically different, and the carved stone in the eleventh-century church which records the burial of 'two Innocents and Saint Sidonius' refers to a different saint: this was the Provençal Sidonius, believed to be the blind man healed by Jesus, who drifted miraculously to the coast of Gaul in an oarless, sail-less boat along with Lazarus, Martha and the three Marys.

The lake of Avitacum was 'seventeen stadia' (two miles) long. The Lac d'Aydat is only half a mile long, and all the other natural lakes of the Auvergne are smaller. Perhaps Sidonius had been describing the villa of his dreams . . . Leaving the phantom Avitacum, we cycled on to Arvernus, noting the implausible inconvenience of living fifteen hilly miles from the city in an area devoid of Roman roads. That evening in the hotel, I looked at the maps I had brought in preparation for the visit to the *oppidum* of Gergovia.

❋

The quietest and flattest route out of the city appeared to run through the charmless suburb of Pérignat. The road skirts a large plain, partially industrialized but mostly vacant. On my printout of the nineteenth-century État-major map, a faint caption explained this surprising emptiness four miles from the city centre. There, sprawling at the foot of Gergovia, with a network of pale blue lines indicating drainage channels, was the 'Ancien Lac de Sarliève'.

The 'former lake' at the foot of Gergovia had been drained by the Gauls a century before the Roman conquest. Sidonius's letter mentions a 'subterranean tunnel' by which the river left the lake: this was probably a relic of the old Roman drainage system. In the days of the first barbarian invasions, when infrastructure fell into disrepair, the channels had become blocked and the lake had returned. When Sidonius arrived in the 460s, the lake had been standing on the southern edge of Arvernus for more than a hundred years. It remained there until it was re-drained by a Dutch engineer in the seventeenth century.

The size of the lake and the local topography match the description in the letter. The foundations of a Roman villa at Le Pré du Camp, recently spotted from the air between a housing development and a road junction, could well be those of Avitacum itself. The archaeologists have found unusually little evidence of imported marble. 'My poor huts and hovels', wrote Sidonius, 'unenriched by the rigour of exotic marble, nonetheless convey a certain civic chill'.

In the noise and gracelessness of that *zone industrielle*, I heard the voice of Sidonius Apollinaris: he was vaunting the makeshift splendours of his earthly paradise in euphemisms wryly redolent of the Golden Age of Latin literature. It took this visit to the outskirts of Clermont-Ferrand to excavate the subtle ironies of the text. To a guest arriving from Lugdunum, the villa might have been a splendid sight in the middle distance; close up, there were signs of penny-pinching and decay: the lack of costly marble ('neither Paros, Carystos, Proconnesos, Phrygia, Numidia nor Sparta have installed their mosaics of varied stone'), no saucy coloured frescoes on the bath-house walls, a portico 'propped up with rounded wooden pillars instead of desirable monolithic columns', the winter dining-room 'often stained with black soot'.

The undrained lake of Sidonius's day was nothing like the leisure lagoon at Aydat: lashed by the wind, it spattered the house with spray. Some stretches of the shore were clogged with reed, sedge and algae; others were slimy and voraginous (full of bog-holes). The disagreeable details are almost smoothed away by the gracious prose, but the smile can be seen wilting on the visitor's face: would it really be possible to sleep through that chorus of frogs, cicadas, swans and geese, cocks crowing at dead of night, 'prophetic ravens saluting the purple torch of rising dawn in three-part harmony' and the 'frequent nocturnal song-contests of the unsleeping Tityri* of our hills'?

The *oppidum* of the Arverni on the mountain above the villa had been abandoned centuries before when the Gaulish confederation was crushed to form the foundations of the three Roman provinces, Gallia Aquitania, Gallia Belgica and Gallia Lugdunensis. (Fig. 2.) Now, in the interminable sunset of another empire, the seeker of domestic bliss had to make the best of a bad job. For Papianilla, the daughter of a Gaulish emperor, perhaps the bitterest blow was the loss of privacy. The grove by the lakeside was open to the public, and much of the estate had passed into the private ownership of those insomniac shepherds.

✿   ✿   ✿

Sidonius eventually earned the admiration of his Arvernian princess. In 469, the Bishop of Arvernus died. Impelled by a sense of patriotic duty (and certainly not by personal inclination), Sidonius agreed to take his place. The Church represented tradition and continuity. In the parts of Gaul that were now controlled by Visigoths and Burgundians, it was the only stable expression of Roman authority, and its bishops had the trust of the common people. Unless a bishop was openly antagonistic to his new overlords, he could act as an

---

* Tityrus is the pipe-playing shepherd of Virgil's *Eclogues*.

intermediary between the barbarian kingdoms and what remained of a Roman state.

Reshelving his beloved Roman poets, Sidonius forced himself to study the inferior prose of the Gospels and the Christian liturgy. Though he was embarrassed by his unworthiness, he made a good impression. Arriving one day at the Saint-Cyr monastery in Arvernus, he found that 'someone had maliciously stolen the book he used to conduct the service'. 'Yet he was so well versed in the ritual . . . that he led the service without pausing for a moment.' Since the future Saint Sidonius lacked the usual credentials and was neither an eminent theologian nor likely to become a martyr, this feat of memory would be hailed as a minor miracle: 'It was a source of wonder to everyone present, and they thought that it must be an angel speaking rather than a man.'*

Six years later, with an army of the ever-expanding Visigothic kingdom at the gates, Bishop Sidonius organized the resistance of the besieged city of Arvernus. It was the last stand of the Roman Empire in southern Gaul against the barbarians. Five hundred years before, on the mountain of Gergovia above the villa of Avitacum, Vercingetorix had won a victory over Julius Caesar. Knowledge of the location of Gergovia had been lost, and Sidonius had always avoided the dangerous field of History. ('Historical writing begins with a grudge, continues with drudgery and ends in hatred.') He was unaware, therefore, that he was fighting the second Battle of Gergovia, but he knew that he was standing in the footsteps of his ancestors.

Like Dardanus, Sidonius lived in the ruins of a world which was still in the process of vanishing and which would continue to vanish for the next five hundred years. Except when writing to other bishops, he showed no interest in that theological controversy of almost inde-scribable complexity called the Arian heresy: to the 'Arian' Visigoths, Jesus of Nazareth was a mortal man who had been born at a certain earthly moment; to the Roman Church, Christ was eternal and of the same essence as God. The practical function of condemning 'Arians' was to establish an absolute distinction between Christianity and Judaism, and, as the empire decayed, to affirm that the cultural wall between Romans and barbarians stretched through all creation.

---

* Gregory of Tours, *Historia Francorum*, II, 22.

The Sidonius who risked his life to defend Arvernus was the heir to a different tradition. When the Arvernians surrendered to the Visigoths, the root of his grief was not the victory of unorthodox Christianity but the sight of the Arverni – 'the brothers of the Latins and descendants of the Trojans' – reduced to starvation. Though he owed his authority to the Roman Church, he was acting like one of the priestly scholars of ancient Gaul.

Druids had formed the political, religious and intellectual bedrock of the Gaulish federation for at least eight hundred years. Outlawed and persecuted by imperial decrees, they had come to be seen as a subversive sect of mad magicians, but it was the institutions of the Druids that would guarantee the long-term stability of the Church in Gaul. The ecclesiastical boundaries which survived until the French Revolution were the tribal boundaries set and maintained by Druids. Their schools were the forerunners of universities and monasteries; important elements of their liturgy and rituals survived in the Christian Church. Like Sidonius, they had sometimes stood between two opposing armies to prevent a bloody conflict. They, too, professed a belief in the immortality of the soul.

※

Sidonius in his villa and Dardanus in his mountain retreat had no long view of the road ahead. For all they knew, the end of civilization and time itself was at hand. In 403, Jerome had rejoiced in the fact that, even in Rome, the old pagan temples were 'covered in soot and cobwebs'. Their stone gods were visited only by 'hornèd owls and birds of the night', while 'the crowds hurry on past their half-ruined shrines to the tombs of the martyrs'. In 472, Sidonius observed a similar situation in Visigothic Gaul, but the abandoned temples were those of the Christian faith:

> Diocese and parish lie desolate and untended. One sees the rotten roofs of churches fallen in, the flapping doors with their hinges torn away, the approaches of basilicas obstructed by prickly brambles, and, saddest of all, cattle recumbent in courtyards half open to the air and munching the grass that grows up around the altars. And this desolation reigns not only in the rural parishes, for even the congregations of urban churches are dwindling.

Yet in some parts of Gaul, even in those which had fallen farthest from the heights of imperial grandeur, there were signs of a brighter future. After his appointment as Bishop of Arvernus, Sidonius made a return journey to his home town of Lugdunum. By the cemetery where he had witnessed the desecration of his grandfather's grave, a new church had been built. The Bishop of Lugdunum had asked him to write a dedicatory poem that would be inscribed on a wall at the far end.

The foundations of the church were excavated in the 1970s. The ground plan was marked by coloured plastic blocks in a 'jardin archéologique'. As in the days of Sidonius, there is a view over Lyon towards the Alps, with 'the noisy public highway on one side and the Saône running up against the Rhone on the other'. The gaudy virtual reality of Sidonius's poem completes the fifth-century scene:

> High stands the shining church, undeviating in its rectitude. Its towering front faces the sunrise of the equinox. Within, the light sparkles and the sun is enticed to play on sheets of sun-coloured gold. Vault, floor and windows are bright with varied marble, and beneath the multi-coloured paintings, a mosaic of vernal green makes sapphires bloom in a field of verdant glass. The entrance is a triple portico set on proud Aquitanian columns; a similar portico stands beyond the atrium, and the middle portion of the church is filled with a forest whose pillars of stone stretch far away.

While the villa at Avitacum was a parody of Roman luxury, the new basilica at Lugdunum was the ultimate ideal home, with marble walls and columns, its treasures untainted by irony, 'for here is the place that all men seek, and the way that leads to salvation'. It had been built on the site of an earlier church, which probably replaced an even earlier Celtic temple. The neighbouring cemetery is such a confusion of pagan and Christian cremations and inhumations that archaeologists have been unable to distinguish the periods to which they belong. With its artificial forest and spangled meadow, the basilica itself might have been inspired by a Gaulish shrine or a Druids' grove.

It was only when measuring the angle of the foundations that I noticed Sidonius's luminous mistake. He naturally assumed that, like most Christian churches, the basilica faced due east, towards the rising sun of the equinox. In fact, the church was aligned so that the sun which shone through the middle of the forest of pillars on a particular day of the year was the pagan sun of the winter solstice. The alignment is so precise – with a tangent ratio of 11:7, which is the ratio of half a circle's circumference to its diameter – that the Druidic nature of the design is beyond doubt.

❃

Except in costume dramas, no age is consistent with itself or privy to its own history. The Christians of Lugdunum were praying in a church which had been constructed according to the beliefs and practices of another religion. For its unknown architects, 'the way that leads to salvation' lay in a different direction. Before the Druids, in times older than legend, there had been the builders of dolmens and menhirs, then a nameless Bronze Age civilization of which only a few mysterious place names and implements had survived the Celtic invasions. The gods and language of the Celts were disappearing in their turn, but the Roman deities who had usurped their shrines had been defeated by Christ, and now Christ himself, as Sidonius feared, was about to be 'ambushed' by heretical Goths.

The only unbroken line which runs through that muddle of traditions is a profound sense of place. When a home in Gaul could no longer be called home, by some mystical triangulation of geography, history and faith, somewhere in the great temple of Nature might be found 'the place which all men seek'. For some, it would be a portal to a better world, for others, the earthly paradise itself.

Four hundred years after the death of Sidonius, in the environs of 'Theopolis', five stone coffins on an east–west alignment were found under the rubble that had fallen from the Rocher du Dromon. In Charlemagne's empire, early Christian burials had acquired an aura of the days when Jesus and his disciples walked the earth and sailed to the coasts of Gaul and Britannia, and so it was presumed that, long ago, a saint and his followers had been buried in that remote spot. A small chapel was built for the pilgrims who came to the 'City of God' in search of a miraculous cure.

An undocumented excavation in the 1950s revealed the top of a staircase which is thought to have led down to the original, unexcavated crypt of the fifth-century mausoleum. The diminutive seventeenth-century chapel which stands there today is still occasionally visited by pilgrims, but there is no longer any trace of Dardanus and his household. Neither they nor the sainted Sidonius, whose remains were venerated in the church of Saint Saturninus in Arvernus, had discovered the terrestrial paradise, but in the ruins of the world they had known and in the blessed ignorance of death, they became the trusted guides who might show others the way.

3

The Invisible Land of the Woods and the Sea

I was walking as fast as I could in total darkness along a road near the coast of north-western Brittany. I had a bottle of water, a handful of cooked chestnuts and a leather bag containing some recently published American novels, most of which were set in the Wild West, present as well as past. This was in the late spring of 1987. It was half-past two in the morning and there was no moon. There were, I knew, every five hundred yards or so on either side of the road, small hamlets and isolated cottages, but no lights were visible. After climbing the hill out of Lannion, I still had ten miles to go. I was wearing a green Loden coat (which, at that time, was practically a uniform of French scholars). In effect, the coat was black, and I was hoping that my thumb would be sufficiently luminous to be noticed by a passing driver.

Seven hours before, I had been sitting in an elegant Second Empire drawing-room near the Place de l'Étoile in Paris, eating a comfortingly maternal but stylish Provençal stew composed primarily of chestnuts, the traditional staple of much of southern France. The Sorbonne Professor of French Literature – officially a friend but still mostly a mentor – had produced some unheard-of wine from 'derrière les fagots' which had the savour of a lost manuscript. I had come to Paris to collect some more books from a publisher in a street near the Odéon who flatteringly supposed that I might know which novels were worthy of translation into French. Those reader's reports were my only source of income. The return train fare from Lannion to Paris had already consumed more than half a dozen novels.

My plan was to take the midnight train from the Gare Montparnasse and arrive at Lannion in time to catch the first morning bus to Tréguier, a mile from the cottage we had borrowed. Since a second magical bottle had just been uncorked, this seemed an especially good plan. Claude (as I was not yet quite able to call him) stubbed out his *bidi* and exclaimed, 'Le train de minuit? Ah non! Mon cher Graham . . .' The train would stop at every station, and I would be unable to read or sleep for the clucking of Breton fishwives and their hens. Claude's wife, who came from Aix-en-Provence, objected to this Parisian caricature of savages infesting a remote peninsula. 'Mais si,' he insisted, refilling my glass: the aisles would be clogged with drunken fishermen and their lobster pots. 'Et la puanteur! . . . Non. On va vous trouver un hôtel.'

I pointed out that Margaret was expecting me back by morning, and so Vincenette was sent to check the train times. She returned with the timetable and a small bag of chestnuts. A taxi was ordered and paid for, and I left just in time to catch the earlier, slightly faster train to Brittany. The taxi driver who took me to Montparnasse had his own opinion of the revised plan: Lannion was a long way from Paris; he doubted that there would be a taxi at the other end, if they even *had* taxis there. 'You should have taken the midnight train. That way, you could've slept on the train and arrived in the morning.'

✿

Rennes, the capital of Brittany, lies far to the east of the Breton-speaking region. It was once a border town between the empire of Charlemagne and the petty kingdoms of Armorica. (Fig. 4.) Culturally and geographically, it seems closer to Paris than to the granite land of ragged coasts and gloomy forests, of 'Celtic' monoliths and the chapels of seven thousand local saints.

After Rennes, the 'train express régional' was almost empty. (The TGV network had yet to reach Brittany.) I changed at Plouaret for a rhubarb-and-custard-coloured diesel train which sounded like a very large and reluctant lawn mower. The only *puanteur* was that of the diesel fumes. I reached Lannion without having seen or heard a single hen. I had no intention of taking a taxi, which would have cost at least another two novels. In any case, the station forecourt was deserted. Half an hour later, I was out on the open road.

Several sections of the D786 from Lannion to Tréguier follow the line of a Roman road, but to someone who has suddenly lost the power of sight, no road is straight. In a novel, the stranger in a Loden coat would have struck a match, spotted the metallic sheen of a hazel stem and cut himself a handy walking stick with which to tap his way confidently along the asphalt. Instead, I limped along with one foot on the road and the other brushing the verge. At that rate, it would take nearly four hours to reach the cottage, with one chestnut every thirty minutes.

Somewhere before, or possibly after, a hamlet called La Ville Blanche, a light swept over the trees up ahead. A long, low van squealed to a halt. The passenger door was pushed open by a man in an oilskin cap. He inspected my face, gestured to the rear of his van and said, 'I warn you: you might not want to ride with me . . .' I took this to be a reference to my incongruously metropolitan appearance and told him that anywhere closer to Tréguier would do nicely. I clambered aboard and was hit in the face by a powerful smell of putrefaction. The dustman was delighted: 'Heh heh! Impressive, eh? It's waste from Lannion – mostly meat and veg.'

The stinking missile surged through the night and the miles fell away with merciful speed. The jolly dustman dropped me off on the main road, half a mile from the cottage, still chortling: 'Hein? C'est votre femme qui sera contente de vous revoir . . .' ('Your wife'll be glad to see you, eh?')

Tottering down the dark lane towards the hamlet of Le Guindy, I could smell the pigs from the other side of the little river. Since the pigsties were invisible from the cottage, the inexplicable stench had occasioned some anxious investigations of our primitive sewage system. A light was shining from one of the cottage windows. A minute passed, during which I became aware of my aura, then Margaret opened the door and uttered a phrase normally addressed to someone who has arrived late rather than several hours early: 'Where have you *been*?'

✽

The cottage in Le Guindy was dark even in the daytime. It crouched under a wooded slope on the cold side of a horseshoe valley. In Wales or western England, the valley would have been called 'World's End'. In Brittany, the name is applied to the entire western third of the peninsula: Finistère or *finis terrae*, with its innumerable bays and inlets, frayed and gnawed at by the sea. The valley was formed by a tidal tributary of the River Jaudy, which ferries the mud of the ocean seven miles inland. Here, the two traditional divisions of Brittany come together – Armor, the land of the sea, and Argoat, the land of the woods. The place had been chosen several years before by a Professor of French from Long Island as a textbook example of Breton culture:

> People think they know the country because they've seen a postcard and eaten in a *crêperie*. The French! . . . The French have no idea. You know Brittany? I'll show you Brittany. Take the cottage. Stay there as long as you like.

Professor Raymond Poggenburg had an unerring sense of typicality. Our immediate neighbour was a spindly woman dressed eternally in black. She was neither friendly nor hostile: she never communicated with us in any way. When she passed us in the lane, it was as though she believed herself to be invisible. The hospitable matriarch of the hamlet, Angèle Le Dû – whose name means 'dark' or 'black' – lived in a larger cottage on the corner. She explained to us that the silent one, her servant, spoke only Breton. Enthroned by arthritis, Mme Le Dû had afternoon tea served to us in a lamp-lit room filled with carved wooden objects and albuminous photographs of ectoplasmic figures who looked as though they predated the invention of photography.

Just before we arrived in Le Guindy, Mme Le Dû had had a nearby fountain restored. Its stone surround was only four feet high: veiled by the dripping ferns of the hillside, it looked like the monumental gateway of a dwarf's mansion. The spring was said to have been blessed by the patron saint of Brittany, Saint Yves,* but the ulterior and perhaps only purpose of Mme Le Dû's act of devotion was to confront the drinkers who staggered home from the Bar du Guindy with a reminder of their disgrace.

The professor, the son of an encyclopaedia salesman, had 'sold' us the hamlet as a place of tremendous significance. Had we but eyes to see, what might we not learn? . . . After a few weeks in what had

---

* Pronounced to rhyme with 'eve': 'Saint Yves était Breton, / Avocat et pas larron: / Chose rare, se dit-on.' ('The Breton Saint Yves, / It's hard to believe, / Was a lawyer who didn't thieve.')

seemed the dullest of backwaters, I began to think that he might be serious. This inconspicuous cul-de-sac was strangely important in Breton history. I later realized that this in itself was typical: we could have lived almost anywhere in western Brittany and still found ourselves at a nodal point of Armorican culture. Historical interest in Brittany is not concentrated in a few prestigious sites but scattered throughout the peninsula. With few exceptions, the prehistoric stones, sacred wells and Christian crosses commemorating forgotten battles or marking the graves of unknown heroes are so common as to be unremarkable, like the illiterate Breton lairds who could barely be distinguished from their serfs.

The lower part of the hamlet was called Le Merdy. In French, the name suggests 'Shitty Place', but before Parisian cartographers imposed their insulting orthography on Breton place names, it was the *maer ty* or 'steward's house'. A few minutes' walk downstream stood the manor which the steward had served. It was famed for two valiant knights who had fought the English and a medieval bully who was buried in a peat bog. His tortured spirit was said to live on in the guise of a large, presumably toothless black mastiff which had a nasty habit of jumping out at passers-by and knocking them over.

Saint Yves himself was born one mile to the east of the cottage in 1253. He was a relative latecomer to Brittany. Before him, beginning in the fifth century, flotillas of saints, including Tudwal, the first Bishop of Tréguier, had sailed with their flocks from Ireland, Wales and Cornwall, supposedly fleeing Saxon invaders. Eventually, so many seaborne immigrants had arrived that the Armorican peninsula was renamed 'Britannia minor' or Lesser Britain. Their boats, which legend said were made of stone, pushed up the long estuaries into the forested interior, where, typically, the saints were directed by wood-dwelling swineherds to the secret places which became their hermitages.

These expatriate explorers turned inwards from the stormy sea and headed for the low, heathy 'mountains' of central Brittany. They followed the old Roman highways which intersected at crossroads deep in the woods. Those who made landfall above Tréguier would have passed under the diminutive *oppidum* upstream of Le Guindy until the tug of the tide abated and they smelled soil and leaf mould instead of brine. None of the primitive parishes, which date from the 500s, were centred on a port, and none of their place names refer to the sea by which the saints and their followers had arrived. The maritime tribes known to Caesar as the Armoricans – 'the people by the sea', whose navy had ruled the waves from the mouth of the Loire to the coast of Britain – became the people of Argoat, the land 'by the woods'. The sea retreated into legend and, like the Breton fishermen's cottages with their windowless seaward walls, the peninsula turned a blind eye to its own geography.

❉   ❉   ❉

Nothing explains this strange desertion of the Breton coast – neither piratical raids nor a changing climate. No reliable records have survived. The evidence, if it can be called that, consists of the lives of the saints, none of whom were ever canonized by the Catholic Church. Their miracles (crossing the ocean on a leaf, turning pagans into stone) were considered too miraculous and their very existence was in doubt. The oldest hagiographies were written three centuries after the fabled migrations. The 'saints' themselves are so numerous that there must have been, on average, one saint for every two square miles. In reality, they were probably figments of collective memory conflated with local gods from Celtic or even older times.

Until the age of migrations, the history of Brittany had been the history of Gaul. Armorican tribes had fought in the pan-Gallic coalition against the Romans. After the conquest, Armorica had taken its place in the empire as a part of Gallia Lugdunensis. The Roman road on which I had hitched a ride was one of several links in the northwestern sector of a network which covered most of Europe. When Gaul was being swallowed up by Visigoths and Franks, 'Little Britain' had become a desirable destination. Sidonius Apollinaris knew a 'king of the Bretons' called Riothamus. He wrote to him in 472 on behalf of a friend whose slaves had been lured away to Armorica. Evidently, in those days, the far west was a land of opportunity, ripe for colonization and safe from barbarian invaders.

As the empire decayed, Armorica turned its back on Gaul. The scanty records suggest that it was ruled by regional 'kings' or 'chieftains' who spoke a language more closely related to British than to continental Celtic. Its contacts with the expanding kingdom of the Franks were sporadic. In the mid-500s, the Franks began to establish border forts and watchtowers in the region later known as the Breton

March. From then on, Brittany was practically an island, and so it would remain until the rickety but long-lived Duché de Bretagne was defeated in 1488 and incorporated into the Kingdom of France in 1532.

✿

Even indoor historians have resorted to physical geography to explain this exception to the national narrative. In the geo-historical view, the original sin of isolationism was committed by the Armorican Massif, which includes the Vendée, the Cotentin peninsula, the Channel Islands and the western borders of Normandy. The geographer Vidal de la Blache described Brittany in 1903 as 'a two-hundred-and-fifty-kilometre wedge between the English Channel and the Atlantic, heading out ever farther from the main routes of the interior and continental France'.

The other ancient land mass which dominates the geological map of France is the Massif Central. Between the two lies the watershed region of the Seuil du Poitou (the Poitou Gap). Here, the lanes are a poorly mapped maze. Panels by the side of the main roads which show the local section of maze look like diagrams of printed circuit boards and have to be photographed or memorized if the 'shortcut' is not to add several hours to the journey. To the north and west, 'the rocks grow darker, the trees close ranks, the fields and meadows break up into smaller units and take cover behind the hedges'. Instead of winding lanes, there are deeply shaded tunnels of vegetation called *chemins creux* (hollow ways), which stretch for miles without any visible exit.

These are the outlying defences of an enormous natural fortress. Its approaches were once protected by forests: Andaine, Brocéliande, Héric and Molac. But even when the forests had wizened, the bare moors and eroded mountains offered few vantage points from which to survey the whole country. The Monts d'Arrée, which are the highest hills in Brittany, never exceed thirteen hundred feet. No cols or passes connect one tight valley to the next, and no great river provides a convenient route to the interior. It is easier to plot an unexhausting cycle route through the Alps than it is to find a comfortable passage from one end of Brittany to the other.

This obstructive topography had a peculiar result. When the

Revolutionary government began to quantify its resources at the end of the eighteenth century, western Brittany was found to be one of the most densely populated regions in France, yet much of it appeared to be deserted. There were twenty-five thousand hamlets, farms and isolated cottages, which accounted for two-thirds of the population. The average settlement contained only twelve inhabitants. They were bedded down in muddy hollows like Le Guindy where enough vegetable matter could be collected to produce fertilizer for the thin soil. Sometimes, the only clue to a human presence was the smell of pigs.

✻

Brittany's 'non-nucleated' pattern of settlement made it virtually unconquerable. Nature had created the ideal habitat for hermits, smugglers and guerrillas. In few regions are geology and society so obviously connected. The rock is mostly schist, which requires regular manuring, and granite, from which nothing sprouts but standing stones. In porous limestone country, where the water seeps away into sponge-like caverns, humans congregate around the rare sources of water. On the impervious bedrock of Brittany, water is always close to the surface and settlements are smaller and more scattered.

While the population was hidden from view, the land itself seemed to vanish. Nearly all of Finistère and the Cotentin peninsula, which account for about half the coastline of the French mainland, are missing from French maps of France until the late sixteenth century. Sailors had always known that a promontory stretched for a hundred miles or more into the Atlantic Ocean. But the Roman geographer Strabo doubted its existence, and so it seems did every French map-maker until the late Middle Ages. It has been suggested that the expanding Kingdom of France was so slow to claim and conquer the West because this cartographic cloak of invisibility blinded it to its size and territorial importance.

In the blank spaces on the map and in the silence of history, almost anything can be imagined. The 'land of myth and legend' has been fictionalizing itself for the last sixteen hundred years. Its forests were the settings of medieval romances which are now an ineradicable part of its 'heritage'. Its innumerable micro-cults with their shrines to unofficial saints and deities have never quite been stifled by incredulity.

Near the northern edge of the forest of Paimpont, which is one of the largest remnants of the primeval Brocéliande Forest, the ruin of a prehistoric chambered tomb has been identified for more than a century as the tomb of Merlin the Enchanter. Prayers are regularly inserted into a cleft of the granite rock. On Easter Day in 2006, I unfolded one of those slips of paper. It was written neatly in French and signed with a woman's name:

> *Dear Merlin,*
>
> *You have made me happy. Please give me some magic spells so I can make others happy too.*

The Merlin who is supposed to have lived and died in the Brocéliande Forest was no more real than the Lady of the Lake. Even his name is a fabrication, a dainty alteration of the original British 'Myrddin' with its unfortunate hint of *merde*. But the wizard lives on in the minds of his devotees, and so the only prayer a historian could offer up would be a kind of sacrilege: 'Dear Merlin, though it would mean denying your own existence, please give me some hard facts so that I can share them with other people.'

❅ ❅ ❅

As though by magic, a figure emerges from the forest – a small man with a swarthy face, weighed down by a shield and a sword. He has waded through swamps and clumped along old Roman roads. Though timorous by nature, he has a cheeky sense of humour, which probably explains why he has been sent to this God-forsaken land a hundred miles north of his native Aquitaine. The name of this jesting chronicler is Ermold or, as he signs his published works, Ermoldus Nigellus.

'Little Black Ermold' is not the sort of emissary from the past a historian might have chosen: his four-part chronicle, *Poem in Honour of Louis, the Most Christian Caesar Augustus*, is written in flowery, singsong Latin verse which matches his talent for warping the truth. But until the late ninth century, Ermold is the only direct witness to Brittany who is not a ghost of legend. Only he can speak with the authority of a man who has muddied his boots on Breton soil.

Since the days of Sidonius, the Germanic tribes known as the Franks have established an enormous realm called Francia. In 818, four years after the death of Charlemagne, the Frankish king and

'Emperor of the Romans', Francia covers an area equivalent to most of modern France, Germany, the Low Countries, northern Italy and territories as far east as Bohemia. Charlemagne's son, Louis the Pious, has conquered Barcelona – 'a den of Moorish bandits', according to Ermold – and the country of the 'rabid Basques' beyond the Pyrenees. Only one part of ancient Gaul has held out against the Franks and retained its independence.

Louis the Pious, the first of thirty-five kings and emperors to be crowned at Reims, has discovered that his father's claim to have subjugated 'all of Brittany' is a vast exaggeration. ('All of Brittany' is the phrase routinely used whenever Frankish soldiers exchange blows with border Bretons and conquer a few feet of bog.) Frankish power in fact extends no farther than the no man's land called the Breton March, whose first governor was Charlemagne's general, Roland, the hero of the eleventh-century epic poem, *La Chanson de Roland*, who was killed by 'Saracens' (Basques) at the Pass of Roncevaux in 778.

This natural buffer zone, which still served a strategic purpose in the Second World War, was a waterlogged, unproductive swathe of country running from the tidal island of Mont-Saint-Michel to Rennes, then down the Vilaine to the river port of Redon and the coast near Vannes. Defence policy on both sides of the March consisted of launching occasional border raids, with the Bretons agreeing in principle to pay tribute or to show loyalty to Francia, for example by refraining from laying waste to Frankish lands east of the March and around the estuary of the Loire.

❋

Part Three of Ermold's chronicle describes an expedition led by Louis the Pious in 818. A Breton king called Murman (or Morvan), whose stronghold stood somewhere north of Vannes among trenches and swamps, was refusing to pay tribute to the Franks. In the usual way of propagandists operating as historians, Ermold justifies the invasion by dividing the people of Brittany into two contrasting groups: the inherently honourable natives and a noxious immigrant population of evil opportunists. This is one of the essential texts of early Breton history and the most detailed secular evidence for the legendary migrations.

In days gone by, that country was conquered by a hostile race which skimmed over the sea in their stealthy little boats. The Britanni, who came from the outermost edge of the world, are called Brittones in the Frankish tongue. Lacking land and battered by wind and rain, they took possession of farmland, though they did pay tribute to the Gauls, who, of course, were the inhabitants of the country in the days when the Brittones were driven here by the waves.

In this politically expedient view, the 'hostile race' which refused to bow to the Carolingian empire was not authentically Gaulish or Armorican. While the Franks were conquering territory to the south and east, the asylum-seeking Brittones had been left to breed and multiply until 'they filled up the fields'. The native population had been swamped by aggressive foreigners who, in their 'ignorance' and 'arrogance', dared to attack the Frankish state.

This crucial historical document is, by its nature, extremely suspect. Legends of migrant saints and reports of British mercenaries brought across the Channel by the Romans in the fourth and fifth centuries were used to justify annexation. Since Armorica could claim the honour of being the only true remnant of independent Gaul – and since the Franks themselves were immigrants from beyond the Rhine – it was necessary to prove that the ancient land had been corrupted by aliens. The Brittones, 'baptized and anointed with oil', could not be reviled as pagans; however, says Ermold, they were 'Christian only in name'.

Brothers rape each other's wives and they all live incestuously together, behaving in unmentionable ways. They make their homes in briar patches and sleep in bogs. They also delight in scavenging like wild animals.

This was the imperialist Frankish view, which Ermold puts into the mouth of Lantpreth, Count of the Breton March. Ermold was writing in Strasbourg, to which he had been banished for making an 'offensive' remark about King Louis. (He tells us this himself, without specifying the offence.) The king was not noted for his laxity or his sense of humour: his first act as emperor had been to purge his court at Aachen of debauchees. But having reached this delicate point in the narrative, Ermold was warming to his task . . .

The Frankish ambassador, an abbot whose estate borders King

Murman's domain, is about to obtain the king's submission when Murman's bewitching queen reminds her drunken husband of his duty:

> Thereupon, from the bridal chamber, with venom in her heart, issued forth the cunning wife of Murman, imploring his embrace. First, she kissed his knee and then she kissed his neck. Another kiss she planted on his beard and pressed her lips to his mouth and hands. She twirled and turned around him and he felt her practised touch. The artful woman yearned to serve him . . . At last, the wretched man grabbed hold of her, squeezed her with his brawny arm and, yielding to her desire, found pleasure in the actions of his wife.

This lingering scene of conjugal (and, therefore, legitimate) sex in which the muscly brute is expertly reduced to a state of post-orgasmic quiescence was hardly a dish to set before the Pious One. Even more imprudently, the recently disgraced Ermold steps through the frame of his narrative and we are listening to a living witness of that dark and distant world on the edge of the empire.

✻

He appears as though in an ancient photograph. The year is now 824. Six years after the defeat of King Murman, the Franks have invaded Brittany once again. This time, they are led by Louis's son Pippin, ruler of the sub-kingdom of Aquitaine. The details are smudgy, but the image contains clues which allow it to be traced to a particular region.

> Under Pippin's command, the Franks marched along wide roads, and the realms of the Bretons, criss-crossed in all directions, lay open before us. I fought there myself, with a shield on my shoulder and a sword strapped to my side, but no one suffered from my blows. Seeing this spectacle, Pippin burst out laughing and said, in amazement, 'Put that sword away, brother, and stick to words.'
> Then the Franks spread out through the fields and woods and the trembling swamps, and the population was obliterated, all their livestock perished, the wretched prisoners were led away and hacked to death.

This postcard from the early ninth century appears to depict a region just beyond the western border of the Frankish empire. The 'wide roads' suitable for marching are certainly Roman; the fields and livestock indicate agriculture, but there are also woods and swamps – all of which suggests the Breton March in the watery area south of Redon, where several Roman roads intersected.

Drafted into the Frankish army for this latest harrying of the Bretons, Ermold pops up in his own poem in an oddly self-incriminating cameo. The savage police action on the borders proves that Louis's defeat of Murman had been an episode rather than a conclusion, while the farcical ineptitude of the sword-wielding scribbler hardly inspires admiration for Frankish military efficiency.

In the background of Ermold's selfie can be seen the horrors of war – the destruction of livelihoods, the killing of prisoners, the vicious humiliation of a culture. Ermold had grown up by the River Charente, several days south on the same Atlantic coast, and his eccentric eulogy of Louis the Pious expresses something akin to ethnological interest and the empathy of a traumatized conscript.

> While the countryside filled with Frankish soldiers, the Bretons took to secluded paths in the woods. They sought out the food they had placed in swamps and ingeniously stored in furrowed earth.* Those poor wretched men were rounded up, along with every cow and calf. There was no escape; no clever tricks could hide them. . . .
>
> Wherever one looked, there was a Frankish soldier destroying treasures. As Caesar [Louis the Pious] had instructed, they respected the churches, but all other buildings were consigned to the flame-vomiting pyres. . . .
>
> A few of you Bretons appear in the distance, camped among thorns or dense bracken, giving battle only with a cry. Like the oak leaf which falls at the coming of frost, or in autumn showers, or when it rains on the warmest days of summer, the pitiable Bretons filled up the bogs and swamps like slaughtered beasts. There were violent skirmishes along the narrow paths, but those who were shut up in their houses offered no resistance.

✢

---

* An aromatic fatty substance known as 'bog butter', produced from either milk or meat, is sometimes found in Irish, Scottish and Scandinavian peat bogs, often in wooden containers. Most specimens date from the Iron Age. Ermold's text is the only contemporary written evidence of the practice, and the only sign that it was common in Brittany and in a much later period.

With this, the vision dissolves and the chronicle moves on to King Louis's pious mission to reform the monasteries and to proclaim the Christian unity of the empire. There is no further trace of Ermold, our principal guide to this period of Breton history.

Like some devilish enchanted manuscript, this priceless document not only reveals our ignorance of early Armorica, it half-erases what we *did* appear to know. Those glimpses of the Breton borderlands are blurred by Frankish propaganda and the spurious justification of military aggression. They therefore beg the question: did those migrations from Britannia and Hibernia ever take place on such a scale?

There *is* a historical reality behind the legends, but it belongs to a much earlier period, when the Bronze and Iron Age peoples of the western coasts traded precious metals, jewellery, tools and eventually wine. Ireland, south-western Britain, western Gaul and Galicia were the trading nations of a Celtic Mediterranean. Busy sea lanes connected Fisterra, Finistère, Land's End and Hibernia. In that lost world of commercial and cultural exchange, Armorica had been the crossroads of an Atlantic civilization.

Centuries later, when Gaul had become Francia and a curtain had descended between the Armorican Massif and the rest of the continent, a folk memory of that long-lasting civilization survived in tales of noble pioneers and holy migrants. Like the Stone Age menhirs which were carved into the shape of Christian crosses, the stories were reworked for a new, more inward-looking age. As the peninsula turned in on itself, legends of inspired adventurers gave a sense of common heritage to those scattered, land-locked settlements whose inhabitants were trapped by mud and rain in their tiny domains for months on end.

When France itself, that *finis terrae* on the edge of a continent, had come to view itself as the centre of the civilized world, and the shadow of the Eiffel Tower fell across the country as far as the western coasts of Finistère, Brittany would be seen as the opposite of what it once had been – monocultural, mono-ethnic, never changing. The strength of that dispersed society lay in its ability to resist conquest, but this was also its weakness. Even in the days of Ermold, the food 'placed in swamps and ingeniously stored in furrowed earth' implied a mole-like existence in murky hollows and leafy tunnels which could easily become a prison.

Not long after we left Le Guindy, the TGV finally reached Brittany. Many small communities that were bypassed by the new rail system felt the fear of increasing isolation. Homemade signs appeared on country roads protesting at this new invasion of Brittany by France.

The high-speed trains would cut through the capillary networks maintained by women like Angèle Le Dû. The French capital would suddenly be much closer in time, and in that backwater which revealed its fascination to us only in retrospect, the fountain of St Yves, the haunted dog and the silent servant would seem quaint and pathetic. A few months later, and I would not have met the happy dustman or navigated a Roman road in darkness, and I would have returned to the cottage in Le Guindy still smelling of a tobacco-scented drawing-room in Paris.

4

Time Machines

In works of fiction, time machines usually arrive at a particular historical moment and in a place where everything, except the machine itself, is in keeping with the period. The efficiency of time travel is greatly exaggerated: a road through time never leads to only one past.

Approaching Reims after a long day in the saddle with the hardest part yet to come – the rush-hour traffic and a maze of streets – something like a hallucination appeared on the horizon. It was the kind of mirage that can be produced by exhaustion and wishful thinking. At a quiet crossroads in open country, a smooth, straight track cut south across the chalky plain: it ran for about three miles on precisely the desired trajectory. At its distant terminus, amid the smudge of city buildings, rose the two towers of the Gothic cathedral.

I had noticed the track on the Michelin and IGN maps as a broken line labelled 'Ancienne voie romaine'. Usually, 'former Roman roads' are either undetectable or impassable, but in this case, the surface was firm and dry with a strip of low grass in the middle. It offered such a convenient shortcut to the centre of Reims that it was a surprise to see it so wonderfully deserted.

I stopped to take a photograph of the vision. Apart from the vapour trail of a jet, there was nothing to place the scene in the twenty-first century. This was Reims in the early Middle Ages – a huddle of hovels at the focal point of Roman roads leading north to the Channel ports and the Rhineland, and south to the Mediterranean and Rome. It could easily have been the place which the Romans called Durocortorum were it not for the white edifice which dominated the hovels like a twin-towered lighthouse on the edge of a sea of clouds.

The old road to Reims was a sign of continuity: it joined the empire of Caesar and Augustus to the Middle Ages and now to the present day. But as I raced to catch up with Margaret, I saw the cathedral shift slightly to the left. In that almost perfect scene of Roman exactitude, the religious centre of Reims was misaligned, or perhaps aligned on an earlier axis. An hour later, funnelled into the city by the successor of the ancient road, we arrived, as the Roman engineers intended, at the commercial hub of Durocortorum, now the Place du Forum. The original heart of the Remi's *oppidum*, where the Gothic cathedral stood, lay three hundred metres to the south. Only the tops of its towers were visible above the Bistrot du Forum and the offices of the Crédit Industriel et Commercial.

On the glass door marked 'Réception', a scrap of paper indicated that the hotel would reopen 'later'. A large dog was slumbering on the carpet. When I tried the handle, it twitched an eyebrow. I could hardly expect it to open a locked door, and so we left the bicycles in the courtyard and went to wait in the cathedral.

For an indeterminable length of time, we sat in a silent daze which might have passed for prayerful contemplation. Whenever I closed my eyes, the road was still spinning out its yarn. A priest was arranging some heavy glinting objects at the high altar; a small group of nuns gravitated imperceptibly towards the transept. Otherwise, the nave was empty, and yet, by some trick of the stonework, the vault was filled like the concourse of a railway station with the murmur of many voices.

✢

Two thousand years ago, beneath the roofs of an arcaded temple, there was the whisper of running water. A sacred spring lay at the centre of the *oppidum*. When Julius Caesar convened a council of the Gauls at Durocortorum in 53 BC, he would have visited the shrine and washed in the holy waters. After the pacification of Gaul, the temple became a bath house where travellers scrubbed and anointed their weary bodies. Acts of purification which are now performed in the privacy of a shower cubicle were not considered sacrilegious. After the bath house had fallen into ruin, a basilica was built on the site. It was there that Clovis, King of the Franks and founder of the Merovingian dynasty, was baptized by Saint Remi in 496.

The shrine expanded like a tree adding growth rings to its trunk. The only surviving son of Charlemagne, Louis I ('the Pious'), received the imperial crown from the hands of Pope Stephen IV at Reims in 816. By the Treaty of Verdun in 843, the Frankish empire was divided among the three sons of Louis le Pieux. The western third became the Kingdom of the West Franks, which ended a few miles east of Reims, but the power of its rulers was confined to the region of Paris. The rest of the kingdom was a puzzle of semi-independent fiefdoms.

The Carolingian empire had been more than just a tangle of transient borders. Haunted by the memory of greatness, the rulers of the politically fragmented realm of Francia knew that the Church and its institutions were the only guarantee of their spiritual and political authority. At the hub of long-distance roads, close to several borders, Reims was becoming one of the great centres of learning in northern Europe.

In the late 900s, three centuries before work began on the Gothic cathedral which replaced it, Archbishop Adalbero transformed the basilica into a state-of-the-art monument to the glory of God and the miracles of human ingenuity. The old Gallo-Roman crypt was excavated and restored. Treasures taken by invading Norsemen were replaced. The interior was darkly lit by windows which recounted the lives of Christian martyrs, and because Adalbero believed in the power of sacred noise, at certain times of day, according to an earwitness, the building shook to the sound of 'bells bellowing like thunder'.

The ecclesiastical library at Reims, which had once held little more than a basketful of mouldering parchment, was served by five or more scriptoria where monks traced the fading characters of ancient manuscripts – the word of God in Greek and Latin, the convoluted commentaries of the Church Fathers, the undoubted lives of saints. The older monks could remember scraping away at pagan parchment so that it could be reused. Now, those inky scrawls were being recognized as precious clues to the past. In the more advanced institutions, trained scribes copied miscellaneous texts from heathen times which few could decipher and even fewer understand.

*

Wandering scholars who entered that echoing palimpsest of stone saw wonderful things even before they began to explore the library catalogue. At the far end of the nave, clouds of vapour billowed up into the vaulted gloom as though the Roman bath house was still in use. Sunbeams pierced the painted windows and sent green, blue, red and yellow jewels dancing like moths across the floor. In one corner, the hours of day and night were measured by a 'mechanical clock' – a special kind of sundial which had no need of the sun.

At certain predetermined moments, the clouds would explode with a polyphonic din. This was not the wheeze of an organ's gasping bellows; it was the voice of the Holy Spirit: 'In a strange and wonderful manner, the wind emerging from violently heated waters' was impelled through 'brazen tubes' to burst out of 'many holes' as 'melodious cries'.

This is how the cathedral school at Reims advertised its excellence to the world, and especially to its rivals at Laon and Auxerre. The amazement of visitors is easy to imagine because the reality is just as baffling today: what was a steam-powered mechanism doing in a pre-Gothic cathedral six hundred years before the harnessing of steam? A fragment of the later Renaissance seems to have broken away like an exotic island from a disintegrating continent and drifted back to the barren shores of the tenth century.

These anachronistic devices from a time yet to come – the sunless sundial and the steam-driven organ – disappeared from the cathedral in about 1050. We know that they existed: these and other curious inventions are mentioned in letters written by their creator and in a remarkably rational account of his life composed in 996 by his pupil, Richer of Reims. But other mind-boggling marvels have either passed unnoticed or been consigned to the medieval museum of crazed misconceptions. The problem is that most of these miraculous contraptions were described only later, in the credulous idioms of the eleventh and twelfth centuries.

Modern historians have been no more inclined to examine these childish tales for clues than a detective would bother to obtain a witness statement from a monkey or a parrot. It can be as hard to interpret them as it is to make sense of the stories told by the stained-glass windows in the nave of Reims Cathedral. Those implausible tales are closer to us in time but more remote in mentality, for they belong to a period when the superstitions of the common people were settling like bats on every rafter of every church in Christendom.

✿ ✿ ✿

One day in the year 955, just before dawn, some monks were heading for the Benedictine abbey at the remote but prosperous town of Aurillac in the Auvergne. Near the hamlet of Belliac on what is now the Route des Volcans, a boy who was supposed to be guarding a flock of sheep was observing the sky through a shepherd's whistle – a tube of elder from which the pith had been removed. Intrigued by the sight of an infant astrologer, the monks stopped to question him. The boy gave his name as Gerbert and explained that he was counting the stars.

This local legend may be true in substance if not in detail. The boy who became the first French pope proudly confessed to his 'obscure birth': he had neither fortune nor noble lineage, and perhaps no living parents. A shepherd whose only company other than sheep was the starry flock above may well have thought to use his elder whistle as a sighting tube. This is more believable than the other folk tale according to which, when the boy was born, a cock crowed three times and was heard as far away as Rome.

The monks hastened on to Aurillac. Soon after, some wise men came out of the town and led the star-gazing shepherd back to the monastery. Thirty years later, Gerbert wrote to his beloved 'lord and father', the Abbot of Aurillac, perhaps remembering the mists which cling to the granite hills: 'Blind fortune envelops the world in its heavy fog.' Thus the future pope denied the role of divine providence as far as his humble self was concerned. Mere chance had delivered him to the abbey of Aurillac, which boasted a scriptorium and a library. In that miniature universe, he found the untranslated knowledge of several centuries lying about like an abandoned banquet.

Eleven years passed happily in the study of rhetoric, Latin grammar and logic. Gerbert grew in wisdom, and, as the Gospel says of the adolescent Christ, 'all who heard him were amazed at his understanding'. He would normally have been trained for ordination as a priest, but Gerbert's teacher cleverly decided to leave him untethered: having taken no vows, he would be free to browse among the secular ruins of the pagan past. It was in this opening of doors to the pre-Christian world that Gerbert chose to see the hand of God. He wrote to his pupil and friend, Otto III of Germany, two years before ascending to the papal throne in 999:

What more evidence of the divine can there be than that a man, as if by hereditary right, should seek to recapture for himself the treasures of Greek and Roman wisdom?

❊

When Gerbert was on the verge of manhood and had gobbled up all that the library of Aurillac had to offer, the abbot one day received the visit of Ramon Borrell, Count of Barcelona, who was on a talent-spotting tour of religious establishments. The omnivorous student was in need of fresh pastures, and perhaps, as a chronicler stated more than a century later, the boy had become something of a nuisance '*pro morum insolentia*' ('by the insolence of his manners' or 'the strangeness of his behaviour').

Since Gerbert's teacher was not a man who selfishly clung on to his favourite pupils, he inquired of the visiting Count whether there were 'any in Spain who had attained to excellence in the sciences'. The name of Atto, Bishop of Vic, was mentioned. A few days later, when the Count rode south towards the valleys between the Pyrenees and the Mediterranean, his train included an excited young man who saw treasures of the mind gleaming on the horizon.

If the roads were passable and bandits were busy elsewhere or had recently been hanged at crossroads, the Count of Barcelona and his retinue would have reached the sea in less than a week. At Narbonne, they turned south along the coast then cut inland at Perpignan. After fording the torrents which rush down from the snowy peak of the Canigou, they climbed the valley of the Tech to the Col d'Ares, which now marks the border of France and Spain. In crossing the pass, they entered a fortified buffer zone between Christians and pagans that was neither Francia nor Hispania.

The Spanish March, roughly equivalent to modern Catalonia, had been created by Charlemagne at the end of the 700s. It divided the kingdom of the Franks from the Saracens who had conquered most of the Iberian peninsula. The March was now ruled by the Count of Barcelona as an independent territory. A few miles to the west began the vast Caliphate of Córdoba. There on the frontiers of Christendom, the future pope looked over to another world and felt its powerful fascination. The Saracens, who followed Muhammad, were known to have commerce with demons, who provided them with them infallible incantations, but they also possessed works of science, cartography and philosophy which had been lost to Christians in the fall of Rome and Byzantium.

The prodigy from Aurillac was taken to the monastery at Vic, but the intellectual riches he amassed during his three years of study suggest that he spent most of his time at the Benedictine abbey of Ripoll in the hills to the north. The library at Ripoll contained almost a hundred volumes (more than the Vatican in Rome), including translations of Arabic manuscripts. Reports that Gerbert managed to creep across the border into the Caliphate itself are barely credible: a diplomatic passport would not have been issued to an adolescent monk from Francia who spoke only Occitan and Latin. But like a trading vessel moored off the coast of a new continent, the abbey had secret lines of communication with the enemies of Christ. Copies of manuscripts found their way to Ripoll from the great library at Córdoba, which was said to contain six hundred thousand works listed in a forty-four-volume catalogue.

❁

Gerbert left Ripoll at the end of 970 having mastered mathematics and other forgotten arts. There are two different versions of his departure. According to Richer of Reims, who owed his information to Gerbert himself, he persuaded Bishop Atto and the Count of Barcelona to take him on their mission to Rome. He was introduced to the Pope, who was delighted to meet such a knowledgeable young bird shimmering with rare erudition. The Pope recommended him to Otto I, the Holy Roman Emperor, as a tutor for his son. Gerbert, however, had met an archdeacon from Reims, who told him of that famous Roman city and its library, of Adalbero's recent improvements to the cathedral and his desire to educate the clueless clergy of the diocese.

The other version, though flagrantly ridiculous in some respects, is illuminating in its own garish way. It was written by the English chronicler William of Malmesbury, in about 1125. Parts of William's history are based on first-hand accounts. His main source is thought to have been an old monk of Malmesbury Abbey called Eilmer who had visited Reims Cathedral when the evidence of Gerbert's genius was still on display.

In Spain (says William), Gerbert had lodged with a Saracen philosopher who, in exchange for various gifts, allowed him to read all his books, except one. This forbidden tome, which 'contained the knowledge of his whole art', naturally became an obsession with Gerbert. Having 'procured a certain intimacy' with the Saracen's daughter, he enlisted the girl's help in sedating her father with wine. Then, sneaking into the philosopher's bedchamber, he stole the book from under his pillow and headed for home.

> Shaking off sleep, the Saracen pursued the fugitive by reading the stars – an art in which he was well versed. The fugitive, looking back, discovered his danger by means of the same art. He hid himself under a nearby wooden bridge, hanging from it and embracing it so as to touch neither earth nor water.
>
> His eager pursuit thus frustrated, the Saracen returned home. Quickening his step, Gerbert arrived at the sea, where he called up the Devil by incantations. He promised to serve him for all eternity if he would defend him from the Saracen (who was once again in pursuit) by transporting him to the opposite coast. This the Devil did.

William of Malmesbury artfully concludes his tale:

> No doubt one of those vulgar people who like to undermine the reputation of scholars will regard this as fiction. . . . But in that case, why, when he was close to death, did Gerbert mutilate his own body [to escape eternal torture] unless he was conscious of having committed some extraordinary crime?

This musty anecdote, like an old attic, contains some peculiar but ultimately familiar objects. When William wrote that Gerbert and the Saracen plotted their course 'by reading the stars', he was echoing Gerbert's astronomical investigations (of which more in a moment). But what gave him the idea of that ingenious hiding place, the wooden bridge, which allowed Gerbert to elude his pursuer? Why would the man of science have suspended himself from a wooden structure, 'embracing it so as to touch neither earth nor water'?

The same text asserts that Gerbert had learned from the Saracens 'the meaning of the song and the flight of birds'. To William and most of his contemporaries, those studies in natural mathematics inevitably evoked the pagan practice of divination, in which the real Gerbert had no interest.

William's colleague, old Eilmer of Malmesbury, had visited Reims Cathedral when Gerbert's fame was at its height. Back in England, the young Eilmer had 'fastened wings to his hands and feet . . . and, collecting the breeze on the summit of a tower, flown for more than a furlong' (one-eighth of a mile) before crashing to the ground. 'He used to relate that his failure was caused by his forgetting to provide himself with a tail.' This is exactly what was said of the Andalusian scientist and inventor Abbas ibn Firnas, who died in the Caliphate of Córdoba about fifty years before Gerbert was born.

Unlike Eilmer, who broke both his legs in the attempt, Gerbert was not crippled: for him, the experiment was probably either successful or purely theoretical. It is also possible that William misinterpreted a manuscript illustration like those of the Amiens illuminated manuscript (c. 1300), in which Gerbert d'Aurillac is shown stealing the Saracen's book and operating his steam organ. In some neglected parchment, there might yet be found a depiction of a monk 'embracing' a wooden frame 'so as to touch neither earth nor water', preparing to fly back to Francia on his maiden flight.

❋

Later that year, transported by the Devil, a horse or his own two feet, Gerbert arrived in Reims on the Roman road from the south. He had an unparalleled acquaintance with astronomy, geometry, music and mathematics, and a passion for imparting this knowledge to his pupils. He had learned from the Greek and Roman orators the art of reasoning: with a few simple axioms and a love of truth, even 'people of lesser comprehension' could grasp difficult ideas. The point, Gerbert wrote in a letter of 982, was not to fill the air with empty sounds but to reach the verifiable truth by the shortest path: 'Instead of using many words, we should stick to facts.'

Under Gerbert's tuition, carpenters were set to work on intricate devices which, once assembled, seemed to acquire minds of their own. A single-stringed instrument called the monochord demonstrated the mathematical basis of musical harmony. Ungainly contraptions made of rods and tubes and little wheels measured the height of distant hills and the width of unbridgeable rivers.

Though they were fashioned by human hands, some of those mechanisms appeared to be operated by invisible demons. Gerbert was later said to have learned from the infidels the art of summoning spirits from hell: the proof was that he could perform calculations which exceeded the capability of any mortal. A shield-maker was instructed to divide a plank of wood into twenty-seven compartments. Tokens made of horn were then inscribed with curlicues which represented the nine magic numerals. These Saracen figures, according to Gerbert, could express all possible numbers. His pupil Richer was one of the first to describe this intelligent machine, the *abacus*, with its Arabic numerals, which 'multiplied and divided numbers so enormous that one understood them faster than one could express them in words'.

I Ꞇ Ꝣ Ꝩ Ꝩ ♭ ꓶ 8 9

The apprentice wizard with his stolen book of spells was turning the cathedral at Reims into a laboratory and observatory. High up among the arches of the vault, there was an opening through which the light of a certain constellation would shine. Far below in the nave, a polished disc divided into hours and days was tilted up towards the heavens. Some instructions have survived in a letter sent by Gerbert to a monk at the Benedictine abbey of Fleury-sur-Loire in 978. The metal tube attached to the disc was to be used to locate the pole star:

> If it is the pole star, you will be able to see it all night long; if not,
> it will soon be invisible through the tube because its position will
> have changed.

A pointer was then aligned on a second star which, as it moved around the pole, would indicate the passage of time.

This *horologium nocturnum* or nocturlabe was undoubtedly the 'clock constructed on mechanical principles' which Eilmer of Malmesbury saw in Reims Cathedral. Another 'night clock' made by Gerbert was displayed in Magdeburg Cathedral. For at least another century, these marvels were treated as unique creatures incapable of reproduction, and yet they solved one of the basic practical problems of monastery life – how to keep track of time in the hours of darkness. The unreliable drip of a water clock, the burning of a calibrated candle, the measured singing of psalms or the crowing of the cock were replaced by a beautiful computer which even the dullest monk could be trained to use.

*

Because all these inventions had previously existed in ancient Greece and Rome, Gerbert is often disparaged as an imitator. But sometimes it takes a genius to follow an instruction manual, especially one produced by an extinct civilization. He tracked down the manuscripts in which the devices were described; he begged monks in other monasteries for copies of manuscripts, suggesting how they might circumvent a ban on lending or copying texts. At no point did he show any desire to obtain biblical or ecclesiastical writings. His devotion was to the discovery and elucidation of the laws which govern the universe. The instruments themselves, once they had been used to test and demonstrate the principles, served as bartering goods.

After learning that a monk at Trier had access to an epic poem called *The Achilleid*, he promised to send him a model of the heavens in exchange: 'The sphere is now being polished in the lathe and skilfully covered with horsehide.' It would be 'equipped with a horizon ring, marked in many beautiful colours' and calibrated to the local latitude – which is why the process would 'require a year's work' (for a complete cycle of astronomical readings).

This amazing instrument, which could predict the position of any star 'without the aid of a teacher', is the first armillary sphere known to have existed in Christian Europe since Roman times. William of Malmesbury pictured it as a prophetic 'talking head'. In an age when no distinction was made between astronomy and astrology, an ability to foretell the cosmological future was certain proof of divinatory powers:

> He cast for his own use the head of a statue, which, by a particular
> inspection of the stars when all the planets were at the start of their
> course, began to speak – but only if asked a question and then either
> yes or no. 'Shall I be Pope?' Gerbert would ask, and the statue would
> answer, 'Yes'.

William of Malmesbury looked back on this early Age of Reason with wonderment and fear. This was a secondary purpose of Gerbert's wonders – to impress the poor souls of the diocese who came from the surrounding villages to seek relief from scrofula or toothache, to cure a blind baby or because they had been terrified by the sight of great armies fighting in a fiery sky, portending hailstorms or plague. No one who saw the melodious clouds of steam burst into the vault of the basilica could have doubted the existence of another world.

The organ itself has no known precursor and may be an original invention of Gerbert. Some Roman authors had described organs played by a water pump or the 'wind' produced by bellows, but Gerbert's instrument is the first to use steam. The principle itself had been revealed in a work which he might have seen in Arabic translation in the library at Ripoll.

If there was a single book of secrets which he might have stolen from a Saracen philosopher, it would have been Hero of Alexandria's *Pneumatica*. This first-century physics textbook contained a range of 'temple wonders' with full instructions: a trumpet which sounded when a temple door was opened; a vending machine or 'sacrificial vessel' which dispensed an exact measure of holy water when a coin was introduced; and some novel uses for the vapour which rises from heated water: an artificial blackbird was made to sing and a ball rotated when the vapour was channelled through metal tubes.

For a brain like Gerbert's, it would have been child's play to combine two of those ancient blueprints and invent the world's first steam organ. At the time, the mathematical basis of music was uppermost in his mind. But if he had happened to be thinking about velocity instead of harmony and rotating balls instead of blackbirds, the highways radiating from tenth-century Reims might have seen the first sputterings of an industrial revolution and a sight even more incongruous than a velocipede on a Roman road.

✿ ✿ ✿

Apart from an unhappy spell as Abbot of Bobbio in northern Italy, where the monks were surly, corrupt and set in their ways, Gerbert remained at Reims until 997, latterly as archbishop. He continued to collect manuscripts, but there are few further signs in his letters of scientific experiments. He called himself 'an ex-teacher' and longed for 'the guaranteed leisure of study'. Unfortunately for him, his love of practical solutions made him an able politician. In league with Archbishop Adalbero, he used his growing reputation to secure the election of Hugues Capet, nephew of Otto I, as King of the Franks in 987. Along with all his other achievements, he thus helped to found the Capetian dynasty which, in one branch or another, held the Crown of France until the Revolution.

This world of peripatetic scholars and potentates which embraced Saracen Spain, Germany, Rome and even England should be pictured as a geologist pictures a landscape. Different eras coexist and seem to come in the wrong chronological order. Borders change from one decade to the next. In the tenth century, the great drift of progress had barely begun to smooth away the chaos. Political entities had yet to stamp their mark on every 'citizen'. With hindsight, Gerbert appears to have been a one-man Renaissance and a figment of fantastic tales, but he was more exemplar than exception.

The tales of sorcerers and demons that were written long after his death have been discarded as superstitious drivel, which is understandable because the evidence is caked with fallacies. The telling clues take the form of an impossible event, a strangely worded phrase or some other sign that the storyteller had no idea what he was recounting. Most of the legends concerning Gerbert were fed by folklore, monastery gossip and a hasty reading of his letters. They were supposed to explain the incredible rise of Gerbert d'Aurillac: how did a humble shepherd from the depths of the Auvergne ascend to the papal throne if not by the power of the Devil?

In the late 1100s, the Welsh courtier and diplomat, Walter Map, believed or pretended to believe that he had found the answer. At noon one day, Gerbert walked out of Reims to a nearby forest. He was shabby, unshaven and desperately poor, having recently been rejected by the girl of his dreams. He came to a glade in which a woman of matchless beauty was seated on a silken carpet next to a huge pile of money. This was Meridiana, a woman of voracious sexual appetite and formidable powers of seduction, who could see into the future and the past.

Meridiana had remained a virgin because she was waiting for a man who would be worthy of receiving her gift. That man was Gerbert d'Aurillac, who, by following her nocturnal instructions, 'rose in glorious triumph to the highest pinnacles of fame'. In return, the future pope gave himself to the enchantress 'under the shade of a gnarled oak'.

This half-baked fantasy is speckled with fragments of reality. We know from Gerbert's letters that he owned a seventh-century compilation of works by Roman surveyors or *agrimensores*. Here were all the formulae which allowed the wide world to be measured and mapped. In Reims, he lived at the centre of a compass-like road system. Those straight lines on the plains of Champagne were an image of his own mind, impatient with meandering and delay. They were also a full-scale demonstration of ancient surveying.

It would have been an obvious test of the principles described by the ancient *agrimensores* to walk south from the cathedral for about seven miles to the place where the Roman road from the Marne valley looks down over Reims. At noon (the *hora meridiana*), the shadow of the sun cast by a gnomon (the upright blade or spindle of a sundial) would point due south to the heart of the city. This imaginary north–south line is the meridian which provides the basis of a land survey.

The road runs through a forest which forms part of the plateau called the Montagne de Reims. Its name is Forêt du Chêne de la Vierge (Virgin's Oak Forest). For many centuries, the eponymous oak was hollowed out to receive an image of the Virgin. Local people and pilgrims would take scrapings from the tree to use as charms and remedies, and when the oak had been whittled to death, the statue of the Virgin was removed to another gnarly oak in the vicinity.

Somewhere on the northern edge of that forest, where the road from Épernay drops down towards Reims, the future pope lay down with an enchantress and the real Gerbert d'Aurillac brought the forgotten art of surveying back to northern France.

✷

Hugues Capet died in 996. His successor to the Frankish throne, Robert II, expelled Gerbert from Reims and gave the archbishopric to his own protégé. Banished from Francia, Gerbert was invited to Germany by the sixteen-year-old Holy Roman Emperor. Young Otto III had been charmed by the cheerful omniscience of his father's tutor. He begged him to come and 'add the flame of your knowledge to our little spark that we might rekindle the blazing genius of the Greeks'.

On the death of Gregory V in 999, Gerbert was elected Pope at the behest of Otto III. Both men saw Rome as the capital of a new Christian empire. Gerbert then took the name Sylvester II, in homage to the pope who had been the mentor of Emperor Constantine.

At Reims, Gerbert had lived in the middle of an archaeological site; at Rome, he found himself in a vast wonderland of ruins. In the gloating idiom of William of Malmesbury,

> He discovered by the art of necromancy the treasures formerly buried by the inhabitants, and, scraping away the rubble, made those treasures serve his own desires.

Translated into the language of reason, this means that Gerbert was one of the first people to take a serious scholarly interest in Roman antiquities.

Though most of the hare-brained accounts of Gerbert's schemes and theories are probably too garbled for the original reality to be retrieved,* one of the most preposterous contains so many concrete traces that it should no longer be dismissed as fiction, especially since those traces are still visible today.

According to William, Gerbert was particularly drawn to the Campus Martius next to his home at the Vatican. There stood a statue which appeared to be pointing at something, and on its head was a bizarre inscription: '*Hic percute*' ('Strike here'). Supposing this to be the clue to a great treasure, citizens of Rome had hammered the head repeatedly, to no avail.

Gerbert, says William, noted the spot where the shadow of the statue's finger fell at noon and marked it with a post. After dark, he returned with a servant and a lantern. Then he 'opened the earth' by some magical means (presumably a spade), and revealed the entrance to a palace in which everything was made of gold – the roofs and

---

* Immediately after the bridge episode (p. 63), Gerbert reaches the sea (coming from Ripoll, this would have been the Mediterranean at Narbonne) and persuades the Devil to transport him to the opposite coast (the Atlantic). From Roman geographers and his own travels, he knew that Narbonne lay at the eastern end of the narrowest crossing of the Western European isthmus, and that the rivers Aude and Garonne were navigable for much of their length. He had also read about the canal-building schemes of Nero and Charlemagne. This coast-to-coast transportation by the Devil may be the earliest expression of the dream that was eventually realized in the Canal du Midi, opened to traffic in 1683.

walls, some golden soldiers playing dice, and a golden king and queen sitting at a banquet of golden delicacies. Light was supplied by a small *carbunculus** of the finest quality. In the opposite corner, a boy was holding a stretched bow.

Convincing himself that 'in a booty of such magnitude, a small theft would go unnoticed', Gerbert's servant reached out to snatch a golden knife from the table . . .

> In an instant, all the figures started up with a loud clamour, the boy released his arrow at the glowing *carbunculus*, and suddenly everything was plunged into darkness. . . . Their boundless avarice unsated, they departed thence, the lantern directing their steps.

Incredibly, this appears to be, in essence, a true story. The Indiana Jones-style defences are remarkably similar to Hero of Alexandria's hydraulic anti-burglar device in the *Pneumatica*, which Gerbert might have used to burglar-alarm the treasury of Reims Cathedral or the room in which he stored his manuscripts.† As for the battered 'statue' in the Campus Martius, it is described in a manuscript which Gerbert entrusted to a monk from Aurillac – the ninth-century copy of an ancient codex containing books xxxii to xxxvii of Pliny's encyclopaedic *Natural History*.

In book xxxvi, Pliny explained the function of the Egyptian obelisk (the 'statue') erected by Augustus in the Campus Martius. A golden ball which cast a shadow in the shape of a human head was placed on top of the obelisk. At noon on the shortest day of the year, the shadow fell precisely across a certain bronze line set in the stone pavement. The purpose of this gigantic gnomon, according to Pliny, was to measure the length of the days and nights.

The origin of the popular superstition and the 'Strike here' inscription can be seen nearby on the base of the column of Antoninus Pius.

---

* A reddish, fiery-coloured gemstone (garnet, ruby, etc.) or, literally, a small burning coal – perhaps from an experiment described in a lost version of Hero of Alexandria's *Catoptrics* (a treatise on the propagation of light and the use of mirrors).

† An apple sits on a pedestal near a Hercules with a stretched bow. 'If anyone should raise the apple slightly from the pedestal, the Hercules will discharge his arrow'. There may be an echo of this in Gerbert's papal decree commanding that if anyone should try to 'seize as booty' the monastery of Langogne, 'they shall be pierced by the javelin of divine curses'.

The bas-relief shows a personification of the Campus Martius supporting the solar obelisk. Another figure holds the rod and insignia of Antoninus. To the peasants of early medieval Rome, ignorant of imperial symbolism, it would have looked as though the top of the obelisk were being struck by a very large hammer.

The obelisk collapsed several decades after Gerbert's death. A section of the meridian or noon line itself was rediscovered in 1748, and the bronze inlay, as well as the signs of the zodiac, can be seen today in the cellars of no. 48, Via del Campo Marzio. To Gerbert, searching pagan manuscripts for devices with which to measure God's creation, that shining strip of metal would have been worth a palace of gold.

✻

In 1003, only four years after his election, and before he had reached the age of sixty, Gerbert fell ill while celebrating mass. A few days later, he died in the Lateran Palace. His last papal letters sound like a farewell to that brief Age of Reason when science cohabited happily with Christian observance. Shortly before his final illness, he had written to the Archbishop of Reims on the subject of a local controversy. The last rites were being refused to certain inhabitants of Reims who, because of a harmless superstition, longed to be laid to rest in the old burial ground of Saint Remi which stood outside the city walls on the Roman road to the east. For the scientist-pope, the yearnings of suffering humanity were more sacred than the dogma of God's Church:

> By apostolic authority, we command therefore that the dying be not prejudged, and that the Eucharist be denied to no one who professes repentance at the point of death. To all who so desire let interment be granted in the ancient cemetery of Saint Remi without opposition so that the living might possess the certain expectation of being buried and the dead rest in peace in the place for which they long.

The shepherd from the Auvergne was buried in Rome in the Basilica of St John Lateran. In the early 1100s, it was noticed that, despite the absence of humidity and even in sunny weather, his tomb exuded drops of water. No one sought a simple explanation for the phenomenon of condensation: the sweating tomb was still held to be a sign of Gerbert's demonic dabblings five hundred years after his death. Even today, there are pilgrims who peer at the cold stone on which they breathe and believe that the drops of moisture on its surface signify the imminent death of the Pope. It was not until 1648, when emergency repairs were carried out to the nave and portico of the basilica, and the tombs of the popes were disturbed, that there was the first hint of a rational approach to the mysteries of Nature.

The canon who supervised the opening of Gerbert's tomb confirmed the 'sweating' of the stone: it would have been imprudent to deny the miracle. He did, however, venture to propose an empirical explanation for the belief that the corpses of saints gave off an 'odour of sanctity':

> His body was found intact inside a marble sepulchre, dressed in its pontifical finery. . . . Coming into contact with the air, the body crumbled to dust and all around there was a sweet and pleasant odour. This may perhaps have been caused by the perfumes which had been used in the embalming.

      ✿   ✿   ✿

Without the chill that spreads through the bones after a long and energetic journey, it would have been hard to keep track of passing time in the cathedral. From outside in the square came the tolling of a bell. Worshippers were arriving for the evening service. We stood up and, as we headed for the west door, found ourselves walking on the light-projected image of the labyrinth which had been set into the marble of the nave in 1286.

The labyrinth partially covered the old west entrance of the basilica of Gerbert's day. It was intended to commemorate the completion of the main body of the new Gothic cathedral. In the four corners were mosaic figures of the four architects and in the centre the Archbishop. The blue stone sets of the labyrinth were hacked out and removed in 1779 on the orders of the canons because children and idlers were using the labyrinth as a racetrack during services.

The labyrinth's itinerary is aesthetically pleasing but the puzzle has little intellectual interest. Unlike a maze, in which it is easy to get lost, a labyrinth has only one path from start to finish. Its complexity is an illusion. If Gerbert had lived to see it, he might have thought it a parody of mental effort and the quest for truth. As he admonished the slothful and rebellious monks of Bobbio in 984, 'Those who make a pretence of seeking God do not deserve to find him.'

Ignoring the meanderings of the labyrinth, we walked out into the square and made a beeline for the hotel, which, thank God, was open.

5

Cathar Treasure

Just before Christmas 1243, a heavy bundle was lowered under cover of darkness from the tower which dominated the isolated *pueg* or rocky cone called Montségur. For several months, the fortress on 'safe mountain' had been horribly overcrowded. More than four hundred people were living in that aerial prison: farmers, shepherds, craftsmen and their families; lords and ladies whose estates had been confiscated by brutal, bearded knights from the Kingdom of France far away to the north. The tower was garrisoned by local knights and sergeants; there were also some strangely sanguine characters who might have been taken for pilgrims or priests since they carried paper books written in Occitan in the pockets of their blue hooded coats.

That dizzying platform created by a quirk of geology might have been the pinnacle on which the Ark had come to rest. There were no lepers, Jews or clerics among the throng, but otherwise it was a cross-section of the society which had thrived for many centuries in the valleys and uplands between the plain of Toulouse and the foothills of the eastern Pyrenees.

The siege had been surprisingly desultory: for much of the time, the soldiers of the King of France were no more menacing than a well-fed wolf passing along the edge of woodland in the daytime, but now that winter had set in and the foreign army had stripped the countryside of its crops and robbed the forests of their squirrels and grouse, supplies were running low. The two men who followed the heavy bundle a few moments later on ladders or ropes must have been glad to feel the cold air of mountain pasture on their faces. They would have been even more relieved to find that the sentries on duty at the foot of the *pueg* were men from Camon – a village which lay twelve miles to the north in the country of Olmes, whose southern approaches were guarded by Montségur.

Dividing the bundle into two, they skirted the sleeping camp of huts and tents and hurried away from the tower along a valley to the south. When the valley began to climb, the tower would disappear behind the haunch of a hill. It would remain out of sight until they were much higher up the pass. If anyone had set off in pursuit, the fugitives would show up against the snow. One of the men was an ordained 'Perfect' of the heretical Cathar faith. Having mastered its most arcane doctrines and renounced marriage, fornication and meat, he was deemed to be '*engal so dels angels*' ('equal unto the angels') and assured of resurrection. The other man was a deacon who had been responsible for Cathar affairs in the region of Toulouse. If he had stayed in that conquered city, he might now have been a smear of ashes on a market square or a carcass manacled to a wall, macerating in its own excrement.

The precipices were patrolled by demons who were sometimes seen in the mist, flinging wicked souls to their doom, but the slopes of the valley were like guiding hands, and the tracks of animals in the snow showed where it was safe to walk. Six miles from Montségur, the two men reached the Col de la Terme or Col de la Peyre, from the stone (*peyre*) which marked the boundary (*terme*) of the land of Olmes. This cradle in the mountains was the lowest crossing of the ridge which separated Olmes and its southernmost watchtower, Montségur, from the valley of the Ariège.

For the shepherds who spent half the year in the high mountains, the cols were like village squares where news could be exchanged without fear of being overheard. Ever since the Pope and the King of France had launched a crusade against the heresy which had spread from the East like a mysterious plague, the Occitan-speaking towns and villages of the south had taken on the air of catacombs. Some families had installed walk-in cupboards where a tall man could stand upright and secret panels through which the heretics could slip away into a neighbouring house. In the hamlets which straggled down the limestone crags, one person's sun terrace was the ceiling of another's *foganha* – the fire-lit kitchen which was the hearth and hub of every home. At any moment, a corner of the roof might be raised and a face would peer down into a room where men in blue tunics were eating a mountain trout (which has no soul) or preaching to a believer kneeling with her palms and forehead pressed to the floor.

❋

Once over the Col de la Peyre, in the pink light of dawn they could see the miniature *pays* of Aillon to the east and the much larger mass of Sabartès to the west.* The *pays* of Sabartès was the upland part of the County of Foix; its borders were set by Nature whereas those of Foix existed primarily in charters and deeds of sale. To the north, beyond Toulouse and Carcassonne, the world was a blank. The men and women of Sabartès always went south for seasonal work; they crossed the larger cols on the southern horizon which were called *ports* because they served as portals to another realm. The Sabartésiens looked to Cerdagne and Roussillon, to Catalonia and Aragon, to the sunny lands of sugar, dates and wine, where the Pope and the King of France were powerless to impose taxes or to prise the thoughts from an innocent heart.

Without descending all the way to the river, the men turned west in the direction of Tarascon and Foix. On the ridges beneath them, 'castles' that were little more than rubble walls jutted out of the forest. Some had been reduced to ruins on the orders of the Inquisition; others were inhabited for only part of the year by lords who were almost as poor as their servants. The territory visible from each tower was a *châtellenie*, the smallest division of a *pays*. Where a hill or an outcrop interrupted the line of sight between one tower and the next, there were cavities and fractures in the rock which, on closer inspection, proved to be drainage holes, stairs and crenellations. These half-prefabricated fortresses were the inexpensive castles known as *spoulgas*. A curtain wall and a wooden door would transform a cavern into a bastion stretching far under the mountain. Several *spoulgas* are named in charters of the time as significant defences. Many have yet to be rediscovered.

It was to one of those sepulchral citadels that the men were heading. Somewhere in the *châtellenie* of Châteauverdun, between the Col de la Peyre and the valley of the Ariège, they clambered up the

---

* A *pays* (from *pagus*, whence 'pagan' and 'peasant') was once the region occupied by a tribal group, with distinct natural and sometimes administrative boundaries.

side of a cliff and deposited their burden in the *spoulga*. A wooden chest would have been cumbersome on such a journey, and so the 'treasure' (described as such in a deposition made the following May) was probably wrapped in cloth or leather. It would have to be made safe from scavengers and rodents and pushed into one of the deeper recesses of the grotto in case a shepherd searching for a lost sheep should happen to look up at the cliff and notice the glint of gold.

*

Three months later, soldiers were still camped at the foot of Montségur. When the snow had melted, hundreds of resinous pines were felled, and after a few days of sawing and hammering, an enormous catapult was wheeled up to the foot of the *pueg*.

It was thirty-six years since Pope Innocent III had ordered a crusade against the heretics who threatened to supplant the Catholic Church in the Languedoc and to cut off an important source of revenue. Philippe Auguste – the first King of the Franks to call himself 'King of France' – had authorized an autonomous army of crusaders to serve as the advance guard of the Inquisition. He preferred to acquire territory by marriage and inheritance. In his eyes, even the province of Poitou was 'so remote' that controlling it directly from Paris was out of the question. At twice the distance, the Languedoc was an alien realm on the edges of Christendom.

Most of those mercenary adventurers came from Normandy and Picardy, the Paris Basin and the lower Loire. Their reward would be a place in heaven and whatever land they could seize. For the next twenty years, the County of Toulouse and its satellite seignories were ravaged by bloodlust and greed. The people of the Languedoc were starved, stripped, burned and subjected to humiliating surgical alterations. No distinction was made between Cathars and orthodox Christians. The crusaders behaved as though the entire population of the Occitan-speaking lands were composed of heretical pacifist vegetarians who denied the efficacy of baptism and communion, and believed that the earth and all things in it were creations of the Devil.

The gigantic balls of stone that were lobbed onto Montségur in the spring of 1244 were the thudding finale to the annexation of the Languedoc by the Kingdom of France. When this last outpost of resistance surrendered, about half of the besieged recanted and were pardoned or given some light penance. The remaining Cathar 'Perfects' and a few of their male and female converts – more than two hundred people – were led to a meadow below the *pueg* and burned to death.

❧

Tourists to 'Cathar Country' are invited to imagine this scene of horror as they enjoy the region's natural attractions. The thought of unspeakable torment serves as a condiment for the delicious spectacle of ruins suspended in mid-air. The thirteenth-century reality is not so easily recaptured. According to a heretic sympathizer who had seen an unrepentant Cathar incinerated in the town of Pamiers, 'when the ties that bound his hands were consumed by fire, he brought his hands together as though he were praying to God'.

The words 'as though' have a certain poignancy . . . When life has been swiftly extinguished by smoke and carbon monoxide, the limbs of a burning body flex and may well appear to move by voluntary action.

In the absence of actual footage, there is a reliable recording of the sound. In 1320, a man accused of heresy had been summoned to appear before the Bishop of Pamiers. A friend in Tarascon advised him to 'tell his Lordship the exact truth':

> He replied by blowing into his hand to simulate the fire and to indicate that, if he did tell the truth, he would be burned.

The sound produced by blowing into a cupped hand evokes a roaring furnace rather than a sputtering bonfire. This would be consistent with the benign purposes of the Inquisition: by that late stage of the crusade, the intention was not to torture but to purify, which is why heretics who were found guilty *post mortem* were disinterred and cremated.

As for the 'treasure', it may have been retrieved by four Cathar Perfects. They had hidden themselves in one of the subterranean passages under the castle of Montségur. On the night before the surrender (15–16 March 1244), they slithered down the *pueg* on ropes. A witness who was interrogated that April said that 'this was done so that the Church of the heretics should not lose its treasure, which was concealed in the woods'.

It was inevitable that the treasure of the 'mysterious' (and extremely well-documented) sect which seemed to threaten the existence of the Catholic Church and whose rituals can be traced back to the earliest days of Christianity would eventually be identified as the Holy Grail. One of the sergeants who had defended Montségur claimed that the treasure had consisted of 'gold, silver and an incalculable sum of money' (*'pecuniam infinitam'*). Another witness stated that the four fugitives had headed south to Caussou – which implies a crossing by the Col de la Peyre – and then on to Prades and Usson in the *pays* of Donezan.

Their final destination would have been Piedmont or Lombardy, the home of the Cathar Church in exile. This was not the easiest route to the east, but it was a logical choice if it had to include a detour into the *châtellenie* where the treasure had been stored. None of the witnesses explicitly stated that the treasure was recovered. It may still be there in its *spoulga*. Whatever the last resting place of the Cathars' hoard, such is the power of the fictitious Holy Grail that it will always lend a peculiar glint to the limestone crags of the Ariège.

✿   ✿   ✿

Some time ago, I acquired a taste for apparently futile journeys of discovery. It began with inscrutable prehistoric dolmens and continued with various sites which the Celts had for some reason named *mediolana* or 'middle sanctuaries', the principal characteristic of which was that there was nothing of interest there to see.

A treasure hunt for a non-existent treasure was as good a pretext as any for a journey of serendipitous discovery. It would be a liberation from the chivvying lists of guidebooks, and the quest would have a pleasantly ascetic purity. All archaeologists know the hypnotic pleasure of sifting evidence until nothing is left in the riddle. 'When you have eliminated the impossible, whatever remains, however improbable, must be the truth', says Sherlock Holmes. Replace 'improbable' with 'banal' or 'disappointing', and this would be a good description of much historical investigation.

The futility, of course, is only apparent: without the distraction of a goal, the mind becomes receptive to all sorts of uninvited information, just as averted vision allows the light of a faint star or galaxy to fall on the sensitive periphery of the retina.

Before setting off, I reviewed the lack of evidence:

None of the ruins advertised as 'Cathar castles' belong to the period in question. They were rebuilt as border forts after the Treaty of Corbeil (1358), which established the frontier between the kingdoms of France and Aragon. Of the villages where the Cathar heresy took hold, only a few foundations and scatters of rubble remain.

The 'Cathars' never called themselves 'Cathars'. They were 'good Christians', 'good men' or 'good women', and their followers were 'believers'. 'Cathar' was a colloquial term for heretics. Two twelfth-century theologians supposed that 'Cathari', 'as the common people say', came from ancient Greek and meant 'the pure ones'. But the common people knew nothing of ancient Greek. The word was derived from the Low German for 'cat': the Cathars were 'cat people' because heretics were believed to worship the Devil in feline form.

The mythification of Montségur, that 'holy mountain, protesting and impregnable in the clouds', began in 1870 with a hallucinatory history written by a French Protestant pastor, Napoléon Peyrat. In 1933, by dint of much pseudo-research, a German writer, Otto Rahn, identified it as the Holy Grail of medieval romance. (As though in punishment, Rahn, whose sympathies were liberal rather than fascist, won the admiration of Heinrich Himmler, who funded his search for the Holy Grail and made him an officer in the SS.)

'Grails' *are* mentioned in witness statements obtained by the French Inquisition, but these '*graals*' or '*grazals*' were the wide-mouthed jugs used to contain flour rather than the bread of the Last Supper or the blood of Christ. If Rahn had consulted one of those repositories of arcane erudition called dictionaries, he might have discovered that '*trésor*' then referred simply to the money and valuables of an abbey or a church.

The only positive sighting of a treasure was recorded by an English-speaking visitor to Montségur in 2009. The visitor's landlady told him that her grandmother had discovered a cave beneath the castle: a flight of stone stairs led to a cellar in which she had been surprised to find '*un énorme saucisson*'. Assuming that he had

misheard, the visitor asked his landlady to point to the word in
his French–English dictionary, and she was able to confirm that
her grandmother had indeed stumbled upon 'a giant sausage'.
Perhaps this was a confused memory of an article or a talk which
had mentioned the Cathar who took the treasure with his compan-
ions to Usson ('*avec ses socis à Usson*'). A sausage would have been
a curious trophy for a vegetarian sect to treasure.

✳

Pilgrims who place their trust in inspiration rather than in a reinvented
'pilgrim way', and who follow the urgings of topography and terrain,
will sooner or later find themselves on a genuinely ancient route. Just
before we left for the far south, I noticed that a thirty-mile section
of the itinerary I had devised was spelled out in the records of the
Inquisition. Naturally, it took a more dramatic form. A Cathar convert
who was questioned in 1321 overheard a warning given to a hunted
heretic:

> Trust not the words of a treacherous priest, but tell Pierre Maury
> that if he finds himself at the Col des Sept Frères, he should flee
> to the Col de Marmare, and if he is at the Col de Marmare, he
> should flee to the Col de Puymorens [on the road to Spain], and
> he should not stop there either, but keep on fleeing.*

A Sabartésien could have covered that distance in a day. Walking
fifty miles between sunrise and sunset was an unremarkable achieve-
ment. (This also happens to be the average daily distance a reasonably
fit touring cyclist can tolerate on a journey of two or three weeks.)
Men and women walked many miles to buy and bring back oil, wine
or fish, to visit the hot baths at Ax-les-Thermes or to be questioned
by a bishop at Pamiers or Carcassonne. Motion was their measure of
time and distance: references to leagues or to hours and minutes are
rare. A certain conversation 'lasted as long as it takes to walk the
distance a man can throw a stone'. Two men 'remained with the
heretics for as long as it takes to go from Ax to Savignac'.

Historical time was foreign to their thinking. Two generations

---

* See Notes for Travellers, p. 397.

after the mass burning of heretics, when Cathar missionaries had begun to creep back into France from Lombardy and Sicily, and the Inquisition, like a poisonous plant, appeared in the higher villages every summer, no one ever mentioned or alluded to the destruction of Montségur. The crusade against the Cathars might as well have happened on the other side of the world in a different age.

Even within a single lifetime, few written or mental records were kept. A witness could sometimes date an incident to a particular season – for example, 'when the leaves were appearing on the elms' (but this was only because the conversation had taken place under the elm where village meetings were held). However, the witness would be unable to say exactly how old she was or how long she had been married. It was as though the world had begun in infancy. Before that, there was Eden, and somewhere in the future, the Day of Judgement.

The landscape in that part of France can seem oblivious to the passing centuries. The pastures of upland Sabartès are largely unchanged. Some parts are wilder than they were seven centuries ago and probably as sparsely populated as in the aftermath of the Black Death (1348): watermills have disappeared from the mountain burns; wheat, oats and turnips are no longer grown on high terraced slopes. The tarmacked road which leaves Montségur for the Col de la Peyre ends after two miles. In the forested pass, it is easy to catch sight in the mind's eye of two hooded figures in dark-blue coats briskly ascending the valley some distance up ahead. It was in places such as this that a person walking from one village to the next would encounter a 'good Christian' disguised as a pedlar and be drawn by his jokes and riddles into a risky discussion of God and the human soul.

At the col itself, time rushes back to the present. To a fourteenth-century eye, the scene on the other side might have been an engraving in a pedlar's almanac or the dream of some terrifying paradise. A blinding white expanse carved into gigantic steps and embankments has eradicated more than four square miles of pasture and forest along with all the subterranean watercourses and caverns. On dry days, clouds of white dust sweep across the Trimouns Quarry. The biggest talc mine in the world takes its name from the 'three mountains' it has partially pulverized. The fabled treasure of the Cathars may have rested and even remained under this vast obliteration until, a hundred years or a few months ago, it was scraped out of its shattered *spoulga* and carted off in a spoil bucket swinging from an aerial cable.

For some reason, the memory of such spectacular, photographable sites becomes increasingly abstract, while insignificant corners glimpsed in passing, stared at while devouring some food or noticed only because a bird or a butterfly happened to settle there, return much later in vivid detail – a cemetery wall, an unrepaired field-gate, a sudden view of mountains. Scenes of insignificance are rare in documented history but common in the records of the Inquisition, because it was in such quiet corners of ordinary lives, seventy years after the burning of heretics at Montségur, that strange events began to take place for which the Catholic Church had no credible explanation.

❊   ❊   ❊

In the valley of the Ariège, the oldest villages stand well above the flood plain and can easily be missed by a traveller intent on reaching Tarascon or Ax. In one of those vertiginous settlements, a widow fell off a wall in her garden. This happened in Ornolac at harvest time in 1317. There was nothing unusual about the accident: most gardens were terraced, and people were forever falling off steep slopes or being toppled and even partially buried by minor landslides.

As Guillemette Benet picked herself up, she noticed a red stain spreading on her clothes. In the twinge of panic before she realized it was just a nosebleed, she saw life flowing out of her body and cried, 'The soul! The soul! It's nothing but blood!'

The following Easter, Guillemette was walking into the forest when her son-in-law Raimond called to her and asked her to go home and look after his son. The baby was close to death and all hope had been given up. She watched over the baby from morning till night, and as she gazed at the limp form in the dying light she knew that she would soon be present at the great mystery of life:

> I kept watching to see whether anything would come out of the child's mouth when it died . . . I saw nothing come out but air.

Like the Virgin Mary, who was said to have given birth to a child before she had known a man, Guillemette was troubled by these things and 'pondered them in her heart'. Her observations were at odds with what the Church instructed her to believe, and it was some relief to know that she was not alone.

✿

When the official truth is supernatural, the everyday becomes extraordinary. Common incidents seemed disturbingly abnormal. From the snowy *ports* which formed the southern battlements of the *pays*, to the narrow Pas de Labarre which led out to the lowlands north of Foix, people wondered at the evidence of their eyes, and when they described these incidents to the Inquisitor at Pamiers, it was as though they were reporting a miracle.

One day, almost the entire population of Ornolac (about fifty) had gathered to watch a grave being dug on the south side of the little church. (Both the church and its cemetery are still in use.) The *bayle**
was struck by the quantity of brittle white sticks that were being extracted from the soil, and the thought rushed into his mind with such urgency that he voiced it in front of the assembled villagers: 'How could the souls that used to be in those bones ever go back into them?' The Church taught that there would be a resurrection of the body, but the worm-nibbled relics in the cemetery soil had moved only because of the gravedigger's spade.

These heretical musings might have been the direct result of Cathar indoctrination, but it would probably be fairer to say that the reform movement found fertile ground in the stony fields of Sabartès. Pastoral communities were less superstitious than lowlanders in arable country who never left their native village and rarely saw strangers. Anything that was unconfirmed by daily experience was likely to be questioned. For a Saracen fortune-teller – even one equipped with a mysteriously twitching magic wand and a book in Arabic characters – a Sabartésien (in this case, a man from Ax-les-Thermes) could be a difficult customer:

> I greeted [the fortune-teller] in the usual way and said, 'You ought to know why I've come', and he said, 'I'm not God, am I?' . . . Then he said I either had a wife or a fiancée. And when I told him neither was true, he said, 'Well, someone's trying to find you a wife', and I said, 'That's news to me.'

---

* A *bayle* was a headman, comparable to a village mayor. His was the lowest rank of local authority, below the *seigneur* (usually absent) and the *curé*.

Centuries before education created a religious and intellectual divide between the sexes, young women could be just as sceptical as their husbands and brothers. At the church of Sainte-Croix near Merviel, Aude Fauré, who had only recently married, heard about a pregnant woman who had given birth in the street. 'Then I started thinking of that disgusting thing that comes out of women when they give birth.' The next time she saw the priest raise the host above the altar, the thought seemed to cloud her vision: how could the Lord's body have been 'smeared with all that filth'? And how could it ever be true that His body was a loaf of bread which a woman had baked in an oven and given to the priest?

Far from the towns where the Church and the monastic orders had an eye in every home, the Cathars feasted on these crumbs of disbelief, and although their sermons were whispered in cellars and attics, their words were more resonant than those of a priest in a cathedral.

There was little a village *curé* could do to stifle these thoughts, other than to bar the door of the church which the villagers had built and to refuse absolution. In the pre-industrial world, long hours were spent talking. When the sun was out, the people of the Pyrenean foothills sat in front of their houses, making and mending, eating snails or sheep cheese or some freshly baked flour cakes. Settled on a sun terrace, at a window or by the fire, they picked the lice off each other's heads, and the conversation, amplified by the walls and limestone cliffs, was punctuated by the snap of nails. Distinctions in the social hierarchy were so slight that news and ideas could spread like the wisps of a grain of incense dropped onto a burning candle.

The Cathar Perfects who had grown up in the region knew how much value was attached to a good conversation topic. They encouraged people to complain about the tithes that were exacted by the Church. They told jokes and mocked the sacraments, and their comic repertoire was as familiar to many people as the Catholic creed. Only when they stood before the bishop in his palace did some converts and sympathizers realize that not everyone found their axioms amusing:

> 'Even if the body of Christ was as big as Mount Bugarach, there
> are so many priests they would have gobbled him all up long ago!'

'Christ was created just like the rest of us, by fucking and screwing!'

Q: 'Did you ever say that the world has no beginning and will never end?'

A: 'Not as far as I recall, but sometimes when I was working I might have said, as a joke, "*Tos temps es, e tos temps sira, qu'home ab autru moilher jaira.*" '*

Q: 'Did you say that when someone is on the point of death, one might just as well stick the holy candle up his arse as put it in his mouth, as is currently the practice?'

A: 'No, I didn't, but my late brother-in-law Bernard Masse maliciously claimed that I'd said it even though I hadn't.'

✺

It was about twelve months after Guillemette's gardening accident that Jacques Fournier, the Bishop of Pamiers, a graduate of the University of Paris, launched his forensic crusade. His model inquisition, which ran from 1318 to 1325, concentrated on the 'little people' who had been exposed to the heresy. A revival had been started in the early 1300s by a lawyer from Ax-les-Thermes, Pierre Authié, but he and his brother had been burned to death. Since then, several inquisitions seemed to have stamped out the vestiges of Catharism and other deviant sects. Fournier was a farmer hoeing a field which had already been cleared by fire, decapitating the little weeds that had sprouted from the ash.

The trials were conducted according to enlightened, Christian principles. With the exception of one extraordinary case (p. 92 n.), Fournier never used torture or even the threat of it, knowing – unlike some modern inquisitors – that torture was incapable of producing the truth. Instead, he would first interview the witnesses and then cross-examine the accused before they had been able to learn what the witnesses had said. In this way, in the course of five hundred and seventy-eight interrogations, conducted in Occitan and translated into Latin, he ignited feuds and spread the contagion of suspicion and fear throughout the *pays* of Sabartès.

---

* 'For all time that is and all time yet to come, men will lie down with other men's wives.'

While Fournier interrogated prisoners in his palaces near Pamiers and at Foix, the Cathars were still active in the field. They were just as determined as Fournier to protect the interests of their Church, and they, too, were trained in pedagogical techniques.

The general Cathar strategy was to divide the sacred teachings into the 'exoteric' (for public consumption) and the 'esoteric' (reserved for initiates). The exoteric curriculum was the shopfront display. In a cheerfully permissive society where sex was acceptable provided that both partners enjoyed it, a religion which insisted on total abstinence could never rival the established Church, and so, in contradiction of their creed, the Cathars permitted practically everything – lying under oath (especially to the Inquisition), making the sign of the Cross (if this was done to wave away the flies), eating meat (if the animal had been killed by a Catholic) and having sex (preferably not with one's wife or husband – marital sex was more sinful because the two partners 'mingled their bodies' 'more frequently and with less shame').

The 'esoteric' teachings were alien to the region and more cautiously dispensed. They originated in the Cathar schools of Lombardy and their authorities were the Gospel of John, the Book of Revelation and the writings of early theologians. They claimed precise knowledge of the unknowable (the seven heavens through which a soul would pass in seven days), and, in glaring contrast to Sabartésien custom, they demonized women. Because the Devil had tricked his way into paradise by disguising himself as a beautiful woman, a female soul had first to migrate into the body of a man before it could be escorted to paradise by forty-eight angels.

The esoteric doctrine which found most favour in Sabartès was the heresy of Manichaeism. This was the belief that the material world, including human bodies, had been created by the Devil. Manichaeism solved a common paradox and was sometimes used by the Perfects to sow doubt in the minds of Catholics. In the right conditions, a thought which had flitted through the mind like a cloud passing over the mountain tops would begin to thicken and cast a dark shadow.

In the village of Caussou through which the fugitives from Montségur had passed eighty years before, four men were sitting in the *foganha* around a blazing fire. This was in the Christmas of 1321. The snow was falling thickly and the owner of the house was praying for better weather. 'Come, my good fellow,' said another man. 'It's just the weather doing what it does, bringing the cold and then the flower and the seed. There's nothing God can do about it.'

The room fell silent. Then the first man said, 'It's bad to talk that way. If He wanted to, God could make the sun shine this very moment.' But the sun didn't shine and the snow kept falling. No one said another word because they knew where this conversation led: if God was good and could do as he pleased, why *didn't* he make the sun shine? Why did it sometimes snow after Easter, flattening the wheat and burying the food of the cattle on the high pastures? If a benevolent deity had created all things in heaven and earth, why were there creatures such as lice, vipers, bears and wolves? Evidence of evil was all around. Every snowstorm and hailstorm and every wolf-ravaged sheep confirmed the active presence of a malign god.

✣

When the snow was blanketing Caussou, the Bishop of Pamiers had completed the fourth year of his inquisition. Guillemette of Ornolac had been sentenced to 'the Wall' (incarceration in one of the Bishop's prisons); she would be freed after two years but condemned to the shame of wearing two yellow felt crosses on her clothing like a leper or a Jew. The *bayle* of Ornolac spent almost eight years in jail. The man who had questioned the efficacy of holy candles was released after ten months. Aude Fauré, who was unable to believe that the body of Christ could be a loaf of bread, was sentenced to a complicated calendar of fasts, confessions, visits to the Bishop and pilgrimages to Le Puy, Vauvert and Rocamadour totalling more than one thousand miles.

In the history of the French Inquisition, these were light sentences. Only one Cathar heretic was burned – a convicted murderer who had escaped from Carcassonne jail. But with his spies and informers, Bishop Fournier had poisoned the whole diocese, pawing through the litter of ruined lives, peering with feline acuity at every crack and inconsistency, and enabling the envious and the spiteful to destroy their enemies.

In the longer term, he provided historians with a unique treasure, boosted the tourist economy of the Ariège *département*, and ensured that the persecuted 'pure ones' would shine like saints. The spirit of the people themselves tends to be ignored because our own inquisition of the past exaggerates the importance of institutions and because remoteness from the centres of power is equated with ignorance and insignificance.

The men and women who hopefully assured the Inquisitor, 'I believe whatever the Church tells me to believe', knew that they were caught between two institutions – Catholicism and Catharism – which demanded obedience and sacrifice to an arbitrary set of beliefs: the triune God, the immortality of angels, conception without intercourse, the miracle of transubstantiation. The old tale of Church and State bringing order and reason to a small, benighted population is false in spirit and in detail. The established Church, the Kingdom of France as well as the Cathar Perfects were purveyors of chaos and irrationalism.

The harmless mystics of Cathar legend would have been unrecognizable to the people who knew them. Heretics and clerics alike were hated for 'ruining the whole *pays*'. One of those cloaked custodians of a secret treasure can be seen at work on his sacred mission in the village of Arques, near Rennes-les-Bains, in 1307. A woman called Sibille Peyre had a sick daughter. Little Jacqueline was less than a year old and although a convert was supposed to be able to understand and respond to the ritual of the *consolamentum* or 'heretication', the Perfects, whose supply of willing adult souls was dwindling, had begun to appear after dark at the death beds of children and babies like the owls which were believed to perch on the roofs of dying people to take their souls to hell.

The Cathar equivalent of the last rites involved a particularly harsh form of fasting called the *endura*. Sibille was told by the Cathar Pierre Maury that if she gave food to Jacqueline, she would endanger the baby's soul. This is a scene to inspire a change of heart in any modern fan of the Cathars.

> After he and my husband had left the house, I suckled my daughter because I could not simply watch her die. When my husband returned, he told me to be sure not to give the little girl any milk since she had now been received and would be in perdition if she broke the fast. I told him I had already suckled her after the heretication, which greatly disturbed and distressed him. Pierre Maury comforted him, saying that it wasn't his fault, and also that certain

people who ought to know better would never become good Christians. Then he said to the little girl, 'Your mother has been very bad!'

He told me I was a bad mother and that women were demons. My husband was in tears, shouting abuse and threatening me. At that moment, he stopped loving the little girl and me, and this went on for a long time until he recognized his mistake.

The little girl lived for about a year and then she died. But she wasn't hereticated again. When Gaillarde Escaunier heard what I'd done to my daughter – feeding her after the heretication – she became a great friend and wanted to start eating meat again. I gave her the meat myself. And my husband as well as all the other believers were very upset, especially Pierre Maury, who said [of Gaillarde Escaunier], 'That wicked old woman! She wants to go on living; she isn't disgusted with this world; she wants to eat meat! She'll never do anything good again!' But he never said any of that to her face.

*

The Cathar's temper tantrum at the baby's death bed was not untypical. The 'good Christians' did not take well to questioning and often found the Sabartésiens irritatingly disputatious. As a young man, Maury himself had been warned to watch his mouth by Pierre Authié, who spearheaded the revival of Catharism:

> You've been asking a lot of questions, Pierre. In future, when you meet a good man, don't ask so many questions. . . . You might be questioning one who doesn't know the answers . . . and since they have to tell the truth, you'd be catching them out – which is a sin.

Witnesses were intimidated and silenced. At least three were murdered by the Cathars to prevent them from talking to the Inquisition. One man, a notorious chatterbox, was found with his windpipe 'broken and staved in'.

In the light of this sinister oppression, the fabled treasure assumes its real form and the enchanted realm of 'Cathar Country' takes its proper place in French history. In all the dealings of the Cathars, there is a clinking of coins and precious metals. Merchants, artisans and minor aristocrats were persuaded to part with huge sums of money. In northern Italy, the Cathar diaspora lived in wealth and comfort.

One 'heretic treasure' consisted of silver plate donated by the faithful. Another was said to be worth sixteen thousand *livres tournois*. The 'treasure' held in Toulouse, Mirande and Castelsarrasin amounted to 'a hundred thousand *livres*'. The smaller of the two sums would have bought about fifty thousand sheep or four hundred townhouses. To the Cathars, a holy grail would have been useless except as bullion.

The treasure smuggled out of Montségur is a shining example of the primitive economy of the Languedoc. Banking operations in Lombardy were more sophisticated, but in the Languedoc, wealth still had to be physically transported. The expanding kingdom of France, with its burgeoning bureaucracy and its expensive wars of conquest, was increasingly reliant on taxation and the frictionless circulation of money. An occasional chest secreted in a *spoulga* or bouncing along a highland track on the back of a mule was no longer a prize to tempt an invading army of crusaders. Most of the coins used by the Languedoc Cathars were, significantly, the currency of cities in that foreign land to the north: *parisis* (the Paris pound) and *tournois* (the Tours pound, soon to be called the 'franc').

Money had already imported its own morality. Theft by the State on a massive scale was justified by the outlawing and vilification of a section of the population. Intolerance and fear fed by false rumours oiled the wheels of repression. The latest expulsion of the Jews in 1306 and the dissolution of the allegedly sodomitical order of the Knights Templar in 1307 were intended to replenish the coffers of King Philippe le Bel. His son, King Philippe le Long, hoped that some phantasmical treasure hoarded by leper hospitals would provide an equally sudden source of revenue.*

With its combination of fabulous wealth, supernatural power, genocidal hatred and beautiful scenery, it is no wonder that the Cathar myth appealed to Heinrich Himmler. It still attracts, not only psycho-tourists in search of an earlier self, but also Aryan supremacists. The tangle of Cathar schools of thought lends itself to a variety of

---

* In 1321, a leper from Pamiers was made to confess to a ridiculous plot supposedly hatched by the King of Grenada and 'the Sultan of Babylon': they had conspired to poison all Christians by contaminating wells with the powdered body of Christ (the host) and an extract of snake, toad, lizard, slow-worm, human excrement 'and much else besides'. This was the only occasion on which Bishop Fournier used torture: he was acting under strict orders from the French authorities.

ideologies, and not all those ideologies are travesties of the historical reality.

In fourteenth-century Sabartès, some of the more cosmopolitan adherents – a travelling salesman from Lombardy, a corn factor in Ax-les-Thermes, or a shepherd who had worked and lodged with Muslim 'infidels' – believed that 'God loves Saracens and Jews as much as he loves Christians'. But practically all the ordained Cathars approved of crusades against the infidel and purges of the Jews. They were quite certain that 'no Jewish soul has ever been saved or ever will be saved'.

*   *   *

In Ax-les-Thermes, there was great excitement about the imminent invasion of the Tour de France. It was mid-June and the town was not yet suffering from the annual scourge of tourist fatigue. As we sat in the square, dangling our feet in the sulphurous waters of the Bassin des Ladres (named after the crusaders who returned from the Holy Land with leprosy), it was easy to imagine the stoical cheerfulness of the people of Sabartès in the periods of grace between inquisitions.

We left the town on 18 June, following the trail of the treasure-bearers to Usson. Like them, we were fleeing to the east: a few hours behind us, the great storm of 2013 was washing away roads and houses and depositing immovable boulders on pasture and ploughland. Several farmers in the valleys of the upper Ariège would be facing ruin. In the aftermath of the deluge, a Cathar missionary might have found an audience receptive to tales of the evil god who rules the material world.

Two years later, a congregation which included clerics, local dignitaries, neo-Cathars, Occitan separatists and journalists gathered in the little church at Montségur and in the square outside. The fifty-fourth Bishop of Pamiers was to apologize on behalf of the Catholic Church for the persecution of the Christian Cathars. With a gap of almost eight hundred years and a mountain of medieval records that no one could be expected to have read, there was an air of historicidal fantasy about the ceremony.

The Bishop, who was born at Pamiers, wisely chose not to question the popular perception of the 'pure ones'. When the congregation processed to the field where the Cathar heretics are said to have been burned, he carried a shepherd's crook as a sign of humility. But he did take the opportunity to remind his flock that mortals can be as blind to the present as they are to the past:

> We do not know how the future will judge us. This very day, men and women are drowning as they cross the Mediterranean. Perhaps one day we shall be accused of inhumanity and rebuked for our indifference.

In the *commune* of Montségur, nearly half the eligible population voted for the National Front in the presidential elections of 2017. Without the Bishop's innocently blissful demeanour, his reminder might have been taken for a political statement. In some minds, the South of France was experiencing an invasion of infidel refugees from the lands of Saracens and Moors. Many of the congregants were simply hoping for a sign that the Church was no longer at war with individual consciences. As Christians attending a Christian service, they would receive the renewed and lasting reassurance that Good would triumph over Evil and the consolation which history seldom provides.

6

The Tree at the Centre of France

I first saw the tree one evening on a beautiful *Carte ecclésiastique* of 1624 showing 'the archbishoprics and bishoprics of the Kingdom of France and adjacent principalities which form part of the Gallican Church'. The map was curiously old-fashioned for the time and no doubt deliberately antiquated. The doctrine of Gallicanism asserted the independence of the French king and clergy from the Pope in Rome. Accordingly, each cathedral city was labelled with its Gallo-Roman as well as its modern name, to stress the ancient pedigree of the Church in Gaul.

The dainty groups of spires which symbolized the cities were positioned more or less correctly, but the shape of the land mass owed as much to Ptolemy as to seventeenth-century cartography. France had been squared off so that awkward corners such as Finistère and the region of Montségur had been swallowed by the sea or engulfed in pillowy black mountains. Fluvial arteries followed their own imaginary topography through a land teeming with trees. A forest covered Lorraine and the north-east. What remained of Brittany was barricaded to the south by a non-existent mountain range near the mouth of the Loire. In the silken seas, creatures of the deep outnumbered ships: the basilica of Agathopolis (Agde) was about to be thrashed by the tail fin of a whale with a double blowhole, while a monkey-faced leviathan forged its way down the Atlantic coast towards a three-masted galleon.

The oddest feature of the *Carte ecclésiastique* was not immediately conspicuous, but once spotted, it was impossible to miss, like a familiar face in a crowd. In the centre of the map, where six rivers had their source, a giant tree dwarfed the neighbouring cathedrals of Avaricum Biturigum (Bourges), Ratiastum Lemovicum (Limoges) and

Augustonemetum Arvernorum (Clermont). The tree appeared to be growing out of something that might have been a dais or the base of a chalice. Its branches twirled upwards like flames and burst into an almost perfectly spherical display of foliage. The mountains and rivers, cities and islands were all clearly labelled; only the tree at the centre of France was unnamed.

Presumably, the 'gentlemen of the General Assembly of the Clergy of France' to whom the map was dedicated knew what this arboreal Goliath represented. The two-stepped plinth was detailed enough to suggest the drawing of a real structure, and I had a vague sense of having seen the figure somewhere before. When I looked at the map the following morning, half-expecting the tree to have shrunk to a normal size or disappeared, the answer came quite naturally and, with it, the idea for an expedition.

The sails of the ocean-going galleons were filled with an easterly breeze, but they belonged to the fantastic margins of the map. France was still a kingdom or a collection of provinces in search of its own identity, and the secret of that identity lay somewhere in the undiscovered interior, where a giant tree cast its shade over a peaceful realm of pasture and hedgerows, at the farthest point from the monstrous sea.

✽

Ever since Norman knights had conquered Sicily from the Arabs in the late eleventh century, and crusaders captive or convalescent had learned to appreciate the delights of a Moorish garden, ornamental horticulture had spread through Europe like a new religion. Miniaturists and weavers recreated the original horticultural masterpiece described in the Old Testament, and the walled gardens in which *châtelains* and *châtelaines* strolled among the idle beauty of flowers resembled the pages of an illuminated Book of Hours. The Garden of Eden was mapped with dreamlike precision, sometimes with scale-bars and keys to show exactly where the events of Genesis had taken place. Usually, the garden was sited in Arabia, Mesopotamia or Palestine, and in the midst of the garden, at the source of four rivers, stood the Tree of the Knowledge of Good and Evil.

A priest who inspected his copy of the new *Carte ecclésiastique* would have recognized at once the umbilical tree at the heart of creation. In this Gallican Genesis, the mother of all trees grew, not in the Holy Land, but in the navel of France, equidistant from the Mediterranean, the North Sea, the Atlantic Ocean and the Alps. The heart of Christianity had shifted to the west, and the kingdom which had once been without form and void was now a garden of delights under the stewardship of the Church and the King.

This cartographic cohabitation of the real and the symbolic was intriguing. The *Carte ecclésiastique* placed the Tree of Knowledge in what seemed to be a particular location, somewhere beneath the northern slopes of the Massif Central. It was possible, of course, that the artist had simply sited the tree in a conveniently uncluttered section of the map, but it was also possible that a tree of geographical or transcendent significance had existed somewhere in the triangle formed by the cities of Bourges, Limoges and Clermont – in which case, some trace of it might be found on other maps of the time . . .

*

The first map of France to show small towns and tributaries as well as cities and great rivers was the *Nova totius Galliae descriptio* (1525), drawn by a mathematician called Oronce Fine. Unfortunately, his map was quite treeless, and the next detailed rendering of the whole kingdom – Jean Jolivet's *Vraie description des Gaules*, published post-humously in 1560 – was largely copied from Fine's map and equally parsimonious with vegetation. But Jolivet was a native of Bourges and had undertaken some on-the-ground research of his own, which is why the central portion of his map includes a feature unknown to his predecessor. Between the upper reaches of two rivers, a peculiar leaf-shaped tree with a curving trunk was growing on a grassy mound. It appeared again in the 1570 edition, this time surrounded by something like a low wall or palisade.

From then on, the tree cropped up so often that I wondered why I had never noticed it before or seen any reference to it. Seventeen maps spanning eighty years (1560 to 1637) showed it in slightly different forms and locations – sometimes near Guéret, sometimes near Aubusson, but usually at the crossing of speculative lines of latitude and longitude. This tree must have lived in the minds of educated people for the best part of a century. After 1637, it never appeared again and played no further part in French history.

I would have consigned these cartographic gleanings to the ever-growing 'unsolved mysteries' folder were it not for the caption in French or Latin which accompanied the tree on most of the maps: '*Ulmus haec quatuor collateralium provinciarum fines attingit*' ('This elm touches the frontiers of four adjacent provinces'). In some cases, the four provinces were named as Auvergne, Berry, Bourbonnais and Limousin. This allowed the search area to be narrowed down to the frontier region called the Marche where the cultures of northern and southern France and their language groups – *oc* and *oïl* – came together.

The problem was that no such intersection had ever existed. After the disintegration of Roman Gaul, provincial boundaries had been so fluid and their evolutions so complex, dragged about by inheritance, purchase, litigation and encroachment, that, even if the geodetic skills had existed, it would have been impossible to define their meeting point. And at what stage of the expansions and contractions of Gallia, Francia and France had it seemed possible to define the geographical centre of the kingdom?

The functional evidence amounted to this: the tree had been an elm and it had stood somewhere in the northern Marche. Armed with this flimsy intelligence, I began to devise an itinerary based on whatever scraps could be found in the medieval records. The obvious place to start was the earliest detailed guidebook to the whole kingdom – Charles Estienne's pocket-sized *Guide des chemins de France*. It had been published in Paris in 1552, at about the time when Jean Jolivet was creating his map. The guidebook was patently erroneous in several respects and I was not expecting it to be of much practical use.

✿

Charles Estienne was one of the few publishers who were authorized to call themselves 'Imprimeur du Roi' (Printer by Appointment). He had studied anatomy and botany and practised medicine. His illustrations of the human nervous system were the first of their kind. As a young man, he had travelled to Germany and Italy. Now in his late forties, he was a seasoned armchair traveller. Instead of crawling over the surface of the mutating kingdom, he sat in his shop in the Latin Quarter behind the Rue Saint-Jacques like a spider at the heart of a trembling web of information.

In a short preface, he explained how he had set about his task and to what extent his guide could be relied upon:

> Given the diversity of opinions concerning distances and journey times on each route . . . it seemed sufficient to indicate the lodging and eating places so that each person might set off according to his convenience, being assured that, should he take lodging elsewhere, he will be in danger of receiving ill treatment.
>
> That said, I beg you to excuse the spelling of the names: I was forced to seek the aid of divers writers such as messengers, merchants and pilgrims, and the result is inevitably uneven . . .
>
> As for uncertainty about the bounds and extent of the regions, it is well known how variable they can be depending on the *apanages* [fiefdoms granted by a sovereign] and changes of prince. Therefore he begs you be content for the time being with what is said of these regions herewithin.

All guidebooks feed on their predecessors, sometimes to the point of plagiarism. The task facing the author who had virtually nothing to plagiarize is hard to imagine, yet Estienne's pioneering guide remained in use, with or without its author's name, and despite its errors and omissions, for over two hundred years.

His sources were handbills and booklets sold to pilgrims (or people travelling as such), lists of place names scribbled on scraps of paper, and crude maps drawn by pedlars and messengers. It was not always possible to tell to which place a caption was supposed to be attached, and then the places would appear out of order in the guide. Soiled manuscripts in half-legible cursive Gothic produced some garbled names: 'Crigny' for Origny, 'Saint Lir' for Saint Cyr, 'Mons ouveru' for Montfleury. Sixty years after the discovery of the New World, the internal exploration of France was barely under way. But the mistakes are easy to correct, and although the picturesque details are few and far between, this sixteenth-century Michelin guide and TripAdvisor can still be made to function like a magic carpet.

> Ribécourt windmill [near Noyon]: *See the mounds of Roland. Pass along the hedges of Ribécourt and leave it on your right. Boot yourself for the bad path in winter.*

> Mailly [near Châlons-en-Champagne]: *Fine open country with small descents and climbs made dangerous by thieves.*

> Neuville [near Bar-sur-Seine]: *Here one begins to see houses covered with hard, thin stone.*

> Le Chesne rond [near Dijon], *where the gallows stand, and from which point in good weather one can see Mount Bernard* [Mont Blanc] *and the mountains of Germany.*

> Briançon: *Nearby is a rock or mountain with a hole through the middle by which Caesar entered Gaul.*

Since Estienne's routes are purely verbal, I plotted them all on a map (fig. 6). Of the five routes leading through the middle of France, the one which seemed most likely to pass near the umbilical tree was the 'direct path' from Paris to Tholoze (Toulouse). After Orléans, it went south to Issoudun, marked '*g.*' for *giste* (a place to sleep). On the following day, it crossed a forest to Saint-Chartier, marked '*r.*' for *repeue* (meal). The next *giste* was at Lissaunay, thirty-five miles from Issoudun. (The guide generally assumed a day's journey – with or without a pack animal – of about thirty-five miles.) Then came a place called 'Le Mats sainct Paul'. At this point, the list of place names was interrupted by an unusually long paragraph:

> *See the elm & stone which mark the beginning of the Marche & divide four ways, being those of Berry, Lymosin, Bourbonnois & Auvergne, & beneath which it is said that four princes of those four lands in days gone by conducted negotiations, each one on his own ground.*

The elm and the stone reappeared a few pages later in the preface to the Limousin section. This second text seemed to have come from an earlier age when the four princes or lords were still meeting at the tree:

> *Within the Matz sainct Paul, three leagues from Nostre Dame de Lasangy & an abbey called Prebenast, there is a large stone which one climbs on a step in order to preserve the memory, & also a tall & ancient elm which marks the bounds of the lands of Berry, Lymosin, Bourbõnois & Auvergne, so that the four lords of the said lands, according to common report, might hold discussions together in this place, each remaining on his own soil.*

✤

I read these paragraphs repeatedly as though they were letters from a long-silent friend. This was unquestionably the tree I had seen at the centre of the *Carte ecclésiastique* and the other maps of France. The discrepancy between the two paragraphs hinted at two different sources: the tree and the stone either marked the meeting point of four provinces or, 'in days gone by', they had stood at the crossing of four ways leading to or from each province. It was unclear whether or not 'four princes' were still keeping up the tradition.

In the solitude of central France, in an obscure hamlet with no other claim to a traveller's attention, a simple ritual was performed. On Estienne's route, Le Mas Saint-Paul lay approximately halfway between Paris and Toulouse: perhaps the act of stepping onto the stone commemorated the successful completion of the first two hundred miles. 'It is said' and 'according to common report' suggested that the ritual had its origin in a local legend which told of a lost age when the princes of neighbouring provinces had lived in harmonious peace.

Intertribal meeting points marked by a tree or a stone are common in pre-modern history. Truces were sealed there, trade deals concluded and prisoners exchanged. These were invariably places which had long been considered sacred. 'Le Mas Saint-Paul', I discovered, had never been a settlement of much importance.* The latest IGN map showed it as two distinct hamlets – Le Mas and Saint-Paul – comprising fewer than forty houses. The hamlets were separated by hedge-lined fields and connected only by a track. But I also discovered that the little chapel of Saint Paul had been a place of local pilgrimage until the late nineteenth century: the waters of its well were believed to have the power to cure children of colic.

A healing spring at an early chapel normally indicates a pagan site that was Christianized some time after the fourth century. The earliest written record of Saint-Paul dated only from the mid-eleventh century, when a woman called Aina bequeathed the chapel and all its woods, meadows, ponds and streams, along with a watermill and a serf called Gosbert, to the Abbey of Déols near Châteauroux. Neither this nor any other document mentioned a meeting of four provinces, and the deed stated unambiguously that the chapel stood '*in pago Lemovico*' (in the region of Limousin).†

This silence of the records was surprising. The borders of the Limousin and the Auvergne had been matters of intense interest since the twelfth century. In 1154, two years after marrying Queen Eleanor of Aquitaine, Henry Plantagenêt, Duke of Normandy, became King Henry II of England. This powerful alliance of two monarchs placed much of western France under the control of the English crown. Territorial complexities and disputes tend to produce detailed documents, but in the mazy history of those central duchies, counties, baronies, seignories, dioceses and parishes, there was no trace of a quadrivial intersection, only the usual confusion of buffer zones and enclaves.

There remained the more promising clue of the 'four ways'. An ancient path rarely disappears completely. It might have degenerated into an overgrown bridleway or evolved into a four-lane *route nationale*,

---

* In this part of France, 'mas' was a collective term for the land and buildings owned by a family or a small clan.

† The *pagus* or *pays* of the Lemovici (the Gaulish tribe whose name meant 'People of the Elm').

but the descendant of a Roman or Gaulish road can nearly always be found on a large-scale modern map. Yet in the lattice of lanes in the vicinity of Saint-Paul, there was no sign of a significant crossroads.

An expedition now seemed inevitable. It was too much to hope that the tree would still be there: disease has decimated the elm population and the oldest living specimens in France sprouted in the late eighteenth century. But the ritual stone itself might have a tale to tell. I began to plot a route, hoping that the stone could still be found and that, if it did have a tale to tell, it would be in a language I could understand.

※　※　※

The difficulty of planning a bicycle expedition should always be underestimated: otherwise, the task would be too daunting. The route has to be worked out months in advance; then, as the day of departure draws near, news comes of a road closure, a rail strike or an unexplained decision to exclude bicycles from a particular train service, and a whole section of the beautifully balanced itinerary has to be reconstructed.

The plotting itself has the tidy complexity of an equation or a puzzle. The variables or clues are gradients, road surfaces, traffic density, availability of food and lodging, and the limits of comfortable endurance. In this case, I had the bones of an itinerary in the *Guide des chemins de France*, and by a happy coincidence, though most of the places were different, the distances between hostelries in the present were very similar to those specified by Charles Estienne in 1552. It seemed that, in the world of unmotorized transport, the bicycle had simply enabled our sluggish species to keep up with its fleet-footed ancestors.

Those ancestors must have had a peculiar sense of convenience. Logically, the itinerary included abbeys and hospices, where travellers might be fed by benevolent monks, but unlike the touristy routes proposed to modern pilgrims, it omitted almost every place of interest: it bypassed the pretty town of Sainte-Sévère, steered clear of Guéret and contrived to miss out Aubusson. For some reason, wherever possible, it avoided river crossings, keeping instead to soggy watershed lines. The Roman roads used by nineteenth-century stonemasons who walked to Paris from the Creuse ran several miles to the west. It was as though some terrible calamity had occurred so that travellers bound for Paris or Toulouse had to thread their way obscurely through a post-apocalyptic landscape like fearful children avoiding bullies on the way home from school.

It was only after extending the search for a plausible itinerary several decades before Estienne's guide that I realized that the calamity had actually taken place and that its name was the Hundred Years War. Departure would now be delayed until I could work out our date of destination.

*

A strictly chronological history, with its unstoppable baggage-train of documents labelled with their correct address in time, can be a poor guide to the past. The series of Anglo-French wars and dynastic struggles called the Hundred Years War had ended in 1453, ninety-nine years before Estienne published his guide. The initial conflict was caused by Philippe VI's confiscation of the Duchy of Aquitaine from the English in 1337. Edward III of England, claiming to be the rightful King of France, invaded with an army of longbowmen, against whom the best defence was to run away and hide, leaving the countryside to the enemy (a tactic known as *terre déserte*). In the mid-fourteenth century, the English had controlled the port and hinterland of Calais, much of Brittany and a rectangular swathe stretching from the marsh-lands south of the Loire to the Pyrenees. (Fig. 5.)

The accidental legacy of the English would be the dream of a united and eternal French state. In the final phase of the war, after the victory of the resurgent English under Henry V at Agincourt near Calais in 1415, when most of the northern half of France had fallen to the English, that dream was so potent that on the eastern edges of France, in the Marches of Lorraine, a girl born on the banks of the Meuse was inspired by saintly voices and national sentiment to drive the English out of France and to have a French king crowned at Reims. Twenty-two years after Joan of Arc was burned by the English at Rouen in 1431, France had recovered Normandy and the wine-growing region of Gascony, purchased the Dauphiné and established an eastern border along the 'four rivers' – Escaut, Meuse, Rhone and Saône.

A long-distance historian might be tempted to say, as though speaking for a nation, 'Thank God the War's over.' But for the populations who were now notionally at peace, the aftermath of the Hundred Years War was another hundred years of poverty and unrest. Decades of conflict, famine and disease had weakened the power of the monarchy and created a mosaic of kleptocratic feudal statelets. Many regions were cut off from the rest of the country by bands of feral soldiers and peasants in revolt, and by the disappearance of roads which had been left unrepaired for generations.

When Charles Estienne published his guide in 1552, it was possible to imagine, at least in the heart of Paris, that the dream of unity had come true. The Ordinance of Villers-Cotterêts in 1539 had made the dialect spoken in the Île-de-France the official language of the kingdom. Paris, which had been ruled for sixteen years by the English and their Burgundian allies, was the political, religious and intellectual capital. Forests haunted by highwaymen had been cleared. The whole country was open for business and – a new concept – journeys for pleasure. But the guide also warned of 'brigands' and 'perilous passages' as far north as Villers-Cotterêts and the outskirts of Paris in the environs of a paltry village called Versailles. Traced on a map, many of Estienne's *'chemins de France'* prove to be cul-de-sacs ending on the edge of trackless zones, two of the largest of which – Upper Normandy and western Gascony – were the areas most recently occupied by the English. (Fig. 6.)

In the *Guide des chemins de France*, the Hundred Years War was not even a footnote. The brief account of Normandy said nothing of the half century of English occupation, and no one would have guessed that the 'fortified town' of Calais was still an English possession: 'from there in clear weather one can see the opposite shore and the tail end of England'. Though the guide included Orléans, Rouen and Lorraine, Joan of Arc was never mentioned. There were references to Charlemagne and Roland, but by far the commonest historical figure was Julius Caesar. It was as though little of lasting significance had occurred since the end of the Gallic War.

In the centre of that kingdom, four lords or princes had met or were still meeting under an ancient tree where geography and politics were in perfect accord. When we left the Anglo-Scottish border in the summer of 2018 for the land that was about to be severed once again from England, I still thought of that leafy enigma as the Tree at the Centre of France, but the closer we came to the region in which it had grown, the harder it was to believe in the reality of its timeless world.

✿

At the Gare d'Austerlitz in Paris, we boarded the slow train to La Souterraine. From there, we cycled east to Guéret, the former capital of the Marche province, now the administrative centre of the Creuse *département*. Twelve years before, a broken gear-cable had forced us to spend the night at Guéret in a fetid hotel. The hotel was unrecognizable: it had been purged and modernized by a new owner. Portraits of the Buddha now smiled serenely on the clean efficiency. From our room on the top floor, between the houses across the street, I could see green hills to the north shimmering in the heat haze. I studied the itinerary with the usual misgivings that precede enactment. Transposing Estienne's route into the twenty-first century had produced an unusually convoluted travel plan.* If anyone asked where we were heading, it would be hard to give a simple answer.

> Guéret [460] – r. F. Roosevelt [399] – D4 [443] – rndbt Intermarché [392] (2.8) – under bridge on L – 'Pommeret' exit – D100 – *Creuse* [311] – Ajain [473] (13) – Loubier [468] – Roches [474] – Châtelus-Malvaleix [412] (27) – St-Dizier [341] – D3 – *Petite Creuse* [283] – **Prébenoît** (abbaye) [288] (34) – le Chalet [329] – D3A – ✞ [370] – ✞ [395] (check track) – Viviers [402] – Puyssetier [371] – **St Paul** [338] (41) – La Cellette [351] – ✞ [373] – (turn down lane, 500 m. [374]) – **Le Mas** [383] <> la Jarousse [402] (see road N twds La Châtre) – St Paul [338] – Tercillat [392] <> Pré du Moulin [358] (48) – Maison Rouge [423] <> CREUSE / INDRE – ✞ [437] – Chez Merlin [420] – Nouzerines [419]: 54

Early next morning, the two women at the reception desk – the proprietress and her assistant – asked where we were headed.

'To Lyon, then up into the Vercors and over to the Alps.'

'You're going to Lyon – today?!'

'Ah, no. That'll take a little longer. Today, we're going to a place called Le Mas Saint-Paul . . .'

---

* For a decipherment, see the Notes for Travellers, p. 397.

I pulled out a copy of the two pages of antiquated French and summarized the contents. 'With luck, the tree or the stone will still be there.'

The friend of Buddha was amused by this latest example of English eccentricity. A potentially non-existent tree in an unknown hamlet must have seemed a poor substitute for the 'unmissable sites' advertised in the neatly stacked brochures. Who would adopt the dubious recommendations of an obsolete guidebook when they were guaranteed a pleasant outing at the Wolves of Chabrière Animal Park or the Giant Labyrinth of the Monts de Guéret? The other woman was being trained in the tricky art of hotel reception. I could see that, at that moment, an outdoor adventure, however pointless, had a strong appeal. She stared at the unfamiliar script with what can only be called a wild surmise:

'Mais c'est la chasse au trésor!'

'En quelque sorte, oui . . .'

'Et qu'est-ce que vous ferez si vous le trouvez, ce trésor?'

'Eh bien, en ce cas-là, je le fourrai dans les sacoches et nous retournerons directement en Angleterre.'*

Both women laughed, probably for different reasons. The occupation of medieval France by the English is more present to French than to British minds, especially in that part of the country, and the idea of English-speaking foreigners riding off with a treasure has a certain historical resonance.

✳

As we pedalled up from the River Creuse on the old road from Limoges, I scanned the swarming hedgerows, partly to reassure myself that I could spot an elm, but also because looking at the roadside rather than the summit makes a long climb seem shorter. There was oak, hazel, field maple, bird cherry, willow, chestnut, walnut, birch and poplar, but no elm, which was odd because the disease-ridden tree still grows vigorously to a considerable height. At several crossroads, we saw plinths and crosses carved out of a single block of stone.

---

* 'It's a treasure hunt!' 'In a sense, yes . . .' 'And what will you do if you find the treasure?' 'In that case, I'll stuff it into the panniers and we'll go straight back to England.'

This was a more promising sign: the crosses were medieval or early medieval and surprisingly well preserved.

The roads grew even quieter. Soon, there was no traffic at all and no one was about – no farmers or dog-walkers, not even a local amateur historian. At a meeting of ways on a straight road far from any other habitation, someone had repainted the faded sign on a roadside house: 'LABORDE, AUBERGISTE'. The former *auberge* was a clue to an old long-distance route. The low hills of similar size had the roundness of the cumulus rising over the hot earth; their slopes were divided into fields by ever more luxuriant hedges, and the tree list grew longer: ash, lime, alder, pine, blackthorn, lilac and acacia. We seemed to have stumbled on an elm-free zone. Perhaps the ancient tree had been chosen for its rarity . . .

The silent ruins of the abbey of Prébenoît, which comes next to Le Mas-Saint-Paul in the 1552 guide, stand just off the road on lower ground beyond the defensive moat that was dug during the Hundred Years War. In 1367, the road through Saint-Paul and Prébenoît had been 'constantly trampled by men-at-arms and foot soldiers'. Two stone columns mark a grand entrance which no longer exists. The surviving, still habitable buildings of the courtyard had the air of an abandoned railway station.

The road climbed gently for three miles; then we were looking down into a diminutive dale where the roofs and walls of Saint-Paul play hide-and-seek among the hedges. At the far end of the hamlet, just before a crossroads, the tiny chapel of Saint-Paul sits lopsidedly on a mound of earth. Its rear end had been used as a barn. The rickety outhouses of a smallholding lay round about. The farm appeared to be derelict and only a brindled cat came to inspect the strangers.

The wizened oak door was locked, but the keyhole was wide enough to reveal a dusty nave with two steps leading up to a crude stone altar. Unless it had been incorporated into the altar, there was no sign of 'the stone which one climbs on a step to preserve the memory', which is only to be expected since dressed stones rarely stay put when the structure to which they belonged has crumbled. Twenty feet above us on the west front, three medieval faces serving as modillions were the only decoration. The least eroded of the three appeared to be smiling.

There was little else to see – some old graffiti consisting of initials scratched on a side door, three iron horseshoes pushed into cracks in the mortar, and the flattened, feathery cape of a dead buzzard. I returned to the front of the chapel. A few feet away among the ivy and the brambles, the noonday sun fell on a pallid, bone-coloured column. Peeling away a flap of bark, I saw on the yellowed wood the pattern of ripples created by the breeding galleries of the elm-bark beetle.

This was probably the first ritualistic act performed at the tree since the late Middle Ages: a spindly man in a bandana pointing a digital camera at some dead twigs and uttering sounds of excitement. Margaret sat on the chapel steps to eat the rice cakes and cream cheese, making the best of a wild-tree chase. Admittedly, it was not the most spectacular monument. This was history in the raw, skeletalized by time, unembalmed by heritage committees. Four hundred years after it disappeared from maps of France, the descendant of the elm looks exactly as it should, throwing up its dead arms in posthumous defiance of the disease. It will have seeded itself somewhere in the vicinity before it died, and one day, when the species has learned to live with its pathogen, a tall and ancient elm will stand there once again.

✿

'Waste of time' is a concept which haunts the mind of any researcher, but time itself is never wasteful. After months of route-planning, I knew that the road through the centre of France had been an artery of the Hundred Years War. Perhaps it was the sight of the ruined sheds of the deserted farm – it struck me more forcefully now that, wherever the centre of late-medieval France might have been, we were standing on a fault line between the two great European powers. After the Treaty of Brétigny-Calais in 1360, the land to the west of the road through Prébenoît and Saint-Paul had been English, not French, and the tree had marked the western edge of a shrinking kingdom. This obscurest of places, to which we had been led by a far-fetched drawing on an antiquated map, had been a nodal point of French history.

We left the chapel to search the neighbouring lanes for the misplaced stone before circling back to approach the chapel from the other direction. The only likely candidate was a curvaceous block of granite dumped in a heap of agricultural rubbish at a meeting of paths to make way for a telegraph pole. We cycled along the continuation of Estienne's route to the north for about a mile before turning back. A road seen but untravelled can exert a poignant fascination, and I was determined to incorporate it into a future journey.

That journey took place sooner than I expected. Hardly any time now seems to have elapsed between that first visit and the second, twelve months later.

After returning to Britain, I discovered a text by the novelist and social historian George Sand. Sixteen miles up the road, at a place corresponding to 'La Poste' on Estienne's itinerary,* there had once stood a cross on a stone pedestal next to a magnificent elm called the Orme Rateau because it looked like a rake. According to Sand, who lived a twenty-minute walk away, the abandoned north–south road 'was formerly one of the great thoroughfares of central France. To this day [1866], it is known as "le chemin des Anglais" '.

At the lonely crossroads near Lourouer-Saint-Laurent, there are wide views in all directions. The iron cross is less than a century old, but the stepped pedestal is still there, with wheel symbols carved on each of its six sides. The cross known to George Sand had apparently replaced the 'very ancient' statues of four saints, one of whom was

---

* Predating the establishment of a state monopoly, the 'postes' in Estienne's guide were not staging posts but farms or isolated houses where a horse could be reshod or a wheel rim replaced.

said to have been active in the Hundred Years War. The stone Saint Anthony had agreed to watch over the pigs of a young swineherd while the boy set off to help expel the English from the nearby town of Saint-Chartier. (This would have been in 1372.) In his modest way, the swineherd did for Saint-Chartier what Joan of Arc did for Orléans. He returned to the elm to find that the wolves and looters who followed the English army had miraculously left his pigs in peace.

This was a compelling coincidence: two ritual sites on the same war-ravaged path were associated with legends which spoke of political unity and the formation of a nation-state. The eroded figures of early saints were often confused with depictions of feudal lords, and vice versa. Until the eleventh century, both were referred to as *domini* ('lords' or 'masters'). Perhaps the stone plinth at Saint-Paul had once supported a similar statue marking a quiet crossroads where travellers were in danger of taking the wrong path and finding themselves in a foreign land.

❁

The warnings in Charles Estienne's *Guide des chemins de France* concerning incorrect distances, misspellings and provincial boundaries would be considered dangerously inadequate by a modern publisher's lawyers. He must have known that this section of his itinerary had been an international frontier and that the Marche through which he cheerfully sent the users of his guide was still the suffering heart of a disunited kingdom.

When the first edition of the guide was published in 1552, the Catholic monarchy was threatened by the spread of Protestantism and in particular by the potential for an unauthorized sect to become a rallying cry for the factions which proliferated in the decentralized state. In 1550, Charles's brother Robert had fled to Geneva under suspicion of Lutheran heresy. Robert Estienne's scholarly editions of the Bible, for which he devised the system of verses and numbers still in use today, were intended to elucidate the word of God, not to confirm the official doctrine of the Church and the monarchy.

Charles Estienne died in 1564. Five years later, when the several editions of his guide were painting a sunny picture of journeys through a largely peaceful kingdom, the route through the Marche was a war path once again: the 'Chemin des Anglais' was the main supply line for Protestant forces recruited in the south. A Huguenot army funded by Queen Elizabeth of England destroyed practically every place between Saint-Chartier and Jarnages, including the abbey of Prébenoît.

In 1572, on Saint Bartholomew's Eve (23 August), Estienne's successor might have heard from his printing shop across the river the frantic clanging of church bells around the Louvre. The wedding of the King's sister Marguerite de Valois to Henri de Bourbon, ruler of the Protestant kingdom of Navarre, had brought Huguenot nobles and their followers flocking to Paris. The royal wedding was intended to douse the fires of religious hatred. But militantly Catholic Parisians seized the chance to purge the capital of Protestants. Several thousand were slaughtered in the night. In the morning, bloated corpses were washing up on the banks of the Seine and a murdered woman hung by her long hair from the stays of the Pont Notre-Dame. A hawthorn tree in the Cimetière des Innocents was miraculously covered in may blossom.

With God's manifest approval, the massacre continued for several days. Over the next month and a half, as false reports spread from Paris faster than the King's messengers, Protestants were butchered in a dozen towns and cities, either by mobs or by local officials who believed that they were carrying out the orders of the King.

✻

The tree which survived into old age on one of the bloodiest roads of a fractured nation symbolized a powerful fantasy. This is one of the earliest signs that a sense of national identity – and of entitlement to certain geometrically justified territorial acquisitions – would be invested in the shape of the land itself. For Charles Estienne, France was 'a lozenge twenty-two days wide and nineteen days long'; for others, it would be the circle, the oval, the square and finally – the modern synonym for France – the hexagon.

The figment of a cosy arbour enclosed by the securely walled estate of a centralized monarchy harked back to the half-imagined days when the soon-to-be-deified Caesar had unified Gaul and the Roman geographer Strabo had detected a guiding hand in the distribution of its natural resources.

The harmonious arrangement of the country appears to offer evidence of the workings of Providence, since the regions are laid out, not haphazardly, but as though in accordance with some calculated plan.

In that Wonderland of conveniently located eating and resting places, with busy roads plied by trans-provincial merchants and drovers, no traveller would ever be lost again, and if they died, they would already be in heaven.

❀

At about the time when the elm of Eden was disappearing from maps, another tree took its place. In the City of Bourges, according to a guidebook of 1643 titled *L'Ulysse françois* ('The French Odysseus'), a lime tree was believed to mark the exact centre of the country. Even two centuries later, 'people come from far and wide to dance around the tree so they can say they have danced in the middle of France'. Bourges had briefly been the capital of Charles VII in 1418–19, when Paris and Reims were occupied by the English and Burgundians. The lime tree had been planted in front of the palatial townhouse of Jacques Coeur, the millionaire merchant who had helped to finance the expulsion of the English from Normandy.

Charles VII owed his coronation at Reims to Joan of Arc. To Jacques Coeur, he owed the means to pursue the war, to fund a standing army and to reorganize the provinces into subservient *parlements*. The umbilical tree at Bourges commemorated the magic fountain of money which had saved the kingdom more conclusively than the saints who instructed Joan of Arc.

This was the tree of a new age, when the princes of separate provinces no longer stood 'each on his own ground'. In 1643, the four-year-old Louis-Dieudonné of the House of Bourbon had just ascended the throne as King Louis XIV. He would be called the Sun King, and around him the increasingly impotent provincial aristocrats would revolve in decaying orbits until they were either absorbed by the Court or cast into outer darkness.

❀   ❀   ❀

This tale of a tree hunt was to have ended here. The file had been closed and the photographs of stones and hedges renamed and backed up. Then, not quite unexpectedly, I saw the tree again – or rather, the ghost of the tree, looking out of place, as ghosts typically do.

I was working my way through the hundreds of eighteenth-century maps assembled by the Bibliothèque Nationale de France on its 'Gallica' website. In the Age of Reason, the country had its now-familiar shape. Whimsical decorations were no longer admissible in serious cartography and the monsters had vanished into featureless seas. On each map, I always scrutinized the area where the tree had stood. Of course, the tree had gone, and yet three of those maps still showed the fictitious meeting point of four provinces.

The first was a map of the areas of Jesuit ministry published in 1705. This might have been stubborn ecclesiastical tradition, but ecclesiastical tradition could not explain the presence of the meeting point on the *Carte des Traites* which showed the zones of internal customs duty. Until the Revolution of 1789, this was the official map of the royal tax authorities. Berry and Bourbonnais, coloured grey, belonged to the free-trade zone centred on Paris; the other two provinces, Limousin and Auvergne, coloured yellow, were classed as 'provinces considered foreign' for tax purposes. The intersection of the four occupied the very centre of the map.

The divisive system of Paris-centric taxation dated back to the Hundred Years War, when the dissenting 'foreign' regions (Brittany, Flanders, Franche-Comté and all provinces south of Berry and Bourbonnais) had been unwilling to fund the failing monarchy. After three hundred years, they were still resisting attempts to impose a uniform tax system. The harmonious 'centre of France', which had once stood on the frontier between England and France, now marked a more lasting division. The lands to the south of the centre were those in which French was still a foreign language. The elm or its offspring must have scattered its seed over two separate and antagonistic zones – the Occitan south and the Francophone north.

The third map was such a brazen retelling of the old tale that, most unusually, I bought a copy of it for twenty euros to have some lasting proof of this overlooked moment in the psycho-history of France. It was a map of the central provinces, drawn in 1763. The map was included in an important new historical atlas by a classical scholar and professor of history who was also one of the royal censors.

A thick stroke of black ink down the centre of the map shows the

Paris Meridian – the thousand-kilometre-long line of zero longitude which ran through the Observatory in Paris. The Meridian was one of the great achievements of the age. The result of precise triangulations and a great deal of leg-work, it formed the basis of the Cassini map of France and, by allowing the size of the Earth to be measured, it gave the world its first universal standard measurement, the metre.

The royal censor must have felt that the incontrovertible, mathematical truth of the Meridian had sinned against the proper order of things. As a scientific fact, the Meridian was detached from history and tradition. And so, forcing science to serve the dream of predestination, he took those four perfectly interlocking provinces and shifted them twenty-four kilometres to the east so that the Meridian would bisect their meeting point.

The site of the Gallican Tree of Knowledge was thus incorporated into the longest '*chemin de France*' of all, as though to prove that a myth of national unity could conquer truth and reason, and that the Paris Meridian itself had been anticipated by the God who created paradise in France and gave the King dominion over all its children.

PART TWO

Louis XIV to the Second Empire

7

A Walk in the Garden

In the days when the quartiers and sub-quartiers of Paris were like a Great Exhibition of the French provinces and *pays*, each one distinguishable by the smells and voices of a particular region or valley, a colony of the Hurepoix *pays* occupied a cluttered street of boarding houses by the banks of the Seine. The Rue du Hurepoix lost its identity after the Revolution when the Quai des Augustins was extended to the Pont Saint-Michel and the houses on the brink of the river were demolished. The street had once marked the northern limit of the Hurepoix itself. To cross the Seine to the spire of the Sainte-Chapelle, which rose above the rigging of the barges, was to leave the Hurepoix and enter the province called Île-de-France.*

Until the Latin-speaking University came to dominate the Left Bank, Paris began on the north side of the bridges. By the late seventeenth century, the Hurepoix, whose enigmatic name was presumed to refer to the bristling hair (*poil*) of the wild boar (*hure*), had retreated to the south. Its frontier was considered to lie at the far end of the Rue d'Enfer, beyond the Royal Observatory, towards the windmills and gibbet of Montrouge. The Rue du Hurepoix then became a typical Latin Quarter encyclopaedia of trades: there were cab drivers and ostlers, wine merchants and poulterers, sellers of soap and perfume

---

* 'France' or 'Francia', the empire of Charlemagne, also referred to the region of plains and plateaux north and east of Paris, hence the place names Châtenay-en-France, Roissy-en-France, etc. The name 'Isle de France' is first attested in 1429, when the English invaders were 'eager to withdraw to the Marches of Northmandy and to abandon their possessions in the Isle de France and round about'. 'L'Isle de' is likely to be Middle English 'litel' or 'littel'. 'L'Île de France' would thus be 'Little France'.

battling with the Parisian miasma of cabbage and manure, and second-hand booksellers whose gloomy bazaars, filled with the detritus and treasures of the bankrupt and the dead, competed with the all-weather hawkers whose book boxes still line the *quais*.

The *pays* of France were originally the *pagi* or sub-tribal territories of Gaul. At the end of the Middle Ages when they were incorporated into the larger provinces, few of the three hundred or so *pays* had any political or administrative identity, yet some of their contours betrayed their earthy origins. Accurately traced, their loopy meanderings have an air of randomness, like clouds in complex weather systems or puddles spreading over uneven terrain. They describe the long and intimate affair of people with their native soil. Only GPS satellites and ground-penetrating radar could now replicate their minute observance of topography and geology. (Fig. 7.)

The Hurepoix covered about six hundred square miles between the royal hunting forests to the north-west, the sandy wastes of the Gâtinais to the east and the windy plain of the Beauce stretching away towards Orléans and Chartres. The tattered edge of an ancient plateau, the Hurepoix is mostly sand, clay and millstone grit on a bed of limestone. Its unassuming rivers – Bièvre, Essonne, Orge and Yvette – trickle down to the Seine through deep wooded valleys, sometimes lingering in semi-stagnant lagoons. Geologically, the Left Bank of Paris belonged to the Hurepoix: the 'hell hole' of the Plaine du Trou d'Enfer near Versailles was probably a sinkhole or limestone cavity like those which threatened to engulf the Latin Quarter until the architect of the Catacombs shored it up with an enormous underground 'cathedral' in the late eighteenth century. Barren outcrops of rock in the hedgeless fields gave some of the plateaux a spartan appearance, but the stony soil saved many a peasant from starvation: about one third of the wine sold in Paris came from the cottage vineyards of the Hurepoix.

✢

The friable and unpredictable terrain accounts for the presence of a colony of the Hurepoix on the banks of the Seine. Such was the state of the roads that unless they lived in the northernmost part of the *pays* at Vaugirard, Gentilly or Issy, merchants from the Hurepoix would not expect to reach home if they left Paris after noon. Until 1738, there were no certified road menders to firm up the carriageway with spoil from the ditches. A freeze followed by a sudden thaw, and a single pothole could morph overnight into a chasm and paralyse the traffic of an entire region. An hour's walk from the centre of Paris, there were not only impracticable areas but also impassable seasons. Between harvest and planting, the 'road' or swathe of land set aside for transit might be marked only by an overturned carriage with broken windows and a crow-pecked horse slumped on the soggy earth.

When the winter wind blew through the huddled farms and villages, a howling could be heard which was not that of the wind. For seven years in the mid-seventeenth century, the Hurepoix was a hunting ground of the infantivorous Beast of the Gâtinais, depicted in engravings as a long-legged she-wolf the size of a horse. The monster's descendants still appear in parish burial registers of the 1690s:

> On this, the third day of February 1693, was buried in the cemetery of Saint-Jean-de-Beauregard a part of the head of Marie Mignet, found in the Marcoussis woods devoured by wolves while keeping the cows, aged eleven years or thereabouts.

The hunting-mad son of Louis XIV bagged more than a thousand wolves between 1684 and 1711, averaging one wolf per hunt. Almost eight hundred of those peri-urban predators had their field of operations within fifteen miles of Notre-Dame.

Even at a distance of three or four miles, the influence of one of the world's biggest cities was imperceptible. The north wind might bring smells of tanneries and human waste, but there were no lights or sounds or sometimes even traffic to guide a traveller. One morning in 1745, a seven-year-old boy walked out of Paris with his uncle to collect payment for work carried out in the village of Issy. It was a journey of about a league (seven stops on the Métro from Montparnasse). The customer paid his bill and was so lavish with his food and wine that when uncle and nephew tottered off for home, the sun had set.

> The wine kept us walking, but the way seemed longer to me than in the morning. Uncle teased me and said I was upset because I wanted a cuddle from my grandmother. After walking for two hours or more we saw a light in the distance. 'Look', said my uncle, 'the

lanterns of the Faubourg Saint-Germain'. As soon as he said it, the light disappeared. We kept walking till we came to a village. It was terribly dark and the whole village was asleep. . . . We knocked on a door and asked how far we were from Paris, and they told us that it was three leagues from there . . .

When they finally made it back to 'our own *pays*' (Paris), they found that the boy's grandmother and aunt had gone to the Rue aux Ours to pray to the statue of the Virgin for their safe return from that faraway land on the doorstep of Paris.

＊

At the time when this tale of war and horticultural conquest begins, the city on the edge of the Hurepoix was a bloated giant. Its population numbered nearly half a million; the Faubourg Saint-Germain alone was larger than any other French city apart from Lyon, Bordeaux and Toulouse. To a native of the Hurepoix, Paris was a pandemonium of traffic jams and violent mobs. In 1610, Good King Henri IV of the House of Bourbon had been stuck in one of those congested streets between a wine cart and a haywain. After his tactical conversion to Catholicism, Henri had restored certain civil rights to Protestants and almost ended the Wars of Religion. But to the psychotic conspiracy theorist who followed his coach from the Louvre, the King was an apostate whose invasion of the Spanish Netherlands constituted an attack on the Pope. His coach had large, unshielded windows and so it was a simple matter to step up onto the carriage wheel and stab the King to death.

Under Henri IV's son, Louis XIII, and the tentacular ministry of Cardinal Richelieu, the Court tightened its grip on the fractious kingdom. The parliament of the États-Généraux was already a largely ceremonial body when it was convoked – for the last time until the 1789 Revolution – in the winter of 1614–15. It sat in the town-house complex which the Bourbon clan had been building for itself next door to the Louvre since 1303. The representatives of the 'three states' – nobility, clergy and bourgeoisie – were little more than house guests of the Bourbons. The powers of their own regional assemblies could be exercised only with the assent of the King's *intendants*.

The old states – or, as they were coming to be known in haughty reference to the Roman Empire, 'provinces' – were fading away into a romanticized past, along with their ancient laws and customs. (Fig. 8.) In regions to the north and east of Paris, where localized peasant revolts were frequent, tighter central control might have been politically justified, but the Hurepoix itself had long been a model of peaceful cooperation. The farmers of the Hurepoix, few of whom owned more than two acres, had been well represented by local councils composed of heads of household (including widows) who each served a twelve-month term. 'More democratic than today's municipal councils' – as the historian Emmanuel Le Roy Ladurie tartly observed in 1975 – these peasant assemblies had cushioned the *pays* to some extent from the effects of state interference and the ever-more intrusive officers of the King.

Small *pays* like the Hurepoix had usually been able to recover within a generation from famine and disease, but now, in the enlarged nation-state, they found themselves exposed to storms coming from much farther afield. The formation of ever-larger political units may have promoted cohesion and security in the very long term, but for peasants who lived within a twelve-hour radius of Paris, it was as though a harbour wall had been demolished and they found themselves in the great ship of state, sailing on an open sea.

✵

For the Hurepoix, the nightmare began in the fifth year of the reign of Henri IV's grandson, Louis XIV. The boy had become king at the age of four in 1643. His mother, Anne of Austria, was regent, and his chief minister was Richelieu's successor, the dictatorial and incongruously affable Italian Cardinal Mazarin. Impervious to the xenophobic and pornographic pamphlets which accused him of usurping royal authority, and revelling in his unpopularity, he behaved like the steward of a private estate. Large parts of the domain were occupied by relatives who paid no rent. On three sides – Flanders, the Rhineland and the Pyrenees – a family of foreigners was building an empire. Expensive wars were waged against the Austrian and Spanish rulers of the Habsburg dynasty, and the people of the Hurepoix, along with their twenty million compatriots, felt the steward's long fingers rummaging in their pockets.

As usual, the trouble began in Paris. When Mazarin tried to tax the previously untaxed nobles of the Parlement de Paris in 1648, they rebelled and the ringleaders were jailed. Street urchins who regularly fought pitched battles with each other were persuaded to smash the windows of Mazarin and his supporters instead. The Parisian Cockney's weapon of choice, the *fronde* or slingshot, gave its name to the uprising, and, since the civil war came to be seen as a farcical national embarrassment, the name 'Fronde' was eventually applied to the five years of chaos which ensued.

The few Paris streets which offered a line of sight of more than a few yards were barricaded with wooden beams, wicker baskets and barrels filled with cobbles or manure. On the night of 5–6 January 1649, when Parisians were taking a break from revolting to celebrate the Fête des Rois (Twelfth Night), Louis XIV was smuggled out of the Palais Royal and rushed to Saint-Germain. This was one of the satellite royal estates whose hastily refurbished palaces would often serve as dismal sanctuaries beyond the reach of a Paris mob. Louis's aunt Henriette-Marie had been given the use of the *château* after her departure from England. Three weeks after Louis's arrival, news reached Saint-Germain that her husband, Charles I, had been decapitated in London.

The civil war in France took a very different form. Religious affiliation was almost irrelevant. The Fronde was primarily a revolt of the nobility against the hated Mazarin, which explains why the principal aggressors – Louis's cousin, the Prince de Condé, and his uncle Gaston d'Orléans – fought for and against the King as Mazarin's influence waxed and waned. Fortified *châteaux* and walled towns had been abolished by Richelieu (a largely symbolic emasculation, since gunpowder had rendered medieval defences useless), but huge tracts were still controlled by provincial 'princes'. No Norman Conquest had ever imposed a coherent feudal regime on the whole country, and as Mazarin tried to pull it into shape, the patchwork realm came apart at the seams.

Between the three of them, the Prince de Condé, his brother and his brother-in-law governed about half of France. From Normandy to Languedoc, uncodified systems of patronage enabled these latter-day tribal kings to convert local insurrections on all levels of society into wide-ranging military campaigns. Peasants and artisans, clergymen and landowners were induced to fight for their own local prince.

Pitchforks and muskets were replaced by cannon. The territory controlled by the Crown changed from one season to the next. At one point, when Guyenne and Gascony had declared their independence, the southern frontier of 'France' was the River Loire. Louis XIV, who had been brought up to think of himself as the supreme, predestined ruler (Dieudonné or 'God's gift' was his middle name), moved about his kingdom like a beleaguered knight on a chess board. In the space of a year, the Court sat at Fontainebleau, Bourges, Poitiers, Tours, Saint-Denis, Pontoise, Compiègne and Saint-Germain.

The worst year in the history of the Hurepoix was 1652. The fields were left fallow because ploughmen kept their horses indoors. Soldiers from the Marches of Lorraine led by the Prince de Condé carted off the harvest. Some of the longest processions ever seen passed through the *pays*: each army was the vanguard of an immense itinerant suburb of vagabonds, prostitutes and thieves, with several thousand cows and sheep bringing up the rear as though a caravan of transhumant livestock had been diverted from the Alps. Farmers saw their daughters tortured, raped and killed, their homes destroyed and the precious vine-shoots chomped by foreign horses. A third of all children between the ages of one and nineteen perished. Some villages lost a greater proportion of their population than in the First World War.

In January 1652, when that lupine camp-follower, the Beast of the Gâtinais, acquired a taste for young human flesh, Louis XIV complained to his uncle Gaston that his troops were 'prowling and pillaging and ruining everything in the Brie, the Hurepoix and the Gâtinais'. In May, he attended the siege of Étampes on the southern edge of the Hurepoix and was nearly killed by a cannonball. In October, Condé's men were finally ordered out of Paris by the Parlement de Paris. They headed north to fight for the Spanish in the Netherlands, leaving behind them 'grande ordure et puanteur'. On the 21st, the fourteen-year-old King re-entered his festering capital through a devastated suburban landscape the like of which would not be seen again until the Napoleonic Wars.

✣

Peace of a sort returned to the Hurepoix. The vine stocks recovered, thatched cottages burned only by accident, the thud of boots and hooves was once again the sound of fruitful labour. Then the sound of lasting change, which had been drowned out by the noise of battle but which had never ceased, could be heard in the scratching of lawyers' quills.

Small farmers saw the land around their little plots swallowed up by government officials, Parisian bourgeois and nobles who had bought themselves out of the bourgeoisie. The great city was remodelling its supply zone. The incomers ignored ancient parish boundaries and rural traditions. Much of the northern Hurepoix was given over to hunting forests and supplies of Vin du Hurepoix dwindled. In some parts, only a fifth of the land remained in the hands of natives.

The wealthier farmers whose sons attended Jesuit colleges in the city had once spoken the same dialect as the poorest peasants. Now, for the first time, agricultural labourers outnumbered farmers. 'Paysan' became an insult and the mud of the *pays* was an emblem of brutishness. And yet, as society solidified into ranks and castes, something of the old self-confident peasantry survived.

On the northern edge of the Hurepoix, a sludgy lane barely wider than a cart led south from Marly across the plain of the Trou d'Enfer towards the *buttes* or hillocks around the village of Versailles. This was in the early 1660s, before the paved carriageway to Marly became one of the finest roads in the kingdom. A heavily laden tumbril was bouncing and slithering along the lane. From the other direction came a gilded carriage drawn by a team of thoroughbred horses and escorted by liveried footmen and guards in uniform. The tumbril groaned and the carriage creaked to a halt. Either the cart or the carriage would have to be pulled off the road into the fathomless mud of the verge.

There is nothing like travelling on a public highway to imbue a man or a woman with a sense of entitlement. The carter showed no sign of moving. One of the guards shouted, 'Can't you see who it is?', but the immovable obstacle only grunted, 'Huh. He can get bogged down if he wants to. He's got more horses than me.' The occupant of the carriage ordered his driver to give way. The painted wheels sank into the mud, the tumbril swaggered past, and the gentleman stood on the rutted road to observe the always interesting spectacle of liveried servants trying to extract a coach and horses from a quagmire.

✿   ✿   ✿

The gentleman who gave way to the carter was by far the wealthiest of the incomers. The lane to Marly ran along the eastern edge of his domain, through some fields acquired or appropriated from an abbey. Those fields had recently been given faux-rustic names such as Pré des Crapaux (Frogs' Field) and Buisson de la Porcherie (Pigsty Thicket). The *château* itself was built on higher ground to the south. A windmill had stood there until his father, Louis XIII, had replaced it with a modest hunting lodge and then a U-shaped *château* which allowed him to prolong his hunting expeditions without having to spend the night in the drovers' *cabaret* in Versailles or ride back to Saint-Germain in the dark.

Louis-Dieudonné, the fourteenth King Louis of the House of Bourbon, was in the process of removing from the landscape half a dozen villages along with their churches and inhabitants. The drovers who had always passed through Choisy-aux-Boeufs on their way to Paris would be forced to take long detours. The 'Petit Parc' in which the gardens were being laid out covered four thousand acres. The whole domain, which he had been piecing together since 1662, would soon be seven times the size of Paris.

The inspiration had come from a housewarming party given by his Superintendent of Finance, Nicolas Fouquet, on 17 August 1661, five months after the death of Cardinal Mazarin. As befitted a Superintendent of Finance, Fouquet was the richest man in France. Arriving from one of the moth-eaten royal *châteaux* of the Paris region at Fouquet's shiny white palace at Vaux-le-Vicomte, the King had toured the gardens with their canals and cascades and thirty-six fountains fed by an underground river; he had promenaded along the gravelled paths, plucked a blushing peach from the sun-warmed walls, seen the new comedy by Molière and watched the firework display with a frozen smile. Three weeks later, Fouquet, who had pictured himself as the natural successor to Mazarin, was lured to Nantes and arrested there by D'Artagnan, lieutenant of the King's musketeers, for misappropriation of public funds.

Fouquet's team of brilliant young architects and designers was transferred *en bloc* to Versailles along with all his rare shrubs and orange trees. Never again would a Fouquet or a Prince de Condé have the power to humiliate the King and send him scurrying about his own kingdom like a famished mouse. As for a new chief minister, the post would be abolished. The King's ministers would advise; he alone would govern.

The fact that it took nearly three years to persuade a jury to find Fouquet guilty was a useful lesson: it showed that the monarchy could still be bridled by institutions of government. Ancient royal prerogative, however, entitled the King to slice through the knot of laws. He commuted the disappointingly lenient sentence of exile to life imprisonment. The former Superintendent of Finance was transported to the lonely fortress of Pinerolo near the Italian border, where he dissolved into legend, served by a convicted conspirator whose face was covered by a black velvet or iron mask.

❖

Though his hair was falling out and the winds always blew sharply along the avenues, the King walked through his gardens without a hat or a wig. Gangs of men black with soil or bleached by lime were working on the Grand Canal and the new fountain of the dragon with its ninety-foot spurt of water simulating blood gushing from the monster's mouth.

Masons and carpenters were hammering away at all the fairy-tale structures required for the Grand Divertissement Royal de Versailles, which had been announced for 18 July 1668. Giant rocks were being levered into place to form a temporary grotto. The high-speed Alpine *glissoire* – a toboggan on rails – had been repaired, and mature fruit trees on which apricots and oranges would be hung were being planted in five avenues forming a star. There was an octagonal ballroom that would never be used again and a *trompe-l'œil* theatre that would be dismantled after the performance of a new comedy by Molière. There were to be palaces, pyramids and miniature mountains of confectionery, and then, to close the festivities, a firework display.

Three thousand guests had been invited. The total cost was rumoured to be half a million *livres*. The actual cost was only a hundred thousand, not counting the grotto. By comparison, the Grand Master of Ceremonies and the King's head doctor each received an annual salary of three thousand *livres*. Prior to its demolition, the entire village of Choisy-aux-Boeufs was valued at 33,175 *livres*.

Two months short of his thirtieth birthday, the King was in excellent health, despite the prognostications of his doctor. Dr Vallot followed him about with his bloodletting pans and the syringes he was forever inserting into the royal bottom – usually in the presence of favoured courtiers – before recording the results in a diary which the King always read. The doctor disapproved of parties. His Majesty was capable of giving up wine for four or five days, but he had a tendency to gorge himself on Portuguese oranges and sugary drinks; he played tennis on a full stomach, danced for hours on end and subjected his quivering constitution to the vertiginous *glissoire*.

The Grand Divertissement, however, seemed to meet with the doctor's approval. It was being held to celebrate the signing of the Treaty of Aix-la-Chapelle, which had ended the latest war with Spain and confirmed the King's recent conquests in Flanders, for which the doctor took some credit: in his opinion, the role of a healthy digestive tract in the winning of wars should never be underestimated.

Louis XIV – the human being rather than the gorgeous tailor's dummy of his portraits – felt at ease in the natural world. He had never liked *bains de chambre* but preferred to bathe in the river. He had (according to the doctor) damaged his generative organs by riding horses instead of taking carriages. The recommended walks which the King later published as a visitors' guide to the gardens of Versailles are three miles long and involve a total climb of over two hundred feet. Through the rain-streaked windows of the *château*, courtiers often spotted him in the distance, striding over the cols and watersheds of his microcosmic kingdom, inspecting the latest works.

✻

On the Grand Canal, the sailors of the Versailles navy were trying out a new ship. From there, the Allée des Matelots led south to the Étang puant. This putrid corner of the park, five hundred yards from the royal apartments, was the septic swamp into which the effluvia of the village of Versailles were channelled. To the nobles who trekked out of Paris to camp in exiguous accommodation, hoping to enhance their standing in the eyes of the King, the pong that rose from the Étang puant was the characteristic smell of Versailles.

Even when a sector was drained and planted with vegetables to create the Potager du Roi (the Royal Kitchen Garden), the Stinking Pond retained its name. This might seem an odd name to attach to one of the largest features of a park which embodied absolute power, but the explicit reminder of the stench of the peasantry was typical of the age of *préciosité*. The booby-trapped form of French promoted by Richelieu's Académie Française with its pedant's delight of finicky rules could be outrageously euphemistic but also exquisitely offensive. As a pseudo-dialect spoken by a tiny élite, *précieux* language was made for sneering at uncomprehending inferiors.

'Let us render unto nature the customary tribute' ('Let's eat').

'Useless one, pray excite the combustible element' ('Valet, please light the fire').

'Summon the bastard of Hippocrates' ('Call the doctor').

'Your dog is ferociously agape' ('Your dog is defecating').

References to bodily functions abound in the *Grand Dictionnaire des Précieuses* of 1660. Less abundant were the facilities offered to ladies and gentlemen on those three-mile walks. The shrubberies and copses as well as the labyrinth with its thirty-nine tinkling fountains and sixteen-foot-high hedges must have been a godsend.

❉

Experiencing the gardens of Versailles through the mind of its creator is practically impossible. For historical verisimilitude, the monotonously manicured expanse is best seen at its worst, when earth-moving machines are churning up the flower-beds of a deteriorated sector. The ground-shaking preparations for the Grand Divertissement of 1668 were nothing out of the ordinary. From 1662 until the death of Louis XIV in 1715, Versailles was a construction site. Almost every day brought a new spoil heap or hole in the ground. Thirteen years and thirty-three million *livres* after the Grand Divertissement, when the formerly seditious nobles of France fought their battles at Versailles with the weapons of gossip and intrigue, courtiers in knee-high boots and tucked-up skirts were still stumbling over a military assault course.

> To reach the cool of shade one has to cross a vast torrid zone after which one is forever climbing and descending . . . The stone chippings burn one's feet, but without the gravel, one would sink into sand or the blackest mud. (Duc de Saint-Simon)

Because of all the digging and upheaval, the air is bad and contaminated by all the stagnant water, which is why everyone who was there in the month of August fell ill, except the King and myself . . . This is a thankless *pays* with nothing but sand and feverish marshes. (Comte de Saint-Mayol)

While he fretted over every detail of the gardens, Louis was hardly bothered by his own body, though he was concerned about the multicoloured discharge from his penis. The doctor had first noticed it in the spring of 1655, when some soiled undergarments were brought to his attention. The King was then sixteen-and-a-half years old. This might have indicated the disease 'which young debauchees contract from shameless women' were it not for His Majesty's personal assurance that 'he had slept with neither girl nor woman'.

Dr Vallot was being tactful rather than naive. 1655 was the year in which the young king began his amorous training with Mazarin's seven specially imported Italian nieces. Known collectively as the Mazarinettes, they were targeted by the trolls of Parisian social media and denigrated for their 'owl-like eyes', 'sooty complexions', 'flat bottoms' and foreign accents. The plan had been to offer the King an outlet for his sexual energy and to prove to the courts of Europe that he was capable of producing an heir. He was started out on Olympe, who was plump and not too pretty, but to the dismay of Mazarin and Louis's mother, he fell in love with her younger sister Marie.

Marie Mancini seems to have possessed the kind of unconventional beauty which aroused the cattiness of women, thereby making her more attractive to men:

Despite her ugliness, which at that time was excessive, he took pleasure in her conversation. She had a dusky, yellowish complexion and skinny arms and neck . . . Her eyes were dull and unrefined but pregnant with softness and vivacity.

. . . He would always take her home, at first following her carriage, then serving as her driver and finally climbing into the carriage beside her. (Mme de Motteville)

One of the provisions of the Treaty of the Pyrenees (1659), which set the border between France and Spain, was that Louis XIV would marry the daughter of King Philip IV of Spain. To serve the national interest, Marie was sent away by her uncle to the Atlantic province of Aunis, where she chose as her retreat the 'sad and solitary fortress' of the silted-up port of Brouage – 'a place without distractions, where I could nurse my melancholy thoughts and where my sisters were bored to tears'.

Louis's long and tearful letters were intercepted by Mazarin, who denounced his own niece as a scheming libertine and pointed out to the King that he was plotting against himself. Years later, Louis would pass the lesson on to his son: 'In giving away our heart, we must remain absolute masters of our mind.' The master of Versailles consoled himself with 'conquests'. According to his sister-in-law, he was 'not fussy':

> Peasant girls, gardeners' daughters, servants, chambermaids, women
> of quality – any woman would do, just as long as she pretended to
> be in love with him.

This is one reason why the subjective reality of Versailles is hard to recapture. Like any cherished garden, the park was imbued with the memory of all the conversations and adventures that had taken place there. That vital aspect of the place may be more accessible to users of the 'lieux de drague' website for 'rencontres libertines', who are advised to frequent the Potager du Roi and the former Étang puant:

> Enter by the wrought-iron gate or the Allée des Peupliers, then
> follow the path to the end, into the woods or the edge of the woods,
> and along both sides of the basin and around the equestrian statue.

✵

A more convenient King's-eye view of Versailles is provided by an oil painting commissioned in the year of the Grand Divertissement. Without the buildings in the foreground, the scene could be mistaken for an Alpine valley near the border with Italy or one of the three-dimensional models of battlegrounds and siege works which informed the King of operations on the frontier. The painter, Pierre Patel, specialized in imaginary landscapes, but in this case, the dizzying intensity of detail functioned as a faithful reproduction of reality.

The Grand Canal leads from the palace of Louis XIII and its recent additions towards a distant range of blue hills. Long escarpments half-colonized by horticulture protect both flanks of the gardens and the Great Park. It looks like a Shangri-la discovered from the top of a ridge in a forgotten valley of the Hurepoix. The hallucinatory quality suggests the visual system of an omnipotent being. For this, Dr Vallot may be partly responsible. Since 1662, he had been administering daily half-ounce doses of his original remedy for headaches and dizzy spells – a decoction of opium poppies, red roses and powdered mother of pearl:

> His Majesty found the remedy so congenial that He earnestly requested that I administer it to Him for the rest of his life, assuring me that He had never taken anything so pleasant.

This was the enchanted domain in which the Grand Divertissement was to be held. The ubiquitous emblem of the radiant sun and the fountains and statues of the sun god Apollo proclaimed that this was the home of the beneficent Sun King. His palace faced the setting sun, so that to the workers who toiled in the gathering gloom, it appeared to be on fire.

Some scholars have searched for a pattern of solar symbols in the grand plan of the estate and the walking tours devised by the King. Though no such pattern has been detected, guidebooks routinely state that the sun sets precisely over the Grand Canal on the King's birthday. The moment when the sun appears to sink into the blood-red canal actually occurs nearly a month before his birthday. The more impressive truth is that the alignment skilfully matched the local topography. Unlike other theme parks of the Paris region – Parc Astérix, Disneyland and France Miniature (but not the Mer de Sable or 'Sea of Sand') – this kingdom-within-a-kingdom was created in collaboration with the wider landscape. This was the Baroque enterprise: to enhance rather than supplant Nature. Versailles was the work of a man who had a soldier's respect for terrain and hydrography – the kind of gentleman-officer who, in line with military protocol, would order his driver to give way to a heavier vehicle on a muddy lane.

If the pink-tinged clouds above the western horizon of the Great Park held a secret significance for the King, it might have been the memory of Mazarin's disappointed niece gazing out over the mudflats of Brouage at the retreating sea. But as he surveyed the installations for the Grand Divertissement like a general on the eve of battle and looked forward to the surprises he had prepared for his subjects, it is more likely that he spared a thought for the unfinished *château* of Vaux-le-Vicomte and the cramped cell in which Fouquet and his masked attendant languished in never-ending darkness.

✲

The association of Louis XIV with the Sun dated back to his first public performance at the end of the Fronde. A year after his re-entry into Paris, he had played the role of Apollo (and several minor roles) in a sumptuous ballet, the *Ballet royal de la Nuit*. It was performed in February 1653 in the Petit Bourbon theatre next to the Louvre, where the États-Généraux had been convened for the last time in 1615. On either side of the hall where parliamentary delegates had sat, the audience was stacked up in balconies like cherubim and seraphim.

In the final act of the ballet, when the witches and werewolves of Night had been banished, Dawn's chariot ushered onto the stage the amazingly costumed Sun King, who addressed the gaping throng: 'Scarce have I begun my vast career, / Yet already I am admired on mountain peaks.' (Bashfulness was not then considered a virtue in a king.) 'And any who refuse to admit my light / Shall feel my heat.' The fashionably historical reference to crusading was also a hint of things to come:

> My shining eye can pierce the heart's abyss,
> Yet pleasure leaves my own heart cold as stone,
> As for passion, I know not what it is,
> And lovely Daphne affects me no more
> Than a tree with an interesting leaf.
>   . . .
> By inclination, I am bound to what must be:
> If it be the will of Him who exalted me,
> Once I have dispelled the shadows that darken France,
> O'er distant lands appearing, my light incessant
> To Byzantium's heart in glory will advance
> And obliterate the Crescent.

(Poetic licence evidently allowed to Sun to reverse its course.)

Two months after the ballet, the Sun King was on the north-eastern frontier, 'dispelling the shadows that darken France' in the trenches of Flanders. It was his first opportunity since the Fronde to practise what became his favourite hobby after gardening and palace design – breaching earthworks, building redoubts, tunnelling, damming, flooding and all the other engrossing techniques of siege craft.

Trench warfare was so much the norm in seventeenth-century France that when the French army was bogged down in the hell of the Ardennes and the Somme in 1915, the *Revue des Deux Mondes* felt it necessary to explain that this 'war of moles' was not some quaint revival of the *ancien régime*: 'These techniques of attack and defence seemed to have had their day, and some people appear to think that war has returned to almost prehistoric methods.'

The trenches were dug at night and sometimes attacked at dawn when they were still full of workmen. Officers were often killed, but kings did not usually expose themselves directly to artillery fire. Much later, during the siege of Besançon, the municipal delegate who crossed the siege works to speak with the French commander was amazed to be asked, 'Why not speak with the King himself?'

Dr Vallot was appalled by his patient's intrepidity. 'I was forced to administer an enema when he was just out of the saddle, still wearing his boots, in the most desolate and inconvenient place in the entire kingdom.' He suffered from fevers, dysentery and constipation. From Sainte-Menehould, he rode through wintry fog for almost thirty miles to reach Châlons. In the valley of the Sambre where Caesar had anni-hilated the Nervii and in the marshes of the Pas de Calais, he breathed in the 'miasma' of putrefaction which was thought to carry death.

There are two contemporary paintings of Louis XIV inspecting the trenches at Douai and Tournai in 1667. I had always assumed these to be propagandist fantasies, but the paintings lied only in the muting of the horror. The proud white horse depicted in oil would have stumbled over the sun-baked ruts of farm tracks destroyed by cannon and squelched through sewage and corpses, bearing the diseased body of a king who, said the doctor, 'with his extraordinary passion for glory, neglected his personal hygiene and health in order to attain the goals that testified to his generous spirit.'

✻

On a day when the fog was rising from the ponds and streams of the Hurepoix, a veteran of the frontier who stood on the Butte de Versailles looking west might have found himself back on the battlefields of northern France. There are few more dissimilar images of France than the gardens of Versailles and the trenches of Flanders. Yet there on the edge of the Hurepoix were bastions and battlements, copses and hedges for cover, and ramparts from which the scene could be surveyed. In the middle distance, miniature ships sailed on a freshly dug canal. The parallel escarpments running to the horizon were buttressed by defensive walls. In the country beyond, the enemy was marshalling its forces . . .

It would be a useful test of the Great Park's military potential to take a hundred schoolboys from the Paris suburbs, divide them into two armies and invite them to stage a battle among the statues and the fountains.

The battleground of Versailles would not have been complete without the loss of life. Almost every day, a worker fell from scaffolding or was crushed by a block of building stone. Many were migrants from the Limousin and Flanders, housed in makeshift barracks. The local area was well represented too. Even at harvest time, men from villages within a ten-mile radius of Versailles were requisitioned to lug stones from nearby quarries (using their own horses) or to smash them into paving slabs. Any who baulked at the task were punished with the lash or imprisonment. Soldiers employed for their siege works experience sometimes went on strike or ran away, in which case they were branded with the *fleur de lys*, their nose and ears were cropped and they were either sent to the galleys or hanged.

Lists of French military disasters do not include the ten thousand soldiers – one sixth of the number that fought in Flanders – who died of malaria, typhoid and accidents while digging the canal that was to channel the waters of the River Eure into the waterworks of Versailles. Designed by Louis XIV's military engineer Sébastien Vauban, the Canal de l'Eure was never completed. The abandoned Maintenon aqueduct is the only monument to the thousands who died for Versailles.

✻

The great day arrived. In the afternoon of 18 July 1668, three thousand people converged on Versailles. Since the guards on duty at the gates were unfamiliar with the insignia of civilian rank, some foreign ministers and ladies of the Court were roughly treated and forced to make way for the guardsmen's own uninvited relatives and friends. As the crowd pushed up against the gates, dresses were crumpled, feathers went flying and the knee ribbon loops called cannons were ripped off.

With all the pushing and shoving, some people missed the afternoon refreshments. By the time they reached the arbour at the meeting of five avenues where the tables were set, the giant melons which had served as couches, the cavernous mountain of cold meats and the candied-fruit pyramids had been ravaged by a mob. After a light collation, the King had ordered the tables to be 'left to the looters' (according to the court historian's account). The resulting stampede and 'the alacrity with which those marzipan *châteaux* and confectionery mountains were demolished provided the Court with an additional amusing *divertissement*'.

Molière's new comedy was performed, with music by Lully, in a magically realistic rustic setting within the semi-artificial setting of the park. Visually, it was twice removed from reality, but the plot was uncomfortably close to home. A rich peasant, Georges Dandin, whose name suggests 'bumbling peasant', has married the daughter of impoverished country nobles. His tarty young wife has set her spiteful heart on having sex with a snooty aristocrat who calls himself Clitandre. Dandin is treated as a jealous idiot and repeatedly humiliated by his snobbish in-laws, the Sotenvilles ('fools in town'). At the end of the play, punished for marrying above his station, he realizes that his only option is to drown himself.

Equating social mobility with petty ambition and ridiculing all but the highest-ranking members of an increasingly stratified society, this bleak farce was the celebration of a purge. In 1666, Louis XIV had launched a Grande Enquête sur la Noblesse. Commoners who had acquired their wealth in vulgar activities such as commerce, manufacture and farming had been ennobled for lending money to the Crown. This meant that they paid no tax; it also meant that the social hierarchy was unbalanced by *nouveaux riches*.

The Great Investigation required them to prove that their family trees had been untainted by plebeian forebears for least a century. Any who were found to have 'usurped' their titles were fined and demoted. However, to prevent this ossification of the social order from blocking the flow of money, they were offered the opportunity to purchase at great cost one of several hundred official but flagrantly spurious positions: Inspector of Wood Piling, Commissioner of the Weighing of Hay, Visitor of Pigs, etc. Later, they would be stripped of these ludicrous positions, which would then be sold back to them at even greater cost to fund the endless wars and building projects.

Perhaps because of all the crumpled dresses and fruity refreshments, the ball was an anti-climax, but the five-course *souper* at which the King was served by noblemen – including the man who had purchased the office of 'Contrôleur de la Bouche du Roi' – was a tremendous success, and the fireworks exceeded expectations. In the afternoon, no one had seen any sign of the usual pyrotechnic apparatus. Now, as the light waned, they milled about, anxious not to miss the spectacle, trying to work out where to stand for the best view, when 'suddenly', according to the authorized account, 'they found themselves surrounded'.

'A thousand flames shot out of the earth': the pipes which fed the fountains seemed to have been commandeered by Fire 'in its war against Water'. Caught in the conflagration, the crowd flinched and swarmed. 'Unable to discover a line of retreat, they dived into the depths of the shrubberies or threw themselves on the ground.'

The war of the elements was over in an instant. The discomfited guests picked themselves up and emerged from the bushes, shaking the dirt from sleeves and bustles, and made their way back towards the blazing, torch-lit palace. Everyone agreed that the dazzling display had been a fitting conclusion to the *fête*.

At that moment, the real onslaught began. The earth shuddered with a great explosion and bolts of lightning split the sky. 'Countless big rockets were shooting out of the tower which housed the water pump.' The tower appeared to have caught fire: it was 'vomiting flames' as though it would never stop. Most of the missiles headed skywards, but some of them swerved and swivelled unpredictably as though they were out of control. The spicy, sulphurous smell of gunpowder filled the air and the cowering horde noticed that the tails of the rockets were spelling out the initials of the King, who had watched the whole flawless operation from his vantage point on the terrace.

The official recorder of the Grand Divertissement concludes his account with an appropriate quotation – perhaps more appropriate than he realized – from the Roman general Aemilius Paulus:

> A great man who can organize a banquet that will delight his friends is no less able to marshal an army that will strike fear into the heart of his enemies.

The King and Queen left Versailles at half-past two in the morning to spend the rest of the night at Saint-Germain. A few hours later, when 'the day, jealous of such a beautiful night, was beginning to reappear', crews of workmen arrived to begin the dangerous work of demolition.

❋   ❋   ❋

I returned to Versailles in 2016 after seeing Pierre Patel's panoptic view of Louis XIV's Baroque paradise and the long valley in which it was set. I had no memory of such a scene, but the paintings of the Sun King in the trenches had proved to be more documentary than fantastic and I was curious to know whether such a landscape could possibly have existed in the west of the Paris Metropolitan Area.

On the 171 bus from Boulogne-Billancourt, two girls on the seat behind were discussing their Sunday outing. It was the sort of intelligently excited conversation between friends which often turns up useful information and so I eavesdropped all the way to Versailles. But as the bus began its final approach on the mile-and-a-half-long Avenue de Paris, and the palace on the Butte de Versailles revealed its vastness, I recognized from my own experience of the place that silencing of the analytical faculties which is almost indistinguishable from boredom. 'C'est énorme!' said one. 'C'est dingue!' said the other. Until the bus reached the stop, nothing more was said.

In the blinding heat of the Great Park, the globe-trotting crowds were slow and listless but, on the whole, quite festive. The electric mobility vehicles were easy enough to sidestep, and city-dwellers were enjoying the expanse of greenery. Unlike the medieval castles which Cardinal Richelieu consigned to history, Versailles, with its thousands of generally well-heeled visitors, can still convey a reasonably accurate impression of its original ambience.

By the reflecting pools on the terrace from which Louis XIV had watched the pyrotechnics, a casually dressed woman was having her photograph taken: she lay on the ground, laughing, balanced on one hip to mimic the recumbent naked statue of the River Loiret. Eight statues around the basins represent the four longest rivers in France – Seine, Rhone, Garonne and Loire – and their tributaries, Marne, Saône, Dordogne and Loiret. The rivers are male, the tributaries female. Cast in bronze by a famous cannon-founder, they were placed there in the late 1680s to symbolize the monarch's mastery of his wide-arched kingdom. By then, he had revoked his grandfather's Edict of Nantes and was making war on his Protestant subjects, billeting thuggish dragoons on Huguenot families and triggering one of the biggest forced migrations in the history of Europe. Pulsating with heat on her bed of bronze water, the nymph of the Loiret might have been a lady of the Court ignoring the tittering servants.

In the avenues and lawns, only the most obdurate invasive species have survived the weedkiller. Biomonotony is the twenty-first century's contribution to the Baroque taming of Nature. The endless rows of trees and statues have a mildly hypnotic effect and the long perspectives paradoxically tighten and compress the view. I retraced one of the King's recommended walks and quite forgot about the painting, until, feeling the need for distance, I climbed back up to the gusty terrace where the windmill and the gallows had stood. The King had once asked his favourite courtier, the ageing Comte de Gramont, to reminisce as they walked on the terrace. Did he remember seeing the windmill? 'Aye, Sire,' said the Count, 'the mill has gone but the wind remains.'

Beyond the park, I saw a landscape which, with the Baroque foreground, looked like the first glimmerings of the Romantic Age. There were the two low escarpments running to the west and the bluish horizon on the far side of Villepreux. The Great Park and the zone of demolished villages were just the eastern end of a half-forgotten *pays* on the borders of the Hurepoix. Its name, Val de Galie, may be either Celtic or Frankish: the meaning of 'Galie' was lost long ago, but the valley is still considered to be a distinct region by people who live there. This was the view that enchanted the father of Louis XIV when he saw it on a hunting expedition. He had no idea, of course, how much of the nation's wealth would be sunk in those muddy fields.

When the brain has been swamped with data, a detail of no apparent importance often bobs up repeatedly like a piece of bright plastic on a flooded meadow. On the bus back to Paris, I remembered the statue of the River Loiret. What was that insignificant stream doing in such august company? Several other tributaries of the Loire are major rivers in their own right – the Allier, the Cher, the Indre and the Vienne are all about two hundred miles long from source to confluence – but the Loiret runs for only seven miles through the suburbs of Orléans. On a fluvial map of France, it would be a dot.

Later, I discovered that the Loiret, a resurgent stream of the Loire, was believed until the eighteenth century to be a great subterranean river which rose in the mountains of the Massif Central or, by some inexplicable quirk of physics, near the coast of the English Channel.

In the reign of the Sun King, France had colonies in India, Senegal and the Caribbean. 'New France' covered about one third of North America and included a territory of over one million square miles between the Great Lakes and the Gulf of Mexico named after Louis XIV. Meanwhile, much of the home country was still *terra incognita*. The colossal Verdon Gorges were known only to a handful of villagers, some of the highest peaks of the French Pyrenees were unscaled by human beings, and a diminutive river on the doorstep of Orléans, sixty miles south of Versailles, was an unfathomed mystery.

Even the territory beyond the hills which form the Val de Galie, and the human beasts of burden who lived there, were as alien to the Court as an abandoned colony. The nobility had been tamed and the peasants taxed to the point of starvation. Councils and parliaments were bullied by royal *intendants*. Yet large parts of the country remained under martial law. In the year of the Grand Divertissement, in the forests to the east of the Landes, the 'Invisibles' were fighting a guerrilla war against the state and its punitive salt tax. Brittany was in almost constant revolt and about to lose what was left of its independence. Soon, the people of the Vivarais above the right bank of the lower Rhone would refuse to have their earnings siphoned off to pay for the Canal du Midi. Thousands would flee into the 'deserts' of the Cévennes, where, thirty years later, the Protestant Camisards would be rooted out and slaughtered by government troops.

In 1675, when the 'Bonnets Rouges' of Brittany and other rebel bands from Normandy to Périgord were pillaging, kidnapping and

burning legal documents, 'security' would be the pretext for neutral-
izing and humiliating the regional parliaments. The Parlement de
Bretagne was evacuated from the city of Rennes to the port of Vannes,
while the Parlement de Bordeaux was ordered to go and sit out the
troubles in Condom. Neither Vannes nor Condom was served by the
network of post roads.

The lack of an effective communication network made the repression of revolts expensive but it also prevented those ragged rebel
armies from joining forces. One day, just over a century after Louis
XIV moved the Court to Versailles, they would come together with
astonishing speed like the coordinated explosions of the firework
display. An apprentice watchmaker from the Rue du Hurepoix would
become the first citizen to stand on the ramparts of the Bastille and
look down over a new world. A mob of angry women would march
out to Versailles to place the Sun King's descendant, Louis XVI, in a
carriage and escort him back to the enormous seething city where he
rightfully belonged.

8

Stained Glass

Travelling around Europe in the late 1970s, I had the good fortune to lose my Interrail card and half the money I was carrying. Somewhere between the Via Nazionale and the main railway station in Rome, my wallet had escaped from my inside pocket. In the police station, I sat in a busy corridor alongside all the other bereft foreign tourists, with that nameless teenage feeling of embarrassment, tearfulness and excitement.

I was tired of sleeping in trains. The journey had turned into a series of uncomfortable city breaks and I had yet to meet anyone interesting. I left my parents' address with a policeman, then cashed some of the remaining traveller's cheques, placing the proceeds in a money-belt my sister had given me and which I had carefully packed away in my bag.

In my new mode of travel, the centre of a city was like the middle of a desert. Back at the station, I caught a north-bound bus *all'auto-strada*. An hour or two later, I was standing at a windblown intersection of the great asphalt network which, with luck, would take me to any part of Europe without the permission of a railway time-table.

That summer was hot and almost rainless. I slept in fields, on people's floors and, once, in the partially walled-off section of a pigsty from which the migrant German farmworker but not the animals had been evicted for my benefit. I was preparing for my final year of French and German at Oxford and felt faintly guilty about lingering in Italy, memorizing Italian words in the order dictated by necessity: *acqua, pane, dormire, serpenti, cinghiali, autostop, polizia*, and so on.

It was not until the penultimate leg of the journey back to Rouen, where I had been teaching at a *lycée*, that I reconnected with French culture. On a *route nationale* near Metz, at one of those open-air, all-weather brothels signposted *aire de repos*, I waited for a ride with a boy who was probably not yet seventeen. I asked where he was headed, and he told me, in a Lorraine accent, 'Ch'pars à l'aventure, comme ça!' ('Wherever I happen to end up'). Since leaving school, he had worked as a butcher's apprentice; now, he was setting out on his Tour de France.

From him, I learned that the expression originally referred, not to a bicycle race, but to the organized circuit of France undertaken by apprentices learning their trade. Aspiring butchers did not normally undertake a tour, but he was an unusually intrepid young man. I envied him his breeziness and hoped that he really was unusual.

We were picked up by a large van which already contained half a dozen hitchhikers feasting on a crate of peaches. There were no windows or benches and I began to long for the cinematic comforts of a train. When the driver stopped to let us stretch our legs, I saw the dreary plains of Champagne that would be such an adventure on a bicycle. A light rain was falling on the outskirts of Reims when I said farewell to the butcher boy. He had already formed an enviably close relationship with the only girl in the group. It was easy to see that he was going to have a fruitful Tour de France.

Even when hitchhiking, it is hard to avoid Paris. I thumbed a ride near Reims and was delivered to the ear-splitting environs of Orly Airport by a man who explained how fortunate I was not to have been arrested or murdered and to be riding in his Porsche. The area was given over entirely to transport infrastructure; a dead body would not have been out of place. I paid my toll to the capital, taking a suburban train to the centre of Paris and then a *train corail* to Rouen, where I returned to the world of nineteenth-century French poetry like a deep-sea fish released from a trawl net.

Years later, when planning journeys from one end of France to another with no professional object, I seemed to be hitchhiking through French history. Most of the places through which we cycled were included on the itinerary simply because they came between start and finish and could not be avoided. They had no clear connection with the established curriculum of French history. If they were known for anything at all, it was usually because they had been obliterated in a war or because someone had been born there and never returned.

The backroads of French history can be very quiet indeed and any travelling companion is welcome. This is how I came to know Jacques-Louis Ménétra, a glazier from Paris. He, too, was on his Tour de France – a very long tour, which lasted from 1757 to 1763. (Fig. 9.) The notes I had collected from various sources with no other aim than to make the cycle trips more interesting had become the groundwork for a social history of France since the Revolution. But I was not convinced that Ménétra was a reliable or representative witness. His three-hundred-and-thirty-one-page manuscript, 'Journal de ma vie' – misspelt, unpunctuated but very neatly written – struck me as the autobiography of a self-satisfied womanizer and rapist, and I was glad that he fell outside the chronological parameters of the book.

Journal of Mylife
Written by me in the year 1764 <u>menetra</u>
all
Without Ostentation And Without Reflexition

———

Writing the truth in my Opinion should not be talking about crests and coats of arms but forgetting what ones ancestors were and not dressing up ones name with those vain titles

The second time I met him was on a research trip to Gaulish *oppida* in 2012. Having kept a note of the places Ménétra had visited, I knew that he had worked for a brief spell in the Gascon cathedral town of Auch, the former capital of the Ausci tribe. Now, as I reread the relevant section of his memoirs, I was not so sure. How did I know that he was untypical and untruthful? He had written his journal 'for [his] own pleasure and the pleasure of remembering', and apparently without ever trying to find a publisher. I had accepted rides from complete strangers without asking questions because I had no choice, yet I was reluctant to tag along with this intensely communicative man from the eighteenth century.

This whole region of French social history is very sparsely populated. For a space of several centuries, Ménétra is the only authentic proletarian whose words are not mediated by other writers or translated into the bourgeois idiom of the author's later self. The Parisian apprentice who fornicated his way around France for six years was the only representative of a vast section of society, and there was no escaping his company. I joined him in Auch, halfway through his tale, where I could be certain of finding at least one part of the scene unchanged since 1759.

❀ ❀ ❀

Apart from a snaky coil of yellow hair caressing the contour of her left breast and a piece of scalloped material resembling an opened corolla, the figure in the cathedral was radiantly naked. Her little finger was slightly parted from the others to hold the cloth in place. It was the only sign that she was aware of her magnificence. The childishly small breasts had the rotundity of the untasted apples on the tree to her right, but there was a weight of promise in the thighs and belly. Her nakedness would remain on view even on a dull day because she was suffused with the light of another world. Anyone who looked up at her from outside in the street would see nothing but the smudges of a butterfly's folded wing.

That autumn day in the ambulatory of Auch Cathedral, Eve's body was almost completely occluded by a man of twenty-one. In size and physique, he would have made a fitting partner. His hands were working just above and between her breasts, his legs brushing against the lower panes of the window as the light played on his face. At the foot of the ladder, a priest was keeping a steely eye on him, but neither the priest nor the naked blonde (his favourite type of woman) could distract him or make his posture more uncomfortable. His landlady in Auch, the wife of his *bourgeois* (the boss), was 'an extremely good sort', as attentive to his needs as to those of her husband, and the *bourgeois* was grateful to him for sharing his remedy for gonorrhoea: 'I think he never realized it was me who'd given them that lovely present . . .'

He kept his tools in the pouches of a leather belt. The only sounds were the tapping of his chisels and glazing hammers, the occasional scrape of the stopping knife and the diamond-cutter. He levered out the old lead and teased the new into place.

> When it comes to painted glass you'll not find anything more beautiful than what they've got in that cathedral. The canons are so

protective they take turns standing guard. When I worked on the windows of that church they were there all the time and never left me on my own and nor did my *bourgeois*.

His job was to repair the cracks in the two-hundred-and-fifty-year-old glass. The strips of lead called *plombs de casse* were minor works of art in their own right: they had to be thick enough to support the glass but subtle enough in their hearts and flanges to preserve the outlines of the figures and – the mark of a true craftsman – to ease the work of future restorers. When he worked on stained glass, he was a member of a large team of craftsmen, some long dead, others yet to be born. Inferior glaziers tackled damaged windows like surgeons patching up soldiers on a battlefield. The trick was to find an accommodation with chance, to turn defects into charms, like the girls of the 'seraglios' of Paris who could make a man tremble and blush even if they were pock-marked or lame.

When I saw the world-famous windows of Auch Cathedral by the Gascon master, Arnaut de Moles, they were crazed with repair leads. Saint Peter had been lobotomized, Christ's head was sliced in two. Some of the buxom Sibyls seemed to have served as practice cuts for butchers' apprentices. But the spidery leads on the body of Eve in the Garden of Eden were noticeably more tactful. Seen from below, the black strips on her chest suggested poorly healed scars, but they showed the touch of a true admirer, respecting the bulge of her breasts and highlighting their perfection. This brazen cosmetic enhancement is probably the only surviving trace of Jacques-Louis Ménétra's devotion to his craft.

※

Ménétra was then in the third year of his Tour de France. He was born in 1738 and grew up by the Pont Neuf in Paris. The *quartier* was a trouble-maker's paradise where riots were often sparked by reports of police brutality. Jacques-Louis fished and swam in the Seine and skated on its frozen surface. He sang in the choir at Saint-Germain-l'Auxerrois, poked fun at priests and made 'Chinese rocket' fireworks which he placed between cracks in the paving and under the seats of peasant women who sold apples on the *quais*.

He learned his trade from his alcoholic father who sometimes beat him and locked him out of the house so that he had to go and sleep under the bridges. His mother had died when he was two years old, but his grandmother and aunt were devoted to him, and his uncle enjoyed the boy's company. One of his treasured memories of childhood was their night-time adventure in the Hurepoix, when they had set off for Paris in the wrong direction.

Even as a boy, he showed a mature appreciation of beauty and was sought after for his skill as a glassworker as well as for the skills he didn't know he possessed. A glazier's work gave him entry to the homes of the rich. Before he turned eighteen, he made the great discovery that a handsome lad could earn a tidy sum by spending some 'pleasant moments' with the mistress of the house after he had polished off her windows.

Fearing his father and the repercussions of amorous adventures in the neighbourhood, he left home in March 1757. One of his cousins had developed a bad case of the 'vapours', which, in Ménétra's coy idiom, means that he had made her pregnant. He packed his bag and walked to the permanent construction site of Versailles, where the King had provided glaziers with work until the end of time. From there, he headed for the Loire Valley, and so began a ragged Tour de France which included several months as a sailor harrying English vessels in the Channel during the Seven Years War.

✻

'Parisien le Bienvenu' – his official nickname as a Tour de France journeyman – always received a warm welcome from men as well as women. He played pranks, organized battles between apprentices of different trades and told funny stories, some of which were true. Ignoring the rules of his guild, he accepted almost any commission. He made little glass boxes and pagoda-style cages to give as presents, concocted potions for venereal complaints and performed conjuring tricks. He had the knack of causing a woman's clothes to fall from her body like leaves from a tree in autumn. Sometimes, he stayed in the hostels (which still exist) for touring apprentices, but more congenial accommodation was usually available from widows and women whose husbands were away on business or at war.

When he arrived at Auch to work on the stained-glass windows, he had just spent six weeks as an odd-job man in a convent at Agen.

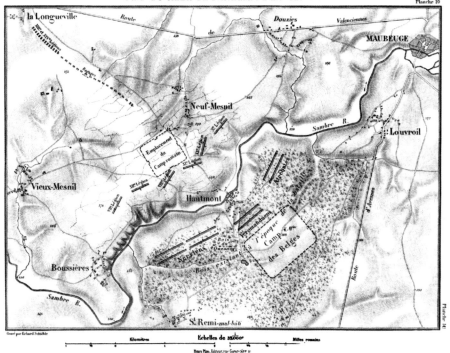

1. Caesar's battle on the Sambre in the second year of the Gallic War (57 BC), reconstructed by Napoléon III and his research team. From the atlas of his *Histoire de Jules César* (1866).

2. The probable site of Theopolis, the lost 'City of God' beyond the carved stone which bears its name (c. AD 414), looking south from the D3 between Sisteron and Digne. The early medieval chapel stands below the Rocher du Dromon near the centre of the picture.

3. Charlemagne's general, Roland, governor of the Breton March, slain by 'Saracens' (Basques) at the Pass of Roncevaux in the western Pyrenees in 778. From the fifteenth-century *Chroniques de Saint-Denis*.

4. Gerbert d'Aurillac, who became Pope Sylvester II in 999, stealing the Saracen philosopher's book and operating the steam organ in Reims Cathedral. From *Abrégé des histoires divines* (Amiens?, c. 1300–10).

5. The Trimouns talc quarry and, to the right of the ropeway trestle, the Col de la Peyre, by which Cathar heretics fled Montségur in 1243.

6. An early sixteenth-century pilgrim – or a representation of Saint James of Compostela – on the church of Saint-Jacques-le-Majeur at Villefranche-d'Allier.

7. The mysterious tree at the centre of France on the *Carte ecclésiastique contenant la description des archeveschés et éveschés du royaume de France et principaultés adjacentes appartenants à l'église gallicane*, by Antoine-Fabrice Des Bleyns (1624).

8. Louis XIV at the Siege of Tournai, 1667. Attributed to Adam Frans Van der Meulen. Tournai, now in Belgium, was a frontier town of the Spanish Netherlands. It was captured by the French after a siege of four days. Trench warfare, which Louis XIV experienced enthusiastically at first hand, was considered an inglorious but effective innovation. The trenches were dug at night. The wooden stakes in the foreground would have been used for gabions and fascines to shield the workers and to reinforce the walls.

9. The Palace of Versailles and the Val de Galie, looking west, by Pierre Patel, 1668.

10. Eve in the Garden of Eden, by Arnaut de Moles, c. 1510,
before its recent restoration, in the ambulatory of Auch Cathedral.
This image has been cropped.

11. *La Construction d'un grand chemin*, by Joseph Vernet, 1774, showing local peasants and their horses conscripted for the *corvée* (road-building duty). 'Grands chemins' were post roads leading from Paris or a provincial capital to a minor town. The rider inspecting a plan is J.-R. Perronet, the King's chief engineer. In this composite scene, one of the stone-arch bridges built by Perronet in northern France has materialized in a landscape reminiscent of the Alpes Maritimes. Milestones were erected every half-league from Paris. The stone at bottom-left is marked '250', which, with the exposed rock of the cutting, suggests the Forez region, home of Abbé Terray, Contrôleur Général des Finances, who commissioned the painting. The man by the stone is wielding a fifty-pound *demoiselle* or *hie* for compacting cobbles. Cobbling was mainly urban but sometimes used to stabilize treacherous mountain terrain.

12. Parisian women heading for Versailles 'to bring back some bread and the King', 1789. Three bewigged *bourgeoises* have either adopted or been forced to wear the cockade of the Revolution. Scythes, axes, forks and clubs have been supplemented with stolen swords, spears, bayonets, a musket and a gun carriage.

13. The Mistral wreaking havoc on the Col des Tempêtes, just below the summit of Mont Ventoux, 1827. A votive offering to the Virgin Mary in the chapel of Notre-Dame-des-Accès in Crillon-le-Brave (Vaucluse).

Ménétra's description of his *modus operandi* is elliptical but basically transparent:

> In my first days there the nunettes hid from me as though I was the Antichrist. They'd given me a little bell I was supposed to ring when I was about to enter one of the dormitories. Since I always liked to make myself comfortable when I was working they got used to me – especially two young sisters who were happy to have me passing from the arms of one to the arms of the other and so they knitted stockings for me and got the other sisters to knit some too.
>
> Whenever anything needed doing in their cell, because they had a say in such matters, they always found work for me and no one ever made such a good job of things as the Parisian – which is why my boss became suspicious. I was very sorry to leave that convent and its good sisters to go and work on the country house of the bishop who is the lord and count of Agen.

In the early Middle Ages, some English women had funded their pilgrimages to Rome by prostituting themselves in every town on the route, which, as Saint Boniface observed in a letter to the Archbishop of Canterbury, defeated the object. 'Go a pilgrim, come back a whore' was a medieval proverb. Though Ménétra considered himself a *bon viveur* who took whatever came his way, he used his body to similar effect. At Nantes and at Nîmes, he lived rent-free for several months with an older woman. As a general rule, the younger the woman, the shorter the affair. He preferred a woman who was either too old to become pregnant or familiar with the prophylactic devices used by prostitutes.

Apart from his preference for blondes – noted by a high-class brothel madam in Paris rather than by Ménétra himself – he was indiscriminate in hunting *gibier* (game). On two occasions, the girl was 'half resisting, half consenting', and it would be hard to guess from Ménétra's only slightly sheepish tone that rape was punishable by death (but only if the victim was a virgin or married, or if the perpetrator was in a position of trust). Once, it was a girl at the hostel in Montpellier masquerading as a boy in order to complete her Tour de France as a tailor. On the other occasion, it was 'an unexpected windfall' on the road from Tours to Angers:

At the entrance to a small wood I saw a little shepherd and a young shepherdess hard at it. I crept up as quietly as I could and when I was close to them I made a noise at which the young man who was naked took to his heels and the young girl covered herself up. My friend ran off after the young man but I amused myself with the girl half with her consent and the rest by force. But then because my friend wasn't trying to make the most of it I thought for a moment and retraced my steps to take my ease again. Being a good Christian I'd heard it said that a sin paid for is a sin half forgiven so I gave her six *sous* and went on my way.

The average daily wage of a manual worker was about twenty-five *sous*. A silver six-*sou* coin, bearing the laurel-crowned head of Louis XV, was considered by one of Ménétra's contemporaries to be a fair price to pay for a 'superannuated' *fille de joie* in a Paris brothel.

Ménétra wrote as though he was talking to fellow journeymen in an inn. He was obviously unaware that readers in the remote future might find his stories repugnant. Life on the road was cheap. In the valley of the Loire on a sunny afternoon, there were apples on the trees, rabbits waiting to be skinned and eaten, and girls warmed up and waiting. An enterprising young artisan could sow the seeds of the nation's prosperity while reaping the benefits of the social and legal subjugation of women, which prosperity would preserve.

❂   ❂   ❂

Ménétra might have been the emblematic protagonist of an eighteenth-century philosophical novel – a glazier letting light into the tenebrous chambers of what would soon be called the *ancien régime*. The houses where he hid from fathers and husbands were rickety warrens knocked together from half-demolished structures belonging to several different centuries, with narrow stairs and ladders and sometimes open drainage channels running through the rooms. But outside, public spaces were being adapted for an urban population which was discovering the pleasures of *flânerie*, mingling with other classes and observing the changing face of the world.

After the endless frontier wars of Louis XIV, the reign of Louis XV was a period of relative peace. In the wealthier parts of France, taxation was the only obvious sign that the nation's financial reserves were perilously low. In 1744, Louis XV instructed his *contrôleur général*, Philibert Orry, to assess the '*facultés des peuples*' (the human resources of the kingdom)

and also to inform me as secretly as possible how much silverware there is, other than what belongs to the Church and to clerics.

During the Seven Years War, with French possessions in North America and India under attack from the British Navy, the King himself had sent all the silver of Versailles, a whole museum of masterpieces, to be melted down at the Mint. When Ménétra helped to glaze the King's fleet at Brest, he received a paltry wage, but when he worked for town councils, abbeys and private individuals, he was paid handsomely. Most of the cities in which he spent more than a few days – Nantes, La Rochelle, Bordeaux, Toulouse and Marseille – were enjoying the newly indispensable luxuries of West Indian molasses, sugar, rum, coffee, coconuts, cotton, indigo and all the other sweet fruits of African slave labour.

The Seven Years War ended in 1763 with the humiliating abandonment to the British of the eastern half of Louisiana, but the domestic building boom continued. When Ménétra arrived in Auch to work on the stained glass, the council had just voted to begin construction of a town hall that would include an Italian-style theatre. He and a coppersmith spent three months providing Montpellier with hundreds of Parisian-style streetlamps made with imported Bohemian glass rather than the usual recycled broken windowpanes. There and in other cities, the old ramparts were being dismantled and transformed into tree-lined boulevards where workers and bourgeois could stroll on sunny afternoons and where Ménétra went scouting for prostitutes and girls out for a good time.

As a native of the imperial capital, he was lionized and quizzed about its fabled sites – the Samaritaine pump, the Place des Victoires, the many bridges and the busy streets. At an inn on the road from L'Isle-Jourdain to Toulouse, he was offered free board and lodging in exchange for his tales of the modern world ('I thought what a handy thing it is to come from Paris!'), 'and all the people who were drinking in the inn and who'd never been out of sight of their village steeple listened to me with wide-open eyes.'

✿

The pre-eminence of Paris is the single most important fact in the political and geographical history of France from the twelfth century to the present. The serving-girl at the roadside inn near Toulouse, whose mother tongue would have been Gascon, was impressed by Ménétra's Parisian patter, which she took to be excellent French. Even on the well-travelled post roads, a Parisian would be greeted like an important visitor touring a remote colonial outpost.

In 1760, the backwoods seemed to begin half a day's ride from Notre-Dame. The impression was confirmed by economic reality. Philibert Orry's survey of human resources suggested that the areas in which most people lived comfortably ('à l'aise') accounted for only one-fifth of the country (predominantly the North, from Normandy to Alsace, but excluding Champagne and including a few wine-growing regions). In most of the South, below a line drawn from the estuary of the Loire to Lake Geneva, the population lived either in 'pauvreté' or 'misère'.

As he drew near to the southernmost frontiers of France, Ménétra discovered what appeared to be the remnants of a barbarian civilization. Like a modern tourist in a third-world country, he was appalled as well as titillated by what he saw. In Bayonne near the Spanish border, he witnessed a picturesque medieval punishment. Some girls who were probably prostitutes had been locked in an iron cage dressed in nothing but a shift. They were being dipped repeatedly into the River Nive. 'You couldn't help laughing when you saw them wriggling about so I asked the local girls if they'd like me to give them a good washing too.' In the papal enclave of the Comtat Venaissin, annexed by France in 1791, he visited the Jewish ghettos of Carpentras and Avignon, where he tried to seduce a Jewish girl with a false promise of marriage. Observing the local custom of playing cruel tricks on the Jews, he stole two chickens from a Jewish man, knowing that because the man was not wearing the obligatory yellow hat he could be robbed with impunity.

Now that inhumanity is implicitly tolerated only at a distance of several hours on a plane, Ménétra's behaviour seems repellently at odds with his stated belief that all men and women were created equal. He was untroubled by the inconsistency. As a citizen of what he saw as 'a free country', he was free to follow his natural instincts. The blame for any injustice lay with the fear-mongering Church:

It's here that fanaticism and superstition are at their worst and the unhappy Jew can't go out without wearing a yellow hat. . . . Oh that so-called tolerant Christian religion! How can you ministers of the altar behave so cruelly? . . . You never stop to think that the Jews are our brothers and equals in the eyes of the Eternal and it's from their religion that you got all your teachings and ceremonies.

Ménétra was writing twenty-five years before the Fall of the Bastille, but a social revolution was already under way. He had read several books (as had almost half the servants and a third of all labourers in Paris), he felt at ease in different social strata, and he believed firmly in his right to pursue happiness on earth. As a choirboy, he had acquired the rudiments of an education but not the fear of damnation. His cheerful blaspheming was quite acceptable to most of the people he met.

While working above the altar in the church at Mondoubleau near Vendôme, his ladder slipped. He grabbed the beard of God the Father but the whole face came away in his hand. The Holy Ghost, who was underneath, slipped his moorings and, as Ménétra crashed to the floor, he snapped off an arm of the crucified Christ before breaking his own leg.

And this is why the good people of that region always hailed me by saying there goes the man who exterminated the Holy Trinity.

※

The division of France into a prosperous, modern North and an impoverished, antiquated South would come to be seen as a natural dichotomy. Examinations of army conscripts in the mid-nineteenth century revealed a North–South divide reminiscent of Orry's survey of 1745, with a southern preponderance of short, dark, illiterate non-French speakers. The linguistic frontier of *oc* and *oïl* would then appear to mark a permanent reality, rooted in racial characteristics.

This division was reinforced by the Paris-centric road-building policy instituted by Orry in 1738, which treated the capital as the heart and brain of the whole country. To foreign visitors, the new roads looked like the tree-lined avenues of an enormous half-deserted park. Superimposed on the maze of tracks and the unconnected mass of rural France in which eighty-two per cent of the population lived, this was the first national network to transcend geography and historical time. Travelling on the post roads, Ménétra was living in the world of coincident but separate spheres which is now a normal part of social life. While nearly half the population was ignorant of the national language, practically everyone he met on those nationwide prolongations of the Paris boulevards could either speak or understand French.

When Ménétra began his four-thousand-mile-long tour in 1757, there were already eleven thousand miles of maintained carriageway. The road-users were not containerized motorists warped by speed and obscured by laminated glass: they were as visible to each other as vagrants and cyclists are today. The coincidences which some of Ménétra's modern readers assume to be novelistic inventions were commonplace. In Lyon, he met a man from Rennes who knew that he had 'croqué' ('had a taste of') two little nuns at Agen. A bootblack who shined his shoes on the Petit-Pont in Paris had seen him in Toulouse. Twice, he was given news of one of the children he had fathered.

Without these glimpses of the corpuscular efficiency of the network, it would be hard to gain a sense of what it was to be mobile and sociable in mid-eighteenth-century France. There was so little traffic that, even close to a city, a roadside family could treat the drained and levelled carriageway as an extension of the farmyard, and yet news could spread at the speed of village gossip. Instead of paying ten *sous* to a postmistress, Ménétra could hand a letter to a fellow traveller and expect to have it delivered a few weeks later to his grandmother in Paris. He could also expect to hear back from her, even when he was on the road.

The post roads not only accelerated the movement of troops and information, they were vital in coordinating an increasingly specialized workforce of craftsmen, engineers and architects. In a land of bodgers and jacks of all trades, a skilled artisan could export his *savoir-faire* to distant provinces and, like Ménétra, leave his mark – and his genes – all over France, from the palace of Versailles to the Château de Crillon, and from the church of Mondoubleau to the cathedral at Auch. Complaints about the hardships of travel are remarkably rare in his journal: the 'atrocious' roads across the marshes of the Vendée and Poitou, the rental donkeys in the Rhone Valley (very slow and temperamental), and a river crossing on the road to Aix-en-Provence, where 'there was neither bridge nor boat but only a tall and sturdy man who carried me on his shoulders'.

The 'magnificent causeways' of the Languedoc on which the English agriculturalist Arthur Young saw women walking barefoot seemed to have been imported from a future civilization. In the Languedoc and other *pays d'état*, which enjoyed a degree of fiscal autonomy, the roads were funded by taxation. In the *pays d'élection*, which were controlled by the King's *intendants*, they were built by local people whose taxes took the form of physical labour: they worked ten hours a day and sometimes had to sleep at the worksite. The institution of the *corvée*, which came into full effect in 1750, required all able-bodied men (including those with a wooden leg) and women (but only spinsters and widows), along with their mules and horses, to devote a week or more in spring or autumn to constructing and repairing the King's highway. In Touraine alone, a quarter of a million people were requisitioned every year.

Ménétra would have seen those grudging amateur road crews struggling with their winches, picks and wheelbarrows, but like most of the people he met, he was resistant to his own and other people's physical suffering. Walking to Carcassonne, he had rescued a woman who had given birth on the road: she had left the coach 'to satisfy some needs' and been unable to catch up. Some time later, he heard from the woman herself at Narbonne that she and the baby were doing well and were about to go and join the father in the Flanders regiment.

❋

Compared to the years of famine, anarchy and mass conscription before and after the Revolution, this was an age of dawning liberty. Under Louis XV and his enlightened reformers, a life of happy security was not an impossible dream, unless one happened to be a Protestant, a Jew, a pauper, an invalid, the tenant of a bullying lord or an unprotected woman. In the temperate, low-altitude France that was becoming familiar to British and German tourists, Ménétra could wend his sunny way like a student on a working holiday, ticking off the guidebook sights – the Pont du Gard, the fair at Beaucaire, the tomb of Nostradamus, the grotto of Mary Magdalene at Sainte-Baume.

Old perils still lurked: wolves came down from the hills on the right bank of the Rhone and highwaymen hid in the woods between staging posts, but the bandits Ménétra encountered were robbers by vocation rather than necessity. When he and the grain merchant who had given him a ride were waylaid on the road to Montpellier, the thieves took his new leather breeches but left him his coat because they noticed a small stain on the front. ('The only reason it was wet was that I'd fallen asleep after drinking the brandy that the driver kept in a gourd.')

In a world increasingly domesticated by progress, a man of *sensibilité* might even befriend one of those howling harbingers of famine. At a *château* in Gascony, the gamekeeper gave him a little wolf cub. 'I kept him for about eight months and he followed me everywhere. . . . He slept at the foot of my bed.' Unfortunately, the wolf cub developed adult appetites and a taste for living flesh and freedom: 'I had to get him muzzled because he started trying to bite the children.'

> They warned me that even though the wolf knew me he might do me a mischief and so I took him to the edge of the Verdun woods and the gamekeeper who'd given him to me shot him with his musket.

✿   ✿   ✿

When the Sorbonne historian Daniel Roche unearthed the three hundred and thirty-one sheets of paper which had somehow ended up in the Bibliothèque Historique de la Ville de Paris and published his transcription of Ménétra's journal in 1982, most historians welcomed this revelation of a lost world, but many were appalled by the glazier's treatment of women and, contradictorily, by his implausible 'fantasies'. Reviewing the edition, an American Professor of History wondered whether one man 'can really have seduced so many women?'

There is no doubt that Ménétra was recounting real events. It would have taken a literary genius to fabricate that café-table chatter with its clumsy non-sequiturs and convincingly unnecessary details. This was not the writerly, epicurean pornography of Diderot or de Sade in which even items of furniture and the natural scenery pulsate with lust. Everything was described in the same relentless, raffish tone

– work, sex, sightseeing, pranks and philosophical opinions. The only woman in Ménétra's journal who might have been at home in an eighteenth-century boudoir novel is a girl he met at a wedding in Angers who had probably read a novel or two herself:

> She asked if I wanted to go with her and in my room while I was still lying down on top of a chest she started pulling on white silk stockings so I could look at them and say if I thought they suited her. It was a risky thing to do and I took full advantage.

Before cycling to Auch in 2012, I reread the journal and was surprised to find that less than one-fifth of it is taken up with fornication. It occurred to me in retrospect that this was not an extraordinary preponderance of erotic exploits. I had more or less deliberately forgotten all the pesterings, the sexual ironies, the propositionings by the respectable and the demoralized which can blight the journey of almost any young person travelling alone.

Except as a source of idiomatic phrases, the libidinous aspirations of strangers seemed to have no connection with the studious purpose of my journey and I had consigned these trivial incidents to a rarely visited part of memory. When the journal was published, some historians were similarly reluctant to accept Ménétra's smutty testimony on its own terms and condemned him as an aberration – as though there were any other direct examples of an eighteenth-century proletarian mind. For all we know, Jacques-Louis Ménétra was typical of an age when physical desire and spending power were acquiring a heightened potential to penetrate class barriers.

Practically all our sources of information on eighteenth-century France are legal, administrative, historiographical or literary. Letters and memoirs are almost exclusively bourgeois or aristocratic. Most of those texts were conceived and written in a study, an office, a library or a cell, which is why they lend themselves so readily to historical writing. It is easy to forget that nearly all were produced by a Parisian elite. This narrow focus of origin is responsible for some of the more peculiar ideas of theoretical social history – the belief, for instance, that it was not until the Victorian age that common people began to love their children and to mourn them when they died.

Perhaps historians are orderly and continent by nature, though there are exceptions. The unintended effect of professional propriety is to whiten the age in which we live. A history of any period also paints a picture of the present, and future historians might be led to conclude that in early twenty-first-century Europe, decency prevailed, exploitation was frowned upon and women were never abused.

I saw the stained-glass windows of Auch Cathedral just in time. In 2013, a campaign was launched to fund a major restoration. Air pollution was dulling the blush and luminosity of the figures' flesh and the wind was rattling their panes. Further damage would be prevented and it would be possible to admire the windows in their original state.

The strips of lead which Ménétra fitted to the face and body of Eve have been taken out and that part of the window's history is now preserved only in pixels. Unlike the saucy girl in the white stockings, who later threatened 'to stick a knife in me . . . if I didn't give her back what I'd taken from her' ('her petticoats were bulging out more than usual'), the Eve of Auch Cathedral has recovered her virginity. But it would be a delusion to think that we know exactly how she looked to a sixteenth-century worshipper gazing up at a lost paradise, or to the man who worked his potent magic on that damaged beauty.

9

Bloody Provence

It was a typical Mediterranean scene, ten miles west of Marseille: the sea hidden by low, mangy hills warped by the heat; the nearness of the coast shown only by the chimneys of oil refineries and heating plants; a computer-generated road system of cyclocidal roundabouts and pinch-points. This was the Estaque, once beloved of Cézanne, Renoir and Braque. There was the inhuman stench of diesel, combined with roadside fennel and mixed with the dust of demolition yards. After two miles on the unavoidable D9, we turned onto the old road to Martigues, with its clumps of flailing bamboo and concrete-block bungalows. Everything seemed designed to magnify the heat. On the old road, the traffic was much lighter and we relaxed into the normal state of watchfulness.

A black car came towards us and accelerated at Margaret, who was cycling just behind me. A second before the missile reached the kerb, she threw herself onto the concrete verge. Deliberate intimidation of cyclists is not uncommon, but this driver appeared to be in earnest. I threw up an arm in protest. The driver braked, swerved and came back at us, then screamed to a halt, perhaps judging the angle of wheel and kerb too tight for a clean hit. While I memorized the number plate, a stocky, brown-skinned man of about thirty leaped out of the car, bristling with unused energy but, as far I could tell, armed only with muscle.

In such cases, I find it best to open the verbal proceedings, but as the shouting began, I realized, first, that he was sincere in his murderous hatred and, second, that although the '13' on the car's number plate suggested a resident of the *département*, he was insulting me in a Romance language that was neither French nor Provençal nor any other I could recognize. Then something happened which I understood only later: infuriated by his anger, Margaret yelled, 'This guy tried to fucking kill me!' He suddenly stopped shouting, got back into his car and screamed off in the direction of Marseille.

After the customary shrugging of shoulders, the *gendarmes* at the nearest police station agreed that this was 'one for Ange'. The man called 'Angel' proved to be a community police officer with the stature of a giant and a passion for American jazz. He brought our bicycles into his office, made out a report and overwhelmed us with sympathy.

A black man laying down the law in a region notorious for racial violence, he could speak with authority on a subject which was beginning to preoccupy academic historians of the Midi during and after the Revolution: the inexplicable intensity of violence in the south-east of France. The image of sunny, thyme-scented Provence promoted by artists and tour operators was false, Ange explained. Many different groups of people lived there, and because they were poor, they found it hard to get along with one another. Holidaymakers such as ourselves could find plenty of safe and pleasant playgrounds in other parts of France.

※

Ange's warning chimed with our previous experience of Provence. For six months, we had house-sat a tiny disused bakery in the village of Bédoin at the foot of Mont Ventoux, 'the Giant of Provence', whose sun-bleached, wind-scorched summit always appears to be covered in snow. The snail-like configuration of the streets was typical of a wine village, curled up against the Mistral, shielding its cellars from the sun. As a result, the bakery was a refrigerator, but outside there were all the ingredients of the Francophile idyll – the rasping song of the cicadas, lavender for photographs and wardrobes, thyme for the pot, and the euphemistically termed 'glass of wine in the hand'. A large shed-like building on the road to Carpentras dispensed the staggeringly cheap product of the Vignerons du Mont Ventoux from something which resembled the nozzle of a petrol pump.

At first, the natives of that fragrant land played the role assigned to them by tradition. Because of the enormous daily outdoor queue snaking around the Préfecture de Police in Paris, and the bureaucratic war of attrition within, we had had to leave the capital before obtaining a *carte de séjour* for Margaret, who held a United States passport. The period of grace had elapsed when we arrived in Bédoin. Legally, she was now *en situation irrégulière*, as the clerk at the Bédoin town hall frowningly pointed out. The mayor was brought out of his office and I recounted our battle with the bureaucrats in Paris. No sooner had I uttered the magic word, 'Paris', than the documents were signed and stamped and we were assured that, during our stay in their little town, the officials of the Mairie de Bédoin stood ready to help in any way they could.

That sympathy for victims of the imperious capital was the last we saw of the reputedly carefree Provençaux. The travelling glazier, Jacques-Louis Ménétra, who repaired storm damage to the church windows in 1761, had singled out 'the good people' of 'that charming little town' Bédoin as 'the best I've ever seen': 'They made us very welcome and did everything they promised.' Whether it was the incessant draught of the Mistral and the onset of unphotogenic winter or the fact that foreigners were still relatively infrequent in Bédoin, the attitude of the people was one of sullen hostility.

One evening at a village *fête*, while we listened to a folk group in the square, some local boys dropped a tear-gas capsule at our feet. Through streaming eyes, I saw a well-dressed man pointing an accusing finger at us. The people around him glowered in our direction and I thought of the lynch mob in Jean Giono's novel of the cholera epidemic in Provence, *Le Hussard sur le toit*. I indicated the tittering juvenile terrorists who were still hovering on the edge of the square and urged him to give chase, but the gentleman and his neighbours turned back to listen to the music.

On a return visit a few years later, we experienced similarly un-accountable acts of animosity on the roads of the Carpentras Plain to the west of Bédoin – not from the migrant fruit-pickers but from National Front-voting natives. In Carpentras itself, in 1990, the old Jewish cemetery was defiled by Neo-Nazis. The white summit of the Giant of Provence looks down over a land of warring tribes and factions. I later became friends with an inexhaustible explorer of French municipal archives who has never ventured into certain parts of Provence because his skin is not white. To some inhabitants of Provence, the song of the cicadas is not the backing chorus of blissful idleness but the sound of seething hatred.

✿

An ungainly pyramidal monument at the end of our street in Bédoin marked the site where the guillotine had been erected during the Revolution. The misspelt inscription (since corrected) was probably engraved by a man whose first language was Provençal. It spoke of 'a year of weeping o'er these terrible ruins' and the restoration of 'justice'.

APRÈS UN AN DE PLEURS SUR CES DÉBRIS AFFREUX

LA LOI RAMÈNE LA JUSTICE;

CONSOLÉS VOUS Ô MALHEREUX

PUISQUE L'ÉCLAT DU CRIME EN PRÉDIT LE SUPLICE

The massacre of counter-revolutionary 'traitors' at Bédoin in 1794 is one of the lesser-known examples of violence in south-eastern France in the Revolutionary period. Historians of the Revolution have been struck by the exceptional ferocity of revolt and counter-revolt in the sphere of influence of Marseille and in towns along the Rhone corridor – Lyon, Nîmes, Avignon, Arles, Tarascon, Aubagne and Aix. The 'phenomenon' of Mediterranean savagery has been explained in various ways: socio-economic disparity, resentment at the previously untaxed aristocracy, the festering conflicts of earlier civil wars, the weakness of the state breeding vigilantism, the old traditions of feud and vendetta.

Anthropological analyses have conjured up an image of the hot-headed southerner which bears a striking resemblance to the stereotypes peddled by eighteenth-century Parisian journalists and orators. The people who would come to be seen as loveable *bons viveurs* were stubborn, ungovernable and unpredictable, a prey to 'unbridled passions' and fratricidal feuds, children of a land cursed by the Mistral and the sudden rains that turn the desiccated riverbeds into deadly torrents.

Studious immersion in a particular age sometimes regenerates the prejudices and mental habits of that period. Perhaps this explains a tendency to look for answers in native characteristics rather than in political events. Or perhaps the series of revolts and *coups d'état* which founded the modern French state is too complex to produce rational conclusions. For six or seven years, the course of French history seemed to change as often as the weather, and even the most flagrant physical realities of the Revolution were inextricable from its fictions.

✵　✵　✵

Within a month of its official date of birth – Tuesday 14 July 1789
– the French Revolution was writing its own history and, despite
confusion about its purposes and means, promoting itself in a vigorous
branding campaign. By 1790, it had an emblem (the tricolour cockade),
a hat (the Phrygian cap), a song ('Ça ira!'), a motto ('Liberté, Égalité,
Fraternité'), a sacred text (the Declaration of the Rights of Man and
the Citizen), a revamped and humanized head of state (Louis XVI,
formerly 'King of France and Navarre', now 'King of the French'),
and a founding event, the Storming of the Bastille, which also gave
the Revolution its iconic building.

Shopkeepers and artisans of the Faubourg Saint-Antoine had spent
that Tuesday afternoon besieging the hulk of blackened stone at the
end of their street, hoping to find arms and ammunition with which
to defend the new National Assembly from a military coup. Built to
keep the English out of Paris during the Hundred Years War, that
monument to arbitrary justice had turned out to contain only seven
sleazy prisoners: four petty forgers, one incestuous count and two
lunatics, all reasonably well looked after. But after the catastrophic
harvest of 1788 and several years of unemployment and rising prices,
the sufferings of the people were real enough. The Bastille was a
necessary symbol of oppression. The torture chambers, the dripping
dungeons and the grizzled prisoner with white hair down to his waist
were theatrical fakes, but when mini-Bastilles carved from the tumbled
stones were carried throughout the land by travelling salesmen dubbed
'Apostles of Liberty', those 'patriotic relics' were paraded in provincial
streets like the reliquaries of saints.

In the provinces, the first rumble of the great upheaval had taken
the form of news from Paris. At Versailles on 17 June 1789, the delegates of the Third Estate – the ninety-seven per cent of the
population who were neither clergy nor nobility – had demanded
equal representation and declared themselves a National Assembly.*
It was widely assumed in the provinces that they would govern under
the benign guidance of the monarch, who had tried, but failed, to

---

* The majority of Third Estate deputies were small-town officials – lawyers, notaries
and magistrates – with prior experience of government. A few were merchants,
manufacturers, bankers, doctors and teachers. Many considered themselves noble,
whether by the purchase of venal offices or self-promotion. Most were, in an etymological but not a Marxist sense, bourgeois.

replace the hated *corvée* with a tax on landowners. On the following Saturday, barred from the parliamentary chamber (allegedly 'closed for repairs'), the delegates had met in a tennis court in a back street of Versailles, and vowed 'never to separate . . . until the Constitution of the kingdom be established on firm foundations.' King Louis had eventually given his approval and a reassurance that the troops who were massing in ever-greater numbers around Versailles and Paris were a simple precautionary measure.

Twenty-four days later, the Bastille fell and, to the astonishment of the National Assembly, an uprising spread spontaneously from six or seven places hundreds of miles apart to cover much of the country. Rumours of an imminent invasion of 'brigands' led by aristocrats and foreigners winged their way with inexplicable speed from mountain plateaux to rarely contacted hamlets crouching in their hollows far from any road or river. There were sightings of suspicious figures, variously called 'bandits', 'Anglais' and 'Mazarines', as though ghosts of half-remembered French history had risen and were on the march. Weirdly, Paris itself was at no point the origin or the destination of these rumours.

This mass peasant revolt is known, somewhat condescendingly, as 'the Great Fear'. The National Assembly itself was in a state of near-panic. Faced with a seemingly simultaneous kingdom-wide uprising, and unnerved by these invisible networks of high-speed communication, previously recorded only in the war reports of Julius Caesar, they, too, imagined a sinisterly coordinated aristocracy 'pursuing the path of anarchy and disorder' to ignite a counter-revolution.

When the peasants set fire to *châteaux*, reaped unripe crops before they could be taken by invaders, and destroyed seigneurial archives, they were ill informed but not illogical. Bands of beggars were a constant threat to small communities, and it was quite true that Britain and Austria were wondering how to prevent the contagion of revolution. The fears of French peasants in 1789 were more grounded in reality than some of the fairy tales which inspire political movements in the digital age.

✻

The smoke pouring from the towers of the Bastille had been the first puff of the volcano; the nationwide uprising was the pyroclastic flow: 'Paris had taken its Bastille; now the peasants would take theirs – all those feudal Bastilles, those castles with their arrow slits and dovecotes lording it over villages and plains' (Jean Jaurès). In the suddenly accelerated vortex of events, the delegates of that disturbingly diverse multitude, the Third Estate, vowed to keep pace with the Revolution. Their serious recognition of the equal importance of the provinces (98 per cent of the population and 99.97 per cent of the land mass) was a revolution in itself.

In the early hours of 5 August 1789, while provincial authorities from Normandy to the Rhone Valley were hanging and beheading riotous peasants, the National Assembly at Versailles boldly voted to abolish several feudal privileges. The King had refused to sign the resolution into law – regardless of which, a few days later, the sputtering of muskets and the slaughter of once privately owned pigeons, rabbits and deer announced that a new age had dawned. Towards the end of that month, the English agronomist Arthur Young, who was on his way to Aix-en-Provence, witnessed at close quarters the effects of unenforceable good intentions:

> . . . one would think that every rusty gun in Provence is at work killing all sorts of birds; the shot has fallen five or six times in my chaise and about my ears. . . . As I am everywhere informed, [the abolition of feudal rights] has filled all the fields of France with sportsmen to an utter nuisance.

The National Assembly continued to issue decrees heralding a series of impressively sensible reforms. Work began on 'an equal, fraternal and useful' division of the kingdom into *départements*,* retaining wherever practical the old provincial boundaries, but reducing their dimensions to a manageable size. The purpose of this administrative masterpiece was to ensure that no citizen would be inconveniently remote from the legal and commercial capital of each

---

* Until 1789, *département* referred only to the apportioning of possessions, taxes, responsibilities and parts of a building, or to the quartering of troops. Most of the original eighty-three *départements* were subdivided into five or six 'districts'. Apart from Paris and Corsica (annexed four months after the Fall of the Bastille), the *départements* were named either after geographical location or, more commonly, natural features: rivers (sixty-two) and mountains or massifs (eleven). Calvados in Normandy was named after a rocky bank four miles off the coast which was normally submerged but shown on the Cassini map of France as an impressive fifteen-mile-long barrier facing England.

region, and, conversely, that no one would be able to escape 'public surveillance'.

On 26 August 1789, the Assembly produced its first version of the Declaration of the Rights of Man and the Citizen. This poignant master-piece of French philosophical prose, drawn up in an atmosphere of impending chaos, would be engraved, not only on souvenir stones of the Bastille, but also, with omissions and modifications, in the mind of every literate, French-speaking citizen.

> Article 1. Men are born and remain free and equal in rights. Social distinctions can be founded only in the common good.

> Article 6. The Law is the expression of the general will. All Citizens have the right to contribute, in person or through their Representatives, to its making. . . .

> Article 9. Every man is presumed innocent until declared guilty, from which it follows that, if his arrest be judged indispensable, any need-less rigour in securing his person must be severely punished by law.

> Article 11. The free communication of thoughts and opinions is one of the most precious rights of Man. All Citizens may therefore speak, write and publish freely, whilst remaining accountable for any abuse of this freedom. . . .

> Article 17. Property is an inviolable and sacred right, of which none may be deprived, unless public need, established by law, evidently demand it. . . .

Before long, it would seem to many of the delegates who enshrined property rights and social distinctions in their Declaration that they were reinforcing a dam and opening its floodgates at the same time.

✻

Even after two hundred and thirty years of analysis, the equations governing the course of the Revolution seem bewilderingly complex. Left behind with a handful of servants in the British embassy, the twenty-four-year-old *chargé d'affaires* Robert FitzGerald struggled to provide the Foreign Secretary in London with a coherent account. By FitzGerald's reckoning, two revolutions had already taken place and a third was on its way:

A most mysterious and impenetrable veil covers all at this moment, and from the dark face of things since the residence of the Royal Family in this Town, most fatal conclusions [must be] drawn: there are few people who do not believe that a third Revolution in affairs will shortly take place, and none who do not suppose it will be more bloody than the two former.

An extraordinary event had taken place, and although the implications were only slowly sinking in, FitzGerald had the distinct impression that a point of no return had been passed.

On Monday morning [5 October 1789], My Lord, we were much surprised and at first much entertained with the ludicrous sight of a female army proceeding very clamorously, but in order and determined step towards Versailles.

Several thousand women armed with knives and broomsticks had surged out of the central markets and invaded the Hôtel de Ville. They were infuriated by the price of bread and reports of an orgiastic banquet at Versailles where the King and Queen had refused to toast the Revolution. After smashing in the doors on the ground floor of the Hôtel de Ville, they tore up whatever paperwork came to hand, saying 'that's the only thing the men have done since the revolution began'.

A collective decision had been made to go and see 'le boulanger, la boulangère et le petit mitron' ('the baker, the baker's wife and the little baker's boy') at Versailles. Women from every shop and market joined the throng as it left the Hôtel de Ville. They marched along the *quais*, past the Louvre and the Tuileries, and spilled out into the open fields of the Champs-Élysées, where the size of this paramilitary shopping expedition became apparent. Estimates varied from six to ten thousand.

Continuing along the river, they trooped through the silent, shuttered villages of Chaillot and Auteuil. Riders coming out from Paris were intercepted in case they tried to close the bridge at Sèvres. They reached Versailles at noon, only to be told that the head *boulanger* (Louis XVI) was out hunting. On his return, the King made some emollient remarks to a delegation of twelve women, one of whom, appointed to address the King because she was young and pretty, fainted and (she remembered) was given 'some wine in a great golden goblet'. The King promised to provide them with flour, while the women outside chanted obscenities about the Queen and called for her head.

A hundred or so women trudged back to Paris in the rain, but most remained in Versailles. Exhausted and muddy, they squeezed onto the benches of the National Assembly, fondled a bishop and made sarcastic remarks while the Assembly conducted its business. Wine, bread and saveloy sausage were rushed into the chamber. The following morning, the reinvigorated mob swarmed into the palace and discovered the bedchamber of Marie-Antoinette a few moments after she had fled into the King's apartments. The Marquis de Lafayette, hero of the American Revolutionary War and commander of the now openly mutinous National Guard, obtained (literally, as it turned out) a stay of execution by agreeing to escort the King and Queen back to Paris.

The 'female army' which re-entered Paris that evening after six hours on the road was preceded by the National Guard. The procession included fifty or more cartloads of flour and grain, the Royal Family sporting tricolour cockades and the freshly powdered heads of two palace guards stuck on pikes. After several speeches hailing the happy day when the monarch returned to his capital, the *boulanger*, the *boulangère* and the *petit mitron* were finally allowed to make their beds in the long-abandoned, morgue-like Palace of the Tuileries.

❊

This 'odd story' or 'curious incident', which used to be treated as a quirky footnote to the main, male narrative, was a founding event of the Revolution just as much as the Storming of the Bastille. The Women's March on Versailles secured an official assurance that the stomachs of the People would be a patriotic priority. It established the political power of the mob (though not the constitutional rights of women, who would not be granted full suffrage until 1944). It won a public declaration of allegiance to the Revolution by the Army and the National Guard, and it forced the King to ratify the abolition of privileges and the Declaration of the Rights of Man. Crucially, it recentred political power in Paris.

Feudal privileges were abolished, but so were the privileges of the provincial states. There was no question now of a confederation of

French provinces with their own administrations and governmental traditions. It was from Paris, the only city to be a *département* in itself, that the Revolution would be exported, with its laws and political assembly, its measures of weight and distance, and its own official form of French. Most of the provincial states had enthusiastically welcomed and even anticipated the reforms, and there was little sense that this imposition of 'unity' would widen fault-lines that had been created long ago by the expansion of the Île-de-France.

The British orator and parliamentarian Edmund Burke, blusteringly ignorant of the geographical and administrative logic of the new *départements*, and mistaking the reform for a 'geometrical distribution and arithmetical arrangement', was horrified that the Assembly had 'chosen to dissever [the country] in this barbarous manner'.* He was crudely enamoured with the image of an 'almost naked' Marie-Antoinette fleeing from 'a band of cruel ruffians', and of the lovely teenage princess he had seen floating 'just above the horizon' at Versailles seventeen years before. But he was right in one respect: 'these pretended citizens' of Paris would 'treat France exactly like a country of conquest'.

The fate of the nation would now depend on the nature of the regime in the capital and, when the mob was not dictating policy, and the devolutionist 'Girondin' faction had been defeated, on the ambitions, prejudices and mental health of an ever-smaller number of individuals.

✿　✿　✿

Popular images of the French Revolution reflect the horror into which it descended: the snickering guillotine and the clacking needles of gore-spattered *tricoteuses* at its foot; the ransacking of churches and the hounding of priests. The 'horrible histories' version of the Revolution presupposes a Burkish empathy with aristocrats (as nobles were now called). The epic slaughter of the Terror (1792–4) and the Revolution's long epilogue, the Napoleonic Wars, are less immediately

---

* *Reflections on the Revolution in France* (November 1790). Burke, who is still often treated as an authority on the matter, probably misinterpreted one of the grid maps of France created by the royal geographer Robert de Hesseln to show the approximate dimensions of the proposed *départements*. The government commission wanted to minimize 'changes to existing customs and relations' and 'never intended that division to be strictly geometrical'.

compelling than tales of mannerly individuals severed from their children and possessions, praying for a Scarlet Pimpernel.

Most of the clichés are false or misleading. Only 8.5 per cent of the guillotined were aristocrats. (Priests accounted for 6.5 per cent and workers for 31 per cent.) The tritely named *tricoteuses* were women who formed their own revolutionary clubs or attended political meetings, where they knitted instead of doodling or taking snuff. Anti-clericalism was widespread long before the Revolution: statues and icons were often flayed or smashed if the saints had failed to protect the harvest. Most of the destruction wrought on religious buildings was the work of speculators marketing nationalized Church property.

Images of violence illustrate centralized policy rather than the acts of individuals: the abolition of monastic orders and nationalization of the clergy; the execution of the King and Queen; the declaration of war on Austria and Prussia and the consequent introduction of 'emergency' measures such as the Law on Suspects (September 1793), which effectively made the entire population guilty of treason until proven innocent.

The Revolution's first anthem shows the same bellicose trend. 'Ça ira!' ('It'll all be fine!'), on a favourite tune of Marie-Antoinette, was a remarkably feeble expression of patriotic fervour – 'The people will distinguish the true from the false'; 'Every Frenchman will do his best / To obey the letter of the law' – until it was politically corrected: 'We'll string 'em up, the aristocrats / And when we've 'ung 'em all, / We'll shove a spade right up their arse.'

In this, the most systematically bizarre period in French history, government representatives were despatched from the capital like missionaries or salesmen, to educate, reorganize and, if the need arose, pacify the provinces. The 'barbaric' dialects and non-French languages of the majority were to be silenced. After the storming of the Tuileries Palace in August 1792, the monarchy and the National Assembly were replaced by a one-chamber National Convention which launched a programme of dechristianization. The nation was to be stripped of every vestige of 'superstition' and aristocracy, even the supposedly nobiliary particle, 'de'.*

---

* These reforms were seriously enforced. A German scholar living in the Rue Saint-Denis, challenged by a guard and asked for his particulars, was forced to reduce his address to 'Rue Nis' – 'because', said the guard, 'we don't have saints no more . . . and we don't have de's neither.'

A new Republican calendar was adopted in 1793, purged of the 'lies and deceit' of saints' names. The fifth day of each ten-day week or *décade* – including one moveable day of rest – was dedicated to a useful animal (silkworm, donkey, shrimp, etc.) and the tenth day to a tool (spade, ladder, watering pot, etc.). Christmas Day was rededicated to the dog. The remaining days were associated with natural products such as flowers, fruits, vegetables, minerals and manure. A whole generation of patriotic babies – usually orphans – started life with names such as Artichaut, Carpe, Coriandre, Oignon, Pissenlit (a cruel name to give an infant),* Prune, and even Sarcloir (hoe) and Pressoir (wine press).

✿

Mass conscription and a growing population enabled the armies of the Republic to lay the foundations of an empire. By conquest or plebiscite, the Austrian Netherlands, Belgium and the Duchy of Savoy became French *départements* in 1792; in 1793, the County of Nice and the Principality of Monaco together formed the *département* of Alpes maritimes. This missionary expansionism far surpassed the dogged territorial acquisitions of Louis XIV. The Revolution was to transcend the old frontiers. In the eyes of Robespierre and other ideologues, the only difference between the enemy without and the enemy within was that the domestic threat was more dangerous and must be suffocated by 'the despotism of liberty'.

On three September days in 1792, well over a thousand inmates of Paris jails and hospitals were butchered. 'News' had spread that foreign armies were advancing on the capital: aristocrats, priests and cut-throats were to be released from prison to murder the families of soldiers who were away defending the fatherland. With the blessing of the Paris Commune, which was now a national government in all but name, massacres took place in several other towns and cities. In Reims, there were decapitations, dismemberments and the brandishing of gory souvenirs: on the Place de l'Hôtel de Ville, the bodies of seven priests, one of them still alive, were thrown onto a bonfire.

As power was sucked into the unstable mass of Paris, the provinces reacted. In 1793, federalist revolts, both republican and counter-revolutionary, bourgeois and proletarian but rarely royalist, broke out

---

* The diuretic dandelion, still known in parts of Britain as the 'pissabed'.

in Normandy, Brittany, the Vendée, the Gironde, the Basque Country, Burgundy, Dauphiné, Franche-Comté, the Massif Central, the Upper and Lower Rhone Valley and Provence. The goal of the so-called federalists was not decentralization but resistance to the Jacobin minority in Paris and its reign of terror. 'Federalism' was a term of Jacobin propaganda, suggesting a treasonous attempt to break up the nation when it needed to present a united front to its enemies.

The crushing of these rebellions against the dictatorship of Paris was justified by a colonialist dehumanizing of the provincial savages. Looking more than ever like a Parisian *coup d'état*, the 'French' Revolution espoused the prejudices of the metropolitan elite: provincials were sly and treacherous, treated their fellow citizens with sadistic brutality and were riddled with medieval superstitions.

Between March 1793 and May 1774, more than one hundred thousand alleged traitors were 'exterminated' (the word was used in orders from Paris) by Republican troops in 'the Vendée'. The Vendée was actually just one part of a killing zone which covered much of western France. Towns were levelled and fields made unfit for farming. To save gunpowder, soldiers stabbed non-combatant citizens with their bayonets. Sometimes, bread ovens and cider presses were used as death chambers.

In Nantes, several thousand prisoners were 'baptized' (drowned) by the government's commissioner, Jean-Baptiste Carrier, in customized barges on the Loire. In Lyon, 1,684 people were executed and the order was given – but only partially carried out – to obliterate the city. It was renamed Ville Affranchie ('Freetown'). In Marseille, which formed a federalist army to support the people of Lyon, the public prosecutor wrote to the Committee of Public Safety in Paris* ('because Paris may serve as a model in all things'), requesting that the Marseille executioner be given guillotine lessons by his counterpart in Paris, who could process twelve people in thirteen minutes – 'or we'll never be finished'. Marseille was renamed, or de-named, Ville sans nom ('Town With No Name').

After the port of Toulon was reconquered from the British, who had been invited to rescue it from the Revolution, several hundred

---

* The Comité de salut public was instituted by the National Convention on 6 April 1793 as the emergency executive branch of government.

people were summarily executed. The young artillery officer who had distinguished himself at the siege was later accused of organizing the execution of prisoners at Toulon. Fortunately for his reputation, Colonel Bonaparte had been stabbed in the thigh by a British sergeant and could plausibly claim to have played no part in the massacre.

❉   ❉   ❉

A special case, because it belonged to the Pope and shared all its borders with France, was the part of Provence which comprised the city of Avignon and the Comtat Venaissin (the County of Venasque). The papal enclave had been the scene of a small but vicious civil war. With its powerful Republican faction led by a former bandit called Jourdan Coupe-Tête ('the Decapitator'), Avignon voted to become a part of France. The town of Carpentras, capital of the neighbouring Comtat, remained loyal to the Pope. The Avignon army laid siege to Carpentras and the National Assembly ended the civil war by annexing the entire papal enclave in September 1791.

In June 1793, this rich domain of bishops' palaces, monasteries and vineyards became the *département* of the Vaucluse. It was annexed partly 'in order to maintain the credit of the *assignats*' – the rapidly depreciating paper currency that was based on the projected value of confiscated religious property.

To the *commissaires* on mission from Paris, Provence was a hotbed of religious fanatics with a climate to match. According to the author of a patriotic guidebook,

> The lethal habit they have in Provence of encasing roads in extremely high mud walls makes travel unbearable. In summer . . . it is not unusual to see men and beasts of burden collapse with exhaustion, heat and thirst, and perish on the spot.

Apart from the weather, the commonest complaint about Provence was the length of the Provençal league. Almost two kilometres longer than the Paris league, it seemed to possess the supernatural power of making space itself expand:

> The traveller finds reality continually contradicted by the informa-tion he obtains along the way . . . Villagers will often tell him that he has but a short league to reach his lodging. Three hours later,

he has still not arrived. . . . It is high time that uniform measures came to the traveller's aid.

The *commissaires'* sense of alienation was exacerbated by the government's policy of appointing only representatives who were foreign to the *département*. This policy, introduced in the summer of 1793, ensured that the *commissaire* would be guided, not by local custom, but by the dictates of the capital.

✿

Étienne-Christophe Maignet, the government's 'missionary' to the *départements* of Vaucluse and Bouches-du-Rhône, arrived that November to bring order to this nest of zealots, thieves and 'moderates'. By the end of the year, the 'hydra' of federalism which had raised its heads in Marseille and Toulon had been crushed. On 22 April 1794, Maignet wrote an assessment of the region formerly known as Provence and sent it to Paris, where it arrived thirteen days later.

> I conclude with a thought you would do well to ponder. The state of these *départements* is not as well known as it should be. Almost everything here is gangrenous: they can be saved only by the most vigorous remedies and an unremitting war on all these scoundrels.
> Greetings and friendship.
> Maignet

It is here that the cheerful and flourishing village – or, as it then was, town – of Bédoin makes its first appearance on the national stage. On the night of 12–13 Floréal in the Year II (1–2 May 1794), as representative Maignet learned a day or two later, 'sacrilegious hands dared to touch the liberty tree' at Bédoin. The tree, which had been ceremoniously planted in the square by the fountain, had been ripped up by the roots and heaved over the town wall into a ditch in the 'Pré aux porcs' (Pig Field). The red bonnet which had perched on top of the tree was found at the bottom of a well. A wodge of papers had been trampled into the sludge at the base of the fountain. These proved to be the latest decrees from Paris, which until recently had adorned the doors of the Maison Commune (the town hall).

Nine miles away in Carpentras, Maignet's agent, Lego, and Louis-Gabriel Suchet, commander of the Fourth Ardèche Battalion, received an order to send troops to the town at the foot of Mont Ventoux 'in a number sufficient to intimidate the aristocracy'. They arrived just before dawn on 5 May, at the hour when the sun-glow behind the mountain makes the white summit look entirely black.

✻

'Liberty trees' had been one of the great successes of the new regime. As substitutes for the traditional maypole, they seemed to appeal to a devotional instinct and were believed to embody, as though by tran-substantiation, the growth of the young Republic. By 1792, six thousand *arbres de la liberté* had been planted in towns and villages all over France. The commonest choice was the poplar because it grew quickly, took up little horizontal space and bristled with twigs from which to hang Republican insignia such as ribbons and cockades. It also had a Latin name, *populus*, which might have meant (but didn't) 'the People's Tree'.

In his report to Paris, Maignet presented this 'overturning of the august emblem of our regeneration' as the final straw. The people of Bédoin had consistently obstructed and insulted the Revolution. The municipal authorities had retained the *fleur de lys* and the coat-of-arms of Louis XVI. The soldiers who were billeted on the town to intimi-date the inhabitants had been overcharged, and on the fourth anniversary of the Fall of the Bastille, instead of voting for the new constitution, the town council had discussed the theft of a bell from a chapel. Maignet reminded the Committee of Public Safety of his repeated warnings. Without 'vigorous action', the region would rise up like the Vendée.

Suffused with a kind of geographical paranoia, Maignet's reports made the well-tended, fruitful *pays* of Bédoin sound like an overseas colony where traitorous savages enjoyed the protection of a white mountain whose name appeared to mean 'suction-cup' or 'air-hole': 'Situated at the foot of Mont-Ventouse [*sic*], surrounded by hills intersected by numerous defiles, this region had everything it took to become a new Vendée.'

There was every sign of a counter-revolutionary plot . . . It would have been powerfully abetted by the situation of the town, which backs on to Mont Ventouse, an enormous, inaccessible mountain.

❄

Lego, Suchet and the Fourth Ardèche Battalion arrived in Bédoin with specific orders to punish the outrage so as to 'freeze with fear the hearts of all who hear of it.' The mayor, Silvestre Fructus, tried to flee in his nightshirt. A shot was fired; his legs buckled with fear, and he was incarcerated with all the other municipal officers in the town hall. The townspeople were herded into the church while 'the filth of fanaticism' (icons, crosses, etc.) was piled up outside and set on fire. A curfew was imposed and all the houses of Bédoin were to be brightly lit. Lego and Suchet sent messages to Maignet in Avignon informing him that no culprit could be discovered and that, consequently, the entire town must be guilty.

The Committee of Public Safety approved Maignet's plan of action on 17 May. The town was renamed Bédoin l'Infâme and the surrounding area declared 'an enemy territory to be destroyed by sword and fire'. On the first day of official 'vengeance', two priests who had been hiding in a barn near Mazan were guillotined. Five days later, on 28 May, the court, which sat in the open air, delivered its judgement: ten people were to be outlawed, fifteen sent to jail and sixty-three executed.

The list of the dead is the posthumous portrait of a socially diverse and well-served community. There were lawyers, farmers, cobblers, weavers, potters, tilers (including the mayor), saltpetre men (who produced an ingredient of gunpowder), millers, bakers, a locksmith, a blacksmith and a surgeon. There were also six aristocrats (two gentlemen and four ladies), six priests and a sixty-five-year-old nun who told the court that she 'preferred the Pope's regime to that of the Republic'.

Sixty-three was too large a batch to process in a single day, and so, observing an *ancien régime* distinction, the gentlemen, ladies and priests were beheaded while the others were shot to the sound of music and the soldiers' cries of 'Vive la République!' The bodies were dumped in a hole in the middle of a field. Then the town, including the hospital, was looted and set on fire with tarry torches.

The church was partially blown up and salt was scattered on the fields. Bédoin l'Infâme was renamed once again: it would henceforth be identified on maps and official documents as Bédoin l'Anéanti ('the Annihilated').

The fire burned for several days. The stores of flour, grain and wine were consumed, as were all the silkworms. One of the silk factories had contained sixty thousand pounds of silk. On 3 June, Maignet's chief administrative officer, a Jacobin and ex-priest, was travelling back to Avignon. 'At a distance of four leagues', probably near Carpentras, he saw 'the revolutionary flames devouring Bedouin l'Infâme, where the counter-revolution had broken out with all its horrors and audacity.'

❊   ❊   ❊

Evidence might conceivably be found in the ashen husk of Bédoin of that proverbial hot-headedness of the South. Someone must have reported the felling of the tree to the authorities in Carpentras. Bédoin certainly had its share of committed 'patriots' who had fought for the Revolution at Marseille and volunteered for the Republican armies. But the question that was never raised by the prosecutors at Bédoin was: why would someone have risked the destruction of their own town by vandalizing the sacred tree?

Similar acts of arboricide had been committed not long before in the villages of Monteux and Crillon without repercussions. A proper investigation might have asked why yet another liberty tree was cut down at Bédarrides *after* the burning of Bédoin. This looks suspiciously like an attempt by patriots to have the town wiped off the map. The only two clues that subsequently came to light both suggested deliberate acts of provocation. Suchet was said to have ordered his own men to be shot at from a window to justify the destruction. A later vicar of Bédoin was told that Lego had paid a local boy to desecrate the tree in order to provide Maignet with a pretext for the purge. (The boy in question was rounded up with all the others and executed anyway.)

After the massacre, letters sent to the National Convention in Paris from the neighbouring villages of Malaucène and Mormoiron and from the town of Lambesc near Aix painted a picture of a unanimously patriotic population, indignant at the perfidy of the Bédoinais:

> We thank you for sending Maignet among us – the virtuous Maignet, whose name strikes fear into the hearts of aristocrats and intriguers ... May all who dare to emulate that land of infamy be reduced to ashes.

> May our *commune* be purged of the foul monsters who persist in sullying the land of liberty.

> Continue, O representative, to smite with the national mace [the symbol of parliamentary authority] all those impious men who yearn to be slaves.

These ludicrously sycophantic letters might have been written by fervent patriots or they might have been dictated by fear of Citizen Maignet or even drafted by Maignet himself, afraid that his killing spree might be deemed excessive, as it eventually was.

It is especially revealing that when the survivors of the holocaust were billeted on the inhabitants of Crillon, Flassan and Le Barroux, there were no reprisals or denunciations. These explosions of violence were shocking precisely because, despite occasional inter-village rivalries and Lilliputian 'wars' inflamed by the political situation, the Provençaux were peaceful and their rebellions infrequent. The obvious fact is that the savagery came from outside. Some of the most brutal of the government's 'missionaries' were natives of the Auvergne – Maignet the butcher of Bédoin, Carrier the butcher of Nantes, Javagues the terrorizer of the former provinces of Burgundy and Lyonnais. Suchet's parents were Auvergnats. All these men were sent from Paris and many were Parisian by birth: Fréron (Marseille and Toulon), Collot d'Herbois (Lyon), Tallien (Bordeaux) and Maignet's agent, Lego.

Under its ideological camouflage, this invasion of supposedly less civilized regions by a belligerent state is the classic drama of colonialization. Some people seized the opportunity to wield power. Others may have felt, correctly or not, like certain individuals after the Brexit referendum, that acts of aggression against traitors and aliens were sanctioned and encouraged by the state.

✿

Five months after the Terror had ended with the guillotining of Robespierre and his followers, the brutal reconquest of a rebellious *pays* in the Vaucluse was condemned by the Convention. It voted to fund the reconstruction of Bédoin and the erection of the pyramidal monument which stands by the fountain. Lego and Suchet served a short prison sentence. Suchet was later celebrated as one of Napoleon's most brilliant marshals. Maignet himself was censured but judged to have acted in accordance with the law. He pursued a successful legal career and served as mayor of his native town, Ambert, where a quiet cul-de-sac bears his name.

Several nineteenth-century historians in sympathy with the Revolution, convinced that its horrors had been exaggerated, claimed that only six, seven or eight houses rather than four hundred and thirty-three were destroyed in Bédoin. This was ideological wishful thinking. In 1843, half a century after the annihilation of Bédoin, Murray's *Hand-book for Travellers in France* described the settlement at the foot of Mont Ventoux as 'a miserable village rising from amidst the blackened ruins of a former town destroyed at the Revolution'.

✿ ✿ ✿

I never did find an explanation for the sullenness we experienced in Bédoin. At the village *fête*, the coincidence of tear gas and two strangers in city clothes might have sparked thoughts of the Parisians who were beginning to buy up old farmhouses to use as summer homes. The recent opening of the small 'Lion' supermarket was a worrying development for the local shopkeepers. The nudist campsite on the lower slopes of Mont Ventoux can't have helped.

I did, however, find a clue to the motive of the man in the black car who tried to kill us on the road to Martigues. Travelling off grid, we caught up with the news only after reaching Paris. The political talk was mostly of President Sarkozy's decision to expel the Roma or Romani. The police had been secretly instructed to clear illegal travellers' camps within three months and to 'prioritize' Roma people. No distinction was made between illegal immigrants and the French Roma, a large majority of whom are sedentary. One of the main groups in France is the long-established Gitan population of the northern suburbs of Marseille and the townships around the Étang de Berre lagoon: Port-de-Bouc, Marignane and Martigues.

At the European Union summit in Brussels, Sarkozy had rebutted accusations by the EU Justice Commissioner that he was illegally persecuting an ethnic minority – something she had thought 'Europe would never again witness after the Second World War'. Sarkozy had sarcastically offered to send the expelled Roma to Luxembourg, the country of the Justice Commissioner. This was on 14 September 2010, the day on which we were attacked by the car driver. The Romance language I had failed to understand was probably the 'kaló' dialect of that area, which is a mixture of Spanish, Catalan, French and Romani.

The murderous motorist had the appearance of a tzigane, and we must have looked to him like white *bobos* (bourgeois bohemians) from the north on a late-summer cycling holiday. We were treating his back yard as a playground while his people were being deported by the fascist president in Paris. When he heard us speaking English, his anger subsided and we were no longer considered to be enemy combatants.

✻   ✻   ✻

Provence, the fourth week of April 1814

In the spring of 1814, when more than a million French citizens had died in wars of conquest started by the Revolution and pursued by its most successful general, the people of Provence were given the chance to avenge themselves on the tyrannical state. The artillery officer who had rescued Toulon for the Revolution in 1793 – and who, as First Consul, had signed a decree in 1802 expelling all 'bohémiens' (gypsies) from the south-west of France – was travelling more or less incognito on the road from Avignon to Aix.

Two weeks before, at the Palace of Fontainebleau, as Emperor Napoleon I, he had signed the decree of abdication. He was to be escorted to Saint-Tropez, where he would embark on a British frigate for the island of Elba. From there, in fine weather, he would be able to see the coast of his native Corsica.

He left Fontainebleau on 20 April with a cavalry escort and the four Allied commissioners. The first part of the journey passed without serious incident. At Nevers, Moulins and Lyon, there were a few, perhaps sardonic cries of 'Vive l'Empereur!' and 'Vive Napoléon!' But as he entered Provence and headed south into the regions which had suffered most from the Republican armies and the seventeen years of mass conscription, the convoy of fourteen carriages, separated now into several groups, was passing through a hostile foreign land.

In a small town south of Montélimar, his carriage was delayed by a torch-lit street party that was being held to celebrate the restoration of the Bourbons. The revellers were crying out, 'Down with the tyrant!' and 'Down with the man who butchered our children!' He spent that night in his carriage and reached Avignon at dawn. He had lived there for a few weeks in 1793 when Provence was being purged of counter-revolutionaries.

On the edge of town, a crowd had gathered. Despite the servant on the box seat who brandished a sword, hands were reaching for the door handle. Breakfast would have to wait . . . The horses galloped out of town, crossed the Durance by the new Bonpas bridge and reached Orgon at eight o'clock. An Italian *abbé* lodging at the inn was surprised to see several coaches arrive with a military escort and mountains of baggage. In one of those coaches, he saw a pale, trembling figure trying to hide behind a general of the former imperial army.

Everyone was shouting, 'Death to the tyrant! Long live the King!' They burned an effigy of him in his presence and showed him other dummies which had been lacerated with sword-cuts and stained with blood. Some of them climbed onto his carriage and shook their fists, shouting, 'Die, tyrant!' Women armed with stones were screaming, 'Give me back my son!' Other women shouted, 'Say "Long live the King", you tyrant!' And he said it, though some of his servants refused.

After Orgon, he borrowed the uniform of an Austrian officer, mounted a small saddle horse and galloped to the viewpoint above Aix where the ruins of the Gaulish *oppidum* can still be seen. Then he rode back to the inn at La Calade. Introducing himself to the landlady as 'Colonel Campbell' (the British commissioner), he asked her to prepare some food for Emperor Napoleon and his escort, to which she replied, 'I'll be damned if I'm going to cook a meal for that monster. I'd like to see him skinned alive for all the blood he's spilled.'

The Mistral was blowing when the convoy reached the inn at La Grande Pugère below the Montagne Sainte-Victoire on the border of the Bouches-du-Rhône and Var *départements*. It was now four o'clock in the morning on 26 April. The sub-prefect who had accompanied them from Aix was giving him news of Marseille: 'English' troops had been rapturously received by the Marseillais, just as the people of Toulon had surrendered their town to the British twenty-one years before. Napoleon interrupted the sub-prefect:

All the way from Fontainebleau to Avignon, I had no cause to complain about the loyalty of the French, but between Avignon and here, I have been insulted and exposed to many dangers. The people of Provence are disgracing themselves. In all the time I have been in France, I have never had a decent battalion of Provençal troops under my command. They know how to shout, but that's all they can do.

In spite of their incendiary reputation, the people of Provence – all those parents of dead sons, the widows and the victims of political purges – had shown remarkable restraint. But Napoleon was appalled by their ingratitude. They were blind to the nation's great destiny; they blamed *him* for the fortunes of war; and, as King Louis XVIII would soon discover, they never paid their taxes. He called them 'rabid dogs' and 'cowards'.

A nasty race, the Provençaux. They committed all sorts of horrific crimes during the Revolution, and now here they are at it again.

The sub-prefect was lost for words. He was glad to be leaving for home. He promised that his *gendarmes* would protect the emperor as far as Saint-Maximin. The route had been changed: Napoleon would embark for Elba at Fréjus instead of Saint-Tropez, probably to avoid the Massif des Maures, where he might be lynched by 'rabid dogs'. The sub-prefect was dismissed and left for Aix with a final message for his compatriots:

You can tell your Provençaux that their Emperor is most displeased with them.

If – or rather, when – he returned to France, he would be sure to take a different route back to Paris and avoid that country of savages altogether.

10

How He Did It

It would have been hard to prove that Napoleon was the son of Jupiter Ammon and Olympias or the grandson of Venus and Anchises, and so some liberated scholars discovered a more convenient miracle. They proved to the Emperor that he was a direct descendant of the Man in the Iron Mask.

The governor of the Îles Sainte-Marguerite had been a man called Bonpart. This M. Bonpart had a daughter. The Iron Mask, who was the twin brother of Louis XIV, fell in love with his jailer's daughter and they were secretly married . . . The children born of this union were spirited away, under their mother's name, to Corsica, where, in the local tongue, 'Bonpart' became 'Bonaparte'.

And so it was that the Iron Mask turned out to be the mysterious, brazen-faced ancestor of the great man. Napoleon was related to the Sun King, which explained why the Franchini-Bonaparte branch of the family bears on its coat-of-arms three golden *fleurs de lys*.

Napoleon smiled incredulously when he heard this genealogical demonstration. Nevertheless, he did smile . . . Anything that established an imperial claim was not to be lightly cast away.

(Chateaubriand, *Mémoires d'outre-tombe*)

In the late afternoon of 27 February 1815, under a cloudless sky and with a light southerly breeze, the *Inconstant* was forty miles out from Elba when it was spotted by the *Zéphyr*, a cruiser of the French royal navy. A handsome eighteen-gun brig, the *Inconstant* was the flagship of the diminutive Elban navy, consisting of twenty-five vessels, seventeen of which served the iron mines. Since the arrival of Napoleon, it had become a familiar sight in the sea-lanes between Elba and the Italian coast, carrying grain, livestock and visitors, most of whom disappeared almost as soon as they landed on the island. After running aground in squally weather, the *Inconstant* had recently been repainted, refitted and – a normal precaution against Barbary pirates – rearmed.

The *Zéphyr* manoeuvred within hailing distance of the *Inconstant*. The men who had been on deck a moment before, making copies of a printed document with drums and benches as writing desks, had gone below. The brig was riding low in the water, but there was no other sign of anything untoward. The *Zéphyr*'s commander asked where the *Inconstant* was bound and 'How is the Emperor?' 'To Genoa, and the Emperor is well', came the reply. Prompted by a man in a grey overcoat who was keeping out of sight below deck, the commander of the *Inconstant* invited the *Zéphyr* to join them. Unfortunately, the *Zéphyr* had business in Leghorn and the invitation had to be declined.

The breeze freshened. Soon, the French cruiser merged with the hills of Tuscany, and the *Inconstant* altered her course some eighty degrees to port. A small despatch boat and a Maltese speronera appeared in the middle distance and then – a rare sight so far out to sea – four feluccas with their white sails shaped like the wings of seabirds. All seven vessels were heading west. If they held to that bearing, they would make land on the French coast somewhere along the quiet stretch of beaches between Cannes and Antibes.

The British Resident on Elba, Colonel Sir Neil Campbell – the Scottish commissioner whose name Napoleon had borrowed during his nightmarish journey through Provence – had returned from Leghorn just too late to see the miscellaneous flotilla sail from Porto Ferrajo at dusk on 26 February. Officially, Campbell was to remain on Elba 'so long as Napoleon himself should desire the protection of his presence'. Unofficially, he was to organize patrols of Elba's harbours and the outlying islets, which, on the chart, looked to Campbell like stepping stones to Rome and Naples. In the terms of the Fontainebleau Treaty, Napoleon was not a prisoner, and 'a person in his situation' should not be 'deprived of sea excursions in the vicinity of the island for the fair purposes of recreation'. In any case, as the Foreign Secretary explained to a House of Commons which found the treaty dangerously lenient, it was 'absolutely and physically impossible to draw a line of circumvallation around Elba'.

Ten months earlier, in the first days of exile, Campbell had been given an accelerated course in empire-building. Shortly before disembarking on 4 May 1814, Napoleon had sketched a flag for his island kingdom (white, with a diagonal red stripe and three imperial bees on the stripe). Before breakfast, he had inspected on foot the fortifications and storage facilities. After breakfast, he had toured the interior on horseback, evaluated the iron mines, 'then ascended a number of hills and mountain-tops upon which there are ruins', humming Italian songs as he walked. Before the week was out, he had conceived a comprehensive programme of administrative, economic, industrial and military reforms, planned improvements to the road system and the water supply, and chosen a residence for himself.

At the end of that first week, he had ridden with Campbell 'nearly to the summit of the highest hill above Porto Ferrajo, from whence we could perceive the sea in four different quarters'.

> After surveying the scene for some time, he turned round to me and smiled; then shaking his head, he observed, '*Eh! mon île est bien petite.*'

To the south-west, towards the Isle of Montecristo, they could see an almost uninhabited rock of four square miles. Though Pianosa had not been 'given over to the possession of Napoleon', he annexed it anyway, colonized it with a garrison of Polish lancers and their horses, and made arrangements for the growing of corn. He laughed as he told Campbell of his new acquisition: 'All of Europe will say that I have already made another conquest!'

That had been the honeymoon period. Campbell had enjoyed Napoleon's company, as most people did. On the frigate which brought him from Fréjus, the deposed Emperor had charmed the British crew. Even the grumbliest of them all, the boatswain Hinton, had raised a toast to 'Boney' and wished him 'better luck next time'. Campbell had been happy to answer his detailed questions on the cost of running a ship-of-war, the training of recruits, and the devices by which ropes on British vessels were worked on the lower deck, so that fewer men were exposed to gunfire.

In December, he wrote sadly but with a twinge of suspicion in his diary, 'He has gradually estranged himself from me, and various means are taken to show me that my presence is disagreeable.' The imposition of stiff imperial protocol had made pleasant chats impossible. Campbell supposed that Napoleon had credited the rumours that the British were intending to send him to Fort George in the Moray Firth or to St Helena in the South Atlantic. Or perhaps it had something to do with the 'mysterious adventurers and disaffected characters' who had been arriving on the island.

When the flotilla was on the point of setting sail on 26 February, Campbell had been relieved to learn in Leghorn that the King of Elba's latest scheme had nothing to do with conquest or revenge: the Imperial Guard had discovered a surprising passion for horticulture. To the delight of the Elbans, those grizzled veterans of Austerlitz, Jena and Borodino were wielding trowels instead of bayonets, digging flower-beds in front of their barracks and planting avenues of trees with tidy gravel paths. Napoleon had evidently decided to create a miniature Versailles for his island empire in the Tyrrhenian Sea.

The news reached Campbell on 6 March. About eleven hundred Elban, Corsican, French, Neapolitan and Polish troops, along with a contingent of secretaries and servants, had landed at Golfe Juan near Antibes. They had set off into the interior, following the edge of ravines, climbing up into the mountain garrigue on mule tracks still covered with snow. Louis XVIII was informed of the landing on the afternoon of 5 March. The rest of Paris heard about it on 7 March in the official *Moniteur*. A royal decree on page three ordered all civil and military authorities 'and even simple citizens', to 'fall upon and arrest' the 'traitor and rebel', Napoleon Bonaparte.

Fog on the coast and storm clouds over the Dauphiné Alps temporarily disabled the telegraph. Two more days passed before details of the incredible invasion were transmitted. Bonaparte, whose men, said the *Moniteur*, were deserting him in droves, was heading for Grenoble. The Grenoblois had 'spontaneously' rushed out into the streets 'in complete unanimity', begging for permission to fight the tyrant. By the time these lies were printed, Napoleon would be within a day's march of Lyon. Fresh copies of his proclamations had been printed at Gap on 6 March and were fluttering about the south of France as though they had been dropped from the air:

Soldiers, we have not been beaten! . . . In my exile I have heard your voice. I have returned to you in spite of every obstacle and danger . . . Victory will march in double-quick time and the eagle will fly with the national colours from steeple to steeple to the very towers of Notre-Dame. Then will you be able to show your scars with honour and boast of your great deeds . . . And in old age, surrounded and honoured by your fellow Citizens, you shall say with pride, 'I, too, was a soldier of that *Grande Armée* which entered twice within the walls of Vienna, which took Rome, Berlin, Madrid and Moscow, and delivered Paris from the stain of treason and occupation by the enemy.'

After ten months under a feeble monarchy, with the same heavy taxes and rumours that feudal rights were to be restored, there was a surge of popular support for the miraculously reincarnated hero – especially in regions such as Champagne, Lorraine and Burgundy which had suffered the humiliation of seeing Prussians and Cossacks on French soil. In contradiction of the *Moniteur*, Grenoble was in a state of near-rebellion, and so, to prevent a battle in the streets, a detachment of the Fifth Regiment had been sent out to intercept Napoleon.

On the windswept plateau near the village of Laffrey, where the road begins its long descent to Grenoble, an overweight man with a sallow complexion and a bad cold stood in front of his miniature army. He was wearing the grey overcoat that was familiar from sixty battles and a thousand engravings. 'Here I am, soldiers of the Fifth!' He began to unbutton the overcoat . . . 'If there is a soldier among you who wishes to kill his Emperor, he may do so!'

Three separate witnesses of the scene felt 'electricity' in the air. Cries of 'Vive l'Empereur!' exploded like a thunderclap. Not long after, Napoleon entered the city of Grenoble surrounded by weeping soldiers and ecstatic peasants who had left their crofts and hovels like disciples of Christ.

Between Elba and Paris, as Napoleon boasted a few days later, not a single shot was fired. The only loss of life occurred on 19 March at Pont-sur-Yonne in a peculiar incident which was soon forgotten.

Nothing was said of it in the *Moniteur* and very few of Napoleon's biographers mention it.

They arrived at Pont-sur-Yonne in fading light. A boat carrying troops and supplies had moored safely upstream of the bridge to wait for daybreak. With his usual pugnacious *bonhomie*, Napoleon mocked the boatmen for being 'afraid of getting wet' and called them 'marins d'eau douce' (landlubbers). An hour after midnight, he rode off towards Paris while the soldiers, enthused by his swashbuckling audacity, ordered the boatmen to sail on in total darkness. Some wooden piles had been submerged by the swollen river. The boat struck them and sank. The battalion commander, four officers and forty-one soldiers were drowned.

That morning's *Moniteur* announced that, in view of 'the present crisis', the King was removing himself 'to another part of the kingdom'. However, he would soon be back to restore 'peace and happiness'.

The Tuileries Palace had only just been vacated when the ladies of Napoleon's court assembled in the rooms of state to greet the returning emperor. The husband of Empress Joséphine's niece recorded the scene. The ladies were lamenting the fact that the imperial bee had been replaced on all the furnishings by the *fleur de lys*: the vast carpet in the Throne Room was covered with them. Then one of the ladies noticed a *fleur de lys* which had curled up at the edges. She pulled at the patch of cloth, the flower came away, and underneath was the original bee: 'Thereupon, all the ladies set to work to sounds of general merriment, and in less than half an hour, the carpet was imperial once again.'

The following day's *Moniteur*, looking exactly the same as usual, but dictated by a different head of state, announced on its front page that 'the King and princes departed in the night' and that the Emperor was back:

> His Majesty the Emperor arrived this evening [20 March 1815] at 8 o'clock in his palace at the Tuileries. He entered Paris at the head of the same troops who had been sent out that morning to bar his way.

A second brief paragraph recorded a new land-speed record for marching troops:

The brave battalion of the Old Guard, which accompanied the Emperor from the Isle of Elba, will arrive here tomorrow, which means that they will have covered the distance between Golfe Juan and Paris in 21 days.*

🐝 🐝 🐝

The Napoleon who returned to Paris in March 1815, promising a people's referendum on the constitution, was not the Napoleon who had left for Elba in May 1814. The new citizen-emperor had magicked himself across the sea and from one end of France to the other to become the embodiment of the Republic. He was now the friend of the oppressed and the nemesis of the *ancien régime*. Crippled by obesity, Louis XVIII and all the other addled vestiges of feudal privilege who had 'forgotten nothing and learned nothing' had melted away at his approach.

The terminal disaster of Waterloo was less than three months away, yet this messianic Artful Dodger who bloodlessly reconquered France with a small band of adventurers would be the longest-lived of Napoleon's incarnations. The French Enlightenment's model student, he showed how a man of (supposedly) humble origins could apply a few logical precepts like the equations used by gunners to calculate trajectories and turn himself into a cannonball that would pulverize whatever obstacles society and foreign powers could put in his way.

Along with haute cuisine, haute couture, Impressionism, Existentialism and Deconstruction, the practical wisdom of Napoleon Bonaparte is one of France's most enduring cultural exports. The number of lunatics who mistook themselves for Napoleon is tiny compared to the host of entrepreneurs and fantasists who believed that they could profit from his *modi operandi*. Somewhere in that plethora of Napoleons – each one visually dissimilar because he could never bear to pose for more than a few minutes – might be found

---

* The journey took nineteen days: Napoleon landed at Golfe Juan on 1 March at 5 p.m. and set off for Cannes at 11 p.m. He arrived in Paris at 9 p.m. on 20 March. The account subsequently dictated to the *Moniteur* by Napoleon reduced this to 'eighteen days' and observed that 'the distance [about 560 miles] would normally be covered in forty-five days'. He also reduced the size of the invasion force (about eleven hundred) to an even more impressive six hundred.

the secret formulae for gaining influence, wealth and even happiness. Something other than random events and luck must account for the fact that History itself had apparently been monopolized and directed by Napoleon Bonaparte for twenty-two years.

Illiteracy was no obstacle to the propagation of the legend. Paintings and prints, cutlery and crockery, bottle labels and above all tobacco boxes depicted his many avatars: the young artillery officer who rescued Toulon from the British, the twenty-seven-year-old general who liberated Italy from the Austrian Empire, the conqueror of Egypt at the Battle of the Pyramids, the First Consul enthroned by the mob and then the self-crowned Emperor of the French, the builder of monuments and plunderer of treasures, the Mosaic provider of a legal code, the scourge of Prussia and terror of the Iberian Peninsula, the Homeric hero who left Moscow a smoking ruin and lost half a million men to snow, wolves and Cossacks in the most glorious defeat of modern times.

The image of Napoleon as the prime fixer first burgeoned in Britain. For two years (June 1803 to August 1805), on or near the site of Caesar's camp at Boulogne-sur-mer, his army had watched the English coast. With the 'Corsican ogre' on the doorstep, it was vital to know the mind of the possible future conqueror of Albion. Lieutenant J. H. Sarratt's three-hundred-page tirade of 1803 – *Life of Buonaparte, in which the Atrocious Deeds which he has perpetrated in order to attain his Elevated Station are faithfully recorded, by which means Every Briton will be enabled to judge of the disposition of his Threatening Foe and have a Faint Idea of the Desolation which awaits this Country should his menaces ever be realized* – offered a dictator's manual of dirty tricks: invest heavily in spies; unexpectedly outnumber the enemy; send battalions on suicide missions by inspiring them with brandy and the promise of plunder; never be a hostage to truth (exaggerate your victories and frighten the enemy with false reports).

When the threat of invasion had passed and exile enhanced the aura of the fallen hero, H. Scott's 'impartial account of that Extraordinary Personage', ending prematurely with his 'retirement to the Island of Elba' (London, 1814), presented him as a nineteenth-century Caesar:

> A complete victory over all our passions is allowed to be one of the
> most difficult attainments, yet it is affirmed that Bonaparte has

reached it. He is abstemious in his meals, and none ever beheld him in the smallest degree intoxicated with liquor. His friends are numerous; of minions he has none; and by virtue of a rigorous silence, he more effectually preserves an inviolable secrecy, than can be done by other men who are hypocritically talkative. He has no taste for the enjoyments of the table, for the fair sex, nor for the fine arts. These would reduce him to the rank of ordinary beings, while his main object has ever been to be above them.

In France, where rectitude and moderation would rarely be considered the foremost qualifications for premiership, Napoleon came to be seen as the model leader. He was the man whose patriotism was served by wiliness and steely charm combined with ruthless determination – which is why the epithet *'napoléonien'* is applied to Presidents Mitterrand, Sarkozy and Macron rather than to General de Gaulle.

The Napoleon of the English-speaking world had a very different career as a life-and-business guru, the super-efficient citizen whose spartan virtues were geared to the furthering of his own interests. The maxims of Napoleon – nearly all apocryphal – were staples of inspirational literature from Samuel Smiles's *Self-Help* (1859) – *'Impossible*, said he, is a word only to be found in the dictionary of fools' – and Orison S. Marden's *Pushing To The Front* (1894), to Dale Carnegie's *How to Win Friends and Influence People* (1936) and Napoleon Hill's *Think and Grow Rich* (1937).

In later manuals such as Jerry Manas's *Napoleon on Project Management* (2006) and William Dietrich's *Napoleon's Rules: Life and Career Lessons from Bonaparte* (2015), Napoleon is the man who crossed the St Bernard Pass without a car ('The Alps do not exist') and who 'ran an entire empire without e-mail, telephones or computers'.

Donald J. Trump's ghostwritten *The Art of the Deal* does not mention Napoleon but he is there in spirit: 'If you're going to be thinking anyway, you might as well think big.' Invited by President Macron to pay homage to Napoleon's tomb at Les Invalides in 2017, President Trump, despite confusing Napoleons I and III, retained the impression of an all-round great man who was magnified even by his failures:

Well, Napoleon finished a little bit bad. . . . So I asked the president, so what about Napoleon? He said, 'No, no, no. What he did was incredible. He designed Paris.' . . . The street grid, the way they work, you know, the spokes. He did so many things even beyond. And his one problem is he didn't go to Russia that night because he had extracurricular activities, and they froze to death.

I first encountered the life- and profit-enhancing Napoleon when Proctor Jones, a gentleman-publisher from San Francisco, sent me an English translation of a book by Napoleon's longest-serving secretary. The memoirs of Baron Agathon Fain, completed in 1829, were credibly presented as a 'business-school textbook' for the 'modern executive' and cannily retitled, *Napoleon: How He Did It*.

This was potentially a more useful book for aspiring CEOs. In most manuals, the pulp of history is trimmed off and the apocryphal maxims served up as nutritionless stones of 'wisdom'. But in Fain's book, Napoleon's daily practices were described in raw detail. The son of a roofer and by training an archivist, Fain was neither blinded by admiration nor distracted by gossip. He marshalled his facts like a zoologist observing an extraordinary animal. And so the question arose: if the ingredients of success were extracted from Fain's memoirs and others of the time, paraphrased and presented, as it were, *au naturel*, would they still be useful for CEOs? Failing that, would they help to explain how a Corsican artillery cadet created and ran the largest European empire since Charlemagne? (Fig. 10.)

OFFICE WORK

- When faced with a mountain of paperwork, arrange all the papers in a single pile. Starting at the top, scatter the documents with a sweep of the arm until the pile is a manageable size. Do not retrieve documents from the floor.

- Never look at the same document twice. Retain only your first impression. The time saved will more than make up for the inevitable misconceptions and mistakes.

- Remove any article of clothing which restricts movement and throw it on the fire.

- Do not be a slave to meal-times. Have a chicken roasting on the spit night and day. If necessary, eat the meal in reverse – dessert first, hors-d'oeuvre last. A meal should never take up more than twenty minutes. If stomach pains and vomiting result, eat less often.

- Your mind is a file cabinet. Only one drawer should be open at a time. To sleep, close all the drawers.

PERSONNEL MANAGEMENT

- It is not enough to judge people by their actions: judge them only by their latest action and constantly revise your judgement.

- Always patch up quarrels before the other person leaves the room, but not by agreeing with him.

- Never promote a man who listens to his wife.

- Expect the impossible. (Do not use the word 'impossible'.)

- When addressing staff, lean on the mantelpiece with the candelabra above to create the 'light of inspiration' effect.

- Express yourself in proverbs, but remember that the man who obeys his own maxims is a man who walks with his feet tied together. 'Misfortune is the midwife of genius' is a good proverb for the soldier.

PUBLIC RELATIONS

- Perform small but memorable acts of private charity and have them widely reported.

- Design uniforms yourself, making heavy use of gold; distribute medals and meaningless awards; devise a memorable logo.

- Newspapers are to be written, not read. When one of his younger secretaries read the morning papers to him, Napoleon would say, 'No, not the *Moniteur*. I already know what's in it.'

- Do not take too many prisoners: you may be forced to kill them, damaging your reputation and inspiring sympathy for the enemy.

- Practise religious tolerance. (Arresting Pope Pius VII was a political matter.) To imams assembled in the Great Pyramid, Napoleon said,

'Glory be to Allah. There is no god but God; Mahomed is his prophet, and I am one of his friends.'

INTELLIGENCE AND PLANNING

- Consult experts – always more than one at a time. Choose advisors with opposing views and pretend to be convinced by the most preposterous argument.

- Beware of meetings and committees. The result of deliberating, consulting and speechifying is that the most pusillanimous course of action is adopted. Energetic decision-making is the mark of the wise leader.

- Encourage gossip.

- Use spies (especially pirates and smugglers) rather than ambassadors, who are expensive and not much good for anything.

- Talk to anyone with practical knowledge of a subject regardless of rank or status and including enemies and would-be assassins. The moment a person ceases to provide useful information, end the conversation.

In the field, precepts and routines are subject to the infinite variables of circumstance and human behaviour. The dramatic encounter with the Fifth Regiment on the plain of Laffrey, for instance, was not as simple as described above and almost everywhere else.

1. Forewarned by the advance party, Napoleon knew that his force outnumbered the royal troops. At the town of Corps, he slept well – as he always did, even during battle – and set off at dawn for Laffrey.

2. An aide-de-camp was sent to parley with Major Desessart, the commander of the royal troops in Grenoble. It transpired that Desessart was reluctant to initiate an armed conflict and that some of his soldiers had been heard shouting, 'Vive l'Empereur!'

3. Napoleon delayed the advance on Laffrey, however, until confirmatory reports had been received from defectors and civilians.

4. Major Desessart was warned in writing that he would be 'held account-able to France and posterity for any orders he issued'.

5. The advance guard, refreshed and ready, having travelled in *diligences* (public coaches) requisitioned at La Mure, moved into position – Corsicans on high ground to the left, Polish lancers filling the flat meadow to the right.

6. At one o'clock, the main performance began: the tricolour was unfurled, the band struck up the 'Marseillaise', and the Emperor appeared at the head of his cavalry.

7. With the stage set, Napoleon delivered the short speech which he had had a night and part of a day to prepare. He appears to have borrowed the famous scene in Lucan's *Pharsalia*, where Caesar offers his bared breast to the soldiers' swords. The speech was followed by two minutes of silence. Then, as though arriving at a village *fête*, the opposing troops began to mingle, exchanging news, greeting old acquaintances and reminiscing about battles and campaigns. One old soldier came up to the Emperor, raised his musket and rattled the ramrod in the barrel to show that he had had no intention of firing it.

8. As usual in moments of high tension, Napoleon became extremely loquacious, though he was too emotional to speak in complete sentences. This was of little consequence because the drama now had its own irresistible momentum.

The 'Flight of the Eagle' from Elba to Paris was a masterclass in applying the principles of successful leadership in real situations. The lessons were, first, that acts of conspicuous bravery must be thoroughly worked out in advance, and, second, that the basic narrative of the operation must be reducible to a single memorable scene. The simpli-fied version dictated by Napoleon and printed in the *Moniteur* is the one that has prevailed.

Contrary to later claims that Napoleon was diminished by his ten months of exile, the remainder of the journey back to Paris confirmed that all the old tricks and tactics were working as well as ever.

MAINTAINING THE LEGEND

When he arrived at the Hôtel de la Poste in Avallon on 16 March, he told the mayor that 'three thousand songs' had already been written in his honour since he landed at Golfe Juan. No one seems to have asked how he knew.

A veteran with 'a crooked face' called Eugène Gagniard turned up at the hotel: 'Still chewing tobacco, I see, Gagniard?' said Napoleon. A face distorted by a habitual wad of tobacco – and perhaps a hint from one of the local officers – enabled him to demonstrate that famously infallible memory for the names and faces of common soldiers which had often earned him the adoration of his men.

CHARM

Few business manuals try to convey that most precious 'secret of success', perhaps because what was charming in one age is repellent in another. For Napoleon, physical contact was a vital management tool. When he talked to subordinates, to soften the order he was about to give, he would place his hand on the man's cheek or pat his shoulder. To gain his attention, he would kick his feet. When explaining something which he thought should be obvious, he would tweak the man's ears or pull his nose.

He often appeared before soldiers *en déshabillé* or in a dressing gown, as he did at Avallon. Sometimes, he received ambassadors while taking a bath. Before he left Avallon, people of all ages and classes – Bonapartists as well as Royalists – gathered in the courtyard. Napoleon appeared on the balcony for a curtain call and the crowd 'gave every sign of satisfaction'. 'The mirror which had received his Caesarean reflection' was preserved as a relic and would be admired by a stream of lesser celebrities, from Eisenhower to Salvador Dalí, until 2018, when the hotel closed its doors.

FOCUSING ON THE LONG TERM

The lethal incident at Pont-sur-Yonne came two days later, when, having goaded his men to sail on in the dark, he lost forty-six of them to the river. The policy might not be spelled out in a management manual, though it is common enough in practice. The mass drowning was one of the acceptable costs of a strategy which consisted of narrowing to almost nothing the gap between conception and execution. On the race back to Paris, the overriding criterion was speed. The loss of forty-six men was unfortunate, but it did not invalidate the principle.

Successful speculators know that if the odds have been calculated with sufficient accuracy, a strategy consistently applied will eventually yield a profit. Even in the brief period between Elba and Paris, it gave an excellent return. Napoleon had left the island with his dwindled stock of gold coins packed in trunks and hidden under books. Less than three weeks later, he had the material and human resources of a nation at his disposal.

A businessman who would like to hear Napoleon's secrets from the horse's mouth but who baulks at the thirty-two-volume *Correspondance de Napoléon Ier* can gain a good idea of the hopelessness of the task on pages 17 to 275 of volume xxviii. The letters dictated by Napoleon at the Tuileries Palace in the spring of 1815 cover everything from the cost of saddles, the upgrading of uniforms and the manufacture of muskets to the securing of the borders, the repression of a new civil war in the Vendée, and the budget for 1815.

Considering Napoleon's reorganization of the entire country in the thirteen weeks leading up to Waterloo, there is nothing eccentric about the whirlwind office management techniques recorded by Baron Fain. At that level of efficiency, it is not surprising that, after tidying up what remained of the empire, Napoleon was able to materialize at Charleroi and cross the Sambre on 15 June when 'Lord Vilainton'* was preparing for a glittering reception in Brussels. By Wellington's clock, time had moved at a slower pace. The news reached him at the ball. Giving his best impression of Francis Drake at Plymouth Hoe with the Armada bearing down, he asked his host for a map and, behind the closed doors of his study, exclaimed, 'Napoleon has humbugged me, by God! He has gained twenty-four hours' march on me.'

Napoleon's plan was to drive a wedge between the two Allied

---

* 'Vilain ton': 'poor taste'.

armies on the northern frontier of France.* It was a position he had
often engineered and he had every hope of success.

On 16 June at Ligny to the north-east of Charleroi, the Prussians
were heavily but not disastrously defeated. Wellington had remained
at a distance, perhaps because his army was still assembling. On the
following day, he withdrew to a ridge at Mont-Saint-Jean near the
village of Waterloo. Napoleon established his headquarters three miles
to the south at a farm by Plancenoit. All night long, the rain hammered
on the tents. It was not until nine o'clock in the morning that the
downpour became slightly less torrential and Napoleon ordered his
troops to move into position on either side of the main road to
Brussels.

An exhibition devoted to 'Napoleon the Strategist' was held in the
Musée de l'Armée at Les Invalides in 2018. On display was practically
everything required to plan a successful campaign – the artillery and
tactics manuals which Napoleon had studied at military school, relief
maps folded into travelling cases, a collapsible table and chair, a spyglass
and a multiple-choice quiz on a video screen: *'The enemy is approaching:
Napoleon wants your advice.'*

I chose to advise the Emperor on the Ulm campaign, which led
to the defeat of the Austrian army at Austerlitz in 1805. After the first
four questions, I felt I had earned a pat on the shoulder: Napoleon
was in complete agreement with my advice. The answers, in fact, were
blindingly obvious, given the principles laid down on the display
panels: split the enemy and attack the weaker of two points; attack
the rear; delay the decisive action until the enemy's intentions are
unmistakeable; as in chess, never lose sight of the ultimate goal.

It was then that I made the fatal mistake: I assumed that among
the obvious manoeuvres, there would be one daring and disorienting
stroke of genius. And so I advised Napoleon – counter-historically, as
it turned out – to march on Vienna instead of consolidating his posi-

---

* The strength and composition of the armies according to the most detailed estimates were: Wellington, 106,000 (45% German, 35% British, 20% Dutch-Belgian);
Blücher, 50,000 (Prussian); Napoleon, 72,000 (French, with some Irish, Polish,
Piedmontese, Swiss, as well as volunteers and conscripts from the former Belgian
and German *départements*).

tion . . . I had fallen into the trap of supposing that there must be a trap, which is why I scored only four out of five on the quiz. Napoleon later pointed out to me, in an imaginary conversation, that Lord Vilainton had acted with similar false subtlety when he deployed his troops to the west of Brussels to block the routes to the Channel ports, suspecting that Napoleon's advance on Brussels was a feint.

The remarkable fact is that, although Napoleon was a skilful deceiver and especially good at feigning weakness, his tactics were commonsensical applications of the rules he had learned as a student. One of his main innovations was to divide his armies into highly mobile units who could live off the land instead of dragging huge, unconcealable baggage-trains across the countryside. Even when he outnumbered the enemy, he favoured tactics normally used by smaller forces – inviting engagement on complex and difficult terrain, hiding in woods or behind hills, stretching out his battle lines over distances which the marching enemy could barely cover in a day. Though he had at his command the largest population of any nation in Europe including Russia, numerical superiority was no longer an essential advantage.

Why it took so long for the armies of Europe to digest and implement the methods of Napoleon, the exhibition did not explain. Were they prisoners of military tradition or blinded by the blindingly obvious? On 18 June 1815, when the three armies converged on the heights of Mont-Saint-Jean near the village of Waterloo, ten years had passed since Austerlitz and many lessons had been learned by his enemies. Even then, if one of Napoleon's generals had not defected, if Marshal Ney had acted with average competence and Marshal Grouchy had followed orders, his most famous battle might have been a victory and not, as Wellington confessed, 'a damned nice thing'.

On the evening of 20 June, the Emperor who had been seen leaving the battlefield in tears reached the hilltop cathedral town of Laon on the road to Paris with about three thousand men. There, he completed his first account of what he called the Battle of Mont-Saint-Jean.

When composing his *bulletins de l'armée*, like a screenwriter adapting a convoluted novel, Napoleon would sometimes speed-dictate a first version to the furiously scribbling scribe. While his abbreviations were still decipherable, the scribe would dictate the text to a second man. This tidied version would then be read back to Napoleon, who would re-dictate it with improvements. At Laon, when the two-man word processor produced the final document, the description of the Battle of Waterloo sounded like the work of a Julius Caesar strongly influenced by the Romantic Movement.

The decisive incident had taken place at Mont-Saint-Jean. General Grouchy had unaccountably failed to stop a Prussian attack on the right flank of the French. Seeing the British retreat under heavy bombardment, the reserve cavalry, 'in a fit of impatience of which there are many disastrous examples in our military annals', charged the British infantry. The remaining French cavalry rushed to support their comrades while the Prussian attack on the right flank continued.

Three hours later, despite the premature cavalry charge, the battle appeared to have swung in favour of the French. The sun was setting when a last-minute charge by Wellington's men forced a sudden retreat. The French regiments in the rear saw the soldiers running past and thought they glimpsed some veterans of the Old Guard, which never retreated . . . There were cries of 'All is lost!' and 'The Guard is repulsed!' Napoleon received reports that provocateurs had been posted in several places to shout, 'Sauve qui peut! ('It's every man for himself!')

> When it noticed this astonishing mêlée, the enemy created an opening for its cavalry columns. The chaos increased. The confusion of night made it impossible to rally the troops and show them their error.
>
> And so it was that, at the close of a battle and the end of a day, when mistakes had been rectified and greater success was assured for the morrow, all was lost by a moment of terror and panic. Even the service squadrons who stood at the Emperor's side were tumbled and muddled by those tumultuous waves and the only possible course of action was to follow the torrent. Munitions and baggage stranded on the far side of the Sambre and everything on the battlefield remained in the hands of the enemy. Our right-flank troops had to be left behind. There is no need to say what the bravest army in the world becomes when it loses its shape and cohesion.

Those 'tumultuous waves' and that shattered army of heroes were the fruit of long years reading Ossian, the Celtic warrior-bard whose songs of poignant catastrophe, 'rediscovered' by the Scottish poet James Macpherson, Napoleon carried into battle and on his final voyage to St Helena. His self-exculpatory dispatch on the Battle of Waterloo is in some ways just as fantastic. Yet this battle report in poetic prose is the authentic sound of Napoleon's dictation voice. Even in the aftermath of the most obscene and irreparable disaster, like one of the mist-enshrouded warriors of Ossian, he could hear the ultimate victory of his reputation.

It would be repeated and amplified by the century's greatest poet, whose father, Léopold Hugo, had fought, destroyed and massacred for Bonaparte and the Republic in the Vendée and Spain. While Napoleon was at Waterloo, General Hugo was defending the frontier town of Thionville a hundred and twenty miles to the south-east. He was still holding it three months after Napoleon had sailed for St Helena.

> A spyglass in his hand, he could sometimes observe
> The centre of the struggle – a dark, bristling point,
> The terrible living thicket of the mêlée –
> And sometimes the horizon as dark as the sea.
> In sudden joy, he cried, 'Grouchy!' – It was Blücher.
> Hope changed sides; the battle changed its soul.
> The roaring throng grew larger, spreading like a fire.
> The English battery flattened our formations.
> The tattered banners were shivering on that plain
> Of which nothing remained but a flaming abyss. . . .
> He saw those regiments made of granite and steel
> Melt like wax candles in the breath of a furnace . . .
> Saw them all – men, horses, drums and flags – flow away
> Like a river . . .
> Those veterans of Friedland and of Rivoli,
> Knowing they celebrated the day of their death,
> Saluted their god, who stood upright in the storm,
> And cried with one voice, 'Vive l'Empereur!'

WAR GAMES

Five thousand miles and ninety-three days from France, on a rat-infested volcanic island in the South Atlantic, Napoleon and General Gourgaud, a thirty-two-year-old veteran of Austerlitz, Saragossa, Wagram and Borodino, were crossing a field in which some cows were grazing.

According to the thirteen-year-old daughter of Mr and Mrs Balcombe, who lived nearby at the Briars, a cow – probably sick or separated from its calf – spotted the intruders, lowered its head and charged at Napoleon. 'He made a skilful and rapid retreat, and, leaping nimbly over a wall, placed this rampart between himself and the enemy.' Meanwhile, General Gourgaud, who had raised his sword and placed himself between the Emperor and the cow, shouted, 'This is the second time I have saved the Emperor's life!' (He was alluding – as he often did – to the lunging Cossack he had shot with his pistol the previous year at the Battle of Brienne.)

When the emergency was over, Miss Betsy Balcombe observed to her friend Napoleon that the cow had calmed down as soon as he disappeared behind the wall. 'She wished', Napoleon explained, 'to save the English government the expense and trouble of keeping me'.

• Always keep both flanks in sight. The most destructive attacks come from the flanks, not from the front.

• No tactical decision should be made without reference to the predetermined path of retreat.

A few weeks before, in October 1815, Betsy had been appalled to learn from her father – who seemed strangely unruffled by the news – that the man-of-war which had been announced by the alarm gun on Ladder Hill was carrying the infamous ogre Bonaparte. William Balcombe was the East India Company's purveyor of supplies to St Helena. The house assigned to Napoleon at Longwood had proved to be riddled with rot, and so the ogre was offered the hospitality of the Balcombes' summer house in the grounds of the Briars. He accepted with gratitude and on condition that the family's routine would not be disturbed.

The younger of two sisters, Betsy was the sort of intelligent, independent child who makes rude faces behind the backs of boring visitors. She soon forgot her childish fears. Before long, she was calling her new playmate 'Boney'. She had seen the name on caricatures in the illustrated papers and on a toy, which, out of exuberance rather than unkindness, she showed to the Emperor: a wooden Napoleon strode jerkily up a ladder labelled with the names of all the countries he had conquered, then tottered down the other side to land on St Helena. Napoleon was delighted with her impudence – and by her proficiency at French. He helped her with her translation exercises, teased her without mercy or condescension, and thought of his four-year-old son, whom he would never see again.

Betsy Balcombe's recollections of her famous friend, published in 1844, are among the most illuminating memoirs of Napoleon. Why they have been treated in such a cursory fashion by Napoleon scholars is hard to say. Betsy was often allowed to remain in the room when the adults were discussing adult affairs, but in most studies of Napoleon's life, she is sent to bed just when things are getting interesting. Books about Napoleon are usually written by men (in the current century, ninety-four per cent), and perhaps the observations of a teenage girl, recalled by a forty-year-old woman, are thought to be of minor importance. Napoleon himself hated the British custom of separating the women and children from the men at the end of a meal so that the men could drink themselves into a stupor.

Some of the most clear-headed first-hand accounts of Napoleon's battle tactics can be found in Betsy's recollections of shenanigans at the Briars. Unlike some of Napoleon's generals, she did not have a reputation or a political career to defend, and her memoirs were not ghost-written. As one of the very few people who engaged in physical combat with Napoleon, she should be considered an authority on Napoleonic strategy.

One day, having been pestered several times, 'Boney' finally consented to play the game of blind man's buff. Slips of paper were handed out and – she suspected, by imperial sleight of hand – Betsy received the slip on which the fateful words '*la mort*' were written. Napoleon tied his cambric handkerchief tightly over her eyes, then waved his hat in front of her face. Betsy flinched . . . 'Ah, leetle monkee', he said in English, 'you can see pretty well!' A second handkerchief was tied over the first, and the game began.

The emperor commenced by creeping stealthily up to me, and giving my nose a very sharp twinge; I knew it was he both from the act itself and from his footstep. I darted forward, and very nearly succeeded in catching him, but bounding actively away, he eluded my grasp. I then groped about, and, advancing again, he this time took hold of my ear and pulled it. I stretched out my hands instantly, and in the exultation of the moment screamed out, 'I have got you – I have got you, now you shall be blindfolded!' But to my mortification it proved to be my sister, under cover of whom Napoleon had advanced, stretching his hand over her head.

We then recommenced . . . He bantered me in every possible way, eluding at the same time, with the greatest dexterity, all my endeavours to catch him. At last when the fun was growing 'fast and furious', and the uproar was at its height, it was announced that someone desired an audience of the emperor, and to my great annoyance, as I had set my heart on catching him and insisting on his being blindfolded, our game came to a conclusion.

- Attack is the best form of defence.

- Cover your advance. At Waterloo, the French reserve cavalry had attacked without a defensive screen of *tirailleurs*. Shielded by the front rank (in this case, Betsy's older sister Eliza Jane), Napoleon was able to hold off the counter-attack until help arrived in the form of a visitor – another difference with Waterloo, where Marshal Grouchy failed to turn up.

On another occasion, to entertain Betsy's two little brothers, one of Napoleon's servants captured four mice and harnessed them to a tiny carriage. Frozen with terror, the mice refused to advance. The Emperor was begged to intervene. He pinched the tails of the leading pair, 'and immediately the whole four scampered off, to our great amusement, Napoleon enjoying the fun as much as any of us, and delighted with the extravagant glee of my two brothers.'

- 'Men [and mice] are activated by two levers: fear and self-interest.'

- It is sufficient to apply the stimulus (threats, punishment or tail-pinching) to the front rank: the second rank will follow their lead.

- Good soldiers are made by training and severe discipline. Love of the fatherland and national glory are not essential.

Writers of Napoleonic life- and business-manuals, as well as biographers of Napoleon, should never forget that they are dealing with a strategist. Betsy usually knew when she was being teased – but not always. For example, she records as a fact that, when Napoleon had moved to the house at Longwood, he had a ditch dug so that he could take a walk without being gawped at by sightseers. In reality, the defensive ditches were the work of the governor of St Helena, Hudson Lowe – a petty and malicious man who saw it as his duty to spoil his prisoner's little pleasures.

To Betsy, it was as though the character of a fairy tale had materialized in her home and could be questioned about his actions in the tales she had read. Was it true that he had 'turned Turk' (become a Muslim) in Egypt? ('I always adopt the religion of the country I am in', he told her.) Was it true that he had butchered Turkish prisoners at Jaffa and euthanized his own plague-ridden soldiers in the hospital? (He answered only the second part of the question.)

It is impossible to know how far this self-made hero of implausible adventures can be trusted. There was one question which Betsy had hesitated to ask, because surely the Retreat from Moscow must be a painful memory. But Napoleon himself brought it up when he was testing her knowledge of European capitals. At the word 'Moscow', he 'fixed his piercing eyes full in my face' and demanded, 'Qui l'a brûlé?' When she pretended not to know, he said, 'laughing violently', 'Oui, oui. Vous savez très bien, c'est moi qui l'ai brûlé!'*

The story was too good – or bad – to be true. Moscow was burned by fleeing Russians. But Napoleon was playing to his audience, and he had a legend to maintain. He had happily conspired with Betsy when she decided to frighten her timorous little friend, Miss Legg, who believed everything her nursemaid had told her about that monster Bonaparte.

He walked up to her, and, brushing up his hair with his hand, shook his head, making horrible faces, and giving a sort of savage howl.

---

* Who burned [Moscow]? . . . Come on now, you know very well – I did!'

The little girl screamed so violently, that mamma was afraid she would go into hysterics, and took her out of the room.

The howl, he explained to Betsy, when he had failed to frighten her with the same performance, was the sound a Cossack soldier made when charging at the enemy.

General Gourgaud noted in his diary on 22 December 1816 when Napoleon and his servants had moved into the house at Longwood: 'The Emperor is growing impatient, wondering when the Misses Balcombe are going to arrive. He keeps looking at the road through his spyglass.'

With the ocean all around, a close horizon could be a comfort as well as a reminder of captivity. As he re-dictated his accounts of battles, justifying his actions, the panorama of the past expanded, as mutable as a dream. The Empire, especially in the last two years, had been a brilliant illusion – the island kingdom of Elba and its diminutive 'navy'; the command performance at Laffrey; the 'Messiah of the Revolution' and his army of disciples; the evacuated royal palace and the bees on the carpet.

So much of the Republic and then the Empire had been a mirage, and it seemed increasingly unreal as he vanished into his own story. But the destruction of the illusion was real, and so were Betsy's tears when the Balcombes left St Helena for good and returned to England in March 1818.

> He walked with us in his garden, and with a sickly smile pointed to the ocean spread out before us . . . and said, 'Soon you will be sailing away towards England, leaving me to die on this miserable rock. Look at those dreadful mountains – they are my prison walls. You will soon hear that the Emperor Napoleon is dead.' I burst into tears, and sobbed, as though my heart would break.

Napoleonic manuals should reserve a final chapter for the art of coping with defeat, and to the delicate stratagems required to inspire affection and dedication to a cause other than profit and self-advancement.

> He affectionately embraced my sister and myself, and bade us not forget him; adding that he should ever remember our friendship

and kindness to him, and thanked us again and again for all the happy hours he had passed in our society.

A few English travellers who were on their way to admire the wonders of the Ganges or who were returning home called in at St Helena to see another wonder of the world. . . .

Napoleon found these visits rather painful, but he did agree to receive Lord Amherst, who was returning from his mission to China, and he enjoyed the company of Admiral Sir Pulteney Malcolm.

One day, he asked the Admiral, 'Does your government intend to keep me on this rock until I die?'

The Admiral feared that it did.

'In that case', said Napoleon, 'my death shall come soon.'

'I hope not, Monsieur', said the Admiral. 'You will live long enough to record your great deeds. They are so numerous that the task of writing them will ensure you a long life.'

Napoleon did not take offence when the Admiral addressed him simply as *Monsieur*. In that moment, he showed his true greatness. It is fortunate that he never wrote the story of his life. He would only have diminished it. Men of his stamp should leave the recounting of their memories to the anonymous voice of populations and centuries – the voice that belongs to no one.

Only we common people may talk about ourselves, because, otherwise, no one would.

(Chateaubriand, *Mémoires d'outre-tombe*)

11

The Murder of Madame Bovary

Louis XVIII's successor, the stubbornly anachronistic Charles X, who believed in the divine right of kings and the necessity of stifling civil liberties, was deposed in July 1830 by a brief but bloody revolution of workers and intellectuals. He returned to his former home in exile at Holyrood Palace in Edinburgh and was replaced by a 'Citizen King'. Louis-Philippe was a member of a cadet branch of the House of Bourbon. It was hoped, however, that, as a modern constitutional monarch, this scion of an ancient dynasty would be amenable to liberal reforms which would please almost everyone and allow the bourgeoisie to enjoy its share of power.

Ten years on, with rising urban unemployment and a dangerously politicized workforce, 'the bourgeois monarchy' made an attempt to unite, mollify or divert the fractious nation with an image of its glory. In May 1840, the request was conveyed to the British parliament by the French ambassador in London and instantly granted: the ashes of Napoleon would be shipped to France. Inflammatory rumours of a vacant tomb and the flight of the eagle to New Jersey would be quashed once and for all, and a new age of cross-Channel cooperation would begin.

Forty-three days after setting sail from St Helena, the frigate *Belle Poule* dropped anchor in the roadstead of Cherbourg. The six nested coffins were transferred to a steamship, the *Normandie*, which entered the Seine at Le Havre and corkscrewed its way between the chalk cliffs to the point where the river became too shallow for sea-going vessels. At Val-de-la-Haye, a paddle steamer with an unromantic name suggestive of a pleasure boat on a municipal lake – *Dorade n° 3* ('Sea Bream no. 3') – was waiting to ferry the immortal remains of Napoleon to Paris and Les Invalides.

Seven miles upstream, the fifth largest manufacturing city in France was almost ready to prove itself worthy of a great state occasion. Since the accession of Louis-Philippe, Rouen, the capital of Normandy, had been transformed with the help of British and Irish technicians and labourers into a Lancastrian mill town – but a mill town with blackened wattle-and-daub instead of blackened red brick. The view from the hills around Rouen was the vision of an industrialized Middle Ages – the spread of the suburbs, the crowded docks, the rivers of coal smoke rising into a leaden sky and the new cast-iron spire, 'like a sky-bound railway track', three-fifths finished and destined to make the Gothic cathedral the tallest building in the world.

The cotton mills of Rouen produced the tough cotton print fabric called *rouennerie*. Not all those mills were fully mechanized, and much of the cotton was still being spun in villages of the Seine-Inférieure *département*. But industry had already brought with it the maladies of mass production. The worry now was not the weather but the fluctuating price of cotton. Wealth had produced an underclass of wage slaves. There were bankruptcies, forced sales and sudden redundancies. Machines had been smashed and, that year, the organized strikes in Rouen and the satellite towns of Louviers, Darnétal and Sotteville had proved that the misery of factory workers could be harnessed for political ends. The troops and national guards who lined the banks of the Seine that foggy morning in December 1840 were not there just to pay homage to the Emperor.

Emergency regulations were in force. All traffic had been banned from the centre of the city. The streets were to be left clear of chairs and benches; there would be no climbing on monuments or trees; and guns were not to be fired from windows or in public spaces.

The crowd which gathered at dawn on 10 December was the largest ever seen in Rouen. The iron suspension bridge had been wrapped in violet drapery studded with thirty-six thousand imperial bees in gold cloth. Twenty thousand metres of material had been produced for the hangings of the triumphal arch. Every few minutes, a cannon was fired from the belvedere of the Côte Sainte-Catherine. When the convoy was rounding the last bend before the bridges, and the cathedral bells had begun to toll, workers were still putting the finishing touches to the decorations.

Dorade n° 3 was escorted by a flotilla of seven steamboats. At

Val-de-la-Haye, its captain, 'trusting to his own artistic initiative', had
festooned his boat with flags, shields and symbols, 'all in the worst
possible taste', according to the local reporter. The Prince de Joinville,
the son of Louis-Philippe who commanded the convoy, had ordered
all the frippery to be torn down. *Dorade n° 3* had been repainted stark
black: the catafalque and flag were the only adornments apart from
a simple altar from which clouds of incense rose and mingled with
the black plumes gushing from the funnel.

The local captain knew his public better than the Prince de
Joinville. The *Journal de Rouen* reported the next day that when the
convoy materialized from the fog, 'the niggardliness of the trappings
caused widespread dismay'. In its 'naked setting', the cenotaph 'was
painful to behold and, it must be said, formed a jarring contrast with
all the pomp and ceremony for which our city footed the bill'.

The imperial fantasy made the reality hard to stomach. This
funereal commemoration of Napoleonic glory by an unpopular
monarchy was marred by the presence of the man himself, his death
now finally undeniable. Cries of 'Vive l'Empereur!' were heard only
twice – from the old soldiers standing to attention on the bridge who
had struggled into their mothballed uniforms, and the notoriously
seditious pupils of the Collège Royal de Rouen who were under very
strict instructions.

The Republican-leaning *Journal de Rouen* saluted the patriotic
fervour of 'those young voices': 'It was a sacred vow to avenge one
day the shame we are made to suffer'. Napoleon had understood that
'France was predestined to lead the world, not in order to exploit it
but to enlighten and energize it'. The lesson, said the editor, was
sorely needed in this utilitarian age when devotion and self-sacrifice
had given way to personal ambition and greed. The *patrie* had been
superseded by the *home* (a word recently borrowed from the English),
and the motto of this reign of mediocrity was 'Each to his own and
every man for himself'.

Nonetheless, the day when the mortal remains of Napoleon came
to Rouen would leave a lasting memory, and it was a cause of celebration that with a crowd the size of an army occupying the city, there
were only three accidents to report: the guard whose arm had been
blown off by a cannonball, the patriot who had been trying to plant
a flag on the roof of the gunpowder magazine when he fell to his

death, and the bystander who was so engrossed in the erection of a statue to Napoleon that he slipped off the quayside and sank without trace.

❊ ❊ ❊

The part-time national guards had arrived in Rouen from the farthest corners of the *arrondissement* 'with the most laudable zeal' to line the banks of the Seine alongside the army regulars. A contingent had come from the village of Ry on the eastern edge of the *département*, in the agricultural region called the Pays de Bray, from an obsolete word meaning 'muddy'.

The Ry contingent included the twenty-eight-year-old village doctor, who also sat on the municipal council. Unlike his neighbours and fellow councillors, the chemist and the notary, Eugène Delamare was a man of progressive political views. Standing with soldiers who had fired on striking factory workers, he must have felt some discomfort at abetting this appropriation of Napoleon by the bourgeois monarchy. As a freethinker, he would certainly not have enjoyed the spectacle of the Archbishop of Rouen granting absolution to the people's Emperor. His second wife, the eighteen-year-old daughter of a farmer, had recently returned to her village three miles up the road to tell her friends about her new life in Ry, and when the bell had tolled for vespers, she had declined to join them at the service, saying that 'her husband had never blackened the doorstep of a church'.

As the convoy steamed off towards Paris, Dr Delamare journeyed back to Ry, either on the plodding mare he used for his rounds or, since (according to the newspaper) a freezing mist was descending over the Normandy plateau, in his cabriolet. None of the three coaching routes from Paris passed through Ry. It would be six years before the village innkeeper launched his twice-weekly service (Tuesdays and Fridays, departing at 6.45 a.m.) 'in a suspended carriage' painted bright yellow.

Delamare's arrival in Ry in the summer of 1835 had coincided with the opening of the first proper road, grandly titled 'Chemin de Grande Communication', which was the lowest of the three categories of road. Until then, as the local council had complained to the Préfecture in Rouen, it was 'impossible' – as it still is on some of the twisting, hedge-lined lanes – 'for a rider or a pedestrian to pass alongside a carriage without being exposed to perilous danger'. That year, railway surveyors had come to the villages on the edge of the Forêt de Lyons, prospecting a possible route for the line from Paris to Le Havre, but hopes were now fading that they would choose the quiet valley in which Ry and Blainville awaited the arrival of the modern world.

After twelve miles, the *route nationale* from Rouen veers to the south and a narrower road branches off across flat fields before winding down into the valley of the Crevon.

✻

Fifty years later, when Ry had acquired a direct link to French history thanks to Dr Delamare and his wife, the rural hinterland of industrial cities was coming to be seen as an attraction rather than as a zone of social and economic stagnation. Even then, the son of the chemist, Jouanne Jr – a more forward-thinking man than his monarchist father – struggled to promote his slumbering 'town' as a tourist destination to readers of the *Journal de Rouen*. In his famous novel, *Madame Bovary* (1857), the Rouen novelist Gustave Flaubert was believed to have described a domestic drama which had taken place there, and it was a shame that he had felt it necessary to paint a rather unappetizing picture of the place.

> The little town of Ry, which the author depicts as an isolated village with nothing to offer but boredom, is not as dismal as his assertions might lead one to believe. For the man who cherishes the charms of the countryside, it holds many a seduction. There are fine walks to be had in the vicinity and also eminently picturesque sites which could give the beauties of Switzerland a run for their money, not to mention the fact that this is one of the healthiest of resorts.

To the enlightened chemist, it was a sign of progress that the two houses in which Dr Delamare had lived had been demolished to make way for more modern buildings.

> Thus, as you may see, everything has been transformed, and come the day when the railway network of the Andelle valley is complete, this undeservedly obscure little town will rapidly become the goal of numerous excursions.

For Eugène Delamare, as for Ry itself, the age of prosperity was slow in coming. As he neared the end of his sixth year as a country doctor, it even seemed to be retreating. The road from Rouen led past a huddle of low thatched hovels, then the covered market and the church with its Renaissance wooden porch. From there, looking down the Grande Rue, which was the only street, one could see with the naked eye the far end of the village where the little River Crevon burbles down from Blainville and Catenay through the water-meadows.

He passed the chemist's shop with its iridescent display of porcelain jars and glass carboys filled with coloured liquids, and then the house with a garden ending at the river where he had lived with his first wife. He had married Louise Mutel shortly after taking up his first post as an *officier de santé* at the village of Catenay, to which his parents had retired. The bride was five years older than the bridegroom and described on the marriage contract as a 'property owner of independent means'. It was a sensible match, probably arranged by Eugène's mother. A year after the wedding, Louise suffered a miscarriage. Eight months later, just after her thirtieth birthday, she died.

There had been some acrimony in the division of the inheritance: the case had dragged on for several months, to the profit of his neighbour the notary, M. Leclerc. Either those 'independent means' had been exaggerated, or the mother, brother and sister-in-law of the deceased felt justified in reducing or withholding his share. He had since remarried and moved to a smaller house. It stood opposite the notary's office and the inn. He turned into the alleyway beside the house, stabled the mare and announced his return to Delphine and the maid. By then, the paddle-steamer bearing the remains of Napoleon was another twenty miles closer to Paris.

✱

A life of modest distinction had once been a realistic dream for the son of Monsieur and Madame Delamare. When he was born in 1812, his parents were wine merchants in the Rue des Arpents in Rouen. The business had prospered, and they were able to send their only son to the prestigious Collège Royal, formerly the Collège Impérial and now the Lycée Corneille.

The state-controlled *lycées*, instituted under Napoleon in 1802, were a solid grounding for a career of respectable hardship. In

1979–80, when I taught at that bastion of the Rouen bourgeoisie, it still had the air of a monumental barracks: a grand entrance on a steep and narrow side-street, spartan classrooms painted battleship grey and a decaying Jesuit chapel. In a cobbled courtyard, the pupils sheltered from the rain under lean-to roofs. University graduates who looked like nineteenth-century caricatures of starving bohemian students were charged with the thankless task of imposing discipline while they prepared for a fiercely competitive teaching examination which few of them would pass. One evening after lights out, I was taken up to the dormitories, which smelled of socks and the rabbit stew that was served at almost every dinner. I saw the urchin-like *internes* peering out of the gloom in obvious need of a bedtime story.

The *salle des fêtes* next to the headmaster's study was decorated with enough portraits of former pupils to illustrate a history of French culture: writers (Corneille, Fontenelle, Bernardin de Saint-Pierre, Flaubert and Maupassant), artists (Corot, Delacroix and Marcel Duchamp), and a pantheon of other luminaries including La Salle, the explorer of the Mississippi Basin, and the poet and Resistance fighter Jean Prévost. It conveyed the rare impression of a self-confident provincial capital shining with its own light despite its proximity to Paris.

The only surviving example of Delamare's intellectual attainments – a letter written in 1848 (p. 231) – suggests a mind muddled by haste and distraction, ignorant of syntax and impatient with punctuation. But no matter how mediocre the pupil, the Collège Royal would provide him with a lifelong network of useful contacts. Eugène was a contemporary of Achille Flaubert, the son of the nationally famous chief surgeon at the Hôtel-Dieu in Rouen. The boys' mothers were close friends. It was almost certainly because of Mme Delamare's association with the Flaubert family that when he left the *lycée* at the age of seventeen in 1829, Delamare was able to study under Dr Flaubert at the Hôtel-Dieu.

His goal was to qualify as an *officier de santé*. The 'health officer', instituted to cope with the carnage of the Revolutionary Wars, was an inferior grade of doctor. He was not licensed to perform major operations: most of his work was humdrum and repetitive – bone-setting, bloodletting, tooth-extracting. His social status was equivalent to that of a village priest or schoolmaster, but unlike the teacher and the priest, he was financially dependent on his impoverished flock. Fifty centimes – the price of a basic meal – was the usual payment for a visit, but with no insurance or sick leave, bedridden peasants would often have to pay in kind. An *officier de santé* was rarely short of fruit, chickens, animal feed, firewood and spare furniture, but he never grew rich.

For much of the nineteenth century, politicians and public health experts justified this penny-pinching exploitation of a vital resource:

> Country dwellers have a purer way of life than townspeople and therefore have simpler maladies which require less training and treatment. (1803)

> Poor and simple patients need doctors who are similarly poor and simple. . . . Being of humble birth and obtaining his qualification at little cost, the *officier de santé* is able to content himself with modest remuneration. (1847)

This was the voice of the smug gerontocracy which ignored the growing population of educated young men with no outlet for their energy and skills. As one of Balzac's characters predicted in 1840, this compressed mass of underemployed intellects would 'explode like the boiler of a steam engine'.

After the usual five years of study, Delamare graduated as an *officier de santé* at the age of twenty-two. The diploma cost two thousand francs, which was ten times the annual pension of a retired soldier. At about that time, Dr Flaubert made him an interest-free loan of three hundred francs. It was typical of his generosity and also good professional practice. Surgeons often kept in touch with former students who might bring them instructive or even lucrative cases. Delamare would indeed provide a case of absorbing interest, though it was Dr Flaubert's younger son, Gustave, who would profit from it. The loan was never repaid, but three hundred francs was a trivial sum compared to the lasting benefit of the Flauberts' connection with the Delamares and the unhappiness that would be visited on Delamare's descendants.

✻

Dr Delamare's catchment area was large enough to make life irksome – especially in winter and at harvest time, when the farm tracks were claggy – but too small to provide a decent living. The population of Ry was stagnant until M. Hommais, who lived next door to the chemist, opened a cotton mill which fed the factories in Rouen, when it increased from under five hundred to just over six hundred. The population of all the villages served by Delamare amounted to about four thousand, but another student of Dr Flaubert, Henry Laloy, had moved to the village, so that even if every single person in the area required medical attention and was able to pay, and if, exceptionally, no one used the services of faith-healers, charlatans and *rebouteurs* who treated people as well as animals, he would be lucky to make a thousand francs a year.

His neighbour, Henry Laloy, despite being two years younger than Delamare, had the pick of the better class of patient. When he came to Ry in 1841, Laloy already enjoyed an international reputation for his thesis on Dr Flaubert's discovery of a cure for pseudarthrosis (the failure of a fractured bone to fuse). He also had the distinction of being married to a Parisienne. The two men were not on speaking terms.

A few miles to the west, towards Rouen, Delamare's constituency met that of Laloy's father. Laloy Sr was a cheerful man who would come tripping down the lane, singing comic arias of his own composition. His nephew once heard him perform his ribald version of *Paradise Lost* as he entered the home of a farmer who had just suffered a stroke: 'Up and down the angel swings, / And then he flings himself down, / Eyeing up Adam / And inspecting Eve from top to bottom.'

The nephew, Jules Levallois, who became a noted literary critic, was a pupil at the Collège Royal in Rouen. He spent his summer holidays with his aunt and uncle and came to know almost everyone in the area, including the innkeeper and the chemist of Ry. His memoirs, which are uniquely and verifiably accurate, contain the only physical description of Eugène Delamare.

The description dates from a slightly later period, shortly after the death of Delamare's second wife. On a sunny afternoon in May or June 1848, Jules and his uncle were crossing the wheat fields near Martainville. In that open expanse, a dark smudge in the distance is the only sign that the deep vale of the Crevon lies three miles to the east.

A silhouette rose up against the sky. Coming towards us we saw a horse which made me think of Rocinante and a rider who could easily have served Gustave Doré as a model for his *Don Quixote* illustrations.

The melancholy figure slumped over his skeletal nag stopped to exchange 'a few insignificant, desultory words', then ambled off towards Ry.

'Did you recognize him?' asked my uncle. 'That's D . . . the doctor. You've heard about the misfortune that struck him.'

In the spring of 1848, few people knew the circumstances of the doctor's 'misfortune' – the disgrace and suicide of his young wife. Nothing had appeared in the newspapers, and beyond the immediate family, only the Laloys, the Flauberts, and the chemist and his son were familiar with the details. But a generation later, several 'witnesses' who had read Flaubert's novel of 'provincial manners', *Madame Bovary*, could recount with remarkable precision the tale of the oblivious, boring husband and the passionate, brown-eyed adulteress who frittered away a non-existent fortune in promissory notes and poisoned herself with arsenic when the bailiffs descended like demons.

✣   ✣   ✣

Delamare's second wife, Delphine Couturier, was the youngest daughter of a farmer at Blainville. The village was a five-minute walk from Catenay, where Delamare's parents lived and where he had begun his career as an *officier de santé*. He would have seen the girl and perhaps treated her when she was twelve or thirteen. The Couturiers owned the land they farmed and could afford to send Delphine to a village *pension* for *jeunes demoiselles* and then, according to her classmate Adèle, because 'the food left something to be desired', to a convent school in Rouen.

Little more than a year after settling his dispute with the family of his first wife, Eugène married Delphine on 7 August 1839 at eight in the evening (a normal time of day for a wedding). She was seventeen; he was twenty-six. There are no portraits of the bride and, of course, no photographs. In 1878, her friend Adèle was asked by her son, a professor of medicine, what she remembered of the presumed model for Emma Bovary. She was loath to discuss the shameful subject, but she did confess that a portrait in the Musée des Beaux-Arts in Rouen of a pretty young woman with crow-black hair and a porcelain complexion reminded her of Delphine – 'but without the innocence'.

Jules Levallois, who met her many times, never confused Delphine Delamare with a fictional character. In the summer holidays of 1847, he saw her 'almost every day'. She did not strike him as the sort of woman who would inspire or become embroiled in a passionate affair:

> Hers was surely not a *figure à passions*. She was blonde with blue eyes and she had a *teint de Normande* [a pale complexion verging on deathly white], which, towards the end, had a tendency to blotchiness. I cannot say whether or not she dressed with irreproachable elegance. What I do know is that her clothes were, as we say in our part of the world, *voyant* [gaudy]. She had a particular predilection for pink dresses. I could not vouch for her intelligence.

The Delamares' house in the Grande Rue was fairly well appointed. The dining-room looked onto the street. It had embroidered muslin curtains and a green rug, ten tapestry chairs, two flower vases and a round walnut table with a draughts board. There were four engravings on the wall, subjects unknown. Upstairs, the bed in the blue bedroom had a baldachin of gilded brass with a fringed silk canopy, a dressing table with a mirror, a marble-topped chest-of-drawers, six coffee cups and two silver-plated candlesticks. A smaller bedroom, perhaps used by the maid, contained a painted wooden bed, a mahogany bureau, a wash basin and a glass coffee machine. In summer, when the windows at the back were opened onto the long, narrow garden, the two hundred rose bushes 'in superior varieties' might have attenuated the smells of the village and the doctor's preparations.

In Balzac's *Scènes de la vie privée* (1830), the cosy new world of 'private life' swarms with clues to a personality. But it would have taken years for a young wife to transform a rented house into a personal statement. The dowry of the first Mme Delamare probably accounts for the furnishings that were not second hand; others were heirlooms and payments in kind. There is no sign of a piano in the after-death inventory. The bookshelves were dominated by dictionaries, general histories and medical textbooks. One hundred and nineteen fascicles of the *Journal de médecine et de chirurgie* 'for practising doctors' lined the walls of the consulting room. Among the surgical equipment, like a primitive household god, was a phrenological head – a fleshy young face on one side, a hellish mask of bone on the other – which eventually found its way to the Musée Flaubert in the Hôtel-Dieu at Rouen.

Apart from Lamartine's *Souvenirs d'Orient*, the only whiff of Romanticism is the work of a forgotten novelist published in Paris in 1835. In *Julia, ou l'Amour à Naples*, a young married girl with blue eyes, blonde hair and a pale complexion unexpectedly triumphs over her sultry, ebon-haired rival by devoting herself to the cause of love with 'a passion as virtuous as illegitimate passion can be'.

✿

Social life in Ry was limited but in one respect more varied than it would have been in the city. *Officiers de santé* were not allowed to take holidays and it is doubtful that Delphine ever saw Paris, let alone Naples. But the scarcity of educated people meant that even a doctor, a teacher, a chemist or a village notary would be invited to parties at the manor houses of the minor rural nobility. Levallois, who was a guest at most of the *châteaux* in the area, suggests that Delphine was on intimate terms with Baron Boullenger, who lived in retirement with his wife and three daughters a short walk away at Saint-Denis-le-Thiboult.

People of all classes met at fairs, auctions, funerals and weddings, which could last for two days. A girl two years younger than Delphine who lived eight miles away at the Château d'Écalles and whose name happens to have been Esther de Bovery (not an uncommon surname in Normandy) explained at a trial where she was called as a witness that she had danced with the local chemist at the wedding of her father's tenant 'because there were only farmers at the *fête*'.

At Blainville, Delphine had her childhood friends and her family. Her older brother Ulysse and his wife were in the fancy goods business, selling trinkets and drapery at all the town and village fairs. A typical evening at home would be spent playing draughts, dominos or cards with a few neighbours: Jouanne the chemist (tolerated by Delamare despite his monarchist views); Louis Campion, a bachelor in his early thirties whose father owned some land around Ry and who, like Delamare and Jouanne, sat on the local council; and the notary's clerk, Narcisse Bottais, who studied law in Paris in 1841–2. His tales of student life in the Latin Quarter might have spiced up the evening conversation.

Bottais left Ry in 1843 for the neighbouring Oise *département*, where he married in 1846. Much later, one of his friends told an interviewer that 'we occasionally talked about Mme Delamare, of whom Bottais . . . had a fond memory'. Delphine was remembered as the person who had taught Bottais a pleasantly unexciting form of cribbage called thirty-one: 'This game, unknown at Formerie, was played only at the home of M. and Mme Bottais and then at their friends' homes.'

The only notable event occurred on 29 November 1842. Nearly three and a half years after her wedding, Delphine gave birth to a girl. She was christened Delphine-Félicie-Augusta-Alix. Twelve weeks later, despite Dr Delamare's antipathy to the Church, the baby was baptized at a full public service.

The unnecessary expense of a baptism would usually indicate high social status or aspirations to gentility. The parish register for this period records only one other baptism at Ry – the daughter of the Delamares' next-door neighbours, Henry Laloy and his Parisian wife. According to Levallois, each doctor kept to his own 'clan' or coterie, and it is only to be expected that their professional rivalry extended to their social life.

✿

Life went on, the seasons changed. The store of apples in the Delamares' cellar (listed in the inventory) grew and diminished. The notary's clerk left for Formerie, where he married the daughter of an army captain. The son of M. Jouanne qualified as a chemist, and Dr Delamare was re-elected to the council. In 1841, the year of the census, Delphine, described as a 'ménagère' (housewife), had acquired a new maid, Cézarine Durand, who was sixteen years old. The cotton mill run by M. Hommais ensured the availability of young women who might be glad of more congenial indoor employment.

For a novelist who considered style superior to subject, a place like Ry was a blank canvas on which timeless phrases could be worked into a *tableau*: 'Sitting in her armchair by the window, she saw the people of the village passing on the pavement.' History was a product of the city. In 1843, at the new railway station on the Left Bank, the

Rouen section of the line from Paris to the sea was inaugurated. The valley of the Crevon had been left to its leafy lanes: the closest station to Ry lay thirteen miles to the south in the valley of the Seine.

Even in Rouen, news of national interest was in short supply, and so the trial at which Esther de Bovery was cross-examined in late February and early March 1845 filled the *Journal de Rouen* for several days and was comprehensively covered in the Paris *Gazette des Tribunaux* and even in the British *Spectator*. It was the biggest event in Rouen since the return of Napoleon's remains. Despite the freezing temperatures, crowds gathered in the streets around the Palais de Justice and had to be prevented by armed soldiers from invading the courtroom.

The case concerned a M. Loursel, who was a chemist at Buchy, eight miles north of Ry. He was accused of murdering his simple-minded wife with arsenic. The prosecution depicted him as a cold-blooded Lothario who had formed a romantic attachment to the pretty young lady from the local *château* after meeting her at the farmers' dance. Mlle de Bovery had been touched by the chemist's concern for her fragile health. Horrified to learn of his arrest, she had exchanged some passionate, platonic letters with the accused, who had led her to believe that 'only the slenderest of threads held him back from suicide'.

To her mortification, those cries of an innocent soul were read out in court. The emotional messages she had sent to a married man without the knowledge of her parents had an air of amorous intrigue. It was as though a character from one of the serial romances which occupied the bottom of every page in the *Journal de Rouen* had migrated to the news section:

> I may have acted improperly [she told the court], but I have been cruelly punished for it . . . God knows my feelings were pure! . . . I had honourable intentions: I did not want his mother and child to lose him! If there are sensitive souls in this court, they will understand me, I am sure! . . . And then, I was in the country, left to my own devices, alone with my imaginings . . .

The case was of special interest to the doctor and the chemist of Ry. A friend of Mlle de Bovery's father had been a witness at Delamare's first wedding and both men were personally acquainted with Loursel.

They would have followed the trial intently, up to the moment when the defence counsel, Maître Senard, a friend of the Flauberts, secured the acquittal of Loursel with a blazing speech worthy of the last chapter of a novel.

Compared to this drama of love and poison, the incidents which composed the insipid gruel of gossip at Ry were even more insubstantial. Even if something newsworthy was happening in the village, so much of life was lived behind muslin curtains that the developments in the doctor's household were probably known only to the notary and his client.

*

In July 1843, Delamare borrowed six thousand francs – a colossal sum for a country doctor. The annual rent on the house was four hundred francs; the maid would have received about one hundred and fifty francs a year. In 1845, he borrowed a further two thousand five hundred francs, and in 1847, one thousand two hundred. Including the unpaid loan of three hundred francs from Dr Flaubert, Delamare's debts totalled exactly ten thousand francs.

This unexplained spate of borrowing is a material link between the real Delamares and the fictional Bovarys. Flaubert later claimed that his story was '*totally invented*', but this was in exasperation with readers who imagined that a novelist simply rummaged about in the charity shop of *faits divers* until he found a ready-made tale. Along with the many coincidences of name and location, letters to his friends Maxime Du Camp and Louis Bouilhet prove that the drama at Ry was a starting point. 'Have you made a decision?', Du Camp asked him in 1851. 'Is it still Don Juan? Or is it the story of Mme Delamarre [*sic*], which is really splendid?' In 1855, when the novel was more than half written, he wrote to Bouilhet: 'I fear that the end – which in reality was the fullest part – will be too skimpy in my book.'

The story of Mme Delamare had come, not from a newspaper but from his family – perhaps his brother Achille and certainly his mother, the *confidante* of Mme Delamare *mère*. Gustave's niece Caroline remembered:

> In my childhood, an old friend of our family, Mme Delamare of Catenay, would come from time to time to see my grandmother

[Gustave's mother]. She had lost her son, who was an *officier de santé* and a former pupil of my grandfather. He was a *brave garçon* who had been very unhappy in his home. . . . I am convinced that *Madame Bovary* had its origin in the scandal that was caused by the misbehaviour of Mme Delamare, the daughter-in-law of the old lady I knew.

The bills for fancy goods and fabrics which rain down on Emma Bovary are the ostensible cause of her suicide. The inventory made after Delamare's death includes what some proponents of the Delphine = Emma thesis have taken to be an extraordinary number of women's *chemises* – eighty-three of them, valued at two hundred and twenty francs. These were cotton undergarments which covered the whole body. Some were for daytime wear, others, of thicker cloth, served as pyjamas. A recent study of cotton manufacturers in the Nord *département* found that the average number of *chemises* 'per wardrobe' in 1831 was 'nearly fifty'. Delphine's entire stock of *chemises* would have required laundering after little more than a month. The maid might be ill or the *lavoir* frozen over, and in those circumstances, eighty-three was not altogether excessive.

Delphine's dresses, pink or otherwise, are not detailed in the inventory. Perhaps baulking at the complex taxonomy of women's apparel, the notary and his clerk merely noted 'a great quantity of very fine table and body linen'. In 1847, the cost of a top-of-the-range woman's outfit sold by a reputable Parisian tailor was just over four hundred francs (dress of Italian shot silk, overcoat with frills and flounces, hood with artificial flowers, lace-trimmed *mantelet*, and parasol with ivory handle). But most women would have bought the material and worked from a pattern in a fashion magazine or had the dress made up by a seamstress. Unlike Emma Bovary, who has to deal with the usurious draper of Yonville, Delphine had the advantage of a brother and sister-in-law in the fancy goods trade.

If she was overspending, so was her husband. Some of that 'very fine body linen' was his, and the debts were all in his name. Levallois, who saw the doctor on his decrepit mare, might have been surprised to learn that he also owned two pedigree hunting dogs as well as two pairs of pistols and a double-barrelled fowling piece. The Don Quixote horse suggests parsimony rather than penury or at least indifference to the suffering of an animal. The poor thing is listed with the contents of the stable in Delamare's after-death inventory: an iron-hooped wooden bucket, a pitchfork, a saddle, an oat-tub, and 'a mare with bay brown coat, past all work, and afflicted with pursiness [short-windedness], valued at a hundred and fifty francs'.

Dr Delamare was not, as would soon become clear, an unobservant man, nor was he inclined to turn a blind eye to bad behaviour. He would have known if his wife was threatening the household with financial ruin. In any case, there is no record of a forced sale or a bailiff's warrant. Everyone later accepted that his wife had committed suicide, but debts can hardly have been the reason.* Something else must have made that *brave garçon* unhappy in his marriage.

✧

The other vital component of the story known to Mme Flaubert, her two sons, Gustave's friends, Dr and Mme Laloy, the chemist and his son, who confirmed the suicide by arsenic, is the 'misbehaviour' of Delphine.

Levallois's aunt predicted that Delphine would 'come to a bad end' because she was 'une évaporée' – a giddy, light-headed girl. The word was applied to both sexes, but in the feminine, it had connotations of tartiness and loose morals. Her school friend insinuated as much when she said that Delphine lacked 'innocence'.

As Mlle de Bovery had discovered at the Loursel trial, it did not take much for a woman to lose her reputation. Maxime Du Camp, who was familiar with the story but not the woman, decided that the doctor's wife, 'an unbeautiful little woman whose spotty, freckled face was framed by dull yellow hair', suffered from 'one of the forms of the hysteria which afflicts anaemics' – 'nymphomania and maniacal profligacy': 'Since the only treatment she received was good advice, she did not make a recovery.'

Even supposing that 'vapourishness' led to adultery, what amorous opportunities were there in the valley of the Crevon? There was the

---

* Cash was scarce in rural parts and most people lived on credit. Some of the ten thousand francs might have been borrowed in anticipation of the sale of his late father's house at Catenay. When Delamare died in 1849, his assets and the sale of his possessions were enough to ensure that, unlike the orphaned daughter of the novel, Mlle Delamare would have a small annuity and a dowry including a field and half a house in Rouen as well as some silverware, jewellery, toys and dresses.

notary's clerk, who had 'un bon souvenir' of the housewife who taught him a card game. There was Louis Campion, who began to sell off the small family estate after his father's death in 1847. When he died of consumption in 1868, Campion was selling flowers in the streets of Paris. And then, down the lane at Saint-Denis, there was Baron Alexandre Boullenger, a former *procureur général* (chief prosecutor) and mayor of the village who, according to an obituary, was 'leading a patriarchal life divided between literary pursuits and the sweet charms of family'.

Despite Levallois's hint that 'the syllabic harmony of the name "Boulanger de la Huchette" [Emma Bovary's first lover] corresponds almost exactly to the name of the real person', one hesitates to impugn the memory of the Baron, who was thirty-one years older than Delphine and whose bronze bust, paid for by public subscription, still sits on a plinth above the entrance to the town hall of Saint-Denis-le-Thiboult. This beloved benefactor had 'left his wife and child' during the cholera epidemic of 1832 and 'spent entire days with the priest of his parish in wretched, abandoned hovels where he tended the unhappy victims with his own hands'.

We don't know, and perhaps there *was* nothing to know: Maxime Du Camp imagined a giddy young woman flouncing about the muddy lanes in a pink dress, frantic to spend money and have sex with any presentable man who was not her husband. Levallois's account is obviously more credible, and in its oblique reference to *Romeo and Juliet*, it contains a clue more compelling than a coincidence of names:

> My cousin [Laloy] and D[elamare] were doctors in the same place: they lived next door to one another but never spoke. Each had his own clan, rather like the Montagues and Capulets. I might add that my aunt said of Mme D[elamare], 'She's an *évaporée*: she will come to no good.'

The sectarian division at Ry, which would become flagrant during the 1848 Revolution, is reflected in the fact that, while Delphine was a familiar daily sight, her husband was seen so rarely that Levallois's uncle was unsure whether or not his nephew could recognize him.

Even if there was never a Romeo in Ry, a 'light-headed' woman with a tendency to ignore the proprieties might have found it hard to observe the village battle lines, and a sour husband whose whimsical young wife drew attention to herself with 'gaudy' dresses might have preferred her to stay at home instead of socializing with the enemy. A woman's light relief could be a husband's bitter torment.

✻

These were difficult times for husbands, when women were beginning to enjoy a certain social, though not legal, independence. Coincidentally, there was a similar household not far away at Croisy-la-Haye, on the other side of Saint-Denis. A well-to-do young farmer, described as 'sombre and taciturn', lived with his wife and their two children in what appeared to be wedded bliss. Mme Laquerrière was said to be 'of a very happy-go-lucky disposition', and when she lay dying in agony on the afternoon of 12 August 1847, vomiting a whitish substance and screaming, 'My poor children, must I leave them?', no one suspected her of suicide.

The case came to court in August 1848: the 'dissembling' husband had given himself away by clumsy denials. It was three long years since the Loursel case had filled the papers, and the *Journal de Rouen* might be forgiven for revelling in the details. First Buchy, now Croisy . . . That obscure valley in the Pays de Bray was turning out to be a hotbed of uxoricidal poisoning. 'How little we know of what goes on in a household!' the prosecuting counsel was quoted as saying.

The arsenic – normally used to dress wheat to prevent smut disease – had been supplied by M. Jouanne, the chemist of Ry. And the doctor who attended the dying woman and who suspected arsenic poisoning was Eugène Delamare, the *officier de santé* of the same village. It was a tribute to his expertise that Dr Delamare had drawn the correct conclusions from the appearance of the body, the nature and location of the pain, and the colour of the vomitus. In such cases, autopsies and chemical tests were invariably conclusive, but in a living patient, it was notoriously difficult to distinguish the effects of arsenic from those of cholera and of other poisons.

By chance, the recent April 1847 fascicle of the *Journal de médecine* to which Delamare subscribed had listed the antidotes to be administered in cases of arsenic poisoning. If only the doctor had been summoned in time, he might have saved the poor woman.

✻   ✻   ✻

Delphine turned twenty-six on 17 February 1848. Five days later, a battle broke out in the centre of Paris. After catastrophic harvests, a cruel winter and a decade of policies calculated to improve the lot of the very rich, the bourgeois monarchy was foundering in corruption, debt and unemployment. Cavalry and cannon rattled through the streets to find them blocked with barricades. When the July 1830 revolution had deposed Charles X, a new regime had been waiting in the wings. In February 1848, the curtain went up on an empty stage. Though the customary elements of a Paris insurrection were present – the smashing of streetlamps, the gouging-up of paving stones – it was a sign of the people's desperation that this revolution was taking place in winter and in heavy rain.

On 24 February, Paris fell to the mob. King Louis-Philippe signed his abdication, and a large, pear-shaped man called 'Mr Smith' took a city cab to Dreux before sailing for Newhaven, never to return. A provisional government was declared. On 25 February, the rioting spread to Rouen. Workers rampaged through the city shouting, 'Vive la République!' and, 'À bas les Anglais!' In 1843, there had been violent demonstrations against the British engineers who had raised the Union Jack above the tricolour at the inauguration of the railway. Now, British looms were smashed, and two arches of the new wooden railway bridge, the Pont aux Anglais, were set on fire.

On Sunday 5 March, the *Journal de Rouen* reported the provisional government's declaration of universal male suffrage. In Rouen, the 'Marseillaise' was sung at both theatres before and after performances of *Les Diamants de la couronne* and *Une femme à deux maris*. The weather was overcast and rainy; the temperature ranged from one to five degrees centigrade but it was probably colder still in the valley of the Crevon. At some point – to judge by the case at Croisy, it would have been around the time of the evening meal – Delphine Delamare ingested arsenic in the form of powder.

For the farmer's wife at Croisy, the time between ingestion and organ failure had been about seven hours. Symptoms – usually nausea, stomach pains, vomiting and diarrhoea – appear early enough for action to be taken. As he had demonstrated at Croisy, Delamare was familiar with the signs, but perhaps on that rainy Sunday evening he was out visiting a patient. It was only when 'the sickness had declared itself with extraordinary violence' that Dr Laloy Sr (as he told his nephew) was called to the house in the Grande Rue. The words 'violence inouïe' suggest the later stage of poisoning at which convulsions begin. This would have been an hour or so after midnight in the early hours of Monday morning.

✿

At ten o'clock on Tuesday morning (7 March), Dr Delamare and the village schoolmaster M. Durier walked to the *mairie* by the covered market and declared the death, 'yesterday, at three o'clock in the morning', of Delphine Delamare *née* Couturier, 'of no particular profession', 'aged twenty-seven years' (she was twenty-six and eighteen days old), 'born on the seventeenth of February 1821' (she was born in 1822), married to Eugène Delamare at Blainville-Crevon 'on the tenth of August 1839' (they were married on 7 August).

Delamare was not the first or the last husband to forget his wife's date of birth and the date of their wedding anniversary. The situation was hardly conducive to accuracy. One might have expected to see the signature of Jouanne the chemist on the death certificate. His name is also absent from the burial certificate, on which her age was given as 'about twenty-eight': it was signed only by the priest, a day labourer and a blacksmith. There appears to have been no funeral.

It is often asserted that a Catholic priest would not have permitted a woman who had killed herself to be given a Christian burial. Most priests had abandoned that dogmatic cruelty. The official guidance now stated that 'a church burial is not refused to those who commit suicide in a fit of frenzy or in any other sickly excess or in a state of insanity'.

A pyramidal gravestone, which was later broken up and either lost or stolen as a souvenir before the First World War, was erected near the church door, probably by her own family:

Ici repose le corps de Delphine COUTURIER,
épouse de M. DELAMARE, médecin,
décédée le 6 mars 1848.
Priez Dieu pour le repos de son âme.

✿

In cases of death by poisoning, including suicide, the Code Civil stated that an autopsy should be carried out and a report compiled by a police official and a fully qualified doctor or surgeon (rather than a simple *officier de santé*). The *procureur du roi* would then endorse the report and authorize the burial. In rural parts, where there might be some delay in fetching an expert from the city, the burial could proceed immediately, provided that the body could easily be exhumed. This is what happened both in the Loursel case at Buchy and in the Laquerrière case at Croisy.

Curiously, there is no record of an exhumation or an autopsy, and nothing appeared in the local papers. On the day before Delphine died, the national press had covered a minor case of arsenic poisoning in a small village four hundred miles away in the Tarn. The more sensational death by arsenic of a doctor's wife in the Rouen *arrondissement* would have filled several columns in the *Journal de Rouen*. The reporter might have drawn attention to the remarkable fact that this was the third such case in five years in the same small valley.

Perhaps it was just as well for Delamare: a bereavement is harrowing enough without a police investigation. The unexpected death of a lively twenty-six-year-old woman certainly had elements to interest the public prosecutor's office. This was the second time that Delamare had lost a wife prematurely. On the first occasion, there had been legal squabbling over the inheritance. It could also be established that he was familiar with the symptoms of arsenic poisoning and yet had failed or been unable to administer the remedies in time.

For the Jouannes, too, the silence of the judiciary would have come as a relief. The usual questions would have been asked. Had the sale of the arsenic been recorded in the chemist's register? Had it been 'denatured', as required by a recent law, with an iron oxide pigment to prevent its being mistaken for a harmless substance such as powdered sugar? In 1890, an anonymous letter in the *Journal de Rouen* (later known to have been written by Jouanne Jr) insisted that Flaubert had been wrong to state that the doctor's wife had 'found the arsenic in the chemist's cupboard'. It had come from 'a collection of miscellaneous drugs which her husband had stored away in an attic'. No attic store is mentioned in the after-death inventory of Eugène Delamare.

Delphine had died at a moment when the usual formalities were likely to be overlooked. The decision to launch an investigation lay with the *procureur du roi*. The *procureur du roi* (or, as he now was, *procureur de la République*) answered to the *procureur général* – a powerful post which had once been occupied at Rouen by Baron Boullenger of Saint-Denis. On 4 March, a day before Delphine fell ill, when communications had only just been re-established between Rouen and Paris, Jules Senard, the friend of the Flauberts and defender of Loursel, was appointed *procureur général* in a public meeting reminiscent of the 1789 Revolution. Before an ecstatic crowd, Senard hailed the return of freedom and democracy and marvelled at 'the series of strange, swift and miraculous events' which had 'smashed and borne away a throne . . . and snatched me from the routines of private life'.

The entire administrative structure was being dismantled and reformed, propped up in the meantime by *commissaires* appointed by the government in Paris. An intoxicating air of anarchy was everywhere, even at the *lycée* in Rouen, where a pupils' revolt had to be put down. The Préfecture felt it necessary to remind citizens that not *all* laws had been abolished. Faced with these earth-shaking events, the prosecutor's office had little time for cases which presented no threat to public order. The adulterous, spendthrift wife of a respected and well-connected village doctor had killed herself, and there was no reason why anyone should be troubled any further by the tragedy. The story that was told by Mme Delamare *mère* to her friend Mme Flaubert had the sad ring of truth.

✿   ✿   ✿

Less than a fortnight after Delamare buried his second wife, the ten-man Ry municipal council suffered a devastating coup. In a purge of bourgeois councillors, six members were deposed, including Hommais the mill owner, Leclerc the notary (denounced as a 'bad patriot') and Jouanne the chemist, who had sat on the council since 1831.

Nearly all the new councillors were proletarian – a blacksmith, a butcher, a miller and a tailor, and the man who drove the Ry–Rouen *diligence*. Only one bourgeois had survived the purge, and this, it would soon appear, was the man who had engineered it: the village doctor, Eugène Delamare.

As in a spy novel, just when the case has been closed, a light falls on the most elusive character. He is sitting in the house in which his wife died in convulsions a month before. His five-year-old daughter is upstairs with the maid in the small bedroom, or perhaps she has gone to stay with her grandmother. For once, there are no farming accidents or paupers' diseases to attend to. He has the time to write to the Préfecture in Rouen about the vital matters which have been weighing on his mind.

He writes as the 'citizen president' of a new committee, the Club de la Fraternité. These revolutionary 'clubs' were set up to gather intelligence on the local community, to root out political incorrectness and to feed the authorities with reports of counter-revolutionary activities or opinions.

> *Citizens,*
>
> *I am surprised to learn that among the citizen mayors who have been removed from office, Grandin the mayor of Boissay of the canton of Buchy has been retained, which is all the more surprising since a report was filed and he was denounced as an anti-Republican . . . The citizen mayor has set himself up as president and eight members appointed through his influence must have some amicable arrangement with the Blainville committee which is made up of* Legitimists and Monarchists. *I have seen their list and I can assure you it's worthy of them.*
>
> *I am not the sort of citizen who informs on other people. I know the opposition party which is the reason why Grandin is still mayor, and the epithet I'd use for this is* nepotism. . . . *This man has always been the dogsbody of ministerial deputies.*
>
> *I hope, Citizens, that you will find this information useful and do justice to our sacred cause with the shortest possible delay. . . .*
>
> *Some true Republicans are asking themselves how such enemies can be retained.*
>
> *Greetings and fraternity*
>   *Delamare, Citizen president of the Club de la Fraternité*
>   *Ry, 8 April 1848*

This sly, sardonic letter was a vicious piece of work. The revolution in Rouen was sliding towards anarchy or a workers' state. In that volatile climate, a denunciation could lead to public disgrace and even violent retribution.

Delamare had not been crushed by the death of Delphine. His main target, Grandin, was the brother-in-law of his first wife and one of the parties to the legal dispute over her estate. Blainville was the home of his second wife. Most of her family still lived there. Far from being an enclave of legitimists and monarchists, Blainville had declared its support for the new regime in a noisy public ceremony nine days before Ry.

The Robespierre of the Crevon valley was carrying out his own domestic purge. He was what the political discourse of the time called a *déclassé* – an exile from his own social class. He was alienating his relatives, the bourgeoisie to which the Laloy clan belonged, as well as the two remaining friends who had played cards with Delphine. This unintended self-portrait is the photograph of a stranger. It has nothing of Mme Delamare's *brave garçon*, nor of Dr Laloy's pitiful Don Quixote, nor especially of Delamare's supposed literary likeness, the hapless, well-meaning Charles Bovary.

If this letter had been written in normal circumstances, it might have invited a diagnosis of paranoid delusions caused by grief. But in those months of liberation and with the bloody repression of workers' riots in Rouen (April) and Paris (June), even some moderate republicans discovered in themselves an unsuspected propensity for violence. In 1848, the ranks of revolutionaries included many country doctors – the most poorly paid members of the professional class, exploited by the state like the paupers whose sufferings they witnessed and only occasionally alleviated.

For an *officier de santé* whose first wife had left him poorer than he had anticipated and who had remarried for what he might have hoped would be pleasure, a flighty wife who wore pink dresses and gadded about with the reactionary bourgeoisie could be a source of intense exasperation.

Delamare was re-elected to the council by the expanded electorate. He was still a councillor when Louis-Napoléon Bonaparte, a nephew of the Emperor, was elected President of the Republic in December, promising to eradicate poverty and to uphold the rights of property owners and the Church. The dates on which Delamare attended council meetings are all we know of his activities until 7 December

1849, when he died 'unexpectedly' at half-past five in the morning. The death certificate mentions neither illness nor accident, and so the likeliest cause of death is suicide.

✿ ✿ ✿

La Véritable 'Madame Bovary'
Journal de Rouen, Saturday 22 November 1890

Should you be wandering one summer's day and happen to find yourself in the large village of Ry on the confines of the Vexin and the Pays de Bray, you will be struck by its resemblance to the place so minutely described by the novelist. . . . This secluded little place, which is connected to the outside world only by a *diligence* service (the last working *diligences* in the region), is the forgotten corner where that lamentable drama took place which gave the novelist his theme. . . .

And if you ask the old people about Mlle C[outurier] . . . the real Mme Bovary will appear in their conversations just as she was immortalized by Flaubert – a pretty brunette, gay and fond of dancing . . . Bored and romantic, she lost herself in books.

It was after the publication of this article that the knowledge spread beyond the valley of the Crevon and the parallel world of Gustave Flaubert began to spawn chimeric beings that were neither real nor entirely fictional. The *diligence* driver, M. Thérain, who was still in business, remembered Madame's insatiable appetite for romantic novels, which he used to bring back from the *cabinet de lecture* in Rouen: 'The bill was still unpaid when she died.' Augustine Ménage, who had served Delphine as a maid for a few months in 1841, was photographed in front of her house in her Sunday best and received fifty centimes for every postcard that was sold of '*Une ancienne servante de Mme Bovary*'. Augustine was interviewed so many times that she began to sound like a writer: 'She had such a sweet voice that it made you want to bend down and pick up all the words that she said.' Never would she forget the terrible scene (seven years after she left the doctor's household), when Madame had taken the poison: 'It was so much sadder than it is in the story!'

In a bizarre reversal, the chemist, Jouanne Jr, who had recognized Ry in Flaubert's novel and who had personal knowledge of the poisoning, became a living facsimile of Flaubert's freethinking, cliché-spouting chemist, M. Homais. His advertisements and prospectuses for his philanthropic institution and his patent remedy for lameness in livestock, his devotion to the progressive new Emperor Napoléon, his promotion of the Crevon valley as the Switzerland of Normandy – all this might have come straight from the novelist's research files. Instead of the father serving as a model for the character, the character served as a model for the son.

❊

The Delamares' daughter, Alice-Delphine, married a Rouen chemist in the village of Blainville in 1860. The couple had only one child. Lucie Lefebvre, born in 1861, was the last direct descendant of Eugène and Delphine Delamare. As an adult, she was never allowed to forget it.

In 1931, a journalist tracked her down to 27, Rue Stanislas-Girardin in Rouen, two streets from the Musée Flaubert, which had opened in 1923. Mlle Lefebvre lived alone and had never married. She had tried to lead a simple, quiet life, but after the death of her parents, there had come the great surge of interest in 'the real Madame Bovary', and she had been pestered by scribblers and gossips and literary tourists.

The journalist who visited her in 1931 must have been courteous and reassuring. The old woman begged him not to write about her until she was dead, and thanked him for his promise – which she considered a great favour – by sending him a copy of her family tree. When the journalist published it in 1954, thirteen years after Lucie's death, he added the names of the fictional characters to their alleged models.

The shame and fear of exposure which the journalist saw in the tearful eyes of Lucie Lefebvre belonged to the extended legacy of Gustave Flaubert as much as the rebranding and Bovarization of Ry. Under the moralizing empire of Napoléon III, the author of *Madame Bovary: moeurs de province* had been prosecuted for 'insulting public and religious morality and decency'. The son of Dr Achille Flaubert had been successfully defended by Jules Senard, but naturally, the novel remained on the Catholic Index of Proscribed Books. Lucie's grandmother was the heroine of an obscene publication, and her own life had been 'tarnished', she told the journalist: 'She had never felt at ease, there had been so many whisperings all around her . . .'

Private life, which the *Journal de Rouen* in 1840 had associated with selfish insularity, had become a fragile retreat from a widening world. Nothing now would occur independently of history. An individual could be picked out of the mass, and it would be as though the walls of her home had been demolished – which is what happened to Lucie Lefebvre's quartier along with half of Rouen in 1944 when Allied bombings left the gutted cathedral looking down over a flaming sea of rubble.

For the granddaughter of Delphine-Emma Delamare-Bovary, that life of intrusive phantom realities had started early. What Flaubert had taken to be a true story was itself a work of fiction – a tale told by a country doctor to his mother to explain how he had lost that wife of whom she disapproved and who had made him so unhappy.

12

Miss Howard's Gift to France

The historical fate of the Englishwoman who was the Empress-in-waiting of France for four years is a lesson for peddlers of fake news. Ignore the naysayers; never give up; posterity will believe you.

The most polite sources, rehashing earlier reports and therefore not really 'sources' at all, describe her as a 'courtesan' and 'adventuress'. A recent history with good credentials states that she was the daughter of a Brighton publican and that, despite her lucrative 'charms', she probably never had much money of her own: no doubt she was simply 'a channel for secret donors'. Other accounts have her serving behind a bar or selling oysters in the streets of London while her father plied a murky trade as a boatman on the Thames. Almost none of this is true.

Propagandists and enemies of Napoléon III have left us a selection of racy factoids from which a butler's-eye-view biography could be pieced together. The landlord's daughter hooked herself a champion jockey by the name of Jem, became ridiculously rich, then netted a famous Frenchman when he was down and out in London, and ended up with her own palace not far from Marie-Antoinette's Petit Trianon. Yet still she wasn't happy.

In France, she was known as 'Miss Howard' – pronounced to rhyme with 'boulevard', the 'h' and the 'd' being silent.

> HARYETT, Elizabeth Ann [known as Lizzie Howard] (bap. 1823?, d. 1865): courtesan . . . like most of her kind, of obscure origins . . . By 1840 she was among the most sought-after whores in London.
> (*Dictionary of National Biography*, 2004)

This Victorianly hoity-toity entry – apart from the hurtful and inaccurate 'whore' – is based on four books, none of them entirely reliable. They include a study of Victorian pornography and a compendium of tittle-tattle published under the *nom de plume* 'Le Petit Homme Rouge'. The Little Red Man was the impish bringer of bad news who appeared on critical occasions in the Tuileries Palace over a period of three hundred years to warn of the imminent demise of a regime – not quite a full-time job but fairly regular employment all the same.

The dignity of history demands a seemly awareness of its underside and a contrasting respect for the men who controlled or perverted the destiny of nations. Courtesans are known to have driven their besotted slaves to acts of desperation – a daring theft, a murder, a leaking of state secrets, a *coup d'état*. They belong to the cast of minor characters, which includes adventuresses, assassins and little red men, who seem bent on making a mockery of history.

In the opinion of the distinguished Victorian historian A. W. Kinglake, it was quite possible for one man to belong to both categories – jester and man of destiny. That 'venturer of the December night', Louis-Napoléon Bonaparte, was the individual he had in mind – one of that 'small knot of middle-aged men who, in the winter of 1851, were pushing their fortunes in Paris'. In London, where Kinglake knew him personally, the nephew of Napoleon I was forever 'contriving scenic effects and surprises in which he himself was always to be the hero'. Despite 'the seeming poverty of his intellect' and 'his blank wooden looks', he charmed, befriended and, when destiny demanded it, betrayed.

It would be an insult to Kinglake's objectivity to point out that, while tutoring her in history, he became infatuated with 'Miss Howard' and that she found those 'blank wooden looks' eminently worthy of her kind attentions.

BONAPARTE, Louis-Napoléon (b. Paris, 1808; d. Chislehurst, 1873): adventurer, gigolo and convict; Emperor of the French.

The assertions of a published historian not only have to be verified, they must also *look* like the truth. Here, the son of Napoleon's brother Louis and of Joséphine's daughter by her first marriage presents a tricky conundrum. If his deeds are accurately described, the account will inevitably sound like fake news put about by his detractors.

Growing up in Switzerland on his mother's estate by the shores of Lake Constance, Louis-Napoléon was a slim footnote in his uncle's epic: the merest abridgement of the tale would have erased him. He was like a figment of someone else's dream, destined for greatness but starring in a play which had yet to be written.

His personal attributes were not those a serious writer would have chosen for a hero. He looked good on a horse, but his legs were too short and when he dismounted they retained their bandy conformation. His eyelids drooped and he had glassy eyes so that no one could tell what, or whether, he was thinking. His nose was more psittacine than aquiline: Victor Hugo likened him to 'a sleeping parrot'. By a cruel irony, he had a slight German accent, pronouncing '*république*' as '*ripiblique*'. His desire to do good – a trait he had been told he shared with his uncle – was genuine and appealing, but the concomitant of his sympathy for the suffering masses was a sensibility so acute that, in later life, his English doctors found it almost impossible to catheterize him.

Strasbourg, 1836

Louis-Napoléon's first performance on the stage of History was announced by the Strasbourg–Paris telegraph. The despatch arrived at the transmitting station on the roof of the Louvre late on 31 October 1836:

> This morning, at about six o'clock, Louis-Napoléon . . . hav gai d
> th conf ce of artillery colonel Vaudrey, passed through the streets
> of Strasbourg with a section of . . .

This much got through to Paris when the fog rolled down from the Vosges. King Louis-Philippe and his ministers had to wait until ten o'clock the following morning to read the sequel, when the mail coach (the only service that was allowed to put its horses to a gallop) squeezed through the congested streets around the Louvre and pulled into the courtyard of the General Post Office in the Rue Jean-Jacques-Rousseau:

> . . . its regiment to cries of Vive Napoléon! They presented them-
> selves at the barracks occupied by soldiers of the 46th regiment to
> incite them to revolt. . . . Thanks to the loyalty and sincere devotion

of our troops that imprudent young man was arrested along with his accomplice.

He had, in fact, eight accomplices, plus the regiment which had been subverted by its Bonapartist commander, Colonel Vaudrey. The Young Pretender, now aged twenty-eight, had prepared the ground by sending copies of his *Manuel d'artillerie* to every artillery regiment in France. It was a stunningly detailed work of scholarship with tables showing the speed of certain rivers, the specific weight of twenty-three species of wood, the correct temperature and type of water to be given to horses, and so on. Nothing had been forgotten, yet something seemed to be missing. It was the work of a military man whose weapons of choice were the paper knife, the steel pen and the blotting pad.

A street map of Strasbourg would have been useful. He was hampered not just by his determination to avoid bloodshed but mainly by his decision to advance on the quarters of the 46th Regiment along the corridor-like courtyard which separated the ramparts from the barracks. In that tight space, only the laughable device of arranging his men in order of height, with the tallest at the rear, would have shown the strength of his invasion force.

Crammed together like passengers in a mail coach, attackers and defenders were unable to point a musket or swing a sabre, even if they had wanted to injure their comrades. The whole operation was so improbable that the false report which spread through the writhing mass had the distinct ring of truth. 'Soldiers, you are being made fools of! . . . He's an imposter,' shouted the colonel of the regiment. Another officer took up the cry: 'That's not the nephew of Napoleon: that's Colonel Vaudrey's nephew. I'd know him anywhere.'

The London *Times* drew the moral four days later:

> Playing at kings and queens and princes is a pastime harmless enough within the precincts of a private dwelling. But it is preposterous to find these . . . persons presuming on their purely adventitious distinction for the insane purpose of agitating France and Europe. They may be assured France laughs at them.

Words never applied to Napoleon Bonaparte peppered the editorials of the European papers: 'ridiculous', 'impish', 'hare-brained' and 'silly'. Because Bonapartism was still a potent political force, the errant nephew was left at liberty on condition that he deport himself to the United States. He spent ten weeks in New York City, then sailed back to Europe.

In October 1838, having inherited a fortune from his mother, he was living in London at 17 Carlton House Terrace overlooking The Mall and St James's Park. He went riding in Hyde Park, joined several clubs and hunts, wintered in Leamington Spa and undertook a fact-finding tour of industrial England. In Birmingham, he attended the Hippodrome and was acclaimed as the principal attraction. At the British Museum, he was given his own private room. There and in his study at Carlton House Terrace, he sat for hours every day, plotting the future history of France.

Boulogne-sur-mer, 1840

It is unclear from the subsequent interviews at what point the employees of the Commercial Steam Navigation Company became aware of the extraordinary nature of the excursion. *The City of Edinburgh*, a wooden paddle-steamer which normally ran a cross-Channel Rye–Boulogne service, had been chartered on 6 July 1840 by Mr E. Rapallo, 'a member, it is believed, of the Stock Exchange', at a cost of £400, 'to go on a party of pleasure wheresoever he and his friends should desire'.

Mr Rapallo lacked neither money nor friends. The steamer left St Katharine's Docks on 5 August with about fifty passengers of various nationalities, along with twelve beautiful horses, two brand-new carriages, some servants and grooms and a cook. The luggage included twenty-four cases of wine, spirits, beer, ginger ale and soda water, and an eagle in a cage. Several more passengers boarded at Deptford and then at Blackwall.

Captain Crowe was under the impression that the destination was Hamburg, but at Gravesend, he was 'informed that the gentlemen had changed their minds and had resolved to visit the coast of France'. Still more passengers were taken on at Margate, and if the captain had remained unsuspicious until then, he would have realized, as he headed out into the Channel with a pistol at his head, that he had entered someone else's version of reality. The excursionists were coming out from below dressed as soldiers of the French 40th Regiment, currently stationed at Calais.

Shortly after midnight, *The City of Edinburgh* anchored a mile off the small fishing port of Wimereux. Two hours and four boat trips later, the landing party set off along the coast road to the south. Above them to the east rose the Colonne de la Grande Armée, marking the site of the enormous campground where Napoleon's army had prepared to invade England in 1803–5.

The intention was to win over the garrison at Boulogne, then to march to the column, which the Prince would ascend by the internal stairs with a morsel of meat attached to his hat. The eagle would fly to the top of the column to show that, while the remains of the Emperor were returning from St Helena, a living Napoléon had 'come from exile with nothing but love and reconciliation in his heart'.

In Boulogne, a few people were up early enough to witness the dawn invasion. One of those early birds happened to be a correspondent of *The Times*:

> I had a peep at Louis Napoléon. Poor devil! he looked awfully excited. His followers are fine-looking fellows. They appear to be the dare-devils of all nations – Poles, French, Swiss, and, some say, English. The latter statement I do not believe.

There was a scuffle with soldiers of the local garrison. Louis-Napoléon produced his pistol and, to his great distress, accidentally shot one of the soldiers in the lower jaw. The invasion party then went running through the streets, shouting, 'Vive l'Empereur!' The *sous-préfet* of Boulogne tried to stop them but was poked in the chest by a gilt eagle affixed to an imperial banner. Meanwhile, the servants were knocking on doors, distributing printed proclamations and scattering money to the generally sympathetic crowd of onlookers.

Finding the gates of the upper town locked, they proceeded in a spirit of heroic desperation to the Colonne de la Grande Armée, which was closed to the public. The Prince declared himself willing to die at the foot of his uncle's monument but was persuaded to make for the cliffs instead. Down at the harbour, the lifeboat of the Humane Society was boarded by so many fugitives that it sank. The Prince himself, who was a good swimmer, was found clinging to a buoy about one-eighth of a mile from the shore. From there, he was taken to the prison in the Château de Boulogne and, at his request, reunited with his eagle.

At the Conciergerie in Paris, out of respect for his name, he was tried by the court of the Chambre des Pairs, which sentenced him to life imprisonment. He did not defend himself but expressed remorse for injuring a French soldier, pleaded for his fellow conspirators and re-asserted his mission – to restore the empire and the sovereignty of the people. He was led away under cover of darkness to the fortress of Ham in a treeless marsh in central Picardy. The eagle was not allowed to join him: it was tied to the bars of the Boulogne abattoir, somehow freed itself, was recaptured by a restaurateur from Arras and later sold to a coal merchant, who had it stuffed.

For the next six years, the nephew of Napoleon studied at what he stoutly called the University of Ham. He conducted chemical and electrical experiments, created a flower-bed for botanical research on a parapet of the fortress, began a biography of Charlemagne, wrote a pamphlet on sugar-beet and another pamphlet on founding a company to cut a Pacific–Atlantic canal across Nicaragua. He re-designed Paris using a street map and coloured pencils. Eventually, he was allowed to ride a small horse around the courtyard. He had the companionship of two of his fellow conspirators, a young beagle called Ham and, when she came for his laundry, the twenty-year-old daughter of a local weaver, by whom he had two children. As he wrote in the preface to his treatise, *Extinction du paupérisme*, published while he was in prison, 'it is natural in misfortune to think of those who suffer':

> Crushing men as well as raw material in its cogs and wheels, industry depopulates the countryside and gathers the population in airless spaces, enfeebling minds as well as bodies, and then casting them out into the street when it can find no further use for them. . . .
>
> Society is not a fictitious being: it is a body of flesh and blood which can thrive only if all its component parts are in a perfect state of health.

Ham–London, 1846

On 27 May 1846, the Member of Parliament and *bon viveur* the third Earl of Malmesbury, was driving home down Jermyn Street in Piccadilly when a shabby-looking man dashed across the road and stopped his horse. The sight was so shockingly unexpected that when the Earl mentioned his encounter that evening to an *attaché* from the French embassy, the man 'dropped the lady who was on his arm and made but one jump out of the room. . . . I never saw a man look more frightened.'

A few nights later, after visits to the barber and the tailor, the prisoner of Ham was sitting, as he had often done before, in the salon of Lady Blessington at Gore House (on the site of the Royal Albert Hall). His immediate audience was a tall and thrillingly intelligent Englishwoman of twenty-two who had been introduced to him as Miss Harriet Howard. In his latest incarnation as an escaped convict, the thirty-eight-year-old nephew of Napoleon Bonaparte struck her as a sensitive man with a frank and honest face. Perhaps it had something to do with the loss of his facial hair.

As he had just explained in an article for the newspapers, he had shaved off his beard and moustaches and completed his disguise with a workman's smock, a clay pipe, a pair of clogs and a large plank of wood, previously in use as a bookshelf. On the morning in question, repairs were being carried out to the fort, but most of the workers were busy enjoying the drink generously provided by the Prince. The Prince himself was seriously indisposed, as anyone could tell from the lump in his bed and the convincingly human smell produced by his latest chemical experiment.

He was passing the first guard with the plank on his shoulder to hide his face when the clay pipe fell from his mouth. In an act of *sang-froid* of which he was especially proud, he stopped to pick up the pieces. Then he walked through the gate and began to clump along the road to Saint-Quentin. A carriage was coming out of the village of Ham. He dumped his bookshelf in a ditch and leapt into the carriage, which was driven by his valet.

At Saint-Quentin, he took the post-chaise to Valenciennes, showed his borrowed Belgian passport to the station official and, after acting inconspicuous for seventy-five minutes on the north-bound platform, took the 4.15 Paris train to Brussels, where he changed for the port of Ostend. At about that time, the governor of Ham discovered the deception. But Ham was a good fifteen miles from the nearest telegraph station . . .

Next day, the Prince was in London, arresting the Earl of Malmesbury's horse, and writing to the Prime Minister and the Foreign

Secretary to apprise them of his return and his peaceful intentions. The Foreign Secretary, Lord Aberdeen, no doubt mindful of the spinning weather-cock of French politics, notified him that 'his sojourn could be disagreeable neither to Her Majesty the Queen, nor to Her government'.

London–Paris, 1846–8

Louis-Napoléon's new acquaintance, the handsome and witty Miss Howard, had her own dramatic tale to tell. The daughter of a Brighton shoemaker called Haryett, she had run away from home at the age of fifteen, impelled by a passion for horses and the stage. The man of the moment, Jem Mason, who had just won the first Grand National steeplechase on a horse called Lottery, offered – or was persuaded – to set her up in comfortable rooms at 277 Oxford Street near Grosvenor Square (in the old numbering).

Using Jem's brougham and his numerous contacts in clubs, casinos and dressing rooms, 'Miss Elizabeth (or Harriet) Howard', the raven-haired 'orphan' with the face of a Greek statue, secured some minor roles in the sort of West End plays in which, according to one theatre critic, 'the exhibition of a boarding-school for young ladies is the main object of attraction'. She made her debut in *The Love Chase* at the Haymarket in January 1840, and despite stage fright and excruciatingly bad acting, 'at the fall of the curtain Miss Howard was tumultuously called for'.

To the self-liberated convict, this winsome yet majestic young woman was an angelic apparition whose beauty was enhanced by her humble origins, her interestingly louche circumstances and by one radiant quality which proved that she was destined to play a leading role in his rise to power.

Miss Howard had left her jockey for a wealthy middle-aged officer in the Life Guards. Major Francis Mountjoy Martyn was in need of a hostess to entertain his friends at Rockingham House (23 Circus Road, near Lord's Cricket Ground). Since his wife was unable to bear children, he also required a son to whom he could leave his considerable fortune.

It was while playing the fleeting role of Third Apparition in *Macbeth* at Drury Lane in the spring of 1842 that she discovered she was pregnant.

Be lion-mettled, proud, and take no care
Who chafes, who frets, or where conspirers are:
Macbeth shall never vanquished be until
Great Birnam wood to high Dunsinane hill
Shall come against him

For appearances' sake, the baby boy was baptized with her father's surname and registered as her brother. The grateful Major honoured their agreement by endowing her with a fortune which, even in a melodrama, would have strained belief.

Apart from all her other attractions, Miss Howard, at the age of twenty-two, was immensely rich. She owned houses and building plots in the heart of the City of London, in Mark Lane and Gracechurch Street, among some of the most expensive real estate in the British Empire. Thanks to the Major, she had the services of a skilful and devoted financier, Nathaniel Strode, to administer her portfolio, the value of which was increasing by the day.

Louis-Napoléon was living on bankers' loans, the remnants of his inheritance and the proceeds of the auction at Christie's of his Napoleonic heirlooms. He lost two thousand pounds to a swindler and was supporting the two children he had fathered at Ham, as well as some of his disgraced confederates. Before the Boulogne fiasco, the annual income from his inheritance had been a paltry hundred and twenty thousand francs. Much of that inheritance had now evaporated.

Harriet and Louis-Napoléon became lovers and business partners overnight. A promissory note took the place of a marriage contract, and she agreed to fund his *coup d'état* habit. Her first known contribution to the restoration of the French Empire was a tidy one million francs, the loan being secured by one of his few remaining assets, an estate at Civitanova. Similar sums would follow.

In early February 1847, Louis-Napoléon moved to rooms at 3 King Street, off St James's Square. The earliest surviving blue plaque in London records his tenancy: 'Napoleon III. Lived Here, 1848' (*sic*). A year later, Harriet moved to 9 Berkeley Street, a short walk from King Street. It was then that she studied history under the leering eye of A. W. Kinglake and engaged other tutors to fill the gaps in her education. She was preparing for life as a consort while caring for her own son and the two children brought over from Ham.

A young Frenchman, the son-in-law of a former Prefect of Police, saw them both together and wondered how anyone could imagine that this convict, ladies' man and mountebank was the future of France:

> Picture to yourself an ugly and vulgar little man with big moustaches and piggy eyes . . . living openly – and scandalizing the prudish English – with a fifteenth-rate actress called Miss Howard, who is actually very beautiful.

❉

It was in central London, the green room of the French political drama since the days of the Revolution, that Louis-Napoléon Bonaparte finally became a serious contender for a lead role in French history. The revolution of February 1848 revealed to him the formula for conducting a successful coup. Previously untested in any major European nation, the magical device was called universal suffrage. All that was needed now was enough money to pay for a nationwide advertising campaign.*

On 27 February, he travelled overnight to Paris. The cobbles which had been used in the barricades were still being re-laid. The head of the provisional government, Alphonse de Lamartine, told him that now was not the time and reminded him that the *loi d'exil*, which prohibited Bonapartes from entering France, was still in force. He sailed back to Folkestone on 2 March, a few hours before the deposed King Louis-Philippe disembarked at Newhaven as 'Mr Smith'. His visit had been a calling card rather than an attempted coup: it indicated his willingness to serve and, as he pointed out in letters to the French and British papers, it proved that he had learned to conduct himself with moderation.

Harriet Howard's money was put to work. Napoleon Bonaparte had dreamt of conquering England by occupying London and dealing 'a deathblow' to the nation's 'funds, credit and commerce'. Now, a fortune based on the London property market was to pay for all the

---

* On 5 March 1848, the provisional government of the Second Republic instituted 'direct and universal suffrage' (excluding women, the army, the clergy and men under the age of twenty-one). The electorate increased from about two million (since 1831) to almost ten million. In the United Kingdom, the right to vote was extended to men of twenty-one and over and to women over thirty (with property qualifications) seventy years later in 1918.

paraphernalia of a modern election campaign: posters and propaganda sheets; vignettes of himself and his uncle; little flags, medals and imperial eagles to pin to hats and lapels. Commercial travellers would be employed to hand out free copies of his works and to purchase advertorials in local newspapers.

In England, he had successfully exhibited himself as an affable celebrity-about-town, 'a balloon-man', in Kinglake's testy expression, 'who had twice had a fall from the skies, and was still in some measure alive'. In France, where the turmoil of revolution had created a yearning for a new Napoleon, the balloon-man's shimmering canopy soared over towns and fields from the plains of Picardy to the canyons of the Mediterranean Alps. Peasants in the Ardennes recognized in that floating fantasy a fabulously rich friend of the poor. The young Hippolyte Taine heard them saying, 'He'll pay for the government and there'll be no more taxes!'

To radicals whose comrades died on the barricades in June when the working-class factions were crushed, the man who had languished in the dungeons of a heartless monarch was a bona fide socialist: without his moustaches, he had easily passed for a worker. To the clergy, he would be the saviour of the Church. To republicans, he would stand up to Britain and Russia and realize the Napoleonic dream of a United States of Europe with Paris as its capital. To monarchists, he was an airy vessel who could easily be steered and, when the time came, deflated.

On 4 June, in elections to the National Assembly, Louis-Napoléon topped the poll in four *départements*: Charente-Inférieure, Corse, Seine and Yonne. (Multiple candidacies were permitted.) The Assembly voted to repeal the *loi d'exil*. When new elections were held in mid-September, he was elected in the same four *départements* and in the Moselle. On 24 September, he arrived at the Gare du Nord, which was only two years old and already overcrowded. He checked into a hotel on the Place Vendôme and, two days later, made his first appearance at the Assembly. Victor Hugo saw him take his seat: 'He seems lost for words rather than taciturn.' He was said to be 'very poor', and in the following weeks, it was noticed that 'he always came to collect his pay as a representative on the very day it came due'.

✿

That autumn, a friend of Harriet Howard known only as 'B. B.' told Captain Denis Bingham (who recorded it in his diary) that he had met 'Mrs Howard' 'in a railway-carriage going down to Dover':

> She had with her all the ready money she could scrape together, and her jewels, and was on her way to Paris to lay her wealth at the feet of her lover, who, as they say in France, had the devil by the tail, and was surrounded by adventurers as needy as himself.

If Harriet had 'scraped together' all her 'ready money', it would have taken up most of the guard's van. The kind-hearted courtesan donating her savings to her hero and immolating her respectability on the altar of his ego is such a deeply imprinted image that it takes the brute force of financial fact to erase it. Captain Bingham, who had first-hand knowledge of the workings of the Second Empire, was convinced, as were several other people, both British and French, that Louis-Napoléon 'would in all probability never have recovered the Imperial crown but for the aid of a member of the English *demi-monde*'.

The private papers that were found in the Tuileries Palace in 1871 after the fall of the Second Empire show colossal repayments made to Miss Harriet Howard. The earliest receipt, dated 25 March 1853, is for the one million francs secured on his property at Civitanova, but this was probably not the first loan. In July 1851, after his election as President of the National Assembly, he was being sued by a money-lender in the Palais-Royal. The word at the Paris Bourse was that his English mistress had gambled away his money on the stock exchange and was threatening to leave him if he refused to cough up. This seemed to confirm the rumour that he was planning to prorogue the Assembly and conduct a coup in order to pay off his mistress's debts with public funds.

The summary of repayments up to 1 January 1855 shows a total of 5,449,000 francs. Ten monthly instalments of 58,000 francs were still outstanding. Her trustee, Nathaniel Strode, received a further 900,000 francs between 1862 and 1864. The grand total was therefore close to seven million francs. In 1847, when Miss Howard first allowed her lover a glimpse of her treasure chest, seven million francs was equivalent to fourteen per cent of the annual budget of the city of Paris (which was already undergoing massive redevelopment), five per cent of the monetary reserves of the Banque de France and more than half a per cent of total government spending.

The returns on her amorous investment were spectacular. In the presidential election of December 1848, he won almost seventy-five per cent of the vote and came first in all but four *départements* (two in Brittany, two in Provence). For the rural three-quarters of the population, 'Napoléon' and 'Bonaparte' were the only recognizable names on the ballot. Apparently, it made sense to vote for a living legend. Local dignitaries who feared the scourge of the 'red' urban proletariat were only too happy to guide the hands of illiterate voters.

✣   ✣   ✣

As the President's mistress and chief financial backer, Harriet Howard was a permanent member as well as the hostess of his small inner circle. They met at her house at 14 Rue du Cirque. Across the road in the grounds of the Élysée Palace was a garden door which allowed him to slip away into his domestic haven. There, he could smoke his endless cigarettes, enjoy the company of Harriet and the dog Ham, and plot the shortest route to absolute power. Later, a tunnel was dug which eventually became an underground garage, used by President François Hollande when visiting his mistress at 20 Rue du Cirque.

In 2014, the President of France was more roundly criticized for riding to his trysts on a scooter than for conducting an affair with an actress. In 1849, Louis-Napoléon's ministers, whom he was about to sack *en bloc*, disapproved of his illicit *ménage* with an Englishwoman, mainly for political reasons. They presumed that the three children living at the Rue du Cirque were the offspring of Harriet and Louis-Napoléon. Her own child, Martin, always believed himself to be a Bonaparte.

That year, the artist Henriette Cappelaere was commissioned to paint two portraits: one of his mistress in an imperial pose (identified only as 'Madame H . . .') and one of his doe-eyed beagle with the fortress of Ham and a stormy sky in the background. When 'Madame H . . .' appeared in person at the first review of troops after the election, the feeling among *boulevardiers* was that 'Louis-Napoléon isn't such a dimwit after all: he's brought back from London the most beautiful horse and the most beautiful woman!'

In the provinces (which meant anywhere beyond the outer

boulevards of Paris), Miss Howard was a public relations liability, as the boldest of his ministers warned him before they were sacked. During an official visit to the Loire Valley for the opening of the Saumur section of the Tours–Nantes railway, the devoutly Protestant civil servant whose house at Tours was requisitioned for the President's mistress complained that his virtuous abode had been 'sullied' by the 'unmarriageable' companion of the head of state. In rage and at great length, Louis-Napoléon wrote to his chief minister, Odilon Barrot:

> Along with the cares of government, I have the misfortune to possess in my own country, from which I was absent for so long, neither close friends nor childhood attachments nor relations to provide me with the comforts of family life . . . I believe I may be forgiven an affection which harms no one and which I do not seek to publish.
> . . . Pray inform the gentleman that I keenly regret that a person of such pure devotion and elevated character should have found herself in a house in which hypocritical virtue reigns under the mask of religion.

Harriet Howard is usually dismissed from histories of France at this point, just when the President's advisors were beginning to worry about her political influence and ambitions. The British ambassador, Lord Normanby, recognized her as a key player in the new administration. Overlooking her social status, he made sure that she and his wife became friends. The Minister of Foreign Affairs, Alexis de Tocqueville, suspected the Englishwoman of interfering in international affairs and believed that she had persuaded the President to send the French fleet to the Dardanelles to join the British fleet in support of Turkey against Russia.

General Fleury, who had known the Prince in London and spent many an evening at the Rue du Cirque, found her 'noble and gracious', 'generous and disinterested in her devotion', 'incomparably beautiful' and 'intelligent'. Her imagination, 'like that of all her countrywomen' was 'inflammable':

> We considered her influence dangerous from every point of view . . . Had she been French and therefore more conversant with our language, and if, instead of being a courtesan, she had occupied even

the smallest place in polite society, she might have reigned as a new Pompadour.*

✿

On 2 December 1851, the double anniversary of the Battle of Austerlitz and Napoleon I's coronation, Louis-Napoléon fulfilled his pledge to save the nation from politicians. The National Assembly was occupied by troops, and the people of Paris were informed by posters that a socialist coup had been narrowly averted. Much of the work had already been done – newspapers censored, councils purged of 'reds', army officers bribed, martial law imposed and a nationwide network of spies established. Sixteen members of the Assembly were arrested; others, including Victor Hugo, were forced to flee the country. Twenty-seven thousand arrests were made; almost ten thousand 'traitors' were transported to penal colonies in Algeria and Cayenne.

Eighteen days later, the people of France were asked if they would like to delegate to the President 'the powers required to establish a constitution' – a question paraphrased by Victor Hugo in *Napoléon le Petit* as, 'Do the French people mean to place themselves, bound hand and foot, at the discretion of M. Louis Bonaparte?' Seven and a half million people (ninety-two per cent of votes cast) voted 'yes'. One and a half million abstained.

Though the advent of another dictator called Napoléon was scarcely good news in London, there was some relief that the dangerous experiment of universal suffrage had produced a strong leader instead of anarchy. It was reassuring to note that a population could be coaxed into near-unanimity.

At this pivotal moment in European politics, the Brighton shoe-maker's daughter became an intermediary between the two great powers. The Earl of Malmesbury, who was Foreign Minister in 1852, has been credited with expediting British recognition of the French Empire, yet his private secretary found it impossible to obtain an audience with Louis-Napoléon. The subject of discussion was to be the embarrassing clan of exiled agitators led by Victor Hugo who were broadcasting to the world from the island of Jersey, disseminating

---

* The Marquise de Pompadour was the 'official mistress' and unofficial chief minister of Louis XV. The Élysée Palace was originally her residence.

their counter-propaganda in hay bales, sardine tins, false-bottom trunks and paper balloons. After being put off repeatedly, the private secretary finally found the key to the presidential door:

> I called on Mrs. Howard, toadied and flattered her, stating that I was in a great hurry to get back to London, and only wanted to see his Highness the President for two minutes. She sent off an orderly at once, and before night I received an invitation from Louis Napoleon to accompany him out shooting, to say my say at 5.30, and dine afterwards.

This was in September 1852. In November, a month before Louis-Napoléon Bonaparte was proclaimed Emperor Napoléon III,* Harriet Howard was still the principal source of reliable intelligence: Malmesbury, whose spies had shown him several plans for a French invasion of England, was informed that 'the army is peaceably inclined, and that Mrs. Howard, the President's mistress, declares he has no wish for war.'

❊

Like an expanding government department, Harriet had begun to acquire other properties in the vicinity of the presidential palace: a detached house at 26, Avenue des Champs-Élysées and then a large vacant plot at the other end of the avenue, a stone's throw from the Arc de l'Étoile. The plot is currently occupied by a Zola-esque symbol of the exorbitant Second Empire: Cartier jewellery at the front, Valege lingerie at the rear and a money-changer in between.

She may still have been hoping to become Empress Harriet or Elizabeth, but her lover, whose casual affairs she had treated as peccadilloes, had become more infatuated than usual with a twenty-three-year-old Spanish noblewoman. As a French-speaking, God-fearing virgin, Eugénie de Montijo was deemed a suitable match by his ministers. To Harriet, the girl's virginity was a serious threat: her resistance would have him rushing straight up the aisle. She told an English friend in a letter, 'If the fair Infanta has not yielded, marry he may . . .'.

---

* Napoléon II would have been the son of Napoleon I and Empress Marie-Louise, twice proclaimed Emperor by his father, in 1814 and 1815, but never crowned. He died at Schönbrunn Palace in Vienna in 1832.

Louis-Napoléon was trying to secure Harriet's agreement to a separation, without quite desiring it himself. She wrote to her friend in June 1852 from the house in the Rue du Cirque:

> His Majesty was here last night, offering to pay me off: yes, an earldom in my own right, a castle, and a decent French husband into the bargain . . . Oh! the pity of it all! I could put up with a dose of laudanum . . . The lord almighty spent two hours arguing with me . . . Later, he fell asleep on the crimson sofa and snored while I wept.

The 'castle', which she bought with her own money for 575,000 francs as 'Mrs Elizabeth Alderton' (her mother's maiden name), was the crumbling and verminous Château de Beauregard, built in the seventeenth century on the hill to the north of Versailles. She decided to have it rebuilt in the monumentally frivolous style soon to be called 'Second Empire'. A further 955,000 francs were spent on enlarging and landscaping the domain, which occupied nearly five hundred acres between Versailles and Saint-Cloud. The perimeter wall alone cost 800,000 francs.

While the *château* and the estate were being transformed, she installed herself in the ground-floor apartments of the royal palace of Saint-Cloud. There was no longer any doubt that he would marry Eugénie, but as a co-founder of the Second Empire, she demanded the title 'Comtesse Elizabeth Haryett de Beauregard'. The noble Beauregard families who already existed in various parts of France were outraged, but she refused to accept a different name: 'Beauregard suits me, Beauregard sounds just like me. I shall be Lady Fairlook or no lady at all!'

The Emperor married Eugénie de Montijo on 29 January 1853. They spent their honeymoon at a small country house in the Parc de Saint-Cloud because Harriet had failed to move out of the palace in time. The thousands of spies employed by the new regime had already spawned a mirror network of double agents, which is how Harriet's only surviving letter to her lover, written on the occasion of his wedding, came to be published a few weeks later on Jersey by an exiled republican militant:

> Sire, I am leaving. I would readily have offered myself up for polit-
> ical necessity, but I really cannot forgive you for sacrificing me to

a whim. I am taking your children with me and, like Joséphine, your star.

I ask only for a final meeting so that I can bid you an eternal farewell. You will not refuse me this, I hope.

There were to be many farewells, some of them lasting several weeks. He would escape from official functions for an hour or two and return to the party or the ball in a much better mood. To the relief of his wife and ministers, Miss Howard finally gave up in May 1854, when, for the sake of her son, she married a young Cornishman to whom she had been introduced by Lord Normanby. The marriage was announced in *The Gentleman's Magazine* with sarcastic inverted commas and a reminder that, even in marriage, she would never be respectable:

> Lately, at St James's Piccadilly, Clarence Trelawny, esq. . . . to 'The Countess of Beauregard' (better known to fame as Miss Howard).

❋   ❋   ❋

In May 1855, the house in the Rue du Cirque was swarming with manufacturers from all the major industrial towns of Britain. They had come to register with the exhibition agents who had rented the premises a few hundred yards from the sparkling new Palais de l'Industrie between the Seine and the Champs-Élysées.

France and Britain were fighting as allies in the Crimea. The Paris Exposition Universelle was an emulation of the London Great Exhibition of 1851 and a celebration of the flourishing Empire and its commitment to peaceful international trade. Napoléon III and Empress Eugénie had visited England in April; a return visit by Queen Victoria in August was to seal the rapprochement.

At Boulogne on the morning of 18 August, he rode up to the Colonne de la Grande Armée to see the royal yacht steaming into the harbour where, fifteen years before, he had clung half-naked to a buoy. He kissed the Queen on both cheeks and rode beside her carriage to the station. It was dark before they reached the palace of Saint-Cloud through cheering crowds, past window displays devoted to Victoria and Albert, and Union Jacks flapping from balconies, 'amidst the roar of cannon, bands & drums'.

Victoria was thrilled by Paris, 'so white and bright' in the smoke-less air, 'and everything so different to England, – so gay & lively'. The Emperor himself drove them everywhere – 'along the Beautiful Boulevarts, the Rue de Rivoli – quite new, the Emperor having cleared away many streets, making the new ones quite magnificent.' They crossed the Place de la Concorde, 'where poor Louis XVI, Marie-Antoinette, & so many others were guillotined.' On the Pont au Change, he pointed to the Conciergerie and said, *'Voilà où j'étais en prison'*.

She was made 'quite jealous' by the grand and spacious palaces and the dainty comforts of their home-from-home at Saint-Cloud. At Versailles, she saw Eugénie 'looking really like a Fairy Queen'. Most of all, she was impressed by the gentleness and charm of her host: 'Isn't it odd?' she remarked to the Foreign Secretary, 'the Emperor remembers every frock he has ever seen me in!'

On Friday 24 August, in the church of Les Invalides, they gazed down on the porphyry sarcophagus of Napoleon Bonaparte. Since the tomb was still unfinished, the coffin containing his remains was displayed in a side-chapel:

> and there I stood on the arm of Napoleon IIIrd, before the coffin of his Uncle, our bitterest foe! I, the granddaughter of that King [George III], who hated Napoleon most & who most vigorously opposed him, & this very nephew, bearing his name, now my nearest & dearest ally!! 'God save the Queen' was being played on the organ at the time of this solemn event. Strange & wonderful indeed!

✳

Second Empire France belongs to the physical history of the modern world. Materially, much of it still exists: there are very few Second Empire ruins and even fewer archaeological digs. The photographed faces stare back at us, unsurprised by the process of being captured on a collodion plate in less than a second. We know what Harriet Howard saw through her lorgnette when she examined the Emperor for the last time at the Théâtre Italien in 1865 ('dirty white hair and face, watery, swollen eyes, and arched back'). There are people alive today who heard first-hand accounts of life in the Second Empire or who received from a grandparent a coin bearing the laurel-wreathed profile of Napoléon III which was handed to them by a waiter or a shopkeeper in imperial Paris.

The last mystical vapours of the Middle Ages should by now have disappeared – the bewitching power of rumour, profound ignorance of the past, belief in a paradise on earth. Warring provincial kingdoms, barbarians from beyond the Channel and the Rhine, crusades at home and abroad were now the stuff of storybooks and national heritage. Purges in the Second Empire were political rather than religious.

The top hats, crinolines and horse traffic have gone, but the sights on Victoria's tour of Paris are instantly familiar. Around the Élysée and the Rue du Cirque, the 'very well-kept' troops admired by the Queen have been replaced by sauntering heavies on the look-out for terrorists and sexy female tourists, and laden with the kind of weaponry which the French army would discover only near the end of Napoléon III's reign in the form of the rapid-fire *mitrailleuse*, which they mistakenly used in close-combat training. Native Parisians and immigrants were already being shifted out of the city and packed like gunpowder into shanty towns and dismal suburbs.

The new world order proclaimed by Louis-Napoléon in his pre-Empire speech at Bordeaux in October 1852 was acquiring an appearance of solidity: cooperative nation states would replace coercive empires and there would be such a weighty balance of power in Europe that, as Chancellor Bismarck and several political observers warned, any attempt to upset that balance would be 'a catastrophe for humanity'.

The dreams and legends which had once defined the mindscape of each semi-autonomous *pays* had been concentrated and weaponized by universal suffrage. Democracy had installed a dictatorship. Almost the entire adult population of France had chosen to place a 'man of destiny' in the Élysée. Peasants, factory workers, shopkeepers and bourgeois, as well as Queen Victoria, were entranced by what she called his 'power of fascination':

> That he is a very extraordinary man, with great qualities there can be no doubt – I might almost say a mysterious man. He is evidently possessed of indomitable courage, unflinching firmness of purpose, self-reliance, perseverance, and great secrecy; to this should be added,

a great reliance on what he calls his <u>Star</u>, and a belief in omens and incidents as connected with his future destiny, which is almost romantic.

✿

The realization of his dream had spawned a world of phantom realities. The 'Star', whose progenitor lay in Les Invalides among the mutilated veterans of his campaigns, had decreed the establishment of a police state in which people would be free to vote for their enslavement. Louis-Napoléon's later attempts to liberalize the Empire and to create the semblance of a parliament to match the Londonesque parks and 'squares' (pronounced *skwar*) of the new Paris, were frustrated by the ministers he appointed himself.

Harriet Howard had been his consort in the period when, according to the Bordeaux speech, 'the Empire [meant] peace'. Her successor, Eugénie, deflowered and disillusioned by a man who always smelled of other women, turned out to be a hawkish advisor. She championed the persistent foreign policy based on trivial perceived insults which had prevailed since the invasion of Algiers in 1830. The disastrous attempt to establish a Catholic empire in Mexico (1861–7) was one of her pet projects.

Without Eugénie, he might have 'resisted the bellicose notions which had taken hold of a section of the population' (as he put it in a book attributed to his secretary in 1872: *Les Forces militaires de la France en 1870*). He would not, he thought, have launched a suicidally inept attack on Prussia in July 1870. And when the Prussian counter-offensive turned into a war of conquest, he would not have obeyed the Empress-Regent's instruction to remain on the battlefield 'for honour's sake'. When the news reached Paris that the Emperor and over one hundred thousand French soldiers had surrendered at Sedan on 2 September, she was so enraged by his betrayal of the legend that she shouted at her ministers:

> A Napoléon does not capitulate . . . Why did he not get himself killed? Why did he not have himself buried under the walls of Sedan?

He had, in fact, exposed himself to enemy fire with precisely that in mind.

After the Prussian siege of Paris (September 1870 to January

1871), one third of France was under enemy occupation, Alsace and much of Lorraine had been annexed 'in perpetuity', and the capital had suffered three weeks of heavy shelling. (Fig. 11.) After its recapture by French troops from the revolutionary Commune (March to May 1871), Paris was a panorama of devastation. The Tuileries Palace was a husk; the Champs-Élysées resembled a building site after an earthquake. The demolition of the palace left a vast, vacant space in front of the Louvre.

The Tuileries Palace has yet to be rebuilt, but practically all the city which Louis-Napoléon had planned in prison at Ham was restored well in time for the 1889 Exposition Universelle and the first centenary of the Revolution. Thanks to sandblasting – a technique invented six weeks after the Battle of Sedan – many Second Empire buildings now look almost as they did when they were a few days old. With its boulevards and avenues, balconied limestone apartment blocks and manicured squares, much of central Paris is still a monument to the Second Empire.

The Avenue Victoria kept its name, but since France was once again a republic – the third, declared two days after the Battle of Sedan – 'Napoléon' was expunged from the street map of Paris, and, of course, there was never a Boulevard, Rue or even Impasse Harriet Howard. It was not until January 1987 that Napoléon III made a discreet return to the city. Perhaps at the behest of President Mitterrand, the taxi-congested strip of cobbles in front of the Gare du Nord was renamed 'Place Napoléon III'. An appropriately ambiguous space, this open-air waiting room is not quite a street and hardly a square. Its transient population is predominantly British and French. There are pickpockets and swindlers, railway workers and refugees, business people and tourists checking their passports and luggage, smoking the first cigarette on arrival or the last before leaving.

✻   ✻   ✻

It took a while to find the grave of Harriet Howard in the semi-urbanized village of Le Chesnay, twenty minutes by bike from Versailles. The 'Plan du cimetière' is wordless and the recumbent gravestone self-effacing: 'Comtesse de Beauregard / née Howard / 1822–1864.' It was carved more than forty years after her death to accompany the gravestone of her son, Martin, who squandered his huge inheritance. 'Howard' was not her maiden name and both dates are incorrect. She was born in 1823 and died of cancer at the Château de Beauregard in 1865.

Higher up the hill, in a tidy zone of social housing, just off the unremarkable Avenue Miss Howard, stands a rare example of a Second Empire ruin. The facade of the central bay, shored up by a brutal concrete buttress, is the only remnant of the Château de Beauregard. It was occupied by the Prussians in 1870 and the Nazis during the Occupation. The cherubs on the pediment have been used for target practice; the stone clock face in the centre has been smashed. This unnamed relic is flanked by a Franprix mini-supermarket and a Presse-Tabac; the forecourt is an obstacle course of cars and bollards. The whole incongruous assemblage could be a conceptual memorial to the rummage heap of recent history to which a historian is supposed to bring some kind of order or, failing that, signage.

Louis-Napoléon, who never visited the Château de Beauregard, was happier writing history than making it. The archaeological explorations which he funded lavishly as though they were military campaigns are one of his greatest gifts to France. He sent a colonel and an admiral to London to interview boatmen and to spy out the place where Caesar might have crossed the Thames. He identified Boulogne as the bridgehead for Caesar's raids on Britannia, and he confirmed Hautmont near Maubeuge as the scene of the Roman victory against the hedge-building Nervii: 'To this very day, the fields by the Sambre are divided by hedges of a similar kind.'

He knew that the shapes and substance of the land itself are as important to historians as they are to tacticians. With its meticulous maps and diagrams, his two-volume *Histoire de Jules César* is a major contribution to the discovery of ancient Gaul, though some French scholars are still reluctant to accept any information that came from the pen of a dictator. It can be hard to ignore the imperial dream which permeates the material detail like mist evaporating over a battlefield. In the illusory weight of the layered past, he saw the work of Providence. In his view, there was no such thing as a 'spontaneous event': Caesar, Charlemagne, Napoleon and his nephew had been the messianic envoys of Providence – men who had come from beyond the Rhine and the Alps to save humanity from barbarism and oblivion.

Much of his life had been spent as a foreigner. When he entered France, it had been as an interloper and aggressor. He refused to believe that the people of France had directed their own destiny. He and the other outsiders had 'shown them the way'. He quoted approvingly his uncle's surprising assertion in his precis of *The Gallic War* that 'the principal cause of the weakness of the Gauls was their lack of any national or even provincial spirit'.

It is ironic, then, that his greatest archaeological exploit was the excavation of Alise-Sainte-Reine in Burgundy. He plausibly equated the place with Alesia, the *oppidum* where a third of a million warriors had come together under their elected leader Vercingetorix to drive the Romans out of Gaul. No such demonstration of pan-Gallic national spirit would ever be seen again, not even in the nationalistic Second Empire.

If France was a creation of Providence, only a chosen one could fully comprehend it: with such an autocratic assumption, it was inevitable that parts of that fractious and multifarious land would remain obscure to its last emperor, as they would to later 'providential' leaders who, like General de Gaulle, were inspired by 'a certain idea of France' and who chose to believe that 'France is only truly herself when she occupies the leading rank'.

✣

When Bismarck released him from captivity, the former Napoléon III, suffering more than ever from chronic urological disorders, made his way to England to join the Empress and their son. They rented a house called Camden Place in the pretty village of Chislehurst, nine miles south-east of central London. Camden Place was Miss Howard's final, unintended gift to France: the house belonged to her trustee, Nathaniel Strode, who had decorated it 'in the French style' and was glad to be of assistance to his client's erstwhile lover and beneficiary. Strode himself continued to live at Camden Place until the Empress let it be known that his presence was *embarrassant*.

He walked to the village and the common, witnessed the enigmatic ritual of cricket, developed his idea for a European League of Nations, and perfected his inventions – an economical coal-stove for the poor and a new type of mortar. Despite the South Eastern Railway company's offer of a special train, he sometimes travelled up to London on the regular service: 'More than once he was noticed sitting unobtrusively on a seat at Chislehurst station, or standing almost unobserved on the platform at Charing Cross.'

Private detectives hired by the French government lived in the windmill on the other side of the cricket ground. They kept a daily list of visitors to Camden Place. Every morning over breakfast, Louis-Napoléon would read a copy of the list provided by a double agent. Mysterious confabulations were held in his study, and it was a sign of the extreme sensitivity of the project that Eugénie had no inkling that anything was afoot.

The plan was to take a villa on the Isle of Wight, ostensibly for his health. He and his confederates would go sailing in the Solent and along the coast. On a day when conditions were favourable, they would prolong the excursion to Ostend, from where they would travel down through Germany and Switzerland to the property of his cousin Jérôme on the shores of Lake Geneva. Jérôme's steam yacht would ferry them over to Thonon on the French side of the lake. Then General Bourbaki, the military governor of Lyon, would ensure that the next stage of the journey would be as smooth and triumphant as Napoleon's return from Elba.

Flattering intelligence from loyalists in France suggested that an imperial coup was a realistic possibility. The only snag was the past and future Emperor's state of health. It was an essential part of the plan that he should ride at the head of his troops rather than enter Paris as an invalid in a carriage.

He was in constant pain from gout, bladder stones and the effects of an enlarged prostate. On 11 December 1872, to test his readiness, he saddled up and set off for Woolwich in the fog, but the pain was too great. For years, he had refused treatment; now he was forced to submit to the cruel comforts of modern medical science and that final outrage to the maker of history – death, which arrived shortly after the second operation.

He was buried at St Mary's in Chislehurst on 15 January 1873. Fifteen years later, his remains and those of their son were transferred to Farnborough in Hampshire, where Eugénie had founded an abbey to serve as an imperial mausoleum. The granite sarcophagi were donated by Queen Victoria.

The previous ruler of France, King Louis-Philippe, had been

buried fifteen miles away at Weybridge, but his body was returned to France in 1876 and reburied at Dreux. Louis-Napoléon is still at Farnborough, and, because he has yet to fall into historical and political irrelevance, will stay there for the foreseeable future, two short train rides and a boat trip away from the country of his childhood dreams.

PART THREE

The Third, Fourth and Fifth Republics

13

Savage Coast

The only outsider known to have seen the great trading city of Corbilo, which stood somewhere on the River Loire, was the merchant-explorer Pytheas of Marseille in the fourth century BC. Two centuries later, while trying to discover the routes by which British tin and gold reached the Mediterranean, the Roman general Scipio Aemilianus met some natives of Corbilo in southern Gaul. None of them would divulge its location, and when Julius Caesar made similar enquiries in the first century BC, he found the Atlantic tribes equally taciturn. The name itself appeared to have fallen out of use.

Since most long-distance trade routes were maritime, the likeliest location of Corbilo is the mouth of the Loire. The untranslatable name may be Celtic, or it may belong to a language of the prehistoric peoples who migrated to the Atlantic coast when the Celts arrived from the east with their superior technology. A trace of it seems to survive in the name of a half-submerged island, the Banc de Bilho, which was attached to the mainland until deep dredging began in 1940. It can be spotted just upstream of the last bridge over the Loire – the soaring parabola of the Pont Saint-Nazaire, which is more dangerous to cross on a bicycle than a mountain pass in a storm.

Six hundred miles from its source in a rarely visited region that was unmapped until the mid-eighteenth century, the longest river in France broadens into an oceanic estuary. The views of grey and distant shores and the swirling, labyrinthine currents narrow the gap between the present and the irretrievable past. An endless cycle of change reconfigures the river at its mouth. Charts of the estuary were revised, on average, once every ten years and sometimes annually. In 1756, lighthouses were built to guide ocean-going vessels bound for Nantes through the tenuous channel between the sandbars. The trick was to align the slowly blinking eye of the Tour d'Aiguillon on the rocky headland of the Pointe d'Ève with the white beam of the Tour du Commerce which stands, incongruously inland, among suburban houses like a blind old mariner in a retirement home.

✣

When the estuary lighthouses were built, several stretches of the granite coast to north and south, between Quiberon Bay and the Île d'Oléron, were already known as the Côte Sauvage because of the lurking shoals, the lack of safe anchorage and the crashing of the breakers scouring out the caverns and the coves. The name acquired another connotation in the 1840s, when a new breed of traveller felt the centrifugal force which still flings an unusually large proportion of the population to the edges of the continent with buckets and fishing nets. They came from the cities of western France, from Nantes, Tours and Poitiers and even from Paris, to take the waters and to breathe the life-preserving air. For those ruddy-cheeked pioneers, one of the attractions of the Atlantic seaboard was the novelty of an older society with its ruined citadels, quaint customs and antiquated forms of speech. The friendly savages of the fishing ports of Pornic, Saint-Gilles and Les Sables-d'Olonne served as guides and messengers, waiters and chambermaids, and their native costumes provided a picturesque foreground for the wild Romantic seascape.

The bathers were soon followed by another sub-species of *Homo modernus*. This type of visitor was drawn by the dolmens, menhirs and 'Druidic' circles of Brittany and the Vendée. They, too, came in search of an undiscovered France, but their interest was scientific rather than hygienic. In those crude stone monuments and in the weather-tanned faces of the Armorican peasants they saw evidence of an ancient civilization which, once the data had been collected and the analytical tools refined, might prove that the history of France stretched far back in time beyond the days of Julius Caesar and Pytheas of Marseille.

Some of those scholar-tourists were as excited as children when they first see the ocean and its outlandish creatures. The brittle remains of the dolmen builders themselves were sometimes unearthed by quarrymen and geologists. A handful of educated men, their senses sharpened by the highbrow science of anthropology, had become convinced that ancestors of those proto-Frenchmen had survived the ebb and flow of populations, and that fossils of flesh and blood were perpetuating their primitive race in the nineteenth century. Some went so far as to believe that this hitherto unrecognized cohabitation of distinct anthropic species presented a threat to modern civilization. Of course, it never occurred to them that they themselves might be part of the threat.

⁂ ⁂ ⁂

A moonlit mountain covered in trees materialized above the dark line of a coast. The eight surviving crew members of the three-masted merchantman the *Saint-Paul*, and her captain, Emmanuel Pinard, had spent twelve days crossing the Coral Sea in a longboat from the Louisiade Archipelago (named after Louis XV) on the eastern edge of New Guinea. They had caught exhausted seabirds, which they baked in the sun, chewed briny flour and slaked their thirst with their own urine.

Thirteen months before, on 6 August 1857, the *Saint-Paul* had left Marseille with a cargo of wine for Bombay. From Bombay, they had sailed to Hong Kong to recruit three hundred and seventeen 'coolies' for the gold fields of New South Wales. (Fig. 12.) Slavery had been abolished in the French colonies in 1848, but cheap labour was still a lucrative business for a tight-fisted captain.

On such a long voyage, a calm sea was more worrying than a storm. The wind had dropped and the already stingy rations were halved. With a crew of twenty sailors and more than three hundred mutinous migrant workers, Captain Pinard had decided to risk a shortcut by steering a speculative course through the fog-shrouded reefs of the Louisiade Archipelago. He had run aground and wrecked his ship on a tidal island within paddling distance of the Île de Rossel, whose black inhabitants were reputed to be among 'the most inhospitable in the world'. A landing party had gone ashore. Several of them had been captured and were presumed eaten.

While fleeing from the cannibals, the fourteen-year-old *mousse* (the cabin boy) had been hit on the head by a basalt stone and staggered back to the shore just in time to see the longboat pulling away without him. He managed to splash out to the boat and clambered aboard. Captain Pinard's report to the ship's owners is understandably mendacious in several respects. He claimed to have told the coolies of his plan: they were to stay on the wreck while he and the crew set off in the longboat in search of help. According to the cabin boy, he left them to their grisly fate while they were fast asleep. A later rescue mission found only one of them alive.

Captain Pinard was nearly two hundred miles and two degrees of latitude out in his calculations. Only much later would he learn that the moonlit mountain stood between Cape Direction and Night Island on the Cape York Peninsula of north-eastern Australia. The men went ashore to look for water. Still suffering from his head wound, the cabin boy struggled to keep up. He found the men at a parched waterhole. They refused to share what little water they had been able to scoop up. Overwhelmed by exhaustion, he slept for several hours, and when he returned to the beach, he saw nothing but the wide horizon.

The cabin boy's name was Narcisse Pelletier. He had left Saint-Gilles in the Vendée at the age of twelve, lured by sailors' tales of strange lands and wonderful adventures. Though some attempt had been made to regulate the training of young seamen, a *mousse* was often little more than a dogsbody and a whipping boy. One of his principal functions seemed to be to satisfy the savage instincts of the adult sailors. On his last ship, the *Reine des Mers* of Bordeaux, the second mate had stabbed him with a knife, but even that had not deterred him.

Seeing a white creature of indeterminate sex, three naked women ran away screaming into the thorny woods. After a while, two men armed with bows and arrows cautiously approached. The boy offered them his white handkerchief and his tin cup. In exchange, they gave him water, nuts and coconuts which had been brought by the sea. One of the men, Maademan, having no family of his own, instantly adopted him as his son. For the next seventeen years, the Narcisse Pelletier whose name was recorded in files at the Ministère de la Marine ('shipwrecked and disappeared', 'believed dead') and in anxious letters from a shoemaker and his wife in Saint-Gilles, ceased to exist. He had been replaced by Amglo, the only white-skinned member of the Uutaalnganu people.

A day would be spent fishing with spears and the next day repairing canoes, making arrows or visiting the hunting tribes who lived in the hills. The Uutaalnganu were nomadic but never travelled more than six or seven miles from the centre of their domain. He acquired the habits and tastes of his family and lost all conscious memory of his mother tongue. He learned to use the serrated edges of shells to cut down trees and gouge them into ten-man boats. Shards of glass and the iron hoops of shattered barrels occasionally washed up on the shore and then a canoe could be made in days rather than months. He was rarely ill. Infections might have been caused by the incisions that were supposed to cure pains, but there were none of the dubious refinements of the popular medicine practised on the Vendée coast, where magnetism and spiritism, horoscopes and witches were trusted more than qualified physicians.

His nose and right ear were pierced so that he could wear the cylindrical shell and the hollow stick of wood. Decorative raised scars on his chest and arm were produced with pieces of broken bottle. After several years, his father, Maademan, married him to a little girl from a neighbouring tribe who found his white skin frightening and repulsive. The girl was far too young to conceive: the marriage, like his scars, was a token of his naturalization. Sometimes, he saw in his mind's eye a harbour and a church with a steeple, but they belonged to such a dead and distant time that he was unable to distinguish them from a dream.

✻

When Narcisse Pelletier was born at Saint-Gilles on New Year's Day 1844, the town was adapting to its new identity. In the mirror held up to it by the outside world, it could see itself, not as the main settlement of a *pays* that could be crossed on foot in half a day, but as one of the up-and-coming resorts on the Côte Sauvage which, apart from fish and crustaceans, had several other, previously unmarketed commodities to offer: sand, waves, air, wild flowers, ozone, local characters and 'views'.

In August 1845, the front page of the Paris magazine *L'Illustration, journal universel*, was devoted to the 'Iowa Indians' who were being displayed by the American painter George Catlin in a travelling 'museum'. The magazine also turned its spotlight on internal exoticism. There was a drawing of two Vendée peasants – a woman with a white apron and a conical hat, and a milkmaid with a yoke and an interest-ingly short skirt which left her calves and ankles entirely naked. These two natives of the Savage Coast were being examined by visitors from a distant metropolis – a lady in a voluminous fur mantle which looked like a bear costume without the head, and a gentleman wrapped in a winding sheet like a Bedouin with an ignited cylinder of tobacco leaves protruding from his mouth.

The first sea-bathing establishment at Saint-Gilles was opened in July 1863. By then, these French but foreign incomers were a common sight. They poked their noses into every corner of the natives' lives, even into their boats and cottages. They pestered fishermen and pilots, asking the names of fish and fishing boats and about the heathen practice of luring ships onto the rocks with lanterns tied to the horns of oxen to simulate a boat bobbing about on the ocean. They sought out curious superstitions regarding the shape of clouds and the colour of the sea, and were delighted to learn, for example, that the wife of a fisherman would secretly attach a lizard's tail to her husband's trou-sers to bring him luck.

The most intrepid visitors ventured into the hinterland to hear first-hand tales of the swamp-dwelling tribe of Colliberts or *huttiers* who used vaulting poles to move about their wetlands and slept on floating beds. The Colliberts had a surprisingly erudite explanation of their ethnic and cultural difference: many centuries ago, when the Roman legions were ravaging Gaul, they had retreated into the Poitevin marshes and thereby retained their independence. Something about this artful adaptation to a difficult environment struck the tourists as 'primitive'.

✳

The sub-group of scientific visitors first came to the attention of the Vendéens at about this time because of their odd behaviour. Men in top hats and black frock coats were seen staring at local people and making unflattering sketches of them on a drawing pad. Staring at people was not considered particularly rude – except by the British, for whom the land beyond the English Channel was a frontier terri-tory of the Dark Continent itself. The Reverend George Musgrave, in his *Cautions for the First Tour* (1863), advised anyone staying in a hotel with a female relative to carry a small hammer, a box of tacks and some paper with which to cover up the holes that would have been bored in the communicating door by a bug-eyed Frenchman.

The scientific voyeurs were unusual in two respects: they stared at men as well as women, and instead of feasting their eyes on shapely waists and well-turned ankles, they showed a strange predilection for ugliness and deformity. One of the most active of these connoisseurs of human eyesores was Anatole Roujou, a geologist and naturalist born in 1841, whose most respectable claim to scholarly fame is his role in introducing the work of Charles Darwin to his sceptical compatriots. Darwin himself wrote to thank Roujou for his support in 1872:

> It has delighted me to find that you are not shocked at the belief that man is a modified and wonderfully improved descendant of some lower animal-form.

Roujou's favourite hunting grounds were remote and rocky parts of central Auvergne (he taught at the University of Clermont-Ferrand), the mountains and borderlands of Brittany, and the slum-suburbs of Paris. In such wild districts, specimens could be found of a rare sub-type of human, perhaps dating back to the Quaternary Period – thick-lipped, with dark or yellowish skin, limited intelligence and 'an occasionally sinister expression'. Some of those semi-troglodytic 'residues of very primitive inferior races' still practised flint-knapping. Other scholars likened this 'Australoid' type to the aborigines of the Cape York peninsula and the neighbouring Melanesian archipelagos. They carried clubs of holly sticks with which, when drunk, they beat each other senseless, and their children fled at the sight of a stranger. Roujou's pencil sketches of degenerate types, which he insisted were 'not exaggerated', supported his colleagues' analysis.

Professor Roujou himself was not an outstanding example of a superior species. An official assessment by his University called him 'scruffy and insolvent'. Applied to a studio photograph of Roujou held in the Cantal departmental archives, his own anthropometric criteria would suggest a cephalic index of 76.9, which would place him at the very bottom of the dolichocephalic or 'long-headed' group of humans. The lower part of the face has a simian bulge, and the expression is both sly and confused, which could be an inherited trait or a result of thinking beyond his intellectual means.

He was one of several eminent thinkers who had realized that, instead of undertaking a long and perilous voyage, a student of human evolution could find a lifetime's supply of specimens on his doorstep. The field guide published by the anatomist Paul Broca, a founding member of the Paris Anthropological Society (1865; revised edition, 1879), urged the collecting of brains as well as heads. 'The head should be opened as soon as possible, because in warm countries, the brain will begin to soften within twenty-four hours.'

Fresh brains were harder to come by in France. However, tourism was beginning to provide anthropology with useful data. Postcards depicted the people of Saint-Gilles and Les Sables-d'Olonne in salacious or comical poses, performing daily tasks among the seaweed-strewn boulders in their Sunday best. Some of the photographs were captioned with amusing samples of their barbaric speech. As Dr Broca explained,

> Travellers [in France] are often able to procure from photographers in the towns they visit collections of photographs depicting the natives. These photographs, having a picturesque purpose, are not as valuable as those produced according to our instructions. They are, nonetheless, interesting ethnographic documents and should be collected and preserved.

❉   ❉   ❉

The *John Bell*, a British lugger employed in the pearling industry, had been lying at anchor off Night Island. Trade with the 'savages' of Cape York Peninsula had recently picked up – knives, biscuits and tobacco were the most coveted items – and it had become safer for ships plying the Great Barrier Reef to replenish their supplies of fresh water. As an extra precaution, on 12 April 1875, when a boat was sent ashore from the *John Bell* to the wooded islet where some naked savages had been seen, it was manned by a crew of black Australians.

They returned with astonishing news: one of the savages was a white man. The master of the *John Bell* sent the boat back to the islet with some rare and dazzling items of cheap merchandise and a promise that more treasures would be made available if the white savage came back to the ship alone. Amglo suspected that the black sailors were cannibals, but he was ordered by his father to go and fetch the promised gifts.

In this devious fashion, the white man of the Uutaalnganu, who had twice been left to die by a French captain, became a prisoner of the British. He stood on the deck of the *John Bell*, a revolver pointed at his head, and watched in terror as the ship made sail. To prevent a rescue attempt, muskets were fired over the heads of his family, who were pleading for his return.

✻

As the ship sailed on to the settlement of Somerset on the Torres Strait, Amglo understood that he was not about to be eaten. He felt the anguish of separation and, for the first time in seventeen years, the discomfort of clothes. According to an eyewitness, he 'crouched about here and there' like a 'savage'. For a man who was experiencing extreme disorientation, he was incredibly resilient. He showed the sailors his scars and his distended earlobe with evident pride, but his identity was a complete mystery until he heard the word 'Frenchman' and nodded his head. He still had no exact sense of the time elapsed and simply believed himself to be very old.

At Somerset, he was entrusted to the resident magistrate. Since he was determined to escape back to his family, he had to be tethered. He spent most of each day 'perched on the rail fence of a paddock like a bird . . . casting quick, eager, suspicious glances around him on every side'.

On the steamer to Sydney, Amglo was befriended by a thirty-four-year-old lieutenant of the Royal Engineers who had studied in Paris. John Ottley – the only man who never called him a savage – began to tease out and nourish the few shrivelled remnants of French which floated to the surface of Amglo's mind. He also had the foresight to record about a hundred words of the Uutaalnganu language before Amglo 'professed to have forgotten the remainder'. His eyesight 'was little short of marvellous': he correctly identified some minute specks on a distant island as the canoes of a certain enemy tribe when 'we were quite unable, even with our most powerful glasses, to make out what these specks really were'. More remarkable still, the concept of private property was quite alien to him:

> At times I found him a serious nuisance owing to the fact that . . .
> he seemed to think that we ought to hold things in common. Coming
> down to my cabin he used calmly to annex anything that struck his

fancy and shewed his annoyance when I took things from him and locked them up in my trunks.

Every year, the French consul in Sydney had received a letter from a poor family in the Vendée asking for news of their son. It occurred to the Consul, as he tried to interview the white savage, that there might be a connection. He retrieved the latest letter and read out the name of the lost cabin boy and the name of his village. Then he watched as Pelletier suffered the agony of a slow rebirth. He sat with his head in his hands, tortured by missing memories, cupping a hand to his ear, shielding his eyes to stare into an invisible distance, beckoning with his arms to urge the memory closer.

On the eighth day, he found that he could trace letters on paper. The words were almost unintelligible. They would turn out to be the first draft of an account which the French consul would send to the castaway's parents in Saint-Gilles, who mistook it at first for a cruel joke:

naci narcise peletier desaingile

*le capitane lecete du sa*vage *gesus gacet aborte*

duloranx genesupa pale parle fanrce gesuparle

sovage genesue nore genesue vivant vele vouvle

papa done abore*

After more than a month in Sydney, he was put on a warship bound for Nouméa, the capital and only town of the French penal colony of New Caledonia. From Nouméa, on 11 July 1875, he wrote again, in a more recognizable script, to announce his departure for France on a troopship of the French Navy:

Mon cher Père et ma chère mère et maisfrère, Je vous ècrie une autre foi. Je vous enbarsse De tout Mon coeur. ci vous ête vivant.†

---

* Retranscribed from the original. To judge by the orthography of his later letters, the sense would be: 'Narcisse Pelletier of Saint-Gilles. The captain left me with the savages. I looked for dirty water to drink. I cannot speak French, I can speak Savage. I am not dead, I am alive. They did not want to give me water to drink.'

† Translation: 'My dear father and my dear mother and my brother. I am writing to you again. I kiss you with all my heart, if you are alive.'

It was a shame that Lieutenant Ottley could not have sailed with him. He had observed that confused but gifted mind as it refocused on the past. The captive was impressively good-tempered despite his abduction, but it was clear to Ottley that this man of two worlds would not be returning to civilization on its own terms:

> On one point I was quite satisfied – namely that it would be an exceedingly evil day for his old captain, should he ever have the misfortune to come across the cabin boy he had deserted so many years before. Pelletier never disguised his intention of killing him if he ever had the chance.

❋

The timing could not have been better. A Frenchman was arriving from a blank space on the map with intimate knowledge of an undocumented tribe just when the science of anthropology was celebrating its status as a full-blown academic discipline. A Museum of Ethnography had been founded by Dr Ernest Hamy, noted for his observation that the heads of Australians were significantly similar to Neanderthal skulls. The museum would be housed in the new Palais du Trocadéro by the Seine. Its displays of native dress, including several examples from the Côte Sauvage, would be one of the main attractions of the 1878 Exposition Universelle.

The man from cultural outer space might have been a flesh-and-blood creation of his fellow Vendéen, Jules Verne (born in Nantes on an island in the Loire), whose bestselling tales of castaways and colonial adventures advertised the romance and entertainment value of primitive races. While Amglo / Pelletier was crossing the Atlantic, the popular press was announcing the imminent return of 'the French Robinson Crusoe' or 'the Australian Savage': 'Attention all novelists, dramatists and lecturers!' trumpeted the reporter of *L'Univers illustré*. 'Setting aside the matter of skin colour, he gives every appearance of being an authentic savage' and 'will probably soon be on view in Paris.'

In the seventeen years of Pelletier's absence, anthropologists had collected enough data to develop the general theories that would be the pride of the new discipline. Physical examinations of army conscripts enabled them to divide the country, along a rough diagonal from Brittany to the southern Alps, into two distinct zones:

predominantly short, dark people below the line, and a taller, lighter-skinned population above. This was rich soil for conflicting explanations of human diversity. The puniness of recruits from infertile, hilly regions might be caused by environment, by historical incursions of superior races, by evolutionary inferiority or by the atavistic recurrence of primitive traits.

Like any field of salaried intellectual endeavour, anthropology was riven by controversies. Theories were wielded like axes, to gain territory or destroy a rival, and the social mobility which had allowed men such as Anatole Roujou to rise in the academic hierarchy was like the grating of bone against bone. The proliferation of types and sub-types demonstrated the discipline's sophistication. Only a generation before, likening clod-hopping peasants to cavemen or apes had been a journalistic joke. Now, social class was just one of the criteria by which the population could be divided up – race, skin colour, physiology, educational attainment, language and political tendency.

It was an early sign of the great flowering of theorized prejudice that would curse the twentieth century. A colonialist view of humanity, turned against the tribes of France itself, had a powerful appeal for men who had lived through the Prussian invasion and the monstrous anarchy of the Paris Commune. It had seemed quite fitting that those low-browed, prognathous-jawed socialists who had done more than the Prussian army to destroy civilization had been deported to New Caledonia, the land of anthropophagous living fossils.

Arthur de Gobineau, author of the viciously racist *Essai sur l'inégalité des races humaines* (1853–5), blamed the Franco-Prussian catastrophe and its aftermath on the pollution of the white, aristocratic 'Aryan' race by interbreeding with 'Gallo-Roman plebs'. Privately, he was haunted by the possibility that, because his mother's family had lived in the colony of Saint-Domingue (Haiti), his own blood might be tainted.

Anthropologists are only human. Roujou himself had lost his family home at Choisy-le-Roi during the troubles of 1870–71, and his insulting caricatures of 'inferior types' were an expression of his fear and hatred of the lower orders. He had the additional unhappiness of knowing that his superiors at the University of Clermont-Ferrand deemed him socially backward: 'Compromised by his bad wife, he is an embarrassment to the staff and faculty of the University.' 'A bad teacher but original scholar . . . It would be in our interests to remove him.' After 1888, Roujou was permanently 'on leave for reasons of health'. For his admirers, it was a sad irony that, in 1904, when his racist theories were finding an enthusiastic new army of supporters, he was found dead, 'clutching in his stiffened hand an uncompleted manuscript'.

※

After one hundred and twenty-nine days at sea, on 13 December 1875 Pelletier's ship sailed into the forest of masts beneath the cliffs which guard the port of Toulon. He saw the prison from which all the remaining convicted Communards had been shipped to Nouméa the year before and the mangled skeleton of the ironclad which had exploded in the harbour that October. One of his brothers was waiting at the dockyard to accompany him to Paris, where he was to meet various officials. The railway journey from Marseille to Paris now took only seventeen hours.

If his memories were clear enough for a comparison, he might have been struck by the now ubiquitous crinolines sweeping the pavements and the dragonfly figures spinning the pedals of velocipedes, but the shock was social rather than scenic. In his last letter home, sent from Rio de Janeiro, he had described the unpleasantness of conversing with the ship's officers: 'They have no pity for me, for the suffering I've had since I stayed with those savages, but I don't get on badly with the sailors.' His only friend had been a young French conscript returning from Nouméa to Saint-Gilles who had known M. and Mme Pelletier and assured him that his parents were alive and well.

Under a clear and chilly Parisian sky, he and his brother visited the offices of the *Constitutionnel* newspaper near the Palais-Royal. 'The cabin boy from Saint-Gilles' told his story to a reporter, including his double abandonment by the French captain (which should have led – but didn't – to a judicial investigation): 'He is a strong lad, rather stocky, but well built. His long sojourn with the savages has in no way harmed his intelligence.'

The story was printed on page three along with items of equal interest – the fireproofing of the Mont-de-Piété (the municipal pawn-broker) in the Marais, the refurbishment of the abattoirs at La Villette, the official visit of an important Tunisian mufti 'who wears a superb oriental costume', and the trial run of a silent, condensed-air omnibus which covered the distance between Porte Maillot and Place de l'Étoile in only seven minutes.

Five days later, Pelletier was admitted to the Hôpital Beaujon and examined for a painful ulcer on his thigh. 'Pricked with a bone by the savages of Australia' was the diagnosis. It was then that he was finally seen by a certified anthropologist, Arthur Chervin, an expert on craniometry and the mechanics of stammering. It would be another five years before Dr Chervin's brief verbal observations were reported in the Anthropological Society's journal. They were published at the end of an article 'On a Frenchman named Narcisse Pelletier who lost his language among the Australians'. The subject of the article was the tenuous and 'artificial' nature of acquired 'civilization':

> I must say that this individual made a rather pathetic impression on me: he was very suspicious, sly and probably mendacious. Moreover, he was not very intelligent, though he spoke French perfectly well.

The 'individual' from the other side of the world was left in the waiting room of scholarship with his scars and distended earlobe. The discipline had already refined its specializations to a point where entire areas of knowledge could be discarded as uninteresting. Perhaps this reflected the general lack of political interest in the colonies, or perhaps, as a local reporter suggested in the Nantes newspaper, *L'Union bretonne*, a few months later, it was the depressing conclusion to be drawn from Pelletier's adventure – that 'education leaves such shallow traces in a man's mind' and that there was 'nothing deep-rooted and essential in the fact of being French.

*

The journey from Paris to Saint-Gilles was still quite complicated. The station would not be opened for another six years. After a long day travelling back in time – from railway carriage to stagecoach to local taxi or farmer's cart – anyone might have agreed with Arthur de Gobineau, despite his hysterical conclusions, that

> Paris and the remainder of the territory are separated by an abyss. Another, very different nation begins at the very gates of the capital.

On 2 January 1876, a day after his thirty-second birthday, coming from the east along the Rue du Calvaire towards the steeple of Saint-Gilles, Narcisse and his brother noticed groups of people standing by the roadside. Several carriages had driven out to meet them. His brother went ahead to prepare their mother for the shock of happiness. Though he had not been seen at Saint-Gilles since 1856, Narcisse was recognizable as his mother's son. The door of the house by the harbour was left wide open to the street, and the whole village saw the boy and his parents locked in a joyful embrace. A report written by a local carpenter would be reproduced in the national papers a few days later: 'None of the many friends who were there could bear the sight without shedding torrents of tears.'

A towering pyramidal bonfire had been built. As the sun sank over the ocean, the family were invited to light the pyre. Guns were fired in the air and the local *château* put on a display of fireworks and lanterns. When the fire had died down, the villagers danced in the dark around the glowing embers. 'And this', said the carpenter, 'is how our friend Pelletier was welcomed back to his native land after seventeen years of absence'.

※ ※ ※

Six miles from the port of Saint-Nazaire, the disused lighthouse of the Tour d'Aiguillon can be reached by a narrow cliff path which climbs and plunges along the headland of the Pointe d'Ève. A hundred feet below, small deserted coves appear between the hanging trees. The long shore of the Vendée coast on the other side of the estuary can easily be pictured as a Pacific atoll.

A local woman saw us sitting with our bikes beneath the lighthouse and warned us that if we ventured much farther along the cliff, we would fall to our doom. For some people, a bicycle automatically evokes thoughts of injury and death. In the late nineteenth century, there were fears that velocipedists, by bringing back into use the enormous bottom muscles and elongated arms of our simian ancestors, represented a regression of the species.

The bungalow at the foot of the tower was built for the lighthouse keeper in 1857, when Saint-Nazaire was being developed as the port of departure and arrival for the first transatlantic service between France and Central America. The job of the 'guetteur' or 'garde de signaux' was to maintain the beacon and to communicate by semaphore with the ships negotiating the sandbars. The authorities at the Ministère de la Marine et des Colonies had deemed it appropriate to offer the man who had been lost to civilization for seventeen years a refuge far from human habitation where he might imagine that he was still marooned on the other side of the world.

The lonely lighthouse keeper repetitioned the Ministry and was moved inland to the Tour du Commerce and then, in 1878, to the port itself, where he was employed as a clerk at the harbour office. A retired surgeon from Nantes, Constant Merland, interviewed him at length and published a book – *Dix-sept ans chez les sauvages* – the proceeds of which were intended to provide Pelletier with a small income.

He seems to have reintegrated himself into society quite successfully. He had a friend from Saint-Gilles who sold sail cloth, and, in 1880, he married a local seamstress, Louise Mabileau. He hated to be pointed out as 'the Savage', but was resolutely polite to journalists. The roguish reporter from the *Figaro* who saw him 'dressed like a worker in very clean blue jacket and trousers and wearing a sailor's straw boater' wanted to know if Pelletier had tasted human flesh. He seems to have found the wordless response of the 'ex-savage' disconcerting:

> There is nothing negroid about the lips, and yet they curl up and contract into a strange and characteristic rictus. Pelletier's laugh is no longer quite that of a civilized man . . . There is something abnormal and savage about it.

The conscientious ethnographic account of Pelletier's adventure by Constant Merland was not reviewed in the Anthropological Society's journal until 1911, when it was dismissed as worthless because it had not been written by an anthropologist. The writer of the review, a native of Saint-Gilles who claimed to have witnessed Pelletier's homecoming, suggested that his apparently painless reintegration into his lowly stratum of French society proved that 'the Neolithic mentality is not as far removed as is generally believed from that of most modern peasants in Savoy, Auvergne and Brittany'.

Working as a clerk at the busy harbour office of Saint-Nazaire, Pelletier might have wondered whether he would one day see the name of the man who had stolen half his life on one of the forms which passed across his desk. Captain Emmanuel Pinard had done well out of the East Indies trade in luxury goods and cheap migrant labour. He had retired to a pleasant *quartier* near the docks in Le Havre. He also owned a property in Paris, at 86, Avenue de la Grande-Armée near the Porte Maillot station on the circular Petite Ceinture railway.

For a man with the trained vision of Narcisse Pelletier, it would have been a simple matter to pick out from a crowd the unforgotten face of an old captain, and then the newspapers would have had a story worthy of the front page – a retired master mariner killed by the arrow of an Australian savage in the heart of the imperial capital. But Pinard had died a year and three months after Pelletier's return, and although the question of the cabin boy's abandonment had been raised by the Maritime Prefect of Toulon five days after the arrival of Pelletier's ship in 1875, nothing came of the enquiry. The dossier might yet be reopened if the Ministre des Outre-mer (formerly, Ministre des Colonies) decides to award a posthumous Légion d'Honneur to the cabin boy who revealed to the world an unknown Australian people and then, despite himself, as the captured son of Maademan, provided an unparalleled insight into the tribal ideologies of the French Third Republic.

✻

Pelletier's place of birth is a day's ride from Saint-Nazaire, through the marshy *bocage* where thousands of his great-grandfather's generation were massacred by government troops in the Vendée war of 1793–4. The fishing port of Saint-Gilles now forms a single *commune* with its agricultural neighbour, Croix-de-Vie. There are seafront promenades and a wind-lashed beach which is moderately popular in summer. The seaside shops sell postcards of windsurfers, bathing huts and seagulls, the traditional white cottages and windmills of the Côte Sauvage, and the *paludiers* with their donkeys who still work the salt marshes.

Among the pictures of lotioned bodies basking in the sun, it was impossible to find a postcard of the half-naked man with the piercings and the surgical scars. Saint-Gilles's most famous native lacks the attributes of a marketable historical figure. The two women in charge of the Office de Tourisme were unable to tell me where the Pelletier family had lived: they supposed that it must have been in the old part of Saint-Gilles. But they were keen not to disappoint an inquisitive visitor. As we headed for the door, one of the women almost apologetically proffered what sounded like a coded message: 'Il y a des sardines par terre . . .'

Outside, at intervals of a few hundred feet, groups of sardine silhouettes had been pasted onto the pavement. When the once buoyant fishing and cannery industry declined, the sardine with its colourful collectable tins was chosen to become the prime cultural icon of the Vendée coast. The 'atypical and enriching' sardine itinerary comprises twenty-eight historical information posts in the form of mooring bollards. Narcisse Pelletier has been relegated to an outlying group of four in a new housing development at the antipodes of Saint-Gilles, nearly two miles from the railway station.

The pedestrianized Allée des Histoires Extraordinaires features 'the young cabin boy who spent seventeen years with the savages' (indigenous Australians are clearly not expected to visit), the seventeenth-century sailor from Les Sables-d'Olonne who became a slave of the Pasha of Marrakech, the beached killer whale, and 'the monkey from the sea'.

The 'monkey' was a female chimpanzee preserved, presumably for a zoo, in a barrel of brandy which washed up near Saint-Gilles in 1908. It was the most notable event since Pelletier's homecoming. The corpse, which can still be seen at the Maison du Pêcheur, and the drunken sailors who found it, became a tourist attraction which soon eclipsed the 'white savage', who had died at Saint-Nazaire on 28 September 1894 at the age of fifty.

A fortnight after Pelletier's early death – caused, it was later said, by homesickness or the curse of an aboriginal sorcerer – a Jewish army officer who lived on the Avenue du Trocadéro in Paris was falsely accused of spying for Germany. As the member of a race which was believed by many high-ranking officials and intellectuals to lack the genetic characteristics of the true Frenchman, Alfred Dreyfus, a proud and courageous patriot, was judged on fabricated evidence to be a traitor to the fatherland. He was publicly humiliated and deliberately exposed to violent crowds shouting, 'Death to the Jews!' Jews accounted for less than a quarter of one per cent of the population, but they were multiplied and magnified by Catholic myth, popular prejudice and pseudo-science.

Pending permanent deportation, Dreyfus was incarcerated on the Île de Ré at the southern end of the Côte Sauvage. Then, since the penal colony of New Caledonia was deemed insufficiently hellish, he was transported to the Îles du Salut off the coast of French Guiana. The steamship chartered for the purpose by the French army was the *Ville de Saint-Nazaire*, which Pelletier would have seen many times entering and leaving the mouth of the great river.

Even before he left French waters, Alfred Dreyfus was a long way from the France which seemed to much of the Western world to epitomize modern civilization, with its Impressionist painters and Symbolist poets, its scientists and intellectuals, its City of Light dominated by the gigantic elegance of a wrought-iron tower which commemorated the centenary of the French Revolution and the triumph of Reason. From the storm-ravaged Côte Sauvage, France might have appeared in its geographical reality as a nation of many tribes inhabiting part of the isthmus which forms the farthest edge of Asia, waging a self-destructive war in defence of a national identity which might prove to be no more than skin deep or a suit of clothes that could be discarded and a language soon forgotten.

14

Keeping Track of the Dead

We were travelling on the stopping train from Saintes to Niort through the quiet countryside of northern Saintonge in western France. Like many underpopulated regions, it owes its peaceful appearance not to war or environmental degradation, but to a long and devastating rural exodus. War itself had only transitory effects: Saintonge was always geographically, culturally and politically fragmented – Plantagenet and Capetian, Protestant and Catholic, French-speaking in the north and Occitan-speaking in the south. As the Saintonge 'Territorial Coherence Development Plan' launched in 2008 points out, the principal threat to its convivial communities is a lack of public services.

Somewhere after Saintes, a garrulous but moody man in his early thirties boarded the train. From his monologue, I gathered that he had been away from home for some time – perhaps in the army or some other institution. In answer to his question, I denied that I was 'Anglais', wondering whether he would think of 'Britannique' or 'Écossais'. This nationality guessing game passed the time and seemed to have a calming effect on him, though at one point he did become quite agitatedly insistent that I must be German.

We had covered most of Europe as far as the Balkans and had started on the Baltic states when the train pulled into the town of Saint-Jean-d'Angély, the small 'capital' of northern Saintonge. As the name of the station appeared in the window, he said, to no one in particular, 'That's odd. It's still here. I thought it would have been wiped off the face of the earth by now.'

Saint-Jean-d'Angély was never destroyed but several nearby villages were, in Allied bombing raids during the Second World War. One of those villages was never rebuilt and only a grassy drystone wall survives. Another passenger took exception to the man's opinion of Saint-Jean. He had grown up there and thought it 'quite a nice little place'. Before a territorial dispute could break out, a bicycle carelessly parked by a boy who had gone to sit in the next carriage clattered onto the floor and nearly hit the returning native. He dropped to his knees and began to deflate one of the tyres. I tried to stop him; our hands touched, and he looked over at me with a happy expression on his face. 'I *have* to do it,' he explained. 'It's a question of morality.' In keeping with the nationality game, I asked, 'That's an example of French morality, is it?', at which he looked even more delighted and shouted, '*Oui – la revanche!*'

After more than a century, the word *revanche* (revenge) still has a precise historical connotation. He was referring to what is generally understood to have been a nationwide upsurge of indignation at the Prussian appropriation of Alsace and Lorraine in 1871. 'Revanchisme' was supposedly the spirit that inspired the *poilus** who marched off to war in 1914, though many of them had little idea why they were fighting. Politically, it was associated with the sabre-rattling ex-Minister of War General Boulanger, who stirred up anti-establishment and anti-Semitic nationalism on the Right and then on the Left in the late 1880s. But in 1914, few people cared much about a frontier province which had been acquired in the seventeenth century, whose inhabitants spoke a language which sounded like German and which, before its annexation by Prussia, had accounted for more than one third of the Jewish population of France.

In the first weeks of the war, while French troops occupied the watershed line of the southern Vosges and moved into Upper Alsace, thousands of Alsatians in France and the colonies were rounded up as potential enemies and placed in concentration camps from Finistère to Gabon.

To the man on the train, *revanchisme* was a historical joke. Living in the twenty-first century, he had a more complicated sense of national stereotypes. The thought of war against Germany seemed to remind him of the other great player in the military and political history of

---

* In the late nineteenth century, 'poilu' ('hairy one') was a popular term for a rough-and-ready, no-nonsense man of the people. In the First World War, it became the common name for the be-whiskered French infantryman, the unbowed, unshaven descendant of the Gaulish warrior king Vercingetorix.

modern France. As he left the train before Niort, he stopped in the doorway and pointed at me in triumph: 'I've got it! . . . You're *Russian!*'

❋

The First World War is such a battlefield of narratives – recorded memories, family legends, old and new propaganda, political appropriations of commemorations and monuments – that it can be hard to know what was real at the time. Landscapes littered with concrete bunkers, pillboxes and shell craters can be used to picture the horror, but those landscapes have been transformed by a hundred years of agricultural upheaval. Even before the war, deforestation had turned parts of Picardy and Flanders into scenes of treeless devastation.

At the outbreak of the First World War there were almost six million farms in France, almost forty per cent of which covered less than two-and-a-half acres (not much larger than a football pitch). In 1913, 37.4% of the active population was engaged in agriculture. That figure had fallen to 9.5% in 1975 and to 3.6% in 2010. By then, the average farm covered 136 acres.

The declining birth rate and the vine-killing phylloxera epidemic of the 1860s and 70s had quietened the countryside. Rural industries were concentrated in urban zones. Specialization and the contraction of space by road and rail turned France into a simplified wall chart of regional produce. A handful of powerful village cheeses came to dominate whole regions. Calvados overflowed the Calvados *département* and even the borders of Normandy. Seven or eight 'traditional' wine-growing areas supplied the entire country and practically all the northern vineyards disappeared.

The landscapes of the First World War also changed in retrospect. Tourists who flocked to Flanders after the armistice were thrilled by the sight of red poppies cloaking the fields of slaughter. The belief arose that the flimsy yet tenacious wild flower had thrived in the blood and bone meal of the fallen. In fact, that living emblem of redemption was a commercial crop: it had long been intensively cultivated from the Nord *département* to Alsace to produce cooking oil and, combined with olive oil, hard soap. It was particularly valued because it could be planted as part of a cereal crop-rotation system without the need for a fallow year.

Symbols of patriotism are always fed by fantasies and misconceptions. Lived experience and acquired knowledge diverge rapidly. Not long ago, it was common to hear first-hand accounts of the Second World War. Elderly men in towns and villages along the Allied invasion routes would recite saucy snippets of vernacular American picked up from GIs. Family-run hotels from Normandy to the Vosges decorated their lounges and dining-rooms with photographs of the ruins from which their establishment had risen.

I never heard any echo of the newsreel footage of grateful citizens cheering Allied tank crews. Often, there was a note of bitterness and even mild hostility. Under the Germans ('Nazis' was rarely used), many of them had known privation and peace. In 1944, they witnessed the high-altitude carpet-bombing of civilian targets and, in some rural districts, looting and sexual violence. 'I know we had to be liberated, but did they have to destroy so much?' was a typical comment.

Only once did I hear an eyewitness account of the First World War. The ninety-year-old owner of the Paris apartment block in which we were living – an impeccably dressed gentleman with a ramrod-straight back – invited us to a lavish May Day lunch with his wife. He kissed Margaret's hand, offered her his *hommages* and suggestively presented her with a bottle of Saint-Amour. Halfway through the meal, he left the table. The maid was sent after him, but it was too late: to the anguish of his wife, he returned to the dining-room in the full uniform of a *poilu*, magnificently preserved and worn with a mixture of pride and self-mockery.

Apparently, despite the horrors, he had had quite a merry war. In contradiction of commemorations and TV documentaries, neither he nor his wife had painful memories of the time. The only reason his uniform was taken from him by his wife (as the maid informed us on the stairs the next day) and reduced to ashes in the stove was that he had been flirting with a young American woman. We had probably seen the last World War I uniform to be deliberately destroyed in a conflagration.

✻   ✻   ✻

The story of the Great War was being written before it began. More than five hundred published writers are said to have been killed between 1914 and 1918. When they marched into battle, they were acting in a drama they had written themselves, and their view of the war would be respected, either because it showed how this unfathomable cataclysm could be integrated into the ideological history of France or because the highly sentimentalized form of writing then in vogue was felt to be appropriate to veneration of the dead.

The prologue had ended with the return of Alfred Dreyfus from Devil's Island in 1899. The world knew from Émile Zola's open letter to President Félix Faure ('J'Accuse!') that his military trial for espionage had been a sham and that an innocent Jewish soldier and patriot had been shamelessly sacrificed to save the real culprit. It was less widely known beyond France that many 'anti-Dreyfusards' were convinced by the evidence that he was indeed the victim of a high-level conspiracy, but they also believed that when the army, the Church and society itself were under threat from Jews, Freemasons, Protestants and socialists, the material evidence was immaterial. For the sake of the fatherland, it was essential that Dreyfus be found guilty.

In 1899, the military court scandalously upheld the original verdict. The 'pardon' granted ten days later by President Émile Loubet was a gesture, not an acquittal. Dreyfus was finally rehabilitated in 1906 and supporters of the Third Republic celebrated the victory of liberal values with what anti-parliamentarian and monarchist groups felt to be vengeful fervour. To the intellectuals of the Ligue de la Patrie Française (a riposte to the Ligue des Droits de l'Homme) and the proto-fascist Action Française, the Third Republic was a left-wing dictatorship with its own secular creed of 'human rights'. Its law on the Separation of Churches and the State (1905) was seen as the beginning of an anti-clerical purge of schools and government institutions.

With its nine Presidents and fifty-nine governments between September 1870 and August 1914, the Third Republic had proved to be a supple and resilient institution. It had survived the demagoguery of General Boulanger, the bombs of anarchists – one of whom stabbed President Carnot to death in 1894 – the accusations of corruption and ideological warfare, and even the Dreyfus Affair. Its 'patriotic', anti-Semitic enemies would have to wait for 1940 and the advent of a puppet regime to celebrate its downfall.

✽

On 28 June 1914, the heir to the Austro-Hungarian throne was assassinated by a Serbian nationalist in Sarajevo. The European alliances went into action like the sluggish but ultimately unstoppable pistons of an over-geared machine. Austria-Hungary declared war on Serbia, Russia mobilized in Serbia's defence, Germany declared war on Russia, and France remained true to the Franco-Russian alliance. On 1 August 1914, three days before Britain declared war on Germany, the French armies of land and sea, including the colonial forces, were mobilized and 'all necessary animals, conveyances and harnesses' were requisitioned. Some isolated communities were perplexed: the mobilization posters did not reveal the reason for the war or the identity of the enemy.

In cities, the immediate effect was an almost unanimous political and social truce, sensitively dubbed a 'sacred union' by President Poincaré. Nationalists and socialists, Catholics and Protestants, workers and peasants would be united by 'the eternal moral power' of 'le droit' – an impressive but airy term implying legal justice or simply the fact of being right no matter what.

In the intellectual world, the desire to tease a moral truce out of the muddle of ideologies had given rise to a quasi-religious or explicitly Catholic cult of the 'sacred soil' of France. In a book-lined study on a Paris avenue, with a backdrop of paintings and mementos, recollections of a provincial childhood could conjure up the vision of a pre-industrial Eden. A great simplicity shone forth: French history was reduced to a mantelpiece platoon of heroic figures – Vercingetorix the proto-Republican, Clovis I the anointed King of the Franks, Joan of Arc the saviour of France and nemesis of an alien race.

To Maurice Barrès, the anti-Dreyfusard writer of faux-Realist novels, including the trilogy *Le Roman de l'énergie nationale*, the hallowed plot which stood for the whole Garden of France was Lorraine, the lost land of whispering poplars, misty lakes and shimmering peaks (Sainte-Odile and Sion). In his pugilistic imagination, Lorraine was ethnically cleansed of Germans and Jews. The true Lorrainer wore his *képi* at a jaunty angle; he had springy tendons rather than mechanical Teutonic muscles, and he fuelled his chauvinistic fervour with Gallic wine instead of Hunnish beer.

For the spiritually and politically confused young novelist Ernest Psichari, whose *L'Appel des armes* (1913) briefly inspired the generation that would be decimated by the war, France was the old province of the Île-de-France – the mossy, bread-scented villages blessed by the angelus bell; the friendly haystacks and apple trees; the willowy meadows where healthy, pipe-smoking hunters shot plover, pheasant and woodcock, and where 'race is in tune with the landscape'.

The post-Dreyfus association of modest, mostly northern landscapes with the soul and *terroir* of the fatherland was so enduring that the mere fact of evoking sylvan scenes of childhood in a temperate province came to be equated with nationalism. Purged of irony and pacifist sentiments, Marcel Proust's Lower Normandy in *Du côté de chez Swann* (1913) and Alain-Fournier's Bourbonnais in *Le Grand Meaulnes* (1913) are still misrepresented in coffee-table books and politicians' speeches as hymns to 'national identity'.

The truce which President Poincaré called the 'sacred union' was elusive. When the poet and essayist Charles Péguy, a socialist and a Catholic, combined republican patriotism with the cult of Joan of Arc, he caused confusion on both sides. Nationalistic writing appeared to require belligerence, a wilful ignorance of history and a hallucinatory narcissism inherited from the Symbolists. In this, the anti-Dreyfusard fallacy prevailed: certain 'truths' were held to be immune from evidence.

Ernest Psichari had developed his mystical idiom while serving as an artillery lieutenant with the Colonial Army in the French Congo. His *Terres de soleil et de sommeil*, published in 1908 when he was twenty-five, said nothing of the widely reported brutality of French administrators and rubber and ivory exporters. It was the role of the empire to save the French soul: 'Africa is one of the last resorts of national energy, one of the last places where our finest feelings can still assert themselves.' If only there could be a war 'to raise up our hearts and fill us with enthusiasm'. 'Such moments in the life of a people seem to sum up in themselves the whole spirit of the race.'

Patriotic intellectuals – though not Maurice Barrès, who was too old to be conscripted – would soon be donning their uniforms as though dressing for dinner. Chronic insecurity about the shape and destiny of France would be cured by a rapid victory. France would recover not only its lost territory but also its imaginary unity. All along a narrow zone from the Channel to the Rhine, drugged and drunken soldiers would smell the ether drifting over from the German lines while patriotic wine and brandy, as well as commonly dispensed derivatives of a foreign species of poppy, would sustain the vision until the very last moment.

✿   ✿   ✿

The first enormous battle for the 'sacred soil' of France took place ten miles north of the border in the Belgian province of Luxembourg. It was centred on the village of Rossignol, which means 'nightingale'. Few French people have heard of it: there are no national commemorations and the Battle of Rossignol is rarely mentioned in the same breath as Verdun, the Somme or Passchendaele.

More French soldiers died at Rossignol on 22 August 1914 than on any other day in French history, before or since. More than twenty-seven thousand were killed in twelve hours, which is about half the number of American soldiers killed in Vietnam from 1959 to 1975. The average death rate was two French soldiers every three seconds. Statistics can have a mildly anaesthetic effect on the imagination, but this one translates itself easily into the sinister crepitation of a ticking clock.

A hundred miles to the south-east, the opening French offensive on the crest of the Vosges was proving inconclusive. The industrial city of Mulhouse was captured on 7 August to national jubilation and lost again two days later. The storming of the Vosges was dictated by symbolic rather than strategic goals. The French commander-in-chief, Joseph Joffre, had no overall plan. He believed in the 'attaque à outrance' (attack at any cost) and in the legend of the *furia francese* – a barnstorming obliviousness to impossible odds. The expression was originally applied by Italian chroniclers to a rearguard action fought against the Kingdom of Naples in 1495.

In most situations, Joffre's orders amounted to a slap on the back and a dig of the spurs. 'Attack the enemy wherever you encounter him' was the usual command. This daredevil policy was not exclusively French, but the French army applied it with exceptional rigour. The 1914 field manual for 'large units' seemed to have been written for medieval knights:

> He who would conquer must push the attack to the end, without
> mental reservation. Victory is won only at the cost of bloody

sacrifice. Any other notion must be spurned as contrary to the
very nature of war.

A battle is a moral contest. . . . It follows that the winner of the
contest is not the one who has suffered the smallest number of losses
but the one whose will and moral courage are the stronger.

The German plan was to sweep across northern France, arcing
south on parallel trajectories: on a map, the curved arrows looked like
sickle blades. The largest, westernmost sickle would sever Paris from
the Channel and the South. In Lorraine, the Germans were surprised
to see their plan so ably abetted by the French. While the *poilus*
advanced across fields mysteriously dotted with striped wooden posts
– unaware that they were operating in areas regularly used for long-
range target practice – huge numbers of German troops were moving
west through Luxembourg and Belgium.

This was the enduring weakness of the kingdom created by the
Paris monarchy. Fed by four great rivers, with arteries running north
and south through convenient geological gaps and a monocratically
centralized road and railway system, the city which had fallen to
Romans, Franks, Vikings, Normans, Burgundians, English and
Prussians was open to conquest as well as trade.

A hundred years after Napoleon's first abdication, the northern
frontier was still defended mainly by mud. By early September, the
government would have fled south to Bordeaux while German and
Allied armies fought along the Marne, twenty-four miles from Notre-
Dame and within the range of a Paris taxi cab, six hundred of which,
meters running, delivered soldiers to the front.

All of this was predictable and had been predicted by the
Germans. French intelligence and reconnoitring were so poor – and
considered less important than fighting spirit – that General Joffre
was unaware of the most ominous development: Germany had
already called up all its reserve troops. He imagined his attack on
the Vosges stretching out an ever-thinner line of Boches along the
Belgian frontier while his own men looked down over the Rhineland
and prepared to celebrate an early end to the war. If Joffre had been
able to draw, if only in his mind, a map of German and French
positions, he might have recognized the old invasion routes laid
down long ago by geography and signposted in the present by

battlefields, cemeteries, memorials and farm names dating from the disasters of 1814, 1815 and 1870.

✿

At dawn on 22 August 1914, a seven-mile-long procession of infantry, cavalry and artillery was clattering across the narrow bridge over the Semois at Breuvanne, seven miles north of the French border. The procession was composed primarily of the illustrious Third Colonial Infantry Division, commanded by the much admired and bemedalled General Raffenel, who had last seen action in Tonkin (North Vietnam) twenty-seven years before.

Raffenel had received secret orders to march into Belgium to counter the westward advance of the Germans. After marching for a day and half a night, his men had snatched four hours of sleep, then set off without a proper meal. Breakfast was ten miles away, in the town of Neufchâteau. They were expecting to encounter their first Germans a few days north of Neufchâteau.

In a change to the grand plan, Crown Prince Wilhelm, commander-in-chief of the German Fifth Army, had cut south, with the Fourth Army protecting his right flank. When the Third Colonial Infantry Division crossed the Semois, heading for the village of Rossignol, German troops had already spent a second night at Neufchâteau on the far side of the Forêt de Chiny. Information supplied by observation planes and reconnaissance patrols had been digested and they were now awaiting fresh reports of French movements.

A hot day lay ahead, but dense fog would linger until noon, preventing further reconnaissance from the air. As the first French soldiers reached Rossignol on the southern edge of the forest, they came under rifle fire from a patrol of uhlans (lancers), who galloped away into the woods.

The Ardennes – known to Caesar as the Arduenna Forest, in which an entire tribe could remain hidden – was the most difficult sector of the Belgian frontier, especially for officers who thought that a proper battle always included a cavalry charge. (It was, ironically, a French general who said of the Charge of the Light Brigade at Balaclava, 'C'est magnifique, mais ce n'est pas la guerre!') The forest was clogged with undergrowth, obstructed by gullies and hummocks and also by livestock fences, which would give the troops their first combat experience of barbed wire.

Viewed from the panoramic ridge to the south on the minor road from Breuvanne to Mesnil, the battle zone has a benignly bucolic appearance with its gleaming meadows, the sparkle of distant windows and the Styx-like meanderings of the Semois. But the soft banks of the streams had been loosened by a recent downpour. Before long, the unmistakeable madder-red trousers of the *poilus* would no longer be a serious liability. German sharpshooters set their sights on the mess-tins which glinted on top of the soldiers' rucksacks.

The First Regiment of the Colonial Division was ordered to advance into the forest: they would be preceded by their officers, as tradition demanded. The regiment was formed of three battalions, each consisting of more than a thousand men. The tail of the first battalion had just disappeared among the trees when the crack of rifles was heard and then the rattle of machine guns. This should have suggested to General Raffenel, as it did to some of his officers, that they were dealing, not with a small band of snipers, but with a large, well-organized force which had already dug itself into defensive positions on either side of the Neufchâteau road.

Along that blind corridor and on the old Roman road to its left, the French soldiers experienced a textbook demonstration of enfilading fire: the entire length of the battalion was exposed to the German guns. The other two battalions were sent in along the same corridor, obstructed now by the dead and the dying. The screaming wounded helped the German marksmen find their targets. Shortly afterwards, a few mutilated remnants stumbled out of the woods: the battalion commanders and most of the officers were not among them.

A visibly ruffled General Raffenel conferred with his subordinates. It was inconceivable that an entire regiment could cease to exist in a matter of minutes, and so the Second Regiment, comprising all the remaining infantry of the Colonial Division, was ordered into the woods. Most of them would be dead by ten o'clock, before the sun had penetrated the fog.

✲

From a knoll on the east side of the road, General Raffenel's field glasses showed him the gun carriages of his artillery stretching all the way back to Breuvanne. They were being pounded by the German guns which had somehow established themselves on the ridge above Rossignol. The battery of the Second Artillery Regiment commanded by Ernest Psichari had crossed the Semois, but the bridge had been blown up and what remained of the Colonial Division was cut in two.

Raffenel and his officers were confronted with a situation beyond experience. A catastrophic anachronism had occurred: a Napoleonic army had blundered into the twentieth century, unaware that battle-fields had become inaccessible to human beings. Technology had rendered all those military landscape paintings and papier-mâché models obsolete. No telltale cloud of smoke gave away the position of a marksman whose high-velocity bullets caused deep, gaping wounds. Machine guns fired ten bullets a second. Cannon stabilized by hydraulic recoil brakes launched their shells repeatedly without the need for readjustment. A shrapnel shell could miss its target and still destroy a dozen men with its shockwave, bursting eardrums, perforating bowels, rupturing eyeballs and testicles, collapsing lungs.

French soldiers were constantly incapacitated by the inflexible chain of command. When its commander had been killed, a battalion was duty-bound to keep attacking: any other course of action had to be authorized by a superior officer who might be several miles from the scene of battle. Significant deviations from established practice would require the approval of General Joffre at his headquarters eighty miles away in Vitry-le-François. Semaphore flags, despatch riders and carrier pigeons had obvious disadvantages in a war zone; telephone calls had to pass through the local exchange. Eleven days after the Battle of Rossignol, Joffre would dismiss one of his most effective generals, Charles Lanrezac, for ordering a tactical retreat instead of a suicidal advance.

A general who showed initiative in the field might be relieved of his command; a *poilu* might be shot. Officers had to stand where their men could see and hear them: on 15 August, at Dinant on the Meuse, the first casualties of a platoon which stormed the bridge had been the sergeant and the lieutenant – an aspiring writer and graduate of Saint-Cyr called Charles de Gaulle. This is why, on the afternoon of 22 August, in the burning husk of Rossignol, where 'every house, corner and pile of rubbish was disputed', Ernest Psichari was standing like a beacon in front of his gunners when a bullet pierced his head.

Officers were primed by military tradition for a hero's death. If propaganda helped to win the war, they did not die in vain. A septic corpse slumped in a trench would be a sight to stir the stomach, not the soul, but when Lieutenant Charles Péguy lost his life on 5 September, two miles north of the Marne in open oat fields, the witness of his death could describe it for a newspaper almost exactly as it happened (though he did, in a later version, soften the description of a bullet's impact):

> Despite our cries of 'Get down!', Péguy was still standing upright in the glorious madness of his valour. . . . And the lieutenant's voice could still be heard: 'Shoot! Shoot! For God's sake!' . . . He drew himself up as though to defy the machine guns, inviting the death he had glorified in his verse. At that moment a lethal bullet shattered the hero's head and smashed that noble and generous brow. He fell without a cry, having been granted, in the barbarians' retreat, the ultimate vision of approaching victory.

✳

Now that so much of First World War history is familiar in the form of numbers, it seems incredible that the realization was delayed by a lack of accurate statistics. It had only recently been noticed, after parliamentary questions, that no proper records had been kept of the astounding number of soldiers who had died of disease since the 1870s in colonial campaigns in Algeria, Tunisia, Morocco, Dahomey, Sudan, Cochinchina and Tonkin.

The desirability of keeping a running total of the dead had never been strongly felt. No one knew that more than a quarter of Frenchmen between the ages of eighteen and twenty-seven would die in the next four years. The newspaper-reading public did not expect reports to be accompanied by sums and percentages. Figures supplied by the army had been considered sufficient. Wounded and 'missing' were often lumped together with the dead. This should have produced inflated figures, but professional pride and a concern for morale tended to produce a downward adjustment of the numbers. General Headquarters had enough on their plate, and when the official policy was 'attack whatever the cost', no one was keen to inspect the itemized bill.

There was not even a set policy for identifying the dead. The nickel alloy or aluminium identity disks were sometimes collected but sometimes left on the body or taken as trophies and mementos. A thin metal disk was easily lost in the carnage and corroded quickly. Of the ninety-eight soldiers buried with Charles Péguy, thirty-four are unidentified. Yet another young writer, Alain-Fournier, was killed near Verdun on 22 September. When his body was discovered in 1991 in a grave which contained shreds of the red trouser material that was used in the first twelve months of the war, his name tag was illegible. His identity was confirmed by his dental record. The method was first applied in 1919 to the nameless dead and to soldiers suffering from amnesia, but it was useful only for identifying officers since the average *poilu* could not afford dental treatment.

❊

Perhaps the first man to grasp the numerical enormity of twentieth-century warfare was the commander of the Third Colonial Division. General Raffenel's itinerary during the Battle of Rossignol can be retraced on the ground from brief reports of sightings, but in that innocuous landscape, his footsteps seem to have fallen in a different dimension. The only actual signs of violence and upheaval are road-side trees lacerated by hedge slashers, the spoil heaps of mole tunnels and the makeshift shrines to recent car-crash victims with their photographs and plastic flowers.

At noon, Raffenel was still with his officers near the forest edge. General Montignault had assured him that the artillery could hold Rossignol indefinitely. Shells roared dangerously low over their heads; some exploded nearby, killing several horses. The shelling was coming from the south-east, and so it was assumed that French gunners were targeting German positions in the forest, unaware that their commanding officers were in the line of fire. Then one of the officers picked up a shiny object like a large metallic mushroom and recognized the percussion fuse of a German shell . . .

According to Raffenel's chief of staff, his face had 'a sunken, collapsed appearance'. He showed signs of disorientation and was unable to keep still: 'he seemed to be looking for someone or something without knowing who or what it might be.' He gave no orders and, what was even more disturbing, listened meekly to his officers' suggestions. The lieutenant suspected that the general no longer knew where he stood in the chain of command.

At about 2.15 p.m., Raffenel wandered off into the woods. He must have crossed the Roman road, then headed south, out of the forest, with the sounds of battle to his left. At 3 p.m., Colonel Lamolle of the Colonial Infantry saw him on his own with a rifle in his hand. He had waded across the Semois and his uniform was wet and muddy. His face was pale; he no longer looked like himself. In spite of this, 'he was very calm and not at all depressed'.

The colonel persuaded him to rest in a nearby wood. A few minutes later, he disappeared again. Incendiary shells were annihilating Rossignol and the Germans were moving south and west of Breuvanne, encircling the village. Meanwhile, the general was heading for the higher ground to the south. From the Breuvanne–Mesnil road, where an orientation table now stands, he would have gained a comprehensive view of the battlefield and seen what no one had ever seen before: a relatively small area of about three miles by four in which approximately forty thousand French and German soldiers had died since daybreak. The artillery column that was stuck on the road to Rossignol was a motionless mass of metal and humanity. In the marshy fields to the west of the road where the batteries had tried to escape the German cannon, the heads of horses could be seen jutting out of the mire.

After 6 p.m., not long before bugles sounded the cease-fire, remnants of the Third Infantry Regiment were retreating west along the road to Frenois, collecting the wounded. A captain spotted General Raffenel lying perpendicular to the road with a hole in his head. A German sniper might have shot him from less than half a mile away, but there is no suggestion in the captain's report that his face had been blown away by a high-velocity bullet.

French officers usually carried a Lebel 8mm revolver. Raffenel's peculiar state of calm was probably pathological and his restlessness a form of ambulatory mania, but there was a certain logic in his movements. He had deserted his command and retreated from the enemy; he had then surveyed the slaughter for which he would be held responsible. The captain who found him noted that 'his field glasses and his revolver were gone'. They might have been stolen by a German soldier, but enemy units were still some distance from the road. It is more likely that the equipment was salvaged by one of the stretcher parties after the general had atoned for his failure and spared the army the embarrassment of a court martial.

✿

That evening, the unprecedented concentration of heavy weaponry and unprotected troops was seen to have created some extraordinary *tableaux*:

> Certain parts of the battlefield presented the unforgettable spectacle of thousands of dead standing upright in several ranks, held in position by corpses which acted as flying buttresses, placed one on top of the other at various angles ranging from horizontal to sixty degrees.

The following morning, the former village of Rossignol offered another preview of twentieth-century warfare. *Revanche* was as much an obsession for the German army as it was for the French, but it took a more virulent form. Ever since the Franco-Prussian War, it had been an accepted fact in Germany that every French and Belgian citizen considered himself an irregular (the word would now be 'terrorist'): German soldiers expected to be shot at by civilians and, if captured, horribly tortured and killed. Thirty years later, the same myth was used by the Nazis as a weapon in the 'war of annihilation' (*Vernichtungskrieg*).

There is not a wisp of evidence that Belgian civilians took up arms against German soldiers at Rossignol. The French wounded were shot, the people of Rossignol were rounded up and penned in the church, and two thousand six hundred captured soldiers were confined to a watery meadow on the edge of the village, where they spent three nights and two days before being deported to camps in Germany.

On 25 August, accused of firing at German soldiers, one hundred and twenty-two villagers, including one woman, were marched to the railway station at Marbehan and loaded into cattle trucks. The youngest was sixteen, the oldest eighty-two. It was a short journey to the town of Arlon, where the military tribunal decided that a trial was pointless. By the buffers at the far end of the station, they were shot in batches of ten. The only woman, Marie Huriaux, was made to watch the entire operation. She was the last to be shot. Poor-quality photographs taken by a German soldier show a group of officers and men in casual poses looking down at what might be mistaken for a defensive wall of sandbags.

The meadow on the edge of Rossignol was later renamed Camp de la Misère, from a field used by the Prussians for the same purpose in the aftermath of the Battle of Sedan. The information panel which stands there now, based on interviews and research conducted by the new village priest who arrived a few months later, notes with a proper sense of what survives a few moments of terror, 'This massacre created 64 widows and 142 orphans'.

❊

News of the worst disaster in French history – appropriately modified – reached the Paris newspapers in the form of a war communiqué on 25 August:

East of the Meuse

Our troops advanced through exceptionally difficult terrain. Vigorously attacked on the outskirts of the woods, they were forced to fall back after a fierce battle south of the Semoy.

. . . Our cavalry was entirely unscathed; our artillery asserted its superiority. The physical condition and morale of our officers and soldiers could not be better.

As a consequence of the new orders, the fighting will take on a different aspect for a few days, and the French Army will remain for the time being on the defensive. When the commander-in-chief decides that the moment has come, the army will once again launch a vigorous attack.

We have suffered heavy losses. It would be premature to attach a precise figure to them, as it would be to number the German losses. We can say, however, that the German army has been dealt such a blow that it has been forced to give up its counter-attacking manoeuvres and to occupy new positions.

Rossignol accounted for more than one tenth of the estimated quarter of a million French soldiers who were killed in the months of August and September 1914. The German commanders were briefly stunned into inactivity. When the fact of their appalling victory had sunk in – thirteen thousand German soldiers killed and yet the battle won – they abandoned the original invasion plan and moved south towards Paris in the wake of the retreating French army.

The Germans were weary, outnumbered and over-confident. After six days of slaughter on the Marne (6–10 September), the French armies and the British Expeditionary Force had stopped the advance on Paris. The German armies were pushed back to the River Aisne. The northernmost outposts of French-held territory were now Soissons, Reims and Verdun. The long stalemate was beginning, when the entrenching tool, the wire-cutter and the gas mask would be vital equipment and the capture of a ruined farmhouse in a quagmire would be front-page news. (Fig. 13.)

The battle which saved Paris would be called – as though in incredulity – 'the Miracle of the Marne'. The first to describe it as a miracle was Maurice Barrès, a *député* since 1906, in one of his journalistic paeans to racial superiority (*L'Écho de Paris*, 22 December 1914). Joan of Arc had risen again from the flames, this time with a British Expeditionary Force at her side – for 'let it not be forgotten that her dream, once France was delivered and at peace, was to ride with the English to the defence of Christendom'.

On the other side of no-man's-land, wrote Barrès, Odin and the other pagan deities were 'presiding over interminable massacres and drinking sessions', but 'the warrior virgin who shows us the path by which the invader will be expelled also shows the universe the heroic and benevolent face of valour *à la française*'.

Barrès was not entirely convinced by his own rhetoric, but it accurately reflected the dream-world of French commanders. The gods of both sides counted – if they counted at all – in very large round numbers. The armies of the Western Front prepared for a war of attrition, as though the fields would be watered and fed by blood and steel, and the dead would endlessly rise again from the shell craters.

✻

Towards the end of 1915, the General Headquarters of the French Army began to notice gaping discrepancies between different sets of statistics. Until then, government ministers had been provided with convincingly precise casualty figures, divided by rank, type of wound and cause of death, and based on reports from various sources: hospitals, regiments, local *gendarmeries* and the État Civil (Registry Office). They were consistent in only one respect: the total was always underestimated and sometimes almost halved.

The official reorganization of war statistics took effect on 1 July 1916, four months into the ten-month-long Battle of Verdun, in which French and German casualties may have exceeded one million. When Joffre's replacement, the twinkly-eyed General Nivelle, blithely proposed in the spring of 1917 to smash through the German Hindenburg Line north of the Aisne by sheer weight of numbers, he promised that only ten thousand men would be killed or wounded. This tidy, heartless sum was considered reassuringly modest.

The road which runs along a narrow plateau of silt and limestone between the valleys of the Aisne and the Ailette is called the Chemin des Dames. The 'ladies' are usually said to have been daughters of Louis XV, but 'chemin des dames' is the name of several other ancient routes. The *dames* were the fairies who had inhabited the land before the soil of France was sacred to a Christian god.

The attack was launched on 16 April 1917, when the enemy and the landscape had been softened up by rain, a late fall of snow and several million shells, including phosgene gas shells. At the eastern end of the Chemin des Dames, tanks were used for the first time by the French. They were disabled by German artillery and anti-tank ditches. At the western end, the village of Laffaux – one of the few destroyed villages in the area to be rebuilt after the war – seemed to have been stamped into the ground by a gigantic boot.

Some futile massacres still have their defenders, but by Nivelle's own reckoning, the Chemin des Dames offensive was a catastrophe. He was out in his calculation by a factor of fourteen. The army's own post-war estimate was 138,589 killed or wounded, which would equate to seventy-eight French casualties for every yard gained. They included more than seven thousand Senegalese riflemen and about one thousand Kanaks from New Caledonia who had recently completed their training at Fréjus on the Côte d'Azur. A month later, Nivelle was dismissed and replaced by Philippe Pétain.

The figures supplied by the army were angrily disputed by *députés* who were alarmed at the sudden increase in mutinies and desertions.

There were fears that exhaustion, dashed hopes and militant socialism might bring the war to a premature end and provoke a revolution. But at least this time there was a general consensus that precision mattered and that something ought to be done to lighten the immense shroud of mourning that weighed down on the whole country.

✻ ✻ ✻

Thanks to the work of the Service des Renseignements des Familles and the Service Général des Pensions and their army of stenographers, the 'first casualty of war' made a long but ultimately spectacular recovery. On the Chemin des Dames today, in the cemeteries where Christian and Muslim graves are intermingled, the almost overwhelming organization of the dead shows the power of statistical truth. While the Douaumont Ossuary north of Verdun covers the carnage of one hundred and thirty thousand unidentifiable soldiers with reinforced concrete like the temple of a terrifying Moloch, the cemeteries of the Chemin des Dames have the intimacy of individual grief.

In the early spring of 1920, in the little town of Molières (Tarn-et-Garonne), Maria Aussignac received a letter from the État Civil. She was informed that the remains of her son, along with those of his brother-in-arms, had been identified. They were to be exhumed on the afternoon of 22 March and transferred to the military cemetery at Laffaux. She was provided with the name and address of the man who owned the quarry in which the bodies had been found and also of the mother of her son's comrade.

She resolved to make the long journey to Laffaux with her husband and promised to write to the mother of the other soldier, who lived in a village near Bayonne, five hundred miles from the Chemin des Dames.

The quarry was in a strip of rugged terrain naturally pitted with tunnels and caves. German machine-gunners had survived there in surprising numbers despite the shelling and the gas. The land is now severed from the Chemin des Dames by the N2 *route nationale*, but it can still be reached by stony field tracks running from Laffaux and L'Ange gardien.

On his last spell of home leave, Frédéric Aussignac had told his mother all about his best friend, Jean-Baptiste Prudet. During the Battle of Verdun, he had pulled him to safety more than once, which is why Jean-Baptiste called him 'l'Infirmier' (the Nurse). Returning to the front in January 1917, Frédéric had been overjoyed to find that his friend had signed up with the same battalion so that they would not be separated in battle.

On 29 March 1920, Maria Aussignac described her visit to the battlefield in a typed letter to the parents of Jean-Baptiste. It was published by his great-nephew in 2014. Belligerence and xenophobia survived the war and even flourished, but so did love, forgiveness and a yearning for truth. There was no mention in Maria Aussignac's letter of the sacred fatherland, the hated Hun or the folly of war.

> You might ask what there was to find after three years. Let me say at once that our dear boys were in one piece and perfectly recognizable. . . . The first one to be exhumed had 971 on his tag – we do not know who he is – then the second was 956 (your son) and the third 957 (mine). All three were on top of other bodies but I can tell you that they were very well preserved. They passed a sheet under them and pulled them out of the quarry and we were able to examine them there at our ease. We kept the two boys with us for as long as we wanted and then they put them onto a wagon and we went with them to the cemetery at about 4 o'clock on Monday evening.
>
> At the cemetery we placed them in their coffins and arranged them ourselves, acting in your place, and we had the idea of cutting a piece of cloth from his greatcoat, which I am sure will be a precious memento, especially for his *maman*. . . .
>
> They are on the edge of the big avenue in the middle of the cemetery, and your son's cross is number 1 and ours is number 2. It was all over at 7 o'clock but you can imagine the state we were in. The owner of the quarry kindly gave us a bed for the night and on Tuesday we went to put flowers on both their graves with the only greenery we could find – a holly plant which had sprouted again in what had once been a garden, and after one last prayer we parted from them with very heavy hearts and left them there in their dear graves.
>
> God has answered our prayers, when you think of how many people can find nothing at all. . . . And since our dear children did not want to be separated from each other, I hope, dear friends, that you will not separate them in your prayers.

15

Mount Inaccessible

In the bishopric of Gratianopolis, hard by the borders of the diocese of Die, in the land which is known to its inhabitants as Treves, there is a very high mountain which looks over to a neighbouring mountain. Its name is *Aequa illi*, because it is 'equal' to the other one, though inaccessibly high. From the opposite eminence, a clear spring can be seen tumbling down the craggy stairs of stone, and at the highest point of the summit there flourishes what appears to be a grassy meadow on which shining white sheets are sometimes observed, spread out to dry as though by washerwomen. The meaning or purpose of this is easy to seek but hard to discover.*

Word of an Inaccessible Mountain in a hidden massif somewhere west of the Alps reached the outside world in about 1211. The collector of folk tales Gervase of Tilbury probably never saw 'Aequa illi' with his own eyes. Nor, it can be assumed, did later chroniclers who described it as having the shape of an inverted pyramid or a giant mushroom. The visibility footprint of Mont Aiguille is small considering its height (nearly seven thousand feet) and its unmistakeable shape. The monolith which soars above the forested slopes is the last bastion of a Cretaceous plateau that was eroded on all sides until only a slender mesa remained like a sky-borne island from a vanished continent.

Nothing more was said of the Inaccessible Mountain until

---

* Gratianopolis = Grenoble; Treves = Trièves (a *pays* within the Vercors); the 'neighbouring mountain' is Le Grand Veymont; Aequa illi (in one ms.: Aequa villa) may reflect the local name, 'aiguille' (needle), or, if originally *aquae*, a belief that the mountain was the source of a river or the home of the rain.

November 1490, when the twenty-year-old Charles VIII of France was travelling from Grenoble to Notre-Dame d'Embrun, one of the most important pilgrimage sites of the Middle Ages. The carriageable road was the 'Chemin de Gap' (part of the future Route Napoléon), but the royal party must on that occasion have taken the longer route which runs above the brawling torrent of the Drac.

After the village of Monteynard, where the road bends to the north, one of the most distant views of Mont Aiguille reveals its eerily anomalous cone jutting out of a range of ragged mountains nine miles to the south-west. It seems to belong to a different landscape: to educated people who read about the miraculous mountain, and perhaps to the few who saw it, that obelisk of white limestone called to mind the earthly paradise of Dante's *Purgatorio* – a lush garden at the top of an impossibly steep eminence. A local legend spoke of the lamb that was flown by an eagle from the stable in Bethlehem to the lofty peak. (It can be seen in clear weather in the form of an erratic limestone boulder on the strip of green at the summit.) When the eagle touched down and the lamb began to graze, the stony soil put forth a carpet of flowers. The heavenly scent sometimes wafted down to the valley below. It was said that if a human foot should ever sully that sacred field, the lamb would turn into a satanic, hornèd ram.

Charles VIII decided that the mountain must be climbed. After twenty months of preparation, a team led by the King's trusted chamberlain, Antoine de Ville, set off to scale the unscalable peak. It was the first recorded rock-climbing expedition in French history. Along with several porters and de Ville's valet, the team included the King's 'escalleur' (a roofer), a master carpenter and a master stonemason from Montélimar, and, most importantly, two priests. 'By means of subtle engines' (ropes and ladders), they reached the summit on 26 June 1492 – a month and a day before Columbus set sail for the New World.

As they pulled themselves up over the last shelf of rock, they were amazed to behold spread out before them a beautiful flowery meadow 'half a league long and a crossbow's range wide' and, miraculously, 'a fine herd of chamois with their young'. Startled by the creatures from another world, one of the young chamois jumped to its death. After this calamity, de Ville commanded that the remaining chamois were not to be slaughtered. Three large crosses were erected, masses were said, and the mountain was baptized 'in the name of the Father, Son, Holy Ghost and Saint Charlemagne' Agulle Fort – which is what 'the people of the country' already called it.

The Inaccessible Mountain was then left alone for another three and a half centuries. Because some 'fleurs de lys' had been found on the meadow – probably the elegant St Bruno's lily (*Paradisea liliastrum*), which still thrives on the high plains of the Vercors – the mountain was declared to be an emblem of royal power. In 1701, it was included among the Seven Wonders of the Dauphiné as a monument to Louis XIV: 'No mortal can attain the pinnacle of glory to which he has elevated himself.' An engraving showed an upside-down mountain with the motto '*Supereminet invius*': 'Inaccessible, it (or he) reigns o'er all.' Fantastic though the engraving was, the otherwise authoritative *Statistique du département de la Drôme* (1835), written by a native of the *département*, stated that Mont Aiguille, 'unlike other mountains, is much narrower at its base than at its summit'.

This was published a few months after the mountain had been climbed for the first time since 1492. One team, led by a priest, left the final ascent to a man who found bare feet more adhesive than hobnail boots. The second team consisted of seven local men who all reached the summit, where they sang the 'Marseillaise', danced a rigadoon and played *boules* with some of the stones, thereby claiming the emblem of monarchy for the secular Republic.

No vestiges were found of the three crosses or the herd of chamois: the only living creatures were the black crows which flapped around the limestone cliffs. Both teams, however, were surprised to discover evidence of human habitation – 'the sparse remains of an old drystone building' and, in a cave beneath the summit, marks made by a stone hammer and 'the rubble of a structure which must date back to very early times'. The crude vaulted chamber, which was invisible from below, might have been the home of a Gallo-Roman hermit or the last hiding place of a refugee from some long-forgotten war.

✻

Mont Aiguille is a miniature of the whole massif. Approached from any direction, the walls and battlements of the Vercors plateau look like the fortifications of a gigantic *oppidum*. From certain streets and windows in Grenoble, an intergalactic Noah's Ark seems to have landed just beyond the suburbs.

The plateau as a whole was nameless until the early nineteenth century, when geographers and geologists gave it the Gaulish tribal name of one of its *pays*, the Vercors. Despite its proximity to Grenoble and the main route to Provence, the Vercors was almost absent from French history. For an unknown reason, it was a blank on the map of seasonal migrations. In the third or fourth centuries, Roman roads had served a quarry on the western side of Mont Aiguille, but it was not until 1851 that the first modern road was gouged through the gorge of the Grands Goulets, connecting the cliff-hanging village of Pont-en-Royans with the interior.

Later in the century, other dizzying 'balcony roads' provided an alternative to the tracks used by pack mules, whose corpses could be seen dotted about the gorges until the torrents swept them away. Even the famously inaccessible village of Rencurel was connected by road to the valley of the Isère: it was no longer necessary to travel there by wicker basket. (The basket was suspended from a pulley which slid along a rope and deposited the visitor on the far side of an abyss.)

The roads of the Vercors are still often closed by rock falls and subsidence, entailing day-consuming detours. Some of the tunnels are no more reassuring and not much wider than a disused mine shaft. In the dark interior, there are unrepaired potholes and abrupt changes of gradient, but what strikes fear into the heart and lungs of an unmotorized road user is the rumble of a vehicle entering the tunnel half a mile behind. A solitary motorbike engine can sound like a tank squadron.

The Vercors first appeared in guidebooks – Baedeker's *Southern France* and Murray's *Handbook for Travellers in France* – in the early 1890s. By the 1920s, the village of Villard-de-Lans above Grenoble was attracting skiers and tubercular children who were believed to benefit from the bracing air. But most of the shepherds, farmers and foresters of the Vercors were left in peace by the outside world. When, for several years in the 1940s, there were no tourists at all, and Mont Aiguille was like the keep of an impregnable citadel, they were sometimes cut off from the land below, and when they looked to the heavens, it would be as though the fairies who spread their sheets on the mountain top were coming to the aid of mortal beings.

All at once, a great white flower bloomed in the dark blue of the sky. It did not appear to have fallen but to have come from nowhere, conjured out of nothing by a sign and a sound; and then came another and another . . . ten, twelve, maybe twenty. The wind of the plateau caught them and pushed them hither and yon, forcing them to perform a strange aerial ballet. It was a sight of astonishing and quite unexpected beauty.

❊   ❊   ❊

Peace was declared on 22 June 1940, forty-three days after Hitler's invasion of the Low Countries and eight days after German tanks rolled into Paris.

There was general relief that the war was over and that Paris would not be destroyed. Only Churchill had wanted to 'fight to the last Frenchman'. The phrase was invented by a German propagandist but it expressed the British Prime Minister's reckless wish:

> I urged the French Government to defend Paris. I emphasized the enormous absorbing power of the house-to-house defence of a great city upon an invading army.

Queueing up to be imprisoned, the French army had been released from its duties on the Maginot Line – the epically useless line of fortifications from the Channel to the Alps which had been designed as though for a high-tech re-enactment of August 1914. The 'English' soldiers (a third of whom were French) had sailed from Dunkirk, leaving behind the thirty-five thousand unsung French who had heroically held off the Germans until the evacuation was complete. Approximately one thousand British soldiers died and sixteen thousand French.

To the six million civilian fugitives who fled south only to return to their ghost towns a few weeks later, it was an article of faith that France had been betrayed, not defeated – betrayed by the English, by Communists or Fascists and, naturally, by the Jews. The 'abandoned populations' may not have 'put [their] trust in the German soldier', as they were instructed to do by a poster which showed a laughing Nazi officer pampering timid French infants, but most people were thankful for the eighty-four-year-old hero of Verdun, Maréchal Pétain, who would protect the fatherland from Hitler and spearhead the hunt for scapegoats.

In the opera house of the frilly spa town of Vichy, the Assemblée Nationale voted on 10 July 1940 to establish the État Français, bringing to an end the Third Republic. Parliament abolished itself by a majority of 569 to 80 and invested power in a single head of state. In official photographs, the grandfatherly Pétain looked like a cut-out figure from a Fascist history of France, a semi-decrepit Napoléon with a pair of gloves in one hand and a walking stick in the other. The blandly named 'French State' still had a small army of about ten thousand for keeping order at home, but its fleet at Mers-el-Kébir on the Algerian coast near Oran had been hobbled by British battleships and planes with the loss of over one thousand French lives, confirming the suspicion that 'Albion' was as perfidious as ever.

✻

A Demarcation Line seven hundred and fifty miles long divided the former territory of France into a Free Zone, an Occupied Zone and several 'forbidden' zones, which, from April 1941, included the entire Atlantic seaboard from the Pyrenees to Belgium. France was now about half the size of Spain. Its coastline had shrunk from two thousand miles to less than four hundred.

This humiliating subtraction created a puppet nation which resembled a vassal kingdom of medieval Occitania. In 843, the Treaty of Verdun had divided the empire of Charlemagne longitudinally into three kingdoms so that each grandson had roughly equivalent natural resources and a similar range of climates. (Fig. 4.) In 1940, the latitudinal division of France ensured that practically all the heavy industry and its raw materials as well as the richest agricultural land were in the Occupied Zone. The Free Zone was self-sufficient in inessential produce such as apricots, chestnuts and sheep cheese, and its nugatory assets could be sucked out whenever its parasitic overlord felt the need.

On 30 October 1940, six days after shaking hands with Hitler at the railway station of Montoire-sur-le-Loir in a La Fontainesque scene of the goose meeting the fox, Pétain made a radio broadcast. He called the dismemberment of France a 'sincere' and 'constructive' 'collaboration', free from 'any thought of aggression'. It was an opportunity for the nation to purge itself of Communists and other undesirables. This would be the next stage in an 'immense effort of regeneration' which would save 'la France éternelle' from total extinction.

The État Français had already demonstrated its servile independence by enacting anti-Jewish legislation, beginning with the denaturalization law of 16 July 1940, many months before its masters demanded such 'regenerative' measures. Within three months, the French press would be reporting some spectacular advances. Jewish students were noticeable by their absence in the Quartier Latin, and the new telephone directory showed an almost fifty per cent reduction in the number of Blochs, Dreyfuses, Lévys, Rothschilds and Weils.

✿

The first organized resistance to the occupiers took the form of aid rather than aggression, and much of it was centred on the Demarcation Line between the 'Zone O' and the 'Zone Nono' ('occupée' and 'non occupée'). (Fig. 14.)

Jews expelled by the Reich had been heading for the Pyrenees and Spain long before the outbreak of war. Blown by the chill winds of hatred, some had been edging their way across Europe since the mid-1930s. At the Demarcation Line, they met Jews from Alsace-Lorraine and especially from Paris, which accounted for three-quarters of the total.

The Free Zone in the south was only marginally safer than the Occupied Zone in the north. Food and jobs were scarce, and the Vichy regime feared a flood of immigrants. The État Français did not wish to become what General Doyen, chief delegate to the German Armistice Commission at Wiesbaden, called a *déversoir* (an overflow outlet) for unwanted Jews.

Some people who found themselves living on the Demarcation Line risked their liberty and asked for nothing in return, but the refugees also had to deal with officious *gendarmes* and village mayors, corrupt border guards, experienced professional smugglers, and con men who left their clients in open country, assuring them that they had crossed the line. The busiest crossing points were along the northernmost sections. At its eastern end, the line would become an impenetrable barrier at the end of 1941, when Switzerland closed its doors.

Prices were pegged to the increasing danger and the customer's presumed assets. When the round-ups and deportations began in earnest, some gangs of *passeurs* operated like underground travel agencies. One group, according to a German spy, offered a basic trip across the Demarcation Line for two thousand francs. The full excursion from Paris to the Free Zone in a heavy goods vehicle departing from the Brasserie des Arcades in the Rue du Louvre cost as much as twenty thousand francs, which was the annual salary of a middle-ranking civil servant.

The most reliable *passeurs* were those who already belonged to an organization and had a certain *esprit de corps* – priests, doctors, postmen, electrical engineers and railway workers. Users of the SNCF network today will not be surprised to learn that for every needlessly obstructive, shoulder-shrugging jobsworth, there was more than one railway employee who asked for nothing better than to bend or break the rules for the benefit of a complete stranger.

Moulins had become a border town for the first time since the Middle Ages: the Free Zone began on the other side of the River Allier. On certain days at the Gare de Moulins, a vigilant *gendarme* or Gestapo officer might have noticed that the station was unusually busy or suddenly overstaffed with drivers, firemen, mechanics, maintenance workers and ticket collectors, all wearing the regulation uniforms and armbands.

A train would trundle slowly off across the Allier on the branch line to Commentry with extra passengers squeezed into the concertinaed gangway between carriages, crouched in a goods wagon, the baggage compartment or the coal bunker. Once the train was out of the station and clanking through the freight yard, men, women and children would clamber aboard or cling to the carriage door until the train had crossed the river.

> A driver who knew what was going on would slow his engine and create an artificial fog by opening the steam purge valves, and then whole groups of twelve or fifteen people, including numerous women, would take advantage of the snail's pace of the train to jump off and run away.

❁

Armed resistance in the early days of the Occupation was predominantly urban. It was also small-scale, sporadic and, in the eyes of expatriate French officers like Charles de Gaulle, disastrously amateurish. Some French Communists had gained experience of clandestine operations in the Spanish Civil War, but since the Soviet Union had signed a non-aggression pact with Germany, it was only when Hitler launched his land-and-air invasion of Soviet-held territories on 22 June 1941 that Communists were ordered by Moscow to take up arms against the Fascists.

On 21 August, at Barbès-Rochechouart in the Paris Métro, a German naval cadet was fatally shot while boarding a first-class carriage on line 4. Later that evening, two soldiers were fired on at Bastille. These were the first 'terrorist' attacks on German personnel in France. In the land of historical make-believe, it was the beginning of a tale of valiant resistance. In reality, it produced the unanswerable and unremitting response: the commander of Greater Paris announced that all prisoners of Germany or the État Français would be considered hostages and that anyone attacking German personnel or property would automatically be treated as a 'Jewish Bolshevik'.

A week later, a French court condemned three Communists to death for the murder at Barbès-Rochechouart. Hitler was outraged by this undervaluation of a German life: for every soldier killed, at least fifty hostages should be executed, then a hundred on the next occasion. He saw no reason why measures applied on the Eastern Front to stamp out resistance should not be used in France. The order was issued on 16 September 1941, with the Führer's own handwritten addendum:

> One must bear in mind that in the countries affected [by conspirators], human life has absolutely no value and that a deterrent effect can be achieved only through the application of extraordinarily harsh measures.

A month later, the military commander of the Loire-Inférieure *département* was shot by three Communists near the cathedral in Nantes. In accordance with the new law, fifty innocent hostages were shot dead.

News of these acts of terrorism and their consequences was

conveyed to the population by the wheedling voice of collaborationist journalism. *Le Matin*, 'the best informed of all French dailies', condemned this 'stupid and monstrous murder' of a German officer as an attempt to 'damage the prevailing relations between French and Germans'. The reprisals were 'harsh but necessary'. By contrast, the indiscriminate British bombing of Le Havre, which had killed French civilians, was an act of barbarism. Maréchal Pétain was quoted on the front and inside pages: 'I protest with all my heart as a Frenchman and a soldier.' 'At the armistice, we laid down our arms. We do not have the right to take them up again to stab the Germans in the back.'

These official appeals for patriotic collaboration with the Nazis, which now seem patently poisonous, were served up in a rich sauce of Parisian wit, trivia and public information. In the week of the Nantes assassination, *Le Matin* contained the usual horoscopes and gardening tips, cartoon strips and anecdotes. There were reports on the Maréchal's charitable initiatives and on humanitarian experiments with tobacco substitutes to ease the pangs of rationed smokers. Cheerfulness in adversity went hand in hand with intimidation. Decensored anti-Jewish books were now freely available again in bookshops. Jews (surnames beginning H to M) were to present themselves at the census office. As a reminder of recent legislation, there were notices of death sentences passed on men in provincial towns and villages who had failed to surrender a hunting rifle.

All over France, wall plaques and roadside monuments bear witness to acts of courage and heroic incompetence, some of which resulted in the salvation of fugitives, others in the massacre of civilians. There are no monuments to the innumerable acts of rebellion perpetrated by graffiti artists, printers and distributors of clandestine news-sheets, ornery ticket inspectors and careless waiters. Acts of micro-resistance served as a form of psychological self-preservation and probably had a more consistent and enduring effect on German morale.

Many a soldier's long-anticipated furlough in the City of Light was marred by the behaviour of a contemptuous Parisienne at a pavement café or a pickpocket in the Métro who knew his way about a German uniform. Even before he noticed that his wallet was missing, a Nazi officer might find himself, as he left the Métro, walking over a carpet of discarded tickets folded into a 'V' for victory or the double-barred Lorraine Cross of the Free French Forces.

* * *

In London, at 4 Carlton Gardens, the headquarters of the FFF, the 'traitor' Charles de Gaulle (as he was invariably named in the French press) was imposing himself as the leader of a government in exile. His battles were being fought on a vast theatre: he had enemies in the present but also in the future. Like bullfrogs waiting for a fly to free itself from a spider's web, Churchill, Roosevelt and Stalin all had designs, it seemed to him, on the future French Republic. Considered 'difficult' by the British, he was often kept in the dark and consulted only after the fact. He was not, after all, an elected leader, but he knew the value of a nation's self-respect.

De Gaulle's immediate task was to unify, from a distance, the politically and temperamentally disparate Resistance groups operating in France. Their ineptitude was an affront to a trained soldier. Operation plans were left on trains; lists of names and code names were kept in drawers; information was conveniently centralized in a few locations. Some groups were drilled by soldiers as though they expected to put up a good fight against a professional army; others were an assortment of hoodlums, desperadoes, drug-dealers, romantics, readers of spy novels, and spies. The 'French' Resistance included Spanish Republicans, Jews of several nations, East Europeans and Russian deserters who had been forced to fight for the Nazis. There were schoolboys and women – many women, in fact, some of them in command of men. Few had any special training and, it was assumed, would be unable to withstand torture.

Jean Moulin, a former *préfet* who had already survived imprisonment and 'rough treatment' by the Nazis, was appointed de Gaulle's plenipotentiary. He was first parachuted into France, landing somewhere in the Alpilles of Provence, on the night of 1–2 January 1942. His mission was to persuade the three main resistance groups to join forces in a 'Secret Army'. As a diplomat and administrator, Moulin was magically effective. When he dropped out of the night sky again fourteen months later, on 19 March 1943, and landed in a field by the Loire twelve miles north of Roanne, he was in command of a

Resistance that was as ready as it could be to assist the expected invasion by the Allies.

Moulin and his fellow parachuter, Charles Delestraint, military leader of the Armée Secrète, had the advantage of high-grade intelligence from London. The codebreakers of Bletchley Park were busy decrypting the telegrams of the Japanese ambassador to France. It would be a few more weeks, unfortunately, before they received the telegram in which the ambassador clearly implied that the entire Resistance network was an open book to the Gestapo.

✿

The situation in France changed radically in the autumn of 1942. On 8 November, the territories controlled by the Vichy regime in North Africa were invaded, from Algiers to Casablanca, by Anglo-American armies under the overall command of General Eisenhower. An Allied landing on the Mediterranean coast of France now seemed imminent, which is why, three days later, the Free Zone ceased to exist. All of France came under direct German rule, apart from an area east of the Rhone which was entrusted to the Italians. The Führer himself, like a landlord asserting his right of access to a tenant's home, assured civilians and Maréchal Pétain in a letter to the newspapers that the German troops passing through the Free Zone 'have orders to importune the French people as little as possible'.

It was then that men in offices in Carlton Gardens and Whitehall began to study relief maps of France. A number of thinly populated plateaux in southern France were identified as 'natural fortresses'. On those aerial redoubts, Resistance groups could be supplied from the air and trained in the use of machine guns and explosives by parachuted British officers. This colourful concept evolved into the Plan Montagnards: the 'mountain people' would distract and delay the Wehrmacht as it rushed to defend the Mediterranean coast. They might also help to block the subsequent German retreat along the Route des Alpes and the valley of the Rhone.

The names of these 'fortresses' were Beaurepaire, Glières, Valensole and Vercors. The Vercors seemed particularly auspicious. It looked down on Grenoble and over to the Alps in the north-east, towards the Rhone in the west and Provence in the south. The Isère and the

Drac served it as a moat, and its upland meadows offered several likely landing strips and drop zones.

The idea had such a Buchanesque appeal to French and British strategists in the dullness of wartime London that it retained its cheering plausibility even when Moulin and Delestraint had been arrested – one in a doctor's house near Lyon, the other at La Muette on the Paris Métro – when the Resistance was fragmented again into disconnected groups, and when the Wehrmacht in Grenoble had shown that it could rumble rapidly up to the edges of the plateau with heavy machine guns and flush out or burn to death in their hiding places the partisans and terrorists.

✿

With its large student population and dissident professors, the city of Grenoble had a reputation as the intellectual capital of the French Resistance. Allied airmen, prisoners of war, German pacifists, Jews and Polish refugees were given shelter and false identity papers and then helped on their way. One escape network was operated by the Church of Scotland minister Donald Caskie (nicknamed 'The Tartan Pimpernel'), who communicated by the valley of the Isère with Chamonix, where two lacy, tea-drinking ladies from the North of England restored fleeing POWs with soup and missionary hymns before sending them over the mountains with a local guide.

Since the start of the war, the population of the Vercors had more than doubled. On the plateau and in villages around the foot of the massif, primary school teachers and municipal secretaries with access to official stationery and printing equipment were prolific producers of forged documents. Priests christened Jewish children and provided them with certificates of baptism. Several thousand Jews spent the entire war safely in derelict farms and outhouses, in village shops and post offices, and in the sanatoria to which sickly children had been sent since the 1920s. Fifty-one Jewish fugitives lived at the tuberculosis preventorium in the hamlet of Prélenfrey. A doctor regularly cycled up from Grenoble to visit the children – an inspiriting or excruciating ride, depending on the weather, of eighteen miles, with a final climb of five miles on a gradient of eight per cent.

The *pays* of Royans and the lands beneath Mont Aiguille had centuries-old traditions of Protestant resistance. Gestapo informers were met with a solid wall of silence. Yet word of the Vercors spread far afield. Perhaps because the health resort of Villard-de-Lans had been promoted before the war as 'the children's paradise', Jews in the East heard of a promised land beyond the Alps, a 'new Palestine' fenced in by dark pine forests and watched over by snowy peaks.

Communities which were used to being cut off by snow and landslides, who had generators, limitless wood piles and blacksmiths, and who knew that a couple of steel-frame bicycles could carry as much food and fuel as a two-door Renault, were well equipped to support a growing population. When the Reich imposed the Service de Travail Obligatoire in February 1943, thousands of young Frenchmen came to camp in the heart of the Vercors where they scrounged and scavenged like forest rodents, happy to live as full-time boy scouts rather than as serfs in a German factory.

These *réfractaires* supplied the Resistance with its foot soldiers. The boys of the Vercors thought themselves particularly favoured. They were ordered to prepare a landing strip, and it was rumoured that General de Gaulle himself was going to land there to proclaim the Republic, which meant that they would be present at the dawn of a great uprising and would enter Grenoble as Napoleon had done on his return from Elba. When the cornucopia began to fall from the air – boots and blankets, bazookas and grenades, playing cards and cigarettes, as well as bandages and surgical instruments – it was obvious that men in high command in London and Algiers believed them to be a well-drilled guerrilla force. It was a flattering and unnerving estimation.

✻

The choice of the Vercors as a diversionary redoubt in the Allied invasion was partly inspired by a thrilling reconnaissance report written by an architect and mountaineer called Pierre Dalloz. The idea had come to him in March 1941, when he and his friend Jean Prévost were cutting down a dead walnut tree in the grounds of his villa above Grenoble. The villa looked over to the Belledonne range where the high Alps begin. To the right, the white cliffs rising out of the woods were a permanent temptation for a rock-climber. Beyond, on the road to Saint-Nizier, stood the ruined Tour sans Venin, the 'venomless tower' where no snake was ever seen, one of the Seven Wonders of the Dauphiné. Within the rock itself, barely a quarter of a mile away but on the far side of the torrential Furon in its twisted gorge, there was another Wonder, the Cuves de Sassenage – a subterranean network which inexplicably filled with water on the day of Epiphany and which was said to be the palace where the mermaid-fairy Mélusine had been imprisoned.

Dalloz's friend, Jean Prévost, was what used to be called an all-rounder before 'Renaissance man' appeared. He looked like a film star in the role of a PE instructor. He had a square jaw, a broad forehead and blue eyes. He swam, sailed, canoed, fenced, played rugby and had frequently out-boxed Ernest Hemingway, whose novels, as a literary editor, he helped to introduce to the French. He was a poet and a novelist and soon to become a prize-winning scholar. Two years later, in June 1943, General Delestraint would appoint him one of the two military leaders of the Vercors Resistance.

Prévost was in Grenoble with his wife, a Jewish doctor, to conduct research for his thesis on Stendhal. Though the report on the Vercors was the work of Pierre Dalloz, Prévost's presence electrified the familiar scene. 'From that day on', Dalloz remembered, 'I had a vision of the Vercors as a kind of island on *terra firma* . . . protected on all sides by a Great Wall of China.'

The report was written like a tourist brochure for commandos. It included a captioned map, a recent guidebook and some photographs. 'No natural citadel in France', wrote Dalloz, 'can compare with the Vercors'. The massif is enclosed by a rocky ridge, so that 'an attacker would be faced with an almost impenetrable wall'. Eight roads lead to the interior. Clinging to the edge of 'vertiginous escarpments', they pass through tunnels, across 'balconies hanging in mid-air' and over death-defying bridges. 'The military value of such country is glaringly obvious.' A few sticks of dynamite could easily bar the roads to armoured vehicles.

In this way, a Free France could be created in the enemy's rear from which the following could be launched:

- harrying raids

- a national call to arms

- large-scale operations

The report was flown out with General Delestraint from a field in the Jura on the night of 12–13 February 1943. In London, it was read by de Gaulle and the man who answered directly to the head of the Special Operations Executive (SOE), Brigadier Gubbins. Churchill himself was aware of the plan. It meshed with the strategy which he and Roosevelt had agreed to implement in August 1943: when D-Day arrived, 'air-nourished guerrilla operations in the southern Alps' would detain a certain number of German units and prevent them from reaching the Normandy beaches.

The Plan Montagnards was officially approved and a coded message was issued by the SOE from a flat at 64 Baker Street near Madame Tussauds. On 25 February, a stationary cyclist on the Vercors plateau turned the cranks of a Pedalator while a wireless operator listened to the BBC's short-wave French service. The words that gave the go-ahead came through like the voice of an oracle speaking from deep within a cave: '*Les montagnards doivent continuer à gravir les cimes*' ('The mountain people must continue to scale the peaks').

It would not have taken a code-breaking genius to suspect that this message, like the later '*Le chamois bondit*' ('The chamois leaps'), referred to a Resistance operation in the southern Alps: a short-wave frequency indicated an audience beyond the range of long and medium waves. But since the idea was to divert German forces, secrecy was not an overriding concern.

There is no sign that the officials who approved the Plan Montagnards had taken account of the two caveats at the end of Dalloz's report. First, the element of surprise was essential and so the increasingly 'turbulent and conspicuous' Vercors *maquis** would have to be trained to carry out covert operations. Second, 'a quick exit from the Vercors' must be guaranteed because of the inevitable reprisals. The point, however, as Churchill insisted at a meeting in Downing Street on 27 January 1944, was that 'brave and desperate men could cause the most acute embarrassment to the enemy'. The Resistance groups should be supplied from the air and then left to their own devices.

✿   ✿   ✿

---

* *Maquis* is the dense, thorny scrub of Mediterranean regions and especially Corsica. In the Second World War, it was applied to remote and inaccessible areas in which the Resistance conducted clandestine operations and, by metonymy, to the *résistants* or *maquisards*.

The white globes descended in serried groups. It was possible now to make out the orb of the parachutes and, beneath them, a dark, elongated mass which might have been a human being. Then came a dull thud – two, then ten, then twenty all at once. The great white flowers shrivelled up and lay flat on the ground. The miraculous cargo had landed.

The first major parachute drop was made on 13 November 1943 by a British Halifax bomber out of Algiers. The *maquisards* were forewarned by a message from the BBC: '*Nous avons visité Marrakech*'. The drop site was the rocky plain of Darbounouse, below the line of passes which runs along the spine of the Vercors, under the shadow of the Inaccessible Mountain's neighbour, Le Grand Veymont.

When American Dakotas joined the operation, they flew too high and scattered the canisters over such a wide area that the separate components of a machine gun or a weapon and its instruction manual sometimes landed several miles apart. Parachutes failed to open; a house was demolished and its occupant badly injured. Photographs of the drop zones show plumes of dust where the canisters crashed and exploded.

Despite the disappointments and anger at the unintended bombardment, the drops were important for morale. Since the arrests of Moulin and Delestraint in June, the Vercors *maquisards* had been out of contact with the rest of France. Remote communication was possible with Algiers but not with groups elsewhere on the plateau. Each pack of Lucky Strike cigarettes that fell from the sky was a reminder that they had not been abandoned. It was easier to be optimistic than in the dismal days of the Free Zone. The BBC and the counter-propaganda newspaper, *Le Courrier de l'air*, printed in London and 'brought by the RAF', reported heavy German defeats on the Eastern Front and the bombing of Berlin in which thousands of German civilians were killed.

The same news was picked up by German soldiers listening to the BBC. The war had been a happy hunting ground for sadists, but most combatants were frightened, unstable young men who had seen and perpetrated terrible acts. As love of the Führer rotted away, it turned into savage hatred of the enemy.

❋

The military commander in Grenoble, Karl Ludwig Pflaum, was the former head of the psychological test centre in Munich. He had fought on the Eastern Front, despite which, from an operational point of view, he appeared to be in a good state of mental health. In January 1944, after several acts of sabotage in the Vercors and the surrounding region, Pflaum took personal charge of all anti-partisan operations.

Two German officials, accompanied by a journalist and an interpreter, had decided to take a motor tour of the Vercors. At the eastern end of the spectacular Gorges de la Bourne, they had been ambushed and captured by some partisans. Next day, four German soldiers in a Peugeot 202, sent in search of the missing tourists, came under machine-gun fire near the top of the Col de Rousset. Three escaped; one was injured and later shot dead.

Pflaum knew that the arming of the Vercors presented a serious threat, and so he seized the chance to mount a full-dress rehearsal. Roadblocks were blasted away, telephone lines were cut and hostages taken. Alpine troops in white camouflage scrambled up to positions above the partisans while observation planes circled over the villages. On 22 January, half of Les Barraques and Rousset were burned to the ground. Seven days later, Malleval was utterly destroyed.

As D-Day approached, de Gaulle remained enthusiastic about the Plan Montagnards in spite of the blitz on the Vercors and follow-up raids by the dreaded French Milice (the paramilitary arm of the Vichy regime). The British were generally sceptical about the benefits of isolated redoubts, but Eisenhower was keen to use whatever help the Resistance could provide, though it would be impossible to support their efforts. Even if they failed, as they inevitably would, they would help to persuade the Germans that the Allies had decided to invade from the south. The deception would be all the more convincing because this is what the *maquisards* themselves had been led to believe.

❖

On D-Day (6 June 1944), at Bush House in London, the voice of General de Gaulle announced with long, funereal vowels that the 'Battle of France' had begun.

For the sons of France, whoever and wherever they may be, their simple and sacred duty is to fight with all means at their disposal, to destroy the enemy which stifles and sullies the fatherland.

The Vercors was silent, waiting for the promised paratroops. There was no sign yet of an Allied landing in the south. Anxious telegrams were sent to Algiers. Marcel Descour, regional chief of staff of the Armée Secrète, reported that all drop zones on the plateau were ready to receive supplies by day or night.

Vercors 2000 volunteers to arm. Initial enthusiasm waning through lack of arms. Extremely urgent send men, arms, petrol, tobacco, 48 hours max. Possible [German] attack in force. Effective resistance impossible present conditions. Failure will result in merciless reprisals. Disastrous for Resistance in region.

This cry for help was transmitted on 10 June. That day, fresh from a massacre of civilians at Tulle, a detachment of the 2nd SS Panzer Division, which had been ordered north to join the battle in Normandy, entered the village of Oradour-sur-Glane west of Limoges (confusing it with Oradour-sur-Vayres) to investigate terrorist activity. After crippling the men with gunshots to their legs, they spent several hours killing six hundred and forty-two people – nearly the entire population. The village was burned to ashes, including the church, in which all the women, children and babies had been locked.

A day later, Descour reiterated his request for '*maquis*-type weaponry' and reminded Algiers that 'the order to mobilize was given with a formal assurance that arms would be supplied'. At that moment, a Resistance stronghold on Mont Mouchet in the Margeride mountains of Auvergne, for which de Gaulle had harboured particular hopes, was being smashed like a wasps' nest dug out by a badger.

The redoubt plan was proving horrifically futile. 'Natural fortresses' were no more effective against a modern army than the *oppida* of the ancient Gauls. The Glières plateau in Savoy had already fallen to SS units and French Milice at the end of March. As the Vercors waited to play its role in the Battle of France, it was an open secret in London and Algiers that, unless the *résistants* were ordered to cease all activity and go into hiding, they and their civilian supporters would be slaughtered.

No orders to that effect were issued. Churchill and de Gaulle both knew that the Vercors Resistance was practically defenceless. But in the month that followed D-Day, the skies above the valley of the Isère were empty, apart from the German spotter planes which flew low enough to identify individual villagers as they scurried for cover. The shifting command structures of the Forces Françaises de l'Intérieur and Allied Headquarters in North Africa and Britain generated misunderstandings, disagreements and failures of communication, but no administrative or temperamental spanner in the works can account for the continuing abandonment of the 'Montagnards'.

Broader considerations may have had a cumulative effect without noticeably influencing any particular decision. Both Churchill and de Gaulle understood the propaganda value of a heroic band of freedom-fighters defying the evil foe on a sacred mountain. The Plan Montagnards served Churchill's ambition to 'set Europe ablaze' and de Gaulle's determination to fan the flames of patriotic fervour. On the other hand, as victory in Europe appeared certain, there was the future of France to be considered. There were already worrying signs of 'national committees' and 'free republics'. Well-trained guerrilla units with heavy weapons might coordinate local uprisings and the Allies would liberate France from the Nazis only to be confronted with a triumphant Communist regime.

✻

A preliminary attack on Saint-Nizier on 13 June gave General Pflaum and his superior officer, Generalleutnant Niehoff, a precise measure of the partisans' strength. It was followed on 22 June by an air-supported raid on the western rim of the Vercors. From then on, most of the telegrams sent to Algiers and London begged for the bombing of an airfield at Chabeuil eight miles to the east on the edge of Valence. Sixty planes had been spotted; others were hidden in nearby woods. From Chabeuil, the bulwarks of the Vercors looked more than ever like the walls of a prison.

On the night of 28–29 June, the longed-for reinforcements landed on the plateau: an American team of fifteen commandos led by Lieutenant Vernon Hoppers from South Carolina and an Allied team of eight, led by two Englishmen – a former bank clerk and a former estate agent. They were mobbed and fêted by a grateful population.

Wine was brought up from cellars and babies were held out to be kissed.

The twenty-three special operations experts were assumed to be heralds of the great invasion from the south – about which they could provide no information. Their mission was to train the *maquisards* in guerrilla tactics. Two weeks later, on 12 July, German planes bombed villages in the heart of the plateau while the machine-gunners on the roof of the planes picked off fleeing villagers. Guerrilla tactics were of little use against aerial bombardment, but there were still reasons to be confident. Jean Prévost and his unit had been rooting out all the young men who had yet to be conscripted, and the Vercors Resistance now numbered more than four thousand.

Excitement reached its peak on the morning of 21 July, when a flotilla appeared in the southern sky: coming from that direction, it could only be the Americans . . . The peculiarly elongated shape of the aircraft was explained when gliders were released and came to land at several points around the village of Vassieux. As the planes wheeled away towards Chabeuil, the black crosses on their wings were plainly visible.

※

The telegram sent from the Vercors later that day would not have surprised Allied Headquarters in Algiers and London since they had been kept fully informed of reconnaissance flights from Chabeuil and the recent build-up of German forces in the area.

> *Enemy troops parachuted Vassieux. Request immediate bombardment [of Chabeuil and Saint-Nizier]. Had promised to hold out three weeks. Time elapsed since organization put in place: six weeks. Request resupply men provisions equipment. Morale of population excellent but will quickly turn against you if you do not take immediate measures and we will agree with them when they say that the people in London and Algiers have failed completely to grasp our situation and are now considered to be criminals and cowards. We repeat – criminals and cowards.*

The 21st of July was the day on which the city of Caen in Normandy was finally liberated, more than six weeks after D-Day. Three thousand French civilians had died in the battle; three-quarters of the city was erased. This would be the pattern: first the destruction of the built environment by Allied bombs and tanks; then the mopping up of enemy units and occupation of the ruins.

In the Vercors, the annihilation came after the fighting. The German paratroops, arriving in advance of the ground forces, had orders to kill anything that moved. Some of the survivors would remember the screaming of cattle or the howling of a shepherd's dog. Families were rounded up and sent down to cellars into which grenades were tossed. Soldiers identified as 'Mongols' (probably Turkic conscripts and volunteers from the Ostlegionen) inflicted death with maximum humiliation to the victim and intolerable pain to the loved ones who were forced to look on.

Suspected partisans and partisan sympathizers were strung up with wire, executed with flame-throwers or subjected to elaborate butchering techniques. Few parts of the Vercors plateau are unfouled by some ineradicable act of cruelty. A visit to the small Musée de la Résistance at Vassieux can make a black cat sitting on a hay bale in an open barn look like a guilty sadist, and it takes a fast descent off the plateau by the hairpin bends of the Col de Rousset, with the fragrant air of Provence rising in sudden gusts, to blast away the horror.

Much of the fighting was centred on the passes, which offered good defensive positions and a choice of escape routes. But with Focke-Wulf fighters strafing the strategic points, local knowledge of the Vercors's topography and its secret places was as useful as a lucky charm. It was only at the Pas de l'Aiguille, where the summit meadow of the Inaccessible Mountain looks down on the grassy plain, that a besieged group of *maquisards* survived the machine guns and explosives. In darkness, they escaped to the world below, where, according to Lieutenant Hoppers, 'the entire Isère valley was guarded by one German every fifty metres'.

On 23 July, François Huet, the army officer who had taken over command on the plateau, ordered the *maquisards* to disperse and disappear. A telegram was tapped out to London:

All have courageously done their duty in a desperate struggle and weighed down by the sadness of being outnumbered and abandoned at the point of battle.

Two days later in Algiers, General de Gaulle offered the Provisional Consultative Assembly a modified version of events:

As I speak, the enemy is attacking the Vercors massif. . . . Despite its ferocious repression of defenceless populations, the enemy in no way has the upper hand.

✿

Jean Prévost and some of his unit had walked and crawled up the ridge to the east of the incinerated village of La Chapelle. They hid in a cave called the Grotte des Fées ('Fairies' Grotto'). It stands out against the dark pine forest like a whitewashed house: the mouth of the cave can be seen for about a mile along the narrow valley of the Vernaison and from every bend of the road which climbs the opposite slope. Perhaps it was protected by its visibility. Six miles up the valley, on 27 July, a cave that had been turned into a field hospital was located and plundered by six German soldiers. The walking wounded were taken prisoner, then shot. The stretcher cases were machine-gunned where they lay.

For a man of action, a week of inactivity in a cave was tantamount to torture. Prévost had buried his portable typewriter somewhere in the valley and was unable to add the finishing touches to his study of Baudelaire's poetic tricks and techniques. He and six comrades, including a local woman, left the cave on 31 July. He seems to have been making for the home of his friend, Pierre Dalloz. There is a logical route to Sassenage along the ridge, avoiding roads as far as Saint-Nizier. After Saint-Nizier, a forest track leads to the perilously narrow Charvet bridge across the Furon torrent. The sheer rock face on the far side belongs to the cavernous palace-prison of the fairy Mélusine. His friend's villa was less than half a mile to the north-east.

On 3 August, at the town hall in Sassenage, a rural policeman reported the discovery of five machine-gunned bodies at Pont Charvet. One of them had been found sprawled on the rocks beneath the bridge. The deaths of 'persons unknown' were recorded. They appeared to have died two days before. 'No. 5' was wearing a khaki jacket and shorts. There was an old scar on his forehead. 'Height approximately 1.7 metres, brown hair, blue eyes, average nose, wide face, very pronounced corpulence.' In 1947, this victim of a German ambush was identified as Jean Prévost.

The mention of 'corpulence' is surprising, but Prévost's diet, like that of most *maquisards*, had been practically medieval – days of nibbling nuts and berries, with an occasional feast of slaughtered cow or sheep. His admirers later imagined that he had flung himself into the torrent: it would have been a poetic leap in keeping with that vertiginous world. 'A true poem achieves its dark and melancholy beauty', he had written in the final pages of his *Baudelaire*, 'only by removing from the threat of death its violence and crudity'. But the parapet of the bridge was barely knee-high and the force of the bullets could easily have propelled a large body into the abyss.

✿   ✿   ✿

Grenoble, evacuated by the Germans on 21 August, was already under the command of the Forces Françaises de l'Intérieur when troops of the American 36th Infantry Division officially liberated the city on 22 August. On their rapid advance up the Rhone Valley and the Route Napoléon, the support of local Resistance groups had been decisive. In the Vercors, six hundred and thirty-nine combatants as well as two hundred and one civilians had died in the biggest anti-partisan operation of the war in France. But the French, British, Polish, Spanish and Ukrainian *maquisards* were still there, fighting alongside the GIs, when the last German forces were driven back from the northern edges of the plateau at Voreppe and Voiron.

Many French people heard of the Vercors only after it had become the symbol of a country under siege and its isolation was a memory. Inaccessible places now existed only in the dreams of fugitives. A monument in the village of Gresse-en-Vercors, adorned with the chamois emblem of the Vercors Resistance, represents Mont Aiguille, not as the sentinel of an impregnable fortress, but as a broken column, the classical symbol of a life cut short.

The Occupation had been a foretaste of the modern state, from which no secrets are hid and which, in its bureaucratic omniscience, could never again be trusted. Even for Donald Caskie, the Scottish minister in Grenoble who helped hundreds of Jews and airmen to escape, it was not easy to detect the hand of God in the randomness of injustice. The Tartan Pimpernel's thrilling account, which includes his torture in the prison at San Remo, is broadly accurate but the details are always artfully arranged as though a crime scene were being covered up. 'Straight at home and gay abroad', Caskie had habits of concealment which served him well as a *passeur*, but he was visibly extracting from his novelized experience the comforting moral which events had refused to produce.

> History does not so much play tricks upon a man, as confound him so that he is suddenly launched into the violently inexplicable. Poor chap, he must rely on a rickety bicycle. Eventually he finds that God can do more with a man on a 'rickety bike' than a tyrant can do with armoured divisions.

For a man of faith whose conception of history included eternity, this was undoubtedly true. It was also literally true for the Jewish children who were protected by the geography of the western Alps and cared for by a doctor who cycled up from Grenoble. This contemplative and practical kind of truth eluded many of the Resistance leaders who squabbled bitterly for half a century over the awarding of medals and the historical importance and ideological purity of their particular unit.

✻

As head of the Provisional Government of the yet-to-be-declared Fourth Republic, General de Gaulle visited Grenoble on 5 November 1944 to present the city with the Croix de la Libération. He urged its population to contribute to the moral, social and economic regeneration of France. 'It must no longer be the case, *n'est-ce pas?*, that a fraction of the French nation should feel itself to be foreign to the nation.' 'All French people born on our soil must without exception be integrated into the Fatherland.'

There were so many 'fractions' in the nation that it must have been hard to tell whether this was a reference to the Jews, whose nightmare was still being brought to light, to the Communists who had pelted the General's car with missiles that morning, or even the Pétainistes, whose beloved Maréchal had called for the 'sacred union' to be restored in very similar terms.

The 'inexplicable' violence of history had not ended with the Occupation. Between the Liberation and the proclamation of the Fourth Republic in October 1946, France was not a happy home for people who had offered comfort to strangers or who had pitied and prayed for the oppressor. The Pimpernel of fiction had operated during the Terror of 1792–4, when the guillotine was purging the

nation of its past. No Pimpernels were in evidence during the 'épuration sauvage', when unregulated courts of Communist *résistants*
tortured and executed 'traitors' – at least ten thousand but perhaps
many times more. The list of those who could be accused of 'collaboration' by the improvised courts was virtually endless: shopkeepers,
hoteliers, civil servants, printers, factory workers, policemen, but not
the Stalinists who had silently supported the Pétain regime in the
early days of the Occupation.

Reconciliation was not in the air while France was still at war.
Almost sixty thousand French civilians had been killed in American
and British bombing raids. The tonnage of Allied bombs dropped on
France was seven times greater than that which fell on the United
Kingdom. An Englishman who had seen the destruction on both sides
of the Channel found the German bombing of London 'tentative and
amateurish' by comparison.

The sphere of state influence now extended far above the mountain tops and into the lower stratosphere. East of the Rhine, no place
was safe. Between July 1944 and January 1945, more than four hundred
thousand German civilians were killed by high-altitude bombing
campaigns carried out with the explicit intention of damaging morale
and inciting the population to revolt. Though their families had
probably perished in the rubble and been consumed by the flaming
air, the German prisoners of war who helped to rebuild the villages
of the Vercors might have considered themselves fortunate.

16

Martyrs of the Tour de France

It was Stage Fifteen of the 2004 Tour de France (Tuesday, 20 July): Lance Armstrong had just taken the leader's jersey from the young French rider, Thomas Voeckler, who had held on to it for ten days of heroic suffering. The *peloton** – reduced by injury and exhaustion from the original 189 to 160 – had covered 182 kilometres in the hot sun, from the vineyards of the Vaucluse, up onto the plateau of the Vercors, through La Chapelle and Les Barraques to the holiday resort of Villard-de-Lans. The mountainside was littered with a picnicking throng as in the days when Alpine villagers congregated at lonely places in the hills where a heavenly visitation had occurred.

Saddled by journalists with the sobriquet 'the housewives' favourite', Voeckler had the requisite look of unrewarded valour. He was nine and a half minutes down on the leader and therefore, barring a miracle, out of contention. His 'Brioches la Boulangère' outfit – advertising a cloying breakfast 'treat' of factory-produced *madeleines*, free samples of which were now splattered over 182 kilometres of tarmac – resembled a fool's motley. The diminutive rider who 'carried the hopes of a nation on his shoulders' was a tortured ballerina strapped to a metal frame and streaming with tears of sweat. Some of his fellow riders shunned him as a self-serving show-off, but Voeckler in defeat was at the peak of his popularity. It was almost disappointing to see, as we left the press enclosure, that the martyr was making a speedy recovery.

Standing on an inflated plastic podium, Armstrong was adorned with the golden yellow jersey to a recorded fanfare and muted acclaim. We left immediately afterwards: the crowd was already flowing downhill and

---

* The *peloton* is the main pack of riders; literally, a ball of wool – hence 'platoon'.

the only lodging we had found was 50 kilometres away on the other side of Grenoble. The unrelenting descent from Villard-de-Lans to Sassenage through the Gorges du Furon was clogged with cars and camper vans, but a hundred or so cyclists were also 'falling off the mountain' (pro-cycling parlance for fluent descending at top speed).

Two cyclists whizzed past, then another close behind. I pulled out to overtake a camper van and felt the breeze of a swarm humming past with barely an inch to spare. Many of those riders were wearing the colours of their favourite team. I was impressed by their fearlessness: no doubt they were inspired by the recent spectacle of professional excellence, or perhaps this was the inherited spirit of the Vercors Resistance . . . Another group zipped past at well over 50 kph; some of them were holding a conversation as they plummeted down to the valley.

There was no question that this was dangerous: no one can tell what a tired or distracted driver might do. But the riders were clearly familiar with the conditions, and the cycling body has an amazing memory for the slightest twist and undulation of a road. On a difficult descent, a local cyclist can often serve as a safe guide to the angles and braking points and will happily 'tow' a stranger down to the foot of the mountain. I relaxed the brakes, hoping to tag on to the rear of a cyclist who was sitting upright, hands off the bars, performing a rotational stretch.

The stretching cyclist swerved and disappeared round the next bend. I pulled on the brakes and felt the ominous juddering which can occur when the bars of an accelerating bicycle are gripped too tightly. A light rain was beginning to moisten the road.

Hands trembling, I squeezed to a stop at a point roughly opposite the Pont Charvet where Jean Prévost was gunned down. There was a dizzying view of Grenoble and the valley of the Isère, still some distance below. Margaret arrived after coasting down at a cheerfully sensible speed. The rain was now falling quite heavily. She pointed to a rider skimming past in the pink jersey of the German T-Mobile team, and it was suddenly obvious that these were not local cyclists but Tour de France professionals who had finished the stage and found it more pleasant and convenient to cycle to the hotel than to sit in a team bus stuck in a traffic jam.

✧

Finding oneself in the midst of an off-duty Tour de France *peloton* is not completely out of the ordinary. From the very beginning, the Tour de France was conceived as a free public spectacle and a kind of collective endeavour. The Tour was not just a publicity stunt dreamed up by the cycling correspondent of *L'Auto* in its circulation war with *Le Vélo*, it was a three-week-long wake-up call to the country, starting at the Réveil-Matin ('alarm-clock') café at Montgeron on the edge of Paris at 3 p.m. on 1 July 1903.

The editor of *L'Auto*, Henri Desgrange, was a Parisian, a Republican and a Dreyfusard. In his front-page editorial on Day One of the Tour, he pictured 'his' riders 'burned by the sun and buried in night's shroud', flaying themselves all the way around France in six uninterrupted stages with an average length of 407 kilometres. As they hammered their steeds along obscure country roads, by the banks of slow and silent rivers, they would encounter 'the useless, the inactive and the slothful' and make them ashamed of their 'benumbed muscles' and 'fat paunches'. By sheer example and osmosis, they would rouse the towns and villages of provincial France, 'still fast asleep in their old ideas and theories', converting them to more progressive views and, of course, inducing them to take out a subscription to *L'Auto*.

Any bicycle owner could take part and although no amateur 'touriste-routier' has competed in the Tour de France since the 1930s, anyone can ride on the same roads and on a very similar machine. To the frustration of the wealthier teams, limits are still imposed on the expensive enhancements that would create too wide a gap between a Tour rider and a normal cyclist.

The expanding budgets of mid-life-crisis cyclists have allowed the sport to progress to heights of technical sophistication which Henri Desgrange would have considered cheating. He refused to allow derailleurs to be used, forcing riders to remove and reverse the rear wheel in order to change to the other gear. Each rider had to make his own repairs, and if the broken part proved unrepairable, it could be replaced but had to be carried all the way to the finish, which is how the Belgian Léon Scieur (a.k.a. 'the Locomotive') did irreparable damage to his spine by cycling with a buckled wheel on his back for 210 kilometres from Hirson to Dunkirk.

Desgrange might have approved of modern amateurs who prefer to wreck their knees rather than add an unprofessional-looking third chain-ring (which eases the climbs and weighs less than a small GPS unit), or those who literally kill themselves when competing in the theoretically non-competitive Étape du Tour, which allows mere-mortal cyclists to ride a stage of the Tour de France on closed roads. In the mind of Desgrange, the Tour was not primarily an exercise in physical self-aggrandizement but a healing of wounds – which, naturally, entailed a great deal of suffering and injury. Each Tour was a patriotic ritual intended to overcome the evils of a recent past by an energetic communion with the geographical realities of France.

The winner of the first Tour in 1903 was Desgrange's personal favourite, Maurice Garin, an Italian immigrant whose compatriots were the targets of xenophobic violence. Garin's victory was a triumph for Republican national unity. From then on, each Tour would be a state-of-the-nation report, a celebration of victory or atonement for failure. In 1919, when the cobbled lanes of the Ardennes were still bomb-cratered and forty-eight previous participants in the Tour were dead, Desgrange, finding the pre-war itinerary 'ridiculously short', more than doubled the length of the Tour in the hope that it would become 'an appalling calvary' to exorcize the horrors of the Great War. 'The chain of traditions that was broken by the filthy Boches' would be mended and the riders – some of whom had served in a cycling regiment – would 'preach a magnificent crusade throughout a war-torn land'.

✳

This mystical function of the Tour can be baffling to foreign spectators who brandish the flags of their own country and cheer riders because of their nationality. Most of the millions of spectators at the roadside are indiscriminate in their applause. The point, for Desgrange, was not to win but to suffer in the attempt. His was the convivial patriotism of a man whose country had suffered undeniable humiliations. Foreign riders were welcomed as a kind of expeditionary force that would fight alongside the home-grown riders. Two Germans took part in the first Tour, when Alsace-Lorraine was still a territory of the German Empire. Josef Fischer from Munich was honoured with a portrait on the front page of *L'Auto*. This was one of the Tour's inspiring lessons: the secret of a nation's happiness and prosperity was its ability to be magnanimous in defeat.

Desgrange himself had been a champion cyclist, but his principal asset was his Hugo-esque talent for quickening the pulse of a working-class and *petit-bourgeois* readership. As he watched the riders assemble for the first Tour in 1903, he gazed inwardly at 'the endless white road which stretches out before them' and recalled his own missionary years of adventure and discovery when he left his comfortable home in Paris for the provinces. He knew that he and his associate, Géo Lefèvre, had harnessed a powerful spirit which 'passes our understanding'. Political travails were just a surface manifestation of something far deeper, something which could work its magic only because the ostensible aim – determining the winner of a bicycle race – was a matter of trifling importance.

> I began to miss the days when I, too, was riding on the long roads, seeing phenomenal sunsets from the saddle of my frail machine, when I was lost under the starry sky and found myself the next morning – with only myself to thank for it – in new lands, where people spoke differently and the gentle-eyed peasant seemed to wonder where that man who came out of the darkness had started his journey.
>
> Now here they are, one foot on the pedal, the other on the ground. . . . A few minutes later, I see a cloud of dust rising in their wake, and that cloud is travelling at a terrifying speed.

❀   ❀   ❀

It was such a novelty and such an obvious fact of human existence that, although it made a profound impression on the millions who read about the Tour, it passed without comment. In 1903, for the first time, places of no apparent importance were randomly, it seemed, extracted from the geographical mass and haloed with the aura of a historical moment.

Until then, the only otherwise anonymous locations to enter common consciousness were battlefields, scenes of robberies or assassinations, or the places where a miracle had been witnessed. All other fleeting coincidences of time and place, apart from those described in literary works, were locked up in individual experience and belonged to the unobservable substrata of history.

Desgrange's descriptions of the Tour's itinerary, published before each stage in *L'Auto*, resembled the stagecoach traveller's guides and roadbooks of the eighteenth century, but without the robber-infested forests and gibbets at crossroads. Calling out onto the streets and roads of France a greater number of people than had ever assembled at one time, he democratized and dignified the spaces in which they lived their lives. The heroes they had read about in a Paris newspaper would be coming to their little corner of the world from far away, caked with dust under a blazing sun or surging through the night in the dazzle of a carbide lamp.

This is an extract from the itinerary of the sixth stage of the 1904 Tour, which ran from Nantes to Paris:

> The route is slightly undulating but generally flat: here is the Beauce with its immense and shadeless plain.
>
> After Patay, which is in the Loiret, it passes through Guillonville and Gaubert, where the steeple of the Free Evangelical church rises up like a directional signpost. At Cormainville, on the edge of the *pays*, be sure to take the well-made road on the right to Sancheville and Villars . . .
>
> Then comes Montainville, of 'Bang! bang! It was fated to be' fame,* then Boncé and Dammarie. Skirting Corancez, a little village of sad notoriety,† it continues through Morancez, past the church and the great oak of Le Coudray, and enters Chartres by the *faubourg* of Saint-Brice. . . . A visit to the superb establishment of the Auto-Garage on the Place Saint-Michel is not to be missed . . . The checkpoint is at the Grand Café de France . . . Then come the Cachemback barracks and the Restaurant des Carnutes (Mme Guérin). . . .
>
> The route reaches Gallardon by a steep descent which bottoms out at a tricky level crossing and the station of Pont-sous-Gallardon. Proceed with caution and go slowly through Gallardon (avoiding the longer way round). . . .

✻

---

* A music-hall song.

† Two years before, a widower of Corancez had killed five of his six children and the family dog with a hammer after learning that his lover would never marry a man with so many children.

One of those chance alignments of a moment and a place can be seen in a rare early photograph which shows the riders out on the road. (Plate 20.)

This is Stage One of the second Tour de France (Paris to Lyon, via Moulins). A drama is in progress: the riders are hoping to slip across a level crossing before the road is blocked by an enormous covered wagon pulled by two carthorses, only one of which is visible. The place is unidentified, but we know that the leading rider in the group of four is the eventual winner of the stage, Maurice Garin.

In pre-television days, the photograph – probably taken for the thirty-centime commemorative brochure (now unfindable) – will have been pored over and pumped for its secrets. The three leaders are wearing the white jerseys of the Garin team sponsored by La Française, a bicycle manufacturer and shareholder in *L'Auto*. The car in the foreground is recognizable from a sketch in *L'Auto* as the luxury four-seater Cottereau of M. Ouzou, a former racing cyclist, owner of a garage and driver of the Tour officials. The outskirts of a village or town lie just up ahead at the top of a rise.

The road has been dry for some time: despite the absence of mudguards, there is no spattering of dirt on the riders' bottoms or the horse's legs. To the left of the road, large sheets have been hung up on a long washing line.

The stage began at nine o'clock the previous evening, 467 kilometres and seventeen (for Garin) or twenty-six (for the last man) hours from the finish line in Lyon. The sun rose shortly before six o'clock, somewhere after Nevers, where they crossed the River Loire. Thus, only about two hundred kilometres were ridden in daylight. The shadows of the riders are short and fall to their left. Given the approximate time of day and the direction of travel, they must now be heading east, on the section between Moulins and Roanne.

The three La Française riders are down on the drops (hands on the lower part of the bars for acceleration and speed). A raised hoof shows that the carter has decided not to give way and lose momentum before the incline. The rider in black is sitting up, resigned to the obstacle or unwilling to risk a dash past a blinkered horse. The finishing times at Lyon and the race report in *L'Auto*, based on telegraphic despatches, point to Michel Frédérick, the Swiss rider on the Peugeot team. He will reach Lyon thirty-eight minutes behind the leader.

This scene snatched from oblivion, where four modes of transport span the centuries – horse, railway, bicycle and car – may well preserve the critical moment at which Frédérick lost the race. The angle of the sheets on the washing line suggests a still day with just a light headwind. Even if Frédérick is stuck behind the wagon for less than a minute, this will be enough to give three riders pacing each other (riding in close formation to reduce wind resistance) a definite advantage. At an average speed of 28 kph, it will be all but impossible for a single rider to close the gap.

The place itself is hard to pin down. The oblique intersection of road and railway is not shown on any map: only the lines of the national network were recorded, and this appears to be a single-track branch line serving a local factory. But there are other clues in the short climb and the sheds and houses at the top of the photograph.

As a historical geographer once wrote, the rural landscape of France 'resembles a big picture book of its own history'. Below an imaginary east–west line running south of Moulins, roofs are invariably angled at thirty degrees and covered with rounded 'Roman' tiles; north of the line, they have a forty-five-degree slope, more suitable for thatch, and a covering of flat tiles or slates.

The village clearly belongs to the southern half. The riders are passing through an ancient but still discernible boundary zone where domestic architecture, farming practices, legal traditions and the merging of dialects from the language groups of Oc and Oïl reflect a cultural divide. The Tour has either crossed or is about to cross the boundary of the Allier and Loire *départements*, which traces the medieval frontier of Bourbonnais and Forez. The village is likely to be Saint-Martin-d'Estreaux, built on an outlying hillock of the Monts de la Madeleine: it has no fewer than four knitwear factories, which might account for the railway, the heavy wagon and perhaps the long washing line.

From here on, the riders will be in the Midi. The air will be warmer and probably already is: two of the riders in white have left their jerseys flapping like spinnakers despite the loss of aerodynamic efficiency.

✻

The great cultural divide between north and south was still an active fault. Fifty-two kilometres after Saint-Martin, a car and a motorcycle drew alongside the riders. The men in the car warned them that they would 'never get beyond Saint-Étienne'.

On the next stage (Lyon to Marseille), they passed through the gas-lit streets of industrial Saint-Étienne and began the long climb to the summit of the Col du Grand Bois (or Col de la République). The 'great wood' had been planted half a century before to shield the imperial post road to Marseille from drifting snow.

Once over the top, they would catch the first pale smudge of dawn over the Rhone Valley, but in the pitch-black forest, the darkness was complete. The leading rider was a local boy, Antoine Faure. Forging ahead, he noticed that the road was lined on both sides by about a hundred men armed with stones and clubs. A moment later, the *peloton* behind him was a tangle of metal and limbs, and a voice was shouting, 'Come on, lads, kill 'em!'

Some of the riders were badly beaten; Garin would finish the stage with only one functioning hand to grip the bars. Standing up in M. Ouzou's car, Géo Lefèvre fired several shots from his revolver. The mob of 'savages' scattered into the woods while a gaunt-faced individual yelled at the officials, 'You see number 58 – Faure of Saint-Étienne? He's the one we want to win!'

This rustic conception of sport was quite in keeping with the persistent tradition of village battles and inter-regional wars. It can still be witnessed in some out-of-the-way parts, especially the Auvergne (which the Tour avoided until 1951). In 2015, the Auvergnat rider Romain Bardet had to ask his loyal supporters not to shower the British champion Chris Froome with urine. Death threats were now delivered electronically instead of face to face.

To the men from Paris in their shiny cars, it was as though the Tour had inadvertently revived some primitive state of medieval autarchy. In *L'Auto*, Desgrange condemned the 'band of Apaches' but was secretly delighted. A fortnight later, he penned an obituary of the Tour:

> The Tour de France is over, and I fear that its second edition will also be its last. A victim of its own success, it will have been killed off by the blind passions it unleashed, by the insults and filthy suspicions we have had to suffer.

The Tour officials were suspected of arranging for the sponsors' team to win; the riders were accused of cheating (taking trains or being towed by cars); some spectators had behaved abominably. It was left to the inscrutable Union Vélocipédique de France, in a show of sporting rectitude, to disqualify several riders, for no specified reason, including Maurice Garin and his younger brother, César.

Desgrange knew perfectly well that the nation would demand an encore. The battle of the Col de la République was precisely the kind of exotic, anachronistic conflict that would give the race its mythic aura. Those 'blind passions' were the blood of the Tour. For one summer month every year, whether or not it cared about the final standings, republican France would be presented with the dramatic spectacle of its most ancient rituals and religious impulses, still spinning out their tales in the twentieth century.

✿   ✿   ✿

The photogravures and telegraphed despatches from distant locations signalled the greater connectedness of the nation. The provinces were no longer coloured prints on a wall or pictures on a biscuit tin. Even before *congés payés* (paid holidays) and subsidized train tickets were introduced in 1936, the whole country was being opened up to vicarious exploration. In 1929, the magic lantern of the camera was joined by the miracle of the TSF (Télégraphie sans fil), and the illusion of reality was more potent than ever.

On 12 July 1929, listeners tuning in to the wireless at seven o'clock in the morning heard the sound of a man sobbing uncontrollably somewhere in the Pyrenees. Victor Fontan, who was said to resemble a Pyrenean smuggler (sly but rugged), had set off from Bagnères-de-Luchon at 4 a.m. as the leader of the race. A cavorting dog or gaping pothole had snapped the front forks of his Elvish bicycle at a hamlet called Le Pont-de-Cazaux. The race officials caught him in the beam of their headlamps: 'The man was desperate, staggering along like a drunkard, incapable of making a decision.'

Despite the unholy hour, a local man was there to offer him his old boneshaker, and Fontan had set off again, shouldering his broken bicycle. As they passed him in the car, the officials overheard him muttering, 'What's the point? It's useless.'

After six kilometres of purgatory, a garage-owner found him a less clunky machine, adjusted it to his height and watched him pedal off into the dawn, tears coursing down his face. Fontan was not a wilting lily: in the war, he had been wounded twice, nearly drowned and walked all the way across Hungary. He had ridden the previous stage, as *L'Auto* had exhaustively reported, with 'congestion in the kidneys and the lower abdomen'. He clawed back a few minutes on the short but savage Col du Portet-d'Aspet and the gentler but interminable Col de Port, but on the flat and peaceful banks of the River Aston near its confluence with the Ariège at Aulos, he threw in the sponge and sobbed into a microphone.

The recording has not survived, but the report in *L'Auto*, copies of which arrived on doorsteps all over France a few hours later, conveyed the scene with the usual epic realism, which is still the standard idiom of the Tour de France with its 'legendary stages' and 'mythical climbs'. Despite the increasing speed of transmission, there was still a magic in remoteness, and the information traversed the intervening space, thick with classical verbiage and tangled with countless other half-remembered tales of heroic mortification:

> . . . He fell too low from too great a height and disappeared, unaware of the fact that, throughout that day, hundreds of thousands of people wanted to know what had become of him. . . . He is a noble example to his French comrades, who should follow his lead a little more often.
>
> ('The Tragic Fate of Fontan', *L'Auto*, 12 July 1929)

❉

One of the first riders to be mythified while still alive was Eugène Christophe. An intensely practical, virtually unstoppable competitor, Christophe had spent much of the war as a travelling bicycle-repair man cycling along behind his regiment, and then as a fitter and welder of Peugeot aircraft engines. Before shaving off his handlebar moustache, he was known as 'le Vieux Gaulois', and then, when he became the first wearer of the leader's yellow jersey, as 'le Canari'. Fans usually called him 'Cri-Cri'.

In 1913, Christophe was barrelling down the 2,115-metre-high Col du Tourmalet in the Pyrenees, ahead of all his rivals, when the forks of his Peugeot bicycle gave way. The official story was that he had been hit by a car. The real culprit was the frame itself, but denouncing the shoddy workmanship of the sponsor's product was out of the question. Shedding tears of rage, Christophe lugged his ailing bicycle down the mountain for ten horrendous kilometres, searching for a shortcut because the mule tracks seemed to be in a better state than the road. He reached the little black village of Sainte-Marie-de-Campan, found the forge and mended his forks while three Tour officials looked on, as he put it, 'like marble statues'.

The man himself can be seen in a short documentary film made in the 1960s. Halfway up the mountain, the aged Christophe stands in the swirling fog, pulling energetically on a short cigar and talking in a gruff Parisian accent. With his round glasses and black beret, he looks like a stern abbot. As he talks, the fog thickens.

> This is where my forks broke, do you see? Here, on this very spot.
> Yes, yes, this is where it happened.

The crux of the story is that a boy – whose leathery-faced later self is brought out for the documentary – worked the bellows while Christophe hammered the glowing rod of metal into shape. The rule that no rider should accept help had been broken, and the time penalty as well as the three-and-a-half hours he had lost to his rivals ensured that Christophe, one of the finest riders of his generation, had no hope of winning the stage or the race. He rode for another thirteen years but never won the Tour de France.

A wordy plaque, now streaked with tears of rust, was later riveted to the wall of the forge, explaining what had happened. Despite losing several hours, 'Eugène Cristophe [*sic*] did not abandon the trial he should have won, and in this way provided an example of sublime willpower.' Much later, another memorial was erected at the site of his accident, near the first hairpin bend after the ski station of La Mongie, then another plaque in the village, and finally, in 2004, an alarming statue of a fork-waving Vulcan in bulgy modern cycling shorts which misses the point of the story by depicting Christophe 'victorious in the face of bad luck'.

✢

Roadside memorials to tragic mishaps belong to a tradition which is sometimes thought to have become so detached from history as to be irrelevant or extinct. In 1905, the Separation of Church and State had enshrined the secularism of the French Republic in law, but two-thousand-year-old customs and beliefs were not expunged by an act of parliament any more than pagan practices had been eradicated by the Christianization of Gaul.

When they referred to his trial on the Tourmalet as a 'calvary', neither Christophe nor Desgrange intended to Christianize the incident or to magnify the Tour with sacrilegious imagery, but religion and its rituals were vivid in their minds and in those of the millions who spent long summer days waiting for the Tour to go by.

In a land where the journeys of saints or their relics were marked by chapels and healing springs, where a saint called Bonnet had carried his own head from the Alps of Savoy to the estuary of the Gironde, leaving a trail of place names, there was a satisfying resonance in the thought of a man whose name means 'bearer of Christ' shouldering his burden and accepting his ordeal, speaking, more or less, the words of Jesus at the Last Supper: 'When you've started a job, you have to finish it, *no matter what.*'

The popular nature of these 'holy sites of cycling' struck me when descending from the hills above the vast reservoir of Serre-Ponçon towards Gap and the Route Napoléon. I was looking for the exact spot where, on Bastille Day 2003, the Basque rider Joseba Beloki had come to grief on what had seemed, on television, a relatively unproblematic stretch of road. With Armstrong hot on his wheel, he had crashed for no obvious reason, sliding across the road on his hip and breaking his pelvis. Beloki had finished third in 2000 and 2001, and second in 2002. Now, his Tour was over. He never fully recovered.

Quite unexpectedly, on the edge of a stony field, there was a crude painted sign attached to a fence post embedded in a ball of concrete. More than two years had passed and the post had fallen over, but the sign was still legible: 'Chute Beloki' (Beloki's Fall).

This monument to the martyred cyclist looked like a home-made Station of the Cross – 'Jesus takes up His cross', 'Jesus falls for the first time', 'Jesus falls for the second time', etc. Typically, this was the first stage in the evolution of a hallowed site – a makeshift memorial or an accumulation of votive offerings to a wandering saint. Most such marks of veneration left no lasting trace; others became the objects of local or even long-distance pilgrimages.

The religious parallels are obvious in the rare cases where the death of a rider is commemorated: the Tom Simpson memorial on Mont Ventoux or the winged statue of Fabio Casartelli at the Col du Portet-d'Aspet.* There is also a chapel in Armagnac on the site of a Gallo-Roman villa dedicated by the cycling fan, Pope John XXIII, to Notre-Dame des Cyclistes, where the jerseys of famous Tour riders hang from the walls and roof beams like trophies in a Gaulish temple.

❧

These sainted sites are normally associated with an extraordinary test. Pitted against the gods of wind, rain, gravity or, latterly, highway engineering, the sacrificial hero is defeated in his vain but ultimately edifying mission.

By definition, the memorial tends to occupy an inconvenient or downright dangerous position. Just after a blind corner on the precipitous eastern descent of the Col d'Aubisque, a plaque marks the spot where Wim Van Est, the first Dutch rider to wear the yellow jersey, went sailing off the edge in the 1951 Tour. A teammate, staring into the abyss, saw a giant 'buttercup in the grass'. Coincidentally or not, the forgotten name of the place is Aipourette, from the bright-yellow bog asphodel which grows there. Miraculously alive, Van Est was pulled out of the void with a stretchy rope formed from his team's entire supply of inner tubes. 'He survived the fall but lost the yellow jersey.'

Visiting these secular shrines along the old pilgrim routes of the Pyrenees is a perilous exploit in its own right. Fifty kilometres east of the Tourmalet, on the Col de Menté, where the road doubles back on itself with a nasty off-camber tilt, the Spanish rider Luis Ocaña won a painful moral victory over his rival Eddy Merckx in 1971 by earning himself a place in the martyrology of the Tour. The annually refreshed flowers and chalk markings on the tarmac were eventually replaced by a plaque affixed to a rock wall.

---

* Though the cumulative total of kilometres cycled (excluding the 5,668 non-finishers) is well over fifty million, only four riders have died on the Tour de France: Tom Simpson, of heart failure in 1967; Fabio Casartelli, from a crash in 1995; Francisco Cepeda fell off the Galibier in 1935 (puncture caused by an overheated rim); Adolphe Hélière died during a rest day in Nice in 1910 (swimming too soon after lunch).

MONDAY, 12 JULY 1971
TRAGEDY IN THE TOUR DE FRANCE
ON THIS ROAD TRANSFORMED INTO A TORRENT OF MUD BY AN
APOCALYPTIC THUNDERSTORM, LUIS OCAÑA, THE YELLOW
JERSEY, SAW ALL HIS HOPES DASHED AGAINST THIS ROCK.

The favourite among failures was 'the Eternal Second', Raymond Poulidor. 'Poupou' (a name he hated) was celebrated until his death in 2019 – and probably will be for years to come – as the champion who never won the Tour de France and never even wore the yellow jersey. One untypically congratulatory plaque commemorates the spot where he launched an attack and won the stage; it goes on to state, however, that, once again, 'he finished second in the Tour de France'. Another plaque, by the side of a drainage ditch on a peaceful stretch of tree-lined road in the Tarn, explains that

HERE, ON 14 JULY 1968,
RAYMOND POULIDOR,
HAVING BEEN RUN OVER BY A MOTORBIKE,
LOST ALL HOPE OF WINNING THE TOUR DE FRANCE.

The most successful riders are absent from the martyrology. There are no plangent memorials to the rare but spectacular misadventures of the Belgian 'Cannibal', Eddy Merckx, the unshakeable shadow and nemesis of Ocaña, Poulidor and all the other luckless aspirants to eternal glory.

✿

When Desgrange and Lefèvre summoned half the population of France to an annual ceremony of circumambulation, they created a simple, capacious structure in which incidents and emotions naturally arranged themselves into a familiar story. All French citizens, male or female, who plan their year around Easter and Ascension, the Tour de France and Christmas, know that this never-ending passion play is only superficially connected to the world of professional sport.

The organizers themselves celebrated the *lanterne rouge* – the rider who came last, hanging off the back like the red lamp on a train – and, in 1956, 'the Unluckiest Rider', who received a twenty-thousand-franc prize, no doubt deepening the despondency of all the other unlucky riders who failed to win it.

Unlike the national football team, the Tour de France *peloton* has never been representative of French society, and in the crowds which line the route, black faces are noticeably rare. Until 2020, no French-born rider of African or Asian parentage had ridden in the Tour. That year, Kévin Reza, born in Versailles of Guadeloupian parents, made an attempt to follow the example of other sports by proposing a modest demonstration of support for the Black Lives Matter movement. The insultingly cursory response of the organizers and sponsors, and the mere handful of riders who wore homemade BLM masks, proved that the official veneration of the republican Henri Desgrange was not even skin deep.

The folk traditions echoed by the Tour belong to the provincial France of the early twentieth century, which is not fundamentally dissimilar from the France of the present day. Though the Tour is apolitical, it mirrors the political world. Like the most popular Tour riders, some of the most popular Presidents of the Republic spent years in the wilderness. François Mitterrand faked his own assassination and was reincarnated as 'Tonton' (Uncle), whereas the law-abiding and record-breakingly unpopular Emmanuel Macron is tainted by his aura of effortless success.

Riders and teams from other traditions have struggled to understand this aspect of the national narrative. When the pharmaceutical dulling of pain became a matter of political and legal concern, the most commonly expressed view in France, but not in the French press, was that the organizers were to blame for subjecting the riders to such a harrowing ordeal. Before the Festina doping scandals of 1998, when another 'housewives' favourite', Richard Virenque, found instant redemption by shedding tears of shame in a police car on live TV, it was already an accepted fact among the Tour-watching public that, just as all politicians are corrupt, all professional cyclists take drugs.

The cult of heroic failure might explain the great mystery of modern French cycling: why has no French rider won the Tour de France in the last thirty-five years? A winner can be exciting to watch, impeccably polite and even able to utter a few words of French in his victory speech, but when he steps onto the podium on the Champs-Élysées, framed by the Arc de l'Étoile, he stands there as an imposter.

The beneficiary of other riders' suffering, he receives his reward on earth without having passed through martyrdom.

Bereft of the yellow jersey, French riders have concentrated instead on the clownish red-and-white polka-dot jersey which is awarded to the rider who amasses the most intermediate 'mountain points'. As though pre-despairing of overall victory, Richard Virenque, Laurent Jalabert and Thomas Voeckler would surge ahead of the *peloton*, attacking early enough on the stage to be virtually certain of failing tragically within sight of the finish line. The lone effort leaves the hero too exhausted to be a serious contender on the next day's stage.

The role of *baroudeur* (someone who fights a hopeless battle for honour's sake) calls for a grimacing face, a lolling tongue and a flapping jersey, and when the camera zooms in to catch the moment at which the rider is swallowed up by the pack, he draws his hand across his throat in an act of symbolic self-decapitation.

✿

Even for the least partisan spectator, the drama demands an Evil One. In folk religion, the Devil was a sartorially sophisticated yet strangely gullible trickster whose powers were almost equal to those of God and who enjoyed sporadic mastery over the physical world, especially the wild and rugged parts of nature. The rider who unwittingly played this role for most of a decade was Lance Armstrong, commonly referred to as 'le Monstre'. Before there was clear evidence of doping, his miraculous recovery from cancer was already talked about in France as a suspect form of resurrection.

In his final incarnation in the archives of the Tour de France, 'the Monster' lives on in outer darkness. The official *Guide historique* to the 2003 Tour, for instance, in which Beloki broke his pelvis, shows Armstrong as the winner, but with a line drawn through his name – and through his alone, though eight of the top ten riders in the list are known to have used performance-enhancing drugs. The cartouche in which the winner's face normally appears is blank.

In his early days, the One Whose Face Must Not Be Shown had found European cycling to be governed by recondite rituals designed to infect foreigners with a crippling inferiority complex. Yet few riders conveyed such an inspiring sense of the Tour de France as a self-destructive act of homage to the land itself. A man who could earnestly say of Mont Ventoux, 'I do not have a good relationship with that mountain', would have delighted Desgrange. The original unbroken lap of the entire sacred land mass had long since been fragmented into comparatively pain-free stages so that the annual map of the Tour's itinerary now looked like segments of spaghetti stuck to the bottom of a pan. (Fig. 15.)

For Desgrange, each journalistically exaggerated adventure had evoked the spirit of a place, like the *genius loci* which once took the form of a pagan deity or a saint. Along with all the other riders (including Maurice Garin) whose names were struck from the official record, Armstrong cheated and was punished, but his balletic bike-handling, enhanced by the collective elegance of the *peloton*, produced a beautiful choreographic collaboration with the geography of France.

✻

No well-balanced human being should try to emulate a Tour de France winner, but any cyclist can perform a *pas de deux* with the same terrain and feel the distinctive character of a place and a *pays* in the swirl of the winds and the persuasion and resistance of the gradients.

The Tour de France generates countless examples of this dance of mortals and the four-dimensional land. Each micro-event is trivial in itself, but like 'Beloki's Fall', it can reveal the depth and complexity of the relationship.

Cycling down to Gap and the Route Napoléon in search of the accident scene, I had found the descent surprisingly simple: the curves of the old road, sculpted and smoothed by centuries of use, had a particular rhythm which could be picked up like a tune. No obviously dangerous stretch had appeared, and the houses of Gap were already in sight when the bicycle suddenly hesitated and shimmied like a startled horse. The road had straightened out after a hairpin bend, yet there was something about its conformation which disturbed the rhythm of descent.

It was at that precise spot that Armstrong had avoided the falling body of Beloki and cut a straight path across the stony field, leaping over a drainage ditch to re-join the race after the next hairpin bend while the commentator, who seemed to be witnessing a wavering of reality, screamed, 'I don't believe what I'm seeing!'

Later, I looked at old maps of the area: the road before the bend was Roman; it was directly aligned with a ford over the Torrent de la Combe while another track cut south to what became the Route Napoléon. The bend itself did not exist until the 1950s, when engineers eased the gradient for the convenience of drivers and the inconvenience of a farmer whose field was cut in two. The 'improvement' upset the cadence of the ancient path. Beloki had crashed at the moment when the original trajectory was interrupted and he was teleported several centuries into the present.

Armstrong, who lost only a few seconds and saw his main rival removed from the race, had instinctively ridden the older route, across the field cleared of its erratic boulders by generations of peasants, across the pebbles pulverized by glaciers, over the alluvium of the torrents and then the drainage ditch which prevented the meltwater from washing away the soil. Technically, he broke the rule which forbids the cutting of corners, but the manoeuvre was so harmonious with the lie of the land and the spirit of the race that he escaped the prescribed punishment.

※　　※　　※

On 4 September 2011, on our way to Switzerland, we cycled into Pontarlier, the capital of *absinthe*, in the Doubs *département*. It was a rainy Sunday afternoon and the town centre was deserted, but the long road we had to take to reach the border was lined with hundreds of people. One of the big races in the French cycling calendar, the Tour du Doubs, was finishing at Pontarlier. The riders were approaching the pass of the Cluse de Joux and were expected to come roaring into town within the next twenty minutes.

At the 'Route Barrée' sign, a *gendarme* held up his hand. But when we promised not to dawdle, he waved us through and we began to pedal smartly towards the finish line half a kilometre up the road. A man was standing in the crowd with his young children. I saw him grin and point to the two cyclists with their touring bikes and panniers. He was evidently trying to convince the little ones that we were part of the race. The next few minutes promised to be excruciating.

To play along, I looked behind for the looming *peloton*, then raised my arms in the conventional gesture of triumph. The man cheered and the oldest of the children clapped her hands. Other spectators joined in and we were clapped and cheered until we sailed across the finish line, laughingly acclaimed as the unofficial winners of the 2011 Tour du Doubs. We kept pedalling until we were well out of town.

It is hard to imagine any other professional sport in which two strangers would be allowed to turn up at a major event and win a fictitious victory without being accused of mockery or sabotage. These communal *fêtes* are now strictly secular, but they perpetuate the cheerful and irreverent traditions of religious holidays, carnivals, fairs and processions of relics. The garish *caravane publicitaire* of the Tour de France, which showers the waiting throng with samples of merchandise, is a reminder of the commercial spirit which prevailed at inter-regional gatherings. Parish pilgrimages and village feasts are still popular, and although some French citizens make a point of airing their anti-clerical convictions when visiting churches on 'heritage days' with dogs and frisky children, the religion of the people was never much concerned with theology and clerical politics.

As a concept, religion probably plays a greater role in French society now than it did a century ago. Four-fifths of French people consider it a threat to the Republic and its values. Many of the same people take part in events which are rooted in religious custom. They know that the point of a *fête* is to celebrate conviviality, to buy and sell local produce, and to reaffirm the cohesion of the community. At the three-thousand-kilometre-long street party of the Tour de France, that pleasure of the *fête* is enhanced by the knowledge that someone else has taken on the burden of suffering and that the outcome of the physical contest, with its bloodied heroes and villainous victors, is of no earthly consequence.

17

La République en Marche!

A Credit to the Education System

A young French woman – nineteen years old, white, middle class, tidily dressed – is being interviewed for the evening news programme on M6. She has been positioned at a busy junction by the Place du Général Catroux in Paris, noted for its statues of Sarah Bernhardt and the three Dumas – *père*, *fils* and *grand-père*, the Revolutionary General, symbolically represented by leg irons and broken chains because he was the son of a San Domingan slave.

The chyron at the bottom of the screen identifies the interviewee as Maryam Pougetoux, Sorbonne President of the French National Union of Students (UNEF). As she begins to speak, a black car passes close to her right shoulder before stopping behind a white van at a traffic light across the street, partially blocking the monumental entrance to the Centre Universitaire Malesherbes. The stop light matches the red on the tricolour flags at the double doors of the entrance. The frailty of youth and the vulnerability of a pedestrian add a touch of dramatic tension to the scene. Mlle or Mme Pougetoux (French has no equivalent of 'Ms'), her head tilted up as she addresses a taller interlocutor, is pleading her case to a higher authority – not just the University administration but the law-makers of the French Republic and the early-evening audience of *téléspectateurs* sitting down to dinner.

It is easy to guess why the students chose her as their representative. Magnified by large spectacles, her dark eyes are fastened unflinchingly on the interviewer. She has been instructed to squeeze her argument into the shortest possible space of time. She talks, rapidly, for thirteen seconds, conveying the essential points with the merest smile and raised eyebrow of sardonic disbelief at the wilful deafness of the Macron regime and its apparent resolve to allow market forces to determine access to University education.

The interview is conducted and broadcast on 12 May 2018. Several campuses – Paris, Bordeaux, Toulouse, Montpellier, Grenoble and Nancy – have been occupied by students in protest at the new law on Student Orientation and Success. There is some surprise and disappointment that the Paris-Nanterre campus, with its proud history of activism dating back to May 1968, has remained comparatively quiet, though there have been sit-ins and banners with slogans addressed to the generation which is now in power: 'While they commemorate, we carry on.'

Fifty years ago to the day, students in the Latin Quarter were recovering in dormitories and hospitals from the Night of the Barricades, when riot police truncheoned and tear-gassed the long-haired anti-fascists, who counter-attacked with catapults, cobblestones, nail boards and home-made napalm. On 12 May 1968, workers had joined the students in a general strike that would send General de Gaulle helicoptering off to Baden-Baden to secure the support of the French army in exchange for granting amnesty to the right-wing terrorists of the OAS* who served in the military.

The May 2018 protest is noticeably less inspired by sociological, sexual and political theory. Today's students are concerned about jobs, salaries and pensions. They are less violent and paramilitaristic, and less likely to smoke and drink. However, they use a greater variety of recreational drugs and are probably more prone to false rumours: several decades into the Information Age, baseless theories have never had such an airing. One-sixth of students believe that Aids is a minor illness from which one can recover quite easily. Many students – especially female students – combine their studies with a job, predominantly in the service sector (shop assistant, waitress, cashier, child-minder, receptionist, kitchen assistant, cleaner). A student is also more likely to belong to an ethnic minority, though the precise figure is unknown because the law prohibits the collecting of data on a citizen's ethnic or religious identity.

---

* Organisation Armée Secrète.

Whatever the *téléspectateurs* might think of the student protest, the Union President herself is a shining advertisement for the Academy. Any University lecturer would surely be delighted to have such a cordial and concise young woman in the amphitheatre or the seminar room. Hearing her articulate exposé, an oral examiner or a government minister might consider her a credit to the education system.

Télévoyeurs

That night, and for several weeks after her thirteen-second interview, Maryam Pougetoux is pilloried by prominent left-wing public figures belonging to her parents' and grandparents' generations. The reason for the attacks is her choice of dress, misleadingly referred to as a 'veil', though it covers only her hair, ears and neck, framing her face so that even the sleaziest *télévoyeur* will be forced to concentrate on the parts of her which are involved in the expression of ideas. In 2018, the hijab is more provocative than the miniskirt in 1968, which implied a certain *disponibilité* and willingness to perpetuate social traditions.

A fifty-year-old political scientist who professes to be 'a strict *laïciste*'* (as opposed to 'a strict Catholic'), and who has previously spoken out against the 'ephemeral and caricatural nature' of online polemic, denounces this betrayal of state secularism in a tweet. More attacks follow: two male television commentators call her attire 'the opposite of feminism', a sixty-three-year-old Socialist politician accuses the students' union of 'sullying the battles we fought in the University', and the seventy-one-year-old Minister of the Interior, interviewed on the news channel BFMTV, stumblingly declares the young woman's appearance 'shocking' – though the wearing of a hijab is not against the law – and tantamount to a recruitment drive for Islamist terror groups:

> You see, when my Mum went to church she wore a veil . . . which, as such, was a sign. But it mustn't be the mark of an identity calculated to show that one is different from French society [*sic*].

'La société française' – the expression is dropped into the discussion as something which requires no elucidation, like a *croissant*

---

* From 'laïc' – lay, as in 'lay preacher'. 'Laïcisme' denotes 'the doctrine which excludes religion from all public institutions' (*Trésor de la langue française*).

ordinaire on a breakfast table. But French society has changed since these pundits were in short trousers. The headscarfed woman turns out to be of good French stock. Her great-grandparents fought in the Resistance and her great-grandmother was active in the suffrage movement. Her parents converted to Islam and gave their daughter the Koranic name of the Virgin Mary. Even before the law changed in 1993, permitting parents to choose whichever name they liked (barring risible names such as Clafoutis or Nutella), 'Maryam' was legally acceptable. The Pougetoux family hails from the Corrèze – one of the umbilical *départements* of central France which represent *la France profonde* and which candidates visit during presidential campaigns to prove that they have a grasp of rural affairs and know how to handle a goat and milk a cow.

Faced with this public shaming of her colleague, the national president of the UNEF, Lilâ Le Bas – blonde hair, blue eyes, scarf bunched at the neck but leaving the head uncovered – tries to enlighten the trousered elite. Students are entitled to elect a leader in a democratic vote, and a woman is allowed to define the meaning of the clothes she chooses to wear: 'It is possible to wear a veil and be a feminist', she explains.

'The rules of the public sphere'

Two weeks after the interview, the face of Maryam Pougetoux is displayed on newsstands all over France. It fills the cover of the nostalgically 'anarchic' satirical magazine, *Charlie Hebdo*. 'They chose me as their leader', says the speech bubble attached to a drooling, thick-lipped, simian-featured Maryam. Many readers – but not Pougetoux herself – express disgust at what the cartoonist, Riss (Laurent Sourisseau), must know will be interpreted as a racist caricature in the colonialist tradition.

Raising his mask of irony, the fifty-two-year-old cartoonist and majority shareholder of *Charlie Hebdo* – long hair, floppy jacket, open-neck shirt – responds with an attack on Pougetoux and her union. They have betrayed the principles of May '68. Any citizen exposing herself to public scrutiny 'must observe the rules of the public sphere'. He does not quite say that she was asking for it. He does say, however, that 'a citizen who does not find the rules to her liking can always stay quietly at home.'

To lighten the dogma with humour, he notes that the student union has recently been 'accused of several cases of sexual harassment of its female adherents'. (An investigation by the newspaper *Libération* has uncovered numerous acts of sexual violence, including rape, perpetrated by the union's male leaders between 2007 and 2015. This was the period when, according to one of the victims, 'Men did the thinking, women did the organizing.') The union has hit on 'the perfect solution':

> So as not to tempt the male students of the UNEF, the women will protect themselves by covering up the charms which the men would be unable to resist.

The article ends with a reminder of *Charlie Hebdo*'s political and intellectual heritage: 'Fifty years after May '68, sexual liberation and the emergence of the first feminist movements, the UNEF deserved to be put on the cover.'

'It's hard to be loved by twats'

May '68 had much more to do with the sexual liberation of men than with the rights of women. Men were demanding access to women's dormitories on the ghastly new Paris-Nanterre campus. As consumers of higher education, they were unhappy with the stodgy condescension of the authorities, the concentration camp architecture and the staggering boredom of lectures.

In those weeks of thrilling mayhem, when ideological graffiti flourished as never before – 'It is forbidden to forbid', 'Under the cobbles, the beach', 'A good cop is a dead cop' – access to women's bodies was one aspect of a wider liberation. Looking back on that bleary dawn, when the Paris sun shone through clouds of reefer smoke and tear gas, right-wing commentators in particular frequently refer to 'the burning of bras'. This rending of veils was one of the older generation's gifts to the young people of today, and those hard-won battles must not have been fought in vain.

Charlie Hebdo is a child of that age when the rights of consumers finally prevailed over the prerogatives of tradition. Founded in 1970 to replace *Hara-Kiri*, which had been banned for exploiting the comic potential of de Gaulle's death, *Charlie Hebdo* folded in 1981 but was revived at the time of the First Gulf War. In 2006, the magazine was accused of inflaming religious hatred with its cover of the Prophet Muhammad 'overwhelmed by the *intégristes*' (fundamentalists), saying, 'C'est dur d'être aimé par des cons . . .' ('It's hard to be loved by twats.')

After another cartoon Muhammad appeared on the cover, the magazine's offices on Boulevard Davout on the eastern edge of Paris were petrol-bombed. The next cover showed a man in a *Charlie Hebdo* T-shirt slobberingly French-kissing a bearded Muslim man. The magazine then moved to new offices in a side-street near the Bastille at 10, Rue Nicolas Appert. Five hundred yards away at the Bataclan theatre, on the night of 13–14 November 2015, ninety people would be killed, one at a time, by three French-born soldiers of ISIS.

In the Rue Nicolas Appert, on 7 January 2015, two Al-Qaeda members armed with rifles and their organization's trademark pomposity, after going to the wrong door and then the wrong floor, burst into the editorial room of *Charlie Hebdo* and spent one minute, forty-nine seconds (the title of a book by the cartoonist, Riss, who survived but was seriously wounded), shouting the usual slogans and shooting dead most of those present until the office resembled one of the magazine's gory cartoons. After leaving the building, they shot dead a Muslim policeman who begged to be spared for the sake of his wife and child.

Two women were present in the editorial room. One – a Jewish woman of Tunisian descent – was killed; the other was spared because

> You are a woman and we don't kill women, but you have to convert to Islam, read the Koran and wear a veil.

'Idiots go to war'

Less than a week after the massacre, four million people in Paris and other French cities marched in solidarity against the 'twats'. The rallying cry was 'Je suis Charlie'. The 'Republican Marches' were conceived as a show of unity in defence of free speech, a closing of the ranks against the threat of Islamist terrorism. Because so many people had found *Charlie Hebdo*'s versatile bigotry offensive, the quotation of the moment was 'I disapprove of what you say, but I will defend to the death your right to say it', attributed to Voltaire, but written in 1906 by the daughter of an English Anglican priest.

The organizers of the unity march and the Socialist Party informed the right-wing National Front that their members were not invited: 'We vomit on those who suddenly claim to be our friends', wrote one of the surviving cartoonists. Jewish groups asked why it was only now that free speech was to be defended with righteous rage when attacks on Jewish citizens, cemeteries and synagogues had become so common that more French Jews than ever were emigrating to Israel. French Muslims feared, with good reason, that they would be blamed for the crimes of godless maniacs and that thugs would use the shooting as an excuse for even more Islamophobic attacks.

There was resistance, too, from citizens of no particular political or religious persuasion who were unnerved by the air of compulsory unanimity. They pointed out that atheism, too, requires a leap of faith and that atheists have their own militant factions and inquisitions.

To no one's surprise, the site of the massacre became a shrine, patently Christian in inspiration, but purified by irony. The hands painted on either side of the entrance were copied from Michelangelo's *The Creation of Adam*. The slogan 'Tout est pardonné' ('All is forgiven') was written twice beneath head-and-shoulders portraits of the martyrs. Two other murdered journalists were shown as chortling cherubs enjoying an ambrosial glass of rosé below a dove of peace. There was a stencilled quotation from one of the murdered satirists, 'Charb', dated 2012. It suggested a proudly ascetic existence free from the constraints of earthly possessions:

> I am not afraid of reprisals. I have no kids, wife, car or credit. What I'm about to say may be a little pompous, but I'd rather die standing up than live kneeling down.
> #JeSuisCharlie

When I visited the shrine in 2017, there were only two dissident notes. Someone had drawn little Hitler moustaches on three of the portraits; someone else had scratched a quotation beneath the two cherubs:

> 'GROTESQUE CREED . . .
> IDIOTS GO TO WAR AGAINST OTHER IDIOTS.'
> KAFKA

I took this to be an attempt to reposition the struggle on a higher plane, to ignore the disparity between the weapons of argument – the pen and the assault rifle – and to suggest that belligerence of any creed would never lead to truth and happiness. The attribution to Kafka implied the same aversion to dictatorial dogma as the Hitler moustaches. I later discovered that the words were taken from the song of a white rapper from the French Basque Country who was expressing his hatred of monotheism. 'Monothéiste' is the title of the song.

'Isms' have played an active role in French revolutions since 1789. In a country where ideologies are not automatically dismissed as vaporous abstractions, there is nothing strange about a rap song which rhymes 'monothéiste' with 'Nemesis' and 'apostasie' with 'fusil' (rifle).

Patriotic Terrorism

Among the perpetrators of terrorist attacks in France since the mid-1980s – Marxist guerrillas, fundamentalist Catholics, the far-left Action Directe group, Hezbollah, the Mujahedin, Algerian Islamists, Basque, Breton and Corsican separatists, Greek anarchists, Spanish anti-terrorists, international jihadists and anti-Semitic groups (left wing, right wing, foreign and domestic, anti-Zionist and neo-Nazi) – Islamists occupy a special place.

The fifth and current French Republic was founded by a referendum in 1958 during a horrendous civil war. Many French citizens considered, and still consider, the referendum to have been a disguised *coup d'état*. Almost four-fifths of the electorate voted to bestow enduring emergency powers on General de Gaulle. The constitution, which is still in force, was intended by de Gaulle to turn a national crisis into a 'resurrection'.

The War of Algerian Independence (1954–62), in which more than twenty-five thousand French soldiers and one quarter of a million Algerians would die – in the mountains of Kabylie and Aurès, in the cities of Algiers and Oran, in concentration camps and torture centres – was on the verge of provoking a military coup. De Gaulle decided that he might once again be 'useful' to France. In his first press conference for three years, speaking in his bar-room comic voice and gesticulating like an automated scarecrow, he replied to a journalist who had asked whether 'fundamental public liberties' would be curtailed: 'Why on earth, at the age of sixty-seven, would I embark on a career as a dictator, eh?!'

The journalists laughed and scribbled. No one asked but many wondered what would happen when a less venerable President wielded the extraordinary powers which de Gaulle promised not to abuse. The new presidential regime was installed, and the rebel French generals agreed not to topple the government, believing that, under de Gaulle, Algeria would remain French . . . The war ended in 1962 with the granting of independence to Algeria and the exodus to France of about a million *pieds noirs* (white French Algerians), many of whom had never set foot in France.

Algerian Muslims had always been denied equal rights and treated as an inferior race. In Paris itself, in October 1961, about two hundred Algerians peacefully protesting against a curfew imposed by a Prefect of Police who had helped to populate Nazi death camps were beaten to death and drowned in the Seine by the police. To the disgust of the patriotic terrorists of the OAS, condemnation by the United Nations and the diplomatic isolation of France had been treated as reasons to grant independence to Algeria. They were outraged by the peace agreement which entitled Algerians to work in France without a visa. An inept but bloody bombing campaign ensued and succeeded in alienating public opinion and enhancing the prestige of the unmurderable General de Gaulle.

From then on, 'Arabs', presumed to be generically Muslim, were widely considered to be immigrants, even if their families had been French for several generations. Nationality was increasingly associated with ethnicity. In 1998, France won the football World Cup with a team in which ethnic minorities were unusually well represented: the captain, Zinédine Zidane, was a French-born Algerian Kabyle. I congratulated a French former colleague on France's victory: 'France!' he replied, with audible inverted commas. 'La "France" a gagné, dites-vous? . . .' ('Won by *France*, was it?')

Several of those players came from the neglected Paris *banlieue*, where popular revolts – recognized as such in police intelligence reports – have often been repressed with the same official violence which helped to cause them. Founded in war and unrest, the Fifth Republic has shown a high capacity for absorbing and even partially tolerating violent groups perceived to be essentially French – the terrorist OAS, the incendiary students of May '68, the road-blocking, McDonald's-demolishing farmers of the Larzac. But the Republic can also mete out violence when the threat appears to come from a hostile cultural domain. The rioters in the *banlieue* were white, black and brown, but they were constantly referred to as 'Arabs', and the rise of jihadism seemed to confirm the foreignness of what Minister of the Interior Sarkozy called the *racaille* ('scum'). It became necessary for the state, not just to repress, but to convert the minorities to the state religion of *laïcité*.

'We're Catholic here'

In 2004, the Assemblée Nationale passed a law which put a little more flesh on the bones of the Education Code as it related to secularism and the separation of Religion and State. The new law, which applied to all public schools but not universities, banned 'the wearing of symbols and forms of dress conspicuously demonstrating a religious affiliation'.

This was a very small piece of flesh for very large bones. A report by the Senate interpreted it as a ban on proselytizing but not on 'the discreet and intimate affirmation of faith': pupils should be allowed to wear a jewel-sized symbol such as a medallion, a small cross, a Star of David pendant or a Hand of Fatima, provided that the object itself did not have the power to provoke 'a contrary manifestation'. The critical size of the religious symbol, in other words, would be determined by the ire of a dissenting zealot. Ideally, the symbol would be rendered impotent by near-invisibility: obviously, this ruled out head-scarves. The leaders of Al-Qaeda redeclared war on the Crusader-Zionists and their agents.

✿

On 23 August 2016, four white men are sauntering between the slabs of flesh basking on the beach at Nice. Two are dressed in black shorts, reinforced T-shirts and trainers. One has a tattoo on his arm, shiny bracelets on his wrist and a bunch of small keys dangling from his belt. Broadly speaking, their clothing belongs to the bondage section of the couture spectrum with their straps, studs and buckles, and hard little box-shaped bulges on the midriff and thigh.

All four have the bowed arms of men who lug heavy objects for a living or who build their muscles at the gym. The effect is exaggerated by the bulky appendages – radio, pistol, shotgun, truncheon. This could be an open-air photo-shoot for the catalogue of the Rhinodefense company, which sells uniforms and self-defence equipment to firemen, policemen and, to judge by the online reviews, foreigners and unofficial-sounding customers identified only by forename: 'Handcuffs came without packaging – must be second-hand.' 'I ordered two tear-gas bombs but only one arrived.'

The two men in long trousers and boots are more clearly labelled 'Police Municipale'. All four are standing over a woman who is lying on the hot pebbles of the beach in black leggings and a black halter under a blue beachwear top. She has covered her hair with a matching striped scarf or bandana arranged as a turban. One of the policemen in shorts squats down to write out a ticket which states that the woman has incurred a fine for failing to wear 'correct dress showing respect for *bonnes moeurs* and *laïcité*'. She sits up and pulls the blue top over her head, revealing her bare arms. This seems to satisfy the policemen, who are smiling, not unkindly.

Bonnes moeurs ('good morals' or 'decency') is a slippery concept, undefined in law, but understood to refer to behaviour which is considered acceptable by decent people at a given moment in time. In another age, the blubbery bellies and bottoms of the other sunbathers would have constituted an 'outrage aux bonnes moeurs'.

Six weeks before, on Bastille Day, a mentally unstable Tunisian Islamist with a record of drug use and domestic violence drove along the Promenade des Anglais in a truck, killing eighty-six people, more than one-third of whom were Muslim. It is no wonder that the municipalities of the Côte d'Azur are extremely sensitive to the outward signs of Islam. Several mayors have enacted by-laws banning the wearing of the 'burkini' (swimwear designed for Muslim women).

✵

There was nothing explicitly Islamic about the dress of the woman on the beach. A piece of material folded into a turban might sit quite unprovocatively on the head of a film star or a concierge. On the same day, at Cannes, a former air hostess on holiday with her family from Toulouse was booked by the police in almost identical circumstances, except that she had a little daughter who was in tears and was ordered, bafflingly, to rearrange her scarf as a bandana or leave the beach.

Some people disagreed with the police action, but others shouted at the woman, 'Go back where you came from! We're Catholic here – we don't want any of that!' As a religiously aggravated verbal assault, this was technically an offence, but the headscarf by-law has the boomerang effect of inculpating the target of the abuse. The arrow would not have been fired if there hadn't been a target.

That summer, thirty-two towns on the Côte d'Azur, in Corsica and in the region of Calais enacted the ban: several other women, but no men, were fined under by-laws the legality of which was subsequently found to be dubious. The women at Nice and Cannes were identified as Muslim, not by their clothes, but by the colour of their skin. A racist may not be able to distinguish a recent Arab immigrant from a descendant of French Algerian parents. He may not know whether a particular Arab is Muslim, Christian, agnostic or atheist. But his mental checklist of skin tone and physiognomy will enable him to pin down an individual to a certain stretch of Mediterranean shore. He will never mistake an olive-skinned Provençale for a woman from Lebanon or the Maghreb.

Several French commentators and female politicians found the cultural resonance of these beach scenes disturbing. They belonged to the history of powerful men ordering women to remove their clothes. It was thirty-two years since evening television screens had begun to redden and bulge with nudity. After the inception in 1984 of Canal Plus, which veiled its content from non-subscribers with a teasing curtain of interference, no garment worn by a young woman in a light entertainment programme could be guaranteed to remain on her body for the duration of the broadcast. In the soft-porn gallery of bus shelters, newsstands, shop windows and billboards, nakedness became a virtual attribute of every young woman.

The Socialist Prime Minister Manuel Valls defended the municipal burkini ban and, confused by his recollection of Delacroix's *La Liberté guidant le Peuple* (1830) – also known as *Liberty on the Barricades* – declared that Marianne, the classical Revolutionary personification of the Republic, 'has bare breasts'. 'That, for me, is the Republic.'

What would Robespierre have said?

The First Republic, born in the blood of French subjects, had cleansed itself in a missionary war against foreign hordes and imposed its ideals on half of Europe. The Fifth Republic concentrated its attacks on individual citizens. Its volunteer defenders targeted that sliver of the national Venn diagram which embraces the young, the female, the minority ethnic and the powerless. Secularism proclaimed its good intentions but did nothing to promote integration. Its enemies were to be shamed and silenced.

National Front supporters were wooed with anti-immigrant policies and patriotic gestures such as the Fillon Law of 2005, defined in the statute as 'a response to the challenge of assimilating external populations'. It made the national anthem, 'La Marseillaise', a compulsory part of the syllabus in a surprisingly unmodernized version. Since then, choirs of primary school children have touchingly called for 'the bloodied banner' to be raised on high and the 'furrows' of France to be irrigated with the 'impure blood' of tyrants.

The conflict had spread to the Academy some years before the Sorbonne President of the UNEF was pilloried in the media. University amphitheatres and classrooms had been a generational war zone in the 1960s and 70s. The final-year *lycée* students I taught in 1979–80 still wore polo-neck sweaters, listened to Boris Vian records and occasionally went on strike, barricading classrooms and singing 'Blowin' in the Wind' to the strumming of a Yamaha guitar. At the local university, students asserted their right to be taken seriously by the authorities. A first-year medical student proudly told me of a successful rebellion against a professor who had been prevented from delivering her first lecture by a whispering crescendo of 'À poil! À poil!' ('Take 'em off!') The professor had removed her jacket, blouse and bra, asked whether the conditions had now been met, and was then allowed to continue with her clothes on.

That disputatious generation was now launching its attacks from the other side of the lectern. Veil-wearing students were sometimes singled out and even ejected from a course by lecturers who imposed their own righteous rules in wilful ignorance of the law and the university's regulations.

At Aix-en-Provence in September 2014, an eminent professor of colonial military history was lecturing on the 1789 Declaration of the Rights of Man and the Citizen. He was banging on the desk, emphasizing the key concepts with peculiar insistence – 'laïcité!', 'liberté de culte!' While he banged and vociferated, his eyes were fastened on a girl in the back row of the amphitheatre who was dressed in a chador cloak, which leaves the face uncovered. The girl, who had earned a place at the university under the equal opportunities programme, began to break down under the onslaught. 'Freedom of worship!' thundered the lecturer. The students were stunned. He raged about 'proselytizing' and accused the girl of being 'a Trojan horse of Islamism'. She left the amphitheatre, sobbing, along with some of her friends. Other students stayed behind to question the professor, who defended his outburst and continued his lecture, ignoring the students who called him an 'intégriste de la laïcité' ('secular fundamentalist').

✻

The proponents of militant secularism were annoyed that whenever a professor attacked a Muslim student, the university authorities apologized, usually in private, to the 'Trojan horse'. One aggressive defender of the secularist faith, a self-styled 'gladiator of laïcité', who was hailed by his liberal followers and, embarrassingly, by some far-right anti-Islamists, asked at a freedom of speech conference held at the Folies Bergère in Paris, 'What would Diderot have said?'

One reason people still read the philosopher, encyclopaedist and pornographer Denis Diderot is that we don't know what he would have said – probably something satirical and humane. A more answerable question might be: what would Maximilien Robespierre have said?

In 1794, during the Terror, an agent of the Committee of Public Safety in Senlis had bragged about his local war on religious 'fanaticism'. Robespierre warned him to 'stay within the law, respect the decree which establishes the freedom of worship, and do good without false zeal'. Another man, claiming to represent the commune of Exmes in Normandy, wrote to the Committee to ask whether the crosses which women wore around their necks should be counted among the 'conspicuous signs of religious faith along with crucifixes and icons' and, therefore, destroyed. Robespierre sent the letter on to the chief of police, ordering him to investigate the writer because the man was obviously 'either a fool or a rogue'.

Belleville

For most French citizens in the early twenty-first century, life went on much the same as before. Seen from abroad, France appeared to be suffering from chronic ideological confusion. There were now several groups, soon to be joined by the Gilets Jaunes protesters, fighting for the Republic as they saw it, each battling the other to defend the same sacred fortress. This was the root of the Fifth Republic's durability. Founded in 1958, and now almost as long-lived as the Third Republic (1870–1940), its constitution was based on abstract principles, any one of which – freedom, equality, the religious neutrality of the state – could be reconceived as the fundament of the whole structure rather than as one of several pillars. Meanwhile, social norms could prevail and regimes change without creating a sense that society itself was under threat.

The stability of the French Republic does not depend on the clubby political parties which give British parliamentary politics the air of a long-running soap opera or exclusive sports league. The thirty-nine-year-old President elected in May 2017 was the founder of a brand-new, purportedly all-purpose left-centre-right party called La République en Marche! ('The Republic on the Move!'). The exclamation mark is *de rigueur*.

Campaigning under this soldierly banner, Emmanuel Macron, a graduate of Paris-Nanterre, former investment banker and Minister for the Economy, Industry and Digital Affairs, laid out his presidential wardrobe. The avowedly 'Jupiterian' but centrist, moralizing but modernizing, patriotic but pro-European presidential candidate mobilized a sufficient mass of cynical and grudging Socialist voters to obtain two-thirds of the vote in the second round of the elections in June 2017.

One year into his presidency, Macron had proved himself capable, on occasion, of appealing to people who would never have voted for him. In December, he delivered a genuinely tear-jerking eulogy at the epic funeral of the beloved king of rock and roll, Johnny Hallyday, the least Macronesque personality imaginable. In July 2018, when he welcomed the World Cup-winning French football team to the Élysée Palace with a back-slapping, shouty speech of thanks, his

ratings on the precise national moodometer of CEVIPOF* were
only just beginning to wobble. 'Dégoût', 'morosité' and 'méfiance'
(disgust, gloom, mistrust) were still at the normal high but uncritical
levels.

*

That sunny summer in Paris, in contrast to Brexit London, the mood
was generally positive. The buses, the Métro and most trains were
running. The Mayor of Paris, Anne Hidalgo, had been waging a
humanitarian campaign against the motor car. If the wind was blowing
from the right direction, on a bridge over the Seine, it could seem
quite healthy and desirable, for the first time in decades, to take a
deep breath of nostalgic Parisian air.

Paris had more or less survived the years of gentrification, the
expulsion of cottage industries and the proliferation of office space.
In the old proletarian Ceinture Rouge (the Communist-voting 'red
belt' surrounding the gilded centre), gun fights had been part of the
late-evening soundscape well within living memory. There was still
an intriguing shabbiness about some of the *quartiers* inside the *boulevards extérieurs*. Belleville, a thirty-minute walk from the Gare du
Nord and the Place de la Bastille, was gritty and graffitied, but to the
middle-class pioneers who rented refurbished or newly built apartments in the *quartiers populaires*, it was a place where 'you can still
find the real Paris'.

Bourgeois colonization of Belleville had begun with hand-to-
mouth artists and creators of original glassware and ceramics. Young
professionals and students with parental backing found the 'bohemian'
presence reassuring, and they appreciated the 'mix of ethnicities' (this
referred mainly to food shops and restaurants). The streets still
belonged to the indigenous working-class population, but the incomers
had their own open-air bridgeheads in the pavement cafés along the
main western artery, which preserved the names of the former villages:
Boulevard de Ménilmontant, Boulevard de Belleville, Boulevard de la
Villette.

On 24 July 2018, twelve days after President Macron had fêted

---

* Centre d'études de la vie politique française, now the Centre de recherches politiques de Sciences Po, but identified with the same acronym.

the national football team at the Élysée, about a dozen men and women in their early twenties were sitting in pairs and groups on the bollarded terrace of Le 9B – a designedly cool but low-key meeting place with metal furniture on the terrace and old movie posters and good music within. Here at the corner of Rue Burnouf and Boulevard de la Villette, the pavement bulges out so that customers are protected from the traffic, with the additional buffer of a cycle lane.

The owner had installed wide-angle CCTV to keep an eye on the terrace. Most of the minute-and-a-quarter segment of footage which went viral is one of those impartially filmed sequences which, to a historian in the far future, will be as valuable as a fossil-slab of corals and crinoids swarming with everyday detail.

The time shown on the screen is 18.35. The T-shirts and summery frocks suggest a warm evening. Everyone is talking in non-virtual reality. Two girls are sitting under the tricolour flag which hangs on the front of the café. A woman at the table behind has rolled a cigarette and is asking for a light. The silent footage could be used as a language-learning exercise: 'What do you think the people are saying?' – 'Vous n'auriez pas du feu, s'il vous plaît?' – 'Désolée, je fume pas.' – 'Pas de soucis.'*

The agentless realism is compelling. Twenty-three seconds of engrossing banality have already elapsed when all the heads swivel to the boulevard on the left. Only a razor-sharp security guard would notice that, from one second to the next, a metal ashtray has vanished from the table at the top-right, taken up by the hand of an unseen pedestrian and flung like a discus above the vertical range of the camera. The heads must have turned when the ashtray clattered onto the pavement or struck an obstacle.

Six seconds back in time, a young white woman in a short sleeve-less red dress with a mane of thick black hair can be seen walking purposefully across the top of the screen past a long-haired man in dirty jeans. Words are exchanged, the man walks on, then flings the ashtray and strides back towards the woman in the red dress. When they meet, the woman is almost out of shot, but the blow to her head makes her stagger to the right and sends her hair flailing into view like the wing of a haggard crow.

---

* 'Have you got a light, please?' – 'Sorry, I don't smoke.' – 'No worries.'

The man walks on, job done. The woman stands, motionless, shocked, warily defiant. Four customers, including the woman with the roll-up, remonstrate with the aggressor, who appears to be justifying his attack. Later, when Marie Laguerre, a twenty-two-year-old architecture student, has posted the footage on Facebook (it was given to her by the café owner), the tens of thousands of viewers know more or less what was said. Apparently, he flicked his tongue and smacked his lips, suggesting that she suck his dick – which, in his view, did not give her the right to insult him in public. 'Ta gueule!' ('Shut your face') is what she said in reply, as she always does when this occurs, as it does all the time.

'Bonjour, princesse!'

The aesthetic quality of the video has an electrifying effect. It takes a work of art – in this case, mostly accidental art – to reveal 'the mysteries which run like sap through the narrow channels of the powerful colossus'. (This was the poet Baudelaire, writing about Paris, 'where the ghost accosts the passer-by in broad daylight'.) It turns out, to the surprise of men who cherish women and rush to their defence, that Marie Laguerre's experience of sexual aggression is normal. Four-fifths of French women under the age of seventeen and almost all women who use public transport have suffered verbal or physical abuse. The men had no idea. A new law banning 'sexist outrage' will be enacted, because until then, 'sexual harassment' had to be repeated several times to count as an offence.

If common knowledge can be so recondite and private in the present, what hope is there for a historian? Does society under the Fifth Republic conceptualize itself as it might be represented in a phrase book or a government guide for prospective citizens?

FRENCH AS IT'S ACTUALLY SPOKEN
Common greetings and replies:

> MAN: Bonjour, princesse! – Eh! mademoiselle. – Vous êtes
> mariée? – T'as de jolies jambes. – File-moi ton 06.
> WOMAN: Je suis mariée. – J'ai déjà un mec.
> MAN: Tu baises? – Tu suces?

WOMAN: Ta gueule.

MAN: Salope. – Connasse. – Sale pute.*

Marie Laguerre – she has a name that would suit a comic-book historical heroine – attributes her refusal to keep quiet to her French-Lebanese mother; she is proud of her Arab heritage. Perhaps this genetic twenty-five per cent is detectable on racist radar. The Front National would have preferred her to be entirely French. The party has recently adopted the friendlier name, Rassemblement National ('gathering' or 'union'). It seizes the opportunity to denounce 'immigrants' who abuse women, though the aggressors come in all colours and belong to different classes and professions. Most were born and grew up in France. French women who live and work in London, which has a larger immigrant population, have reported their amazement at being unmolested.

In that temple of democracy by the Seine, the Palais Bourbon, several female government ministers have been whistled at by some of their fellow *députés* for looking too much like women. For all its definitional problems, the headscarf ban is childishly simple; the unofficial dress code is childishly complex and regulated by the neurological responses of the male visual system. High heels, designer jeans, bright colours are likely to provoke ribaldry or censure. The obsolete law forbidding the wearing of trousers by women in the Assemblée Nationale has finally been repealed, but the *pantalon* must be neither too clingy nor too mannish. The main determining factor is the body of the woman herself, which is even harder to regulate.

The question is delicate and confusing. For some women, it is a drab day that passes without what they take to be a public, heterosexual acknowledgement of their physical attractions. But for the younger generation (from the age of fourteen onwards), and for the thousands of online followers of Marie Laguerre, the thought and fact of harassment are cruel shadows stalking the daily routine.

---

* 'Hello, darling.' – 'Oi! Miss!' – 'You married?' – 'Nice legs!' – 'Gimme your mobile number.'
'I'm married' – 'I already have a boyfriend.'
'D'you fuck?' – 'D'you do blow jobs?'
'Shut your face!'
'Cow.' – 'Bitch.' – 'Filthy whore.'

Viol, voile, violence

On 24 November 2018, fifty thousand women and men in about fifty French towns and cities marched in protest at violence against women. Every year in France, a quarter of a million women were attacked by a partner or an ex-partner; ninety-four thousand were the victims of rape or attempted rape. In Paris, thirty thousand marched from the Place de l'Opéra to the Place de la République. Some of the women wore Phrygian caps and convincing cosmetic bruises on their faces.

Marie Laguerre described it afterwards as a 'media fiasco': on the same day, a Gilets Jaunes demonstration sent the camera crews rushing to the Champs-Élysées to capture the scenic violence, the smashing of windows and lighting of fires. This was consistent with the theatrical traditions of French revolutionary history. It had taken years for the Women's March on Versailles in 1789 to be recognized as a founding event of the Revolution; the Storming of the Bastille had its own dedicated publicity organization from the very beginning.

In 2019, on the anniversary of the first Women's March, fifty thousand people processed from the Place de l'Opéra to the Place de la Nation along the Second Empire boulevards where tourists and dandies used to sit at Tortoni's and the Café Anglais spotting the different subspecies of female human and undressing them with their eyes. The march included the Sorbonne UNEF President, Maryam Pougetoux, and the placards proclaimed the diversity of grievances and unity in injustice. *Viol, voile, violence* – rape, the veil and domestic violence:

> I dream of a France in which more attention is paid to women who talk about rape than to men who talk about the veil.

All the protagonists – women, Gilets Jaunes, police and CRS – saw themselves to some extent as defenders of the Republic, but the women were demanding something more than a legislative adjustment. After each major demonstration, another sticking-plaster law was introduced, and the violence continued. The dream was of a revolution beyond the settled storyline of History. The *ancien régime* of the early twenty-first century was not the government but society itself, and the territory to be liberated from the oppressor was not the Hexagon but planet Earth. 'I am not at war', Marie Laguerre told a reporter, 'I'm in the Resistance.'

President Macron had tweeted his support of the first Women's March: 'The struggle against attacks on women is progressing every day, but our society has a lot of ground to make up.' This was politically prudent but also undeniably true. Women in France were granted the vote in 1944, but it was not until 1965 that a woman was allowed to work and open a bank account without her husband's permission. The man was legally the head of the household until 1970. Even then, fraternity prevailed over liberty and equality. But perhaps the energy required to reach such a distant goal was an advantage. In 1789, feudal France had lagged behind its northern European neighbours and yet became an exemplar of revolutionary renewal.

'Vive la République! Et vive la France!'

On the eve of International Women's Day (7 March 2020), the forces commanded by the new hard-line Prefect of Police in Paris, Didier Lallement – a flinty-faced man who was said to have the 'balls' to deal with violent demonstrations – attacked the feminists who were demonstrating against sexual violence. They were kettled, tear-gassed, insulted and pushed into the Métro at Place de la République.

This was one of the last big gatherings before the lockdown. 'Confinement' was announced nine days later, after the municipal elections. For the foreseeable future, abused women would be incarcerated with their abusers.

In a black tie and marginally less funereal navy-blue suit, the President sat next to the patriotic flags of France and the European Union to explain the emergency measures to his 'dear compatriots'. He was installed in the drawing-room of Louis XV's mistress, Mme de Pompadour, which had become the bedchamber of Empress Eugénie, and then the Salon Doré of the Élysée Palace.

It is customary for a French President addressing the nation to end his speech with a formula first used in 1793: 'Vive la France! Et vive la République!' This is the 'Amen' of the national prayer. A less common variant, used by Macron, places 'la République' before 'la France'.

The manner in which the formula is uttered by a President is as distinctive as a handwriting sample. Nicolas Sarkozy delivered it without a pause, like a paperwork-shy despot scribbling his signature on a death warrant. François Hollande gave it a more congenial lilt and, on one festive occasion, cheekily added, 'Et vive Eurodisney!'

With a backdrop of gilded panelling, Emmanuel Macron performed his interpretation of the consecrated phrase like a head waiter delivering an exquisite example of a basic French dish. 'Vive la République!' had the martial ring of a macho Liberty on the Barricades in full battle dress. 'Et vive la France!' came with a softer, almost wistful hint of 'lest we forget'. It evoked the sacred France of sweet meadows and hidden hamlets, the eternal mourning motherland, threatened now by a new enemy. It sounded like a prayer of supplication, and it made the Republic, the fifth in the modern series of governmental systems, seem unimportant by comparison.

The leader of La République en Marche! was left sitting in the ladies' chamber while the 'Marseillaise' began to play. The camera outside in the courtyard panned upwards across the lighted windows of the palace until it showed nothing but a dark sky with a few shreds of bedraggled raincloud like the tatters of a shroud – one of those Parisian evening skies 'from which regrets and memories come flocking down'.* This casting of the televisual eye to the heavens suited the air of unknowing. The presidential announcement had dissolved into questions: How long would the confinement last? How many would die? And, for those who doubted that any government could represent the life of a nation: Whose Republic? And which France?

---

* Charles Baudelaire, 'The Widows', *Le Spleen de Paris*.

14. The mill town of Rouen, capital of Normandy, the cathedral with its new cast-iron spire, and the Seine, from the cemetery of Bonsecours to the south-east, c. 1850. Three steam trains are approaching or leaving the Left Bank station, opened in 1843. In the middle distance, a fourth train is heading for Le Havre from the Right Bank station, opened in 1847.

15. Louis-Napoléon
Bonaparte, 'Prince-President'
of the French Republic, soon
to be Emperor Napoléon III.
Daguerreotype, c. 1850, by an
unknown photographer.

16. 'Madame H…'
(Harriet Howard), the
President's consort, by
Henriette Cappelaere, 1850.
Exhibited at that year's
Paris Salon.

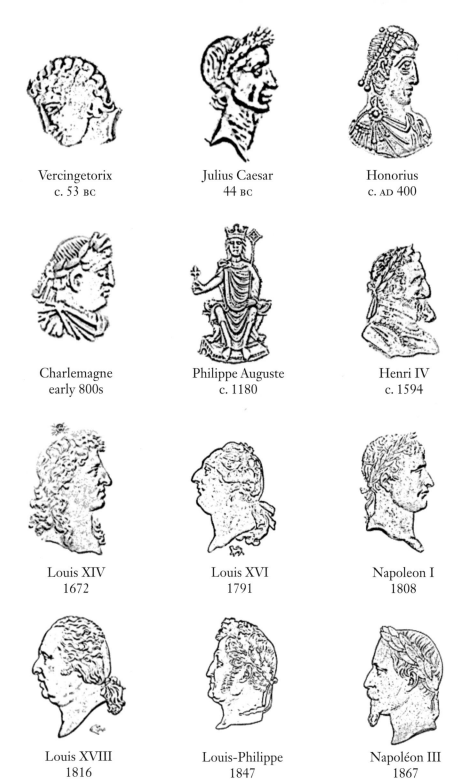

Vercingetorix
c. 53 BC

Julius Caesar
44 BC

Honorius
c. AD 400

Charlemagne
early 800s

Philippe Auguste
c. 1180

Henri IV
c. 1594

Louis XIV
1672

Louis XVI
1791

Napoleon I
1808

Louis XVIII
1816

Louis-Philippe
1847

Napoléon III
1867

17. Rulers of Gaul and France depicted on coins and one seal (Philippe Auguste).

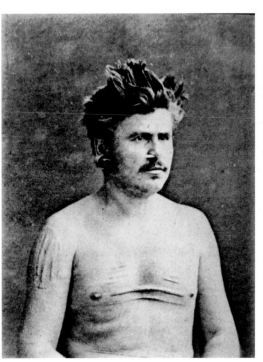 

18. Narcisse Pelletier, 'the White Savage',
in Constant Merland's *Dix-sept ans
chez les sauvages* (1876).

19. Anatole Roujou, geologist
and Darwinian anthropologist
(Paris: A. Bertrand, c. 1872).

20. Stage One of the second Tour de France (Paris to Lyon, 2–3 July 1904), somewhere between Moulins and Roanne in the frontier zone where northern France meets the Midi. The leading rider is Maurice Garin, born in the Aosta Valley (Italy), the first winner of the Tour.

21. Reims after four years on or near the Western Front, looking east towards the cathedral and along Rue de Vesle. The photograph was taken by a member of the American Red Cross on 20 May 1919, more than six months after the armistice. The apparently intact building before the leafy square on the right side of the street, the Grand Théâtre, was an empty shell; it reopened in 1931.

22. Maréchal Pétain on a propaganda poster for the Vichy puppet government by Bernard Villemot, 1943: 'Follow me! Place your unwavering trust in the France that never dies.' The tidy rural scene symbolizing the 'Patrie' (fatherland) is more evocative of the Nazi-occupied zones in the north than of the southern 'Free Zone' administered by Vichy.

23. Mont Aiguille in the Vercors, pictured in *Les Sept Miracles de Dauphiné* (Grenoble, 1701). The motto, 'Supereminet invius' – 'Inaccessible, it (or he) reigns o'er all' – equates 'The Inaccessible Mountain' with Louis XIV. The Vercors plateau was one of the principal 'natural fortresses' of the French Resistance in the Second World War.

24. Outside the offices of *Charlie Hebdo* on 16 October 2017.

25. One of the early leaders of the Gilets Jaunes movement, Priscillia Ludosky, at a Gilets Jaunes demonstration in Paris, 20 January 2019.

18

Demolition

An *aubette* – something of which few French people have heard but which everyone has seen – stands at a secluded crossroads in the Aveyron Gorges, nine miles south of Saint-Antonin-Noble-Val. The usual term is *abribus*, but the Académie Française, in its unwinnable war against linguistic change, has decreed that bus shelters should be called *aubettes* (sentry boxes), because 'Abribus' is a registered trademark.

Given the infrequency of rural bus services, it could be argued that *abribus* is practically obsolete anyway beyond the towns and cities. *Abricycliste* or *abripiéton* would be more appropriate, since a concrete bus shelter, or a hut cobbled together from offcuts by a public-spirited farmer, is often the only place to sit for miles around and the only refuge when the heavens open.

Aubette or 'little *aube*' has another meaning: in Picardy, it denotes the very first glimmer of light at the break of day. The word in this sense is excluded from the Paris-centric *Dictionnaire de l'Académie Française* as 'dialect'. It belongs to the skimpily charted substrata of abandoned but locally evocative words on which 'pure French' was constructed like a business district on an ancient temple complex.

Rural bus shelters might one day intrigue archaeologists. Scattered all over the land, sometimes far from any visible human settlement, they are commonly decorated with primitive hieroglyphics. *Abritaggeur* would be another suitable name. The graffiti, however, tends to be low-grade and unoriginal because no self-respecting tag artist works safely out of sight in a concrete box which requires neither ladder nor abseiling equipment. Like the walls of Pompeii, the *abribus* exhibits a vernacular *florilegium amatorium*: pubescent declarations of undying love jostle for wall space with offers of minority-interest sex and, in a startling number of cases, the name of someone whose mother is said to be pleasuring every male in the community.

✼

It was well past *aubette* (sense ii) when we stopped at the *aubette* (sense i) in the shady gorges on our way to Cordes-sur-Ciel. The daubings were unusually chaste: there was the obligatory zonked-out, joint-smoking face and the circle-A monogram signifying Order and Anarchy – a customary allusion to Proudhon's *Qu'est-ce que la propriété?* (1840):

> Property and royalty have been undergoing demolition since the beginning of the world: just as man seeks justice in equality, society seeks order in anarchy.
>
> *Anarchy* – the absence of a master or sovereign. This is the form of government to which we draw nearer every day.

There was also a warning message in blue paint which I saw there for the first time: 'Macron, on arrive!' ('Macron, we're coming to get you!') It seemed a ridiculous thing to write in a place where no bus was likely to stop any time soon, if ever. On the opposite wall, the same hand had scrawled, in yellow, 'GJ – On lâche rien!' ('We're not giving up!').

The Gilets Jaunes, distinguished by the yellow vests which drivers are obliged to carry in their vehicles, had only recently launched their protest campaign. (Fig. 16.) Graffiti in the provinces normally lags several years behind Paris and the other big cities. Yet the bus shelter was evidence that the movement had already spread across the country. Like the rumour-generated Great Fear of 1789, it had not even waited for Paris to give the order.

This appeared to confirm the reports I had read in the French press. The protests were billed as an insurgency of cash-strapped rural and suburban communities against the plutocratic Macron administration. The two principal grievances were the cost of fuel, especially diesel, and the lowering of the speed limit on two-lane roads from 90 kph to 80 kph. The Gilets Jaunes wanted to be able to drive along the road which wanders blindly through the Aveyron Gorges at 56 mph instead of 50 mph without having to pay a fine which, they believed, would be used to fatten the already bloated bank balances of the rich.

One of the best things anyone can do for a poorly connected community is to use the available public transport or campaign for a better service, yet here, apparently, was an alliance of monads masquerading as 'the people', each possessing his own heavily subsidized and expensively lethal machine, and demanding the financial means to accelerate the decay and obliteration of their communities.

❊

On leaving the *aubette*, as often happens when there has been time to absorb the details of a scene, I noticed that the imp of ironic coincidence had been at work. A few feet away, a galvanized metal pole supported a neatly designed information panel created by a company called 'C'était écrit' ('It Was Written').

The sign advertised RezoPouce (roughly equivalent to 'Thumnet' – a lexical mutant that would horrify the Forty Immortals of the Académie Française): 'the first organized hitchhiking network created by local collectives in France'. A traveller or commuter could obtain an identity card online or at the *mairie* and then wait at certain locations such as bus stops for a driver who had signed up with the network. A contribution to the cost of fuel could then be amicably negotiated. The system was already functioning in well over a thousand *communes* in every region except, for some reason, Bretagne and Pays de la Loire.

Here, I thought, was a cooperative solution to mollify the Gilets Jaunes. But according to both the left-wing and the right-wing press, the protestors who had been blockading roads since November 2018, who had rioted in Paris and defaced the Arc de Triomphe, were a rabble of *ploucs*, *pecnos*, *beaufs*, *olibrius* and *minus* (yokels, clodhoppers, rednecks, nutters and morons). The typical Gilet Jaune was a white man in his forties or fifties who liked to smash up private property and whose favourite comedian was the foul-mouthed clown Coluche – still celebrated long after his death in a motorbike accident for his jokes about Jews, gays, black people and especially Belgians. The Brussels correspondent of *Libération* asked whether there had ever been 'a social movement which has caused so much grief'. In his analysis, the Yellow Vests were nothing but white trash: 'vandals, anti-Republicans, anti-Semites, racists and homophobes'.

Like far-right populist movements in the United States, the Gilets Jaunes feasted on their grievances in what might be termed a perpetual *fête du mensonge* or Festival of Untruth. The expression refers to April Fools' Day in Madagascar but could equally be applied to that state of euphoric indignation in which anything a person wishes to be the case is confirmed by a 'theory'. The more incredible or twisted the theory, the more likely it is to be true: if something has remained hidden – the return of Alsace to Germany, the sale of France to the United Nations, the military compound from which Macron controls the country – it is because the government and the servile media have covered it up. Video footage of the murderous civil war that was raging invisibly in France had been bought up and destroyed by the European Union.

When we reached the former Cathar stronghold of Cordes-sur-Ciel later that day, a friend who lives there in a palatial twenty-first-century medieval *pied-à-terre* told us about the Gilets Jaunes roadblocks she had had to negotiate in the Tarn and neighbouring *départements*. There had been no threats of violence and the proportion of men to women had been roughly equal. There seemed to have been some exaggeration in the press coverage . . . The coordination, persistence and spread of the protests, as well as the violence of the official response, suggested something more than a generalized tantrum of delinquent petrol-heads.

As the riots and vandalism continued, government ministers, journalists and much of the population agreed that the country was faced with an unprecedented uprising compared to which militant trade unions, rioting immigrant offspring, veiled women and even jihadists seemed to belong to a more familiar, even traditional France.

✷   ✷   ✷

If the press unanimously declares a large-scale revolt to be 'a movement unlike any other', it is more than likely that the movement is a popular insurrection which shares traits with most other popular insurrections in French history.

This one was unusual but not unique in that it began in winter and took place mainly at weekends. It *was* unusual in that it manifested itself, not only in city centres with banks and luxury boutiques, but primarily in a sector of the built environment which, though it accounts for more than one-twentieth of inhabited France, leaves little trace in memory and none at all in guidebooks.

The peri-urban or *rurbain* (rural-urban) 'villages' which have been proliferating since the 1970s lie a peristaltic car or bus journey several miles beyond the ring road of the nearest town. They are separated from the traditional centres of population and commerce by fields, post-industrial waste ground and a windy yet acrid zone of single-minded traffic.

The nameless nodal zone may contain prefabricated retail outlets, incubator-like hotels and filling-station restaurants such as the grilled steak dispenser Courtepaille (literally, 'short straw'), with its trademark mock-Gaulish, mock-thatched hut. The vocation of the nodal zone is to ensure that all who enter are ejected as quickly as possible. Anyone who crosses the multiple junctions on foot or on a bicycle might discover that the zone has a transient, unvehicled population with which it is sometimes possible to hold a fleeting conversation: a pilgrim or non-denominational nomad, a failed hitchhiker, a visitor to an out-of-town penitentiary, a passenger who has bailed out after arguing with the driver, a group of scorched migrants or an old person walking a dog through the no-longer-existent countryside.

The village, plonked down on – or, commercially, 'nestling in' – prime monocultural farmland, is announced by the bins of its *déchetterie* (waste-reception centre) and a sign depicting two poorly coordinated infants about to be maimed or killed by a speeding car. Coming after the knotted interchange and before the open country, these villages present their own peri-urban dangers. The main arteries are narrowed by sloping kerbs, street furniture or pinch points positioned so that it is just about possible for an exceptionally skilful driver to squeeze past a cyclist. These 'calming' measures allow a stranger to gauge the prevailing local mood.

Because of the tremendous amount of DIY and small-scale construction which goes on there, strewing staples, rivets and nails in nearly the same density as confetti outside a church, a cyclist with insufficiently puncture-proof tyres is liable to spend more time than most travellers in peri-urban France, but without having to engage, as elsewhere, in a conversation about plastic-versus-aluminium tyre levers and the like, because these noise-enveloped 'villages' are nearly always zones of social silence.

❖

By blocking roads on the outskirts of these commuter villages, the Gilets Jaunes drew attention to *rurbain* France. Newspapers and news sites were full of photographs of untouristy scenes littered with protestors and their camping gear. To educated metropolitans, these post-1960s developments were a blot on the landscape, made worse by their tasteless attempts to deny their unsightliness.

Each living unit had a shrubby garden with an exiguous lawn and a small fruit tree or weeping willow. Some had a basement garage, a veranda on fibreglass pillars with Spanish-style ironwork and some regional garnish such as coloured roof tiles, a slip of natural stone embedded in cement or an ornamental dovecote small enough to frustrate the local pigeons. To many of the lower middle-class families who lived there, saddled with Sisyphean mortgages, they were bastions of comfortable respectability compared to the pre-war terraced houses and post-war Stalinist blocks of the inner suburbs.

The demonstrators' complaints that the French press was run by a snobbish elite in the pay of a small number of oligarchs seemed to be justified. It was hypocritical of the 'elites' to sneer at the villagers' lack of taste, and they deserved the ridicule that was heaped on them by mass-market comedy films such as *Les Visiteurs* (1993). These artificial settlements with no history were created by metropolitan planners and architects, who, instead of allowing their imaginations to run free in the rural location, designed them as though they were extensions of the town's perimeter, which only exacerbated the sense of inconvenient isolation.

Peri-urban France is still expanding. One of the most prolific developers is Maisons Pierre ('Pierre' is the founder's name). The different models of 'maison individuelle' are named after butterflies and moths – creatures which will be exterminated by products used to maintain the garden – and seem to have been chosen from an entomological guide without checking for ambiguities: 'Aporia', a group of the Pieridae family, is also an insoluble logical contradiction; 'Kalima' (Nymphalidae family) is also the Islamic profession of faith in God and his prophet.

The names devised for the new streets refer to history – which is to say, something uncontroversial and extinct, such as the old provinces and *pays* of France or vanished trades and industries – or to the natural world: plant species favoured by planners, flowers and fungi unlikely to be seen outside a shopping bag, and animals unlikely to be seen alive.

✻

At the antipodes of the peri-urban housing estate is a more recent type of development which actually belongs to the same general category – the Plus Beau Village or 'Most Beautiful Village', of which there are now one hundred and fifty-nine. The Plus Beaux Villages de France®, a go-to reference for Francophile magazines, are well worth avoiding when an authentically time-worn equivalent exists in the vicinity, as it often does.

Inspired by a coffee-table book published by Reader's Digest in 1977, the association promotes and modifies villages perceived to be historically interesting and, crucially, photogenic. The mayor and population are invited to join the chosen many, on condition that 'no fewer than thirty criteria' are met. These include 'harmony and homogeneity' of walls, roofs, street lighting, etc.; 'florification'; masking of electrical and telephone wires; organization and control of traffic and parking. If successful, the homogenized village, unrecognizable to the ghost of a medieval inhabitant, will be inundated with visitors far outnumbering any band of knights that ever laid siege to the *bastide* or *village perché*. Cordes-sur-Ciel refused to join, and other *plus beaux villages* have handed back the gift of immortal beauty.

Viewed before the late-morning crowds arrive, the embalmed village appears to have been made ready for a funeral of history, 'transformed by eternity into its final self' (Mallarmé). The same heritage blight has afflicted entire cities and regions, their old buildings painted a single 'authentic' and legally enforceable colour by order of civil servants, their stone walls, which had always been rendered, stripped bare and exposed to the elements.

The Plus Beaux Villages, like the peri-urban villages, are habitats created by committees. The social conditioning is less obvious than it was in the days of Le Corbusier and President Pompidou, when new towns were built for the benefit of the automobile rather than for their indentured chauffeurs. Instead, the inhabitants of the far-flung development, aspirational but stymied, not quite poor but on the crumbling edge of indigence, having missed out on the growth years which TV documentaries call the Trente Glorieuses (1945–75), feel excluded from the cities where the all-powerful Economy digests the products of their labour.

✿

Whether by force of circumstance or a stroke of collective genius, the Gilets Jaunes movement found the epicentres of its viral revolt at one of the most characteristic landscape features of the *rurbain* environment and of twenty-first-century France – the *rond-point*.

France is said to be richer in roundabouts than any other country in the world. No one knows the exact number: fifty thousand is the usual upper estimate. This would make them as numerous as the mysterious subrectangular enclosures of the Iron Age Celts. Future archaeologists may find them just as perplexing.

At the *rond-point*, past and present come together and occasionally collide in a road war of the generations. In France, a vehicle entering another road from the right has the right of way. But on the *rond-point*, which was introduced from Britain in the 1970s, priority is to the left (except on the Place de l'Étoile in Paris). Consequently, older drivers sometimes sail blithely out into the oncoming traffic with the self-assurance of stunt men.

The roundabout epidemic, which has recently spawned some peanut-shaped variations in the west of France, has much to do with the temptingly vacant area in the middle. Of the six billion euros spent on *ronds-points* every year, one-third is devoted to the embellishment of the central portion.

A road-dazed driver leaving the *autoroute* for the puzzle of infrastructure on the edge of a town might be confronted with a hallucination of gigantic nails hammered into a balding lawn (at Rugles) or a stream of small black cars running like ants down a disembodied yellow arm (at Châtellerault). A dangerously distracting wooden chair the height of a three-storey building stands in the middle of a roundabout near Hagetmau in the Landes, commemorating the almost defunct chair-making industry. On the bypass to the south of Rouen at Saint-Étienne-du-Rouvray, the Rond-Point des Vaches was occupied – until the Gilets Jaunes arrived – by five enormous plastic cows. One cow was smashed to pieces, another was removed to an unknown location and the other three were set on fire, leaving nothing but twelve melted hooves.

✧

The Rond-Point des Vaches shot to national prominence just when its principal attraction had been destroyed. The local mayor was furious. To him, the plastic cows were a symbol of Normandy and its agricultural heritage. To the Gilets Jaunes, they epitomized those insultingly expensive attempts by the smarmy elite to persuade the peasants that they were living in Happyland.

The oddly familiar nature of the 'unprecedented' uprising was first observed by pollsters and sociologists. As in 1789, the protesters were more *petit bourgeois* than *paysan* – artisans, tradespeople, clerical staff, public service workers and labourers. They belonged to sections of the population which had always been under-represented in the Assemblée Nationale and regional councils, especially since the withering of the Communist vote and the *embourgeoisement* of the Socialist Party.

Gilet Jaune demography was similar to that of the groups whose existence came to the tardy attention of government ministers across the Channel during the Covid-19 pandemic: single mothers, people who care for children or older relatives, tenants with private landlords, those who do not have the use of a car, the struggling self-employed, temporary and part-time workers.

This, too, was reminiscent of the first Revolution: many of the Gilets Jaunes had never protested before; nearly half were working-class women, who would not normally have had the time or the opportunity to join a movement. (With all those practical skills on offer, it was no great effort to erect a couple of sheds or a marquee in the middle of a roundabout to serve as a crèche.) The right-wing racists, who had enjoyed a disproportionate share of press coverage, soon disappeared from the *ronds-points*. In fact, it proved impossible to connect the Gilets Jaunes with any recognized political group. One of the commonest points of reference was the alliance of Gaulish tribes under Vercingetorix in 52 BC, in part because the shanty settlements on the *ronds-points* were thought to resemble Gaulish villages.

The impressive coordination of unaffiliated groups was particularly confusing to a government steeped in Republican French history which could barely conceive of a revolution that was not inherently republican. More than half the Gilets Jaunes were apolitical: they never thought of themselves in terms of left and right. The only issue on which a large majority (eighty-eight per cent) agreed was the orderly form of anarchy or direct democracy which they called RIC: 'Référendum d'Initiative Citoyenne'. Citizens would be empowered to veto unjust laws that were pushed through parliament by unrepresentative representatives. In this way, the sovereignty of the people would be restored.

✻

Only in films and hasty histories do revolutionaries present a united front. The movement was so multifarious that it was easy to isolate extreme examples and denounce the whole – the weekend anarchists, the anti-globalist vandals, the Jew-haters. The peaceful protestors were mocked for the idiotic fairy tales they 'liked' and 'shared' as the braziers and bonfires burned at the *ronds-points*.

Print journalists blamed social media, 'without which this could not have happened', as though all the other sudden mass revolutions in French history had occurred by magic, with message-bearing crows instead of tweets. But as the skies of social media turned yellow like the heavens before a hail-storm, it became impossible to ignore the similarities to late-eighteenth-century propaganda.

Marie-Antoinette had been accused of bankrupting the state with her frivolous shopping. Brigitte Macron, the unsalaried 'First Lady', was said to be frittering away half a million euros of taxpayers' money every year. The phantom 'foreign invasion' of June 1789 resurfaced as the 'Marrakech Pact' by which the United Nations hoped to reconcile migration policies with human rights: Macron was about to sign the agreement, which meant that France would lose its sovereignty to faceless foreigners.

Tales from the storybook of revolutionary mythology were updated for a credulous modern audience. Wood-block prints had once shown the Paris police kidnapping little boys to drain their blood for a royal princess whose rare medical condition called for human blood baths; now, doctored photographs and videos showed defenceless children being murderously attacked by the CRS.

Some of the false rumours were spurious justifications of irrational hatred, but most were extravagant metaphors of rational grievances and reasonable demands which tended to the general good – equal pay, lower taxes on essential goods, the recognition of child-rearing as a pensionable occupation.

The fake news was truth at one remove, coloured with the outrage the reality had caused. It performed a social function, fostering unanimity in divergent groups. It was patently ludicrous to liken Macron's tax reforms to the 'famine pact' by which the government of Louis XVI had supposedly tried to starve the poor by inflating the price of bread, but no one seriously doubted that the tax reforms favoured the rich, and that the gap between rich and poor was growing ever wider.

✿

Standing in front of the tennis court in Versailles where the delegates of the Third Estate had demanded a constitution based on freedom and equality, two of the founders of the Gilets Jaunes movement read out a joint declaration to the assembled press on 13 December 2018. They were 'not trying to destabilize the state' but to ensure that any future changes to the constitution would be decided by referendum.

The government found this open-air press conference alarming. Instead of semi-literate *ploucs*, they saw two ill-matched citizens sharing a microphone and speaking with one voice. One was a smirky young white man wearing a baseball hat turned backwards, a neatly trimmed beard and a clean new parka. The other was a dreadlocked middle-aged black woman in a tailored cloak.

Priscillia Ludosky had worked in international finance for eleven years at BNP Paribas before setting up her own online organic cosmetics company. Maxime Nicolle was a semi-delinquent influencer addicted to wild but unoriginal theories (gypsies were kidnapping children, Macron was a puppet of the Freemasons, powerful lobbies unmasked by a 'Monsieur X' were about to launch a nuclear war). These two delegates of a movement which had recently mobilized nearly three hundred thousand people in more than two thousand locations and paralysed the island of Réunion appeared to be in perfect agreement on the basic demands.

The State – the so-called 'deep state', which is there for all to see, while the machinery of democracy remains largely hidden through lack of interest – had its own disseminators of *infox* (fake news). The semi-official 'Team Macron' account retweeted miscaptioned images as proof that the movement was dominated by neo-Nazis and that the Gilets Jaunes had set fire to the Jeu de Paume museum in Paris.

The President spoke directly to Priscillia Ludosky, who was unimpressed. He then began a sporadic tour of the country to hear the testimony of local mayors, to thank officials for bearing up in the face of unrest and to remind the Gilets Jaunes that the Republic was a democracy on the local level too. Meanwhile, some prestigious outlets on the Champs-Élysées having been vandalized by anarchist infiltrators, the defenders of the Republic were sent out to protect it in the usual way, with weapons marketed as 'sub-lethal', meaning 'not quite lethal'.

✿

By the early spring of 2019, twenty-four Gilets Jaunes had lost an eye, five had seen one of their hands blown off, hundreds more were severely injured. They included bystanders, journalists, medics and children. The principal weapons were rubber bullets and sting ball grenades, often used at close range and aimed higher than the manufacturer recommended. Facial trauma was especially common.

Violence of this kind had become almost traditional in the *banlieues*; in the centre of Paris, inflicted on peaceful demonstrators in the daytime, it looked shockingly incongruous. When he read the latest report of the United Nations High Commissioner for Human Rights on 6 March, the Minister of the Interior, Christophe Castaner, was surprised to see France cited alongside Haiti, Sudan, Venezuela and Zimbabwe as a country in which protests against 'inequalities' 'are met with violent and excessive use of force'.

Two weeks later, Macron ordered the army's 'Sentinelle' anti-terrorist task force to provide back-up for the riot police. The commanding officer, General Bruno Le Ray, was interviewed on radio and television and let it be known that, in certain circumstances, his men would open fire. This effectively made the point that even in an age of intergovernmental organizations and economic unions, a member state could shut its doors to the world and exercise its sovereign will.

✿

The Yellow tide ebbed; roundabouts were reclaimed. On the outskirts of Rouen, the 'Gaulish village', known to the faithful as 'Notre-Dame des Vaches', was demolished and rebuilt more than once despite the lockdown. The roundabout is now a well-established place of protest. It will be a long time before a herd of plastic cows can stand there again in peace.

The struggle between the government, the orderly and disorderly anarchists, and the anarchic forces of order continues. In June 2020, in response to the Black Lives Matter protests, the Interior Minister advertised the government's 'zero tolerance' of racism by depriving the police of the right to use the 'clé d'étranglement'. The chokehold had proved particularly deadly when applied to minority ethnic suspects. To compensate, the Minister authorized the wider use of the 'shocker électrique' or Taser.

Unplacated, the police then held their own protest marches: why should they be scapegoated for the sins of a racist society? Five days later, on 15 June, the Minister reversed his decision and the police went back to work.

A day before, President Macron had announced a loosening of the lockdown. This time, he sat in front of a casement window which looks on to the private parkland of the Élysée Palace. A fountain was playing gracefully and some pigeons frolicked in the trees. The nation was reawakening in the garden of France. The President appeared to be offering some rhetorical concessions to the Gilets Jaunes. Their labour would be required for the great economic recovery:

> 'Social distinctions can be founded only in the common good.' These words were written by Frenchmen more than two hundred years ago. Today, we must take up the torch and apply this principle in its full force.

He had chosen one of the least revolutionary articles of the Declaration of the Rights of Man and the Citizen of 1789. Everyone could agree, in principle, on the importance of 'the common good', but what about those deep-rooted 'social distinctions'? In 1789, the expression had referred to the grubby servants of the soil, the buoyant *bourgeoisie*, the landed aristocracy and, of course, the King. To the Gilets Jaunes, those divisions were based entirely on privilege and wealth.

Two hundred years must have sounded like a long time to a man who could be voted out of office after only five years in power. Two hundred years was just one-tenth of the lifespan of the nation which had begun to form more than two millennia ago between the Rhine and the western edge of Asia. The end of the story was unknown and its beginning was still being discovered and deciphered. Though the ancestral Gauls were viewed with amused veneration as the long-haired, moustachioed Gilets Jaunes of the Iron Age who stood up to the Roman elite, there was a growing body of evidence that the founders of France were not the Roman conquistadors and merchants who came in search of gold and slaves but the confederation of Celtic tribes that was formed to defeat them.

✿   ✿   ✿

When a political leader repeatedly refers to the history of the nation, this is, historically, a sign of trouble. No one, least of all a busy politician, can possibly grasp the oceanic complexity of accident and desire which fills the centuries. The stone tablets of 'History' are invoked to imply that a questionable course of action has the approval of the gods who govern the destiny of the nation. The subterfuge is more obvious in French, in which *histoire* means 'story' as well as 'history'.

> I say this to you very clearly this evening, my dear compatriots: the Republic will erase no trace nor any name from its history. The Republic will not be toppling any statues.

Macron was alluding to the continuing anti-racism protests which seemed to have taken over from the Gilets Jaunes. He was promising to defend the inanimate guardians of the past, those solidified public history lessons which epitomize resistance to change and ambiguity.

As Victor Hugo suggested several times, a statue's lesson is conveyed, not by the inscription on its plinth, but by the bird which sits on its head. Even a statue contains a multitude of stories. The gilded equestrian Joan of Arc on the Place des Pyramides opposite the Tuileries marks the approximate site of her first serious setback: nearby, at the Porte Saint-Honoré, the Maid of Lorraine was pierced in the thigh by an English crossbow bolt and doubts of her invulnerability began to spread among the soldiers like a disease.

When the statue was inaugurated in 1874, it stood for the defiance of France in the face of defeat by Prussia and the loss of Lorraine. Two decades later, it was appropriated by far-right Dreyfusards and, more recently, by the xenophobic National Front, which still holds noisy rallies at its foot. Millions of TV viewers know her as the iconic 'podium girl' caressed by the swooping aerial camera so that she appears to greet the Tour de France riders as they emerge from the underpass between the Tuileries and the Louvre on their final laps of Paris.

To lovers of *la petite histoire*, that dainty, indomitable figure represents the model herself, the peasant girl who was discovered by the sculptor in Domrémy and brought back to Paris. She was briefly famous and died a pauper. Like Joan of Arc, she burned to death, when the oil heater in her tenement room exploded.

✵

From the Place des Pyramides, the *peloton* skims along the Rue de Rivoli to the Place de la Concorde and swerves up the cobbled Champs-Élysées towards the mother of all *ronds-points*. At the sunset end of the avenue, the Arc de l'Étoile lists the victories of the Republican armies and Napoleon I; at the dawn end, the Obelisk of Luxor recounts the glories of Rameses II.

This unroofed solar temple with its underground chapels – Concorde, Clemenceau, Franklin D. Roosevelt, George V, Charles de Gaulle–Étoile – has hosted triumphal processions by the Grande Armée, the cavalry of Napoléon III, the Prussians, the Nazis, the French and American liberators, the armed forces every Bastille Day and the Tour de France a few days later. It has witnessed the massing of women for the march on Versailles, the battles of Gilets Jaunes, anarchists and police, and, in another department of reality, Jean Seberg hawking the *New York Herald Tribune* and Antoine Doinel stealing a typewriter from an office above the Galerie La Boétie.

Religious monuments are not immune to this endless proliferation of significance. After the fire of 2019, a Parisian journalist called Notre-Dame de Paris 'the soul of France', an eight-hundred-year-old reminder that the nation's history is 'profoundly Christian . . . even if it is buried under a century or more of secularism'.

Notre-Dame is sunk in much older traditions, predating the sequence of events which are recorded in writing and therefore entitled to be called history. Before the Gothic, the Romanesque and the Carolingian cathedrals and the Merovingian basilica, there was a Gallo-Roman church which replaced a Celtic temple. Several centuries before, the temple had probably covered up the traces of a pre-Celtic shrine dedicated to forgotten gods who were prayed to in a lost Bronze Age language.

In the mid-thirteenth century, as soon as the scaffolding was removed from the new cathedral and the adjoining Archbishop's Palace, those buildings, too, began to dissolve into time.

❖

From the higher ground of the Latin Quarter, the smoke could be seen rising against the giant rose window on the south side of Notre-Dame. Down on the quayside, a crowd watched the flames devouring vestments, tapestries, furniture and the irreplaceable archives of the Archbishop's Palace which filled most of the space between the cathedral and the river.

The great cross which had hung on the west front had crashed to the ground and the stained-glass windows of the apsidal chapels created a meaningless mosaic of coloured fragments on the marble floor. In less than five hours, the Archbishop's Palace and the earlier chapel it enclosed had been reduced to rubble. Many of the stones, carved by master masons of the early Middle Ages, had tumbled into the Seine along with the carbonized relics and mutilated statues of saints.

This was in February 1831, during a popular uprising against the Bourgeois Monarchy. In April 2019, live-streaming of the hellishly beautiful conflagration of Notre-Dame proved to the world that a building can be mourned like a human being. The grief and the horror were characteristic of the late Romanticism which was beginning to spread among the general population when Victor Hugo published a peculiarly godless novel which captured the pagan weirdness of that incomprehensible 'sphinx squatting in the middle of the city'.

Reverence for a visually pristine historic structure is a fairly recent development. Twenty years ago, it was easy to find a medieval church or cathedral which had been left in a state of decay and forced to cohabit with shops, sheds, garages, parking spaces and public urinals. Notre-Dame itself is still subservient to the cult of the motor car, begrimed, eroded, shaken by mechanical vibrations. But in 2019, it was as though History itself was at stake. Particles of charred oak beam and roofing lead from the days of crusaders and saints smeared pavements and balconies on the Île de la Cité and the Île Saint-Louis. Almost immediately, before the fire was out, the search for a culprit began.

There were, predictably, false reports of French Muslims cackling at the plight of the infidels' temple, but the image which caught the spirit of that doom-clouded spring was provided by six seconds of zoomed-in footage cropped from the many hours of live coverage. It appeared to show a human figure clumping along the gallery of the triforium above the great rose window of the west front. Just around the corner, in a battle of the elements, a shower of water was arcing onto the oblivious flames. The figure, clad in a yellow vest, passed behind the colonnades and disappeared into an invisible door as though heading for the heart of the fire.

Was this the ultimate act of madness of a popular revolt against a state which lavished millions of euros on an uninhabitable tourist attraction? Had the ghost of Quasimodo returned in a yellow vest to wreak revenge on the elites in the name of a downtrodden populace? The swarming shadows of Notre-Dame had always lent themselves to hallucinations and esoteric theories, and although the truth was obvious and impressive enough – a Parisian fire officer risking his life for a beloved piece of history – an incendiary Gilet Jaune was perfectly congruent with that phantasmal structure.

The mother church of Paris, like Paris itself, is an accumulation of all its earlier incarnations. The thirteenth-century cathedral with its polychrome stonework is long gone, and so is the blackened galleon of the Industrial Age stranded on its island among the filthiest slums in Paris. The nineteenth-century restorer of Notre-Dame, Eugène Viollet-le-Duc, had to work with 'a rubbish dump' of mouldering masonry, a portal smashed by stone-throwing children, and gargoyles which had morphed into featureless lumps of limestone.

Those replacement gargoyles and the medievalized figures introduced by Viollet-le-Duc were re-restored in 1996. When the work of the restorers was unveiled, millions returned to selfie-photograph the national treasure. As they climbed the towers and explored the galleries, several people who had come to know and love the Notre-Dame of

Viollet-le-Duc felt a sense of estrangement and then outrage at the
sly ravages of time. This was the year in which Disney's animated
musical *The Hunchback of Notre Dame* was released. The gargoyles
which had watched the city change beyond recognition were now at
one with modern Paris, and that look of smirking, goofy cuteness was
horribly familiar.

☼   ☼   ☼

All societies live on the ruins of their predecessors, real or imagined.
The Gauls, Britons, Romans, Franks and, until the late Renaissance,
the French believed that their history could be traced back to the Fall
of Troy. Epic devastation was a prerequisite of civilization.

In historical reality, the French nation fell and rose again so many
times that few periods of its art and literature are unmarked by a
nostalgia for material decadence. One of the most beautiful of urban
poems is Baudelaire's 'Le Cygne' (1860), in which the pulverized
building site of Haussmann's Paris conjures up images of black ex-
patriates of the French empire, of 'sailors left behind on an island'
and of the Trojan refugees. In 1871, 1919 and 1946, tourists were
invited to view the wreckage of Paris and provincial towns as though
the nation had acquired an interesting new attraction. 'Coming soon:
picturesque ruins' was a popular graffito on public buildings in
May '68.

In the old Bibliothèque Nationale in the Rue de Richelieu, I
witnessed one of the cherished survivors of the glittering Second
Empire crumbling onto the page in front of me. I was trying to find
and read every poem published in French in the 1840s, and it was
becoming clear to me that Baudelaire had constructed his *Fleurs du
Mal* by rummaging sardonically through the enormous rubbish heap
of contemporary verse. Many of those volumes addressed to 'posterity'
had uncut pages and had probably been read only by their authors.

One morning, I noticed tiny flakes of rust materializing on the
page. I brushed them off, but a few minutes later, the sheet was
speckled anew with metallic punctuation marks.

Directly overhead was one of the nine delicate iron domes of
Henri Labrouste which bathed the *salle de lecture* in an opalescent
light. There was no sound of building work, yet the dome was evidently
disintegrating. I took the open book on which the rust had collected

and walked up to the raised platform of the *hémicycle* where the librarians sat like magistrates. An arm covered in long black lace evening gloves reached out from the lamp-lit gloom and took the book from my hand as I indicated the problem, 'S'il vous plaît, Madame? Le plafond me tombe sur la tête.' It sounded like an unexpectedly useful sentence from a Victorian phrase book: 'The ceiling is falling on my head.'

The librarian of Gothic mien grinned and sounds of muted jollity came from the depths of the *hémicycle*. It was obvious that something would have to be done: perhaps the reading room would be evacuated . . . She took my reader's card, made an alteration in her ledger, and reassigned me to an unoccupied desk about six feet from the drop zone. Kindly, she explained that, knowing my nationality and considering my appearance to be 'Celtic', she had found it amusing that I had accidentally alluded to the meeting of Alexander the Great with some Celtic envoys who assured him that they feared 'nothing, except that the sky should fall in on our heads'.

Not long after, the library was closed to readers; its treasures were transferred to the new Bibliothèque Nationale de France in its four glassy towers by the banks of the Seine at Bercy. In the meantime, so many of the library's holdings had been digitized, far in advance of other national libraries, that I rarely had to visit the place itself, even for such obscure but indispensable titles as the proceedings of the Botanical Society of the Deux-Sèvres *département*. Books, newspapers, maps and prints, all were made available free of charge and without registration, not just to French citizens and employees of academic institutions but to anyone in the world.

*

Writing this book on the border between Scotland and England, temporarily severed from the mother continent, I am struck by the comparative openness of the French state to other countries. In Britain, General de Gaulle's repeated 'Non!' (to 'English' membership of the European Common Market) still resonates, but the nationalism associated with de Gaulle – which entailed saying 'Non!' to many other entities – was always more proselytizing than insular.

I am aware that as a white, male, married, heterosexual, middle-class cyclist with an ability to converse in polite French, I have been spared the hostility I have occasionally seen meted out to other people by civilians as well as by agents of the State, but I was never able or inclined to extract from those experiences a working definition of 'the French'. Its only value would have been to stiffen the prejudices to which any unsettled foreigner is prone.

France the nation is, for the time being, a Republic, as its citizens are constantly reminded. The distinction between the land itself and the reigning system of government has been more consequential than the separation of Church and State. It stresses the contingent nature of that younger sister of the American Republic and has probably attenuated the kind of all-encompassing nationalism which has dogged other European countries and which, in France, still snarls and slavers in the security of its cage.

✿

The land which became France was described by the Roman geographer Strabo as a providentially harmonious whole. Its rivers, plains and mountains were situated so that its natural riches could easily be transported from shore to distant shore and carted off to Rome. Of its population, he knew little, having never visited Gaul, but he was aware of significant differences in language, physical attributes, forms of government and ways of life between the Aquitani, the Celtae and the Belgae.

The collective identity of the ethnically diverse Gauls was first of all a function of geography and subsequently confirmed by commerce, politics and war. Geography had helpfully set the borders of the future Roman province: two seas, one ocean, two mountain ranges and several smaller massifs, and about one third of the course of the Rhine.

Many of those tribal and national borders were zones of transit rather than barriers. Their permeability was vital to the prosperity of Gaul and successive kingdoms, empires and republics. Gaul was the great crossroads of western Europe, the unavoidable *rond-point* by which long-distance trade routes had passed since the beginning of the Bronze Age. The negotiated migrations, the monetary union of the powerful tribes in the east and the pan-Gallic alliance against Rome are among the earliest signs of a European Union.

But if physical geography was the vehicle of predestination, it took a very long way around. More than a thousand years would pass before the square or hexagon of Celtic and Roman Gaul recurred as the shape of a political unity and allowed the land mass to be identified as a coherent, God-given homeland. Now that all countries have been miniaturized by speed, borders are more permeable than ever and 'l'Hexagone' has an increasingly antiquated sound. Even the Tour de France regularly crosses or starts in other countries. France is no longer 'twenty-two days wide and nineteen days long', as it was in 1552, except perhaps for migrants who paddle across the Mediterranean and cross the mountains on foot.

❀

In 2020, one of the dominant expressions of national pride is love of Nature. That love has become one-sided and destructive, demanding for its satisfaction seven hundred miles of *autoroute* and over one hundred public airports. Deranged by human colonization, even the frontiers which once gave an impression of eternity are no longer dutiful guardians of the border.

In June 1846, Victor Hugo delivered his maiden speech in the Chambre des Pairs. He announced to the Lords that an enemy was massing at the frontier: incursions were taking place by day and by night. Swathes of land and even villages and towns had already fallen to the enemy.

> If someone were to tell you this, my Lords, you would not deem it excessive to bring the full weight of our country's power to bear on this terrible danger. . . .
>
> Well, my Lords, I tell you now that that frontier exists and that the enemy is real: the frontier is our coastline, the enemy is the Ocean. . . . The enormous cliff which runs from the mouth of the Somme to the mouth of the Seine is in a state of continual demolition. Dieppe is sinking as I speak.

Interminable histories – as they all literally must be – often conclude *quand même* with a modest prediction, to say, for example, that, in spite of setbacks and shortcomings, the spirit of the people or the political institutions of the country will enable it to weather the storms that lie ahead.

We know already that France will not survive. Dieppe will be covered by the sea and then, like Montreuil-sur-mer today, will find itself several miles inland. It will be swamped again repeatedly until finally it disappears. The Pyrenean forests will burn as they did in the days of Ogmios, meteors will fall, the denuded Alps will continue to rise as Africa pushes into Europe. New cols will be formed by the herculean thrust of tectonic plates, and through those portals, invaders and migrants of one species or another will arrive, just as the Trojan refugees, according to Druids interviewed by Caesar, 'took possession of these empty spaces'.

The length of days will change and time will pass at a different speed. The tale of what was France may then be taken up by geologists and eventually by astrogeologists. Long before that happens, in defiance of the Forty Immortals of the Académie Française, the French language will cease to exist in a recognizable form. The storied past, our home in time these two thousand years, will be locked up in unverifiable legends and unintelligible myths, and historians will have no choice but to set off on the darkening roads that stretch out before and behind us in the here and now.

Notes for Travellers

1. The Hedge

'Cycling with Caesar' would make a good theme for a historical adventure holiday or a series of eight annual expeditions. In the campaign described here (57 BC), Caesar crossed the Great Saint Bernard Pass and reached the lands of the Remi 'in about fifteen days', probably averaging thirty-three miles a day. The arc of destruction passed through Bibrax (Vieux-Laon near Reims), Noviodunum (Pommiers near Soissons), Bratuspantium (Bailleul-sur-Thérain near Beauvais) and Samarobriva (Parc Samara, the recreated Gaulish village on a bike path west of Amiens). The hedge-building Nervii were massacred at Hautmont and the Aduatuci further down the Sambre at Namur. Caesar then took the legions to winter quarters in the Loire Valley before returning to northern Italy.

2. A Home in Gaul

The stone ghosts of Sidonius's villa near Clermont-Ferrand are visible only in aerial photographs. The setting is best surveyed from the towering Arvernian *oppidum* of Gergovia, where Vercingetorix defeated the Romans. From there, it is a pleasantly hilly journey to Aydat and its lake, by which time the volcanoes of the Auvergne Regional Park will have appeared on the horizon. To reach Aurillac by way of Belliac, the birthplace of Gerbert d'Aurillac (chapter 4), aim for the Pas de Peyrol (5,210 feet) and the valley of the Jordanne. The total distance from Clermont-Ferrand is ninety-five miles, but the last forty are all downhill.

3. The Invisible Land of the Woods and the Sea

One of the few places where the valley of the Vilaine looks like a marshy frontier on which a battle might have been fought is on the D176 from La Roche-Bernard by the Château du Plessis. The nearby town of Rieux, south of Redon, was a major junction of Roman roads. The redoubt of King Murman or Morvan may have stood in the region of Langonnet on the Minez Morvan plateau, but any number of fortified sites in southern Brittany fit the description in Ermold's chronicle: 'out-of-the-way paths', 'thorny valleys', 'trackless bog'.

4. Time Machines

On the visit in question, the unpaved Roman road to Reims offered a firm white surface with easily avoidable potholes. On a later visit, after a rain shower, the same road was coated with a deep, clinging paste of chalk and clay which arrested the bicycles after one rotation of the wheels. This section of the Reims–Cologne road begins one mile south of Fresne-lès-Reims where a clump of trees conceals the abandoned fort of Fresne (1878).

5. Cathar Treasure

The curse of the Cathars has caused all treasure maps of 'Cathar Country' to be inaccurate, with sites misplaced and names misspelled. The hiding place in the *châtellenie* of Châteauverdun may have been the twin-chambered Spoulga de Verdun recently rediscovered by rock-climbers. The escape route to the east suggested by the written evidence kept the fugitives within the bounds of Sabartès until Usson (a derelict nineteenth-century spa with the remains of a castle): Montségur, Col de la Peyre, corniche road via Appy, left to the Quié cliffs above Verdun; return to the D20 and continue to Caussou, Prades by the Col de Marmare, Montaillou, Col du Teil, Col du Pradel, Port de Pailhères, Usson – a sixty-mile journey, partly on foot, with another sixty miles to the Catalan coast for a boat to Lombardy.

6. The Tree at the Centre of France

Printed out on a palm-sized piece of paper and used in conjunction with a day's worth of map cut from a Michelin road atlas, these finicky itineraries (p. 106), collated from various sources, can save a great deal of time. In chronically quiet parts of the country, they approximate the directions that might have been given by a farmer, a road-mender or a postal worker. Even if they live locally, car drivers are often unable to provide correct or usable information. The superscript numbers indicate the elevation in metres: muscles are more efficient when forewarned in this way.

7. A Walk in the Garden

The lane in Versailles on which Louis XIV gave way to a carter is now the Rue de l'Ermitage, a narrow road with speed bumps to slow the traffic. Authentically muddy equivalents can be found not far away in the tracks and bridle paths of the Rambouillet Forest.

8. Stained Glass
There are permanent exhibitions of the works and history of the Compagnons du Tour de France in Arras, Bordeaux, Limoges, Paris (a museum at 10, Rue Mabillon, and the carpenters' restaurant at 161, Avenue Jean-Jaurès), Romanèche near Mâcon, Toulouse and Tours.

9. Bloody Provence
The inn where Napoleon presented himself as 'Colonel Campbell' probably stood near La Petite Calade by a crossing of the River Touloubre on the 'Ancienne Route de Paris' which runs parallel to the busy D7N to Aix-en-Provence. A 'cabaret' is mentioned in a road book of 1788 at 'St-Louis' – a name which disappeared after the Revolution. A field name, 'Auberge Neuve', has survived. It was somewhere along this route in 1761, after a thunderstorm, that Jacques-Louis Ménétra (chapter 8) had himself carried across a small, unbridged river.

10. How He Did It
Unlike the Robert Louis Stevenson Trail in the Cévennes, the Route Napoléon sticks to major roads and is unsuitable for donkeys or skittish bicycles. It deviates from Napoleon's route in several places. North of Grasse, it avoids the plunging Gorges de la Siagne, cyclable for three and a half miles from Saint-Vallier, then barred to all vehicles, even those 'of local residents in dangerous climatic conditions'. From there to Escragnolles, the rocky surface is the one on which Napoleon and his landing party marched. The two-hundred-year-old search for the crates of gold coins said to have fallen into the abyss from the back of a lame mule should be abandoned: Napoleon's treasurer Guillaume Peyrusse states in his *Mémorial* that they were unloaded and recovered by himself.

11. The Murder of Madame Bovary
While waiting in Ry for the bus back to Rouen on a market day, lovers of *Madame Bovary* can sit outside one of the cafés frequented by locals – the 'Flaubert' *bar-tabac* rather than the more refined 'Bovary' across the road – and try to identify living avatars of Flaubert's characters.

12. Miss Howard's Gift to France
Re-enactors have occasionally dramatized scenes of military life at the site of Napoleon's Camp de Boulogne, but no one, as far as I know,

has re-enacted his nephew's attempted coup. The Club Nautique of Wimereux offers boats and a splashy 'Marche aquatique' for nine euros. The coast road from Wimereux, which has well-made bike paths on both sides, offers views of England and the Colonne de la Grande Armée and leads straight to the harbour at Boulogne. In the upper town, the castle in which Louis-Napoléon was held prisoner is now the municipal museum. Since 1976, keeping an eagle in a cage can incur a fine and a one-year prison sentence.

13. Savage Coast

Crossing the Loire by the three-lane Saint-Nazaire road bridge (a quarter of a mile, with side winds and a steep climb) is worth it for the short cut, but only in retrospect. There are seasonal bus and taxi services which take bikes but require booking. Thirty miles upstream, a fast and cheerful ferry, the Navibus, carries pedestrians and cyclists across the Loire from the fishing village of Trentemoult to the Gare Maritime in Nantes. The quiet coastal route out of Saint-Nazaire to the west leads to Pelletier's two lighthouses. The harbour office was destroyed in Allied bombing in the Second World War. The cemetery is still there at 47, Rue de la Paix.

14. Keeping Track of the Dead

Roadside information panels are often worth reading or photographing. Many are inaccurate or deliberately flippant, but some display otherwise unpublished material from municipal and personal archives (letters and memoirs, photographs, statistics, etc.). The battlefields of Rossignol and the Chemin des Dames are particularly well served by outdoor documentation.

15. Mount Inaccessible

In the Vercors, winter or summer, wet or dry, it is important to ask locally, on the day of departure, about landslips, rock falls and road works: online information is not always up to date. A 'Route Barrée' sign, however, may apply only to motorized traffic. The GR91 long-distance path as far as Saint-Nizier is probably a close match for Jean Prévost's movements after leaving the cave above La Chapelle-en-Vercors. A paved track branching off the D531 above Sassenage at the 'Pont Charvet' bus shelter (descending, on the right) leads to the site of his death.

16. Martyrs of the Tour de France

Tour de France riders can be seen up close at the end of a hard stage 'warming down' or on a stationary trainer before the start. In 2004, I spent an engrossing twenty minutes watching Eddy Merckx making tender micro-adjustments to his son Axel's clothing and bicycle as he warmed up before the Alpe d'Huez time trial. In the race itself, the climbs are often clogged with spectators. A good alternative is a tight, off-camber bend on a steep descent, late enough in the race for the *peloton* to be fragmented: otherwise, the spectacle is over in a matter of seconds. In the off season, some professional riders reconnoitre the climbs in unmarked clothing. They are easily distinguished from amateurs. They have a fairy-like immunity to gravity and are rarely red in the face; they can eat food and change their clothes while descending; and they invariably return the greeting of a fellow cyclist.

17. La République en Marche!

'This mobile chaos where death comes galloping from every side at once' (Baudelaire) has been transformed by the Mairie de Paris in the biggest social transport revolution since the Métro. All the Parisian sites mentioned in this chapter can be visited on a bicycle in less time than it takes to find a parking space.

18. Demolition

Some *ronds-points* have a green strip marked with a bicycle symbol running all the way around the outer edge of the roundabout. This path of doom should be avoided at all costs: it exposes the cyclist to assault from both sides. As at pinch points, it is safer to occupy the middle of the road. French drivers generally respect a bold, brief assertion of individual rights.

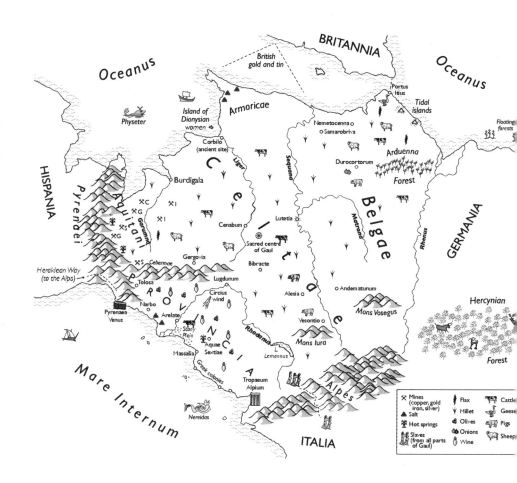

Oceanus

BRITANNIA

British
gold and tin

Oceanus

Physeter

Island of
Dionysian
women

Armoricae

Portus
Itius

Tidal
islands

Floating
forests

Corbilo
(ancient site)

Nemetocenna

Samarobriva

Arduenna

HISPANIA

Pyrenaei

Aquitani

Burdigala

Liger

Sequana

Durocortorum

Forest

GERMANIA

Garumna

×C

×G

×S

×I

×I

×G

Cenabum

Lutetia

Belgae

Rhenus

Heraklean Way
(to the Alps)

Cebennae

Tolosa

Gergovia

Sacred centre
of Gaul

Bibracte

Marona

PROVINCIA

Narbo

Pyrenaea
Venus

Arelate

Lugdunum

Circius
wind

Alesia

Andematunum

Mons Vosegus

Hercynian

Stony
Plain

Aquae
Sextiae

Vesontio

Rhodanus

Mons Iura

Forest

Massalia

Greek colonies

Lemannus

Mare Internum

Nereidas

Tropaeum
Alpium

Alpes

ITALIA

✕	Mines (copper, gold iron, silver)	↯	Flax
▲	Salt		Millet
	Hot springs		Olives
	Slaves (from all parts of Gaul)		Onions
			Wine

Cattle

Geese

Pigs

Sheep

1. The geography, resources and curiosities of ancient Gaul. From the writings of
Caesar, Diodorus, Pliny the Elder, Posidonius, Ptolemy, Strabo and Tacitus.

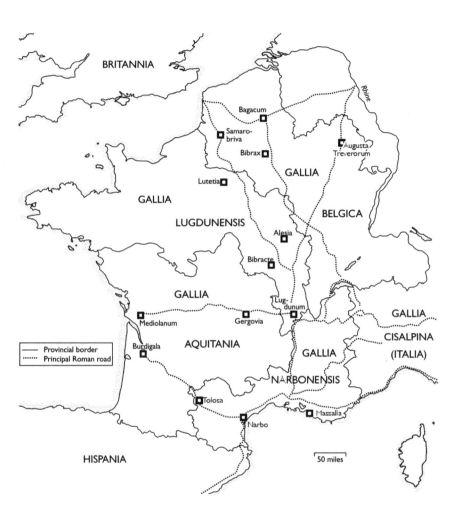

BRITANNIA

Rhine

Bagacum □

Samaro-
briva □

Bibrax □

□ Augusta
Treverorum

GALLIA

Lutetia □

GALLIA

BELGICA

LUGDUNENSIS

Alesia
□

Bibracte
□

GALLIA

Lug-
dunum □

GALLIA

□
Mediolanum

Gergovia
□

CISALPINA

GALLIA

(ITALIA)

——— Provincial border
········ Principal Roman road

Burdigala
□

AQUITANIA

GALLIA

NARBONENSIS

□ Tolosa

□ Massalia

Narbo

HISPANIA

50 miles

2. Gaul and principal Roman roads in 27 BC, when the territory conquered by
Caesar was divided into three provinces: Aquitania, Lugdunensis and Belgica.
Gallia Cisalpina had been conquered in the early second century BC. Gallia
Narbonensis (or Transalpina) had become a province in 121 BC. The borders are
tribal; the division as a whole reflects the skewed Roman conception of Gallic
geography. Caesar's battle with the hedge-building Nervii was fought six miles
south-east of Bagacum (Bavay) near the top of the map.

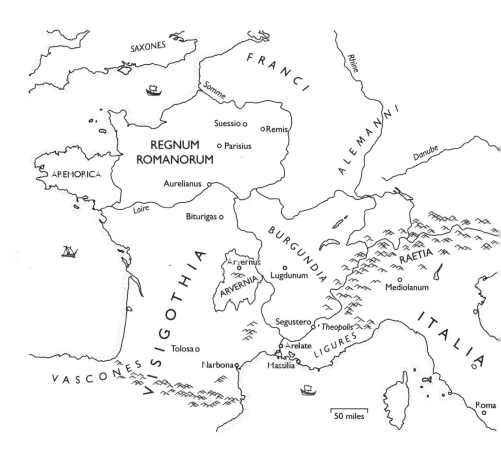

3. Gaul, c. AD 464, when Sidonius Apollinaris lived at Avitacum outside Arvernus (Clermont-Ferrand). North of Italy, the only remnants of the Roman Empire were Arvernia and the brief 'Regnum Romanorum' ('Kingdom of the Romans') ruled by the Roman general Aegidius, then by his son Syagrius, who was defeated by the Franks under Clovis I at Suessio (Soissons) in 486.

4. The Frankish Empire in 843, shared among the three surviving sons of Charlemagne's son, Louis I 'the Pious', by the Treaty of Verdun. This is one of several partitions of Frankish territory. The principle was established in the sixth century, when the heirs of Clovis received roughly equal ranges of climate and resources, with particular regard to olive groves, vineyards, arable land, war horses and any product likely to enhance religious ceremonies.

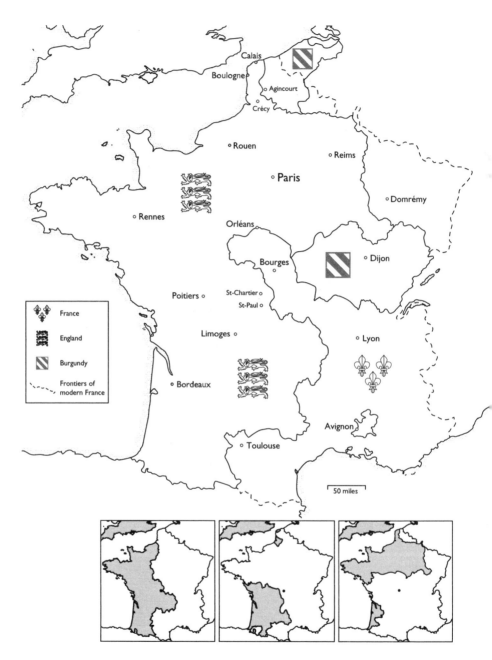

5. English possessions in France, 1154–1558. The main map shows all the territory which ever belonged to the English crown and its Burgundian allies in this period. The three smaller maps show the extent of English possessions (shaded areas) in 1180, 1360–72 and 1429. The black dot marks the site of the tree at the centre of France.

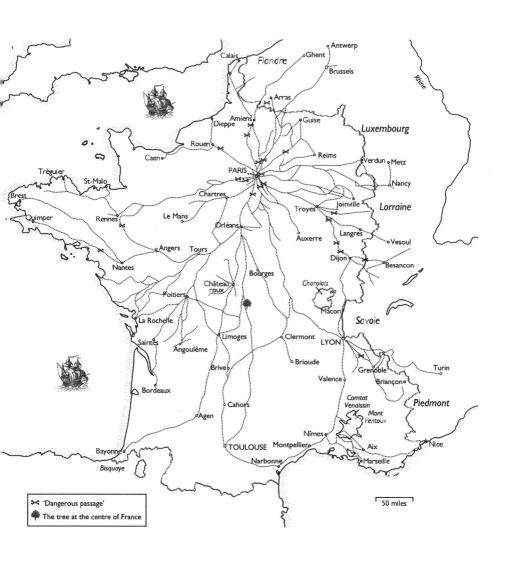

Map labels:

Antwerp
Calais
Ghent
Flandre
Brussels
Arras
Amiens
Dieppe
Guise
Luxembourg
Rouen
Reims
Verdun • Metz
Caen
PARIS
Nancy
Tréguier
St-Malo
Chartres
Troyes
Joinville
Lorraine
Brest
Le Mans
Orléans
Langres
Vesoul
Quimper
Rennes
Auxerre
Angers
Tours
Dijon
Besançon
Nantes
Bourges
Château roux
Charolais
Poitiers
Mâcon
La Rochelle
Savoie
Saintes
Limoges
Clermont
LYON
Angoulême
Brive
Brioude
Grenoble
Turin
Valence
Briançon
Bordeaux
Cahors
Comtat Venaissin
Piedmont
Agen
Mont Ventoux
Nîmes
Bayonne
TOULOUSE
Montpellier
Aix
Nice
Bisquaye
Narbonne
Marseille
Rhine

Legend:

✂ 'Dangerous passage'
🌳 The tree at the centre of France

50 miles

6. Routes described in Charles Estienne's *Guide des chemins de France* (1552).
In the east, France ended at Verdun and Lyon. The 'passages dangereux' in the
guide usually refer to woods and wastelands frequented by 'brigands'. The shape
of the land mass would have surprised Estienne, who had been told that France
had the form of a 'lozenge twenty-two days wide and nineteen days long'.

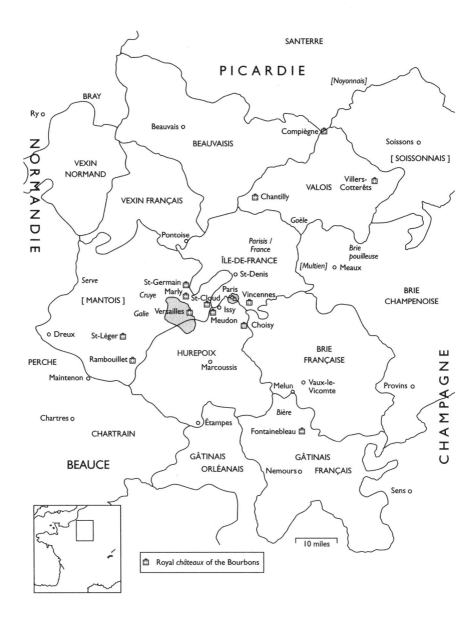

SANTERRE

PICARDIE

[Noyonnais]

BRAY

Ry o

NORMANDIE

Beauvais o

BEAUVAISIS

Compiègne🏰

Soissons o

[SOISSONNAIS]

VEXIN NORMAND

VALOIS

Villers-
Cotterêts 🏰

🏰 Chantilly

VEXIN FRANÇAIS

Goële

Pontoise
o

Parisis /
France

ÎLE-DE-FRANCE

Brie
pouilleuse

[Multien] o Meaux

BRIE
CHAMPENOISE

Serve

o St-Denis

St-Germain 🏰

Cruye   Marly 🏰
        🏰 St-Cloud

Paris
🏰   Vincennes

[MANTOIS]

Galie   Versailles 🏰

o Issy
🏰
Meudon 🏰   o Choisy

o Dreux   St-Léger 🏰

HUREPOIX
o
Marcoussis

BRIE
FRANÇAISE

PERCHE   Rambouillet 🏰

Maintenon o

Melun o o Vaux-le-
          Vicomte

Provins o

CHAMPAGNE

Chartres o

CHARTRAIN

o Étampes

Bière

Fontainebleau 🏰

BEAUCE

GÂTINAIS
ORLÉANAIS

GÂTINAIS
Nemours o FRANÇAIS

Sens o

10 miles

🏰 Royal *châteaux* of the Bourbons

7. The traditional *pays* of the Île-de-France and its supply zone in the
mid-eighteenth century. The large shaded area is the Great Park of Versailles.
The names in square brackets were used by geographers and map makers
rather than by natives. Names in italics indicate subdivisions of larger *pays*.

8. Administrative and historical divisions of *ancien régime* France, based on local and national maps, geographical dictionaries and gazetteers from 1600 to 1753. The darker lines and capitalized names indicate the *gouvernements*, some of which comprised former duchies, counties and bishoprics. Simplified modern maps of these divisions imply a tidy progression from Gallo-Roman *civitas* to *province* and finally *département*. In reality, the legal, fiscal and traditional inconsistencies and complexities are practically undepictable.

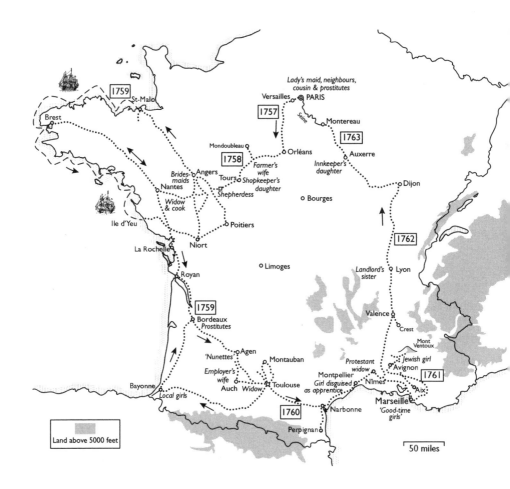

9. The original apprentices' Tour de France, as modified and exploited by Jacques-Louis Ménétra from 1757 to 1763.

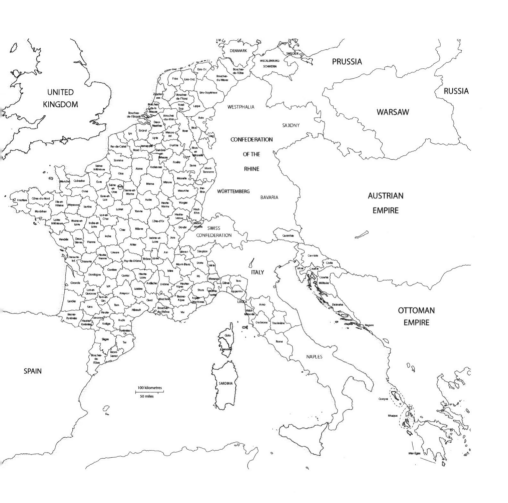

10. *Départements* of the First Republic and the Empire, 1790–1815, from the Revolutionary Wars to the fall of Napoleon. Not all conquered territories were 'departmentalized'. Some *départements*, such as the Catalonian and Greek, lasted barely a year. Ignoring administrative ambiguities, the greatest number of *départements* at any time was one hundred and thirty-four (in 1812). The map shows a total of one hundred and forty-nine.

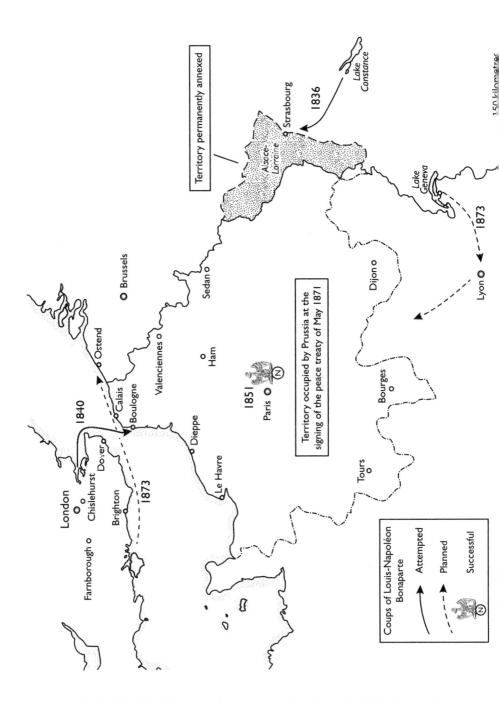

11. Louis-Napoléon Bonaparte's coups, and the aftermath of the Franco-Prussian War. The peace treaty of May 1871 divided the occupied territory into zones. Each zone was to be evacuated by German troops as the corresponding instalment of the war indemnity was paid.

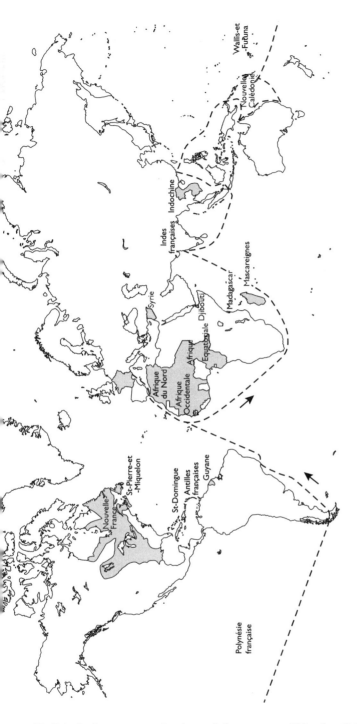

12. Principal overseas territories and the voyages of Narcisse Pelletier in 1857–8 and 1875. The shaded areas indicate French territory from Nouvelle France (1534–1763) to the present (cf. map 16).

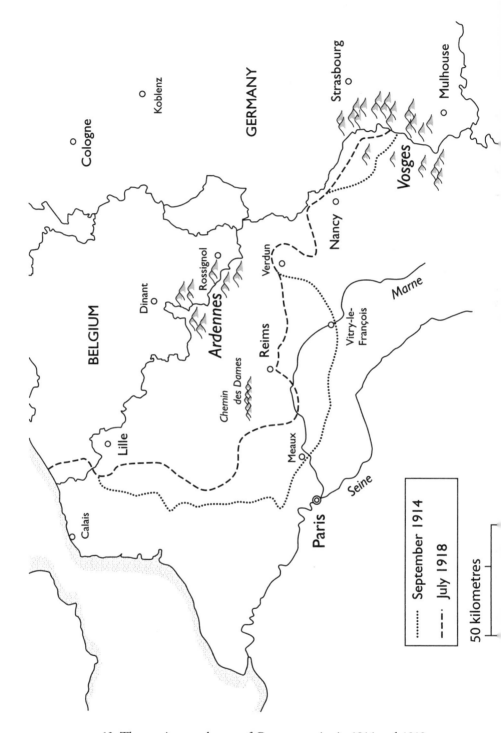

13. The maximum advance of German armies in 1914 and 1918.

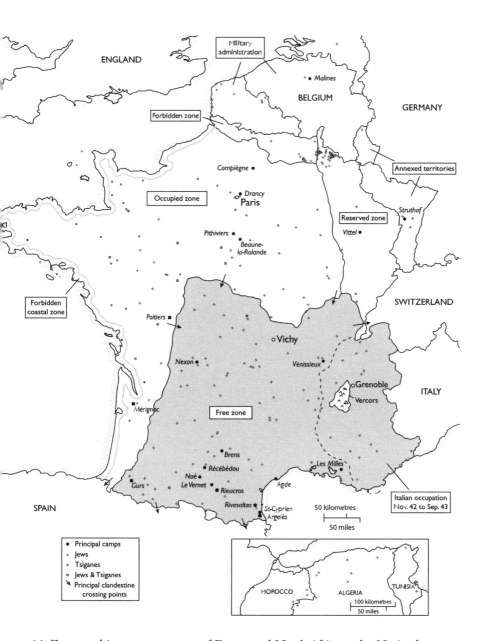

14. Zones and internment camps of France and North Africa under Nazi rule.

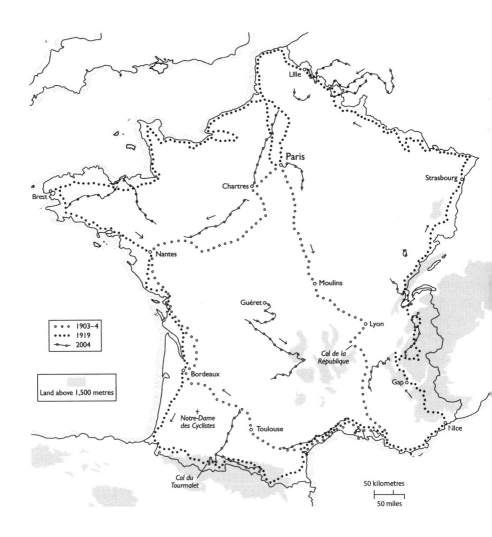

15. The expansion, contraction and disintegration of the Tour de France bicycle
race. The first Tours shadowed the traditional apprentices' itinerary (map 9). In
1919, the Tour became a beating of the bounds. Shortcuts and deviations into other
countries were gradually introduced. After 1958, the itinerary was discontinuous.
Transfers by coach, train and plane now account for at least one third of the
distance travelled by the riders.

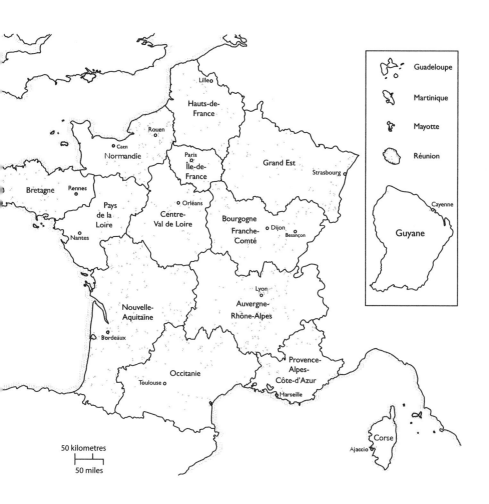

Legend:
- Guadeloupe
- Martinique
- Mayotte
- Réunion
- Guyane

Map labels: Lille, Hauts-de-France, Rouen, Caen, Normandie, Paris, Île-de-France, Grand Est, Strasbourg, Bretagne, Rennes, Pays de la Loire, Orléans, Centre-Val de Loire, Bourgogne Franche-Comté, Dijon, Besançon, Nantes, Nouvelle-Aquitaine, Auvergne-Rhône-Alpes, Lyon, Bordeaux, Occitanie, Toulouse, Provence-Alpes-Côte-d'Azur, Marseille, Corse, Ajaccio, Cayenne

50 kilometres
50 miles

16. Metropolitan and overseas regions after the territorial reform of 2014 (effective from 2016), and the first Gilets Jaunes demonstrations. Each dot represents one or several Gilets Jaunes protests on 17 November 2018 in mainland France as well as Corsica, Guadeloupe, Guyane, Martinique and Réunion.

Chronology

BC

c. 600: Massalia (Marseille) and other Mediterranean trading posts founded by Greek merchants.

Late 6th century: Gaulish 'palaces' in Burgundy, Marne and Rhineland; Greek and Massalian wine imported to central Gaul.

5th century: La Tène ('Celtic') culture spreads along the Danube and the Rhine.

Early 4th century: Gaulish migrations to northern Italy and east through the Hercynian Forest.

387: Celtic occupation of Rome.

c. 325: Voyage of Pytheas of Massalia (Atlantic Gaul, Britain and beyond).

310–260s: Belgic tribes arrive in northern Gaul from the east.

279: Celtic army plunders Delphi.

218: Hannibal marches from Spain to Italy by the Heraklean Way.

196–189: Rome conquers Celtic northern Italy (province of Gallia Cisalpina).

181: Massalia appeals to Rome for help against Ligurian pirates.

125–121: Roman conquest of southern Gaul.

121: Defeat of Arverni and Allobroges; founding of Roman province of Gallia Transalpina (later, Gallia Narbonensis).

c. 120–110: First Gaulish *oppida*; monetary union of eastern tribes.

118: Construction of Via Domitia from Spain to Matrona Pass (Montgenèvre).

113–101: Cimbri and Teutones invade Danube Basin, northern Italy, Gaul, northern Iberia.

102: Roman victory over Germanic tribes near Aquae Sextiae (Aix-en-Provence).

63: Diviciacus the Aeduan Druid asks Roman Senate for military aid.

62–61: Revolt of Allobroges crushed by Rome.

61: Gaius Julius Caesar governor of Gallia Transalpina.

58–51: Gallic War.

57: Defeat of Belgic tribes.

56: Defeat of Atlantic tribes.

52: Pan-Gallic uprising. Roman victory against Parisii at Lutetia. Gaulish victory at Gergovia. *August to September* – Siege of Alesia; capture of Vercingetorix.

43: Foundation of Colonia Copia Felix Munatia, later Lugdunum (Lyon).

c. 27: Gaul north of Gallia Narbonensis divided into three provinces: Aquitania, Belgica, Lugdunensis.

c. 5: Birth of Jesus Christ.

AD

10: *August 1* – Claudius born at Lugdunum (Lyon).

c. 20: Druidism outlawed by Tiberius.

21: Revolts of Aedui.

c. 30: Crucifixion of Jesus Christ.

48: Northern Gauls admitted to Roman Senate.

c. 54: Druidism outlawed by Claudius.

177: Persecution of Christians at Lyon and Vienne.

Late 3rd century: Martyrdom of St Dionysius (Denis) Bishop of Lutetia (Paris) at Montmartre.

354: Baptism of St Martin of Tours.

360: Julian II 'the Apostate', vanquisher of Alamanni and Franks, proclaimed Roman Emperor in Lutetia.

380: Christianity the official religion of the Roman Empire.

382–4: Latin translation of Gospels by Jerome.

410: Sack of Rome by Alaric I, King of the Visigoths; foundation of Lérins Abbey.

414: Marriage of Ataulf, King of the Visigoths, to Galla Placidia, half-sister of Emperor Honorius. Founding of 'Theopolis' in southern Gaul by Claudius Postumus Dardanus and Nevia Galla.

451: Paris saved from Attila the Hun by St Genovefa (Geneviève).

469: Sidonius Apollinaris (b. c. 430) Bishop of Arvernus (Clermont-Ferrand).

Before 474: Arvernian aristocrats abandon 'Celtic speech' (Sidonius Apollinaris).

481–511:	Clovis I, founder of Merovingian dynasty, ruler of expanded kingdom of Salian Franks (Low Countries).
486:	Frankish victory over Regnum Romanorum at Soissons.
c. 493:	Clovis I marries Clotilde, Christian Burgundian princess.
5th and 6th centuries:	Irish, Welsh and Cornish settlers in Armorica (Britannia minor).
496:	Battle of Tolbiac (Frankish victory over Alamanni); Clovis I converts to Christianity.
507:	Alaric II defeated by Clovis I at Vouillé.
511–718:	Fragmentation of Francia into sub-kingdoms ruled by sons of Clovis: Neustria, Austrasia, Burgondia, Aquitania.
c. 529:	Foundation of Benedictine Order.
558–61:	Clotaire I King of the Franks.
c. 570:	Birth of Prophet Muhammad.
c. 573–94:	*History of the Franks* by Gregory of Tours (b. Arvernus, c. 539).
629–34:	Dagobert I King of the Franks.
639:	Basilica at Saint-Denis becomes the royal necropolis; Clovis II King of Neustria and Burgondia (to 657).
c. 708:	Foundation of oratory on Mont-Saint-Michel.
714–39:	Victories of Arab armies in former Roman province of Gallia Narbonensis; incursions in Rhone and Saône valleys.
718–41:	Charles Martel, military leader and statesman, founder of Carolingian dynasty, *de facto* ruler of Francia.
732:	*October* – Battle of Poitiers or Tours: Umayyad Caliphate army defeated by Charles Martel on or near the Loire.
743–51:	Childéric III 'le Fainéant' King of the Franks.
751–68:	Reign of Pepin III 'le Bref', son of Charles Martel.
760–8:	Subjugation of Aquitania by Pepin le Bref.
768:	Pepin's sons, Charlemagne and Carloman I (d. 771), inherit Francia.
768–814:	Charlemagne King of the Franks.
773–804:	Campaigns against Saxons and Frisians.
774:	Conquest of Lombardy.
778:	Army of Charlemagne defeated by 'Saracens' (Basques) at Pass of Roncevaux.
796:	Defeat of Pannonian Avars.
800:	*December 25* – Charlemagne crowned Emperor in the West by Pope Leo III.

814:	*January 28* – Death of Charlemagne at Aix-la-Chapelle (Aachen); Louis I 'le Pieux' or 'le Debonnaire' Emperor (d. 840).
818–24:	Campaigns against Bretons.
840–42:	Civil war (sons of Louis I).
842–911:	Viking base on Île de Noirmoutier: raids on Aquitaine, Brittany, Normandy, Flanders, Paris, Seine and Loire valleys, the Rhone up to Valence.
843:	*August* – Treaty of Verdun: division of Carolingian empire by three sons of Louis I into West, Middle (Lotharingia) and East; West Francia to Charles II 'le Chauve' (r. 843–77) – the first of several divisions.
877–9:	Reign of Louis II 'le Bègue'.
879–82:	Reign of Louis III (jointly with Carloman II).
879–84:	Reign of Carloman II.
c. 880–972:	Muslim enclave in Massif des Maures (Djabal al-Qilâl).
885–7:	Reign of Charles III 'le Gros', King of Eastern Francia from 876.
885–6:	Vikings besiege Paris.
888–98:	Reign of Eudes or Odon.
898–922:	Reign of Charles III 'le Simple' (cf. Charles III 'le Gros', third Emperor in the West).
911:	Treaty of Saint-Clair-sur-Epte: Rollo (Hrólfr), Norse warrior, first Duke of Normandy.
917–54:	Hungarian incursions in Lorraine, Champagne and Burgundy.
922:	Revolt of Frankish nobles.
922–3:	Reign of Robert I.
923:	*June 15* – Battle of Soissons: death of Robert I, imprisonment of Charles III.
923–36:	Reign of Rodolphe (Raoul or Radulf), Duke of Burgundy. Civil war.
936–54:	Reign of Louis IV 'd'Outremer' (raised in Wessex).
954–86:	Reign of Lothaire.
978:	Siege of Paris by Otto II, Holy Roman Emperor (Frankish victory).
986–7:	Reign of Louis V 'le Fainéant'.
987–96:	Hugues Capet King of the Franks, founder of Capetian dynasty.
996–1031:	Reign of Robert I 'le Pieux' or 'le Sage'.
999–1003:	Gerbert d'Aurillac (b. c. 945) the first French Pope (Sylvester II).

1009: Church of the Holy Sepulchre in Jerusalem destroyed by Al-Hakim.

1031–60: Reign of Henri I.

1060–1108: Reign of Philippe I 'l'Amoureux'.

1066: *December 25* – William, Duke of Normandy, crowned King of England.

1098: *March* – Cistercian Order founded at Cîteaux near Dijon.

1096–9: First Crusade.

1099: *June to July* – Siege of Jerusalem.

1108–37: Reign of Louis VI 'le Gros'; Paris the main royal residence.

c. 1119: Foundation of Knights Templar.

1137–80: Reign of Louis VII 'le Pieux'.

1137: *July 25* – Marriage of Louis VII and Eleanor of Aquitaine (annulled 1152).

1154: *December 19* – Henri Plantagenêt, Duke of Normandy, Count of Anjou and Maine, husband of Eleanor of Aquitaine, crowned Henry II of England.

1163–1345: Building of Notre-Dame de Paris.

Late 1100s to 1220s: Cathedrals of Laon, Chartres, Bourges.

1180–1223: Reign of Philippe II 'Auguste', the first to call himself (occasionally) 'Roi de France' instead of 'Roi des Francs'.

1182: Expulsion of Jews from France.

1189–99: Richard I of England ('Lionheart'), son of Eleanor of Aquitaine, Duke of Normandy, Aquitaine and Gascony.

1208–29: Albigensian Crusade against 'Cathar' heretics in Languedoc.

1214: *July 27* – Battle of Bouvines, Flanders (victory of Philippe Auguste over John of England and Otto IV, Holy Roman Emperor); consolidation of enlarged French kingdom.

c. 1220–70s: Cathedrals of Reims, Amiens, Beauvais.

1223–6: Reign of Louis VIII 'le Lion'; conquest of Poitou, Saintonge and Languedoc.

1226–70: Reign of Louis IX ('Saint-Louis').

1233–1329: Inquisitions in Languedoc.

1241–4: Building of Sainte-Chapelle in Paris to house Relics of the Passion.

1243–4: Siege of Montségur.

1257: Foundation of the Sorbonne.

1258: *May 11* – Treaty of Corbeil between France and Aragon establishes Pyrenean frontier.

1270: *August 25* – Death of Louis IX at Carthage (Eighth Crusade).

1270–85: Reign of Philippe III 'le Hardi'.

1282–1390: Building of Albi Cathedral.

1285–1314: Reign of Philippe IV 'le Bel'.

1289: Foundation of University of Montpellier.

1296–1305: French occupation of Flanders.

1307: *October 13* – Arrest of Knights Templar.

1314–16: Reign of Louis X 'le Hutin': slavery abolished in France, serfs allowed to purchase freedom, Jews readmitted.

1316: *November 15–19* – Reign of Jean I 'le Posthume'.

1316–22: Reign of Philippe V 'le Long'.

1322–28: Reign of Charles IV 'le Bel'.

1324: Invasion of Duchy of Guyenne (defeat of Edward II of England).

1328–50: Reign of Philippe VI 'le Fortuné' (first of the House of Valois).

1337: *May* – Philippe VI takes Aquitaine from Edward III of England. *October* – Edward claims the French crown.

1337–1453: Hundred Years War.

1340: *June 24* – Battle of l'Écluse or Sluys (English naval victory).

1346: *August 26* – Battle of Crécy, English victory.

1347–52: Black Death.

1349: Incorporation of Dauphiné.

1350–64: Reign of Jean II 'le Bon'.

1355–8: Reform movement and insurrection led by Étienne Marcel, Provost of Paris merchants.

1356: *September 19* – Battle of Poitiers: Jean II taken prisoner.

1360: Treaty of Brétigny (or Calais): Poitou, Limousin, Gascony, Périgord, Quercy, etc. to England. Introduction of permanent *gabelle* (salt tax).

1364–80: Reign of Charles V 'le Sage'.

1370–74: Du Guesclin Connétable de France: campaigns against English in Normandy, Brittany, western France.

1380–1422: Reign of Charles VI 'le Bien-aimé' and 'le Fol'.

1380–88: Regency of Charles VI's uncles.

1392: First psychotic episode of Charles VI.

1393–1404: Regency council dominated by Philippe le Hardi, Duke of Burgundy.

1394: Seventh expulsion of Jews from France.

1396–1415: Anglo-French truce.

1407: Assassination of Louis d'Orléans, brother of Charles VI. Start of civil war between Houses of Orléans (Armagnacs) and Burgundy (to 1435).

1415: *October 25* – Battle of Agincourt.

1420: Paris occupied by English and Burgundians. *May* – Treaty of Troyes: Henry V of England to inherit the throne of France from Charles VI.

1422–61: Reign of Charles VII 'le Bien-servi' (uncrowned 'Dauphin' or 'King of Bourges' until 1429).

1429: *March* – Jeanne d'Arc (b. c. 1412) meets the Dauphin at Chinon. *April to May* – Jeanne d'Arc at Siege of Orléans. *July 17* – Coronation of Charles VII at Reims.

1431: *May 30* – Jeanne d'Arc burned at the stake in Rouen.

1436: *April 13* – Paris recaptured from English.

1438: *July 7* – Pragmatic Sanction of Bourges: greater independence of Gallican (French) Church from papal authority.

1450: *April 15* – Battle of Formigny (French victory in Normandy).

1453: *October* – France recovers Bordeaux and Guyenne.

1461–83: Reign of Louis XI 'le Prudent', 'le Rusé' or 'l'Araignée'.

1470: First book printed in France (at the Sorbonne).

1472: Siege of Beauvais by Charles le Téméraire, Duke of Burgundy.

1477: Duchy of Burgundy reverts to French throne.

1483–98: Reign of Charles VIII 'l'Affable'.

1485–8: 'La Guerre folle': revolt of nobles.

1488: *August 20* – Treaty of Sablé; subjugation of Brittany.

1491: *December 6* – Marriage of Charles VIII and Anne de Bretagne.

1492: *June 26* – First recorded ascent of Mont Aiguille (Vercors).

1495: *February* – French troops capture Naples: first recorded outbreak of 'le mal français' (syphilis). *July 6* – Battle of Fornovo.

1498–1515: Reign of Louis XII 'le Père du Peuple'.

1499: *January 8* – Marriage of Louis XII to Charles VIII's widow, Anne de Bretagne.

1509: *July 10* – Birth of Jean Calvin at Noyon, Picardy.

1515–47: Reign of François I.

1516–19: Leonardo da Vinci at Amboise.

1525: *February 24* – French defeated in northern Italy (Battle of Pavia); imprisonment of François I (to March 1526).

1532: Union of Brittany to France.

1534–42: Voyages of Jacques Cartier to Canada.

1539: *August* – Ordinance of Villers-Cotterêts: French the official language of all legal documents.

1547–59: Reign of Henri II.

1550: *March 24* – Anglo-French Treaty of Boulogne: France regains Boulogne; English to withdraw from Scotland.

1552: Charles Estienne, *Guide des chemins de France*.

1558: *January* – Calais retaken from England. *April* – François, Dauphin, marries Mary Stuart at Notre-Dame.

1559: *April* – Peace of Cateau-Cambrésis: end of Italian wars.

1559–60: Reign of François II.

1560–74: Reign of Charles IX (Catherine de Médicis regent to 1563).

1562–98: Wars of Religion.

1572: *August 23–4* – St Bartholomew's Day massacre of Protestants in Paris. *August to October* – Massacres in several provincial cities.

1574–89: Reign of Henri III.

1588: *May 12* – Day of the Barricades (revolt against Henri III).

1589: *August 1* – Assassination of Henri III by Dominican fanatic.

1589–1610: Reign of Henri IV 'le Vert-Galant' (first of the House of Bourbon); Basse-Navarre, Foix and Comté d'Auvergne joined to France.

1593: *July 25* – Henri IV abjures Protestantism at Saint-Denis.

1598: *April 13* – Edict of Nantes.

1608: *July 3* – Foundation of Québec by Samuel de Champlain.

1610: Assassination of Henri IV.

1610–43: Reign of Louis XIII 'le Juste' (Marie de Médicis regent, to 1614).

1614–15: Last meeting of États-Généraux (nobility, clergy, bourgeoisie) until 1789 Revolution.

1620: Incorporation of Béarn and Lower Navarre.

1620–29: Huguenot rebellions.

1624–42: Cardinal Richelieu chief minister.

1627: *August* – Siege of La Rochelle, Huguenot stronghold (to October 1628).

1629: Richelieu orders destruction of city ramparts and private fortified *châteaux*. *June* – Capture and destruction of Alès (Huguenot defeat).

1635: Académie Française founded by Richelieu.

1643–1715: Reign of Louis XIV; ministry of Cardinal Mazarin (to 1661).

1648: *August 26* – Day of the Barricades (start of Fronde civil wars). *October* – Peace of Westphalia: France acquires parts of Alsace and Lorraine.

1659: *November 7* – Treaty of the Pyrenees: France acquires Roussillon and neighbouring regions, most of Artois and parts of Flanders.

1661–1715: Conquests in Flanders, Franche-Comté and Alsace; incorporation of Nivernais and Dauphiné d'Auvergne.

1661: *September 5* – Arrest of Nicolas Fouquet, Superintendent of Finance.

1664–1769: French East India Company.

1665–83: Ministry of Jean-Baptiste Colbert: development of road system centred on Paris.

1667–82: Construction of Canal du Midi.

1668: *May 2* – Franco-Spanish Treaty of Aix-la-Chapelle: France retains most conquests in Flanders but returns Franche-Comté. *July 18* – Grand Divertissement Royal de Versailles.

1675: Tax revolt of Bonnets Rouges in Brittany.

1678–9: Peace of Nijmegen treaties: France regains possession of Franche-Comté.

1680: Foundation of Comédie-Française.

1682: The royal court moves to Versailles. *April 9* – Foundation of Louisiana by Cavelier de La Salle.

1685: *October 17* – Revocation of Edict of Nantes.

1702–10: War of the Camisards (persecution of Protestants in the Cévennes).

1715–74: Reign of Louis XV (Philippe d'Orléans regent, 1715–23).

1726–43: Ministry of Cardinal de Fleury.

1738: *June 13* – Introduction of *corvée* (annual road-building duty).

1740–48: War of the Austrian Succession.

1751: First volume of *Encyclopédie* by Diderot and d'Alembert.

1755: *November* – Corsican Republic declared by Pasquale Paoli.

1756: British naval attacks on French ships and imperial possessions: Seven Years War.

1756–1815: Publication of the Cassini map of France.

1763: *February 10* – Treaty of Paris: Nouvelle France (N. America) ceded to Britain and Spain.

1766: Incorporation of Lorraine.

1766–9: Circumnavigation of the globe by L.-A. de Bougainville.

1768: Genoa cedes Corsica to France.

1774: *May* – Accession of Louis XVI.

1775: *August* – Public coaches permitted to use staging posts.

1778: *February* – Benjamin Franklin meets Voltaire in Paris; Franco-American Treaty of Amity and Commerce.

1781: *September 5* – Battle of the Chesapeake (French naval victory).

1786: *August 8* – First known ascent of Mont Blanc.

1789: *May 5* – Meeting of États-Généraux (first since 1614–15). *June 20* – Tennis Court Oath. *July 14* – Fall of the Bastille. *August 4* – Abolition of feudal rights and privileges. *October 5–6* – Women's March on Versailles. *November* – National sale of Church property.

1790: *January 15* – France divided into eighty-three *départements*. *July 12* – Civil Constitution of the Clergy (Church subordinate to State). *August* – Abbé Grégoire, 'Report on the Necessity and Means of Exterminating Patois and Universalizing the Use of the French Language'.

1791: *June 21* – Arrest of Louis XVI and Marie-Antoinette. *August* – Jews granted full citizenship; San Domingo slave revolt (Haitian Revolution, to 1804). *September* – Annexation of Avignon and Comtat Venaissin (later, part of Vaucluse). *October 16–17* – Massacre in Avignon.

1792: *April 20* – War declared on Austria. *September 21* – Proclamation of First Republic.

1793: Counter-revolution in the Vendée and 'pacification' of western France. *January 21* – Execution of Louis XVI. *February 1* – War declared on Britain. *August 10* – Opening of Louvre Museum. *August to December* – Siege of Toulon. *October 16* – Execution of Marie-Antoinette.

1794: *May* – Massacre at Bédoin. *June 8* – Feast of the Supreme Being. *July 28* – Execution of Robespierre.

1795–9: Directoire.

1795: 'White Terror' (Royalist reprisals). *April 7* – Adoption of metric system. *June 8* – Death in prison of 'Louis Capet', aged ten, uncrowned Louis XVII.

1796: *March 2* – Napoleon Bonaparte appointed commander-in-chief of French army in Italy. *May 10* – Battle of Lodi (Austrian defeat).

1797: *January 14–15* – Battle of Rivoli (Austrian defeat). *September 4 (18 Fructidor)* – *Coup d'état*: annulment of elections and repression of monarchists.

1798–1801: French expedition to Egypt and Syria.

1798: *July 21* – Battle of the Pyramids (Ottoman defeat).

1799: *November 9 (18 Brumaire)* – *Coup d'état*: Bonaparte First Consul.

1800: *June 14* – Battle of Marengo (Austrian defeat in northern Italy).

1802: *March 25* – Treaty of Amiens: end of Revolutionary Wars.

1803: *April 7* – Death in prison of Toussaint Louverture, leader of San Domingo Revolution. *April 30* – Louisiana Purchase.

1804: *December 2* – Coronation of Emperor Napoleon I at Notre-Dame.

1805: *October 21* – Battle of Trafalgar (British naval victory). *December 2* – Battle of Austerlitz (Austrian and Russian defeat).

1806: *October 14* – Battle of Jena (Prussian defeat).

1808–13: Napoleon's brother Joseph King of Spain.

1812: *September to October* – French occupation of Moscow. *November 26–9* – Battle of the Berezina: more than 20,000 French killed.

1814: *March 31* – Paris occupied by allied armies. *April 11* – First abdication of Napoleon. *May* – First Restoration.

1815: *February 26* – Napoleon escapes from Elba. *June 18* – Battle of Waterloo. *July 9* – Second Restoration. *October 15* – Napoleon arrives at St Helena.

1815–24: Reign of Louis XVIII.

1818: *November* – End of allied occupation of France.

1820: *February 13* – Assassination of Duc de Berry by Louvel, Bonapartist.

1821: *May 5* – Death of Napoleon.

1824–30: Reign of Charles X.

1825: France recognizes sovereignty of Haiti in exchange for 150 million francs reparation payment to indemnify former slave owners. (Final payment made in 1947.)

1828: *October 1* – Opening of first railway in France (Saint-Étienne to Andrézieux).

1829–50: Honoré de Balzac (b. 1799), novels and studies collected as *La Comédie Humaine*.

1830: *June to July* – Capture of Algiers. *July 27–9* – Revolution. *August 2* – Abdication of Charles X. *August 9* – Louis-Philippe 'King of the French'. *August 25* – Start of Belgian Revolution.

1831: *February* – Riots in Paris (destruction of Archbishop's Palace at Notre-Dame). *July 21* – Belgian independence. *November* – First uprising of *canuts* (silk workers) in Lyon.

1832: *March to September* – Cholera epidemic. *April to May* –

Royalist rebellion in the Vendée led by the Duchesse de
Berry. *June 5–6* – Republican uprising in Paris.

1833:   *June* – Guizot's education law: each *commune* of at least five
hundred inhabitants to maintain an elementary school for
boys (girls from 1836).

1834:   *April 14* – Popular insurrection: massacre in Rue
Transnonain, Paris, by National Guard.

1836:   *October 30* – Attempted coup by Louis-Napoléon Bonaparte
at Strasbourg.

1837:   First railway station in Paris (124, Rue Saint-Lazare).

1840:   *August 6* – Attempted coup by Louis-Napoléon Bonaparte at
Boulogne. *December* – 'Retour des Cendres' (return of
Napoleon's remains).

1845–64: Renovation of Notre-Dame by Viollet-le-Duc.

1847:   *December* – Defeat and capture of Abd-el-Kader, leader of
Arab revolt.

1848:   *February 22–6* – Revolution; abdication of Louis-Philippe.
March to April: Provisional government proclaims universal
male suffrage and abolition of slavery. *June 22–6* – Repression
of popular revolt. *November 4* – Constitution of Second
Republic. *December 10–11* – Louis-Napoléon elected President.

1850:   *March 15* – Catholic Church authorized to run private
secondary schools (Falloux Law).

1851:   *December 2* – *Coup d'état* of Louis-Napoléon Bonaparte
(Emperor Napoléon III, 1852–70).

1852:   Start of *pébrine* epidemic (disease of silkworms).

1853–6: Crimean War.

1853:   *September 24* – France takes possession of New Caledonia.

1854–5: Siege of Sevastopol.

1855:   *May to November* – Universal Exhibition. *August 18–27* –
State visit of Queen Victoria.

1856:   Serialization of Gustave Flaubert's *Madame Bovary*.

1857:   Charles Baudelaire, *Les Fleurs du Mal*. Afforestation of 2.5
million acres of the Landes begins.

1858:   *February to July* – Virgin Mary appears to Bernadette
Soubirous at Lourdes. *August* – Invasion of Cochinchina
(S. Vietnam).

1860:   *March 24* – Annexation of Savoy and Nice.

1860–8: Bibliothèque Nationale, by Henri Labrouste.

1861–7: French intervention in Mexico.

1862:   Victor Hugo, *Les Misérables*.

1863:   Start of phylloxera epidemic (disease of vines).
1869:   *May* – Republican victory in legislative elections.
1870:   *January 2* – Émile Ollivier head of government (to August
        10). *September* – Prussian victory at Sedan; proclamation of
        Third Republic; Siege of Paris (to January 1871).
1871:   *March* – Election of Paris Commune (also Communes of
        Marseille, Saint-Étienne, Toulouse, etc.); National
        Government at Versailles. *May* – Defeat of Paris Commune
        by government troops. Treaty of Frankfurt: France loses
        Alsace and Lorraine; Prussian occupation of northern and
        eastern France.
1871–3: Adolphe Thiers President.
1873–9: Patrice de MacMahon President.
1875–1914: Building of Sacré-Coeur basilica at Montmartre.
1878:   Universal Exhibition; Palais du Trocadéro.
1879–87: Jules Grévy President.
1879:   Government returns from Versailles to Paris. Funding of
        local railways and canals (Freycinet Plan).
1881–1956: French protectorate of Tunisia.
1881–2: Free, compulsory, secular education for boys and girls from
        six to thirteen (Jules Ferry Laws).
1884:   *February to April* – Miners' strike at Anzin (Nord). *March 21*
        – Legalization of trade unions.
1885:   *June 1* – Funeral of Victor Hugo.
1887–94: Sadi Carnot President.
1887:   Creation of French Indochinese Union (Cochinchina,
        Vietnam, Cambodia, Laos).
1887–9: Electoral successes of populist General Boulanger.
1889:   Universal Exhibition; inauguration of Eiffel Tower.
1891:   *March 15* – Paris time imposed on the rest of France.
1894:   *June 24* – President Carnot assassinated by Italian anarchist.
        October 15 – Arrest of Alfred Dreyfus.
1894–5: Jean Casimir-Perier President.
1895–9: Félix Faure President.
1895–1958: Afrique Occidentale Française federation.
1898:   *January 13* – 'J'Accuse!', Émile Zola's letter on the Dreyfus
        Affair.
1899–1906: Émile Loubet President.
1900:   *April to November* – Universal Exhibition; Gare d'Orsay,
        Grand and Petit Palais. *July 19* – Opening of first Métro
        line in Paris.

1901–5: Anticlerical measures (governments of René Waldeck-Rousseau and Émile Combes).

1903: *July 1–19* – First Tour de France bicycle race.

1904: *April 8* – 'Entente Cordiale' agreements between France and United Kingdom.

1905: *August* – Exploration of Gorges du Verdon.

1906–9: Georges Clemenceau Prime Minister.

1906–13: Armand Fallières President.

1909: *April 18* – Beatification of Jeanne d'Arc.

1910–58: Afrique Équatoriale Française federation.

1912–56: French protectorate of Morocco.

1913–20: Raymond Poincaré President.

1914: *July 31* – Assassination of Jean Jaurès. *August 1* – France orders general mobilization. *August* – Battle of the Frontiers (Vosges, Ardennes). *September* – Battle of the Marne.

1916: *February to December* – Battle of Verdun. *July to November* – Battle of the Somme.

1917: *April to May* – Nivelle Offensive: Battle of the Chemin des Dames. *November* – Georges Clemenceau Prime Minister (to January 1920).

1918: *November 11* – Armistice; France recovers Alsace-Lorraine.

1920: Paul Deschanel President. *December* – Foundation of Parti Communiste Français.

1920–24: Alexandre Millerand President.

1923: *January 11* – French and Belgian occupation of the Ruhr (to August 1925).

1924–31: Gaston Doumergue President.

1925: Greatest extent of French colonial empire.

1930–39: Construction of Maginot Line frontier fortifications.

1930: *June 30* – Allied occupation of the Rhineland ends.

1931–2: Paul Doumer President (assassinated by Russian émigré).

1932–40: Albert Lebrun President.

1936: *June* – Victory of Popular Front: Léon Blum first Socialist Prime Minister; introduction of *congés payés* (paid holidays) and forty-hour week.

1939: *September 3* – Declaration of war.

1940: *May 26 to June 4* – Battle of Dunkirk: 35,000 French soldiers captured, 16,000 killed. *June 14* – German army enters Paris; French government to Tours, then Bordeaux. *July 3* – British attack on French fleet at Mers-el-Kébir. *July*

10 – Establishment of Vichy regime (Maréchal Philippe Pétain head of 'État Français'); anti-Jewish denaturalization law.

1942: *July 16–17* – Arrest of more than 13,000 Jews in Paris (Vel' d'Hiv'). *November 8* – Allied invasion of French North Africa.

1943: *February* – Service de Travail Obligatoire. *July 8* – Death of Resistance leader Jean Moulin.

1944: *April 21* – Women granted the right to vote. *June 6* – D-Day (Allied invasion of Normandy). *July 21–4* – Crushing of Vercors Resistance. *August* – Liberation of Paris; purges of collaborators begin. *September 9* – General de Gaulle head of Provisional Government.

1945: *January* – German counter-offensive in Alsace. *April 25* – Maréchal Pétain arrested on Swiss border. *April 30* – Death of Adolf Hitler.

1947: Inauguration of Fourth Republic.

1947–54: Vincent Auriol President.

1954: *May* – French defeat by Viet Minh at Dien Bien Phu.

1954–62: War of Algerian Independence.

1954–9: René Coty President.

1957: *March 25* – Treaty of Rome establishes European Economic Community.

1958: *October 4* – Constitution of Fifth Republic.

1959–69: Charles de Gaulle President.

1959: *July* – Formation of Basque separatist group ETA.

1961: *October 17* – Massacre of Algerians by Paris police.

1962: *July* – Algeria granted independence. *August 22* – Attempted assassination of de Gaulle at Petit-Clamart.

1965: Creation of new satellite towns on outskirts of Paris, Lille, Lyon, Marseille, Rouen. *July 13* – Women granted the right to work and open a bank account without a husband's permission. *July 16* – Opening of Mont Blanc tunnel.

1967: *December 19* – Legalization of contraception (Neuwirth Law).

1968: *May to June* – Student protests and general strike.

1969–74: Georges Pompidou President.

1971–81: Larzac plateau civil disobedience movement.

1972: *October 5* – Foundation of Front National (now Rassemblement National).

1974–81: Valéry Giscard d'Estaing President.

1975: *January 17* – Decriminalization of abortion (Veil Law).

1977: *March* – Jacques Chirac first Mayor of Paris since 1871.

1981: *September 18* – Abolition of death penalty. *September 27* – First TGV rail service (Paris to Lyon).

1981–95: François Mitterrand President.

1982–6: Decentralization laws.

1985: *July 10* – Fatal bombing by French intelligence agents of Greenpeace ship monitoring nuclear tests in French Polynesia.

1989: *March* – Grand Louvre and Pyramid. *July* – Opéra Bastille.

1992: *April* – Opening of Disneyland Paris.

1994: *November 14* – First Eurostar train leaves Gare du Nord for London Waterloo.

1995–2007: Jacques Chirac President.

1996: *January 27* – Last French nuclear test. *December 15* – Opening of Bibliothèque Nationale de France.

1998: *July 12* – French national football team wins the World Cup at Saint-Denis.

1999: *January 1* – Launch of the euro (in circulation from January 1, 2002).

2001–14: Bertrand Delanoë Mayor of Paris.

2004: *March 15* – Islamic headscarves and other conspicuous religious symbols banned in public schools.

2005: *April 23* – 'La Marseillaise' made obligatory in schools (Fillon Law). *October to November* – Popular revolt in Paris *banlieue* and towns and cities throughout France.

2006: *March* – Sorbonne occupied by students, evacuated by CRS.

2007–12: Nicolas Sarkozy President.

2008: *January 1* – Smoking banned in cafés and restaurants.

2012–17: François Hollande President.

2013: *May 17* – Legalization of same-sex marriage.

2014–: Anne Hidalgo Mayor of Paris.

2014: Territorial reform (effective from January 2016): regions of mainland France reduced from twenty-two to thirteen.

2015: *January 7* – *Charlie Hebdo* massacre in Paris. *November 13–14* – Terror attacks in Paris (Bataclan theatre) and Saint-Denis.

2016: *July 14* – Terror attack on Promenade des Anglais, Nice.

2017: Emmanuel Macron elected President.

2018: *July 15* – French national football team wins the World Cup in Moscow. *August 3* – 'Sexist outrage' banned in public places. *November 17* – First nationwide protests of Gilets Jaunes (also Guadeloupe, Guyane, Martinique, Réunion).

2019:   *December 27* – First (retrospectively confirmed) case of Covid-19 in France (northern Paris).

2020:   *September 3* – Hundred billion euro 'green' recovery plan announced by Prime Minister Jean Castex. *October* – Commemorative republication of *Charlie Hebdo* Muhammad cartoons and jihadist murder of a Paris schoolteacher; Macron declares, 'We shall not repudiate the caricatures' and calls for 'unity'.

References

Most of these references relate to only one chapter and can be identified without recourse to a list of Works Cited.

All translations are my own.

Previously . . .

5   Herakles . . . Ogmios: The principal sources are Ammianus
     Marcellinus, Diodorus Siculus, Dionysius of Halicarnassus,
     Lucian of Samosata, Pomponius Mela and Strabo. Full references
     in *The Ancient Paths* / *The Discovery of Middle Earth* (2013),
     pp. 205–6.
5   Saint Christopher: *The Ancient Paths*, p. 75.

1. The Hedge

9   piercing black eyes: Suetonius, 'Divus Julius', 45, 1.
9   'wild men of great courage': Julius Caesar, *De Bello Gallico*, II, 15.
     (Abbreviation: *DBG*.)
9   as he wielded the comb: Suetonius, 45, 2.
10   'They cut notches': *DBG*, II, 17; also Strabo, IV, 3, 5.
10   Roman luxuries: *DBG*, II, 15.
10   'prodigiously large in body': *DBG*, I, 39.
11   Hercynian Forest: Aristotle, *Meteorologica*, I, 13; *DBG*, VI, 25 and 34;
     Pomponius Mela, III, 24–29; Pliny, III, 25 (148) and XVI, 2 (6);
     Ptolemy, II, 14.
11   the Arduenna: *DBG*, VI, 29.
11   Druids, a priestly caste: *DBG*, VI, 13–16.
11   temporary islands: *DBG*, VI, 31; also Pliny, VI, 2, on the Chauci and
     ocean-going oaks, and H. Vansteenberghe, *Histoire de la ville et de la
     seigneurie d'Hondschoote* (1885), p. 8. The hills of French Flanders
     could be mistaken for islands in the fog: L. de Baecker, in *Annales du
     Comité Flamand de France*, IV (1858–9), p. 212.
12   'the most barbarous and remote': *DBG*, II, 4.

12   a river called the Sabis: *DBG*, II, 16.

13   Hautmont, a suburb: Identified by Napoleon I in *Précis des guerres de César* (1836), pp. 39–45, A. von Göler in *Caesars Gallischer Krieg* (1858) and Napoléon III in *Histoire de Jules César* (1865–6). See also T. Rice Holmes, *Caesar's Conquest of Gaul* (1911), p. 671. Abbé Turquin's siting of the battle on the Selle – a trickle of water in a flat plain – was refuted by W. Ernest in the *Revue du Nord*, XXXVIII, 152 (1956), pp. 376–7.

14   Caesar's tactics: Napoléon I, *Précis des guerres*, p. 45.

14   such incredible speed: *DBG*, II, 21.

14   news in Gaul: On the vocal telegraph: *DBG*, VII, 3 and *The Ancient Paths*, pp. 31–7.

15   'So great was their courage': *DBG*, II, 27.

15   Diviciacus the Aeduan: Cicero, *De divinatione*, I, 41.

15   'the dread of death': *DBG*, VI, 14.

16   'unknown and hidden routes': *DBG*, VI, 34.

16   'the central region of . . . Gaul': *DBG*, VI, 13.

16   'written in Greek characters': *DBG*, V, 48.

17   'From that higher spot': *DBG*, II, 26.

18   Menapii and Morini: *DBG*, III, 28–9.

18   'six hundred senators': *DBG*, II, 28.

18   August 1914: On the Siege of Maubeuge, C. Donnell, *Breaking the Fortress Line, 1914* (2013), ch. 10.

18   General Joffre reported: *Historique du 3me Régiment Territorial d'Infanterie* (1915), p. 12.

19   'Caesar's Camps': *The Ancient Paths*, p. 69. Generally, S. Fichtl, *La Ville celtique: les* oppida (2005).

2. A Home in Gaul

21   neighbouring villas: Voroangus and Prusianum on the site of Alès (Gard): *Histoire de l'Académie royale des Inscriptions et Belles Lettres*, III (1746), pp. 260–62.

21   'Sharp-eyed scouts': O. M. Dalton, ed., *The Letters of Sidonius* (1915), II, 9. This edition contains useful notes. (Abbreviation: SA.) The Latin text of the *Epistulae* is edited by W. B. Anderson (Loeb Classical Library, 1936).

22   The quaint customs: Diodorus Siculus, V, 27, 3 and 32, 7; Posidonius, quoted by Strabo, IV, 4, 5.

22   In 414: On the historical background as it relates to Sidonius: J. Harries,

Sidonius Apollinaris and the Fall of Rome (1994); F. Riess, *Narbonne and Its Territory in Late Antiquity* (2013).

22 'unbridled barbarism': Orosius, *Historiae adversum Paganos*, VII, 43, 6.

23 'Situated near town': SA, VIII, 4.

23 'Conscience': R. Verdo, 'Contribution à la toponymie audoise', *Nouvelle revue d'onomastique*, 56 (2014), p. 62; also F. Riess, p. 128.

24 lost to landslips: The 'Pierre écrite' road, absent from the cadastral map of 1814, is shown on Ricard's *Carte de l'arrondissement de Sisteron* (1843).

24 'Claudius Postumus Dardanus': J. Barruol, 'Theopolis en Haute Provence', *Bulletin de la Société d'Études des Hautes-Alpes*, LXIV (1975), pp. 47–54.

25 addressed to Jerome: Letter 129 (AD 414).

25 Augustine of Hippo: Letter 187 (AD 417). Dardanus may have been alluding to Augustine's *De Civitate Dei* ('On the City of God'), but the chronology is unclear.

26 Trophy of Augustus: Pliny, III, 20, with the names of other Alpine tribes.

26 'They have sometimes been seen': Beylet, 'Demi-sauvages de la Provence', *Bulletin de la Société de géographie*, II, VI (1836), pp. 56–60.

26 a refuge or a *locus*: On mystical connotations of '*locus*': M. Varano, *Espace religieux et espace politique en pays provençal au Moyen Âge*, thesis (Aix-en-Provence, 2011), I, 139.

26 unknown to the outside world: *The Discovery of France*, pp. 335–6.

26 Castellum Dromone: G. Bérard et al., *Les Alpes-de-Haute-Provence*, vol. IV of *Carte archéologique de la Gaule* (1994), pp. 179–80; also J. Bromwich, *The Roman Remains of Southern France* (1996), pp. 289–90.

27 'Today shalt thou be with me': Luke 23:43.

28 'gold and silver coins': H. Bouche, *La Chorographie ou Description de Provence* (1664), I, 570.

28 Theous: Abbé J.-P. Papon, *Histoire générale de Provence*, (1777), I, 95; others in J.-J.-M. Féraud, *Histoire, géographie et statistique des Basses-Alpes* (1861), p. 669.

28 '*tauus*' or '*tauius*': See X. Delamarre, *Dictionnaire de la langue gauloise* (2003), p. 292.

29 'I put my horse to a gallop': SA, III, 12.

30 A Roman law: M. A. Esmein, 'Quelques renseignements sur l'origine des juridictions privées', *Mélanges d'archéologie et d'histoire*, VI, 6 (1886), pp. 418–23. Generally, L. Angliviel de la Beaumelle, 'La

Torture dans les *Res Gestae* d'Ammien Marcellin', *Publications de l'École française de Rome. Institutions, société et vie politique* (1992), pp. 91–113; A. C. Dionisotti, 'From Ausonius's Schooldays?', *The Journal of Roman Studies*, LXXII (1982), pp. 83–125 (the torturing of criminals was sufficiently banal to be included in a Greek–Latin primer).

30   'this just and holy man': SA, III, 12.

30   'the scabrous Celtic dialect': SA, III, 3.

30   'blighted with the mould': SA, II, 10.

30   'a name which sounds sweeter': SA, II, 2.

31   his 'affectionate' wife: SA, V, 16.

31   'I am glad to be beaten': SA, I, 2.

31   'silver dishes': Gregory of Tours, *Historia Francorum*, II, 22.

32   'The ice is melting': SA, II, 2.

33   'But I shall say no more': SA, II, 2.

33   Avitacum . . . Aydat: On the Cassini map, Aydat is Aidat. There is no certain etymological link with 'Avitacum': G. Rohlfs, *Studien zur romanischen Namenkunde* (1956), p. 86. C. E. Stevens, in *Sidonius Apollinaris and His Age* (1933), accepted the traditional location but was unable to match the reality with the description.

33   'foamed white against rocky barriers': SA, II, 2.

33   Provençal Sidonius: See L. Levêque, *Un essai d'explication des traditions provençales* (1898), pp. 15–17.

34   The 'former lake': F. Trément et al., *Le Bassin de Sarliève: occupation du sol et paléo-environnement à l'Âge du Fer* (2003). On drainage: Ville de Pérignat-lès-Sarliève, *Plan local d'urbanisme: rapport de présentation* (2012).

34   Le Pré du Camp: B. Dousteyssier et al., 'Les *Villae* gallo-romaines dans le territoire proche d'Augustonemetum', *Revue archéologique du Centre de la France*, XLIII (2005), pp. 115–47 (with maps and photographs). Also M. Provost and C. Mennessier-Jouannet, *Clermont-Ferrand*, vol. 63/1 of *Carte archéologique de la Gaule* (1994), and J. Visser, 'Sidonius Apollinaris, *Ep.* II.2: The Man and His Villa', *Journal for Late Antique Religion and Culture*, 8 (2014), pp. 26–45.

36   'someone had maliciously stolen the book': Gregory of Tours, *Historia Francorum*, II, 22.

36   'Historical writing': SA, IV, 22.

37   'brothers of the Latins': SA, VII, 7.

37   Outlawed and persecuted: *The Ancient Paths*, pp. 191, 250 and 264.

37   'soot and cobwebs': Jerome, letter 107, 1–2 (AD 403).

37   'Diocese and parish lie desolate': SA, VII, 6.

38   excavated in the 1970s: 'Le Parc archéologique Saint-Just':
      http://lyonhistorique.fr/parc-archeologique-saint-just/ (recently
      relandscaped): on Rue des Macchabées by Place de Trion.
      On successive churches: J.-F. Reynaud, *Lugdunum Christianum*
      (1998).
38   'the noisy public highway': SA, II, 10.
39   'the place which all men seek': SA, II, 10.
39   tangent ratio of 11:7: See *The Ancient Paths*, p. 141.
39   five stone coffins: G. Bérard et al., *Les Alpes-de-Haute-Provence*,
      pp. 179–80.

3. The Invisible Land of the Woods and the Sea

44   Saint Yves: The original saying was 'Sanctus Yvo erat Brito, /
      Advocatus et non latro, / Res miranda populo!'
45   fought the English: Maurice and Geslin de Troguindy, at the Bataille
      des Trente (1351) during the Hundred Years War: J. Ogée,
      Dictionnaire historique et géographique de la province de Bretagne (1843),
      I, 409.
45   black mastiff: D. Giraudon, 'Drame sanglant au pardon de Saint-
      Gildas à Tonquédec en 1707', *Annales de Bretagne et des Pays de
      l'Ouest*, CXIV, 1 (2007), p. 67 n.
45   seaborne immigrants: The main primary sources on Breton migra-
      tions are Gregory of Tours, Gildas, Nennius, Geoffrey of Monmouth
      and the lives of the saints: see pp. 13–18 in A. Chédeville and H.
      Guillotel, *La Bretagne des saints et des rois* (1984); also J.-C. Cassard,
      Les Bretons et la mer au Moyen Âge (1998), pp. 15–71; J. Loth,
      L'Émigration bretonne en Armorique (1883).
45   made of stone: E.g. L. Spence, *Legends and Romances of Brittany*
      (1917), pp. 359–60: 'Miraculous Crossings'.
45   *oppidum* upstream of Le Guindy: At Kerdéozer: F. Tournier,
      Fortifications de terre médiévales du Trégor (1994), pp. 225–32.
46   desertion of the Breton coast: J.-C. Cassard, ch. 2: 'La Mer oubliée
      ou l'empaysannement breton'; H. Dubois, 'La Hiérarchie des
      paroisses dans le diocèse de Coutance', pp. 117–35 in M. Balard et
      al., *Villages et villageois au Moyen Âge* (1992).
46   a 'king of the Bretons': SA, III, 9.
47   'a two-hundred-and-fifty-kilometre wedge': P. Vidal de la Blache,
      Tableau de la géographie de la France (1903; 1908), p. 328.
47   'the rocks grow darker': Vidal de la Blache, p. 307.

47   *chemins creux*: E.g. A. Dumas, *Mes mémoires* (1863–84), VII, 97–9.

47   protected by forests: L.-F.-A. Maury, *Les Forêts de la Gaule et de l'ancienne France* (1867), pp. 287–8. Also Victor Hugo's *Quatrevingt-treize* (1874), III, I, 2–3.

48   one of the most densely populated: J. Cambry, *Voyage dans le Finistère* (1798), I, 53–4; J. Peuchet, 'Finistère', *Description topographique et statistique de la France* (1807); B. Lasserre, *Les Cent-Jours en Vendée* (1906), p. 24.

48   missing from French maps: Cf. 'Gallia Novella' in F. Berlinghieri's *Geographia* (Florence, 1480), probably based on portolan charts showing the Cotentin and Armorican peninsulas.

48   the Roman geographer: Strabo, I, 4, 5.

48   slow to claim and conquer: L. Drapeyron, 'L'Image de la France sous les derniers Valois [et] les premiers Bourbons', *Revue de Géographie*, XXIV (1880), p. 5.

49   Ermoldus Nigellus: The Breton episodes belong to part 3 of his *Carmen elegiacum de rebus gestis Ludovici Pii, ab anno 781 usque ad annum 826*, in *Patrologiae cursus completus*, ed. J.-P. Migne, 2nd series, CV (1831), pp. 551–639. There is a good recent edition by T. F. X. Noble: *Charlemagne and Louis the Pious* (2009).

50   the Breton March: Successive frontiers and Frankish fortified posts (*guerches*) are depicted in R. Cintré, *Les Marches de Bretagne au Moyen Âge* (1992), pp. 12–15.

50   natural buffer zone: J.-C. Cassard, 'La Basse Vilaine, une marche de guerre au haut Moyen Âge', *Annales de Bretagne et des Pays de l'Ouest*, CX, 1 (2003), pp. 29–47.

50   Murman (or Morvan): 'Murmanus rex Brittonum' is mentioned in Einhard and the Moissac Chronicle: *Monumenta Germaniae historica*, ed. G. H. Pertz, I: *Scriptorum* (1925), I, 205, 356 and 567. On the location of his palace: P. Guigon, 'L'*arx* de Morvan, les *lis* de Salomon et la *domus* de Gradlon', *Actes des congrès de la Société d'archéologie médiévale*, VII (2001), p. 32.

51   politically expedient: On Frankish views of Brittany: J. M. H. Smith, *Province and Empire: Brittany and the Carolingians* (1992), pp. 63–72; W. Davies, *Small Worlds: The Village Community in Early Medieval Brittany* (1988), pp. 17–22.

53   by the River Charente: Mentioned by Ermold in the first of his poem-epistles to Pippin.

4. Time Machines

58 transformed the basilica: Flodoard de Reims, *Histoire de l'Église de Rheims*, ed. F. Guizot (1824), pp. 225–7.

58 'bellowing like thunder': Richer de Reims, *Histoire de son temps*, ed. G. H. Pertz, vol. II (1845), p. 25 (ch. 23).

59 a 'mechanical clock': William of Malmesbury, *Gesta regum anglorum*, ed. T. D. Hardy, in *Patrologiae cursus completus*, ed. Migne, CLXXIX (1899), p. 1140 (II, 168). (Abbreviation: WM.) Also *Ottonian Germany: The Chronicon of Thietmar of Merseburg*, ed. D. A. Warner (2001), p. 303.

59 'strange and wonderful manner': WM, p. 1140 (II, 168).

60 Benedictine abbey: G. Bouange, *Saint Géraud d'Aurillac et son illustre abbaye* (1870); on Gerbert, pp. 277–93.

60 hamlet of Belliac: On legends of Gerbert's origins: Bouange; J. Havet, ed., *Lettres de Gerbert* (1889), pp. v–vi.

60 'Blind fortune': *The Letters of Gerbert, with his Papal Privileges as Sylvester II*, ed. H. P. Lattin (1961), p. 93. References are to this edition (abbreviation: *Letters*). My translations are based on the Latin edition by J. Havet.

61 'What more evidence': *Letters*, p. 297.

61 Ramon Borrell: Richer de Reims, II, 47 (ch. 43).

61 '*pro morum insolentia*': Hugh of Flavigny, *Chronicon*, in *Patrologia latina*, CLIV, col. 193.

61 'any in Spain who had attained . . .': Ibid.

62 the Caliphate itself: Adémar de Chabannes, *Chronique*, ed. J. Chavanon (1897), p. 154.

62 library at Córdoba: *Œuvres de Gerbert*, ed. A. Olleris (1867), p. xix; also *Autour de Gerbert d'Aurillac*, ed. O. Guyotjeannin and E. Poulle (1996), p. 33; A. Schärlig, *Un portrait de Gerbert d'Aurillac* (2012), pp. 17–19.

62 introduced to the Pope: Richer de Reims, II, 49 (ch. 44).

63 a Saracen philosopher: WM, p. 1138–9 (II, 167).

63 'the song and the flight of birds': WM, p. 1138 (II, 167).

64 'fastened wings to his hands and feet': WM, p. 1205–6 (II, 225). On the tale's plausibility: J. Paz, 'Human Flight in Early Medieval England', *New Medieval Literatures*, 15 (2015), pp. 1–28; L. White, 'Eilmer of Malmesbury, an Eleventh Century Aviator', *Technology and Culture*, II, 2 (1961), pp. 97–111.

64 Abbas ibn Firnas: L. White, p. 100.

64 Amiens illuminated manuscript: *Abrégé des histoires divines*, in J. Pierpont Morgan Library: M.751 fol. 99v (stealing the book); M.751 fol. 100r (playing the steam organ).

64   'Instead of using many words': *Letters*, p. 51.

65   summoning spirits from hell: E.g. Benno of Osnabrück (d. 1098),
      Vita et gesta Hildebrandi; Sigebert of Gembloux (d. 1112), *Chronicon
      sive Chronographia*; Orderic Vitalis (d. 1142), *Historia Ecclesiastica*.

65   'multiplied and divided numbers': Richer de Reims, II, 63 (ch. 54).
      There is no evidence for the story told in 2001 that Gerbert created
      a giant abacus on the floor of Reims Cathedral. See http://www.vlib.
      us/medieval/lectures/gerbert.html (probably confusing abacus with
      clock or labyrinth).

65   'If it is the pole star': *Letters*, p. 38; Richer de Reims, II, 50–61 (chs
      50–53).

65   Magdeburg Cathedral: *The Chronicon of Thietmar of Merseburg*, p.
      303; F. Picavet, *Gerbert, un pape philosophe* (1897), p. 190.

66   tracked down the manuscripts: On Gerbert's collecting: P. Riché, 'La
      Bibliothèque de Gerbert d'Aurillac', *Mélanges de la Bibliothèque de la
      Sorbonne offerts à André Tuilier* (1988), pp. 94–103.

66   'The sphere is now being polished': *Letters*, p. 184.

66   'He cast for his own use': WM, p. 1145 (II, 172).

67   relief from scrofula: Flodoard de Reims, ch. 6 (on 'miracles').

67   fighting in a fiery sky: Flodoard de Reims, p. 541.

67   'temple wonders': Hero of Alexandria, *The Pneumatics*, ed. B.
      Woodcroft (1851), pp. 33, 37, 72 and 103–4.

67   mathematical basis of music: Richer de Reims, II, 55 (ch. 49).

67   'an ex-teacher': *Letters*, p. 53.

68   Meridiana: Gualterus (Walter) Map, *De nugis curialium*, ed. M. R.
      James (1914), pp. 176–83 (IV, 11: 'De fantastica decepcione
      Gerberti').

69   Roman surveyors: *Letters*, pp. 55 n. 5 and 301–2 n. 2.

69   pilgrims would take scrapings: A. Girault de Saint-Fargeau,
      Dictionnaire géographique, historique, industriel et commercial (1844–6),
      II, 228; G.-A. Martin, *Essai historique sur Rozoy-sur-Serre* (1863), I,
      73.

69   'add the flame of your knowledge': *Letters*, p. 295.

70   'the art of necromancy': WM, pp. 1141–2 (II, 169); also *Gesta
      Romanorum*, ed. H. Oesterley (1872), ch. 107. Gerbert had visited
      Rome before – as the Count of Barcelona's secretary, then on a
      book-hunting expedition; on the third occasion, he was ill in bed for
      several months. This episode must date from his papacy, when he
      had the authority and resources to indulge his passion for scientific
      and historical research.

70n. The Canal du Midi: A canal only one-fifth of the total distance would have joined the Mediterranean to the Atlantic. Gerbert might have read about Nero's canal-building projects in Suetonius. It was common knowledge that Charlemagne had ordered the construction of a Rhine–Danube canal. The Aude reached Narbonne until it changed its course in 1320.

71   anti-burglar device: Hero of Alexandria, pp. 62–3.

71   ninth-century copy: *Letters*, p. 53.

71   Pliny's encyclopaedic *Natural History*: XXXVI, 15.

71n. 'seize as booty': *Letters*, p. 338.

72   'By apostolic authority': *Letters*, p. 367.

72   the sweating tomb: First reported in a twelfth-century version of the *Descriptio Lateranensis ecclesiae*.

73   'His body was found intact': *Œuvres de Gerbert*, ed. Olleris, p. cxcviii.

74   'Those who make a pretence': *Letters*, p. 65.

5. Cathar Treasure

75   Just before Christmas: Witness statements edited and translated by Jean Duvernoy in *Le Dossier de Montségur, interrogatoires d'inquisition, 1242–1247* (1998), and M. Roquebert, *L'Épopée cathare*, 4 vols (1970–89), IV: *Mourir à Montségur*.

76   '*engal so dels angels*': E.g. J. Duvernoy, 'Nouveau testament occitan – Rituel cathare', p. 86 in http://jean.duvernoy.free.fr/text/pdf/cledat_luc.pdf.

76   The precipices were patrolled: J. Duvernoy, *Le Registre d'Inquisition de Jacques Fournier*, new ed. (2004), II, 444. (Abbreviation: *RI*.) The Latin texts were published by Duvernoy in 1965. E. Le Roy Ladurie's *Montaillou, village occitan de 1294 à 1324* (1975) was based on a portion of these depositions.

76   walk-in cupboards: *RI*, III, 1242. On domestic arrangements: *RI*, I, 19–20.

76   *foganha*: *RI*, I, 20.

77   borders were set by Nature: Plotting the settlements of 'Terra Savartesii' in the 1272 'Enquête sur les limites du comté de Foix' produces a crazed map of valleys and cols rather than a coherent outline. The Latin document is reproduced in C. Devic and J. Vaissète, *Histoire générale de Languedoc*, VI (1843), pp. 601–3.

77   The territory visible: On the political geography of the Pyrenean 'castles': C. Higounet, *Esquisse d'une géographie des châteaux des Pyrénées françaises au Moyen Âge* (1950).

77   *spoulgas*: F. Guillot, 'Les Grottes fortifiées du Sabartès', in *De la 'spelunca' à la 'roca': l'habitat troglodytique au Moyen Âge* (2006), pp. 87–101.

78   made the following May: Roquebert, IV, 382.

78   Poitou was 'so remote': In c. 1206: see C. Petit-Dutaillis, '*Querimoniae Normannorum*', in *Essays in Medieval History Presented to Thomas Frederick Tout* (1925), p. 117.

79   'the ties that bound his hands': *RI*, I, 151.

79   'He replied by blowing into his hand': *RI*, I, 357.

79   'concealed in the woods': Roquebert, IV, 427.

80   '*pecuniam infinitam*': 'aureum et argentum et peccuniam [*sic*] infinitam' (*infinitam* here is not 'infinite' . . .). Latin texts in Roquebert, II, 531 ff.

81   scatters of rubble: On the 'cleaning up' of Montségur in 1948 by S. Stym-Popper, chief architect of the Monuments Historiques: *Montségur, la mémoire et la rumeur*, ed. C. Pailhès (1995), p. 223.

81   'Cathari': Eckbert of Schönau, *Sermones contra Catharos* (c. 1165), in *Patrologia Latina*, CXCV, 11.

81   'cat people': Alain de Lille (b. c. 1120), *De fide Catholica contra Haereticos*, in *Patrologia Latina*, CCX, c. 366. Also *RI*, II, 787: when 'the inquisitor of Carcassonne died, no one saw him die, and when they went to his death bed the next day they found two black cats, one on either side of the bed'.

81   'holy mountain': Napoléon Peyrat, *Histoire des Albigeois* (1870), I, 365.

81   Otto Rahn: U. Linse, in *Die völkisch-religiöse Bewegung im Nationalsozialismus*, ed. U. Puschner and C. Vollnhals (2012), pp. 552–6. Rahn's *Kreuzzug gegen den Gral* was first published in 1933.

81   'Grails' *are* mentioned: E.g. *RI*, I, 348; III, 1083.

81   '*un énorme saucisson*': shadowtheatre13, 'The Lost Caves of Montsegur', 23 December 2009: http://terraumbra13.blogspot.co.uk/2009/12/lost-caves-of-montsegur.html

82   'Trust not the words': *RI*, III, 814.

82   'the distance a man can throw a stone': *RI*, I, 195–6.

82   'from Ax to Savignac': *RI*, I, 360.

83   'the leaves were appearing on the elms': *RI*, I, 254.

84   'The soul! The soul!': *RI*, I, 256.

84   'I kept watching': *RI*, I, 256.

85n.   A *bayle* was a headman: Le Roy Ladurie, p. 513.

85   'How could the souls': *RI*, I, 246.

85   'I greeted [the fortune-teller]': *RI*, III, 766–7.

86   'Then I started thinking': *RI*, I, 37.

86 His body was a loaf of bread: *RI*, I, 33.

86 they picked the lice: *RI*, I, 269; II, 461, 480, 495.

86 Distinctions in the social hierarchy: Le Roy Ladurie, p. 348.

86 'Even if the body of Christ': *RI*, II, 572; also I, 261 and 263.

87 'Christ was created': *RI*, II, 620–21; also 629–30.

87 '*Tos temps es, e tos temps sira*': *RI*, I, 201 and 205.

87 'Did you say': *RI*, I, 49.

87 five hundred and seventy-eight interrogations: The depositions survived in a Latin copy of the original documents made in c. 1326. An edition was published in 1965 by Jean Duvernoy (with a volume of errata in 1972). *RI* is Duvernoy's three-volume selection in French translation.

88 the two partners: *RI*, II, 572; also II, 616 and 705.

88 tricked his way into paradise: *RI*, III, 843–4.

88 'Come, my good fellow': *RI*, II, 706.

89 flattening the wheat: *RI*, II, 653–4.

89 pilgrimages to Le Puy: *RI*, I, 46.

89 a convicted murderer: Guillaume Bélibaste was burned at Villerouge-Termenès in 1321 on the orders of the Archbishop of Narbonne.

90 'ruining the whole *pays*': *RI*, II, 729 and III, 808.

90 owls which were believed to perch: *RI*, I, 349.

90 'After he and my husband had left': *RI*, II, 575–6.

91 'You've been asking a lot of questions': *RI*, III, 927.

91 'broken and staved in': *RI*, III, 1147–8.

92 sixteen thousand *livres tournois*: *RI*, III, 781.

92 'a hundred thousand *livres*': *RI*, III, 881. Examples of the value of money in *RI*, II, 577 and 587 n. 17.

92 Banking operations: See A. Roach, *The Relationship of the Italian and Southern French Cathars, 1170–1320*, thesis (Oxford, 1989), p. 52.

92 coins used by the Languedoc Cathars: Le Roy Ladurie, p. 444.

92 a leper from Pamiers: *RI*, II, 639.

93 'God loves Saracens and Jews': *RI*, II, 613; also II, 646.

94 'We do not know': S. Lieven, 'L'Évêque de Pamiers demande pardon pour le sort réservé aux Cathares', *La Croix*, 16 October 2016.

6. The Tree at the Centre of France

95 *Carte ecclésiastique*: Antoine-Fabrice Des Bleyns, *Carte ecclésiastique contenant la description des archeveschés et éveschés du royaume de France et principaultés adjacentes appartenants à l'église gallicane* (1624).

Diocesan maps became more common after the États-Généraux of
1614 urged priests to make pastoral visits: F. de Dainville, 'Étude sur
la cartographie ecclésiastique du XVIe au XVIIIe siècle', *Revue d'histoire de l'Église de France*, XL (1954), p. 24.

97   ornamental horticulture: E.g. Denkha Ataa, *L'Imaginaire du paradis et
le monde de l'au-delà dans le christianisme et dans l'islam*, thesis
(Strasbourg, 2012), pp. 188–202.

97   The Garden of Eden: E.g. André Favin, *Paradisus voluptatis longe
late que patens Mesopotamiam, Syriam, Arabias tres & Palestinam*, late
16th c.

97   on-the-ground research: Jolivet's note to readers in his *Vraie
description des Gaules* (1560): 'Following the King's command,
I have visited his kingdoms and provinces.'

98   After 1637: The sample trees are from maps published between 1560
and 1632.

99   pocket-sized *Guide*: *La Guide des chemins de France* (Chez Charles
Estienne, 1552). (Abbreviation: *GCF*.) 'Guide' is now masculine.
There is an edition of the 1553 *Guide* by J. Bonnerot (1936). See
also P. Herrmann, 'Genèse de "La Guide des chemins de France"',
Journal des Savants, 2011, 2, pp. 195–219.

99   the diversity of opinions: *GCF*, ii.

100   with or without its author's name: On editions and plagiarism: M.
Pelletier, 'National and Regional Mapping in France to about 1650',
in *The History of Cartography*, III, pt 2 (2007), p. 1500.

100   His sources: *GCF*, ii.

100   the picturesque details: Estienne, 18 (Ribécourt), 66 (Mailly), 83
(Neuville), 84 (Le Chesne rond) and 154 (Briançon).

100   from Paris to Tholoze: *GCF*, pp. 169–71.

101   '*See the elm & stone*': *GCF*, p. 170.

101   '*Within the Matz sainct Paul*': *GCF*, p. 181.

102   'mas' was a collective term: A. Perrier, 'Quelques noms du vocabu-
laire de géographie agraire du Limousin', *Revue géographique des
Pyrénées et du Sud-Ouest*, XXXIII, 3 (1962), p. 257.

102   chapel of Saint Paul: É. Chénon, *Histoire de Sainte-Sévère-en-Berry*
(1888), p. 404–5; Chénon, 'Notes archéologiques sur le Bas-Berry,
2e série', *Mémoires de la Société des antiquaires du Centre*, XXIII
(1899), pp. 5–6. Also E. Gligny, *Les Noms de lieux de la Creuse* (1976),
p. 75.

102   '*in pago Lemovico*': Chénon, 'Notes archéologiques', p. 7 n.

103   routes proposed to modern pilgrims: On the pilgrim route in *GCF*:
Bonnerot, 10; D. Possot et al., *Le Voyage de la Terre Sainte* (1532;

1890). There were no specific 'pilgrim routes': J.-F. Bergier, review of L. Trénard et al., *Les Routes de France depuis les origines*, in *Bibliothèque d'Humanisme et Renaissance*, XXI, 3 (1959), p. 660.

103 avoided river crossings: Perhaps indicating an older network: J.-M. Desbordes, 'Recherches sur la desserte routière des agglomérations gallo-romaines secondaires en pays lémovice', *Siècles*, 33–34 (2011).

105 feral soldiers: On road travel during and after the Hundred Years War: L.-H. Chaudru de Raynal, *Histoire du Berry* (1847), IV, 78; P. Ducourtieux, 'Les Grands chemins du Limousin', pt 1, *Bulletin de la Société archéologique et historique du Limousin*, LXV (1916), pp. 137–75; É. Levasseur, *La Population française*, I (1889), p. 189. On post-Roman roads: F. Imberdis, 'Les Routes médiévales: mythes et réalités historiques', *Annales d'histoire sociale*, I, 4 (1939), pp. 411–16.

105 the dream of unity: One of the earliest maps of France centred on Paris dates from c. 1460: C. Serchuk, 'Picturing France in the Fifteenth Century: The Map in BNF MS Fr. 4991', *Imago Mundi*, LVIII, 2 (2006), pp. 133–49.

105 'from there in clear weather': *GCF*, p. 25.

106 convoluted travel plan: See 'Notes for Travellers', p. 397.

108 'trampled by men-at-arms': N. de Nicolay, *Description générale du païs et duché de Berry* (1567), ed. A. Aupetit (1883), pp. 86–7.

110 'postes' in Estienne's guide: Herrmann, p. 207.

110 the Orme Rateau: G. Sand, *Promenades autour d'un village* (1866), pp. 199–200; G. Laisnel de la Salle, *Croyances et légendes du centre de la France* (1875; 2013), pp. 79–80.

112 a war path: See É. Chénon, *Histoire de Sainte-Sévère*, ch. 8.

112 a murdered woman: [Simon Goulart], *Mémoires de l'estat de France sous Charles neufiesme*, I (1577), pp. 411–12.

112 Protestants were butchered: See P. Benedict, 'The Saint Bartholomew's Massacres in the Provinces', *The Historical Journal*, XXI, 2 (1978), pp. 205–25, especially pp. 205–10 and 214–15; also *Mémoires de l'estat de France*, pp. 434–77.

112 'a lozenge twenty-two days wide': *GCF*, p. 1.

112 the hexagon: See N. B. Smith, 'The Idea of the French Hexagon', *French Historical Studies*, VI, 2 (1969), pp. 139–55.

112 a cosy arbour: On the 'garden of France' and burgeoning trade: C. Skenazi, 'Une pratique de la circulation: *La Guide des chemins de France*', *Romanic Review*, XCIV, 1–2 (2003), pp. 153–66.

113 harmonious arrangement: Strabo, IV, 1, 14.

113 a lime tree: L. Coulon, *L'Ulysse françois* (1643), p. 430; Du Verdier, *Le Voyage de France* (1662), p. 122; also Jodoci Sinceri in 1649 and

C. de Varennes in 1655. First mentioned by J. Zinzerling in *Itinerarium Galliae* (Lyon, 1616).

113 'from far and wide': A.-A. Monteil, *Histoire des Français des divers états: XVIe siècle*, I (1833), p. 479.

114 the areas of Jesuit ministry: J.-B. Nolin, *Carte des cinq provinces de l'Assistance de France* (1705 and 1709).

114 the *Carte des Traites*: Anonymous map first published in 1760.

114 a map of the central provinces: C. Maugein, ingénieur, *Carte de la Marche, du Bourbonnois, du Limosin, et de l'Auvergne* (1763): no. 5 of 'Provinces de France' in É.-A. Philippe de Prétot's atlas, *Cosmographie universelle physique, et astronomique* (1763–76).

7. A Walk in the Garden

119 colony of the Hurepoix: See Le sieur Jaillot (J. B. M. Renou de Chauvigné), *Recherches critiques, historiques et topographiques sur la ville de Paris*, V (1775), p. 94.

119 'the Marches of Northmandy': Jehan de Wavrin, *Anchiennes* [*sic*] *chronicques d'Engleterre*, ed. Mlle Dupont (1838), I, 283–7.

121 impassable seasons: E.g. C.-I. Castel de Saint-Pierre, *Mémoire pour perfectionner la police sur les chemins* (1715), pp. 2–3 and 33.

121 parish burial registers: J.-M. Moriceau et al., 'Les Loups autour de Paris', in 'Homme et loup: 2000 ans d'histoire': http://www.unicaen. fr/homme_et_loup/cas_loups_paris.php#part4

121 'The wine kept us walking': J.-L. Ménétra, *Journal de ma vie*, ed. D. Roche (1982), pp. 22–3.

122 Faubourg Saint-Germain: J.-L. Dupain-Triel, *Essai d'une table poléométrique* (1782), cit. F. de Dainville, 'Grandeur et population des villes au XVIIIe siècle', *Population*, XIII, 3 (1958), p. 465.

123 'More democratic': E. Le Roy Ladurie, 'Un "modèle septentrional": les campagnes parisiennes (XVIe–XVIIe siècles)', *Annales*, 30–36 (1975) (review of J. Jacquart, *La Crise rurale en Île-de-France*), p. 1402.

124 wooden beams: On the composition of barricades: M. Traugott, *The Insurgent Barricade* (2010), p. 307 n. 35.

124 systems of patronage: S. Kettering, 'Patronage and Politics during the Fronde', *French Historical Studies*, XIV, 3 (1986), pp. 409–41.

125 kept their horses indoors: *Registres de l'Hôtel de ville de Paris pendant la Fronde*, I (1846), p. 398 (23 March 1649); also Le Roy Ladurie, 'Un "modèle septentrional" ', pp. 1409–11.

125 in the First World War: Cf. J. Jacquart, *Paris et l'Île-de-France au temps des paysans* (1990), pp. 253–86.

125 'prowling and pillaging': Dubuisson-Aubenay (F.-N. Baudot), *Journal des guerres civiles*, ed. G. Saige, II (1885), p. 154.

125 nearly killed by a cannonball: *Mémoires de Jacques de Saulx, Comte de Tavannes*, ed. C. Moreau (1858), pp. 139–40.

125 'grande ordure et puanteur': Jacquart, p. 267.

126 Jesuit colleges: Le Roy Ladurie, 'Un "modèle septentrional"', p. 1410.

126 'Can't you see who it is?': J.-P. Jacob, *Le Cicérone de Versailles*, new ed. (1805), p. 169; C. Piton, *Marly-le-Roi: son histoire* (1904), p. 70 n.

127 A windmill had stood there: J.-P. Jacob, pp. 2–3.

127 half a dozen villages: H. Lemoine, 'Un village disparu: Choisy-aux-Boeufs (1163–1686)', *Revue de l'histoire de Versailles et de Seine-et-Oise*, XXXVII (1935), pp. 93–102.

127 transferred en bloc: F. Tiberghien, *Versailles: le chantier de Louis XIV* (2002), p. 194.

128 walked through his gardens: D. Garrigues, *Jardins et jardiniers de Versailles au Grand Siècle* (2001), p. 220.

128 Grand Divertissement Royal: Marquis de Saint-Maurice, *Lettres sur la cour de Louis XIV*, ed. J. Lemoine (1910), pp. 200–209; A. Félibien, *Relation de la feste de Versailles du 18 juillet 1668* (1668).

128 The total cost: Bills for the grotto from *Comptes des Bâtiments du Roi sous le règne de Louis XIV*, ed. J. Guiffrey, I (1881), pp. 191–6 and 302–8 ('Feste de Versailles'). Total expense, including grotto and *glissoire*: 117,000 *livres*. That year (1668), Versailles consumed 300,000 *livres*.

128 three thousand *livres*: V. Richard, 'La Chambre du Roi aux XVIIe et XVIIIe siècles', *Bibliothèque de l'École des Chartes* 170–71 (2012), p. 109.

128 valued at 33,175 *livres*: H. Lemoine, p. 100.

129 a diary which the King always read: A. Vallot et al., *Journal de la santé du roi Louix XIV*, ed. J.-A. Le Roi (1862), p. 26 n.

129 forsaking wine: Vallot, p. 159.

129 the vertiginous *glissoire*: Vallot, p. 88.

129 a healthy digestive tract: Vallot, p. 18.

129 *bains de chambre*: Vallot, p. 92.

129 damaged his generative organs: Vallot, p. 29.

129 recommended walks: Louis XIV, *Mémoires, suivis de Manière de visiter les jardins de Versailles*, ed. J. Cornette (2007); *Nouveau plan des villes, château et jardin de Versailles . . . avec la marche que le Roy a ordonnée pour faire voir le jardin, les bosquets et les fontaines* (1719).

130 *Grand Dictionnaire des Précieuses*: First edition: [A. Baudeau, sieur de Somaize], *Le Grand Dictionnaire des Pretieuses* [*sic*], *ou la Clef de la langue des ruelles* (1660). Quotations are from the second edition (1661).

130 construction site: See F. Tiberghien.

130 'To reach the cool of shade': Louis de Rouvroy, Duc de Saint-Simon, *Mémoires*, XII, ch. 19.

131 Because of all the digging: J.-B. Primi Visconti, Comte de Saint-Mayol, *Mémoires sur la cour de Louis XIV*, tr. J. Lemoine (1908), p. 261; P. de Nolhac, *Versailles, résidence de Louis XIV* (1925), p. 2.

131 'neither girl nor woman': Vallot, p. 45.

131 their 'owl-like eyes': *Satire sur le grand adieu des niepces de Mazarin à la France* (1649), p. 3.

131 producing an heir: S. Perez, 'Passion, pouvoir et vérité à l'âge de la raison d'État', *Dix-septième siècle*, 241 (2008), pp. 617–32.

131 'Despite her ugliness': F. de Motteville, *Mémoires de Mme de Motteville sur Anne d'Autriche et sa cour*, ed. F. Riaux (1855), IV, 117.

131 'He would always take her home': Motteville, p. 143 n.

132 'sad and solitary fortress': *Apologie, ou les veritables memoires de Madame Marie Mancini, connestable de Colonna, ecrits par elle-même* (1678), p. 29.

132 'In giving away our heart': *Mémoires de Louis XIV, écrits par lui-même, composés pour le Grand Dauphin, son fils* (1806), p. 61.

132 'Peasant girls': Élisabeth-Charlotte de Bavière, *Mélanges historiques, anecdotiques et critiques* (1807), p. 62.

133 'His Majesty found the remedy so congenial': Vallot, pp. 80–81.

133 no such pattern: C. Mukerji, *Territorial Ambitions and the Gardens of Versailles* (1997), p. 15.

133 when the sun appears to sink: P. Rocher, 'Soleil couchant dans l'axe du Grand Canal à Versailles', Institut de mécanique céleste et de calcul des éphémérides, Observatoire de Paris, 2010: https://www.imcce.fr/newsletter/docs/newversailles2010.pdf

134 a sumptuous ballet: I. de Benserade, *Ballet royal de la Nuit . . . dansé par Sa Majesté, le 23 février 1653* (1653).

134 'My shining eye': Benserade, pp. 66–7.

135 'war of moles': H. de Varigny, 'Tranchées et mines', *Revue des Deux Mondes*, XXVIII (1915), pp. 197–8.

135 the siege of Besançon: Cit. L. Ordinaire, *Deux époques militaires à Besançon et en Franche-Comté* (1856), I, 496; D. Dee, *Expansion and Crisis in Louis XIV's France* (2012), p. 38.

135 'forced to administer an enema': Vallot, p. 16.

135 two contemporary paintings: B. Yvart, after Le Brun and Van der Meulen, *Siège de Douay (4 juill. 1667)*; A.-F. Van der Meulen (?), *Le Siege de Tournai en 1667.*

135 'his extraordinary passion': Vallot, p. 64.

136 bastions and battlements: C. Mukerji, *Territorial Ambitions and the Gardens of Versailles* (1997), pp. 60–62; also 'Engineering and French Formal Gardens in the Reign of Louis XIV', in J. D. Hunt et al., eds, *Tradition and Innovation in French Garden Art* (2002), pp. 31–4.

136 migrants from the Limousin: Tiberghien, pp. 170–71, 184 and 191. On living conditions generally: J.-M. Riou, *Le Dernier secret de Versailles* (2014).

136 a ten-mile radius of Versailles: Tiberghien, p. 181.

136 nose and ears were cropped: Tiberghien, p. 156.

136 digging the canal: Tiberghien, pp. 165–6.

136 18 July 1668: Félibien, *Relation de la feste*; Marquis de Saint-Maurice, *Lettres*, pp. 200–209.

137 The resulting stampede: Félibien, p. 7.

137 Grande Enquête sur la Noblesse: On the social effects of wealth: R. B. Grassby, 'Social Status and Commercial Enterprise under Louis XIV', *The Economic History Review*, n.s., XIII, 1 (1960), pp. 19–38.

138 spurious positions: For a list covering 1691–1709: J.-G. Locré de Roissy, *Législation civile, commerciale et criminelle*, XI (1837), pp. 178–9.

138 served by noblemen: Félibien, p. 41.

138 'A thousand flames': Félibien, p. 57.

138 a great explosion: 'Fête de Versailles, en 1668', in *Œuvres de Molière*, V (1770), p. 302.

139 'A great man': Félibien, p. 60.

140 'The mill has gone': A. Maquet, *Versailles aux temps féodaux* (1889), p. 9 n.

140 Val de Galie: Maquet, ch. 1; M. Baltus, 'Toponymie du pays de Cruye et du Val de Galie', *Revue de l'histoire de Versailles et de Seine-et-Oise*, XL (1938), p. 3; A. Dauzat and C. Rostaing, *Dictionnaire étymologique des noms de lieu en France* (1963), p. 309.

141 subterranean river: Anon., 'Réflexions historiques sur le Loiret', *Histoire de l'Académie Royale des Inscriptions et Belles-Lettres*, XII (1740), pp. 153–63; A. and F. de Beaucorps, *Étude empirique au moyen de la baguette sur les origines souterraines de la rivière du Loiret* (1900).

141 the Massif Central: *Travaux des années 1900 et 1901 sur les eaux de sources alimentant la ville de Paris* (1902), p. 419.

142 apprentice watchmaker: *Journée de Jean-Baptiste Humbert, horloger, qui, le premier, a monté sur les tours de la Bastille* (1789).

8. Stained Glass

145 manuscript: J.-L. Ménétra, *Journal de ma vie*, ed. D. Roche (1982). (Abbreviation: *Journal.*)

145 'for [his] own pleasure': Transcription of original in G. Ernst, *Textes français privés des XVIIe et XVIIIe siècles*, I (2019), p. 668.

146 'an extremely good sort': *Journal*, p. 74.

146 'When it comes to painted glass': *Journal*, pp. 73–4. On techniques: P. Le Vieil, *L'Art de la peinture sur verre et de la vitrerie* (1774), pp. 216–18. Ménétra's own remarks: *Journal*, p. 138.

147 the 'seraglios' of Paris: *Journal*, p. 149.

147 grew up by the Pont Neuf in Paris: *Journal*, p. 35–47.

148 adventure in the Hurepoix: *Journal*, pp. 22–3.

148 a bad case of the 'vapours': *Journal*, p. 46.

148 Tour de France journeyman: See *The Discovery of France*, pp. 157–9.

148 little glass boxes, etc.: *Journal*, pp. 47, 86, 143 and 257.

149 In my first days there: *Journal*, p. 73.

149 defeated the object: *The Letters of Saint Boniface*, ed. E. Emerton (1976), p. 140 (to Cuthbert in 747).

149 'Go a pilgrim, come back a whore': J. Hobbs, *Mount Sinai* (1995), p. 226; E. Zafra, '"Ir romera y volver ramera"', *Revista Canadiense de Estudios Hispánicos*, XXXIX, 2 (2015), pp. 483–503.

149 preference for blondes: *Journal*, p. 150.

149 punishable by death: *Encyclopédie*, XVII (1751), p. 310: 'Viol'.

149 hostel in Montpellier: *Journal*, p. 87.

149 'an unexpected windfall': *Journal*, p. 53.

150 'At the entrance to a small wood': *Journal*, pp. 49–50.

150 average daily wage: J. Sgard, 'L'Échelle des revenus', *Dix-huitième siècle*, XIV (1982), p. 426; also M. Sonenscher, *Work and Wages: Natural Law, Politics and the Eighteenth-Century French Trades* (1989): on Ménétra, pp. 22–30.

150 a 'superannuated' *fille de joie*: Restif de la Bretonne, *Le Pornographe*, ed. N. Crochet (2011), p. 64. Generally: A. Parent-Duchâtelet, *De la prostitution dans la ville de Paris*, 3rd ed. (1857), I, 27151

151 the '*facultés des peuples*': F. de Dainville, 'Un dénombrement inédit au XVIIIe siècle', *Population*, VII, 1 (1952), pp. 49–68 (with maps); A. Fel, 'Petite culture, 1750–1850', in H. Clout, ed. *Themes in the Historical Geography of France* (1977), pp. 215–45.

151 the King's fleet at Brest: *Journal*, p. 66.

151 construction of a town hall: P. Lafforgue, *Histoire de la ville d'Auch*, II (1851), p. 224.

151 Parisian-style streetlamps: *Journal*, pp. 84–5.

151 on the road from L'Isle-Jourdain: *Journal*, p. 80.

152 Philibert Orry's survey: See Dainville, 'Un dénombrement'; Fel, 'Petite culture'.

152 'You couldn't help laughing': *Journal*, p. 78.

152 the Jewish ghettos: *Journal*, p. 90.

152 'a free country': *Journal*, p. 93 ('je répondis . . . que dans la France l'on était libre').

153 'fanaticism and superstition': *Journal*, pp. 93–4.

153 half the servants: J. B. Collins, *The State in Early Modern France* (2012), p. 219.

153 'And this is why the good people': *Journal*, p. 49.

153 army conscripts: E.g. P. Topinard, *L'Homme dans la nature* (1891), p. 82.

153 Paris-centric road-building policy: E.g. G. Arbellot, 'La Grande mutation des routes de France au milieu du XVIIIe siècle', *Annales*, XXVIII, 3 (1973), pp. 765–91.

154 ten *sous* to a postmistress: *Almanach de la ville de Lyon* (1760), in A. Belloc, *Les Postes françaises* (1886), p. 219; 'Quelques enveloppes postales, XVIIIe siècle' (2007): http://www.corpusetampois.com/che-18-qqenveloppespostales.html

154 his grandmother in Paris: *Journal*, p. 137.

155 'there was neither bridge nor boat': *Journal*, pp. 99–100.

155 'magnificent causeways': A. Young, *Travels in France and Italy During the Years 1787, 1788 and 1789*, rev. ed (1892), p. 45.

155 the *corvée*: A. Conchon, *La Corvée des grands chemins au XVIIIe siècle* (2016), ch. 3; for Tours, see fig. 4.

155 a woman who had given birth: *Journal*, p. 83.

156 'The only reason it was wet': *Journal*, p. 84.

156 'They warned me': *Journal*, p. 122.

157 'She asked if I wanted to go': *Journal*, p. 54.

157 not until the Victorian age: Criticism made by Le Roy Ladurie, *Montaillou*, pp. 307–8.

158 'her petticoats were bulging out': *Journal*, p. 56.

9. Bloody Provence

161 'that charming little town': *Journal*, p. 96.

162 explained in various ways: E.g. S. Clay, 'Vengeance, Justice and the Reactions in the Revolutionary Midi', *French History*, III, 1 (2009), pp. 22–46; P. M. Jones, review of Sutherland (below), *The Journal of Modern History*, LXXXIII, 1 (2011), pp. 177–9; C. Lucas, *The Structure of the Terror* (1973); J.-C. Martin, *Violence et révolution* (2006); D. M. G. Sutherland, *Murder in Aubagne: Lynching, Law, and Justice during the French Revolution* (2009), pp. 11 and 285; M. Vovelle, 'La Place de Nîmes dans les révolutions méridionales', *Annales historiques de la Révolution française*, 258 (1984), p. 450.

163 the grizzled prisoner: *Le Comte de Lorges, prisonnier à la Bastille pendant trente-deux ans*, 2nd ed. (1789): 'Avis de l'éditeur'.

163 'patriotic relics': E.g. J. Charavay, *Catalogue d'une importante collection de documents autographes et historiques sur la Révolution française* (1862), no. 9: 'Les Pierres de la Bastille'.

163n. Third Estate deputies: See C. Lucas, 'Nobles, Bourgeois and the Origins of the French Revolution', *Past & Present*, 60 (1973), pp. 84–126.

164 'the Great Fear': See G. Lefebvre, *La Grande Peur de 1789* (1932); *The Discovery of France*, pp. 142–3 and 375.

164 'pursuing the path of anarchy': Decree of 10 August 1789: *Archives parlementaires de la Révolution Française*, VIII (1875), pp. 378–9.

164 'Paris had taken its Bastille': J. Jaurès, *Histoire socialiste de la Révolution française*, ed. A. Mathiez (1922), I, 310.

165 beheading riotous peasants: See A. Ado, *Paysans en révolution: terre, pouvoir et jacquerie* (1789–1794), pp. 150–51.

165 'one would think that every rusty gun': A. Young, *Travels in France and Italy*, p. 256.

165 division of the kingdom into '*départements*': Assemblée Nationale, 8 January 1790: see especially pp. 119–22 in *Archives parlementaires de 1787 à 1860*, eds J. Mavidal et al., 1st series, XI (1880).

165 Calvados in Normandy: G. de La Rue, *Nouveaux essais historiques sur la ville de Caen* (1842), I, 175–82; *Mercure universel*, 12 April 1791, p. 179; M. Pezet, 'Bayeux à la fin du XVIIIe siècle', in *Mémoires de la Société d'agriculture, sciences, arts et belles-lettres de Bayeux*, VII (1859), p. 143.

167 'A most mysterious and impenetrable veil': *Despatches from Paris, 1784–1790*, ed. O. Browning, II (1910), p. 267 (FitzGerald to the Duke of Leeds, 15 October 1789).

167 'On Monday morning': Ibid., p. 263 (7 October 1789).

167 Several thousand women: 'Déposition de Maillard sur les événements du 5 et du 6 octobre', in J. S. Bailly, *Mémoires de Bailly*, ed. A. de Berville and F. Barrière, III (1822), pp. 406–22.

168 'a great golden goblet': Louison Cabry, deposition in B. Baczko, 'Droits de l'homme, paroles de femmes', *Dix-huitième siècle*, XXXVII (2005), p. 268.

168 fondled a bishop: Baczko, pp. 274–5, quoting depositions by *députés*.

168 saveloy sausage: J.-J. Mounier, *Exposé de ma conduite dans l'Assemblée Nationale* (1789), and *Archives parlementaires*, in Baczko, p. 275.

168 six hours on the road: *Despatches From Paris*, p. 264.

168 cartloads of flour and grain: *Mémoires de Bailly*, p. 116.

168 freshly powdered heads: Chateaubriand, cit. Baczko, p. 259.

168 'odd story' or 'curious incident': A. Cobban, *A History of Modern France*, I (1957), p. 161; D. Johnson, *A Concise History of France* (1971), p. 108.

169 a 'geometrical distribution': E. Burke, *Reflections on the Revolution in France*, 3rd ed. (1790), p. 269.

169 an 'almost naked' Marie-Antoinette: Burke, p. 106.

169 'just above the horizon': Burke, p. 112.

169 'these pretended citizens': Burke, p. 269.

169 *tricoteuses*: *The Port Folio*, XVI (1823), p. 76 n.; P. L. Jacob, *Costumes historiques de la France* (1852), p. 105.

170n. A German scholar: J. F. Reichardt, *Vertraute Briefe aus Paris* (1804), I, pp. 70–71.

170 statues and icons: *The Discovery of France*, pp. 133–4.

170 favourite tune of Marie-Antoinette: Anon., 'French Patriotic Songs', *The London Quarterly Review*, CXXX (1871), p. 109.

171 patriotic babies: Abbé H. Grégoire, *Histoire des sectes religieuses*, new ed. (1828), I, 155. E.g. Archives départementales de la Creuse, 'Les Prénoms révolutionnaires de nouveaux-nés creusois': https://docplayer.fr/49422793-Les-prenoms-revolutionnaires-de-nouveaux-nes-creusois.html; M.-F. Castang-Coutou, 'Prénoms révolutionnaires en Dordogne': http://www.liorac.info/PAGES/prenoms-revolution.php

171 'the despotism of liberty': 'Sur les principes de morale politique qui doivent guider la Convention nationale', 5 February 1794, *Œuvres de Robespierre*, ed. A. Vermorel and F. Cournol (1867), pp. 294–308.

171 On three September days: See P. Caron, *Les Massacres de Septembre* (1935).

171 In Reims: L. Mortimer-Ternaux, *Histoire de la Terreur, 1792–1794*, III

(1863), pp. 325–32; D. M. G. Sutherland, 'Justice and Murder: Massacres in the Provinces', *Past & Present*, CCXXII, 1 (2014), pp. 129–62.

172 Jacobin propaganda: Bill Edmonds, '"Federalism" and Urban Revolt in France in 1793', *The Journal of Modern History*, LV, 1 (1983), p. 28. Also A. Forrest, *Paris, the Provinces, and the French Revolution* (2004).

172 'Paris may serve as a model': L.-M. Prudhomme, *Histoire générale et impartiale des erreurs, des fautes et des crimes commis pendant la Révolution française* VI (1797), p. 128.

173 Jourdan Coupe-Tête: See C. Soullier, *Histoire de la révolution d'Avignon et du Comté-Venaissin*, II (1844).

173 'the credit of the *assignats*': J.-B. Duvergier, *Collection complète des lois, décrets, ordonnances*, 2nd ed. V (1834), pp. 135–6 (1–4 February 1793).

173 'The lethal habit': J. Lavallée and L. Brion de La Tour, *Voyage dans les départemens de la France*, I (1801), 'Bouches-du-Rhône', pp. 42–3.

173 'reality continually contradicted': *Voyage dans les départemens . . .*, II (1792), 'Drôme', p. 21.

174 foreign to the *département*: G. Lemarchand, 'Les Représentants du peuple en mission dans la Révolution française, 1792–1795': review of M. Biard, *Missionnaires de la République*, in *Annales de Normandie*, LIII, 3 (2008), p. 276.

174 'I conclude with a thought': *Recueil des actes du Comité de salut public*, XII (1899), p. 790 (22 April 1794).

174 Bédoin makes its first appearance: On the massacre: É. Le Gallo, 'L'Affaire de Bédoin', *La Révolution française: revue historique*, XLI (July 1901), pp. 289–310; V. de Baumefort, *Épisodes de la Terreur: tribunal révolutionnaire d'Orange* (1875); C. Berriat-Saint-Prix, *La Justice révolutionnaire, août 1792*, I (1870), pp. 418–33; C. Soullier, pp. 193–215.

174 'sacrilegious hands': Baumefort, p. 235.

175 'to intimidate the aristocracy': Baumefort, p. 236.

175 'Liberty trees': 'Arbres de la Liberté', in P. Larousse, *Grand Dictionnaire universel*, I (1866), pp. 558–9.

175 'the august emblem': Baumefort, p. 228.

176 'a counter-revolutionary plot': Baumefort, p. 228; Le Gallo, pp. 293–4. Quoted here from *Gazette Nationale ou Le Moniteur universel*, 9 January 1795, p. 455.

176 'freeze with fear': Le Gallo, p. 294.

176 'an enemy territory': C. Berriat-Saint-Prix, p. 421.

176 The list of the dead: Soullier, pp. 207–9.

177 'At a distance of four leagues': *Le Cabinet historique . . . le Catalogue général des manuscrits*, ed. L. Paris, XII, 1 (1866), p. 300.

177 Suchet was said . . .: 'Réclamations des habitants de Bédoin', late 1794: J. Skinner, *Republicanism and Royalism: The Conflicting Traditions of Peasant Politics in the Department of the Vaucluse, 1789–1851*, thesis (Manchester, 1988), p. 240 n. 59.

177 Monteux and Crillon: Baumefort, p. 33.

177 cut down at Bédarrides: 'Dénonciations contre les Terroristes de Bédarrides', 1795, in Skinner, p. 205.

177 A later vicar of Bédoin: L. de Laincel, *Avignon, le Comtat et la principaute d'Orange* (1872), p. 128.

178 'We thank you for sending Maignet': Le Gallo, pp. 301–2; Skinner, p. 205.

179 his native town, Ambert: Baumefort, p. 222.

179 Several nineteenth-century historians: Notably, for political reasons, Louis Blanc in his *Histoire de la Révolution française* (1856), II, 746. The church was still in ruins in 1821: *L'Ami de la religion et du roi*, XXVII (1821), p. 106.

179 'a miserable village': J. Murray, *Hand-book for Travellers in France* (1843), p. 453. The book was 'the result of four or five journeys undertaken at different times between 1830 and 1841' (p. v).

179 a large majority . . . sedentary: K. Amellal and K. Michel, *Implantation des populations tsiganes dans les Bouches-du-Rhône et patrimoine interculturel* (2013), p. 27.

179 around the Étang de Berre: See M. Alcaloïde and B. Gramond, 'France: The General Situation', in *The Education of Gypsy and Traveller Children* (1993).

180 expelling all 'bohémiens': *Correspondance de Napoléon Ier*, VIII (1861), p. 333 (1 June 1803). Also H. Asséo, 'Des "Égyptiens" aux Rom', *Hommes & Migrations*, 1188–9 (1995), p. 18; E. Filhol, *Le Contrôle des Tsiganes en France* (2013), pp. 13–14; *Nouvelles annales des voyages*, XLIX (1831), pp. 47–8.

180 He left Fontainebleau: A summary in J. M. Thompson, 'Napoleon's Journey to Elba in 1814, Part I', *The American Historical Review*, LV, 1 (1949), pp. 1–21.

181 'Everyone was shouting': J.-B.-G. Fabry, *Itinéraire de Buonaparte* (1814), pp. 44–5.

181 the inn at La Calade: See p. 398. Also L.-A. Fauvelet de Bourrienne, *Mémoires de M. de Bourrienne*, X (1829), p. 231.

181 'I'll be damned': Fabry, p. 47.

182 'All the way from Fontainebleau': Fabry, p. 52.

182 'A nasty race, the Provençaux': L. F. Truchsess von Waldburg, *A Narrative of Napoleon Bonaparte's Journey* (1815), p. 44.

182 Fréjus instead of Saint-Tropez: Sir Neil Campbell, *Napoleon at Fontainebleau and Elba* (1869), p. 192.

182 'You can tell your Provençaux': Fabry, p. 53.

10. How He Did It

183 'It would have been hard to prove': F.-R. de Chateaubriand, *Mémoires d'outre-tombe*, I (1848), p. 362.

183 the diminutive Elban navy: Pons de l'Hérault, *Souvenirs et anecdotes de l'île d'Elbe*, ed. L. Pélissier (1897), ch. 7, pt 6.; Campbell, pp. 343–4, 364 and 381–2.

184 drums and benches: É. Le Gallo, *Les Cent-Jours* (1923), p. 50.

184 'How is the Emperor?': F. Cuneo d'Ornano, *Napoléon au Golfe Juan* (1830), p. 20.

184 'so long as Napoleon himself': Campbell, p. 105.

184 'absolutely and physically impossible': *The Parliamentary Debates from the Year 1803 to the Present Time*, XXX, 426 (7 April 1815).

185 'ascended a number of hills': Campbell, pp. 216–17.

185 After surveying the scene: Campbell, p. 225.

185 'All of Europe will say': Campbell, p. 217.

185 'better luck next time': Quoted by Walter Scott in *The Life of Napoleon Buonaparte* (1832), II, 273.

185 'gradually estranged himself': Campbell, p. 349.

186 Fort George . . . or St Helena: Le Gallo, pp. 41–2.

186 digging flower-beds: Campbell, pp. 369 and 380.

186 'traitor and rebel': 'Ordonnance du Roi contenant des mesures de sûreté générale', *Le Moniteur universel*, 7 March 1815, p. 3.

186 The Grenoblois: *Le Moniteur universel*, 9 March 1815 (letters from Grenoble dated 5 March).

187 'Soldiers, we have not been beaten!': *Correspondance de Napoléon Ier*, XXVIII (1869), pp. 3–4 (1 March 1815).

187 the village of Laffrey: L.-J. Marchand, *Mémoires de Marchand, premier valet de chambre*, ed. J. Bourguignon (1952); Baron G. Peyrusse, *1809–1815, mémorial et archives* (1869), pp. 286–94; L.-J.-A. Randon, 'Retour de l'île d'Elbe' (letter to Stendhal), in 'Le Lieutenant Général Randon', *Revue de l'Empire*, V (1846), pp. 338–9.

187 'electricity' in the air: Marchand, I, ch. 7; Peyrusse, p. 286; Randon, p. 339.

187 Pont-sur-Yonne: A. Rossigneux, 'Napoléon Ier à Joigny, Sens et Pont-sur-Yonne', *Bulletin de la Société des sciences historiques et naturelles de l'Yonne*, LXV (1911), pp. 5–22; *Les Cahiers du capitaine Coignet*, ed. L. Larchey (1883), p. 389.

188 a *fleur de lys*: A.-M. Chamans, Comte de la Valette, *Mémoires et souvenirs du comte Lavallette [sic]*, II (1831), p. 160.

189 The new citizen-emperor: On mutations of the legend: S. Hazareesingh, *The Legend of Napoleon* (2004).

189 'forgotten nothing and learned nothing': Cf. Talleyrand: 'ils n'ont rien appris, ni rien oublié'. Napoleon inverted the phrase in his proclamation to the Army on 1 March 1815, reproduced in the *Moniteur*, 21 March.

189 he could never bear to pose: L.-A. Fauvelet de Bourrienne, *Mémoires*, IV (1829), p. 242.

190 invest heavily in spies, etc.: J. J. Sarratt, *Life of Buonaparte* (1803), pp. 22–9 and 42–3.

190 'A complete victory': H. Scott, *The Life of Napoleon Bonaparte* (1814), p. 231.

191 'ran an entire empire': W. Dietrich, *Napoleon's Rules* (2015), pp. xiii–xiv.

192 'Napoleon finished': *The New York Times*, 19 July 2017.

192 The memoirs: Baron A.-J.-F. Fain, *Mémoires du Baron Fain* (1908); *Napoleon: How He Did It*, tr. D. Raufa (1998).

192 OFFICE WORK: These precepts are derived primarily from Fain, *Mémoires*; Las Cases, *Mémorial de Sainte-Hélène*; A. de Caulaincourt (Duc de Vicence), *Dans l'intimité de l'Empereur*; *Le Moniteur universel*; *Correspondance de Napoléon Ier*.

194 'Glory be to Allah': 'Entrevue de Bonaparte . . . et de plusieurs muphtis et imans dans l'intérieur de la grande pyramide', *Gazette nationale ou le Moniteur universel*, 27 November 1798, pp. 3–4.

194 the plain of Laffrey: see note to p. 187 (the village of Laffrey).

195 borrowed the famous scene: *La Pharsale de Lucain*, tr. J.-F. Marmontel (1766), I, 262–3.

196 'three thousand songs': C.-M. Raudot, *Une heure des Cent Jours* (1833), p. 9; A. Rossigneux, *Une étape de Napoléon Ier, Avallon, 16–17 mars 1815* (1913), p. 6.

196 'Still chewing tobacco': Rossigneux, *Une étape*, p. 9.

196 'gave every sign of satisfaction': Rossigneux, *Une étape*, pp. 17–18; also Lefol, *Souvenirs sur le retour de l'empereur Napoléon de l'île d'Elbe* (1852), p. 14.

197 'Napoleon has humbugged me': *A Series of Letters of the First Earl of Malmesbury*, II (1870), pp. 445–6.

198n. The strength and composition: Capt. W. Siborne, *History of the War in France and Belgium* (1845), pp. 41–50, 583–6 and 589–93.

199   'a damned nice thing': First reported in *The Creevey Papers*, ed. H. Maxwell, I (1903).

199   leaving the battlefield in tears: E.g. M.-L.-G. de Baudus, *Études sur Napoléon* (1841), I, 231.

199   speed-dictate: Comte de Las Cases, *Mémorial de Sainte-Hélène* (1840), I, 247–9.

200   'in a fit of impatience': 'Bataille de Mont-Saint-Jean', *Correspondance de Napoléon Ier*, XXVIII (1869), p. 342.

200   'this astonishing mêlée': Ibid., pp. 343–4.

201   'A spyglass in his hand': V. Hugo, 'L'Expiation', pt 2, *Châtiments* (1853).

202   'a skilful and rapid retreat': Mrs Abell (late Miss Elizabeth Balcombe), *Recollections of the Emperor Napoleon, During the First Three Years of his Captivity on the Island of St. Helena* (1844). (Abbreviation: Balcombe.) See p. 32.

202   'This is the second time': Balcombe, p. 33; also in Baron G. Gourgaud, *Sainte-Hélène: journal inédit* (1899), I, 2 and 531–7.

202   'keep both flanks in sight': Las Cases, I, 247–9; also B. Colson, ed., *Napoleon on War*, tr. G. Elliott (2015), p. 182.

202   the family's routine: Gen. C. T. Montholon, *Récits de la captivité de l'Empereur Napoléon à Sainte-Hélène* (1847), I, 160.

203   blind man's buff: Balcombe, pp. 72–5.

204   captured four mice: Balcombe, pp. 70–71.

204   'fear and self-interest': Bourrienne, *Mémoires*, III (1829), p. 108.

205   Good soldiers: E.g. 'Notes sur l'art de la guerre' (on Gen. J. Rogniat's *Considérations sur l'art de la guerre*), in *Correspondance de Napoléon Ier*, XXXI (1870), pp. 365 ff.

205   defensive ditches: B. E. O'Meara, *Napoleon at St Helena*, (1888), I, 47–8 and 103.

205   'turned Turk': Balcombe, pp. 69–70.

205   prisoners at Jaffa: Balcombe, pp. 217–22.

205   'Qui l'a brûlé?': Balcombe, p. 23.

206   'He walked up to her': Balcombe, p. 31.

206   'The Emperor is growing impatient': Gourgaud, p. 336.

206   'He walked with us': Balcombe, p. 229.

207   'He affectionately embraced my sister': Balcombe, p. 230.

207   'A few English travellers': Chateaubriand, II (1849), pp. 532–3.

11. The Murder of Madame Bovary

209 'a sky-bound railway': Eugène Noël, 'Rouen', *Le Tour du monde: nouveau journal des voyages*, LIV (1887), p. 337.

210 'his own artistic initiative': E.-M. Laumann, *Le Retour des cendres* (1904), p. 116, based in part on local press and Abbé F. Coquereau, *Souvenirs du voyage à Sainte-Hélène* (1841), pp. 153–5.

210 'the niggardliness of the trappings': *Journal de Rouen*, 10–11 December 1840.

210 'It was a sacred vow': *Journal de Rouen*, 12 December 1840.

211 'with the most laudable zeal': *Journal de Rouen*, 10–11 December 1840.

211 'never blackened the doorstep': A.-M. Gossez, 'Homais et Bovary, hommes politiques', *Mercure de France*, 16 July 1911, p. 286 (quoting Dr Brunon).

211 three coaching routes: Blaisot, *Carte topographique et statistique du département de la Seine-Inférieure* (1835; 1844); 'Richard' (J.-M.-V. Audin), *Guide du voyageur en France* (1835; 1840), pp. 31 and 56.

211 'in a suspended carriage': R. Vérard, *Ry, pays de Madame Bovary* (Galerie Bovary, Musée des Automates, 1983), p. 89.

211 'Chemin de Grande Communication': J. Fouché, *Service vicinal, Département de la Seine-Inférieure, carte routière* (1852).

212 'exposed to perilous danger': Vérard, pp. 31–2.

212 railway surveyors: A-J.-C. Defontaine, *Mémoire sur le projet d'un chemin de fer de Paris à Rouen* (1837), p. 21.

212 'The little town of Ry': Jouanne Jr, in G. Dubosc, 'La Véritable Madame Bovary', *Journal de Rouen*, 2 December 1890, p. 2.

213 an *officier de santé*: G. Galerant, 'Un officier de santé nommé Charles Bovary', *Les Amis de Flaubert*, 39 (1970); J. Léonard, 'Les Études médicales en France entre 1815 et 1848', *Revue d'histoire moderne et contemporaine*, XIII, 1 (1966), pp. 87–94.

213 'property owner': F. Clérembray, *Flaubertisme et bovarysme* (1912), p. 47.

214 The boys' mothers: See note to p. 222 ('In my childhood').

215 'Country dwellers': Assemblée Nationale, 10 March 1803 (in Galerant, 'Un officier de santé').

215 'Poor and simple patients': *Annales du Sénat*, V (1864), p. 264 (12 March).

215 'the boiler of a steam engine': Balzac, *Z. Marcas*, in *La Comédie Humaine*, ed. P.-G. Castex (1976–81), VIII, 847.

215 an interest-free loan: A. Dubuc, in *Les Rouennais et la famille Flaubert* (1980), p. 90; Vérard, p. 56.

215 Delamare's catchment area: Deduced from his unpaid invoices:
G. Bosquet, 'Quelques prototypes "traditionnels" de Madame
Bovary', *Les Amis de Flaubert*, 11 (1957). Population figures from
*Dictionnaire général des villes, bourgs, villages, hameaux et fermes de la
France* (1846).

216 Henry Laloy: A. Dubuc, p. 95; P. Berteau, 'Un chirurgien rouennais
du XIXe siècle: le docteur Achille Cléophas Flaubert', *Revue de la
Société française d'histoire des hôpitaux*, 126 (2007), p. 23.

216 Laloy Sr: J. Levallois, *Mémoires d'un critique* (1895), pp. 24–5.

217 'A silhouette rose up': Levallois, p. 27.

217 a village *pension* . . .: her classmate Adèle: R. Brunon, 'À propos de
Madame Bovary', *La Presse médicale*, 1907, pp. 713–15; J. Keller,
'Madame Bovary', *La Normandie médicale*, 1913, pp. 220–23; K.
Feltgen, 'Delphine Couturier, modèle supposé de Madame Bovary',
2016: https://flaubert.univ-rouen.fr/article.php?id=76; G. Venzac,
Au pays de Madame Bovary (1957), p. 206 n. 22.

218 'not a *figure à passions*': Levallois, pp. 27–8.

218 The Delamares' house: Inventories in Clérembray, p. 51; G.
Galerant, 'La Bibliothèque d'Eugène Delamare', in *Les Rouennais*, pp.
97–104; Vérard, pp. 55–60; Bosquet.

219 Baron Boullenger: Levallois, pp. 26 and 28; *Journal de Rouen*,
4 March 1853, pp. 1–2; *Annuaire des cinq départements de l'ancienne
Normandie*, X (1854), p. 558–61; *Bulletin de la Société de l'Histoire de
France*, 1853, pp. 84–5. The character's name is Boulanger de la
Huchette. Baron Boullenger *may* have been known locally as
'Boullenger de la Houssaye' (the name of some land by his *château*).

219 'only farmers at the *fête*': *Journal de Rouen*, 1 March 1845, p. 2.

220 'we occasionally talked': Letter from M. Bellou, mayor of Formerie,
1921, in *Les Amis de Flaubert*, 7 (1955), p. 50.

220 The parish register: *Les Rouennais*, p. 95.

220 his own 'clan' or coterie: Levallois, p. 28.

220 'Sitting in her armchair': *Madame Bovary*, II, 4, para. 1.

221 'I may have acted improperly': *Journal de Rouen*, 1 March 1845, p. 2.

222 Delamare's debts: Vérard, pp. 53–4.

222 '*totally invented*': Flaubert to M.-S. Leroyer de Chantepie, 18 March
1857.

222 'Have you made a decision?': Du Camp to Flaubert 23 July 1851.

222 'I fear that the end': Flaubert to Bouilhet, 9 May 1855.

222 'In my childhood': Published by G. Dubosc in *Journal de Rouen*,
3 May 1922, p. 2.

223 women's *chemises*: Vérard, p. 59.

223 study of cotton manufacturers: M. Kasdi, *Les Entrepreneurs du coton* (2014), pp. 34–5.

223 a top-of-the-range woman's outfit: E.g. *Les Modes parisiennes: journal de la bonne compagnie*, 214 (4 April 1847), pp. 1354–6.

224 'a mare with bay brown coat': Vérard, p. 60.

224 '*une évaporée*': Levallois, p. 28.

224 'nymphomania and maniacal profligacy': M. Du Camp, *Souvenirs littéraires* (1892), I, 319.

225 Campion was selling flowers: J. Toutain-Revel, in Bosquet.

225 'leading a patriarchal life': *Bulletin de la Société de l'Histoire de France*, 1853, pp. 85.

225 'left his wife and child': *Annuaire des cinq départements*, p. 60.

225 'My cousin [Laloy] and D[elamare]': Levallois, p. 28.

226 household . . . at Croisy-la-Haye: *Journal de Rouen*, 25 August 1848.

226 cases of arsenic poisoning: Review of A. Bouchardat, *Annuaire de thérapeutique*, in *Journal de médecine et de chirurgie pratiques*, XVIII (1847), p. 186.

227 'À bas les Anglais!': H. Bouteiller, *Histoire de Rouen, des milices et gardes bourgeoises* (1858), pp. 116–17.

227 the Union Jack: Bouteiller, pp. 112–13.

228 'violence inouïe': Levallois, p. 28.

228 'yesterday, at three o'clock': Vérard, p. 71.

228 'a church burial is not refused': T. Gousset, *Théologie morale* (1845), I, 431; see G. Hervé, 'Petits arrangements avec la mort volontaire', *Interrogations*, 14 (2012).

229 In cases of death by poisoning: *Dictionnaire de police moderne*, II (1823), pp. 739–40 (law of 1817); A.-C. Biret, *Recueil général et raisonné des compétences, attributions et jurisprudence des Justices de Paix*, I (1834), pp. 433–4; C.-J.-A. Bioche, *Dictionnaire des juges de paix et de police*, II (1852), p. 259.

229 an autopsy: An autopsy may have been performed. Levallois's uncle told him that Dr Achille Flaubert himself came out from Rouen. Since Gustave's father had died in 1846, this was probably his brother Achille, who had taken over as chief surgeon at the Hôtel-Dieu. A night-time visit from Rouen when other help was at hand is unlikely, but Dr Flaubert may have been called in later for his expert opinion.

229 a minor case of arsenic poisoning: *Gazette des Tribunaux*, 5 March 1848, p. 456.

229 as required by a recent law: *Recueil des actes de la Préfecture du Département de la Seine-Inférieure* (1875), pp. 98–9.

229　'arsenic in the chemist's cupboard': *Journal de Rouen*, 2 December 1890, p. 2.

230　'the series of strange . . . events': *Journal de Rouen*, 5 March 1848 (Supplément).

231　Club de la Fraternité: *La Fraternité* was a progressive Rouen newspaper: R. Motoike, 'La Franc-maçonnerie rouennaise et la Révolution de 1848', *Annales de Normandie*, XXXVI, 2 (1986), p. 148.

231　'Citizens': Gossez, p. 288.

232　Blainville had declared: *Journal de Rouen*, 18 March 1848.

233　died 'unexpectedly': *L'Impartial de Rouen*, 12 December 1849, in Bosquet.

233　chimeric beings: See Vérard; G. Cléroux, 'De Yonville-l'Abbaye à Ry: une bataille topographique': https://www.amis-flaubert-maupassant.fr/wp-content/uploads/2020/04/yonvillery_cleroux.pdf

233　'She had such a sweet voice': F. Denoeu, 'L'Ombre de Madame Bovary', *PMLA*, L, 4 (1935), p. 1170: from G. Leblanc, *Un pèlerinage au pays de Madame Bovary* (1913).

234　a journalist tracked her down: J.-E. Friederich, 'Ascendance et descendance de Delphine Couturier', *Les Amis de Flaubert*, 5 (1954).

12. Miss Howard's Gift to France

236　racy factoids: E.g. Touchatout (L. Bienvenu), *Histoire tintamarresque de Napoléon III. Les Années de chance* (1874–8), I, 208–10; *Mémoires de Griscelli, agent secret de Napoléon III* (1867), pp. 106–9; H. Fleischmann, *Napoleon III and the Women He Loved*, tr. A. S. Rappoport (n.d.), pp. 98–9.

237　compendium of tittle-tattle: [E. A. Vizetelly], *The Court of the Tuileries, 1852–1870, by Le Petit Homme Rouge* (1907).

237　'venturer of the December night': A. W. Kinglake, *The Invasion of the Crimea*, 6th ed. (1877–88), II, 163.

237　'small knot of middle-aged men': Kinglake, I, 214.

237　'the seeming poverty of his intellect': Kinglake, I, 226.

238　'a sleeping parrot': V. Hugo, *Choses vues*, April 1850 (quoting Comte d'Orsay); also *Châtiments* (1853), III, 1 ('Apothéose').

238　'république' as 'ripiblique': J. M. Thompson, *Louis Napoleon and the Second Empire* (1955), p. 91.

238　to catheterize him: I. Guest, *Napoleon III in England* (1952), p. 194.

238　'This morning': *Le Moniteur universel*, 2 November 1836.

239 'Soldiers, you are being made fools of!': A. Laity, *Le Prince Napoléon à Strasbourg* (1838), p. 59.

239 'Playing at kings and queens': *The Times*, 4 November 1836, p. 4.

240 In October 1838: See Guest, ch. 4.

240 *Boulogne-sur-mer, 1840*: On the Boulogne coup: Cour des Pairs, *Attentat du 6 Août 1840. Procédure. Dépositions de témoins*, III (1840); *Journal de Rouen*, 7 and 8 August 1840; *The Times*, 6–8 August 1840; *Le Moniteur universel*, 7 August 1840; Thompson, pp. 57–9.

240 Mr E. Rapallo: *The Times*, 13 August 1840, p. 4.

240 Captain Crowe: 'Louis-Napoléon's Invasion', *The Examiner*, 16 August 1840, p. 520; 'The Bonaparte Family', *The North British Review*, XI, 21 (1849), p. 97.

241 'come from exile': Cour des Pairs, p. 14.

241 'I had a peep at Louis Napoleon': *The Times*, 7 August 1840, p. 5.

241 a gilt eagle: Cour des Pairs, pp. 45, 151, and 251.

242 the Boulogne abattoir: J. Glikman, *Louis-Napoléon prisonnier: du fort de Ham aux ors des Tuileries* (2011).

242 'Crushing men': *Extinction du paupérisme*, par le prince Napoléon-Louis [*sic*] Bonaparte (1844), pp. 6–7.

243 'the lady who was on his arm': Earl of Malmesbury, *Memoirs of an Ex-Minister*, new ed. (1885), p. 127.

243 Lady Blessington: S. André-Maurois, *Miss Howard: la femme qui fit un empereur* (1956), p. 37.

243 As he had just explained: Letter to editor of *Journal de la Somme*, in *The Times*, 3 June 1846, p. 5; also 9 June 1846, p. 6 (from *L'Écho de la frontière*), and Thompson, p. 70.

243 for seventy-five minutes: Not, as in some accounts, 'a quarter of an hour': see *Bradshaw's Continental Railway, Steam Navigation & Conveyance Guide* (1847), pp. 22–5.

244 'his sojourn could be disagreeable': E. Roth, *Life of Napoleon III* (1856), p. 267.

244 Louis-Napoléon's new acquaintance: See S. André-Maurois.

244 'the exhibition of a boarding-school': *The Times*, 29 March 1842, p. 5.

244 'tumultuously called for': *The Times*, 18 January 1840, p. 6.

244 Rockingham House: A. M. Eyre, *Saint John's Wood: Its History, Its Houses, Its Haunts* (1913), p. 160; Guest, p. 79 n. No. 23 Circus Road is now no. 52.

244 Third Apparition in *Macbeth*: André-Maurois, p. 47. She would also have acted in the accompanying operetta, *The Students of Bonn* (*The Times*, 29 March 1842, p. 5).

245 houses and building plots: Guest, pp. 79 and 163; *Papiers et correspon-dance de la famille impériale* (1871), II, 156; André-Maurois, pp. 35 and 158.

245 Louis-Napoléon was living: *The Times*, 20, 21 (auction) and 29 August 1840 (lease on Brasted Park, Kent); Guest, p. 54.

245 one million francs: *Papiers et correspondance*, I, 157.

246 'Picture to yourself': Alexis de Valon, son-in-law of Gabriel Delessert, 24 June 1848: André-Maurois, p. 55.

246 dreamt of conquering England: I. H. Vivian, *Minutes of a Conversation with Napoleon Bonaparte* (1839), p. 26; Campbell, *Napoleon at Fontainebleau and Elba*, pp. 228–9.

247 a modern election campaign: N. Isser, *The Second Empire and the Press* (1974), pp. 3–5.

247 'a balloon-man': Kinglake, I, 218.

247 'He'll pay for the government': H. Taine, *Du suffrage universel et de la manière de voter* (1872), p. 17.

247 a United States of Europe: Thompson, p. 67.

247 'He seems lost for words': V. Hugo, *Choses vues*, 26 September 1848.

247 'he always came to collect his pay': Hugo, 11 December 1848.

248 'She had with her all the ready money': Captain the Hon. D. Bingham, *Recollections of Paris*, 2 vols (1896), p. 58.

248 the Paris Bourse: *Gazette des Tribunaux*, 7 August 1851, p. 768.

248 summary of repayments: *Papiers et correspondance*, I, 157–60.

248 annual budget of the city of Paris: 'Le Nouvel emprunt de la Ville de Paris', *La Presse*, 27 July 1851, p. 1; C. Nauroy, *Les Secrets des Bonaparte* (1889), p. 38 n.; also B. Marchand, 'Le Financement des travaux d'Haussmann' (2011), p. 3: https://hal.archives-ouvertes.fr/halshs-00583457

249 14 Rue du Cirque: E.g. *Memoirs of Dr. Thomas W. Evans: The Second French Empire* (1905), p. 3; É.-F. Fleury, *Souvenirs du Général Cte Fleury*, I (1897), pp. 82 and 204.

249 Henriette Cappelaere: 'Portrait de Mme H . . .', in É. Bellier de la Chavignerie, *Dictionnaire général des artistes de l'École française*, I (1882), p. 197.

249 'Louis-Napoléon isn't such a dimwit': Fleury, I, 208.

250 'Along with the cares of government': O. Barrot, *Mémoires posthumes*, 2nd ed., III (1876), pp. 362–3; also André-Maurois, p. 69; A. D. Vandam, *Undercurrents of the Second Empire*, (1895), p. 101.

250 Lord Normanby: André-Maurois, p. 65.

250 interfering in international affairs: A. de Tocqueville, *Œuvres, papiers et correspondances* (1951), p. 260.

250 'We considered her influence dangerous': Fleury, I, 204–5; also H. de Viel-Castel, *Mémoires*, II (1884), pp. 111, 162, etc.

251 'Do the French people . . .?': V. Hugo, *Napoléon le Petit*, II, 1.

251 in London, there was some relief: R. Quinault, '1848 and Parliamentary Reform', *The Historical Journal*, XXXI, 4 (1988), pp. 849–50.

251 expediting British recognition: G. Hicks, 'An Overlooked Entente: Lord Malmesbury, Anglo-French Relations and the Conservatives' Recognition of the Second Empire, 1852', *History*, XCII, 2 (2007), pp. 192–3.

252 'I called on Mrs. Howard': George Harris to Lord Fitzharris (James Howard Harris, third Earl of Malmesbury, then Foreign Secretary): Malmesbury, p. 262.

252 'the army is peaceably inclined': Malmesbury, p. 276.

252 26, Avenue des Champs-Élysées: Lot no. 91 in https://www.gazette-drouot.com/lots/2101539

252 a large vacant plot: 154, Avenue des Champs-Élysées: André-Maurois, pp. 159–60, from the archives of Miss Howard's friend, the imperial *notaire*, Amédée Mocquard.

252 'If the fair Infanta has not yielded': André-Maurois, p. 104.

253 'His Majesty was here last night': André-Maurois, pp. 102–3 (in English).

253 The 'castle': M. Fravaton, 'Le Château de Beauregard', *Revue de l'Histoire de Versailles et de Seine-et-Oise*, XII, 1 (1910), pp. 16–45.

253 'Beauregard suits me': André-Maurois, p. 134 (in English).

253 'Sire, I am leaving': In [H. Magen], *Les Nuits et le mariage de César*, par L. Stelli (Jersey, 1853), dated 10 March 1853 (in French).

254 St James's Piccadilly: *The Gentleman's Magazine*, new series, XLII (September 1854), p. 293.

254 the exhibition agents: *Journal of the Society of Arts*, 24 August 1855; 'List of Agents for Exhibitors of the United Kingdom', *Reports on the Paris Universal Exhibition* (1856), pp. 59–60.

254 'amidst the roar of cannon': *Queen Victoria's Journals*, copies by Princess Beatrice: www.queenvictoriasjournals.org Quotations from 18–25 August 1855.

255 'Isn't it odd?': G. Villiers, *A Vanished Victorian, Being the Life of George Villiers* (1938), p. 262.

255 'dirty white hair and face': André-Maurois, p. 212.

256 'That he is a very extraordinary man': 'Memorandum', in *The Letters of Queen Victoria*, III (1908), p. 122.

257 'resisted the bellicose notions': Alfred de la Chapelle [Napoleon III], *Les Forces militaires de la France en 1870* (1872), p. 6.

257 'A Napoleon does not capitulate': M. Paléologue, 'Les Entretiens de l'Impératrice Eugénie, III: Sedan', *Revue des Deux Mondes*, XLIV, 3 (1928), pp. 535–61.

259 Caesar might have crossed the Thames: Napoléon III, *Histoire de Jules César* (1865–6), II, 167.

259 'To this very day': Ibid., II, 110.

259 a 'spontaneous event': Ibid., I, i.

260 'the principal cause of the weakness': Ibid., II, 48.

260 'a certain idea of France': Charles de Gaulle, *Mémoires de guerre* (1954), I, 7.

260 'in the French style': Guest, p. 163.

260 an economical coal-stove: *Œuvres posthumes et autographes inédits de Napoléon III en exil*, ed. A. de la Chapelle (1873), pp. 265–6.

260 new type of mortar: Guest, p. 192. Earlier, he was said to have invented a cannon (the 'Canon Napoléon III') capable of 'killing or wounding a hundred men at once': *Encyclopédie militaire et maritime*, 3rd ed. (1865), III, pt 1, p. 224.

260 'More than once he was noticed': Guest, p. 184.

261 Private detectives: Guest, p. 191.

261 The plan was to take a villa: J. Adam, *Mes souvenirs: mes angoisses et nos luttes* (1873), p. 346; M. Du Camp, *Souvenirs littéraires* (1892), II, 279–92.

13. Savage Coast

265 trading city of Corbilo: Strabo, IV, 2, 1 (from Polybius, quoting Pytheas).

265 Caesar made similar enquiries: *De Bello Gallico*, IV, 20.

265 Charts of the estuary: E.g. *Étude sur les fonds de la Loire, entre la mer et Saint-Nazaire* (1885).

266 Tour d'Aiguillon . . . Tour du Commerce: *Annales maritimes et coloniales* (1831), p. 320.

266 already known as the Côte Sauvage: N. Desmarest, *Encyclopédie méthodique: géographie physique*, III (1809), p. 493 (also in 1782 and other editions); O. Reclus, *France, Algérie et colonies* (1886), p. 254.

266 a new breed of traveller: J. Ogée, *Dictionnaire historique et géographique de la province de Bretagne*, rev. ed. (1843), II, 378; E. Serpeau-Delidon, *Le Guide de l'étranger aux Sables-d'Olonne et aux environs* (1873).

266 dolmens, menhirs: E.g. B. Fillon, *Lettres écrites de la Vendée* (1861), pp. 106–7.

267 the *Saint-Paul*, and her captain: On the shipwreck and its aftermath:
S. Anderson, *Pelletier: The Forgotten Castaway of Cape York*, rev. ed.
(2012), and C. Merland, *Dix-sept ans chez les sauvages* (1876), new ed.
by T. Duranteau and X. Porteau (2016). Also V. de Rochas,
'Naufrage et scènes d'anthropophagie, à l'Île Rossell [*sic*] dans
l'Archipel de la Louisiade', *Le Tour du monde: nouveau journal
des voyages*, 1861, 2, pp. 81–94. For Capt. Pinard's letters to the
owners from Port-de-France (Nouméa), 21 December 1858, and
Sydney, 28 January 1859: http://www.archeosousmarine.net/Pdf/
saintpaul1.pdf

267 'the most inhospitable in the world': Merland, p. 8; also J. Pinkerton
and C. A. Walckenaer, *Abrégé de géographie moderne* (1811), II, 305.

268 a *mousse*: P. Larousse, *Grand Dictionnaire universel*, XI (1874), p. 644
(floating schools for cabin boys at Brest and Toulon).

268 files at the Ministère de la Marine: 'État des marins présumés
décédés', photograph in T. Duranteau and X. Porteau, *Narcisse
Pelletier, la vraie histoire du sauvage blanc* (2016), p. 51.

268 letters from a shoemaker: C. Letourneau, 'Sur un Français nommé
Narcisse Pelletier, qui oublia sa langue chez les Australiens', *Bulletins
de la Société d'anthropologie de Paris* (abbreviation: *BSAP*), 1880,
p. 713.

268 Uutaalnganu people: See Anderson's introduction.

269 In August 1845: A. d'Hastrel, 'Les Bains de mer: La Rochelle, Les
Sables d'Olonne (Vendée)', *L'Illustration, journal universel*, V, 130
(1845), pp. 411–14.

270 a lizard's tail: *BSAP*, 1903, p. 375.

270 Colliberts or *huttiers*: *The Discovery of France*, pp. 39–41.

270 a small hammer: Viator Verax [G. M. Musgrave], *Cautions for the
First Tour: On the Annoyances, Short Comings, Indecencies, and
Impositions Incidental to Foreign Travel*, 5th ed. (1863), pp. 19–20.

271 Anatole Roujou: Obituary by G. Charvilhat, 'Anatole Roujou, 1841–
1904', *BSAP*, 1905, pp. 256–9.

271 'It has delighted me to find': Letter to [A. Roujou], 28 February
1872: *The Correspondence of Charles Darwin*, ed. F. Burkhardt et al.,
XX (2013).

271 'an occasionally sinister expression': A. Roujou, 'Sur quelques types
humains trouvés en France', *BSAP*, 1872, p. 774.

271 'Australoid' type: A. Roujou, 'Sur quelques races ou sous-races locales
observées en France', *BSAP*, 1874, p. 255.

271 they beat each other senseless: Ibid., p. 253.

271 pencil sketches: See 'Les Races d'Auvergne dessinées par Anatole

Roujou', in Archives départementales du Cantal: http://archives.
cantal.fr/ark:/16075/a011350284666y6Yxjm

271 'scruffy and insolvent': F. Huguet and B. Noguès, 'Les Professeurs
des Facultés des Lettres et des Sciences en France au XIXe siècle',
2011: http://facultes19.ish-lyon.cnrs.fr/

272 'The head should be opened': P. Broca, *Instructions générales pour les
recherches anthropologiques à faire sur le vivant*, 2nd ed. (1879), p. 17.

272 'Travellers [in France]': Ibid., p. 8.

272 The *John Bell*: See C. Merland, pp. 120–23.

273 the word 'Frenchman': Merland, p. 122.

273 'perched on the rail fence': *The Times*, 21 July 1875.

273 'a serious nuisance': J. Ottley, letter dated 30 May 1923, in Anderson,
appendix V.

274 French consul in Sydney: G. E. Simon, quoted in Letourneau,
pp. 712–15.

274 '*narcise peletier desaingile*': Photographs of this and the following
letter in Anderson, appendix III, and T. Duranteau and X. Porteau,
pp. 145 and 155. I have used my own transcriptions.

275 'On one point I was quite satisfied': J. Ottley, in Anderson, appendix
V.

275 the heads of Australians: *BSAP*, 1872, p. 774.

275 examples from the Côte Sauvage: *Exposition universelle internationale
de 1878 . . . Catalogue officiel* (1878), II, nos 462 and 464.

275 'the French Robinson Crusoe': X. Dachères, 'Narcisse Pelletier, le
sauvage d'Australie', *L'Univers illustré*, 14 August 1875, p. 523.

275 army conscripts: J.-P. Aron et al., *Anthropologie du conscrit français*
(1972); É. Levasseur, *La Population française* (1889), I, 385–7.

276 'Aryan' race: A. de Gobineau, *Ce qui est arrivé à la France en 1870*;
C. Digeon, *La Crise allemande de la pensée française* (1992), p. 92.

276 'Compromised by his bad wife': Huguet and Noguès.

277 'clutching in his stiffened hand': Charvilhat, p. 257.

277 'They have no pity for me': Photograph in Anderson, appendix III.

277 'He is a strong lad': *Le Constitutionnel*, 22 December 1875, p. 3; also
G. Stenne, 'Narcisse Pelletier', *L'Union bretonne*, 23 December 1875,
p. 2.

278 'Pricked with a bone': Anderson, n. 153.

278 'this individual': A. Chervin, in Letourneau, p. 716.

278 'education leaves such shallow traces': Review of Merland, in *L'Union
bretonne*, 2 August 1876.

278 'Paris and the remainder of the territory': A. de Gobineau, *Essai sur
l'inégalité des races humaines* (1853), I, 161.

279 'None of the many friends': J. Gauvrit, letter to editor of *Le Phare de la Loire*, Saint-Gilles, 4 January 1876: *La Presse*, 9 January 1876.

279 velocipedists . . . simian ancestors: S. S. Buckman, 'Cycling: Its Effect on the Future of the Human Race', *The Medical Magazine*, VIII (1899), pp. 128–35.

280 'nothing negroid about the lips': Anon., 'Un ancien sauvage parmi les Français', *Le Figaro*, 10 July 1878.

280 'the Neolithic mentality': M. Baudouin, 'L'Homme sauvage de Vendée', *BSAP*, 1911, p. 157.

281 Captain Emmanuel Pinard: Notoriété après décès d'Emmanuel Sévère Philippe Pinard (17 March 1877); Dépôt de donation (24 March); Inventaire après décès (18 May): Minutes et répertoires du notaire Eugène Philippe Michelez (étude CXIV), Archives Nationales.

281 Maritime Prefect of Toulon: Préfet maritime Penhoat to Commissaire général de la Marine, 18 December 1875, on enquiry into Pelletier's abandonment: Service historique de la Défense, Toulon, in Chanouga and N. Casanova, *Narcisse: dossier documentaire* (2018), p. 51.

282 homesickness: *Journal des Sables*, 6 June 1954, quoted by Anderson.

14. Keeping Track of the Dead

284 One of those villages: La Crochette, south of Fontenet (Charente-Maritime).

285 concentration camps: Fears of pro-German Alsatians: J.-C. Farcy, *Les Camps de concentration français de la Première guerre mondiale, 1914–1920* (1995), pp. 51–60; J.-N. Grandhomme, 'Les Alsaciens-Lorrains dans les camps d'internement du Finistère (1914–1919)', *Annales de Bretagne et des Pays de l'Ouest*, CIX, 4 (2002), pp. 163–75; J.-P. Grasser, *Une histoire d'Alsace* (1998), p. 92.

286 regional produce: See X. de Planhol, *Géographie historique de la France* (1988), tr. J. Lloyd (1994), pp. 377–8.

286 a commercial crop: J. C. F. Hoefer, ed., *Dictionnaire théorique et pratique d'agriculture et d'horticulture* (1855), pp. 468–70.

288 many 'anti-Dreyfusards': On the intellectual and moral complexities of the Affair: R. Harris, *The Man on Devil's Island* (2010), pp. 7–10.

289 a 'sacred union': President Poincaré, speech to the Assemblies, 4 August 1914: http://www2.assemblee-nationale.fr/decouvrir-l-assemblee/histoire/1914–1918/l-exposition-du-centenaire/le-parlement-s-ajourne-1914/4-aout-1914-la-naissance-de-l-union-sacree

289 The true Lorrainer: Quotations from S. Al-Matary, 'À la frontière

des "races": la géographie morale de Maurice Barrès', *Romantisme*, 130 (2005), pp. 95–109.

290 'race is in tune with the landscape': E. Psichari, *L'Appel des armes* (1913; 1945), pp. 10–11.

290 hymns to 'national identity': See S. Al-Matary, 'Le Siècle du *Grand Meaulnes*: un roman, des cocardes': https://laviedesidees.fr/IMG/pdf/20121005_alain-fournier.pdf and President Sarkozy's speech at the opening of the Musée de la Grande Guerre in Meaux, 11 November 2011.

290 'Africa is one of the last resorts': E. Psichari, *Terres de soleil et de sommeil* (1908), p. 226.

290 'to raise up our hearts': Ibid., p. 20.

290 drugged and drunken soldiers: H. Lacorne, in J. Levine, *Forgotten Voices of the Somme* (2009), p. 77; L. Kamienski, 'Drugs' (2019), in *International Encyclopedia of the First World War*: https://encyclopedia.1914–1918-online.net/article/drugs

291 American soldiers killed in Vietnam: J.-M. Steg, *Le Jour le plus meurtrier de l'histoire de France* (2013), p. 25.

291 'Attack the enemy wherever': Steg, p. 137.

291 'He who would conquer': *Conduite des grandes unités: service des armées en campagne* (*Bulletin officiel du Ministère de la Guerre*, 1914), p. 5.

292 'A battle is a moral contest': Ibid., p. 6.

292 long-range target practice: Steg, p. 141.

293 At dawn on 22 August 1914: On the battle: Rex Beasley, 'Critical Analysis of the Operations of the French Colonial Corps in the Battle of the Ardennes, with Particular Attention to the Operations of the 3d Colonial Division at Rossignol', research paper (Fort Leavenworth, 1933); Steg.

293 the grand plan: On French and German strategies: Steg, ch. 3 and pp. 130–33.

293 'C'est magnifique . . .': J. Ladimir and H. Arnoul, *La Guerre: histoire complete des opérations militaires en Orient et dans la Baltique*, 9th ed. (1857), p. 294.

294 set their sights on the mess-tins: Steg, pp. 217–18.

295 hydraulic recoil brakes: Steg, p. 105.

295 'every house, corner and pile of rubbish': Beasley, p. 41.

296 'Despite our cries': M. Barrès, 'Un témoin [Victor Boudon] raconte la mort héroïque de Péguy', *L'Écho de Paris*, 26 December 1914, p. 1; cf. the later version in V. Boudon, *Avec Charles Péguy* (1916), p. 146.

296 lack of accurate statistics: See J.-J. Arzalier, 'Dénombrer les pertes: les difficultés françaises d'adaptation à la Grande Guerre', in *Les*

Armes et la toge, ed. J.-C. Jauffret (1997), pp. 387–400; A. Prost, 'Compter les vivants et les morts: l'évaluation des pertes françaises de 1914–1918', *Le Mouvement Social*, 222 (2008), pp. 41–60.

297 identity disks: É. Marchal, 'Le Corps identifié', *Corps*, 12 (2014), pp. 37–40.

297 his dental record: É. Dussourt, 'Identification bucco-dentaire et Guerre de 14–18', *Actes de la Société française d'histoire de l'art dentaire*, 11 (2006), pp. 43–5.

297 'a sunken, collapsed appearance': J. Moreau, *Rossignol, 22 août 1914: journal du commandant Jean Moreau* (2002), pp. 70–72.

298 'he was very calm': Beasley, appendix 2, p. 3.

298 probably pathological: Steg, p. 50.

298 'his field glasses': Moreau, p. 106 (Capt. Hartmann).

299 'Certain parts of the battlefield': F. Engerand, *Le Secret de la frontière 1815–1871–1914* (1918), p. 504.

299 expected to be shot at: Steg, p. 191 and ch. 8.

300 'Our troops advanced': 'À l'Est de la Meuse', *L'Écho de Paris*, 25 August 1914.

301 stunned into inactivity: Steg, p. 32.

302 reorganization of war statistics: Prost, pp. 45 ff.; also C. Gué, 'Les Pertes françaises en août et septembre 1914: prévisions et bilans', *Cahiers d'études et de recherches du Musée de l'Armée*, 5 (2004), pp. 315–46.

302 General Nivelle: R. Verquin, 'Le Chemin des Dames: un désastre sanitaire en avril 1917', *Mémoires: Fédération des societes d'histoire et d'archéologie de l'Aisne*, L (2005), p. 144.

304 'You might ask': Maria Aussignac's letter (translated here from the photograph) was published online by Francis Vignacourt in 'Une histoire vraie de 1917 à 1920, de deux compagnons d'armes morts pour la France à Laffaux et du courage de leurs mères' (2014): https://www.retours-vers-les-basses-pyrenees.fr/2015/02/leurs-fils-sont-morts-la-guerreune-mere.html The website includes a link to a ten-minute film based on the letter. The identity papers of Aussignac and Prudet can be consulted in the official database: 'Base des Morts pour la France de la Première Guerre mondiale'.

15. Mount Inaccessible

305 'In the bishopric of Gratianopolis': Gervase of Tilbury, 'De rupe, quae nominatur *Aequa illi*', in *Otia Imperialia*, ed. F. Liebrecht (1856), pp. 23–4 (III, 42).

305n.*Aequa villa*: C. Pignatelli and D. Gerner, *Les Traductions françaises des Otia Imperialia* (2006), p. 542.

305 an inverted pyramid: Les Pères Jésuites du Collège Royal-Dauphin de Grenoble, *Les Sept Miracles de Dauphiné* (1701), p. 1; A. Lancelot, 'Discours sur les Sept Merveilles du Dauphiné', *Mémoires de littérature tirez [sic] des registres de l'Academie Royale des Inscriptions et Belles Lettres*, VI (1729), pp. 760–61.

306 A local legend: Recorded by Rabelais in *Le Quart Livre* (1552).

306 Antoine de Ville: Aymar du Rivail, *De Allobrogibus* (1535; 1844), pp. 119–20 ('Mons Inascensibilis'); S. Briffaud, 'Une montagne de paradis', *Communications*, 87 (2010), pp. 129–35.

307 'No mortal can attain': *Les Sept Miracles de Dauphiné*, p. 2.

307 'unlike other mountains': N. Delacroix, *Statistique du département de la Drôme*, rev. ed. (1835), p. 185. The mountain was more accurately depicted on a map published c. 1620 by Jean de Beins: *Carte et description générale de Dauphiné avec les confins du pais et provinces voisines, le tout racourcy et réduict.*

307 One team . . . The second team: Delacroix, pp. 186–8.

308 seasonal migrations: See Planhol, *Géographie historique*, p. 390.

308 the first modern road: On road-building in the Vercors: A. Joanne, 'Excursion dans le Dauphiné', *Le Tour du monde*, II (1860), pp. 369–418.

308 inaccessible village: *Guide du voyageur dans le département de l'Isère* (1856), p. 521; A. Raverat, *À travers le Dauphiné: voyage pittoresque et artistique* (1861), p. 167.

309 'All at once': 'Lieutenant Stephen' (A. Valot), *Vercors: premier maquis de France* (1946; 1991), pp. 54–5.

309 'fight to the last Frenchman': *Britain and France in Two World Wars*, ed. R. Tombs and É. Chabal (2013), p. 7.

309 'I urged the French Government': Churchill, *The Second World War* (1997), p. 287: at the penultimate Supreme War Council held in Breteau (Loiret) on 11–12 June 1940.

310 Demarcation Line: See É. Alary, *La Ligne de démarcation, 1940–1944* (2003).

310 a radio broadcast: 'Le Maréchal Pétain donne au pays les raisons de son entrevue avec le Führer', *Le Matin*, 31 October 1940, p. 1.

311 anti-Jewish legislation: On internment camps, see fig. 14, based on ajpn.org: https://www.ajpn.org/lieuinternements.html; E. Filhol, 'L'Indifférence collective au sort des Tsiganes internés dans les camps français', *Guerres mondiales et conflits contemporains*, 226 (2007), pp. 69–82; A. Grynberg, *Les Camps de la honte: les internés juifs des*

camps français (1999); G. Megargee, *The United States Holocaust Memorial Museum Encyclopedia of Camps and Ghettos* (2009); J. Oliel, 'Les Camps de Vichy en Afrique du Nord', *Revue d'Histoire de la Shoah*, 198 (2013), pp. 227–44; J. Oliel, 'Les Camps de Vichy au Maghreb', ibid., 205 (2016), pp. 369–84.

311 a *déversoir*: Alary, p. 185.

312 gangs of *passeurs*: Alary, pp. 169–70.

312 Brasserie des Arcades: I. Meinen and A. Meyer, *Verfolgt von Land zu Land: Jüdische Flüchtlinge in Westeuropa* (2013), pp. 206–7. Also, with other examples, Alary, p. 171.

312 the annual salary: R. Rivet, 'L'Évolution des salaires et traitements depuis 1939', *Journal de la Société statistique de Paris*, LXXXIV (1943), p. 105.

312 'A driver who knew': H. Laville, in Alary, p. 120.

313 at Barbès-Rochechouart . . . Bastille: C. Neumaier, 'The Escalation of German Reprisal Policy in Occupied France, 1941–42', *Journal of Contemporary History*, XLI, 1 (2006), p. 119; V. Antelmi, 'Les Incidents dans le Métro parisien sous l'Occupation', in *Métro, dépôts, réseaux: territoires et personnels des transports parisiens au XXe siècle*, ed. N. Gérôme and M. Margairaz (2002), pp. 83–91.

313 'Jewish Bolshevik': Neumaier, p. 119.

313 'One must bear in mind': *Nuremberg Trial Proceedings*, X, 616 (6 April 1946).

313 shot by three Communists: Neumaier, pp. 120–21.

314 'I protest with all my heart': *Le Matin*, 21 October 1941.

314 the week of the Nantes assassination: *Le Matin*, 21–22 October 1941.

315 plans were left on trains: E.g. R. Gildea, *Fighters in the Shadows: A New History of the French Resistance* (2015), pp. 164 ff.

315 The 'French' Resistance: Gildea, p. 205.

316 Japanese ambassador: P. Ashdown, *The Cruel Victory* (2014), p. 48.

316 'to importune the French people': 'Un double message du Führer aux Français et au Maréchal Pétain', *Le Matin*, 12 November 1942.

316 Plan Montagnards: The most detailed scholarly account of the Plan Montagnards and the battle for the Vercors is Paddy Ashdown's *The Cruel Victory*.

317 primary school teachers: L. Yagil, 'Résistance et sauvetage des Juifs dans le département de l'Isère (1940–1944)', *Guerres mondiales et conflits contemporains*, 212 (2003), pp. 57–9 and 68.

317 A doctor regularly cycled up: Yagil, p. 72.

318 a 'new Palestine': Yagil, p. 59.

318   General de Gaulle himself: H. R. Kedward, *In Search of the Maquis: Rural Resistance in Southern France* (1994), p. 175.

319   out-boxed Ernest Hemingway: S. Schiff, *Saint-Exupéry* (2011), ch. 7.

319   'I had a vision of the Vercors': P. Dalloz, *Vérités sur le drame du Vercors* (1979), p. 33.

319   'In this way': G. Vergnon, *Le Vercors: histoire et mémoire d'un maquis* (2002), pp. 218–20.

320   Brigadier Gubbins: Ashdown, p. 35.

320   Churchill himself was aware: At least in July 1944: Conseil National de la Résistance to Churchill, 21 July 1944, in Gildea, p. 357.

320   'air-nourished guerrilla operations': *Foreign Relations of the United States: The Conferences at Washington and Quebec, 1943* (1970), p. 1124.

320   '*Le chamois bondit*': Ashdown, pp. 71 and 169.

320   'turbulent and conspicuous': Vergnon, p. 219.

320   'brave and desperate men': Ashdown, p. 93.

321   'The white globes descended': 'Lieutenant Stephen' (A. Valot), p. 55.

321   '*Nous avons visité Marrakech*': Ashdown, p. 407 n.

322   Pflaum took personal charge: Ashdown, p. 98; Yagil, p. 64.

322   a motor tour of the Vercors: Ashdown, pp. 96–7.

323   'For the sons of France': https://www.youtube.com/watch?v=2S8G VEmjevc (2'35"–2'55")

323   '*Vercors 2000 volunteers*': F. Rude, in 'Le Dialogue Vercors-Alger', *Revue d'histoire de la Deuxième Guerre Mondiale*, 49 (1963), p. 83.

323   it was an open secret: See Ashdown, pp. 113, 122, 162, etc.

324   the longed-for reinforcements: Ashdown, ch. 26.

325   gliders were released: Ashdown, p. 298.

325   '*Enemy troops parachuted Vassieux*': This is the version given by F. Rude, p. 100.

326   identified as 'Mongols': M.-T. Têtu, *Vercors et Résistance* (2006), p. 59, n. 42.

326   a black cat: The cat in question was hunting at La Cime-du-Mas below the Col de Proncel, where 'a few peasants' were arbitrarily shot on 26 July: P. Tanant, *Vercors, haut-lieu de France* (1950), p. 159.

326   'the entire Isère valley': Ashdown, p. 340.

326   '*All have courageously done their duty*': Signed Hervieu; sent on the night of 24–25 July 1944: Rude, p. 107.

327   'As I speak, the enemy is attacking': Rude, p. 108.

327   a field hospital: Ashdown, p. 352.

327   Pont Charvet: A. Guérin, *Chronique de la Résistance*, rev. ed. (2000), p. 1164.

327 The deaths of 'persons unknown': Certificate reproduced in 'Jean Prévost et la Résistance dans la Vercors': https://erra38.fr/manifestations/vercors/

328 'A true poem': J. Prévost, *Baudelaire: essai sur la création et l'inspiration poétiques* (1953; 1964), p. 293.

328 'Straight at home and gay abroad': A. P. Campbell on his BBC2 documentary, in *The Scotsman*, 27 December 2001.

329 'History does not so much play tricks': D. Caskie, *The Tartan Pimpernel* (1957; 1999), p. 20.

329 'It must no longer be the case': The city of Grenoble was awarded the Croix de la Libération. De Gaulle's speech is reproduced on the Order's website: https://www.ordredelaliberation.fr/fr/grenoble

330 'épuration sauvage': See P. Bourdrel, *La Grande débâcle de la collaboration* (2011).

330 The tonnage of Allied bombs: Statistics in A. Knapp, 'The Horror and the Glory: Bomber Command in British Memories Since 1945' (2016): https://www.sciencespo.fr/mass-violence-war-massacre-resistance/en/document/horror-and-glory-bomber-command-british-memories-1945.html

330 'tentative and amateurish': R. Mortimer, in R. Dutton and Lord Holden, *The Land of France*, 3rd ed. (1949), p. xi.

16. Martyrs of the Tour de France

333 front-page editorial: H. Desgrange, 'La Semence', *L'Auto*, 1 July 1903, p. 1.

333 Hirson to Dunkirk: *L'Auto*, 23 July 1921, p. 2: the report calls Scieur 'assez veinard' ('rather lucky').

334 'ridiculously short': H. Desgrange, 'Allons-y!', *L'Auto*, 28 June 1919, p. 1.

334 Josef Fischer: *L'Auto*, 1 July 1903, p. 1.

335 'passes our understanding': G. Lefèvre, 'Veille de bataille', *L'Auto*, 29 June 1903, p. 1.

335 'I began to miss the days': H. Desgrange, 'La Première bataille', *L'Auto*, 2 July 1903, p. 1.

336 'The route is slightly undulating': 'Itinéraire de la sixième étape', *L'Auto*, 23 July 1904, p. 3.

337 commemorative brochure: 'Une plaquette illustrée', *L'Auto*, 24 July 1904, p. 1.

337 four-seater Cottereau: *L'Auto*, 25 July 1904, p. 1.

338   imaginary east–west line: J. Brunhes, *La Géographie humaine*, 3rd ed. (1956), pp. 308–10; *The Discovery of France*, p. 67.

339   'beyond Saint-Étienne': G. Lefèvre, 'Toujours l'aggression de Saint-Étienne', *L'Auto*, 13 July 1904, p. 1 (including the riders' official complaint).

339   The 'great wood': See C. Laboulaye, *Complément du dictionnaire des arts et manufactures* (1872), 'Neige' (unpaginated).

339   dawn over the Rhone Valley: G. Lefèvre, 'La Seconde bataille', *L'Auto*, 10 July 1904, p. 1 (a report written in advance of the facts).

339   'Come on, lads, kill 'em!': *L'Auto*, 13 July 1904, p. 1.

339   'The Tour de France is over': H. Desgrange, 'La Fin', *L'Auto*, 25 July 1904, p. 1.

340   Union Vélocipédique de France: F. Mercier, 'On demande pourquoi?', *L'Auto*, 3 December 1904, p. 5.

340   the miracle of the TSF: On radio coverage of the Tour: C. Thompson, *The Tour de France: A Cultural History*, new ed. (2008), p. 43.

340   'The man was desperate': 'Le sort tragique de Fontan', *L'Auto*, 12 July 1929, p. 1.

341   'congestion in the kidneys': 'La Visite aux coureurs', *L'Auto*, 11 July 1929, p. 2.

342   'This is where my forks broke': https://www.dailymotion.com/video/xknfae (1'49"–1'56"); race reports in *L'Auto*, 10 and 13 July 1913; another interview (not broadcast), 1 May 1968: https://www.ina.fr/video/CAF93017666

342   the site of his accident: Latitude–longitude coordinates: 42.92184, 0.20303.

343   a saint called Bonnet: *The Discovery of France*, p. 117.

343   'When you've started a job': https://www.dailymotion.com/video/xknfae (6'55"–7'00").

343   'Chute Beloki': Location: 44.58059, 6.12515.

344   'buttercup in the grass': For contemporary coverage: https://www.youtube.com/watch?v=TMdYkjNnwjY Location: 42.97452, -0.31807.

344n. Adolphe Hélière died: *L'Auto*, 15 July 1910, p. 3 (contrary to the legend, which blames a jellyfish).

345   'Monday, 12 July 1971': Location: 42.91566, 0.74389.

345   'second in the Tour de France': At the first hairpin bend on the climb to the Col de Portet from Saint-Lary-Soulan: 42.83712, 0.32586.

345   'Here, on 14 July 1968': On the D84 between the Col de Canguilan and Damiatte: 43.68972, 1.99770.

345 'Unluckiest Rider': 'Er liggen miljoenen te rapen', *Gazet van Antwerpen*, 22 June 1962, p. 16.

346 faked his own assassination: See 'The Day of the Fox', in *Parisians: An Adventure History of Paris* (2010).

348 the road . . . was Roman: F. Allemand, 'Note sur la station d'Ictodurum', *Bulletin de la Société d'études des Hautes-Alpes*, 1917, pp. 40–46.

350 Four-fifths of French people: IFOP (Institut français d'opinion publique) poll for *Le Journal du dimanche*, 27 October 2019.

17. La République en Marche!

351 A young French woman: A. Alami, 'The College Student Who Has France's Secularists Fulminating', *New York Times*, 1 June 2018; R. Diallo, 'A Student Leader is the Latest Victim . . .', *Guardian*, 28 May 2018.

352 Today's students: SMEREP, *Santé des étudiants et des lycéens* (2017); V. Monchatre and J. Muller, 'Un tiers des emplois des étudiants ne font pas partie de la formation suivie', *Insee Analyses*, 94 (2019), p. 3.

353 Pougetoux is pilloried: L. Alsaafin, 'French Student on Hijab . . .', *Al Jazeera*, 9 April 2019.

353 'a strict *laïciste*': V. Bloch-Lainé, 'Laurent Bouvet, ma laïcité va craquer', *Libération*, 8 October 2019.

353 'ephemeral and caricatural nature': L. Bouvet, 'Non au bûcher médiatique', *Le Monde*, 18 September 2015.

353 'the opposite of feminism': R. Diallo, 'A Student Leader'.

353 'sullying the battles we fought': 'Polémique sur le voile . . .', *Le Monde*, 14 May 2018.

353 'You see, when my Mum went to church': Gérard Collomb, 18 May 2018: https://www.bfmtv.com/politique/gouvernement/responsable-de-l-unef-voilee-c-est-du-proselytisme-accuse-gerard-collomb_AN-201805180025.html

354 Her great-grandparents: A. Alami, 'The College Student'.

354 'It is possible to wear a veil': R. Dodet and M. Thierry, 'Lilâ Le Bas, présidente de l'UNEF', *Le Nouvel Observateur*, 25 May 2018.

354 'They chose me as their leader': *Charlie Hebdo*, 23 May 2018.

354 'must observe the rules': Riss, 'À propos de l'UNEF', *Charlie Hebdo*, 30 May 2018.

355 An investigation: L. Bretton and I. Halissat, 'Abus sexuels: les témoignages qui accablent l'UNEF', *Libération*, 19 February 2018.

355 'Men did the thinking': 'Polémique sur le voile', *Le Monde*, 14 May 2018.

356 'C'est dur d'être aimé par des cons . . .': *Charlie Hebdo*, 8 February 2006.

356 a *Charlie Hebdo* T-shirt: *Charlie Hebdo*, 9 November 2011.

356 'You are a woman': Sigolène Vinson, interviewed on Radio France Internationale: V. Walt, 'Meet the Women . . .', *Time*, 9 January 2015.

357 'I disapprove of what you say': S. G. Tallentyre (Evelyn Beatrice Hall), *The Friends of Voltaire* (1906), p. 199.

357 'We vomit on those who . . .': 'Willem: "Nous vomissons sur ceux qui, subitement, disent être nos amis"', *Le Point*, 10 January 2015.

359 'Why on earth . . .?': 'Conférence de presse du 19 mai 1958': https://fresques.ina.fr/de-gaulle/fiche-media/Gaulle00210/conference-de-presse-du-19-mai-1958.html

360 'discreet and intimate affirmation': 'Un rappel solennel des valeurs de notre école', A.1: https://www.senat.fr/rap/l03-219/l03-2197.html

360 the beach at Nice: V. Morin, 'Indignation devant les photos d'une femme voilée', *Le Monde*, 24 August 2016; B. Quinn, 'French Police Make Woman Remove Clothing . . .', *Guardian*, 24 August 2016.

362 'We're Catholic here': 'Cannes et Nice: des femmes verbalisées . . .', *Libération*, 23 August 2016.

362 'That, for me, is the Republic': Socialist Party meeting at Colomiers, 29 August 2016.

363 'La Marseillaise': Assemblée Nationale, 11 February 2005: 'Avenir de l'école' (no. 2025), amendment 125.

364 '*liberté de culte!*': J. M., 'Sciences Po Aix: un prof accuse une élève voilée', *Le Nouvel Observateur*, 2 October 2014. This and other cases: P. de Coustin, 'Une enseignante a réprimandé publiquement une étudiante', *Le Figaro*, 25 September 2014; J.-P. Brighelli, *Liberté, égalité, laïcité* (2015).

364 'What would Diderot have said?': 'Toujours Charlie' meeting co-organized by Le Printemps Républicain, 6 January 2018.

364 'either a fool or a rogue': C.-A. Dauban, *Paris en 1794 et en 1795* (1869), p. 411 (24 June 1794); L. Hamel, *Histoire de Robespierre et du coup d'état du 9 Thermidor*, III (1867), p. 605.

366 national moodometer: N. Raulin, 'Enquête Cevipof', *Libération*, 11 January 2019.

366 colonization of Belleville: É. Charmes, *La Rue – village ou décor?: parcours dans deux rues de Belleville* (2006), pp. 22 ff.

367 the minute-and-a-quarter segment: https://www.france24.com/fr/20181005-proces-agression-marie-laguerre-video-paris-harcelement-rue

368 'Ta gueule!': H. Seckel, 'Au procès de l'homme qui avait giflé Marie Laguerre', *Le Monde*, 4 October 2018; J. Deborde, 'Marie Laguerre: accuse les coups', *Libération*, 4 September 2018.

368 'the ghost accosts the passer-by': 'Les Sept Vieillards', *Les Fleurs du Mal*.

368 Four-fifths of French women: A. Debauche et al., *Présentation de l'enquête Virage et premiers résultats sur les violences sexuelles* (2017); A. Orieul, 'Harcèlement de rue', *Terrafemina*, 1 June 2015 (a summary of surveys).

369 Arab heritage: J. Deborde, 'Marie Laguerre'.

369 French women . . . in London: 'Harcèlement de rue', *Le Monde*, 16 April 2015.

369 whistled at by . . . fellow *députés*: E.g. Roselyne Bachelot, Rachida Dati, Cécile Duflot, Nathalie Kosciusko-Morizet, Ségolène Royal.

369 their physical attractions: Similar statements in A. de Villaines, *Harcelées* (2019), ch. 2.

370 a 'media fiasco': F. Marlier, 'L'Année 2018 vue par Marie Laguerre', *Les Inrockuptibles*, 29 December 2018.

370 'I dream of a France': 'Voici les meilleures pancartes de la marche . . .', *Les Inrockuptibles*, 23 November 2019.

371 'I am not at war': https://www.facebook.com/pg/noustoutesharcelement/posts/ 1 August 2019.

371 'The struggle against attacks on women': https://twitter.com/emmanuelmacron/status/1066403238935781378

371 emergency measures: 'Adresse aux Français', 12 March 2020: https://www.elysee.fr/emmanuel-macron/2020/03/12/adresse-aux-francais

372 'Et vive Eurodisney!': Speech on the twenty-fifth anniversary of Eurodisney, 25 February 2017.

18. Demolition

373 *aubettes*: *Dictionnaire de l'Académie Française*, 'Aubette', 3; M. Druon, speech at opening of Académie Française exhibition, Dakar, 23 May 1989: http://www.academie-francaise.fr/allocution-pour-linauguration-de-lexposition-sur-lacademie-francaise-dakar

374 'Property and royalty': P.-J. Proudhon, *Qu'est-ce que la propriété?* (1840), pp. 234–5.

374 protest campaign: See P. Blavier and É. Walker, 'Saisir la dimension spatiale du mouvement des "Gilets jaunes"': https://halshs. archives-ouvertes.fr/halshs-02603206/document

375 *ploucs, pecnos, beaufs*: E.g. D. Robert's preface to J. Branco, *Crépuscule: Macron et les oligarques* (2019).

375 Brussels correspondent: Jean Quatremer, on Twitter, 15 December 2018 and 18 January 2019.

378 *rurbain* France: See J.-R. Pitte, *Histoire du paysage français*, 5th ed. (2012), pp. 317–18 and 352–3.

378 a shrubby garden: Typical features listed in J.-R. Pitte, p. 317.

378 extensions of the town's perimeter: J.-R. Pitte, p. 353.

379 'no fewer than thirty criteria': Les Plus Beaux Villages de France, 'Les Critères': https://www.les-plus-beaux-villages-de-france.org/fr/ le-label/comment-devient-on-lun-des-plus-beaux-villages-de-france/ les-criteres/

379 'transformed by eternity': Mallarmé, 'Le Tombeau d'Edgar Poe'.

379 legally enforceable colour: Examples in J.-R. Pitte, pp. 327–8.

379 exposed to the elements: J.-R. Pitte, p. 352.

380 subrectangular enclosures: These meeting points of earth and heaven remained a mystery until I realized that their lop-sided oblongs could only have been produced by an ellipse, the apparent annual path of the sun: *The Ancient Paths*, pp. 128–9.

380 the *rond-point*: P. Ducamp, 'Pourquoi y a-t-il autant de ronds-points en France?', 1 February 2020: https://www.bfmtv.com/auto/ pourquoi-y-a-t-il-autant-de-ronds-points-en-france_AN-20200201 0029.html

380 peanut-shaped variations: At Nozay (Loire-Atlantique).

380 six billion euros: P. Ducamp.

381 The local mayor: 'Le maire de Saint-Étienne-du-Rouvray veut déposer plainte', *Paris-Normandie*, 21 November 2018.

381 Gilet Jaune demography: L. Rouban, 'Les Gilets jaunes ou le retour de la lutte des classes', *Le Baromètre de la confiance politique*, note 2 (Sciences Po CEVIPOF, 2019); 'Gilets jaunes: une enquête pionnière', *Le Monde*, 11 December 2018.

382 unaffiliated groups: Summary of studies by F. Gonthier and M. Della Sudda in G. Rozières, 'Les Différences entre gilets jaunes des ronds-points, des manifs et de Facebook', *Huffington Post*, 16 November 2019.

383 a joint declaration: Video at https://www.huffingtonpost. fr/2018/12/13/pourquoi-les-gilets-jaunes-de-la-france-en-colere-reclament-un-referendum_a_23617220/

384 set fire to the Jeu de Paume: See 'Fake news no. 4' in http://
lherminerouge.eklablog.com/12-fake-news-macronistes-sur-les-gilets-
jaunes-1ere-partie-par-laurent-a160561002

384 a sporadic tour: M. Darmon, *La Politique est un métier* (2019),
pp. 122–3.

384 Facial trauma: A. Chauvin et al., 'Ocular Injuries Caused by Less-
Lethal Weapons in France', *The Lancet*, 394 (2019), pp. 1616–17.
Statistics on police violence are collected by David Dufresne: see
R. Chalmers, 'Weapons of Peace' (with illustrations), *GQ*, September
2019, pp. 156–67. Articles by Dufresne at https://www.mediapart.fr/
biographie/david-dufresne

384 France cited alongside Haiti: Presentation of report by High
Commissioner Bachelet at 40th session of UN Human Rights
Council, Geneva, 6 March 2019: https://www.ohchr.org/EN/
NewsEvents/Pages/DisplayNews.aspx?NewsID=24265&LangID=E

384 his men would open fire: General Le Ray interviewed on Franceinfo,
22 March 2019.

385 'Social distinctions': 'Adresse aux Français', 13 April 2020: https://
www.elysee.fr/emmanuel-macron/2020/04/13/adresse-aux-francais-
13-avril-2020

386 'I say this to you very clearly': 'Adresse aux Français', 14 June 2020:
https://www.elysee.fr/emmanuel-macron/2020/06/14/adresse-aux-
francais-14-juin-2020

387 the peasant girl: 'Joan of Arc Model Dies', *New York Times*,
12 February 1936, p. 11; T. Gott, 'An Iron Maiden for Melbourne . . .
Frémiet's 1906 Cast of Jeanne d'Arc', *The La Trobe Journal*, 81
(2008), n. 16.

387 a Parisian journalist: A. Poirier, *Notre-Dame: The Soul of France*
(2020).

388 'sphinx squatting in the middle of the city': V. Hugo, *Notre-Dame de
Paris* (1831), V, 1.

389 charred oak beam: A. Poirier, p. xiv.

389 zoomed-in footage: A. Orsini, 'Un "gilet jaune" dans la tour de
Notre Dame pendant l'incendie?', 17 April 2019: https://
www.20minutes.fr/societe/2498187–20190417-gilet-jaune-tour-dame-
pendant-incendie-gare-intox (from 43'20").

389 'a rubbish dump': See J.-B.-A. Lassus and E.-E. Viollet-le-Duc, *Projet
de restauration de Notre-Dame de Paris* (1843).

390 Disney's animated musical: M. Camille, *The Gargoyles of Notre-Dame*
(2009), pp. 350–52.

392 a providentially harmonious whole: Strabo, IV, 1, 14.

392 monetary union: *The Ancient Paths*, p. 180.

393 'If someone were to tell you': V. Hugo, 'Consolidation et défense du littoral', 27 June 1846: *Actes et Paroles*, I, 'Chambre des Pairs', 2.

394 Druids: Timagenes, in Ammianus Marcellinus, *Römische Geschichte* (1968–71), XV, 9, 4–6.

Notes for Travellers

395 aerial photographs: B. Dousteyssier et al., 'Les *Villae* gallo-romaines dans le territoire proche d'Augustonemetum', *Revue archéologique du Centre de la France*, XLIII (2005), fig. 17.

397 a road book: Louette, *Itinéraire complet de la France* (1788), I, 163.

397 Napoleon's treasurer: Baron G. Peyrusse, *1809–1815, mémorial et archives* (1869), pp. 282–3.

399 'This mobile chaos': Baudelaire, 'Perte d'auréole', *Le Spleen de Paris*.

General Index

sexual harassment 355, 368–71
sexual relations 52, 68, 88, 131–2,
146, 148–50, 156–8, 191, 224–6,
249, 252, 269, 352, 355, 368–9,
374
shrines 37–9, 48, 57, 297, 344, 357,
388
Sidonius, Saint, Bishop of Aix 33
Sidonius Apollinaris 23, 29–40, 46,
49, 395
Simpson, Tom 344
slavery 6, 10, 19, 21–2, 29–30, 46,
151, 267
Smiles, Samuel 191
smugglers 48, 194, 311, 340
SNCF railway network 312
Socialist Party 353, 357, 362, 365,
381
socialists 247, 251, 276, 288–90
Sourisseau, Laurent ('Riss') 354,
356
South Eastern Railway company,
England 260
Southern France (Baedeker) 308
Souvenirs d'Orient (Lamartine) 219
Spanish anti-terrorists 358
Spanish Armada 197
Spanish Civil War 313
Spanish language 180
Spanish *maquisards* 328
Spanish Republicans 315
Special Operations Executive (SOE)
320
The Spectator 221
spies 10, 89, 190, 194, 251–3, 282,
312, 315
spoulgas 77–8, 80, 92, 396
SS *see* Waffen-SS
Stalin, Joseph 315
Stalinists 330
standing stones 39, 45, 48, 54, 266

Stations of the Cross 343
statistics 11, 291, 296–7, 301–3
*Statistique du département de la
Drôme* (N. Delacroix) 307
Stendhal (Henri Beyle) 319
Stephen (*or* Étienne) IV, Pope 58
Stevenson, Robert Louis 397
Stone Age 26, 54
stonemasons 103–4, 136, 306
Strabo 48, 112, 392
Strode, Nathaniel 245, 248, 260
Student Orientation and Success
Law (Loi Orientation et Réussite
des Étudiants, 2018) 352
Suchet, Louis-Gabriel 175–9
suffrage 246, 354, 371
Sun King *see* Louis XIV
Suspects, Law on (1793) 170
Swiss troops 198
Sylvester II, Pope *see* Gerbert d'Aurillac
Symbolists 283, 290

Taine, Hippolyte 247
Talleyrand, Charles-Maurice de 441
Tallien, Jean-Lambert 178
'Tartan Pimpernel' *see* Caskie
taxation 92, 114, 123–4, 141, 150,
155, 162, 164, 182, 187, 247,
382–3
telegraph 186, 238, 243, 337, 340
vocal 16
Tennis Court Oath *see* Jeu de
Paume, Serment du
Terres de soleil et de sommeil
(Psichari) 290
Territorial Coherence Development
Plan, Saintonge 284
Terror, the (1792–4) 169, 178, 329,
364
terrorism 178, 256, 299, 313, 317,
323, 352, 356, 358–60, 384

Geographical Index

Acknowledgements

To friends, readers and treasured collaborators, thank you – Kris Doyle and Starling Lawrence; Natasha Fairweather and Melanie Jackson; Gill Coleridge and all at Rogers, Coleridge & White; Paul Baggaley and Philip Gwyn Jones, Nicholas Blake, Camilla Elworthy, Orla King and Nneoma Amadiobi; Ruth Bird, Henry Johnson, Alison Robb and Gerald Sgroi; Anne Hidalgo and the Mairie de Paris; Bernard Cousin; the Cantal Departmental Archives, the Bibliothèque Historique de la Ville de Paris, the Bodleian Library and other institutions credited herein, especially the new and the old Bibliothèques Nationales.